NEW MOON

RICHARD GROSSINGER

Frog, Ltd.
Berkeley, California

New Moon

Published by Frog, Ltd.

Frog, Ltd. books are distributed by
North Atlantic Books
P.O. Box 12327
Berkeley, California 94712

Cover art: "Coniunctio of the Royal Pair over the Lit-up Ravine of Fifth Avenue, New York" from C. G. Jung, *Archetypes of the Collective Unconscious,* translated by R.F.C. Hull (New York: Bollingen Series XX, Pantheon Books, 1959), by permission of Leo La Rosa, copyright Estate of C. G. Jung.
Cover and book design by Paula Morrison
Typesetting and production by Catherine Campaigne

Printed in the United States of America

Distributed to the book trade by Publishers Group West

Library of Congress Cataloging-in-Publication Data
Grossinger, Richard, 1944–
    New moon : a memoir / Richard Grossinger.
       p.   cm.
    ISBN 1-883319-44-7
    1. Grossinger, Richard, 1944–   —Homes and haunts—New York
(N.Y.)   2. Authors, American—20th century—Family relationships.
3. Grossinger, Richard, 1944–   —Childhood and youth.   4. New
York (N.Y.)—Social life and customs.   5. Grossinger, Richard, 1944–
—Family.   6. Resorts—New York (State)—Ferndale.   7. The
Grossinger, Ferndale, N.Y.   I. Title.
PS3557.R66Z468   1966
813'.54—dc20   96-2106
                                        CIP

1 2 3 4 5 6 7 8 9 / 00 99 98 97 96

This book is for my daughter Miranda.

ACKNOWLEDGMENTS

I would like to thank Lindy Hough, Catherine Campaigne, Michael Palmer, Liz Williams, John Hunt, Gerry Rosen, Cindy Frank, Andrew Harvey, and Mary Buckley for comments and suggestions that helped shape *New Moon* through many drafts. I would also like to thank Kathy Glass for her fine editing, the effects of which subtly shape the text, and Paula Morrison for her sensitive and innovative design.

SEA WALL

This present existence begins in the twinkling of babyhood, the signs of which are lost in the babble of languagelessness. Childhood is a memory. It is also a memory of a memory, and memory of a memory of a memory. From this moment, at which the waves part, there are many versions of childhood, memories of memories, echoing without break back into the mist. How many of these memories are true memories, real déjà vu, as opposed to the language of memory in which we recreate ourselves for adult purposes?

Where there is no memory, there is still the intuition of continuity. Memory does not just retreat to a beginning at which it is excised. It combines and overrides; in seeming to go backward it actually goes everywhere, camouflaging our entry point into this narrative. We may have only brief and fragmentary memories of the earliest days of childhood, but our sense of our own eternal beingness is as strong there as it is in memories of yesterday. We seem to ourselves very much as the universe seems to us: originless—sealed by walls of gravity, light, and time-space, or sealed by the warp of consciousness and the fiction of personal history.

We are born into a circumstance of beings. But this is supposition. Our existence could be any number of other things too. This life is shrouded in mystery, certainly all other existences imaginarily lived by the same being too.

For a world of so much light, for such a bright concrete world, this place is a hoax. Only its appearance is bright, only the surface, the textured subsurfaces. Otherwise, we live among shadows.

We project our lives against a vast screen which, although no longer explicitly astrological and feudal, is just as infinitesimalizing.

Other than a biological stream of being, recognized in the laws of thermodynamics and the beating our our heart-lung machines, time does not exist.

As we get older our life spreads out into actual timelessness. The dot of present location erodes; prior decades deteriorate and lose their discrete days, wrapping around the single moments of youth like waterbugs around insects' bodies on the surface of a pond.

Each moment is already eternal. Each moment lives forever; all others are obliterated and absorbed. In breathing we pass from one immortality to another, as phenomena.

NOTES

New Moon began to be written in 1960 when I was sixteen. I worked on it as a novel until 1965. Then I set it aside for twenty years.

I worked on it again from 1985 until 1995, pulling in excerpts from other work done subsequent to 1965. Out of this material I have also drafted two manuscripts in progress—one continuing this narrative and another *(Out of Babylon)* containing fuller stories of my mother, Grossinger's, and my brother Jonathan.

I have always been ambivalent about publishing this material. I offer it finally as a statement of consciousness and memory, not as an autobiography or memoir.

I have changed most names in order to reduce the likelihood of embarrassing people. Some names I have kept in honor of those who have shaped my life and moved me. In either case, there should be no illusion that I am telling anyone's truth but my own.

PART ONE

THE CHILD
IN THE CITY

1944–1956

1

THE BEGINNING

My oldest memory is of seeing an Easter egg in a bush where branches met at its trunk. I had already found the egg once, but the man had rehidden it.

I came back clutching it as he laughed.

That chalky blue is anterior to my life. I touch it yet, unscathed and luminous in my mind.

But the egg was always out of context. Who was that man? Where was a yard with such a bush?

Nanny was there at the beginning. On the first morning of time she ruled the alcove, grinding oranges. She filled a glass decorated with flowers. Tastes flooded my mind.

Nanny slept in a corner of my room. She dressed me, made my food, put me down for nap, bathed me in the tub, and tucked me in at night. I recall her presence as that of life itself: vast and sepulchral, loving me so much "love" was a password between us.

I dwelled on a borderline of wonder and light, my mind a quandary of voices and remote lands. I was the zone of their interference. I was no one in particular.

All afternoon I lay in my crib, waiting for her to come back. I explored the contour of my chest and legs against sheets. I thrashed at the sides. Out the window, brick walls darkened slowly.

Forms flit impalpably through the courtyard. What were these unnamed specters that dwelled among glowing windows, that bore the signatures of knights on horseback, forests of gingerbread?

I chased my balls in their lining. I rubbed light in my eyes. Only the animals on my quilt were loyal—Zebra and Tiger and Bear. My hands underneath, they tussled and made nice with one another, tossing the covers around me until I rolled into sleep.

... awoke with lips and tongue babbling ... the room drained. An opera singer practiced, her trills echoing through the courtyard.

As I rekindle this fragile memory it seems no further from me now than a day later or thirty years later. The agenda has not changed. I am still reaching out from an inchoate reality toward an unknown design. The moment in the crib has stretched, without dilution, over the circumference of my life. And, because there was no other choice, the journey has gone ahead.

Another world stalked me from the beginning, emerging from the background, slipping into the background before I identified it. It was a landscape the same as this one—buildings, blue sky, rooms filled with people—but it was different, its meaning different, me in it a different me.

I faced an adversary who dwelled beyond forgetfulness. Every so often his voice would come chattering through the center of sleep, letting me know he was there. The omen thus delivered, his presence faded. From the opposite horizon another morning began another day.

I felt the reverberation of an earlier, more catastrophic thing. But what could have been antecedent unless it were birth itself?

"It was a horrible experience," my mother later recounted. "It almost killed me. You were black and blue. *I* was covered with blood. He used forceps." The word itself conjured implacable machinery. "You were screaming so—I thought you were dying."

That was *her* story. I have had (all my life) a recurrent dream: an elevator in a hospital, very old, long ago. Unseen, I visit her in her room and wait, expectant in darkness as in a theater. (In later years my wife is there too, about to have our son. These epochal events merge, and I am witness to both as one.)

I have no name for the feeling of this dream; it is just "the feeling." I recognize it as marking the boundary of the knowable world. Words give pale approximations: "homesick" ... "déjà vu" ... "alien" ...

4

"acrid." The sense of premonition is basic . . . footsteps approaching . . . a child who arrives already speaking. . . . I feel I cannot prevent calamity.

And yet I have waited all my life for this being's appearance, long after my two children were born and grown into adults.

Even now I wander, a child-man in a labyrinth of dreams of births of children and old men dying.

At other times I have discovered, in that same birth room, a jungle of orchids, a fountain bursting through the floor, exotic species of water blossoms and long-extinct sea animals quivering in shells—in short, an alien laboratory.

I have dreamed that it was not my mother in the room at all. A replica lay in bed in her place. She had my mother's appearance and gestures. She spoke exactly as my mother spoke. She knew everything about me my mother did.

The doctor attacked me with his knife. I fought him off but awoke with the invisible scar of his strike above my Adam's apple. Plus glimpses of a fleeing stranger.

Other times I cannot find my mother's room and keep returning to crowded elevators, taking them up higher and higher, hundreds of storeys through decorated corridors and ballrooms, each filled with weddings and celebrations.

I remember crawling on a carpet among stuffed chairs. At the end of the room stood bureaus with ivory figurines, flat goblets of colored oil. Golden frames bore etchings of long-whiskered dancing men.

One night Daddy produced a new box—a victrola. He had two records in thin brown envelopes. He set one on a spinning platform and lowered the metal into sound. *"Oh where have you gone Billy boy, Billy boy?"* And . . .

"Cruising down the river / on a Sunday afternoon . . ."

In retrospect I don't see (nor did I then) any ordinary river but, from a 45 degree angle, a cobblestone canal, its banks swarming with adults at carnival. Through a gap in notes of the song swims a giant turtle.

"Charming Billy" emerged from the mists of a bog forest, his name trailing a thousand variants, suspenders holding up his farmer's pants. In the minor chord between "charming" and "Billy" lay a blankness, a hiatus where my heart beat but my mind could not go.

Mommy was a version of the lady with the gem on her forehead on the record album, whose name, I later saw, began with the remarkable letters "Xt. . . ." She was a perfume demon with jet black hair, pearls, dark piercing eyes.

I pulled back from her Noxzema kisses, but she grabbed me, forcing affection, eyes trapping, red nails sharp on my arms till I made a small kiss back. "Don't you love me?" she insisted.

How could I not?

When I visited her in her bed in her chamber I saw the haggard but adorned ruler of a nation at war. I was proud to be associated with her.

Daddy was an odd, infrequent presence in his brown suits and beat-up felt hats, smoking a cigarette and chanting in Hebrew or singing, *"Old Man River, that Old Man River. . . ."* I can remember waiting the whole afternoon to see him and then breaking loose of Nanny (who regarded him with suspicion and held me back), running down the hall and throwing my arms around him as he came in the front door. It was the longest I had stayed on my feet without toppling, and I tumbled into his arms. In great surprise he exclaimed and hoisted me in the air. At least he smelled of other worlds and not like our charnel home.

"The stars above, the one I love, waiting for the moon. . . ."

Our apartment was at 1220 Park Avenue on the corner of 95th. Sometimes wind down the avenue rattled our windows, especially at night behind drapes, but never so fiercely as during the hurricane. Mommy was giddy in preparation, making phone calls, ordering food, warning me to keep back.

The sky blackened. Rain splattered the pavement. Daddy bundled himself, slammed the door, and ran down the street to pick up groceries. As he worked his way back he held onto lamp-posts to keep from being blown away.

Despite Mommy's warnings, I peeked. I saw a man stuck at the corner, his umbrella turned inside out. Sheets of paper danced through air; hurricane spirits rapped on our glass. I kept to the center of the room, filling my scrapbook with cars and trucks from magazines, cutting around tires and bumpers and sticking them two to a page from a jar of white glue.

After the wind, Mommy cried all the time. I heard whimpers, doors slamming, muffled sobs, Daddy's voice cajoling her, then angry, then ghostlike shrieks. Dr. Hitzig came—a fat goblin in a black suit. Mommy couldn't wait for his arrival; she ran down the hall in night clothes. With a steady arm, intoning syllables of authority, he calmed her. I saw him at her bedside, feeling her tummy. The next morning she was gone. Nanny told me she would return with a baby. I was astonished that such mayhem could lead to something innocent. But once I realized another of us was coming I saved a favorite stuffed animal, a bear, for him and was hurt that he didn't take it from me when I held it up to him as he was rushed past me, invisible in his blanket. His name was Jonathan; he was placed on the other side of my room, a china bug, whimpering and then roaring.

Everything was proceeding according to plan.

I planned to hide this brother behind a chair, teach him my words, and surprise everyone with a talking person at dinner. The opportunity never came. The world curved, revealing other contours. The baby was rough and unfriendly; he clung to Nanny, pushing me away.

I used to get lost. These episodes each have a quality of wandering beyond the world to a place nearer home. In the primordial such adventure I strayed from my Nanny at a spot I now recognize as 98th Street by Fifth Avenue. I proceeded in a trance, astonished suddenly to find the sidewalk rippled (I had assumed all pavement was smooth).

I came to an atrium of tulips guarding a silver orb, the reflection of a child passing through an asterisk of light. Flowers stretched above me like trees.

This was the garden, its goblets of water colors. They answered the breeze before the word "breeze."

I waited there, outside time.

Then Nanny came with a policeman.

I felt Richard inside me, inattentive, stumbling, late. I never behaved sufficiently or was grateful enough. I spilled my plate. I dropped my glass on the floor. I fumbled my toothbrush into the toilet. I wet my pants. I cried in my crib until Nanny spanked me. "Mischief, mischief," she scolded. "You're just a big mischief."

My worst was wetting. Too late I felt a trickle down my legs. It was the reddest flower, germinating in my core, engulfing me like a second skin.

Later it turned into a cold wire fence.

She pulled down my pants and pointed to my reddened thighs. "You're going to make yourself sick!"

But I held at the bottom of my heart a wordless directive: there was no way I was going to be tricked into marching down the aisle and putting my neck on the executioner's stone. I would always deviate, procrastinate, divert.

At first I might have seemed to my mother like a generic child. She passed me in her own distraction. Gradually we developed a true antipathy. She would kneel and examine my sores, poke them with her nails. I struggled to get away. She pressed hard on my chest and squeezed along my neck. She held my eyes open and stared into me. I looked back past her.

"What's wrong with him?" she demanded of Nanny.

Nanny didn't know. Then she said, "Sometimes I think he's the devil's own child."

Mommy punished me with quick, sharp slaps, calling out my blame so shrilly my eardrums ached. She grabbed my toys and threw them. She sent me to bed during dinner. She made me sit on a stool facing the wall. Yet I continued to misbehave: broken jars and plates, toothpaste on my jammies, crayon drawings on the wall, water on the bathroom floor.

When she heard me cough, she made me repeat it until my throat hurt. She put her head against my chest; her body was trembling. She thought I had an irregular beat. She asked Nanny to listen. "He may have a weak heart, Mrs. Towers," she said. I pulled free. Mommy's face darkened; she began to cry.

I decided to leave a surprise for her while she was on the phone. I got picture books off her shelves and made them into boats, setting them one by one on the surface of her bath. I was gleeful as I watched them float and sink. When she summoned me I told her calmly I was washing them for her. She whacked me with a hairbrush.

8

Sometimes Mommy would seize me on her lap and sing in another language:

> *"Frerer Jacqua, Frerer Jacqua,*
> *Dormez vous, dormez vous."*

("Are you sleeping, are you sleeping?" she insisted of me in a bemused, slightly out-of-control voice. It was a rhetorical question because I was clearly awake.)

> *"Brother Jon, brother Jon."*

She pulled my face into hers and rubbed our noses together. Then she swung me scarily outward, letting me drop until my head tilted backwards:

> *"Bateau, bateau yey,*
> *O bateau ve san-francez."*

I knew what was coming next. Our boat was in a storm. Were we going to sink and drown?

"Are you going to fall; are you going to fall?" shaking me an extra time and tickling my belly.

Then she shouted, "No!," pulled me back with a rough jerk, and hugged me.

Rescued again!

I was afraid, not as it might have seemed, of Mommy's anger or spankings. I accepted that I was inordinately bad. I was afraid of who she was—who she really was. Although her life was removed from me by a discontinuity of scale and kind, I presumed our kinship. She was the exact mother to punish and correct me. If I wrested myself away from her I was ungrateful, but when I tried to embrace her I felt her unbearable intimacy.

I was trapped in a wavering dance that occupied much of my childhood.

Pushing the carriage with my baby brother, Nanny took me to the playground every day. I mastered the little slide first but eventually got up more courage. Lightheaded, I climbed the stairs and sat at the top. A line of kids collected behind me. They shouted to go; suddenly I flew down the chute. I came to my feet and ran into Nanny's arms.

We walked into the park. I followed squirrels stopping and start-ing along the bushes. When I saw the wagon man, I pleaded with Nanny to buy me nuts to feed the squirrels. She agreed, as long as I didn't sneak any for myself: "Peanuts are poison."

Their forbidden odor rose from a heated bag, elephants drawn on its sides, top tucked in. I unfolded it and crept into the grove, calling gray ones, coaxing them from faraway, tossing one treat at a time. I would keep different squirrels in my mind, tracking their progress, regret-ting their departure if they hadn't gotten any nuts. When the bag was empty I tried without success to get them interested in the spiny brown balls that lay under trees. Then Nanny summoned me to move on.

As we passed the Museum, I wandered in its garden of white stones, hundreds of smooth ones all around, an unguarded treasure. A witch stood beside them, spraying toylike pellets from her purse, yellow and orange, then crumbs and bits of old rolls. Pigeons and sparrows flocked, so many wings she seemed to be growing them from her coat. I tugged on Nanny to go.

We came home by way of Lexington Avenue. Each store had its special smell—a bubblegum of toys, a frosty cavern of roses, a cookie circus with amulets of sparkling sugar and chocolate rings, a restau-rant spewing charcoal from its grates. Nanny asked my help in press-ing the carriage up the steps through the door. I hurried to be good.

Winters were exiles to Pluto. Radiator pipes whined, and wind howled to the verge of a voice in the alleys. Getting warm was my whole exis-tence as I shivered against wet pants. After my bath I wanted to be wrapped in towels forever.

One afternoon Nanny called me to watch as men in trucks hoisted trees by ropes on the center strip. Cabs, cars sped by. The disturbance moved down the avenue, mall by mall, redirecting traffic. At dusk these giants ignited in unison, all the way to the clocktower. Their red, blue, yellow, orange were the most magical colors I had ever seen. Amid traffic signals and car lights, they were fairy tales. Every nightfall they reminded me of who I was.

In the morning, pulling our sled by a string, Daddy took me on the Avenue. Sunshine sparkled so that I could barely open my eyes; the world was etched in exquisite detail, my breath making visible puffs. Sidewalks glittered. Pigeons purred, their feathers clean as pins, gray and white, an occasional black. Awnings were heaped with the aftermath of snow, doormen trying to beat it down with brooms. Scented smoke rose from a chestnut vendor at the entrance to the Park.

We climbed a hill. Inside mittens my fingers glided along a railing, skipping poles. Daddy climbed over, and I ducked. People were sailing—one to a sled, two, three, and four to a sled, tumbling in their woolen coats. I skipped in glee.

Daddy rolled onto the shiny wood, instructing me to lie on his back. I put my arms around his neck. Tobacco-straw from his coat enforced an unusual intimacy. He began slowly, then accelerated as I gripped tight. He hollered out exultation, ice crystals splattering my skin as he pumped his body and urged our wooden frame a little further, a little further. I was a shy recipient of so much labor.

On our walk home, sounds of bells and metal runners evoked gaiety, store windows phosphorescent, dioramas peopled with puppet villages, music everywhere: "Winter Wonderland" and "Santa Claus Is Coming to Town."

Photographs of the time show sedans on the streets, people in shaggy coats. I can't believe I was young so long ago. Those were the Christmas trees of the late 1940s, before anything had happened. They were before television, before I had seen thousands of repetitions of neon. They held the original frosted bulbs of their era.

This, I now know, was after the great war, before the time of formica and vinyl. Every toy was a rough amulet. Every button, colored thread, and wrapped candy bar was an original crafted item. The snow was a wild thing, capable of worlds beyond reference.

My name was Richard, in the ceremony. I dwelled among them then in a rapture of story-book snowmen, wood boats, and plastic farm animals, a charmed miasma not unlike the forest I pictured for Hansel and Gretel—surrounded by stuffed clowns and donkey dolls, toy buses, colored chalk, shiny white schmooes one inside another inside another, treasure balls that unravelled in trinkets of plastic planes and jewelled rings.

In the afternoon I played among colors of my singing top, the bright clown of my jack-in-the-box, the shaggy mane of a rocking horse, red and yellow metal of trucks and trains, molded farm animals, rubber knights and soldiers I set on perches of houses amid trees and birds, Indians and soldiers I wedged onto horses and planted on carpet. My hands ran through them in forays of battle. I tumbled them, twisting fingers through the air. I opened packages of game cards and spread them on the floor, rooster and elephant and mouse. I collected prizes and cartoons from the bottoms of boxes of wrapped candy and Cracker Jacks.

My records were yellow circles of tunes. Shepherds in Bethlehem, a beguiling caterpillar on his mushroom, tinder-box dogs with saucer eyes, loquacious rabbits and frogs—these charmed creatures joined in a medley of songs. In my mind Tweedledum and Tweedledee were chubby decorated ones to whom *"God rest ye merry gentlemen"* was also addressed.

After nap I helped Nanny make dinner, pulling the limas from shells, plunking shiny seeds into the pot, delighting in their tiny pings. The scent of turnips and roast beef enveloped me.

After dinner after playtime Nanny cuddled me in bed.

I had certainly come to a land of lost and faded artisans. Here I was, among their instruments and revelry, part of their clime in a frosted ball.

Existence was as fierce as March wind down Fifth Avenue or wet bedsheets clinging to goose bumps in lost watches of the night. I lay in warm damp islands growing frigid, peering into an unyielding granularity of darkness, a shifting mosaic of hidden and revealed, which was itself everything. And time oozed past me, molecule by molecule.

Life was also as gentle and speechless as the squirrels who came from behind bushes to take in their paws nutted shells. I was vague as the vastness of the City, its edifices around the Park turning to silhouettes against twilight.

I lived in a bottomless trance of chocolate, vanilla, and lime, collecting chips of pink and white quartz, awaiting great celebrations, the green sprinkled cookies of Saint Patrick's Day with its bagpipe parade, the solid chocolate eggs and coated marshmallow peeps of Easter, the orange and black gingerbread men of Halloween with their raisin buttons. Each of those tastes and colors was a land on a sacred calendar through which I was led enchanted and to which I returned in the timeless journey of the sun.

One evening the radio was left on in an empty room. A voice said: "Yet another one fell down the stairs, into the dungeon ... forever!"

"... forever ...!"

My life sank into infinity against this other—obscure, expanding, hostile.

It wouldn't listen. It had never listened. It could do anything to me it wanted, and there was no one to protect me.

Frosty the Snowman sang his jingle in the back of my mind, a mere rattle against the resonance of existence.

Since I couldn't hide I stood in the hallway, screaming, making fists, tearing away, refusing their consolation. They had no idea what I was confronting. My mother, however ominous, was just a lady. The danger wasn't an irregular heartbeat or a spot in my chest. It wasn't polio. It was so much worse than they could imagine. Their shrieks and histrionics were almost comical against such an intruder.

It was my destiny to stand alone in the watchtower.

One day, playing on Park Avenue, I decided I could ride my fire-truck through a bronze plug protruding from the stone of our apartment. I kicked off and rolled its way, then ... a rush of sparkles and pain ... standing outside the door in another body that was screaming, my hand against my head soaked with blood.

Mommy was always scared I was getting sick. On my way to nap she detected a slight limp. My knee was sore and puffy. She kept asking me to walk until I got dizzy and stumbled. I began to feel a bad thing inside me, not the thing she suspected but the thing that turned into a disease with no name. It was sometimes only the echo of a tune.

"He's gonna find out if you're naughty or nice...."

She took me to see Dr. Hunt, a brusque, humorless man who handled my body mechanically, drawing on my skin with his crayon, shining his cold tool in my ears and eyes, listening to my chest and tummy through his probe, finally putting me naked on a metallic stand and turning out the lights. I huddled there shivering while he made pictures of my insides.

These visits filled Mommy with apprehension. I watched her afterward, behind the soundproof window, remonstrating with him. I propelled a small wooden train around the floor wondering if he had glimpsed the thing inside me.

I understood that we were in danger, that most people were our enemies, even Dr. Hitzig and Dr. Hunt. It didn't matter that we pretended to like them. Mommy knew their schemes. Again and again she sniffed stuff from jars and cans. She turned lights off and on. But it was never bright enough to dissolve the foreboding.

Her room was a catacomb of shrouds. It wasn't bandits there that frightened me; it was homunculi amidst garments on the floor, a dead pigeon, a pool of blood, a dried-up witch. Everywhere needed a second glance: the window shades, BMs in the toilet.... Had poison formed overnight on the marmalade? What was that mark on my groin? Did it come off or was it permanent?

I was playing with a submarine in my bath when poison spurted from its seams. I pushed it away and leaped from the tub. Nanny yanked me back and held me there. I struggled, kicked brown water, scratched and bit at her, but she throttled me until all I could feel was the resonance of my crying.

Then I got sick and was put in my mother's bed. I felt strangely protected by its power. Dr. Hitzig viewed me solemnly, running fingers down my cheeks and neck and along my back. He wrote something on a sheet of paper, told a joke in Yiddish, said *"Mazel tov"* to Daddy, and left.

I was fed spoonfuls of horrible-tasting medicine, "Myocin," like dead mice ground up. I went to the hospital, "to have your tonsils out. They will give you something to drink ... and you will go to sleep...."

The serum was bubbly and sweet. I tried to fight, but all of them in white surrounded me.

It seemed as though it might already be the end of life (I had been here so terribly long). In the darkness that followed, figures floated above my cot. I awakened abruptly with a sore throat, gargling and spitting. The nurse insisted I drink a cup of pineapple juice I could barely suck.

Back home I sat on the living room floor, moving Uncle Wiggily's yellow and blue chalkmen across their kingdom of squares.

It's not what I remember but what I don't that threatens me still. Dreams periodically take me back to that old ground-floor flat at 1220. I knock at the door. The present occupants let me in. I see the living room stretching like countryside to my right, the land of bureaus and statues through which the hurricane passed. The hallway to my bedroom curls off beyond, darkened, invisible. Crumbling walls form foyers like rooms in a museum, their lengths draped in hieroglyphic tapestries, gold ornamental ceilings merging with sky.

These spaces are in decay, obscured from current inhabitants. I see through them into other habitations, or merely vacant rooms without end.

I tell the people that something happened to me there once. I want to go back and discover it. They direct me to the oldest sector of the back (which they never use). I start down the hallway. I intend to see where the spell was put on me. I never get there.

Once, grotesque dolls with muttering wooden heads drove me out. More often the interdict is empty … there is nothing at all, just space abandoned, its sterility and disuse marking the closure of a zone of consciousness. I have awakened at that point in inexplicable fright.

On at least two occasions gentle magi have intervened to lead me up the elevator onto the roof where they demonstrated windmills of the future, drawing power from light.

Once, I forced myself down the hallway half-awake, expecting to meet my trauma, but all I saw at its end was Nanny and me on a couch reading together. The scene was bountiful and sunny and betrayed all my suspicions … until I turned and looked the other way and found myself staring into a black light from beyond existence.

I believe the haunting was primordial and did not occur in language. But its vigilance is forever.

The summer of 1949, our Oldsmobile piled with suitcases, Daddy took us to our house in Connecticut. Then he went back to the city to work.

Everywhere flowering trees surrounded castles. Each new morning had adventures. With a shovel I dug rows and put in Nanny's seeds one by one like at the farm in my Little Golden Book. I graded the dirt, and Nanny and I stamped on it.

I tracked caterpillars on branches, ant armies to their mounds. I lay in the grass, staring up at birds. Wind stampeded through branches, fluttering against a shell of blue, each leaf singing a variant of "Cruising Down the River." A breeze of clover curled by.

I saw the world through lollipop wrappers in lime and cherry. I played trucks and boats, hid and refound translucent marbles in dirt, peeled and sharpened sticks into white arrows and made bows with branches and strings. Thin branches whistled like whips. I drew fat boys and girls on the sidewalk with my chalks.

One morning, barely visible leaves emerged from my furrows.

With his tools a workman in overalls put together a Donald Duck bike with training wheels for me. I tore along concrete making up adventures.

"Is Judy there?" I asked her mother standing in front.

Judy was an Uncle Wiggily girl who made figurines of clay and drew perfect pigs with eyelashes. She and her friends were allowed to take me to the playground and candy store.

"She went to the lake today," her mother said. "Is it important?"

I nodded.

I rode around the block again . . . and another time. Each circuit I checked back. "Judy's still not home."

The Good Humor man was there. Judy's mother bought me a toasted almond. I unwrapped the package and bit into its nutty cream.

Holding the stick in my hand, I pedalled slowly to the corner. I turned and stared down the block. The canopy of trees was thick and ominous. I traveled through its tunnel. I turned the corner again and passed my own house.

Judy was standing there alone in the yard. Her presence startled me. I had not expected her so soon. I tore past on my Donald racer, picturing wolves in pursuit. In the distance I heard them calling in bewilderment after me, trying to tell me Judy was home.

My rows had grown into plants with nips of fuzzy beans. I was lying on the ground, my face up close when I heard Mommy's voice.

"Dinner time!"

"It's still sunny," I whined.

The world was bathed in lemon light.

She poured me a cup from a brown bottle. "The days are getting longer." I knew that wasn't the answer. I looked suspiciously at the gold bubbling, drank it in a gulp. Trees rustled on the horizon.

I lay in bed. Fading umber prowled the perimeters. I pushed against it with my mind. I refused its omniscient luminosity. I would not be cozy.

Then from a kingdom of clowns I woke to the whine of Nanny making juice. I was back again, PJs matted to my body. I wandered into morning dripping wet.

Near the end of summer Daddy came. Before I even knew he was back, he had mowed my whole garden. It was hard to tell there was anything but grass. Mommy had one of her rare laughing fits. "He's a city boy," she said. "He doesn't know a tomato from an avocado." Then Daddy got angry at me for crying.

"It's only goddamned string beans. You know how many stringbeans there are in the world? You want more stringbeans, I'll buy stringbeans."

He did in fact return from the store with a huge bagful and dumped them in a heap on the table.

At summer's end we went to a twilight Punch and Judy show. Chains of grape lollipops were distributed at the ticket counter, big children directing. I was sucking my purple when a witch puppet burst in, cackling. My baby brother started crying. Mommy hushed him, but he wouldn't be quiet, so we ran down the aisle, into the night of more stars than I had ever seen, into the car, home.

After the summer, Daddy sold his yellow Olds and got a green Mercury. He took us on a ride into the country but drove fast and curvy. He and Mommy were yelling at each other. In auto smell and cigarette I tasted pineapple and began to cry. "He's carsick, Bob." I gasped and clutched the seat. No matter where I turned, it wouldn't go away. I began to whimper.

Daddy didn't want to stop. His lips were pressed, and he smacked the dashboard. Mommy smiled and teased him. I knew she was reminding him how bad I always was.

I stood by the roadside. At my feet in clover was a bee, spreading lavender grains. I didn't care if he was a stinger; his undulating fur and humming filled my mind. I smelled honey. Far off in the field, bugs and butterflies floated; golden-black susans shone like elfin pots. Then car-tasting liquid poured out of me into the dust.

The dream of my beginning comes in many forms. I recognize it by its simple geometry. In one version I am pursued by bad guys. I am three, and two of them are girls. I am more or less their leader. The pursuit begins somewhere in Central Park outside the playground. I try to throw them off, running into old buildings, along seashore, through exotic shapes, mere abstractions where they should not be able to follow. Yet they always do. And then it is night.

I am discovered by them in a plaza with a fountain. I escape through bushes just before they see me. Days pass.

We are still being chased. The scenery changes. I am becoming more like Richard. We break loose from a grove of trees and take refuge in a stone building, a fort on the Atlantic. A party is in progress inside. I see people against light through a third-floor window. "C'mon," I say.

It would seem that by losing ourselves in the throngs we could throw them off our trail, but instead we climb a fire escape against an outer wall. This is risky. We press ourselves on the wall, and wait. Months pass, and we are bricks. Gradually we are me, fused granule for granule. The pursuers grow close, but I am safe in anonymity. Since they cannot find us, they go into the building.

Alas, when they have shuffled through the entire party and failed to locate us, they look out the window, and there they see us (fine as dust) eclipsed in moonlight.

"Now!" I shout. We break loose and begin to run. They stay a hair's breadth behind us. For days we flee, maintaining a mere step on them. Then we spot an abandoned building and plunge down its stairs into the basement. We hear them on the landing above. We know we had better hide, but where?

There is a corner formed by a base of stairs and the wall, a simple line. We cram into that.

I am not convinced. I tell us to remove the adjacent piece of stone. We do, pulling it back against ourselves and holding it in front so that it seals us into wall. Now we can be here forever. They will never look within stone.

I continue to hold on. They arrive with a flashlight and scan the wall, finally landing on the spot behind which we are huddled. I pull the stone tight so that the space becomes smoother and more cohesive with the existing surface. The three of us are compressed into one. There we sit within, even yet.

One day Mommy took me and the cousins in an armada in two taxis to view one of her favorite alter egos, Mary Martin (as Peter Pan). This was the zenith of the Mommy realm: flying actors, dancing crocodiles, Tinkerbell above a pirate galley. We all cheered for her failing light to be relit.

Another time, she led me silently on the longest walk ever, traipsing determinedly in her black coat into the Park, through tunnels, past lakes with toy boats.

I had never seen any of these places.

We came to a most amazing land—castles, moats, rocky precipices. Its creatures were radiant in cages, lions sleeping motionlessly, bears prowling pale boulders and splashing in a grotto.

Mommy sat on a bench and read while I watched seals climb onto rocks. I scanned the black eagerly, hoping to sight pale flutters before they surfaced with comical snorts. Then—Mommy said okay—I entered the brick castle. In screeching rooms monkeys dashed about, hung from single arms, made faces. I ran back and called her to come. She shook her head and said the smell made her nauseous. When I arrived at the other end, she was waiting in daylight. I reached for her hand.

They held my fifth birthday at 1220. Mommy insisted we wear party hats and carry wands of rainbow maché; she hung masks on the ceiling lights. At each doorbell new aunts and uncles arrived with cousins. I ran to greet them and received perfumed hugs and wet kisses. Jostled among large kids, I tore open wrapping paper to find stuffed animals, trucks, and puzzles.

In a last tiny box (about which Mommy showed unusual interest) there was cotton around a barbell-shaped rattle. She said it was real gold and given to me by Irving Berlin when I was born. He was a famous man from her world. I ran my fingers across the bump his name left.

They brought the dining-room chairs into the living room and set them in a row facing different ways. I couldn't guess the purpose. Then silly music began. Unexpectedly it stopped. The game was to sit in the chairs because they took one away each time while the music played. Everyone pushed and pinched.

I lost my place and sat by the side while Mommy delighted in her role at the victrola, setting down and raising the needle. A man in a clown suit pulled strings of pastel handkerchiefs out of a tube, and my Uncle Eddie blew balloons and twisted them into animal shapes so rapidly that the room was filled with floating creatures as I ran, slapping them in the air. Nanny set a cake with candles in front of me. Mommy held a shining sword. With her weight we came down together through the frosting. Then I filled myself with yellow.

In the summer of 1950 I was sent to a camp in Pennsylvania called Swago. I lived in a cabin with ten other boys and Bob, our counselor, who was mainly concerned with misbehavior and punishments. He would wake "bad" kids in the middle of the night and paddle us with a slipper or belt—the number of blows dependent on the violation. "Crimes" included giggling during silent period, spilling food at a meal, being late, and leaving clothes on our beds. I was the worst offender with my wetting, so I was pulled from sleep again and again, swatted and dragged back into bed. Night became a labyrinth in which I forgot how many times and whether I woke and was summoned or dreamed I was summoned.

Bob warned me to say nothing to my parents. He hung close to us on visiting day. Still I whispered it to my mother.

"That couldn't be true," she snapped, "but I'll speak to the director." Afterwards she told me it was my imagination.

She brought a glider with a propellor wound by a rubber band, slices of balsa wood for the wings, and a green plastic nose. The plane could go higher than gliders we threw. It traveled beyond imagination, chugging gracefully through steppes of sky. No one had seen a prop-driven glider before, and even big kids from other bunks came to watch it sail over the fields.

At twilight we took turns throwing our planes in the air and chasing them. One swooped back into our group and, as we raced together, its wing crushed under our feet. Bob strode into our midst pointing at me. "You broke it," he yelled. "You give him your new plane." Not even my regular one but my propeller. Sorrowfully I went back to the bunk, took it from my cubby, brought it out, and handed it over.

That evening I began coughing. I was coughing and coughing and couldn't stop. I had what they called whooping cough. I was brought to the infirmary and put to bed. I lay there for days.

Plates of hospital food came and went. Leaves burned beyond my window. I heard the shouts of games.

(I have one other memory from Swago—the frog. In coins of dispersed sunlight at the bottom of a pool. . . . "Catch him," I pleaded. An older boy dove down through the water. I saw his fingers reach out as the frog sprang. He grabbed its legs in his hand. He set it in a coffee can and handed it to me. I looked at it resting there in bright silver in undulating ribs of light . . . and I am still looking at it, alive and green, its legs extended, the water unimaginably clear.)

Then Daddy came in his car and got me and took me to the Nevele Hotel, his account. I was filled with joy and relief when I saw them all again. I couldn't believe they were real—Mommy with her famous look, Nanny kissing me, Jonny such a big boy. They were so happy to see me.

That fall I began school at a French academy on Fifth Avenue, but I wet in class, so I was switched to P.S. 6 on Madison. There we painted from jars of colors onto easels, built block villages, and bumped in circle games at recess, pulling hair and tripping each other. Balls from the bigger kids' games rolling into our midst were booted back.

When a bell rang, we lined up and proceeded in rows onto the street. This was fire drill.

There was also an air raid siren. We crawled under desks and covered our heads with our arms. It was like playing warplanes. There was a spooky feeling too, the teacher warning of invisible radioactivity and broken glass flying across the room.

Nanny met me after school. We shopped for groceries at Novack's Market. While she read her list I followed Mr. Novack around. With a long stick ending in a "hand" he plucked boxes of cereal and crackers, cans of vegetables, juices and soups from shelves. All these would be delivered later.

One Saturday afternoon our family went to Palisades Amusement Park. I was put in a chair on a carousel that was supposed to be fun. It began to go fast and zigzag. I got dizzy. My mind came undone in milky rips, each one almost tearing me apart. I saw down dungeon stairs, even worse for their not being there. I struggled out of the chair but was thrown to the ground. Screaming so loud I wasn't me, I tried to get up, but everything was upside-down. I fell. Then the ride stopped, and in a commotion they led me away. Again, vigilance failed.

That spring P.S. 6 had a fair. Colored paper hung from the walls, and booths of cookies and toys filled the recess room. I knew I couldn't visit them all in the short time allotted, so I hurried from thing to thing. I rolled marbles toward holes, bet on paper horses, and aimed balls through rubber-band mazes made of nails in plywood. With my dollar I bought a book called *The Dragons of Blueland*. On its cover a boy in a red and white striped shirt hugged a blue and yellow striped dragon with tiny yellow wings. The dragon was soft and pudgy and hugged back; he had a tiny red horn. All about them five-pointed yellow stars filled midnight blue. I carried this book everywhere. I loved to stare at its map—the train headed to Nevergreen Village, a church with a steeple, tiny cottages, the lighthouse offshore, a snake lifting himself to a cactus, cows sleeping on either side of a squiggly river that wound into mountainous cones, dragons perched on their peaks, a single one (like a blimp) in flight.

Nanny read me the story at bedtime—how the baby dragon found his family trapped in a cave, enlisted Elmer, and flew him on his back over the Spiky Mountain Range. My favorite picture showed the family of dragons: spotted, calico, striped, and otherwise decorated; tumbling, leaping, peeking at their tails through their legs, hopping over one another, rolling onto their backs, prancing on two legs. In a two-page illustration, all the dragons burst from the cave, bouncing and taking flight, Elmer's horns in their mouths.

The men scattered.

A few ended up in the water amid floating hats.

Blueland was immutable and, though my daydreams didn't take me there, they manufactured their own "dragons," their own Bluelands. I couldn't have inhabited this story anyway, but from it I could learn to make other magical countries. Lying in bed, I felt the wind against my body even before I created the creature on whose back I was being carried. The caves in my stories were deeper and more tenebrous than those by the Awful Desert; the horrors I confronted called for a swifter, more daredevil hero than Elmer, whom I became.

I adored the friendly dragons of Blueland, and I wouldn't let Nanny say a word against them or deny their likelihood (as she was wont to do), but my Blueland was a realm a hundred dragon books could not fill, and I went there more and more of the time.

The darkness of rainy days swept into my soul, drips and splashy tires leaving wet masks—the City double with melting colors. My forehead pressed clouds on slick cold.

Jon and I sat beside our record-player, putting on our favorite disks: *"There's a little white duck sitting on the water,"* and *"... among the leaves so green-o."* Blending with the simmer of toast and vegetable soup, these tunes spun webs of afternoons, a symphony of our lives played by pipers in an upholstered box. When a narrator signalled us, we turned pages to follow Bozo the Clown on his travels through Europe and Asia, from the Leaning Tower of Pisa and the Eiffel Tower to the lair of the Wild Man of Borneo with the ring on his nose. In *Bozo Under the Sea* the clown in diving gear visited sea horses, fish with lights, even a great whale. We stuck our faces in a sink of water and mimicked his bubble-filled voice exclaiming, "What could that creature be?" (It was an octopus.)

My favorite record, though, was of Sparky who heard the engine talking through the clatter, complaining that its right rear wheel was coming loose—then persuaded the conductor to stop the train just before they crashed.

All these events make a credible account of childhood.

The radio with the dungeon and the ride at Palisades recall the horror. The toys and records recall the enchantment, the Christmas lights and snowy park the wonder. My mother and Nanny appear somewhat as they must have been.

What is missing is a quality that lies underneath these details, within veils and silhouettes, a cauldron of reality at their core.

When I approach this realm now, I find the barest mists of sensation left, its ambiance vast but thin. The shards of becoming are everywhere and permeate everything, so there is no longer relief or scale by which to identify what actually happened.

I sense a white miasma. It is gaunt as snow, or cream on my mother's face. Ghosts surrounding my bed in the hospital are the white miasma. It glistens and shifts in particles. Then there is nothing. I emerge amid snowy canyons in a place far from home. Villages appear, then whip by so that I cannot enter or approach them.

These vistas could be a movie or an illustration from a children's book. But they are also merely the covering upon another whiteness that seethes and snaps in unlocalized time and space. They exude cold and exile. They are an icicle of panic. They are the world blanching in a pang, and fading.

Then there is a yellow miasma. It pours out of my gut, a field of daisies and insects, an ocean so thick I cannot swallow it, a spinning chamber, a tan Daddy driving the lining of a throat-and-belly car.

The miasma is apple from another planet, buttercup-do-like-butter?, Judy-Judy. It is being put to bed early. It is orange juice. It is buzzing, but I can't see a bee.

In the yellow dream I am trapped in industrial basements, toilets overflowing. I wade through wastewater and urine. Even standing in the shower I am knee-deep in it. Shreds of paper and crud cake about my legs. It is impossible to rinse them because the water is filthy. The drain is clogged.

The blue miasma is the opera singer, the glow of my mother's bedroom. It is twilight in the dungeon. It is the background against which Christmas lights sparkled. If it weren't for the blue miasma, the trees down the Avenue would not have stood in such relief.

The blue miasma is medicinal and bitter, poisonous. It does not have a dream but is the space between dreams, indigo phosphor swirling across landscapes.

In the red miasma Dr. Hitzig arrives with his leather bag to examine Mommy. She wants him to look at me too. For all the years I have been truant I must have spawned fatal diseases. She points to my head and says there is a scar. The all-seeing Hitzig parts my hair and examines my scalp. I think, 'It's just from riding my bike into that fireplug.

It's long healed.' But Hitzig says we have let a disease grow through
our inattention. A monster is arising within my skull, merging with
flesh, incorporating me from my cap and spreading downward. I jerk
away, but he probes me there in his metallic grip. He is going to oper-
ate and cut me away by bits.

Then there is a dream from which I cannot awake, though I tell
myself it's just a dream. I push against its sides, twist, and propel my
body backward through corpuscles of fog. Finally I tumble into a room
I shared with my brother long ago. It is an eddying, shapeless black,
a lesion in consciousness itself.

The Jonny miasma is a suckling presence up against me, jabbing
at me, meeting my eyes, fawning on me in atonement, negating my
existence with a certitude of his own. As often as he dug at me with
his fists, he came whimpering to me for comfort. As many times as he
approached me in intimacy, his tendrils became fangs and he bit me.
He was like my mother, someone I was supposed to love and pretended
to love and couldn't, so I lived in petty strategies of pride and revenge.

Mommy watched my every move and pried into my thoughts. She
was so close to me, so repellent, that she wasn't a person at all. I came
to assume that her qualities in me made me repugnant too. It didn't
matter that I hated her, that she was beautiful.

The summer before first grade we rented another country house, this
one in Long Beach. Every day I played by the ocean. As it crashed in
about me, I sat in the tide with my toys, raking broken shells into a
sieve, collecting and washing them in a Bugs Bunny pail, digging channels and holes for the water to swirl into.

My wind-up plane buzzed on tin pontoons. I would let it go, then
rush through foam to recapture it.

I watched vessels cross the horizon.

Daddy visited his college friends Moe and Nook. Beside the rotating sprinkler Nook's wife, Aunt Alice, served us lemonade. I stared
into jewel-sprinkled grass.

On the way home Daddy and I went into a beach-house and showered off our sand among naked men. I was overwhelmed but comforted by the salty aroma of their flesh. The horror was that they were
almost dead, the drain trapping their skin and hair.

I vowed I would never grow that old.

Then we climbed the steps to the boardwalk and walked along the row of amusement stands. Ignoring stuffed animals, balloons, darts, and turtle races, Daddy said there was "only one real game here." We visited long skeeball alleys with their shelves of porcelain prizes to be garnered by coupons over many visits. He helped me roll wooden balls toward raised pockets with numbers. Targets were circles inside of circles. Within larger circles were smaller circles that made the most points.

The balls were rough and solid, well worth attention. We got ten at a time.

I loved their clatter, the swift notch of a lever releasing new ones, the snugness of their plunk into the center hole, the near misses in adjacent rungs. The moon huge over trees, I pulled sticky paper off a popsicle and sucked its sweet ice, *"The old accordions playing, a sentimental tune. . . . Cruising down the river, on a Sunday afternoon."*

2

P.S. 6 AND BILL~DAVE

In the fall of 1951 I was sent to the new P.S. 6 building on 81st Street. Each morning, Nanny roused me, put out my breakfast and, while I ate, prepared vegetables and a sandwich in wax paper, and fit them into my Flash Gordon lunchbox. Then she took me outside to wait for the wagon.

My classroom was on the first floor facing the yard. We scrambled in and found our places. Chatter was stilled by a clanging bell. From her position beside the flag Miss Tighe led us in the Pledge of Allegiance. Standing in aisles, our hands on our hearts, we recited its words automatically and singsong, "one nation, indivisible, with liberty and justice. . . ."

I sat in my combination desk and chair, watching Miss Tighe's lessons. They were about Dick and Jane, their dog Spot, a cat Puff. We recited their words: "This is Jane." "See Puff jump."

I soon became restless. I wound two pencils in a rubber band into a knot so that they danced weirdly to come undone. Kids at desks around me giggled. My eyes fell on their papers and books; everything was more interesting. I turned pages repeatedly to pictures in the back where I tried to pronounce unintelligible combinations of letters. I drew stick figures, penguins playing trumpets with musical-note q's that became bird double-u's. Part of me merged with how bars between panes of glass cast rhomboids bending from near rectangles to diamonds and creeping across the room.

My mood wandered through tints and luminations. I tracked drones of planes across their entire pitch. "Jane throws the ball to Spot."

Soon my mind was occupied by dragons and magic islands, stories in which I escaped enemies and hunted for treasures. In the forest were castles, giant winged creatures, passages to other worlds. By late in the day storylines crumbled, and mere patterns and colors flowed soporifically by.

A pool appeared under my chair. Kids nearby alerted Miss Tighe. The class stopped, and unhappily I was the center of attention. At first, I didn't experience shame because I didn't identify with Richard. I was on *their* side, laughing at the spectacle.

Meanwhile addition and subtraction were demonstrated on the blackboard; words were spelled, simple sentences sounded out. I was delighted when the single-letter word "a" appeared on an upcoming page. I had been looking ahead to it, wondering what it meant (Miss Tighe purposely not forewarning us). A faint image of that "a" has stood before untranslated symbols and newness of text ever since.

During that year my family moved across the street to 1235 on the corner of 96th. There, on the sixth floor, overlooking a narrow alley, my brother and I shared a room. Our beds were almost touching along one wall, and we had our own bureaus.

Uncle Moe brought a wood-burning kit that released industrial smells as it heated up. Jon and I sat on the rug, etching lines on blocks while Nanny warned us about nipping ourselves with the coil.

Aunt Et and Uncle Hy gave us a black globe with a light in its core to put stars on the ceiling. Uncle Mooney surprised us with a painted turtle in a plastic bowl, a track for him to walk on, and a parasol at the center.

Somehow Timothy escaped. We found him only after pulling up carpet edges and lifting cushions. He had made his way to a corner where his legs plowed sadly against the wall while his little head twisted. We returned him to his bowl and poured in plenty of dried insects. But he got out again, and after three weeks Nanny found him dried up under the radiator.

Jonny and I launched more escapades than Nanny could handle. She was always pulling us apart, taking our cap guns away, making us drink our dinner disgustingly in our milk as punishment.

We hid in closets and behind beds and played pranks on her, misplacing her clothes and medicines and putting plates and silverware in her drawers. She told our mother we were the worst kids she had ever taken care of.

One evening my brother and I decided to save our BMs as a joke. We stored them under his bed. After just a few days a stink filled the room, but the bed was very low-slung, so no one suspected the source.

Our mother collared Mr. Borrig, the superintendent, and he appeared with a plumber in tow. After checking the toilet, the handyman worked his way into the bedroom, yanked the bed triumphantly forward, and announced, "There's your problem, lady."

She stared at me in disbelieving horror. I shook my head in denial.

"It was *him,*" Jon insisted. "It was his idea."

My brother was Mommy's favorite. She trusted him as surely as she despised me. She boasted to relatives how handsome and spunky he was and showed him off everywhere. Compared to such a son I was an embarrassment, not usually worth even mentioning.

As Jon got larger he became an especial nuisance, strutting and boasting in front of me and appropriating my things.

He had an ornery energy about him—a chippiness and pride—plus a vaguely sour, powdery smell that I associated with his banditry. He yelled at me, his mouth spraying spit.

When we played, it seemed as though he made his elbows jab, his knees butt. When I thought he was cute and tried to cuddle him, he gave me sly looks even as he accepted my embraces.

He loved me to challenge him so we could fight. We would shout names at each other and begin hitting.

"Dumb brat!" I screamed as he showed off his boxing style, dancing from atop his bed to mine.

"Pee face!" he retorted wickedly.

I dreaded the intimacy of our bodies grappling. I wanted to throw him off, to pummel him to oblivion. Screams and thuds brought Nanny, then our parents (if they were home). They pulled us apart. To be blamed seemed fair because I knew my dark motives toward Jon. I hated him.

To this day I can picture him, pointing at me, forcing tears, telling. Before the adults, he was innocent as a lamb.

"A born instigator," Daddy said, eyes glaring at me.

"He put my trucks in his toys!" I sputtered. "He stuck out his leg and made me fall. On purpose!" I was the picture of righteous outrage.

Jon shook his head cooly and grinned.

"You're older and should know better," Mommy finally said.

During one particularly bitter tussle Jon and I wrestled each other to a death grip. I wouldn't let go, but I couldn't budge his squeeze.

Suddenly his fingers caught hold of my ear. I shrieked and bit his forearm as hard and deep as I could.

Howling, he reached to the table for a pair of scissors. "I'm going to get you," he shouted. "I'm going to kill you."

As his voice trembled, I experienced throbs of my own rage. I dove at him and wrested the scissors away.

By the time they arrived he was bleeding from a cut on his cheek, and I was sitting beside him crying. The weapon lay on the floor.

I tried to tell my mother what had happened, but she wasn't listening.

She socked me on the head—a hard, painful club. Then she attacked me with fists and elbows, socking again and again, crouching over me as I squirmed along the floor.

I knew she wanted to avenge Jon; she was on his side. I could see Daddy, uncertain what to do. Then he joined in yelling.

"He's an idiot. Let him crawl into his hole."

I stumbled into the closet as she continued to kick and flail at me. Clothing and hangers fell.

"You're the lowest kind of creature alive," he added, "picking on a harmless child."

Inside me a strange, dry voice began to heave in rhythm all by itself. I sat there among the coats, fascinated by the raw cadence of my sobs, calling for my Nanny.

Events of those times included the rare visits of two family members.

Grandpa Harry, a tiny man with a foreign voice, showed up only on Sunday mornings with his chauffeur, Joe. Grandpa was friendly but in a constant hurry, his sole purpose to deposit large boxes of cookies, lox for Daddy, and the same set of fancy chocolate silverware in a flat box covered with cellophane. This included not only knives, forks, and spoons of different sizes, but chocolate pushers. Having presented his gifts at the door, he was usually waving goodbye despite Daddy's protests that he should stop, break bread, and say a Sabbath blessing.

It was a major victory if he took off his hat and progressed out of the hallway to the first chair of the living room.

Uncle Paul, a fat, jolly man, would burst right in, exchanging greetings with Daddy and sometimes even giving Nanny a hug. He arrived at the most unlikely times and, best of all, took me out alone. No one ever said why I was entitled to these adventures, but I assumed it was because I was older.

At F.A.O. Schwartz, Uncle Paul stood beside me as I picked up mechanical fish from the standing pool. "How about *that?*" he pointed across the rear of the store.

Trains wound seamlessly through villages. My eyes went from feature to feature, people in the windows of cottages, a puff of smoke from the engine, the light through a tunnel.

Uncle Paul always concluded our visit by buying me a new game or a boat for my collection (about which he asked quite informed questions: how many tugs? how many barges? how many canoes? any in drydock? any rafts? any ferryboats yet?).

One time, despite his obvious doubts, he honored my pleas to buy a hard plastic man with answers to questions floating in liquid inside him, visible through a plastic window. Another time, he selected a game with presidents' faces on gold coins like real money so that I could learn history. The most special present, though, was when we went to a section at the front of the store and he selected a red motorboat with a real buzzing battery. I was gleeful at how jealous Jonny would be.

At the Penny Arcade we played skeeball and got fortune cards from a glass-enclosed gypsy doll. With cork rifles we knocked down prizes and collected our booty in Uncle Paul's pockets—gum drops, tiny boxes of Oriental cards, puzzle rings, plastic whistles with birds perched on them, packages of miniature books.

To win coupons, we slid a metal puck down a saw-dust surface onto an electric grid beneath bowling pins that lit up scores on a screen as they collapsed upward. Then, together in a recording booth, absurdly out of harmony and tune, we sang my children's songs into a microphone imbedded in the wall—me and Uncle Paul doing "Frosty the Snowman" and "The Thanksgiving Squirrel." I alone knew the words, so he had to race to catch up.

Afterwards, we got to hear ourselves in privacy; then the disk with our voices dropped out a slot.

Uncle Paul visited frequently enough that I always asked when he was coming next. Mommy didn't want to be bothered by questions about him. But his visits were also uncommon enough that I almost forgot about him. He had become a distant memory of something wonderful when suddenly he was back again, interrupting playtime to claim me for an outing.

Miss Tighe set aside a time each day to work with me while the other kids were doing assignments. She went over lessons, reciting sentences to which I hadn't been paying attention, rehearsing the interactions of numbers, shaping my letters with her own hand gently over mine.

I wanted to stay good to reward this attention, but, back at my desk, stories took over my mind; a trickle ran down my legs. Other kids smirked and giggled, holding their noses when they passed me. At lunch a boy purposely spilled his juice on me, then yelled, "Wet pants!" I shoved him. He socked me. Soon I was in the center of a circle, everyone pointing and teasing. My mind tried not to cry, but from somewhere my sobs began until I was dozens of tiny dragons, each with its own wings flapping away.

"Just get up and take this," Miss Tighe would say, pointing to where the bathroom key was attached by a string. "You don't even have to raise your hand." She was granting a privilege. What she didn't realize was that I had no sensation of pee starting, so day by day I disappointed both of us.

One morning, without notice, Mommy packed our suitcases. We were going to Texas, she said, to visit Grandma Sally. In the train Jonny and I kneeled by a window, watching the city sweep by. Soon it was countryside . . . then lights in the dark.

We spent another whole day traveling and, when we awoke in Dallas, everything seemed old-fashioned and warm like summer. We had strapped on our holsters but spotted no cowboys in the streets.

Grandma and Uncle Tom's home was two storeys; it had a yard with a small brambly jungle connecting it to other yards. Using string, boards, and sticks I arranged a makeshift fort from which I spied on activity in all directions.

On his way to work, Uncle Tom drove me and Jonny to a school for little kids. No more numbers and letters, it was back to building block villages and painting on easels. At naptime the class lay on fold-out cots. The teacher read to us from *The Wizard of Oz*.

Late-afternoon yolk flickered on the wall, as radiant figures of a Lion, a Scarecrow, and a Tin Woodman traveled an enchanted forest: a Scarecrow who had been made only yesterday, a Woodman whose joints creaked, a sad Lion.

Oz was the longest story I had ever heard; in fact, it was not a story—it was myself in another version. I adored its characters so much and was so concerned for the outcome of their quest I could barely wait between installments.

Since I was older the teacher kept me up through naptime, reading to me in the backyard. So I heard the story twice, the old parts again with my classmates, then new adventures alone with her under a tree— through the enchanted forest, from jabbering field mice to winged monkeys and—"Richard, today we meet the Wizard himself."

Grandma put surprises at our place settings: look-and-see straws so we could watch our milk spin in circles through Goofy and Donald Duck. For days Jonny and I could not find enough colored fluids to sip. We finally sucked up Kool-Ade out of the sink and began spraying each other. Uncle Tom reclaimed the straws on the pretext they harbored germs.

He took us to a rodeo where cowboys and horses pranced to loud music; men wrestled steers to the ground. He kept asking us if it was exciting enough. Jonny thought so and clapped, but I was silent and sullen, leading him to tease me about being a city boy.

One afternoon, with no more warning than when we came, we got on a train and passed through cities into winter. Only when I was older did I learn my mother had left Daddy, then changed her mind and come back.

When I reentered Miss Tighe's class, everything seemed remote. She said, "Turn to lesson number six on page sixty-two," and I stared at total gibberish. As befitting one who had been in Oz, I spent my days drawing and daydreaming.

I started "group" (that was the name for the day camp we went to at the end of school). At the three o'clock bell we sorted in clumps outside parked station wagons representing different companies (mine was Bill-Dave, the same fleet of drivers who picked me up in the morning). Bill was our fat, friendly ringmaster; Dave was the name of someone fighting in Korea. We were counted, packed into one of two wagons, and driven to the park. A counselor led us to an empty field where we organized games. These included "Capture the Flag," bombardment, volleyball, and kicking a soccer ball toward a gap between two sweaters (with imaginary lines between trees marking "out of bounds").

Bombardment used a soft, fat ball which was heaved at us by the players on the other team. A boundary scratched in the dirt with a stick separated us. If a player was hit, he was "out," but if the ball was caught, the one who threw it was "out." A dare consisted of charging the line to make a target of one's self in order to be in position for a catch. Since a throw had to be from the point of getting the ball (no stepping up to aim!), a close position also allowed a well-targeted return.

I delighted in the solid smack of rubber in the chests of kids who really caught it, the suspense of a quick toss among scattering opponents. I wriggled my body, jumping up and down. Sometimes the ball came my way and, once, I surprised myself by snagging it and holding on. I could barely think straight. "Throw it back!" they shouted. But I didn't want to let go of my prize.

More often I imagined myself transparent and seemed to think that by whirling around I could avoid getting hit. The actual thump always startled me.

Soon after I began Bill-Dave, Mommy wanted me to go on Saturday too. I protested, but she said it would be good for me to be with boys my age. "And anyway all you and Jonny do is fight."

So, I had to get up early and meet the wagon downstairs. I felt my innards tingling with a special Saturday weakness. Wind ripped the gold remains of leaves, it seemed, off the very edge of creation. In football I ran aimlessly among kids.

Some days Bill held treasure hunts. Set loose among fields and copses, we collected colored strings, leaves, clovers, bubble-gum comics, and candy wrappers as per instruction sheets. Soon Bill decided such games could be regular alternatives to sports. "We're going to make you happy yet, Richie boy," he announced, and the kids around him mocked, "Richie boy. . . ."

The most popular activity became "Hares and Hounds." In this event, a team called the Hares (with its counselors) set out across Central Park, drawing chalk arrows on the pavement to signify their actual direction (but also, as camouflage, sending scouts along other roads to leave false arrow trails). After giving the Hares a fifteen-minute head start (counted by the counselor with his wristwatch), the Hounds had to track and catch them and, if there was time, become Hares and hide.

As Hares we would cross the park rapidly, seeking unfamiliar regions, hurrying through tunnels and playgrounds, across the shadow of Cleopatra's Needle, sending scouts to entice the Hounds to dead ends—trails with no more arrows suddenly!

As Hounds we would follow the markings on pavement, dispatching our own scouts to check secondary trails and report back, running to make up ground. Our counselors took these hunts seriously and discussed strategy with the older kids. They were concerned never to be done in by the same counselors who had tricked them before. "Remember the time those pricks crossed that meadow," Freddie said to Wally.

"Do I remember it? I'm going to put those jackasses in a corral and throw away the key. They break the fartin' rules every time."

Once, we spent a whole day looking for the Hares while our counselor cursed and kicked the dust wherever the arrows took us. Every trail, it seemed, led to a dead end or to taunting crisscrosses pointing every which way.

They had hidden in the weather castle on the lake (the path to which we had discounted as an obvious false trail). A custodian, not realizing they were Hares, invited the group for a tour of the equipment, and cookies and milk. Then we suffered the indignity of being hunted down by howling Hares. "Not fair!" we shouted. "You can't go indoors."

They led us to their hiding place. We visited the necromancer's chamber, together this time. With its spinning globes and glowing dials, in my imagination this castle made the winds and rain; its keepers, standing over maps and drums, decided when to send snow through the City.

Late afternoons counselors acted out stories about "the olden days." Bill-Dave Group was founded by a hero named Ranger, but almost from the beginning, he was duped and sabotaged by the Bully. Throughout each episode, as Ranger turned the tables and got sweet revenge, we made faces and cheered his feats. The Bully sniggered away, but he'd be back.

These were lazy, priceless times. I lay with the others in a fort of rock, my eyes on a horizon of buildings. Raptly following the account, I laughed at imitation voices and joined the cheering or moaning at each turn of plot.

At the end of the day a short, round counselor named Bert would drive everyone home while taunting us and giving disgusting accounts of war mutilations, severed arms and penises and other deformities. "You want to talk blood and guts," he serenaded. "I'll give ya blood and guts." He described Japanese and Korean torturers, how they drove stakes through victims' eyes and held them under dripping faucets. Sometimes we convinced him to shut up and put an outer-space adventure on the radio. As our vehicle swerved through traffic, eerie music sent rockets zooming to other worlds. One by one, to hoots and various distortions of our names, we hopped out at apartment buildings.

At home on TV I turned on "Howdy Doody," then the puppets "Kukla, Fran, and Ollie." Daddy knew someone on the show, and he brought home a rubber Ollie dragon I wore on my hand. After Jonny got a Kukla clown, we staged our own performances from behind a living-room table.

I was also loyal to "Flash Gordon," who commanded a rocket ship and fought space battalions. His journeys took him to covens of regal and rhinoceroid creatures, forests of fluorescent snakes and sapphire fruits. Night after night in suspense, I followed his escapades. Then Flash got imprisoned in an acid shower on some sinister world and was pounding the door, screaming to get out. There was a similar story on "The Cisco Kid" in which Indians wrapped a good guy in poisoned blankets. These coverlets were killing him, as he shook violently to get free.

It seemed that an enemy could douse my blankets too. How would I know? Some nights, I kicked my blankets down the sheets, unable to get that squirming man out of my mind. Other nights the threat seemed to come from my own body—my fingers changed shape and size, my feet dwindling to far beyond my torso. Inside my lips and up my arms I felt thick, chalky water pulled as by a magnet. I lay suspended in this trance, testing its boundaries, aware that if I moved abruptly it would go away.

Once, I stayed there long enough that my existence snapped into electricity against a black night. Not only did I feel its sparks, I saw their filaments around me. I struggled to move even a finger. My mind tried to get free, but I didn't regain movement until suddenly I did. Then it was as if it had never happened. Nanny didn't know about these things. Neither did Mommy.

During winter, dusk came early. Bill-Dave kids were beans wrapped in sweaters and overcoats. Our wagon skidded on snowy streets as we squealed and threw our bodies against one another. On cold sunny days we stayed outdoors, sledding, building forts, staging snowball wars that seemed to last a lifetime.

I felt like a soldier in an ancient battle of ice. We had to fight our way sector by sector around the rear of an opposing army, gain high ground among rocks, store enough ammunition (piles of hard snow-balls), and charge their positions, heaving our bullets down on them as they scattered.

Sometimes, though, we were surprised from the flank. Snow was stuffed down our collars and backs. We sought shelter from any bush or tree.

Finally the glow of evening called truce. Then we trooped through the Park, our mittens caked with ice, our bodies throbbing, frost in our pants . . . past the Museum, past the chestnut man, into wagons, home.

On blizzardy or rainy days, we went indoors to any of a variety of sites: a drafty court where we heaved a basketball at chains, the

Metropolitan Museum of Art with its somber suits of armor and mummies, a Planetarium where we could read our weights on the Moon and Mars, the Penny Arcade (handed $2 each in a package of dimes), a roller rink, the uptown Y. . . .

I can remember working my way around the wooden circle of the rink, dodging other skaters, going fast then slow, fast then slow, lumbering toward openings with imagined acceleration, passing through hot and cold drafts, collecting ball-bearings from the floor as piped music replayed yet another same polka . . . waiting for the endless day to end.

At the Museum we chased one another through catacombs and tombs, making werewolf faces and dramatic moans (while kings, queens, and hieroglyphs watched imperiously). Other days, we went in an adjacent door and took our seats in a round theater, a mounted robot in its center.

Celestial music began. The ceiling darkened into New York skyline, then an imaginary starry night. Not only was this a great adventure; it evoked the oldest mystery at my heart. Soaring into outer space, we landed on a Martian desert (the narrator describing its small red sun—two tiny moons rising at nightfall). Afterwards we plunged through Saturn's rings en route to frigid Mimas.

Mean kids and bullies at group enforced a code with sticks and stings from pea shooters. The only antidote to being challenged was to be a spastic (a "spazz!") or a baby. My small size and wet pants qualified me, so I mostly wasn't called on to fight. Instead I was shoved against the side of the wagon as everyone crammed for the best seats. Someone stuck gum on my shirt. A bigger kid elbowed me and then turned away, pretending not to notice ("Geez, I don't know who would have done a dumbo thing like that!"). At cartoons the same kid ordered me out of my chair to go further back. Amused by such antics, the counselors never intervened.

The wish to retaliate smoldered in me. One time, I did swing back, provoking real punches. "Oh, the baby wants to fight!" my tormentor goaded as everyone else went, "Woo-woo." He put up his boxing stance and socked my chest hard. They laughed, made faces, and sang:

> *"Richie is a friend of mine.*
> *He resembles Frankenstein."*

"You think that's funny!" I cried, jabbing at him.

"Harty-har-har!" he countered, slapping my fist away and knocking me in the face while, on cue, they finished their rhyme:

> *"When he does the Irish jig,*
> *he resembles Porky Pig."*

It was better to set anonymous traps. I wedged pencils into seats so they stabbed my enemies. I stole their toy rings, puzzles, and packs of gum. I put rotted food and dirt in their lunch boxes. There was a special delight in watching a prank unfold with absolutely no way I could be found out. I grinned in malevolent innocence.

Hunger was paramount at Bill-Dave. I longed to have money for the ice cream truck, the chestnut man, the pretzel vendor. Rows of nuts and nougats sat in store windows by the magazines, their familiar yet indescribable smells cascading into the street.... Mounds, Oh Henry!, Spearmint Leaves, Butterfinger, Mallow Cup, Clark Bar, Hershey's Krackle, Goobers, Cherry and Grape gums. Each bore some essence of hunger and was capable of filling me with its familiar gist. All afternoon I wanted to bite into their sweetness, every morsel.

Mallow Cups had a sweet, sticky vanilla cream in their hard rippled chocolate. Mounds were soft with sugary coconut. Almond Joys were Mounds with nuts imbedded on top. Butterfingers had a crunchy nougat inside their chocolate, an orangey caramel. Mars Bars held a mocha nutty goo.

The comic names of these foods never struck me as meaning anything else. They were words denoting the fixed universe of particular tastes—Jujifruits, Chunky, Snickers. These stood in their rows in shops, each bar a wrapped replica. I would think a long time about which one to get. Did I want the nuts in the Almond Joy or just plain coconut? I tested each imagined taste in my mind dozens of times before deciding.

Large vending machines flanked the Y's atrium, some with apples, some with ice-cream cups, others with sandwiches. Chlorine from a pool we never saw scented the space. Echoes came from balconies beyond.

We went upstairs to our assigned room, piled our coats on a table, and lined up for games.

I fantasized chocolate-covered peanuts, coated marshmallow bars, black-cherry popsicles, as we played "Snatch the Club" and "Telephone," all of us crammed in, Turkish carpets cushioning walls, pigeons dormant against one gloomy, rain-streaked, dust-streaked window, soot dripping and blowing about the alley. It was as though hunger and sadness ran in a stream together because hunger was so deep it could never be filled and sadness was so faraway I could never understand it.

We raced across the room, twisting and dodging. Light of chandeliers and clatter of play kerned a spell. We sniggered as nonsense syllables came out the end of our whispered chains.

The Y made me sad to the depths of my being.

One day of heavy sleet we went on a tour of the Tastee Bread factory. Everyone was given a shiny white pack of bread, warm from vats of dough. By the time we got home I had only three slices left at the bottom of the wrapper.

Fear remained my closest companion, unconnected either to family strife or daydreaming. It was the dungeon stairs, the hospital, the invisible executioners—and something else again. It was the color of light, the persistence of morning, afternoon, and nightfall, one after another, those same streets, shop windows, shop insides, day after day, hour by hour, relentless, profound—these people, this family, our carpets and furniture, plates and cups, meal after meal, the sound of the carpet sweeper, these same rooms, the rattling elevator up and down and up and down, the black front door. No single thing was that disturbing, but all these things together, unbroken and unending as light seeped and changed, dividing day from night, night from morning, were a march into oblivion.

I woke shivering in the middle of a sleep and staggered into their room, willing to ask even them for help, their husks heaped in murk, Daddy snoring. Alarmed by me standing there whimpering, Mommy jumped out of bed, put on a bathrobe, and hastened me down the hall, turning on lights as we went.

She opened a wooden cabinet and found unfamiliar objects. Out of an ornamental bottle she poured a wee glass of brandy. I didn't want to drink it, but she helped my hand and the bitter gave me such a jolt I stopped shaking and sat down. She was so relieved she began laughing. She laughed so hard tears ran down her face.

I wanted to stay with her there in the light forever.

There was an evening I turned the faucet for my bath and watched water surge out of it against the luster of the tub.

Suddenly it came.

Not the gush—its force, if anything, was elating. It was the sheer fact of being there at all, naked, in relief against white, white stone.

I let out a scream.

My mother and Nanny came running. They looked about in bewilderment. I felt filaments of ice in my belly. I was being blown apart.

"What happened?" my mother shouted.

"I don't know! I don't know!" A word commanded my mind. It was the only one powerful enough. "I have cancer," I said. I didn't want to claim any association with the name. Speaking the word broke a terrible taboo, but the thing inside me was even worse.

"Stop that this instant, and tell me what's wrong! If you think I'm going to tolerate this nonsense any longer you've got another thing coming."

They covered me in my bed with blankets ... and slowly it faded.

Mommy surveyed me lying there. I didn't know what to tell her, so I said I would never be okay again.

"Did you ever hear such nonsense?" she asked, turning to Daddy.

"Talk some sense into him," he insisted.

"If you were poor," she said, "you'd have something to be scared of. If you didn't know where your next meal was coming from, if you didn't know where you were going to live the next day.... You do a million and one things any child would give his right arm for and you're too selfish to appreciate it. How can anyone be so self-centered?"

I tried to say something about how difficult it was at group. I didn't believe that was the cause, but I wanted her to stop.

"Why don't you run away if you hate it so much here? We pay good money for Bill-Dave."

"I was trying to think of a reason."

"Well, I'll give you one: You want attention. You enjoy upsetting me."

"No."

"Don't call me a liar."

Then I heard it again, this time on the victrola—Eddie Fisher singing, *"Oh my Papa...."*

It was as though I recognized the dirge from another lifetime.

"To me he was so wonderful / To me he was so good."

"Wonderful"? "Good"? That's what the words said, but in their tune they betrayed something so eerie and remote it could not be thought.

In the spring at lunchtime I joined a few boys from my class who were also in Bill-Dave. We met three blocks up Madison outside Jessie's "Jip Joint." There we spent our allowances on M&M's, peanut butter crackers, and chocolate bars with letters imprinted in their thin squares, plus occasional toys and tricks, and packs of cards.

Inside of Jessie's we crammed ourselves among bubble gum, old rubber balls, and waxed syrups—packed shelves and cabinets at every level and in every corner. It smelled like hundreds of unopened boxes of puzzles and treats. Our allowances were hardly adequate to such a cornucopia, so we stole from other kids' bankbooks. I took six whole quarters and a fifty-cent piece out of a girl's desk and bought a magical light bulb (that needed only a penny at its base to turn it on). I presented it at Show and Tell, but it wouldn't light, which prompted Miss Tighe to call Jessie and demand he stop cheating children.

In the crowd at Jessie's I attached myself to a red-haired, heavily freckled kid named Phil who was livelier and also goofier than anyone else. He could dart around, stop short, and twist the other way so fast that no one ever caught him. Phil didn't fight much, but when he did, he was surprisingly effective, his quickness making up for size. He was great at faking punches one way and then sneaking a real one in under an opponent's guard. "Made you look!" he shouted.

I could never imitate that, though I tried a lesser version with Jonny.

By hanging around with Phil, I became a member of his clique. In fact, I became his closest sidekick, like Tonto on "The Lone Ranger."

Phil called our club "Throw your lunch in the garbage can." We'd come running out of class at the bell, charge for the nearest city container, open our lunch boxes, and artfully dump their contents into its circumference. We all had similar combinations of white bread and cheese, or peanut butter and jelly, a raw vegetable, perhaps a few cookies worth rescuing. Phil took particular pleasure in splattering a "squushy" tomato against the wire. Sometimes he tossed his cheese high in the air and called out, "Velveeta!" right as it hit the sidewalk.

I received a small allowance, a dime a day, for a snack, but Mommy told me to buy only raisins, never candy. That's what I said I did when she questioned me. I never told her about the club, and I lied about candy. She was uncanny at learning the truth. One day she announced to Daddy at dinner that I was destroying my insides with junk.

I sat there in astonishment, imagining my guts rotting, fearing a summons of Dr. Hitzig—plus a twinge of regret at her picturing innocent raisins while I was betraying her.

At a hint of warm weather in March, Phil brought out a Spaldeen rubber ball. I stabbed at his first throw, dropped it, then heaved it back as best I could. We repeated this ritual many times, as he raced and made leaping grabs.

"Like this," he said, demonstrating how not to throw like a girl. Then he winked and gestured for me to throw it almost opposite where he was. I tried, but it went sideways, rolling down the street.

He tore after it, stopped it on the run, and brought it back. "Up high," he pointed, using his funniest cowboy voice.

I aimed it straight and away from him; he sped down the sidewalk, leaped, caught it, and threw himself unnecessarily onto the hood of a parked car.

Phil was in charge of our whole gang, so we eyed him for instructions. If our cadre at Bill-Dave was winding home in a straight line he would signal a sudden detour past Cleopatra's Needle. We would surge behind him in a screeching circuit. In the tunnel we would answer his howls with our own, kids pretending to be Indians pretending to be animals.

One day Herbie brought a magnifying glass and incinerated ants in the yard. I was amazed at such a feat. When Phil handed the voodoo lens to me in turn, everyone shouted to get the spider. I shifted in obedience and held the glass there. Ambling along, suddenly it scurried, curled, and melted, squirming in a stream of smoke while my friends cheered. Then Billy burned the wings off a fly. For weeks I kept thinking how sad, that poor spider just walking along.

When we went to Phil's house on 91st he sassed his parents (mostly under his breath). His mother called out, "Hello." Phil said, "Hello, ma'am" and then, in a whisper to us, ". . . idiotbrain."

One day, as we poured from the elevator into his apartment, his father intercepted him for introductions to adult company. "Good to meet you," Phil greeted each one, courteously shaking hands. Then he turned to each of us and began shaking our hands: "Good to meet you, Bobby. Good to meet you, Al. Good to meet you, Richie. Haven't I seen you somewhere before?" We galloped into his room for games and comics.

Phil had a collection of Bugs Bunny, Porky Pig, Mickey Mouse, Tubby and Little Lulu, and piles of the best Donald Ducks and Uncle Scrooges. I would grab a stack and shuffle through them, looking for ones I hadn't read. I had seen Bugs and Elmer wrapped to a post with Indians around them, Bugs slicing carrots into a piggy bank (yes), Woody Woodpecker drilling holes and setting funnels in them to catch raindrops (I first had to check inside, but then I remembered), Mickey giving a bath to a yelping Pluto while water splashed all about (a zillion times), Donald raiding a fat red piggy bank that belonged to Huey, Louie, and Dewey (uh huh), Unca Donald who'd rather be boiled in prune oil than crochet to get rid of his nightmares (a longtime favorite), Tubby and Lulu mere eyes in the dark (well worth reading again). Finally here was a new one: Porky carrying Bugs as a little baby in order to get into the theater. The sign beside the blonde cashier said, "Babes in Arms, Free." I set it aside and hastened to find another.

It was a Sunday afternoon's treat to lie there in a group against the furniture, silently reading and exchanging, gorging cookies and ice cream. There was something about the images that made it impossible not to follow them, mesmerized. They were so clean, simple, bright. The trees were bushy, the carrot slices orange, the lightning jagged bright, Donald's eyes so large, his aura so orange-yellow, the snow so white and bumpy—then "Yeek! A Lasso!"

I picked out "Donald Duck in the Golden Helmet."

Donald the museum guard leaned against a statue marked "Prehistoric Cow"; beside him on stilts was an "Old Viking Ship." Next frame, there was the Headless Horseman's toupee, Godiva's laundry bag, the God of Gab. Page by page the story unfolded—an old map with a bit of shoreline, a ship at sea, an iceberg, Crash!, black sky, green waves. Donald's dream bubble had him sitting on the throne, "King of North America: The Viking Kid"; Olaf the Blue's gold helmet rested snugly on his head. Lawyer Sharky—a dog dressed as a sleazy man with bifocals—was after the helmet too; he represented Azure Blue, eldest descendant of Olaf, claiming North America under a 792 law of Charlemagne. I laughed out loud; Phil looked over.

"I'd give the State of California for a hamburger," a famished Donald told Lawyer Sharky.

"I'd give the state of my underpants for your elixir," Phil intoned, grabbing Al's dish of ice cream.

"Hey," snapped Al, grabbing it back.

Phil had a collection of water guns and rifles. We'd choose our weapons—the rifles contended for because they had greater range and didn't require numerous refills at the faucet—and then have a wholescale war, dashing about the room. Nothing like that could ever happen at my house—soaked pillows as shields, hot hisses from light bulbs, everyone shoving at the sink.

The kids in our club collected Flash Gordon cards, a nickel pack a day so as to have enough change left to eat. These were outer-space landscapes and alien court interiors. I valued my set more than anything I had, and I would let other people look at the cards only if I was shuffling through them with my own hands.

Phil said that since Jessie, the stubby, growling proprietor who looked like Iggy from "Little Lulu," was a crook, it was okay to steal from him. In the commotion around the counter Phil had no trouble making off with several packs right from under Jessie's supposed hawk eye.

One day our leader announced he was going to steal a whole box. We waited outside for him, expecting this to be a bluff, but after an interminable period he appeared, clutching the treasure under his shirt: a whole box with dozens of unopened packs. We spent lunch period tearing open our booty and dividing it. Of course, Phil got to choose the best ones.

In the spring we switched to baseball. Phil not only was the short-stop and best hitter, he already knew the names of players on the real teams. Suddenly it was as though Flash Gordon didn't exist.

I preferred planetary landscapes, but the baseball faces were so special to everyone else that gradually I began to collect them too. The men were not as vivid to me as the symbols, the Tiger or Cub in the corner of the card, and the colored backgrounds. I sorted them primarily as reds, oranges, yellows, blues.

We spent hours playing for each others' in games. We would "flip"— the first person putting down heads and tails by dropping his cards in slow spins and the second trying to match the combination on the ground—the cards themselves at stake.

It was a suspenseful business, watching a yellow Gene Woodling or red-orange Turk Lown dance in the air, picture and back flashing alternately, one of which would appear on the ground and determine the winner. If someone put down four tails, that was hard to match. Three tails and a head gave some room for error. If I got to within one card of matching, I was giddy watching the final one spin. When it came up right, I collected the whole jackpot, gathering the cards up, squeezing them into a cube and wrapping them under their rubber band.

There was another game in which, with the flick of a wrist, we sailed cards up to and against a wall in a rotation of two or more players. Anyone who landed a card on another got his own one back and also kept the one he "covered."

Card after card traveled with our distinctive spins. We stared intently as they floated over the landscape of cards, either missing or coming suspensefully close. A perfect shot would cover a good chunk of a card on the ground. Others were too tantalizing to judge.

We would kneel on the ground in serious adjudication afterwards, trying to figure out if certain cards were actually touching or just missing.

During punchball games in the school yard at lunch Phil placed me in the outfield. I was dubious but actually caught the fading Spaldeen after it hit off the high fence above the wall, scattering pigeons. People cheered because such a catch counted and turned a homer into an out. I also grabbed one on a bounce and threw it to a kid who tagged a runner out. At bat, I punched at it and set it skipping along the ground. Phil shoved me so hard toward the wall (first base) that I stumbled, but the ball rolled away, and I got all the way to the pile of coats at second.

That Saturday Daddy responded to my report by driving Jonny and me downtown to his account called Miller's. He bought gloves for us, plus hardballs with knitted seams and a yellow bat. Then he took us to the Park on Sunday. We found a big open area. There he swung my arms with the bat to demonstrate correct form, then lobbed pitches to me.

Gradually I smacked the ball more sharply and further; my brother ran after my hits and brought them back. After Jon's turn with a bat Daddy set both of us at a distance and floated the ball high in the air, calling out my name. To my surprise I turned the right way and caught it. "You're a natural!" he shouted.

Almost as soon as he said that, I developed new abilities. I thought, like Phil, I could run down anything, so I played with abandon, grabbing the ball in the tip of the glove while tumbling, clutching it as I was reaching over my head. "A real natural!" Only the day before I had been lunging and missing in the school yard. How these things were suddenly possible I hardly knew.

Nothing before had been as much fun as baseball. I began playing as often as I could—at school, at group, on weekends. I loved running fullspeed and pulling a hit out of the sky, then shifting my feet and snaring a hard ground ball backhanded.

In class I created a new fantasy that was to last for years. It began with friendly aliens who came to the bedroom window and called me into the courtyard. From there, they transported me to a field. Then they brought down a spherical spaceship as big as city blocks and gave it to me. I pressed its button and shot up into the sky. Earth dwindled against the stars.

I zoomed to Mars (which was uninhabited). Then I changed to longer needle-like engines and blasted out of the Solar System, rocking my desk gently to simulate acceleration.

I was always a step ahead of the plot with dangers and predica-
ments for which I had no ready solutions. With my invincible ship,
there were endless adventures and, as I thought them up, their worlds
became more compelling than school or group.

I took along imagined cohorts, but never Phil and my real friends.
That would have been ridiculous. I picked other people, like Joyce who
drew Donald Duck so well, the girl whose money I stole, Andy because
he had a cute smile and I liked his name, and Joey because I wished
he was my friend during a crime-and-punishment game at his birthday. They made up my crew.

To escape atomic war our group searched for another solar system
with Earthlike planets. We settled there, built houses, befriended and
named strange animals, made up laws, scouted river valleys, invented
a whole civilization. Like Peter Pan we never got older.

Since mere day-to-day life, even on other worlds, became tedious, I
created interlopers with their own terrific machines. Just when our
plight with them seemed hopeless we would discover new powers in
our vehicle or in the resources of our planet.

Every so often we would flee further into the universe.

Traveling at speeds beyond Flash Gordon's and keeping mental
records of landscapes and creatures I discovered, I saw which worlds
had life and experienced how much empty space I crossed to get to
them. My vehicle moved rapidly but not instantaneously. I could always
imagine more space. Sometimes I would spend ten minutes or more
supplying the energy in my head, propelling myself, observing the
minute details of suns and comets as I invented them.

The "tale" was with me for all the years of childhood. In some part
of my mind I knew the condition of our ship and the present map of
the universe, plus the backlog of planets we had visited and colonized;
I could always pick up where I had left off or redo a sequence. In versions months apart I would reformulate the setting in which the outer-
space visitors contacted me, though I never had them return. I also
reenacted our original hair-raising escape many times, mushroom
clouds exploding, parts of buildings flying about like bullets, saving
each startled member of my crew one by one—our great, fiery blasting off ... tearing through Earth's atmosphere toward the stars.

It was comforting to look around the classroom every now and then and imagine these unaware people accompanying me across the heavens. I would reconnect to the story on the van at group or lying in bed waiting to fall asleep.

Rain whipped across a valley of phosphorescent trees. Hedgehogs bounced alongside—our telepathic allies. I called to Andy and Jill to help me. They brought wood from the ribbony forest. Joey had taken the ship and gone back to Earth to rescue Jimmy. The Snellems were searching on the other side of an enormous ocean. Soon their warships would be drawing near.

At night in bed I dug deeper into the covers, as I kindled us into being. Mumby the hedgehog arrived with a message. Andy hurried to interpret it. "Dnt-duh-duh," went the music in my mind. I was checking star-maps in case we had to escape.

Mommy became pregnant again and stayed in bed for months. Finally she left for the hospital and returned with a baby sister named Deborah. It was May of 1952. Our family moved to a bigger place across the hall, 6B overlooking the thoroughfare of 96th Street. Jon and I still shared a room, and there was a nursery behind the kitchen for the baby.

Nanny did not come with us. I heard my mother telling someone on the phone that she was a traitor. She had opened Mommy's mail and spied, even as I was then, from behind closed doors.

I missed Nanny, but I was relieved. Her macabre landscape faded, though its skeleton lingered and, in her absence, grew more profound over the years. Only when she was long gone did I realize she had invoked haunted kingdoms and witches without naming them. Long after I barely remembered her the feelings she inculcated became part of me. She was not only a crone like the one in "Little Lulu" but a denizen of the dungeon itself.

A few weeks later we walked to the corner of 96th and Fifth and met a young pretty lady named Bridey. The wind whipped our jackets and blew newspapers by like racing cars. Bridey held a little hat on with her hand, and Jon and I bounced a ball to keep warm, as she answered my mother's questions in her funny brogue. She was soon hired as Debby's nurse and moved in with us.

Baseball grew in importance and became my counterweight to panics and fears. From the day I took Gil McDougald off a blue card to be my favorite player, I was a pledged Yankee fan. Phil was a Yankee fan too, and I joined him in what grew into a pact of deep loyalty. Mel Allen's voice called us into a greater world: "That ball is going, going, gone!" Such an elating power—the home run that ended discourse in pure sound.

Now, in addition to my daydreams, there was a history of games unfolding. I listened to them on the radio and read box scores in the morning papers.

Uncle Paul bought me Yankee books, and I acquainted myself with past seasons, from when they were called the Highlanders to the eras of Babe Ruth, Herb Pennock, Bill Dickey, Waite Hoyt, Joe Gordon, and Old Reliable, Tommy Henrich. None of these players were still around. Newcomers Allie Reynolds and Vic Raschi now pitched; Yogi Berra was their catcher. They were fighting the Indians for first place, the same Indians they had battled unsuccessfully in 1948. Casey Stengel was the manager. A savvy oldtimer who had never been successful with other teams, he had surprised the world by leading the Yanks to the pennant in 1949 when they beat the Red Sox in the last two games of the season to win by a single game. Rookie of the Year in 1951, Gil McDougald hit a grand slam in the World Series.

The Yankees marked the opening to a world as primeval as the Egyptian tombs and as complex as Jessie's Jip Joint.

At home I made up my own games. I would divide cards into nine-man teams, set one into fielding positions on the carpet, the other into a batting order, make one of my "doubles" the "ball," and play nine innings, with the team of cards at bat swatting the "ball." An out was when the "ball" landed on another card or near an infielder (from where I could toss it onto a part of the first baseman card—or fail for an error). Players took on distinct personalities, as regions of rug became sectors of a grass diamond, the bureaus their bleachers. Few pleasures exceeded the feeling of a seemingly solid hit floating across my room and landing smack on an outfielder's card for an out.

The Major League games on the radio were suspenseful daily rituals. I hurried upstairs from the wagon, heart beating, to catch their endings (sometimes Bert put the game on, but he was a Dodger fan).

A victory by the Yankees would wash out all other sadnesses and disappointments from the day.

Rare games were on Channel 11. They provided occasions to walk down Park to Phil's building and watch with him. We sat in his living room absorbed, from pregame home run contests to postgame interviews.

All through that season of '52 I zealously listened on the radio. Daddy joined me and even put some energy into pulling for the Yanks. He bought Jonny and me Yankee caps and full pin-striped uniforms. He also pulled an old Philco, a red plastic box with a huge battery, from the back of a closet, and I carried it around the house and on walks, trying not to miss an inning.

I don't remember exactly when, but it seemed within a matter of months in 1952 I knew every Yankee and his batting average and home runs.

During spare moments at Bill-Dave (and even whispered in class at school) we played the "Initials" game: L.D., outfielder, Indians?; P.S., second-base, Athletics?; A.S., pitcher, Yankees? (We would never miss a Yankee no matter how obscure.) J.O., infielder, Pirates? Though not a Yankee, Johnny O'Brien was Phil's favorite, the player he imagined and announced himself as, going into the hole at shortstop, making the throw to get the force play with his brother Eddie at second. Neither O'Brien was as good as Phil.

On weekends we'd play in the street, slinging a hardball back and forth, making leaping catches against cars and awnings and calling out plays and players. I tried to claim second base for my position because Gil McDougald played there, but I was better at fly balls, so I ended up in the outfield. I felt reckless pleasure in my Yankee flannels, running across the grass, trapping the ball, relaying it back to Phil. In a game against Leo Mayer I made a running backhanded catch with men on base, and Bill himself ran to my position to shake my hand and call me "a true son of Ranger." Back at the bench Phil quickly reminded me that his specialties—stopping grounders and switch-hitting—were the really hard skills.

On the way home my best friend and I would sit together in the Bill-Dave wagon pretending we were Mel Allen and Jim Woods announcing the innings, complete with introductions, disclaimers, and Ballantine beer ads. We would go pitch by pitch: "Reynolds winds, checks second; now he comes to the plate ... swung on...."

We also had a great rendition of Lou Gehrig's famous speech. I'd speak it, and Phil would do the echoes:

"I consider myself—"

"... consider myself—"

"... the luckiest man—"

"... iest man—"

"... on the face of the earth—"

"... face of the earth."

Then we applauded wildly, other kids joining in. It seemed strange that, when he spoke those happy words to a full house at Yankee Stadium, Lou Gehrig was dying of a terrible disease—strange too that we echoed them so lightly, taking on the role of the doomed man. Yet I felt a sense of honor and importance—and a chill down my spine— as I performed them. It was the most important speech I knew.

3

UNCLE PAUL

I arrived at Miss Hazel's second grade way behind. I couldn't write all the letters and didn't know how to carry over columns in addition and subtraction (I did those problems as if there were no carrying over). I also made puddles. Miss Hazel sat me apart with newspapers under my desk. Close to a wall, I took books off shelves and looked at pictures while the others worked.

On the day of the seventh game of the World Series I felt sleepy, so I was taken to the nurse's office and sent home in a school car. Bridey helped me change into PJs. Under the covers I hugged my pillow, dozing into and out of sleep.

I awoke with a start in the seventh inning. The bases were loaded with Dodgers. As Bob Kuzava came in from the bullpen, I took out his card and reviewed his career. The whole season was on the line, a strange pitcher throwing to the powerful Dodgers.

Then Billy Martin made a lunging catch of a second straight pop-up to end the inning. I cheered out loud.

"Home sick, are you?" laughed Bridey. Ramon, the elevator man, had told her I was playing World Series hookey.

I wore my Yankee pinstripes into the fall at Bill-Dave, my overcoat on top of them, refusing to play soccer or football, holding my glove and ball, willing to have a catch even in the snow. Despite Phil's coaxing and the insistence of Bill and the other counselors, I never gave my loyalty to another sport.

One afternoon the principal called Mommy in for a conference. I learned later he had said that I was either brain-damaged or mentally ill. He required an exam if I were to remain at P.S. 6.

What I remember is a day of no school and a trip downtown in a taxi with my mother—sportive but ominous. We walked around a corner and entered a hospital-like structure. A doctor led me inside, but, to my relief, he didn't ask me to take off my clothes or even have an examining table. Instead we sat on opposite sides of a desk while he set before me a sequence of mazes and puzzles. When I finished more or less solving these he reached into his drawer for a box and, one by one, put down large cards I had to interpret. Then he selected a page of twisted shapes he asked me to sort. I sensed this all had to do with misbehavior, but it was also a game.

I looked at pictures of people peeking around doors, of weird cloud houses and groups of men and women and, as requested, made up their stories and said who I'd go out with and who I wouldn't. I studied a necklace of different colors and shapes of beads, memorized their positions and later restrung them. "Perfect," the doctor acclaimed. "Hardly anyone gets them all." I emerged triumphant and immediately described my success to Mommy.

In the session after lunch, there were no games. I was asked to lie on a cot. A nurse taped wires to my head. I lay there alone, my life revealed in a dense code the stylus translated onto a drum. I hoped my nightmares wouldn't be seen.

Many years later I learned that the tests showed I was normal but emotionally disturbed. At the time Mommy merely said I would be seeing another doctor. Initially I complained because she had scheduled it on my birthday and it didn't sound like much fun. "Sure it will be fun. Remember how much you enjoyed the puzzles and beads."

She took me on my eighth birthday, November 3rd, 1952, on a bus further downtown than I had ever gone. We walked along old-fashioned streets and turned into a seemingly random gate. We found ourselves in a foyer with fancy chairs, New Yorker magazines piled on a table. I read cartoons. Finally a door opened; the doctor gestured me in. Mommy kissed me and left.

It was a ground-floor flat, bookshelves up to its ceilings. A window facing Seventh Street revealed a girl skipping rope; a man strapped to another building washed windows.

The doctor's name was Abraham Fabian. He was tall and resembled Abraham Lincoln. I sat in a chair across from him and, in answer to his questions, gradually warmed to tell him about school, group, and my family. He was cordial and attentive, so I soon confided the thing that excited me most that afternoon: my Uncle Paul was taking me out afterwards. When I exited the office, sure enough Uncle Paul was large as life, reading a magazine. He threw out his arms and greeted me with a big hug. "Richard my boy," he exclaimed. Then he walked over and said hello to Dr. Fabian as though they were old friends.

"Have a good birthday," Dr. Fabian called, as we pushed through the metal door.

Outside, we hailed a cab to Al Schacht's Restaurant. The driver tore uptown in a river of greens, swerved onto a sidestreet, and screeched to a stop.

A doorman led us into an amazing baseball house. Staircase railings were made of bats and balls, and all the choices on the menu were puns on players' names, like Dizzy Trout, Ty Corn on the Cobb, and Yogi Berries. I got a fruit cocktail on ice and was picking out sweet cherries when two tall men in suits joined our table. In answer to Uncle Paul's seemingly silly question, I insisted that I didn't know these fellows. "Sure, you do," he kept saying as I shook my head.

Then he threw up his arms and declared with chagrin, "Why, I was told you knew all the New York Yankees. This is first-baseman Joe Collins and catcher Charlie Silvera." My heart skipped, and I stared again. They were real, the very faces from the cards, dressed in suits and ties. No one I knew had ever had dinner with one of them.

The room was a bustle of activity. I sat watching balancing feats of waiters, meals sailing out of the kitchen. People came up to shake hands with Uncle Paul and his Yankee friends.

The players were large, like cowboys, and they and Uncle Paul talked to each other throughout the meal, never mentioning baseball. Al Schacht, who himself was once a pitcher, pulled up a chair and told jokes. After a while the Yankees began to laugh. Then Mr. Schacht rose to greet a cake of baseball decorations and candles. He led the singing of "Happy Birthday," which even Charlie Silvera and Joe Collins participated in, gazing at me with big grins. I couldn't wait to get to school the next day to tell Phil.

After my first time at Dr. Fabian's I was brought there twice a week by a graduate student from Columbia named Neil. Rescued from the after-school crowd beside the wagon, I pranced alongside my new companion. These were happy journeys through the tunnel beneath Lexington Avenue. Neil bought me science-fiction comics, shared his nickels in candy machines, and played "Initials" and "Geography" (with the last letters of places forming the first letters of other places you had to supply). If we were early, he took me to a nearby cafeteria, ordered desserts, and bought puzzle books. We would sit on adjacent stools connecting numbered dots and solving paradoxes ("What's wrong with this picture?" "Well, the clock has three hands, the table is missing a leg, the dog has the back legs of a rabbit...."). He liked to tease me about baseball, saying I was in love with it. In his challenge of that, he invented a game of him saying words that had nothing to do with baseball and me making up a baseball story about each of them. His first two were stumpers: "paradise" and "florist."

He sat in the waiting room when I went inside. Afterwards, if there was time, he asked Dr. Fabian questions about his own school. Then he took me on the subway home.

Dr. Fabian became the major figure in my life. He never said precisely who he was to me or what his job was, but I understood he was my appointed ally. He reviewed and corrected my arithmetic and spelling, going over the identifying features of parallelograms and trapezoids. Sympathetic about the teasing at school and outraged about my being blamed for fights with Jonny, he was particularly interested to hear about Nanny. Unfortunately, I could remember virtually nothing.

We played War with a deck of cards and Hangman on a piece of paper. He also taught me the game Battleship—a duel of hiding and "shooting" ships by guessing coordinates in grids we drew—and then how to fold sheets of paper into boats and little flat balls that blew up with a single puff.

We used part of each meeting for me to tell him about what had happened to me since I last saw him. I kept him up-to-date on my mother, school, group, Jonny, my fears, and how often I wet both my pants and my bed. He asked very direct questions like, "What do you think at the moment you are wetting?" and "What do you feel when your mother takes Jonny's side?" I was often stumped and silent, but he drew responses by asking me to say the first thing I thought, no matter what it was, and then the thing after that, and so on. These chains of words, like those in the game of Telephone, would lead us in the most unlikely directions, through fairy tales, movies, puns, jokes, advertising rhymes, and just plain nonsense.

After a few sessions Dr. Fabian explained that the true causes of my fears were written out in such a code. "The things you can't tell yourself directly you let dreams and unconscious actions speak. Once you learn what these are, they can no longer harm you."

This was unexpected and bizarre. To me, danger was (as Flash Gordon knew) . . . danger. When someone said, "Down the dungeon stairs with you, into the dark, forever," he meant "down the dungeon stairs." "He" was someone to be fled, resisted. Cancer was cancer, a killer; everyone knew that. Polio was the name of another terrible event. You could hear it in the very word, pretending to be "polo," then tricking you with that evil "i."

"No," Dr. Fabian insisted, "these are threats you've made up to hide other things you don't want to know, that you can't face." He promised that dreams and free connecting would lead us to those things. "What will surprise you is that, as horrible as the things you fear are, they frighten you less than other things you won't face. What will surprise you even more is that when you know those things, both they and your fears will evaporate." He smiled broadly, and I thought of my record called "What Makes Rain" in which gleeful little droplets are converted by the sun into clouds and sing happily as they fall back onto the earth into thirsty flowers, rivers, and seas.

But how could I keep such important secrets from myself? Where inside me would I hide them?

"In wet pants," Dr. Fabian said, "in your daydreams, and in fears themselves."

That made no sense at all.

And why *wouldn't* I tell myself everything? It seemed absurd that some person inside me would conceal things only to my detriment. Finding our way through this subterfuge was a game I was quite willing to play.

In the first dream we studied, I was arranging a chemistry set. The flask suddenly cracked in my hands. I was running down the hall to throw it in the toilet bowl, but I was too late: a burning yellow liquid spilled through my fingers onto me. That, he told me, was urine. Nanny's warnings about infecting myself with my own pee had led me to transform it into an acid I failed to dispose of in time. "This dream by itself doesn't answer the big question," he explained, "but along with others it tells us many important things. Already we know there's a relationship between your wetting and your fear of poisons, but where is your mother? Obviously your anger at her has some place in this too. And what about Nanny?"

I was delighted by his clever deciphering and tested it again and again in my mind. Perhaps I didn't understand its subtlety, but I grasped its simple, raw essence. In fact, I grasped it so profoundly that a part of my life thereafter became interpreting events with symbols as my clues.

I came to see, nothing was what it initially appeared to be. Everything had an edge or an unnoted quality about it. Dr. Fabian was a collector of such shadows.

On a naive level I understood that the urgency of "burning liquid" had nothing to do with chemicals. It was the urgency of my fear of the dungeon—the link between that and my wetting. Both occurred in darkness of sleep prior to dream. Both were beyond my control. By placing a chemistry set in a dream I was trying to gain control over darkness. I couldn't conceive such a connection while awake, but the dream spoke it unmistakably. To everyone's surprise, soon after this discovery my daytime wetting stopped, confirming Dr. Fabian's method.

Week by week a larger dream landscape unfolded. Bob the mean counselor from Swago represented Daddy. My mother was concealed as a giant wounded bird. My brother was a scruffy, black dog who clamped his teeth onto my arm so that I couldn't pull it away. Dr. Fabian was flattered to find himself a magician, then even the General Manager of the Yankees.

From the long line of volumes on his shelf I understood that Dr. Fabian was a kind of spokesman for a man whose name I misread as Dr. Freund because there was a brass plate with that name on the outside of our apartment building. "He lives downstairs from us," I told him.

"Dr. Freud does?"

I nodded.

He didn't correct me.

One day Dr. Fabian asked me an ordinary question about Daddy. When I answered, he startled me by his contrary response. "No, I mean your real father."

I considered this for a while. Was it a trick?

No, not the way he asked it. I grinned playfully and said, "Daddy is Daddy. Don't you know, Bob Towers?" He had never met Daddy, so anything was possible; yet it hardly seemed like a misunderstanding he would have.

"Not Bob Towers. Don't you know Bob Towers isn't your father?"

I shook my head. This game made me goofy. I thought, "Martha Towers, Richard Towers, Jonathan, Deborah. Not my father?"

"I think you know who your father is."

I shrugged and made a funny face. Then I sorted back through my memories until I was drawn to the Easter egg in the bush. I looked at the face of the one who had rehid it. I felt a shock of recognition. He couldn't be just an uncle—this man with the Yankees, who sang with me at the Penny Arcade.... "Uncle Paul?"

"Right. Paul is your father. I asked you because I wanted to see if you knew."

I pondered his claim for a moment. Did I really know, or was it just a lucky guess? Even as I wondered that, I found myself drifting among fragments of near-forgotten memories. Could my mother have really once been married to Uncle Paul?

"Yes, you were their child. Bob is Jonny's father," he continued. "That's why he treats him better than you and why Uncle Paul takes you out alone. Your mother tried to keep him out of your life. But he loved you so much he kept coming, even against her wishes."

I felt daunted by such devotion.

"He's the reason you see me. He found me and pays for me. Your mother would never permit it."

Then he explained how, after the tests at the hospital showed I needed to go to a doctor, my mother decided to get Uncle Paul involved. "Before she learned you were sick she was very jealous of your father. She wanted you for herself. But once you were damaged goods she didn't mind if they shared you."

Revelation upon revelation!

Dr. Fabian had unmasked my father partly because he wanted me to spend more time with him. From then on, Uncle Paul planned an evening together every several months. His phone call announcing the occasion was more glorious than a birthday. "Richard," he would say in his big voice, as if he had just discovered me, "how'd you like to get together?"

"Yay!"

My mother would get me dressed and send me in a cab to the Plaza where he stayed. The hotel had furnished lobbies, massive chandeliers, silent elevators, and decorated, aromatic hallways. I marched through hallways, flaunting confidence. My father met me at the door to his suite.

We ordered dinner by room service. I could choose anything I wanted. I usually had steak or liver and onion rings, pie with ice cream for dessert.

Afterwards, we went out on the town, returning often to the Penny Arcade where we played air hockey and raced each other in imitation cars against landscapes that rolled by on drums.

Once, he took me to the Silver Skates at Madison Square Garden. At the start of the long-distance race he told me to keep my eyes on a contestant he sponsored named Ray Blum. His skater, wearing a blue and white jersey with the name "Grossinger" diagonally across it, dropped behind and stayed in last, even as the contestants entered the final laps. I felt sorry for him. "You watch," Uncle Paul cheered me with a knowing grin. "Ray always saves his run till it counts." I was sure he was wrong; yet almost as he said that, Blum began to pick up speed. He caught the other skaters one by one. We cheered together as he ate up ground in great strides, streaking past the leaders as if they were standing still.

Usually my outings with my father were planned in advance, but on three occasions he surprised me by showing up at P.S. 6 after school. The first time we met the Governor at a cocktail party, then went across the Bridge to the Newark Airport for dinner. They served a dazzling dessert: coconut ice cream balls carried through the dark with sparklers.

After that adventure I looked for Uncle Paul beside the Bill-Dave wagon every day. At times I rushed toward him among crowds of parents, but it was just another fat man.

Then on an afternoon I had forgotten to look he was talking to Bill by the wagon. He hugged me and shouted at a cab. Downtown we attended a rehearsal with Eddie Fisher, after which we dined at a restaurant which had large figures of carved ice around a buffet.

My father was an enigma. While he was grand and important, smelling of perfume and outfitted in the fanciest suits I had ever seen (his initials everywhere), he moved so awkwardly people bumped into him and he was often tongue-tied. When he did speak, he addressed me in baby language. In fact, with his huge belly and soft, round face, he resembled Babe Ruth. Though he had both his eyes, I was astonished to find out that he had lost total sight in one. "A kid shot me with a beebee," he said with somewhat surprising irritation over something that had happened when he was even younger than me.

In the course of our visits he always quizzed me about school work and my family and asked repeatedly whether my behavior was improving. "That's not what I hear from your mother!" he would retort with a wave of a finger. But he'd chuckle.

We'd talk about the Yankees and baseball. He often had inside scoops from the players themselves. If I pressed him too much, he acted as though he were guarding top-secret information and changed the subject. He preferred to describe his own hotel: swimming pools, eighteen holes of golf, skating, and a dining room that could hold ten Plaza dining rooms. He mentioned his wife Aunt Bunny and my brothers Michael and James. "You three will raise some hell!"

I didn't plan on that, but I was dying to meet them.

Though Uncle Paul barely listened to what I said, he was sententiously reassuring, promising that between him and his friend Dr. Fabian all my problems, including my fears, would soon be solved. He had such a warmth and generosity that I wanted to be with him always and I was teary in the cab going home (though he always handed me far too much money for the fare and told me to keep the change). I would return to icy stares from everyone, even Jonny and Bridey. It was as though I had been consorting with a convict. My seeming willingness to "be bought" was further proof of my selfishness and disloyalty.

On holidays Daddy got his Mercury from the garage and took the whole family, Bridey included, three hours through the countryside to the Nevele. The sight of trees and houses put Jon and me in a delighted trance. We raced and tumbled about the lobby and jostled each other as we waited to check in.

Our room smelled like a museum; it had metal beds and a singing radiator. We slept under heaps of covers. In the morning we followed our parents to the dining room; folded cloth napkins made goblets into tall birds beside stacks of hot breakfast rolls and cakes.

The Nevele was Daddy's biggest account and, as the first order of business, he led us into the back room to say hello to Uncle Ben and Aunt Marian, the owners. The space was smoky and crowded, people crouched over ledgers. Like the operator of a Western saloon Aunt Marian rose to greet us with strong handshakes. She gave Mommy a long, concerned hug. "How are you, Martha dear?" Her booming husky voice carried so many nuances. She was a dangerous lady— Daddy's boss, Mommy's confidante, a rival of Uncle Paul. In her presence Mommy acted meek and seemed about to cry.

"She treats me like a dog," she said later to Bridey. "You'd think I was some charity case."

"She acts like Queen Elizabeth," Bridey agreed. "Someone should knock her off her high horse."

All week my brother and I played in reeds where minnows darted; occasional sunnies tantalized—fish too swift to touch. We staged apple fights, climbed small trees, and collected horse chestnuts and rubber molds of cartoon characters from the pottery studio. Then we hiked to Nevele Falls. Eleven school teachers had discovered this site in the woods; the hotel name spelled their number backwards. I loved to watch the water as it roared down rocks and exploded in whirlpools. Jon and I threw sticks and bark into the fast-moving stream.

Back at Ivy's Store we bought puzzle books and baseball newspapers and lay in the lobby reading while Daddy took forever finishing his meeting with Aunt Marian. In a tall red chair under a mirror Bridey wrote to her family in perfect fountain-pen script.

She told us she came from a land where there was fighting and that's why she was with us. We accepted such history as surely as our game board of the Civil War with its bearded faces. It was sad, her having to be away from her sisters and beloved nephews, Margaret and Siobhan, Patrick and Jimmy. She awaited their letters (with foreign stamps) and, after reading them slowly and sometimes tearily, told us about their achievements in the much stricter schools over there.

Yet Bridey was delighted to be in America, and our steak dinners and vacation trips made up a bit for her exile in our mayhem. She wore floral scents, and on Saturday nights policemen rang our doorbell to take her to dances in the Bronx. Jon and I danced around her, teased her, loved her like a second mother, and included her in our prayers at night ("God bless Mom, Dad, Jonny, Deb, Bridey ... "). Gradually, she became part of us, this stranger from *"the place where the dark morn sweeps down to the sea."* She learned our secrets and was sucked into our cabal.

Jon and I commanded a whole repertoire of games, some chummy, others fiercely fought. Part of our life together was deciding which one to play in an empty time. We went from rambunctious sports to shooting galleries to board games, always on the verge of war yet equally in collaboration.

Our mainstay was sockball. With a tennis racquet as our bat, socks tightly wound as our ball, one of us who was the pitcher lobbed it in. The batter aimed for spots in our room.

Singles were drives that bounced uncaught off a thin hollow canopy around the far ceiling. They had to be smacked hard and aimed well. Doubles landed on either Jon's or my bed. Almost always rebounds off walls, they stayed on the bed, and no diving fielder was allowed to dislodge them.

A clean catch, even a rebound, resulted in a double play, though a catch off the canopy simply negated a single into an out.

A waste-paper can placed before the radiator in "deep" center was a perfect triple. One never aimed for triples. They were accidents. To see a sock bounce off the wall delicately into the can was like spotting a four-leaf clover.

The leftfield window had a glass guard set against it at a forty-five-degree angle. Inside it was a home run, either on a soft lob or a carom off a wall. A lob might be defended by a leap, with the ball sometimes accidentally batted down into a double. However, there was one perfect arc, just over the pitcher, soft enough so it didn't bounce off the window back past the guard. The home run was the gentlest shot of all.

Mommy detested sockball and came to recognize its distinctive sound from afar. She charged in, grabbing the racquet away. She thought baseball belonged outdoors, but, more notably, she believed socks were for wearing, not hitting, and she was convinced they went out the window, even though it was shut tight. Because of sockball she never discovered that socks just disappear, like turtles, without explanation. In fact, hers was a self-fulfilling concern because, after she suggested the idea to us, we occasionally opened the window a little bit behind the guard to add drama to home runs. There was a garbage can on 96th Street and, if one of us put it in that, you got credit for winning ten games. Needless to say, it never happened, though, true to form, Phil took up the challenge and landed one so close to it we were amazed. It was special anyway to run to the window to watch a home run sail out of sight and then spot it down on the street. Sometimes a person from below looked up. We interrupted the inning to take the elevator to the street to collect it. Ramon was not amused by the extra summonses, but contrary to Mommy's belief, no one wanted our socks, and we never lost a one.

We set up cowboys and Indians along the end of the hall where there was no carpet and rolled a marble back and forth, trying to knock over each other's warriors. A perfect shot could ricochet one into another and topple two or more. As the field became emptier, the angles more difficult, we frantically rolled back and forth, aiming at the last men, chasing the marble down the hall and around the corner. Sometimes we included farm animals and knights and gave extra points for getting the marble up the ramp into the castle.

We staged epic rubberband fights, ducking behind furniture and firing with our favorite weapons. Mine was a porcelain statue of a stalking tiger I won at skeeball. I strung my "bullets" around its mouth and aimed for Jon's butt along its nose. We sometimes had a free-for-all before bedtime. It was a great pajamas sport, rolling on the rug, pulling our bottoms back up to each other's taunts—and hurried attempts to hit bare bohunkus. When our stockpiles ran out, we collected different colored shots from all over the room and returned them to the ammunition bag.

Other games aroused the grudges and strife that lay just beneath the surface. Jon and I in some sense were born onto opposite teams—deadly opponents like the Union and Confederacy. Sometimes we fought with rubberbands, sometimes with fists, sometimes in currying parental favor.

We seemed to know that finally only one of us could win.

We competed in Chutes and Ladders, Quizkids, and of course Uncle Wiggily's colorful universe. Its board was as intimate to us as our lives, from Wiggily's ramshackle bungalow in the lower lefthand corner—the rheumatoid rabbit setting out with his cane and bag—to Dr. Possum sticking his snouty head out the stone house with the patchwork gray chimney at square 151 in the upper right. In between lay the Skillery-Scallery Alligator with his open jaws, the dreaded Rabbit Hole under the rotted trunk from which ferns grew (back to square 13), the Wibble Wobble Pond (which was either good or bad depending on how far before or after square 60 you drew its yellow card), and the Bad Pipsisewah and Fox Den (I delighted in getting to draw three times in a row when Jon lost two turns).

We competed not so much for fun as from compulsion—to open the board, to see the rigid landscape again, to renew our rivalry. The cards, both white and colored, were utterly familiar. I remember the excitement each time at a drawing 10 or 15, the sinking sensation when Jon got one, the secret pleasure when he fell in the Trap or was sent back to the Bushytail Squirrel Tree after he was almost to Dr. Possum's. No amount of repetition diminished the freshness of those moments. These were the immutable laws—revealed each match—of consciousness itself.

Since each time was different and our personal battle was never resolved, we kept playing, not only Uncle Wiggily but Chutes and Ladders, Sorry, Monopoly—I always with the yellow token, him the red.

I knew his red so well I was reminded of it whenever I saw a bright red toy or picture. Red was a show-off's color—my enemy. I felt a sordid pleasure in knocking red off with a Sorry card just short of Home, then bringing two yellows Home at once with a seven, or watching red slide down the major chute at 87 all the way back to 24—or land on Skeezicks' mouth.

We didn't keep a cumulative score, but my brother and I had a general feeling of who had won more games and who was winning lately. It mattered a great deal; it determined the mood between us, our relative prestige and power. Since the harder games were initially my domain, it was a shock to have him improve and begin to beat me. As he made inroads, he lorded his successes over me.

If I lost, I'd hastily bargain for a new game, all the while trying to maintain a detachment and superiority. Jon liked to savor his victories and prove that I wanted to win as badly as he did. It often took teasing or bribing to get him to play again. "If you win this next one," I'd say, "it counts double."

"I don't care," he'd retort. "I'm champion."

In the summer we returned to the cottage in Long Beach, and Jon and I transferred our tennis-racquet tournament to the front yard, tall bushes serving as home runs. Rolling skeeballs all that July and August, we set our hearts on an electric organ—750 coupons. We came down to a big yellow wall clock that Bridey fancied for the kitchen—only 415.

We also invented a beach game called Ocean Ball, based on home run derbies on TV. We swung fungo at a Spaldeen from a "batting box" of seaweed. Home runs were shots that landed in water of any depth.

As outfielders we guarded the ocean, trying to catch long drives while running through surf. We made (or missed) our catches and then tumbled into waves. Our Philco sat on a blanket in the sand, waiting for Mel Allen (and Ballantine Beer) to introduce the Yanks, a sacred moment.

The Yankees were the one family in which Jon and I were true brothers. Hank Bauer, Phil Rizzuto, and Eddie Lopat were our uncles, Casey Stengel our grandfather. Many afternoons we sat in our room with the Philco, rooting for the home team, Daddy occasionally joining us. Bridey knew the way to our hearts was through baseball, so she would tease us by calling me "Richard McTowers" and Jonny

"Whitey T." (she had a particular fondness for the name Whitey Ford and used it on unlikely occasions). Jon appreciated his nickname and, at its summons, snapped imaginary curve balls for her. We tried to get her even more involved, telling her scores about which she cared little. "It's not an Irish game," she insisted. "And my kinfolk wouldn't want me rooting for Yankees anyway." We thought she sounded hilarious, a character from a fairy tale.

One afternoon Uncle Moe showed up, kneeled down right beside us, and requested an immediate game summary. I told him that Johnny Mize had just missed a pinch homer. Jim Delsing dove into the stands to take it away. Johnny Sain was coming in to pitch.

"Did he buy a ticket?" Uncle Moe asked.

I stared back at him without smiling. This was not a trivial matter, and I was hardly over my disappointment.

"Why, he can't go into the stands without a ticket!"

The third time Uncle Paul showed up after school he grabbed me from behind, as he called out, "Richard the lion-hearted."

I was ecstatic, though I was anything but a lion.

He told the cabbie to make a U-turn and head uptown. We attended a brief business meeting, then caught another cab at rush hour. I thought he was taking me home, but to my delighted shock he said, "Yankee Stadium!" I had seen the Stadium (and the adjacent Polo Grounds) only in the distance from a car. Now the colossus grew larger and larger until it towered over us, banks of lights gleaming against a violet sky. Then we were in the crowd, entering through turnstiles.

We ate dinner at a restaurant right in the ballpark. After that we went to the souvenir stand where Uncle Paul asked me to pick out anything I wanted. There was so much with "Yankees" on it I didn't know where to start. First I got a scorecard and a yearbook. Then I saw a pen-and-pencil set of wooden bats, the pencil the type that you put pieces of lead into; I pointed to that. After Uncle Paul had put down his dollars, I noticed black-and-white glossies of many of the Yankees—Yogi Berra, Mickey Mantle, Gil McDougald, Allie Reynolds. It turned out that twelve came in an envelope—I wanted one of those too. Then Uncle Paul asked the man to throw in an autographed ball and an ice-cream cup. My hands were full as he showed our tickets to an usher. We were led to our seats in the absolute first row behind the home-team dugout.

The lights on the field cast a dream of baseball. Players were warming up so close I sat there transfixed. Then, to my horror, Uncle Paul stood and began calling them. I didn't think they would answer, but Eddie Lopat, the pitcher, jogged over. "What do you think of this weather?" he asked Uncle Paul.

"Colder than a witch's tit," he responded.

I was mortified.

Uncle Paul then coaxed the name of my favorite player—just to hear me say it—for he knew.

I mumbled the answer.

"Well, let's get Gil over here."

"No," I protested, tugging at his sleeve to pull him away, but he was already calling. Finally he got his attention. McDougald jogged from his warm-up, glove in hand, and stood there with us by the railing. He seemed even more radiant than life. My heart was thumping as he asked Paul about his golf game and they talked about holes and shots. This man had both everything and nothing to do with me and didn't even know it. Then I was introduced.

"You play golf too?" Gil McDougald asked.

'Gosh, no,' I thought, but I could hardly mumble an answer. It seemed inappropriate to tell him I played baseball.

Later some friends of Uncle Paul's joined us in the seats behind. "Sorry I couldn't get you any closer," he teased. They laughed and slapped his back. Then all three of them made bets on the game, Paul alone picking the Yankees.

In the eleventh inning Gene Woodling hit one high and far into the lights. I watched the ball disappear against the crowd. Most of the Stadium stood, and the roar grew and grew. I felt excitement all up and down me. This wasn't television; there was no announcer; I was in the Stadium itself!

The men opened their wallets, and each gave a bunch of dollar bills to Uncle Paul. He straightened them into a stack and handed them to me. "Your team won for me," he said.

Then I was put in a cab. Through the swift darkness of the City I stared at an ancient river of lights leading me home.

"The show-off," my mother jeered the next morning. I knew I had been indulged, so it was almost a relief to have her bring things back to normal, to show me the other side of my experience. "Throwing money around, annoying ballplayers at the park where they have to play. What a bigshot he is! Let him have to live with you. Disgust him with your antics. Pee in his bed. Leave him some dripping wet sheets. Then see how much he adores you."

"The man's a sloth," Bob chimed in. "Everything was given to him. He doesn't know how to work for a living. If he weren't giving away free vacations, the players would have him evicted from the park."

"Don't try to talk sense to this kid. He's so gullible he'll believe anything. Just let him be seduced."

"I know, Martha. There's no point in reasoning. He sees what he wants to see."

When I heard this I flushed in anger and shame. I felt exposed in front of them, as though they read my mind. I had betrayed family solidarity. I had violated one of our basic rules by caring for an outsider, by accepting and trusting unwarranted gifts.

"Try the school of hard-knocks for a change," Daddy said, "like the rest of us. No one's out to do you a favor."

"Paul Grossinger was born with a silver spoon," Mommy added. She said he was "a lazy bum, flaunting his parents' wealth."

Daddy compared him to the degenerate kings of England, adding that Aunt Marian had built the Nevele from her own sweat and blood. "No one gave her anything. The man is in the best business of all," he concluded with a flourish, "the inheritance business."

Dr. Fabian likewise was a "no-good son-of-a-bitch who can't hold down a job, a parasite living off other people's money."

They saw these men as my collaborators, enemy agents to whom I was selling family secrets. By contrast *they* were hard-working, devoted parents struggling to pay our bills and teach us the truth about the world.

For hours I sat by the window staring into the flow of activity along 96th Street. There was a random melody to the thoroughfare: teenagers dashing, Puerto Rican women, baby carriages, old men trekking slowly from horizon to horizon, trucks and taxis, horns, every now and then a train bursting up from the tunnel. It held me in a kind of static contemplation beyond a sense of my existence.

Part of me saw my parents' side: I *was* out for myself, even at their expense. Their home was real. Uncle Paul was a cartoon.

My mother tried to reestablish her authority over Dr. Fabian by sending away for a booklet advertised in the *Daily News:* "How to Conquer Your Fears." It was a cute stapled pamphlet with cartoons illustrating individual fears. Each one had a prescribed number of points. Starting with the lowest-rated one, you strove to achieve a better score over weeks by mastering one fear at a time. The highest number was "Fear of Failure," fifty points' worth. I didn't have that one. By comparison, fear of disease was only five. There were also fears I had never heard of, for instance, the fear of being buried alive. That was close to poisoned blankets, and it led me to think about coffins and ghouls. I told my mother not only that the pamphlet scared me but that I knew from Dr. Fabian it wasn't the way you got rid of fears. "The reasons are unconscious," I explained to her. "You can't just tell them to go away."

She was infuriated. "It helps thousands of people but not him," she shouted to no one in particular. "After all, he's not like the rest of us; he's special."

In truth, no one else seemed to act as though Dr. Fabian's symbols existed—not my teacher, not the Bill-Dave counselors, none of my aunts or uncles. Yet over time the power of these codes shot fissures through a world that had seemed sealed by nature.

The unconscious was not obscure at all, not a winged monkey or Indian nickel; it was everywhere I looked. Peeing was not peeing, poison was not poison, and even fear was not fear. The bullies at school and group, who seemed to rule the universe, actually controlled nothing; they didn't even know who they were. P.S. 6 and Bill-Dave were not the monoliths I had imagined, and my mother was no longer either a monster and a tyrant or a compassionate, devoted woman, under attack by ungrateful children; she was trapped in her own fears and doubts, more sphinx than harpy. And Jonny was no hero; he was just as frightened as me. My mission was knowing they all had these secrets of which they were unaware.

Yes, I was behind in class and mean to my brother, but I was a symbol explorer and interpreter of dreams.

I was still in the watchtower, but I was acquiring the tools of a wizard.

Mommy and Daddy grew so self-righteous about their opinion that they made their own appointment with Dr. Fabian. I couldn't imagine what would happen, but I hoped he would convince them. After all, he was the acme of wisdom and good sense. Apparently, they never gave him a chance; the whole time they lambasted him for encouraging insolence in children. Daddy even smashed a lamp while gesturing angrily. "I told Fabian to send me the bill," he recounted later. "The sonofabitch!—he could afford it." When Dr. Fabian related this event to me I was astonished. How could they have been exposed so blatantly without anything changing?

Eventually Mommy did get one day taken away from my time at Dr. Fabian's. She arranged for me to switch to Hebrew School, a ghastly place called Ramaz. Uncle Paul was no help. Since he ran an important kosher hotel, he insisted his son had to attend a recognized Jewish institution.

Men in yarmulkes taught us the Hebrew alphabet and basic words and lectured us on the State of Israel. We read a primer about a pioneer family on a kibbutz. We were asked to memorize events from the lives of Jewish patriots and recite tales of their prowess against their enemies.

At P.S. 6 I was bashful and silent, cowed by swaggering authority. But Hebrew School seemed fake and ostentatious—like a parody of real school. I thought it was humiliating to be there. Since I had nothing to lose, I openly acted the clown, refusing to learn the grammar and disrupting class.

I said I rooted for the Arabs over the Jews. I asked where the cavemen were in the Garden of Eden. I comically mispronounced lessons and threw in the names of baseball players. Finally I was ordered downstairs to the principal's office. "Good," I announced. "I like him. He's a nice guy." The room erupted in laughter.

One day in the gym before classes began, without even realizing what I was doing (I thought I was trying to run faster than I had ever run before), I put my head down and crashed fullspeed into the wall, knocking myself out. I remember sitting on the floor, dazed and crying from the incredible pain. That was my last day at Ramaz.

I had a break of only a month before they reenrolled me, the Park Avenue Synagogue this time. The setting was grander, but I felt the same hierarchy of elders. My teachers boasted xenophobically. I must have heard a thousand times that Jews "made the deserts bloom," that Jews brought civilization to the Holy Land, that Arabs were criminals. At Purim fair, kids and adults threw darts at posters of Nasser and other Arabs for prizes. I couldn't believe that they would do that.

"Arabs are human beings too," I said.

"They're animals," the teacher sneered.

That solidified my opinion of them. I thought such dumb men could have no authority over me, so I continued to rebel and resist. I folded my yarmulke into a boat. I challenged their interpretations of Bible stories. They would become frantic because they thought I was committing sacrilege in the House of God. "Yankee Stadium is the House of God," I retorted.

The rabbis decided I was incorrigible. They told my mother I was an Anti-Semite. I looked it up in the dictionary and agreed that I was against the language and culture of Judaism.

After that I was required only to attend Saturday services. I abhorred those too: having to hold the prayerbook open, stand and sit with crowds of people, pretend to read along. I despised the collective stink of lotions and sweat, the unacknowledged mood of an ethnic gathering, the pretentious march of the loyal students bearing the Torah. I played games based on page numbers, flipping up the corners to see which digit came in the last position (odds and evens fell on the same side of the book only in synagogue).

Yet I willingly accompanied Daddy to his orthodox schul, which was hieroglyphic and old. There was a science-fiction quality to the metal-encased Torah and the rough-throated ram's horn, the impassioned chanting, which at times seemed out of control. For the same reason I went with Bridey to her church. I was moved by the hauntingness of the hymns. My mother, who had no religious interests, accused me of phony superiority and blamed psychiatry for my disrespectful attitude.

There was also a treat after Daddy's services, for he regularly stopped at a garage on Lexington Avenue to bet on Sunday's baseball games. He'd offer me a Chiclet from his yellow pack while he sat there going over the line, occasionally asking my opinion of the starting pitchers. I kept his faith and never told.

In general, Jonny and I relied on Daddy for fun and activity. He was usually good-natured and got involved in household frays only to defend his pride. While Mommy remained in bed all morning, he took us on Sunday-long outings to parks, his advertising accounts, and the Lower East Side apartment where his mother and father still dwelled, tiny brittle creatures like the spiders Coyote found spinning cloth when he climbed the topless tree into the land of the ancestors. They were apparently friendly but almost motionless, and spoke to us in cautions and prayers. "You see what I came from," Daddy would tell us in the car. "I made it through pure guts and spirit."

Our favorite account of his was a kosher delicatessen near his parents' home. Abe Gellis, the owner, a man who looked like the ringmaster at the circus, would reach into every pocket for stacks of flat cardboard which, when dropped in water, turned into colored sponges with ads for his meats.

We were served roast beef sandwiches made of the pinkest, softest slices layered in the world's largest kaiser rolls covered with poppy seeds, separate plates of fat, crispy french fries, bottles of Dr. Brown's orange ("Do they make a sandwich here, Richard ...?"), while the men smoked and talked business—Daddy's booming voice a blend of story and outrage as he serenaded all in earshot with tales of uptown ("The no-good sons of bitches! Abe, are you listening ...?"), and made the Gellises millionaires times over with his promotional plans. Then he drove through the City singing Jolson and cursing the lazy good-for-nothings he had just courted.

Many Sunday mornings when no citywide trip was planned he took us to Central Park. We picked home plate by a vacant tree, and he pitched while we took turns of ten swings. It felt almost major league to be stinging his overhand tosses or catching the line drives Jonny swatted. As I cut off grounders, Daddy would exclaim, "Gil McDougald couldn't have done it any better!"

Sometimes he orchestrated games, inviting in Puerto Rican kids.

They were dubious at first, but a real match with positions was an attraction they couldn't turn down. Daddy was always the pitcher, balancing the teams by playing harder for the losing side, applauding everyone's plays as he umpired.

This was totally out of character for our family. We never talked to anyone; we crossed the street to avoid walking near the kinds of youths he was summoning and later telling, "Son, with that ability you're going to be in the outfield next to Mickey Mantle in a few years." On the way home, sweaty and fulfilled, we stopped at the drugstore for lemonade on crushed ice.

Soon after my sister Debby was born, Mommy took a job running the New York office of the Fontainebleau Hotel, which was in Miami Beach. The position was offered to her from old Grossinger connections (though it helped that she could say the name in flawless French from her childhood in Paris). She answered the reservation line downtown in an office all day, then from an extension at home in the evening right up to bedtime. Her representation of the Fontainebleau became her life calling. She made the booking of rooms into an art, entertaining guests and engaging in eloquent narratives of gossip and intrigue. She often took dinner in bed just to continue in her phone world.

She and Daddy lived at a breakneck pace, catching their shared cab downtown in the morning, arriving home for dinner exhausted. On weekdays they generally ignored us. They were conspiring a mile a minute against some outsider, or enmeshed in monumental fights. These would spring from tense, suppressed voices in their room; then Mommy would begin shouting. Daddy would come running out, her chasing after him. She threw books, ashtrays, and other objects at him. If the skirmish spilled into the kitchen, she would pick up dishes, silverware, even kitchen knives, once actually wounding him. Yet, as Jonny and I would joke, it was lucky she didn't have much of an arm. He would usually go right to the elevator and disappear, either for hours or days, but, when injured, he locked himself in the bathroom. She brought iodine and bandages to the door and seemed genuinely distraught at the damage she had inflicted (though she resumed yelling as soon as he emerged).

In her office at Fifth Avenue and 57th Street she was a different person, thriving on a flurry of paperwork and ringing lines, rushing between file cabinets and the next patron on "hold." Her voice commanded a five-person suite of rooms.

Over the years the "Fontainebleau" on Fifth Avenue was my favorite place to visit her, for she was convivial and affectionate, more likely to order me a hamburger from downstairs than to harangue me over some truancy. By comparison with the second-rate males banished from "headquarters" to New York, she was shrewd and vivacious—in charge, though (I realized years later) paid a quarter of what they were. I watched their baffled looks as she exchanged ironies and twinkles of the eye with her assistant Helen.

At home, she was a one-woman totalitarian regime with an obsessive retention of wrongs done by others, things she considered insults or demeanments against her. Always either preparing for a crisis or having just overcome a crisis, she would set up shop in bed for such long hours we would forget she was even in the apartment. Then she'd summon me or Jonny or both of us to her room for interrogation, or she'd charge out on a foray, looking for misconduct: a toy left on the floor, a rumor of unfinished food on someone's plate; she'd paw through garbage and crawl along the rug in her bathrobe, collecting evidence—telltale candy wrappers, crumbs, baseball cards. We lived in dread of these outings.

The high crime of treason might have been reserved for me, but at another level, both Jonny and I were both truants, and she attacked us as a pair. We had an automatic alert fixed in our minds at the sound of her approach. We would be lying in bed, talking to each other (against the rules), and suddenly she would burst in with a belt and start beating us through the covers. "Do you realize what time it is? Do you realize?"

The punishment never fit the crime. "There's going to be a pogrom in this house," she would announce; then, with swipes and shoves, order us to pull all our games and cards out of closets and drawers and start "cleaning up," which meant throwing out perfectly good stuff. When we played sockball, we had a drill for hiding the paraphernalia instantly if we heard a certain proximity and sound of footsteps.

One rainy day Jonny and I were behaving so silly in Novack's Market that, outside the fish store, Mommy insisted we remain on the street while she shopped there. In our slickers and galoshes we leaned against the plate-glass window, staring at stacks of what used to be living fish and watching lobsters creep on crushed ice beneath the remains of a giant turtle. Suddenly she burst back out at a tremendous clip without acknowledging us. She sure was angry. It was impossible to keep up with her even to share the umbrella.

We followed her from Madison to Park, then up along Park in increasing sheets of rain. She went into a building on 93rd Street. We made the elevator just before its door closed. Only when she took off her rainhat did we realize we had followed the wrong lady. We hurried the three blocks home and stood outside the door waiting for Ramon to deliver our nemesis. She spanked us both, but the worst part was afterwards when she just stayed in her room crying. It was a dirge for the annihilation of happiness forever.

These episodes stand out as myths, tales to be retold years later. The tendency is to define the tenor of growing up in our family by them. They were obviously memorable, but, if anything, they were comic relief to a dark regime. The real pain formed in the shadows within which we lived, a prevalent sense of gloom and impending disaster, a constant reminder to stop being bad, a dearth of hope that it would ever feel any better.

Punishments and spankings were nothing. They were mere outcroppings of moods and circumstance. Every second we lived we were immersed in this realm, mute and invisible. It filled my senses and thoughts. It was the taste of every meal, the melancholy of every bedtime. It was voices, silent more than spoken, filling my head. It was a demonic profundity that matched every gesture I could make and plummeted as deep as I did.

Living in such a milieu was not just shallow harassment; it was like being abducted to another world, like the whole of nature struggling to be born after a thousand years of winter. And no certainty it ever would.

I wished somehow we could just be friendly to each other, that I could feel happy or safe. But things were far too complicated for that. I couldn't even trust my own feelings, let alone those of the others.

After all, if I didn't love Jonny, why would anyone—wet bed, bad grades, and all—love me?

We were the embodiment of tribunal, revenge, and retribution and, despite fancy demonstrations to the contrary, we were quarantined from all other human beings. We hated everyone.

My mother was the official bearer of doom, but doom was all about us. It was the color of the paint, the taste of Sugar Pops, the sound of "One Enchanted Evening" playing in the living room: *"Once you have found her, never let her go"*—another song that meant not only exactly what it said but exactly what it didn't say.

At unpredictable times Mommy was inundated by feelings of tenderness for us and would address us with almost giddy appreciation. We wanted her to stay that way, but it was too much and without context. She'd tell funny stories and display a remarkable memory of all the good things we ever did. But even as she acted friendly, she was challenging us to doubt her, pleading with us not to make a wrong move because then we would be responsible for the return of winter. Her cheerfulness was so fragile that we never completed an episode without the onset of suspicion. "What's wrong? Isn't this all right? Why won't you tell me?" We knew it couldn't last.

No memory of my mother does her justice because the reality contained layers of intimations of ever more subtle layers. She met us with fierceness and vengeance that had no object, merely a longing to set things right in a condition in which something incredible was expected of all of us that we could never enact ... because at times she was so gay we followed her like the pied piper, this woman who turned men's heads on the street.

She was an actress in a 1940s film, playing a heroine who never found the plot, except that she kept on performing her role because people routinely told her how pretty she was, and she never peeked beneath that script, except to light into these wild beasts she had been ceded by mistake as children. It was as though, while she was awaiting some other resolution, our family had grown up around her. My sense of her is as a mourning big as the sky. All the time I knew her she must have held in her mind a magnificent object, like an inexpressible kaleidoscope of all the songs Irving Berlin ever wrote, one "Easter bonnet/girl that I marry/white Christmas" requiem.

The City was my background planet, its twilights of stone shadows, nights of sparkle and clatter—the epic of the Yankees playing on its marquee.

The life of our family was beads strung on a thread of games, walks in the park, fights between Jonny and me followed by reconciliations. We spent long Monopoly afternoons while rain beat on the window ... buying light blue Connecticut and red Kentucky and building houses on them. There were birthday parties, outings with cousins, dinners at Daddy's accounts where the owner came and joined us for a chat. At the table we all told stories from the week. Mine tended to be ironical and downbeat (Daddy called me droll); Jon was almost always triumphant, or outraged if anything went less than perfectly. Debby was quite goofy even as a baby. Daddy would entertain us with the menu, offering insightful comments on our choices and eating styles: "Martha, the way those three attack a basket of rolls you'd think they were just let out of jail." He'd chuckle good-naturedly. "Hey, guys, this fella here loves a saltstick too. Save a couple."

Sunday nights everyone watched Roy Rogers on TV. Pat Brady kicked his jeep. Jon and I chuckled, and Daddy let out a loud laugh: "They know how to entertain, son of a gun!" Then came The Ed Sullivan Show. Eddie Fisher sang, and Mommy was transfixed in delight. When the music announced Daddy's favorite Hebrew ballad, he began first, so Eddie Fisher seemed to join *him* in midstream.

Later, during my bath, I would gather six or seven boats from the hamper and set them in the water with me. As I pulled my body away, displacement set them moving. There was a tugboat and a motorless motorboat, a submarine that half-floated, half-sank, an ocean liner and its lifeboat which raced separately, and my favorite, a sailboat missing its sail which I called *The African Queen* after the movie.

In the opening heat the first one to reach the other end of the bathtub was the winner. Boats would "stick" together and separate; some would move forward for a bit and then drift back. I was not supposed to affect the outcome; yet, as I slid around under them, their whole arrangement shifted, for I was a geography of islands and tides.

Light shone in soapy water as I began the fourth heat, the one in which the winning boat had to touch the drain and then return to start.

Only craft that had contacted the metal circle were in the running and needed to be kept track of.

Over the months, new entrants came and went—canoes and houseboats and barges—but *The African Queen,* paintless and rotted, stayed and held all the records.

I remember outings on the Staten Island Ferry: the rumble of its motor, exploding foam under us, a retinue of white gulls, Manhattan becoming a planet in the distance. Mommy sat with her eyes closed, her silver cardboard reflector open, trying to capture every ember of warmth.

I remember Daddy leading us in prayers as we lit the Hanukah candles: *"Vitzyvanoo, lihadlik nair. ..."* Then he told the story of the Maccabees and their mysterious lantern that ran out of oil but kept burning. We spun dreidels with letters of the Hebrew alphabet. Till bedtime I lay with Jonathan on the floor, watching wax collect in colored piles on the menorah as we bet on which candle would go out first.

For Christmas vacation we drove to the Nevele, my brother and sister wrapped in blankets beside me in the back seat, asleep. My forehead pressed against cold glass, I stared out into the Martian darkness, picturing the alien towns we passed, and tall, slender skaters on the Red Planet's canals. I bundled myself deeper and deeper as I turned us into a chariot and sailed beside Wynken, Blynken, and Nod.

4

CAMP CHIPINAW

The summer after we met as father and son, Uncle Paul decided that I should go to a camp near him, a place known as Chipinaw. Since I had told him about my troubles at Swago, he assured me that no such things would happen. "I'm going to have a bear in the woods looking out for you. If you don't have a great summer," he swore, "he'll spit in the owner's eye."

I smiled stoically.

"And then maybe after camp you'll come and stay with me."

The bear was hardly convincing, but the thought of visiting his hotel was so exciting I agreed to go to camp first. On my suggestion, Uncle Paul and I made up a code (to prevent any counselor from spying on our phone conversations): if I asked him to tell me the names of the moons of any of the planets he would know something was wrong and would come and get me. When I bemoaned missing a whole summer of the Yankees, he promised to get me my own portable radio.

Bridey took me to Rappaport's on the West Side to be measured for the entire red and gray Chipinaw outfit: pants, T shirts, sweatclothes. This was the most exhaustive fitting I had ever undergone. Shirts and shorts piled up atop counters in hills. The performing salesman kept directing me back onto the stool with jokes at which I refused to laugh.

"Why do you have to be so sullen?" Bridey snapped as we walked to the bus stop. "He was such a cheerful chap."

But what did Bridey know about these matters except that she thought he was handsome? It was too much activity, too much focus on my body until I ached and my eyes burned.

A week after second grade ended, Mommy took me in a taxi downtown to the Port Authority where the Chipinaw-bound bus was loading. In a bustle of departing children I kissed her cheek and burrowed aboard into the first empty seat by the window. With a series of war whoops, echoed throughout the bus, the driver made a big turn and headed back uptown. I tried not to get carsick as I watched unknown parts of the city turn old, then to country. Though I didn't take the peanut butter and jelly they handed out, I dozed off, imagining how the grape might have tasted.

I was awakened by everyone singing. At first I didn't understand. They went: *"Ninety-eight bottles of beer on the wall, ninety-eight bottles of beer. If one of those bottles should happen to fall, ninety-seven bottles of beer on the wall."* Eventually I caught on and, as countryside whizzed by, I was one of only three who lasted till *"zero bottles of beer on the wall, zero bottles of beer...."* It was late afternoon when tires crunched into a gravelly lot. "Last stop, Chipinaw," shouted a rising counselor. "We're taking no prisoners, so everyone, alley oop!" We filed into air ripe with buzzing things. The smell was of weeds and manure.

Exuberant counselors sorted us. I was in the youngest group, the Midgets. We were marched across the road downhill to one of four adjoining bunks located in the quadrants of a large cabin. Our individual beds jutted out from the walls—at their heads, cubby-shelves stretching high beyond our reach.

Already in the bunk was a whole new set of parents and kids. I was pulled aside by a giant, perfumed woman who told me she was my Aunt Ruthie. "Here he is," she called out. "I found Richie." She clamped onto my hand and towed me to her son.

Jay had been well coached because he took me right under his wing, leading me from camper to camper: "Artie, this is my cousin Richie." I shook hands. "Barry, I want you to meet my cousin Richie." Then to me, "Barry's my best friend, so you're in with us."

"Hey, Schwartzie, you see this kid here. Well, lay off 'cause he's my cousin, and Barry and I'll kill ya."

Jay was the largest kid I had ever seen, and he made me feel safe. He had a reassuring rubbery smell and a commanding presence. In fact, he was like an adult, shaking hands, initiating hugs of greeting with other campers, organizing matches of Chinese checkers and Stoopball.

Our counselor, Larry, was almost as friendly as Dr. Fabian. He helped me change my sheets and arrange my cubbies, and he coined an identity for our group—we were more than just Midgets: we were the "famous five," and we got our own private nicknames (mine was Sparky) plus special stories at bedtime.

Every day, at the second bugle (the first being the dream-curdling reveille), the whole of Chipinaw lined up in a semi-circle for personal inspection and then flag-raising to the sound of another bugle.

As we hiked to the mess hall in fog, wet grass clung to our sneakers; oatmeal-cocoa steam wafted over us. Waiters brought out industrial bowls filled with sections of orange, jugs of milk, and platters of pancakes and eggs. Since I hated soggy foods and all forms of egg or milk (perhaps from the days of Nanny's leftovers in my milk), I surprised my bunkmates by consuming Rice Krispies straight from the box.

"Gad, he eats them dry."

"That's okay," Larry joked. "Sparky's a horse."

I made a meal out of orange sections, two bowls of cereal, and most of the bread basket.

After breakfast we cleaned our bunks for inspection, then went to the first activity. This varied from day to day. Some mornings we sat in the crafts shop, learning to make wallets and lariats by rotating and tying multicolored plastic strips into box and diamond stitches or molding cups and statuettes out of clay. I loved selecting and cutting bright yellow, orange, and red lengths from the long rolls, and knitting them in different-patterned snakes. Equally magical were the mud figures that turned to stone. Other periods we were assigned to archery, softball, nature, volleyball, and boating, and, after the flag-lowering and dinner, we engaged in freewheeling games like Snatch the Club and Color Tag.

Fragrances of new-mown grass and flowering trees worked their transformation. Thunderstorms passed so close we lay in a blackened canopy of sound. No activities—only Chinese checkers, comics, and Rafter Ball ... Mickey Mouse riding as a ghost on a black horse ... blue night, yellow moon, white clouds. Out the windows came bursts of light; then answering rumbles toppled across Chipinaw. We giggled and threw ourselves on one another, feigning terror.

In the damp undergrowth afterwards, we collected salamanders, plucking soft, wriggling bodies from ferns and dropping them into coffee cans. We transported these to the nature shack, where they were set in a glass terrarium.

Columns of pre-breakfast "spread-eagles" trekking along hillsides, collecting stray wrappers, bottle caps, and bits of foil into garbage bags . . . punching the pocket of my glove and backing up as Jay swung (weeds and moss dividing outfield from trees) . . . thirsty lines at the one cold drinking fountain . . . waiters streaming through swinging doors . . . and then the Midgets' march, the vault of starry heavens after late cartoons—Swago had come and gone in an eternal moment—Chipinaw was profound and real. My toes wriggling in anonymous dirt and dead moths, the gurgle of a rusty shower on my back, I felt camp spreading throughout my being.

Without sounds of traffic, it was hard to sleep, but when the crickets converged, I fell into their directionless call.

The forest primeval was our backdrop. For someone from the city the depth of wilderness was overwhelming. Everywhere the mowed fields ended, woods began with their denizens: clustering ferns, lichens on bark, critters under stones (centipedes and snakes that appeared suddenly, their quick movement ending in camouflage). We investigated these realms with the nature counselor.

His shack was a mournful, spooky place, reminding me of Bert's war stories, smelling like an infirmary but with a faint animal odor, a scent of mineral slime. Frogs were gassed and, still throbbing, turned over on their backbones, their bellies slit to reveal innards and beating guts. Snakes caught by campers summers ago lay dormant in cages or were dried-out skins hung on the walls. Other relics included stuffed skunks and squirrels, pinned butterflies, fish skeletons, and a bear claw. Next to the shack was a cistern of standing water so green and dirty it seemed to drain to the bottom of the earth.

Chipinaw remains an indelible mandala: a mess hall at the top of its hill beside a flagpole and O.D. shack (the letters, I later learned, standing for "On Duty"). Twin rows of bunks ran along the forest, an avenue of tents for older kids to one side, the infirmary behind them (where we lined up every Friday for Aunt Mary to wash our hair, pouring her green antiseptic and running a quick warm hose, grasshoppers and beetles scurrying, my eyes riveted shut). Ballfields, rifle range, archery targets, tennis courts, and stables lay across a narrow road.

In the opposite direction at the end of a dirt path down a wooded slope lay a giant lake. We hiked there single file—moccasins and bathrobes required—towels about our necks. It is a journey I take in dreams. The forest is far denser now, no longer uninhabited. I leave the trail and explore. I discover all sorts of indigenous people: *t'ai chi* masters warming up next to builders of solar yurts taking measurements, dowsers with willow twigs beside slabs of glowing quartz, ginseng and shiitake collectors in Mongolian robes. Their dwellings are wind and rain phenomena, bare facsimiles of huts and cabins. Deeper in are caves to antediluvian worlds, passes over cliffs to captured asteroids, massive amethysts in clusters. None of this did I suspect in childhood. I saw only pine cones amid leaves and dry needles, blueberry bushes, and, once, an orange said to have been left by the Cropsey Maniac, the mythical madman loose somewhere in these woods.

Toward the foot of the hill the first outpost was the swimming counselors' tent. Then came a wooden bathhouse overlooking a cat-tail marsh and a dock area colorfully demarcated into boats at anchor and zones of water, shallow to deep. We were expected to get into still-damp bathing suits and gather in assigned spots. My flesh crawled; my lips felt as though they were daubed in the powdery white that came off the paint.

Midgets populated the shallows and were taught to swim. Beyond, splashes of competitive water sports combined with a medley of shouts and whistles from older boys. I danced in the water, picking up stones with my toes and drawing bubbles with my arms and legs.

We were soon arranged by skill within the territories formed by rows of wooden "eggs" strung together (called lemon lines). I was the only one in the Midgets who didn't progress. I thrashed about, satisfied to pretend while the more precocious of my bunkmates graduated to the intermediate and even into the deep end. It didn't bother me particularly, for not-being-able was who I was. I wasn't a swimmer; I was a puddle creature.

Crows flew from tree to tree along shoreline; darning needles buzzed over lily pads; frogs hopped where you least expected them. Other camps were visible, some of them proximate as stagesets—their landscapes dotted with silhouettes of people doing activities paralleling ours—some mere spots on the horizon. These neighboring realms were also audible as faint recoils of bugles and loudspeakers.

At sea in rowboats we looked down through opacity and saw sunnies hanging, an occasional fleeting turtle or tadpole. It was a spooky darkness, portending the immensity in which one would drown if he fell. Yet it was pregnant with a possibility of life forms: mysterious splashes, giant submerged logs like dragons. If we passed a vessel from another camp, we stared at its occupants in awe as if they spoke a different language. The counselors, like Indian scouts, might greet one another.

An uninhabited stretch of nearby shore was called Pine Cove. There we traveled by canoe for an overnight. The nature counselor, leading the way with his fancy hatchet, instructed us to collect wood and twigs. As these were piled in stacks, he built a fire around the log he had hewed; then he roasted hot dogs and corn in cans. By bedtime the log was disintegrating with a whine. The forest changed from sight to sound, and small animals could be heard running along the pine needles and leaves.

Huddled around the fire, we were told episodes of the Cropsey Maniac, hiding somewhere in these woods. Cut up real bad in a mill accident, his body had been sewn back together by incompetent doctors. Now he prowled the forest, seeking revenge.

As sparks rushed upward into the stars, I invoked the habitable planets I knew and imagined my ship hurtling at tremendous speed through the void. But mostly the bigness overwhelmed me, and I bowed to dizziness and white light.

Even as part of me became a compliant camper, another part rebelled. I preferred to run through unmown fields by the stables, sometimes trying to catch grasshoppers before they flew up. If they jumped, I chased to where they landed, held their rickety beings for a moment. Beside horses and straw, a hose siphoned into a rusty barrel. From puddles formed by its overflow, I rescued flies and other insects by floating leaves to them. Once these creatures started to crawl onto dry ground I tore away from their revival. Such moments of solitude were rare, and usually a counselor came to fetch me back to the activity from which I had wandered off.

I looked forward to rainy-day Rafter Ball in which we flipped a Spaldeen onto the central wood beam in the bunk and counted the bounces as single, double, triple, home run. It took great skill (and luck) to get anything more than one bounce on the narrow board (though once it actually rolled to a stop for an alternate version of a homer).

I also loved the twilight gambol of Color Tag in which a blind-folded counselor would call out a color and everyone wearing that color would have to run between poles without being caught by the other team.

I played many seasons of Roofball, most of them by myself. In this game a Spaldeen was tossed onto a bunk, and it was either caught on the rebound for an out or it landed and then bounced (single . . . double . . . triple . . . home run . . . depending on how long it took to chase it down). The ball could be angled high so that it came back as a long fly ball, or one could attempt to fool oneself (or an opponent) with spins, recoils off pipes sticking through the roof, rolls along seams, or even innocent sequences of bounces that either just hit or just missed the front lip at the last moment.

I learned the bumps and crevasses of the various bunks and used them as different home fields. Counselors would announce a required activity, but I would be camouflaged between the back of a bunk and the woods. The grass was long, the weeds often wet from dew. "McDougald into the hole . . . fields . . . throws . . . gets him!" I would toss it as high as I could, then back up like an outfielder against a wall, coil, and leap at the edge of the forest to meet the apogee of the ball's arc off the roof, stealing a home run and falling into moist foliage. "There's a long drive . . . Mitchell back . . . that ball is going . . . going. . . ."

Sometimes they forgot to look for me, and I played Roofball through a whole period.

I made up another solitaire game in which I would stand at the downhill edge of a long hangar-like building (called "the armory") and hit a ball fungo as far as I could. Over the hedge in front of the girls' dining room was a homer; before the hedge was a triple. Up to the end of the armory was a double. Past the midpoint of the stairs was a single. After each round of swings (depending on how many balls I had) I would retrieve my shots from all over the field. That's when I announced the game to myself, filling the line-up with Yankee subs and farmhands whom I wanted in the major leagues, and playing people in odd positions (Don Bollweg at first, Mickey Mantle at shortstop, Kal Segrist at third). "Gil McDougald leading off. Early Wynn winds and fires. It's a drive down the leftfield line. He turns at first and holds. Now catcher Charlie Silvera." Sweat pouring in my eyes, in the distance I would hear echoes of faraway camp events.

Keeping my game alive on an abandoned field made me real. I set my ritual and separation against the vastness of the landscape. After completing five innings, batter by batter, I'd collapse beneath pine trees and review the action like a sportswriter. I was deliciously AWOL, and alone.

At nap-time after lunch I got to stay indoors playing Rafter Ball and All-Star Baseball, writing postcards, and following the Yankees on the radio. Eager for the score, I'd tear downhill from the mess hall, my body bouncing as my legs almost outran myself, turn on the game in the second or third inning, and lie there on coarse blankets in the sun. This was a time of nostalgia, reading letters from Mommy and Daddy, and aunts and uncles, leisure in which to send them each back a Chipinaw postcard and tell them what I was doing. My messages were short and to the point, like, "I got splinters today," "I am fine," and "I can even reach Boston with my radio." For tear-out camp money (we each had a booklet of different-colored ones, fives, tens, and quarters), visiting monitors sold us candy from a cornucopia of manufacturers' boxes. Nap ended when the bugle sang out, calling us to the next activity.

Radios were strictly forbidden in the mess hall or at any of our activities, but I began setting the Yankees in the outfield of softball games and beyond the fence of the tennis court. At outdoor Sunday barbecues I sometimes had the luxury of the second game of a doubleheader (with its assortment of utility players) beside my plate of hamburger, beans, and potato chips.

On game days I took the radio to General Swim and stayed out of the water listening. If there was a rally, I called out its progress to Yankee fans swimming.

Sometimes, game or not, I just stood by the benches collecting various sizes of rocks and stones and pitching them at trees, announcing strikes and balls depending on whether I hit the target.

Edging along shoreline, I cracked open mussels and threw their goo into the shallows so that small fish gathered and tore it apart. Then I rinsed my hands in the lake.

I saw the rest of Chipinaw cavorting in blue water and, though I wanted to be among their splashes, I continued to honor the dry rituals of my own invention.

Then one afternoon Jerry, the head swimming instructor, asked me to stay after. It was a friendly request. Despite my distaste for their profession I considered the swimming counselors friends. They never forced me to swim, and they let me read comics in the sun in their tent—a spot strictly off limits to campers.

Staring back at me, the rest of the Midgets hiked up the hill. I stood by the grandstand, curious to see what would happen.

Jerry led me into the water behind him and tried to coax me into swimming. I swung my arms in place.

He threw a lemon-line egg over my head and called, "It's hit to the outfield. C'mon ... bring it in. Get him at home." I half-ran, half-paddled to the piece of wood and tossed it to him. He made the tag ... but the runner was safe.

We continued that way several times a week—no talk about swimming, just splashing catches in deeper and deeper water, plays off the outfield wall ... and gradually I was gliding along the water to corral the floating wood. He had this unspoken pact with me that I would pass the test and go into intermediate water. He didn't ask me; he just scheduled it.

On the chosen day I had to jump into the lake and sink beneath my head. I stood on the edge of the dock, goose bumps all over, a wisp compared to the sleek tanks of campers all around me. But I shut off my mind and leaped. Plummeting into bubbles and green light, I glimpsed the muddy bottom for just an instant. I saw my terror clearly— that I'd become so dizzy I'd disappear, that I'd turn into a drowned body floating like cardboard (I saw once along the shore at Long Beach). But these semblances passed in a gasp as I came to the surface, water clogging my nose and throat.

I swam to the far dock.

It was not difficult at all. In one part of me I knew why everyone else simply did it. In another I felt not just myself but a company of fragmented beings borne along the resistance. Yes, swimming was important, but it was also a distraction. Or perhaps it was that I had to be distracted from fantasy in order to do anything real.

One afternoon we had the best adventure of the summer: all four bunks of Midgets hiked together into the forest to pick blueberries. The deeper into the wilderness we went, the more bushes there seemed to be, the thicker with fruit. Our last bush stood in a shaft of sun in a clearing. The bush was so ripe its blue filled the rest of our containers. That night the cooks made us our own pies to the envy of the rest of Chipinaw.

Together with my cousin Jay and his best friend Barry, I made an unlikely partnership—the star athlete; the pudgy mother's boy; and the tiny, day-dreaming child who they competed against and protected. I melded my reality to theirs. I also became the ally to whom Jay confided his fear of the dark, for someone had to slip ahead to turn on the light if we were first back. (The flashlight didn't reassure him at all, and if I held it to my face and made horror masks he actually got scared.) Near nightfall we kept a mutual eye out for the Cropsey Maniac, even as we spooked each other with sudden squeals.

Jay told the rest of the bunk that teasing over my wetting would be avenged. "He can't help it," he said. "How would you like it if it was you?"

Insofar as they were both Dodger fans, Jay and Barry's favorite teasing was to grab each other in ballroom posture and wriggle around in a dance they called "the Gil McDougald." "Stop!" I would protest, but that only made them pretend to kiss like birds.

Saturdays were Chipinaw's official visiting days. All morning we sat through Hebrew services. In relief at their conclusion we mangled the words of the last rousing prayers *("Dy-Dy-Asshole!")*, dissolving in each other's giggles. Parents flooding the campus were already peering impatiently into the armory. As we were set free, all hell broke loose—kids running to their Mommies and Daddies, presents, treats, no activities, do whatever you want.

This was a bittersweet interval. The world was frayed and pregnant with possibility, but it seemed to elude me. Since neither Mommy and Daddy nor Uncle Paul came, I went with Jay's and Barry's families.

This meant dozens of new aunts and uncles and friends from Uncle Paul's hotel.

Aunt Ruthie and Barry's mother, who was her best friend and whose name was also Ruth, flagrantly disregarded the visiting rules. Defying the strict limits, they arrived at odd hours to observe archery, baseball games—and even early enough in the morning sometimes to help us clean our bunk. The Ruths were back every weekend, arriving from Grossinger's Hotel in chauffeured cars with bags of fruit and boxes of cookies and cake. They were not entirely blind to justice and, although they didn't bring quite enough to feed the whole camp, they came surprisingly close. Five huge sacks would be all peaches at just the perfect stage of ripeness. You tore open a different carton of sacks to find grapes, apples, cherries, and the like. I remember the sweet redness of plums, our stolen mess-hall knives splitting watermelons, cutting strings on white boxes of chocolate chip cookies and chocolate-frosted trees, honey and marble cakes.

My mother and Daddy came only once that summer, in the middle, and by then I had an overwhelming nostalgia for them. The very sight of Mommy was heartbreakingly special, her figure in a dark dress suddenly there in the line of parents streaming from the parking lot on visitor's day, like no one else who ever was. Her smile was open and yearning, and she seemed truly delighted to see me. She was the one Jonny and I called Mummsy Wine. There was an ashen sharpness to her, a quality I might call cynicism now—mocking the other parents, talking about their ostentation, their ugly clothes, their Cadillacs—but it was comforting because I heard that voice inside me all the time.

There wasn't much to do with them except walk around aimlessly, though Daddy viewed the facilities with gusto, wishing he could dive into the lake or play a set of tennis. Mommy was on the lookout for notable people from her Grossinger days whom she enjoyed meeting again and introducing to her son. Deep down it was as though she really appreciated Uncle Paul and the fact she was once married to him. Grossinger's had made her important, and she shared that allegiance with me no matter how meager a son I was compared to Jon.

Then, as suddenly as they came, the cult of the parents left. The campus became ordinary playing fields, and the bugle took over our days.

At the end of that summer I didn't go back to the City on the bus. After the other campers left, a large black Caddy came for me. "Ready for Grossinger's?" asked my grandfather's driver Joe, as he wedged my trunk and duffel bag into the car's trunk. I felt memories converging: Oz naptime in Dallas, Hare and Hounds, Daddy's Mercury, the Penny Arcade, the garden in Westport. A muddle of excitement, nausea, and nostalgia, I sat quietly in the back as we bumped along farm roads, past small lakes and bungalows. It was Uncle Wiggily's land, but the cartoon rabbit had been overwhelmed by the vastness of a game board without end. Uncle Paul, once my magical benefactor, was now my father, and his authority was pulling me into a world I both anticipated and dreaded.

We glided up a hill into a cluster of gingerbread buildings. GROSSINGER'S HAS EVERYTHING! proclaimed a large notched sign. I saw small jeeps, some double-parked, others racing around. There were huge gardens and people in groups everywhere. I thought of the color plates in my books—the kingdoms of the Brothers Grimm, the chessboards of *Alice in Wonderland,* the dogs with saucer eyes, the mad tea party. We continued on a short road up to a three-storey white house.

It was a beautiful country dwelling, recalling Aunt Alice's place by the beach, only much bigger. Joe led me in.

I stood in the marble alcove of a palace. Light poured through white curtains onto an orange rug. Then a Creole singsong summoned "Mr. Richard" to the kitchen; there a portly lady named Beulah greeted me with an immediate choice of ice creams. Kitchens in New York were old and gloomy, facing alleys. This one had plants on its window sill, flowers and mint leaves in vases, rows of fancy spices, shiny new pots and utensils on the walls, egg-shaped statues for salt and pepper, a big yellow stove with an overhanging oven. Why did an image of Flash Gordon in the shower of needles flit over me just then?

With a dish of strawberry ice cream and a platter of cookies I sat on a sofa in the living room. Suddenly a blond kid somewhat younger than Jonny burst in the front door and greeted me with a whoop and a finger pointing to stairs up which he sailed.

I found him on the second floor down a hall in his room where he instantly demonstrated a closet filled with toys and stuffed animals—in fact, almost every game ever invented. It was a mess that would have

sent not only my mother but Jon and me into an apoplexy of cleaning up: different seasons of baseball cards randomly strewn, electric
planes, miniature football fields, loose Sorry cards and tokens, ping-
pong basketball, electric boats. As Michael pulled these items out to
show me, soon we had emptied most everything into the room and
were riding elephants and tossing clothing and plastic cars in the air.

We were interrupted by a stern but bemused voice. I looked up and
knew at once this was Aunt Bunny. "Okay, you guys. If you want to
play together, behave. Clean up now. Right away." Afterwards, she led
me away into her room "to get acquainted."

She looked a little like my mother, dark hair, deep eyes, a large
strong face. She was younger, though, and there was an obvious buoyancy and kindness to her. She asked me about camp, so I described
cookouts, salamander hunts, blueberry pie, and learning to swim.
Instead of expecting me to tell her everything was great, she made
faces at most of the activities and said I deserved a badge of honor just
for surviving such a summer.

I smiled bashfully.

Then she planted herself, chin in hands, on the edge of the bed and
asked to my surprise how I liked Doctor Fabian.

"A lot!"

"Is he good on the fears?"

I nodded.

"You and I share that. I don't know if it makes us special people."

"Are you afraid of diseases?" I asked in surprise.

"Every one in the book. Cancer, leukemia, MS; I'm even afraid of
ones people only inherit. Howd'ya like to see your Aunt Bunny as a
sudden dwarf, or a giant?"

I laughed at her expression of mock horror, then said, "Sometimes
I hear about new ones that make me scared. When I see an ad on the
subway, I think about that disease."

She raised her eyebrows and nodded enthusiastically. "It's like it's
on sale. You can't even pronounce the name, but you know what it
feels like to be dying from it just from looking at the picture."

"Yup!"

That evening after dinner, sitting alone with Aunt Bunny in her
room, I betrayed the Towers household. Descriptions of my life there

just poured out of me. At hearing criticism of someone else my mother would have flashed a gleam of triumph, but Aunt Bunny seemed honestly pained and said that my mother was also one of the frightened people but was too proud to admit it.

She and Uncle Paul had a baby Debby's age named James. He was a funny child, cute as a chipmunk, and I carried him around and set him on the floor beside his toys where he made faces and squealed. Michael brought in a record-player and put the needle on *"Jimbo, Jimbo, whatcha gonna doeeoo?"*

Then I was led to my room on the third floor, a large and spooky chamber with a giant radio cabinet and two musty closets filled with paintings, drapes, and other junk, plus deeper closets inside those. I stared in amazement at the quilted double bed with posts. Yet once we moved my trunk in and put my clothes in the drawers, I climbed into the cold sheets and, in total exhaustion (the day had begun at Chipinaw), fell asleep.

In the morning Beulah had a picnic already made for us and, after pancakes and bacon, Aunt Bunny, Michael, and I carted the basket onto a small blue bus. It wound among hills of golfers, down a glen, and then pulled up at a miniature version of the Chipinaw lake.

"This is my favorite spot in the whole hotel," Aunt Bunny announced as we climbed off and walked through gravel to a beach.

From his tiny shack a man gave us fishing rods and a can full of wet leaves and worms. Michael pranced ahead. We got into the green rowboat he had chosen and, with Aunt Bunny on one oar, me on the other, we made our way out to deep water and cast our lines. After a few minutes I felt a tug and pulled my first small fish wriggling and flipping into the bottom of the boat—such a sad thing bleeding on the hook but its yellow fins luminous in my hand as Aunt Bunny undid it. By lunchtime we had six of them.

That whole day my mind was as empty of fantasy as it had ever been. I was delighted by every nuance . . . racing in my sneakers across the beach to get a pail for our catch, setting it beside me on the bus, and handing it triumphantly to Beulah.

Uncle Paul made quite a fuss about our success when its cooked versions appeared on our dinner plates. "Well, I married a fisherwoman." He turned to me. "I bet you didn't know when you came here you were going to have to catch your supper?"

I shook my head. It was silly but so good-humored.

After dinner, Aunt Bunny made popcorn in expanding silver bags. Then she and I set up a board for Monopoly. Michael watched and tried to claim properties and plop down hotels before he knew how. Eventually he was satisfied to let me make the moves and just be on my side. Aunt Bunny had grown up in Atlantic City (on which the game board was based), so she had real stories about Baltic Avenue and Park Place. As we landed on each property, she told what it was like to visit them as a little girl. Some of her tales were real goofy, like her mother stepping in a puddle on Marvin Gardens and splashing her father's new pants.

The next day she led me down a path to the Hotel itself. Lobbies like New York City streets were full of people, most of them in fancy clothes and swimming gear, everywhere greeting and waving. There were rows and rows of indoor shops. On nearby walls hung pictures of baseball players and movie stars posing with Uncle Paul. As we passed offices, people shouted hellos to us. Pointing at me, Aunt Bunny said, "This is Paul's son Richard." The acknowledgments and rough handshakes went on building after building, floor after floor.

The dining room was so large I could not see the other end from the entrance. Tables stretched in all directions. White cloth napkins arranged decoratively in stemmed goblets provided a festive atmosphere like the Nevele, as waiters glided through, bearing trays stacked high with metal-enclosed plates. Uncle Paul had not exaggerated.

After lunch we meandered home by a different route, past a garden around a flagpole, across the edge of a baseball field where men were choosing up a game. I lingered a moment to watch. Then Aunt Bunny and I went to work in the garden behind her house.

I weeded and trimmed with her, picking strawberries, pods swollen with peas, squat tomatoes all shades of pink and red. We put them in baskets and colanders.

The family had a collie named Boy. He became the first animal I met up close. Initially I was cautious, but Boy wasn't. He came right up, drummed his paws, and jumped up on me. It wasn't long before I was wedded to this creature, taking him on expeditions traversing the

Hotel. He ran alongside me and chased the crab-apples and sticks I threw, his eyes meeting mine in hope of action.

I thought how amazed Jonny and my mother would be. To us dogs were alien creatures whose very existence on sidewalks we viewed with contempt, concern if they growled. Here I was wrestling with a huge collie like Lassie while he barked and pawed. I buried my nose in his pungent belly.

The next morning I walked to the Hotel myself. Uncle Abe, the maître d', led me to where family members ate. At a cluster of three tables every boy and girl was a cousin, every adult an aunt or an uncle. Many of them I had met on Saturdays at Chipinaw.

Jay had a place beside Aunt Ruthie and his older brother Siggy. My father's sister, Aunt Elaine, arrived with her kids Susan and Mark. After dessert and getting permission from his mother, Jay led me into the kitchen, which was as busy as a factory: chefs in tall hats, soups and cakes, melon balls and juices crashing onto counters from invisible hands. "We go where we want here," Jay said. "It's not like camp where they order you around." Once again I huddled close to him. The cooks and bakers treated our incursions as an honor, as Jay introduced his new cousin at every station.

We found our way out the kitchen down a back staircase, past the bar, which was dark except for a faint pink glow. We continued through a nightclub behind it, out a stage door into bright sun, along flagstone to an enormous sparkling swimming pool crammed with bathers and sunners, colorful with umbrellas—then through the crowds and piles of folded towels past a basketball game to the edge of a golf course, down along tennis courts and sand-covered pipes of an ice rink to the clubhouse. Everywhere, I saw riotous arrangements of pansies, zinnias, petunias, and other assorted flowers, fountains, gazebos, and wishing wells, trimmed lawns and shaped bushes in elegant circles around cottages.

At the end of our tour my cousin brought me to his own bungalow for mitts, bat, and ball. Then we walked back to the ballfield. As we swatted fungos to each other I was amazed at how many grown men showed up with gloves and joined in. One player commented that Jay slugged the ball like a major leaguer. He sure did. I loved to stand at the end of available space and track his hits coming out of the deep sky.

I stayed a week the first time at Grossinger's. I didn't see much of Uncle Paul, who was hardly ever home, or Jay, who returned to the City, but gradually I explored the entirety of the grounds with Boy. Up beyond our house, at the edge of vast parking lots, we collected old license plates along dirt slopes (a dozen states). Once Boy knew what I was looking for he found great ones, sniffing Mississippi and Georgia out of the garbage. Then we took the bus to the Lake and followed a brook to a small waterfall. There we waded among fish and tiny frogs, turtles of all sizes on the rocks, my pants pulled up over my knees, Boy muddy and splashing.

That night, surveying my caked clothes, Aunt Bunny summoned me into a bathtub with Michael. I was astonished when we were each handed a can of shaving cream. It was part of the ritual—constructing our own floating castles, shooting lather all over each other. When we left, there were three fizzed-out canisters and foam running down the walls. Now that was a real bath!

Each day for lunch I returned to the family section among my new relatives. They encouraged me to sample the menu, so I became more courageous. In the course of a week I tried all manner of unusual foods: mushrooms and noodles, lima beans and groats, fruit with beef, ice cream cakes with lime and bing cherry sections separated by chocolate bread, raspberry parfaits, whipped-cream cheesecakes.

As I walked the lobbies, everyone seemed to know who I was. Strangers greeted me by name. I watched a comedian named Lou Goldstein play Simon Sez with guests. As he tricked them, he made jokes in Yiddish and English, embarrassing his victims further (and yet again) to increasing uproars of laughter. Not far from him people sat at tables playing Scrabble. Someone I didn't know called me over and asked me if I could make any words from his rack. His opponents grumbled and laughed.

"Currying favors with the boss!" a bejeweled lady said.

I told him that "gaze" would get his "Z" on a triple letter score.

"That's my buddy for you."

One afternoon the director of the nightclub joined me at lunch, made a big fuss over me and a promise, and then kept it by showing up at Uncle Paul's after dinner that evening. He led me back to the

Hotel, through a tiny door near the kitchen, then a dark space, then into a room of levers and costumes. From there I could watch the show backstage. I stood alongside the curtain, while dancers, a singer, and then a comedian passed me going to and from their acts. Smoke rose from an invisible audience. Departing in a roar of laughter, the comedian gave me a pat on the backside and asked me to remember him to my father: "Tell him I brought down the house. Don't forget." Then he kissed my cheek and twisted my ear.

In New York I was a bad guy; here I was a virtual prince.

During the week Aunt Bunny never said anything sarcastic. She got angry sometimes, but it was a word or glance, then on to the next thing—no threat of punishment at all on the horizon, no comeuppance in store.

She took us in her car off the grounds to a miniature golf course with animal statues, windmills, and tunnels, each to putt through. Then she bought cotton candy for us. I had never seen a toy golf course or eaten fluff from a silver drum. I also had my first pizza and went to my first drive-in cartoons.

After breakfast one morning, just as I was setting out with Boy, a publicity man in a suit arrived at the door and announced he was taking me to visit my Grandma Jennie. She lived in Joy Cottage, down the hill from my father's. As we walked briskly, he described what a wonderful, generous woman she was. "She can't wait to meet you."

Passing through a small garden and a glass door, we entered a villa with an obscure sweet aroma. We followed a hallway to the end. Grandma Jennie sat in a gold bed in a majestic pink room. "Richard!" she exclaimed, throwing open her arms, her face breaking into a smile. "Welcome home."

'Home?' I searched my memory as though I should remember this—and in a way I did.

Grandma was an older blond woman with a strong, intelligent face. I knew she was famous. Even Bob Towers spoke well of her. I was flattered she was my grandmother and, at her invitation, returned to see her on my own the next day. As I sat on the corner of her bed, we had a serious discussion.

She wanted to know what I was learning in school and had remarkable patience for me to demonstrate simple arithmetic and recite tales of the thirteen colonies. Unlike most others who regarded me only as Paul's son without a past, she had an interest in my other family, including Jonny and Debby. "I want to hear how everyone's doing," she declared. When told my mildest version in deference to her age and stature she urged me to have sympathy for my mother. "Her father was taken ill when she was very young and she was left alone in a boarding school. Her mother treated her very badly. She is married to a difficult man. I'm so sorry she takes this out on you, but you must be forgiving and rise above it." I promised I'd try.

The day I left for home she sent me to the canteen to buy the most luxurious presents I could find for my brother and sister—games, dolls, and stuffed animals. She also arranged for smoked salmon and honey cakes to go back with me for my mother and Daddy. "This way," she remarked, "they'll treat you better."

In a sober end to the summer-long adventure, Joe drove me back to New York. As I watched country change into the outskirts of the City, I felt teary. Streets that had once been second nature now looked harsh and quaint. In the elevator at 1235 I found it hard to greet Ramon. The contrast between his surliness and the gaiety of the Grossinger's staff was too painful. My mind raced as I girded myself for the arrival. My mother was waiting to retrieve what was left of my soul.

I expected her to be furious, so I tried immediately to disguise my mood. But she still had her Chipinaw smile and seemed unusually gay and glad to have me back. In fact, she stayed up late in the living room and told me tales of her own time at Grossinger's, how handsome Paul was then, how she fell in love with him, how much they wanted a child like me. She described the jobs she had done, recounting in a childlike voice how she stood behind the front desk as Mrs. Grossinger and welcomed guests just like Aunt Marian. She asked about the few staff people who were still there from her time. Most of them I had met, and I was able to report that they remembered her and sent their fond regards.

Over those initial weeks back I talked openly (from habit of being at Grossinger's). I considered maybe that in my new outlook from Aunt Bunny and Grandma Jennie my mother might be an ally too. I told her about my problems at school, my frustration with Jonny and, when that seemed to go well, my adventures with Michael, James, and Boy. She heard it all with a show of great empathy. "I know how you feel at Grossinger's," she would say to me. "I was overwhelmed the first few times; it was like fairyland. I never wanted to leave."

One evening, in the midst of a disagreement, she suddenly yelled, "Let him go to his Uncle Paul." This reversion to her old tone startled me.

A day later, rushing to intercept Jonny and me in a shouting match, she scoffed, "Get away from him, Jon. He's got other favorite brothers he plays with now." I burned with guilt. Soon she began to bait in a mocking, singsong voice, "Now go tell on us to Auntie Bunny," Jonny and Daddy staring darts at me, Bridey suitably stolid beside them. For months after, if I appeared too cheerful, she snapped, "Where do you think you are, Grossinger's?"

She had lured me into confession and then used my confession as proof of my disloyalty. Dr. Fabian had warned me about such a trick.

I turned myself into a hardened outsider again, giving them nothing. My mother had the appropriate taunt for that too: "He's only a boarder here, so he'll be treated like a boarder."

I continued at P.S. 6 in third grade and Bill-Dave after school and on Saturdays. In class I would hold open a science-fiction novel or Landmark history book inside my desk instead of listening to the assignment.

I prowled the Louisiana Territories and the Texas Republic, went with Lewis and Clark on their expedition to Indians and unknown rivers, and spied on colonies on Jupiter's moons. I also reviewed collections of box scores and minor league rosters in *The Sporting News,* and Phil and I passed notes about trades and farm players. One afternoon, the teacher confiscated some of my best baseball cards and threw them in the garbage can. Even Phil could not capture them back (if he had, he claimed a right to keep them, like salvage from a sunken ship).

At group Dave was back from Korea and led ambitious outings to the Cloisters, then all the way up to Pelham and Van Cortlandt Park. Hardball remained my best enterprise, and I strived to be good, practicing my swing on the sidelines, figuring my batting average with help from a counselor—rarely over .270, especially with Phil arguing so many of my "infield hits" into "those were really errors!" (he was aiming to bat .500).

Bill-Dave traveled to Palisades Amusement Park where I refused to go on the rides but spent an hour staring at a machine, a claw inside a glass case that, upon the insertion of a quarter, passed over watches, tiny cameras, rings, and other prizes. I longed to have one of those cute cameras, so I tried it but the metal snapped on air and nothing came through the slot. Then I went inside a booth and, after parting with my last quarter, put my eyes in a goggle-cup and watched Woody Woodpecker flash by on cartoon cards. They seemed so simple that I made my own penguin show at home. As I flipped the paper on which I had drawn, musical notes did seem to rise and fall from the trumpets. Bridey was amused.

Some Sundays Phil's father took me and Phil to a batting cage in Long Island where we swung for long nets with different hits and scores marked on them. I loved the feeling of the solid connection of bat and fastball. It reminded me of my record called "Little Johnny Strikeout." Joe DiMaggio, without revealing his identity, approached a kid my age after a game in the Park he happened to watch while strolling by. Johnny had just struck out for the fifth straight time to the taunts of his friends ("Little Johnny Strikeout," the chorus sang, "he can't hit the ball!"). Johnny was on his way home, but DiMaggio convinced him to stay and gave him a lesson. After some whiffs, a bit of batting instruction, and a few hopeful foul tips, suddenly, smack! You can imagine the scene the next day when Joe showed up as a spectator, and, after the taunting chorus, Johnny hit a home run to win the game. Afterwards ("Say, who is that friend of yours, Johnny?"), the Yankee Clipper revealed his identity to the cheers of the kids.

My buddy Neil had graduated, so a variety of other students took me to Dr. Fabian's, mostly a tall girl with a mole on her forehead named Jill. She didn't say much, so I read on the train.

Dr. Fabian was delighted by my time at Chipinaw and Grossinger's and anxious to get a complete account. He thought the changes in my life were positive. Although he was sure we were on the road to success, I knew that nothing had really changed.

There were so many times I experienced the unnamed disease, the feeling of the proximity of the dungeon. Sometimes I whimpered quietly. Sometimes I ran around the apartment. Sometimes I huddled on the bed shaking. I thought, 'I can't die now because I don't know why I'm afraid. I don't know what I'm afraid of. And if I die I'll always be afraid. I'll never find out.'

Dr. Fabian wanted to figure out the symbols behind my panics and, though I welcomed his support, I knew by now, after the bigness of Chipinaw and Grossinger's, there wasn't a symbol. The panic was far too powerful to be reduced to a thing. It was a primal event, like my being at all.

Once I was eating a vanilla ice-cream cup in his office when suddenly I thought its black specks were poison. It seemed such a ridiculous confusion to have in his very presence. I well knew vanilla sometimes had black specks, but I felt a rush of terror. Like any adult he tried to reason with me, without success. Finally, we did free connection on the specks ("seed," "tree," "apple," "orchid," "baby," aha!). He suggested I might be worried about eating seeds and getting pregnant, so he explained the whole process of conception—the role of the penis and the vagina, and the fertilization and growth of the egg, with careful diagrams on the back of a paper on which we had been playing Battleship. This was to establish that boys were in no danger of being impregnated by seeds.

His interpretation of the fear was unconvincing, but the pictures he drew were intriguing. As with the demonstration of Uncle Paul being my father, I couldn't actually tell whether this was something I already knew. If I knew it, I had never thought it. I confided it to Jonny that night in bed. He was shocked and didn't believe me, so he went to ask Mommy. I was sure I was in for big trouble, but she was surprisingly unperturbed. It turned out that he had gotten a wildly inaccurate version in school, and she complimented me for setting him straight.

At Christmas that year I got the only present I wanted—to return to Grossinger's. Uncle Paul invited Larry, my counselor, and his new wife Jackie to take care of me there.

On the much awaited afternoon my mother remained in her bedroom and did not come out to say goodbye, so I hugged Bridey and gave Jonny and Debby kisses. Joe had picked up my counselor first, so he and Jackie were in the back seat when I arrived. We swung down narrow streets onto the highway. In the mountains the world was bright with crystals and dunes.

We arrived at dusk and got directed to our separate rooms on the third floor. In the morning after breakfast we hiked across white powder on the golf course, all the way to the Lake where people sat fishing through holes in the ice.

There was extra excitement that afternoon because Whitey Ford was at the skating rink with his wife. I was anxious that Larry and Jackie hurry through dessert and we not be late. We ran through the lobbies. When we got there, Selma, who was in charge of the skate shop, fitted us herself. It was quite a chore balancing on narrow blades while tiptoeing to the rink. Once on ice, I stumbled along the railing while Jackie held my hand.

Irving Jaffee, the pro, gave me a quick lesson in gliding, which ended with his presenting me, Paul's son, to Whitey Ford. We shook hands with mittens. I edged alongside the blond Yankee, amazed to be looking up and seeing his familiar figure in an overcoat, having him right me when I fell (though he was having a hard time keeping his balance too). Afterwards he conducted a baseball clinic around the fireplace, and I impressed everyone by asking detailed questions about Yankee minor leaguers.

The next day Larry got his movie camera, and we went to the toboggan, a frozen track on the hillside behind the rink. Together we acted out "The Human Cannonball." First, he stood at the bottom and filmed Jackie and me going up the hill on a rope-drawn trolley. We crossed a ramp into an elevated hut heated by a metal-barrel fire. There, a gruff dwarf in ear muffs and a scarf packed people onto long flat sleds and sent them flying out the chute. My boots were lugged forward into Jackie's lap as she gripped them. We shot out the opening and seemed almost to fly, frigid air nipping my ears, my head buried in her coat. We were still zooming as we crashed into bales of hay at the end. Larry ran toward us with the camera. We got to our feet, brushing off the stalks.

On the next trip he sat in the front of the toboggan, bravely holding the lens out.

My hands were numb by the time we raced one another to the canteen and, laughing, burst in the door and ordered sandwiches. The din-

ing area was a bustle of people, the room filled with smoke and conversation. On the way home we passed Grandpa Harry. He stood by
a construction site, observing men putting up scaffolding, yelling orders,
the collar of his overcoat pulled up tight around his chin. "You keepin'
warm?" he asked me. "Look at those gloves. They aren't warm enough!
Are your feet dry? Those boots are no good." He looked at Larry. "Get
him others. Charge 'em to me."

Later I visited him in his room at the rear of Grandma's house
where he sat in stiff dignity in a blue shirt and suspenders, watching
a boxing match on TV. In his heavily accented Elmer Fudd voice he
asked me, how's my mother, how's Bob Towers, does he miss
Grossinger's, do I remember when he and Joe used to come by with
lollipops and chocolate spoons?

I did.

"Your mother nearly bit my head off, that's what!"

Day after day in Uncle Paul's living room, presents piled up for Michael
and James, overwhelming the fireplace, almost a hundred of them left
by guests and clients until they crossed the living room with their bright,
cheerful packaging. I didn't need to have too many be for me. Just to
associate with such bounty delighted me.

On Christmas morning the contents poured out into a full-fledged
toy store. It was too much. Michael got exhausted, then surly as
machines didn't work right or came without batteries. "Junk!" he cried,
throwing things against the walls. Aunt Bunny soon put an end to this
and took us outside to build a snowlady, using some of her old clothes.
Then, to my astonishment, she started a snowball fight with Michael
and me. She got right into the thick of it and hit me three times with
perfect shots.

The visits to Grossinger's were a treachery for which my mother never
forgave me. She had the uncommon discipline to look at me for the
remainder of my childhood as though I were Judas himself.

When I reported my ice skating with Whitey Ford, she subtly nee-
dled Daddy to draw him in.

"Who do you imagine brought ballplayers to Grossinger's in the
first place?" he asked. I had to acknowledge that it must have been

him. "They live off the success of Bob Towers," he said. "And they parade around second-rate idiots like Lou Goldstein in their place. They're going to destroy their reputation in one generation."

"He thinks everything's going to be handed to him, just the way it is at Grossinger's," she rejoined. "Well, it's not. It's dog-eat-dog out there."

"Amen."

I told Uncle Paul about these comments. He heard them unperturbedly, with typical humor and majesty. He said my mother and Daddy were jealous. He was particularly amused by the idea that Bob had made Grossinger's and could do a better job running it. "You tell my old buddy Bob Towers," he laughed, "that any time he wants to set up his own hotel and go into competition with us, I'll be glad to meet him on even terms." He seemed both good-intentioned and delighted at the prospect. "Richard, you should know that people like Bob are second-rate grumblers. They can't be big enough on their own so they just complain about others' success. There's no reason for you to believe him. You're a Grossinger yourself and that's something he can never be." As he savored that for a second, I stared at his gold PG cuff links. "Your mother never wanted to leave. Me, yes! The Hotel, no! Sour grapes. That's all it is."

Sour grapes? I had an image of little blue barrels of candy, and I sensed that Uncle Paul didn't appreciate the degree of oppression I was under. I pleaded to live at his house, but he told me that wasn't possible. "Of course, I want you to, but the law says otherwise, and you and I have to obey the law."

During the next attack I argued back against Mommy and Daddy and defended Uncle Paul. Their screaming got louder and louder until I thought their voices would crack my head. I ran down all six flights of stairs out onto the street. I walked around the block, fantasizing that I'd see the Hotel car and it would pick me up. Every portal and alley attracted me, but in the end, of course, I returned to further punishment.

"How could you scare me like that?" Mommy shrieked.

"Do you know what you're doing to your mother?" Daddy added, turning his back and walking away.

I became the Prince of Darkness in that household, a representative of a foreign, evil country. "The devil," Jonny said in retrospect after we were both grown up. "You were the devil. Everything you did was wrong because you were, like, from hell. All your friends were demons or thieves. You were crazy because you had to go to that doctor all the time. Only it wasn't a real doctor; it was like learning to be more evil. You were always undermining Mom and Dad's authority, explaining why they really did things. You had a way to get at them because you knew all this stuff from the outside. And you had this other family of rich bad guys."

The third time I went to Grossinger's, during Easter vacation, was not so idyllic. I was sent with Gail, one of Daddy's older nieces, and a kid my age also named Richard, the son of one of my mother's friends.

Uncle Paul and Aunt Bunny were traveling in Jamaica with Michael and James, but my mother wanted me to go, partly because they *weren't* there (and because she had made "Grossinger's" promises to the mothers of both my companions). Gail went off looking for boyfriends, so I was left alone with Richard, one of the worst kids I had ever met. He had a "torture kit," as he called it, of pins and blades. He would regularly threaten to "punish" me if I did not show him the proper deference. Actually, except for the occasional sly jab of a pin, he resorted to his tools only once, when I was beating him in Monopoly. Suddenly he grabbed my large bills and properties. When I protested, he took out the kit and began scratching my arm. I called for help, but Bob's niece, who was reading a teen magazine, told us to settle it ourselves. Richard eventually twisted my arm behind my back until I agreed, in increasing pain, that he had won fair and square. From then on I made it clear I needed neither playmates nor guardians.

As for Richard, I knew only that his mother became ill with cancer a few years later, after giving birth to a girl. Her quick death sent my mother into a tailspin of disease panics that led to repeated late-night visits by Dr. Hitzig. Though I was left with a haunted image of that family, I forgot about them as real people until thirty years later an acquaintance became the piano teacher of Richard's grown-up little sister and discovered that her brother had once been my "friend." "Not quite," I wrote to him, explaining why Richard was not a fond childhood memory.

"Your letter gave me the chills," he responded. "Do you know what became of your tormentor? He's now in the upper echelon of counterintelligence for the Army. Obviously, he started young!"

Looking back at my earlier years I am staring into my own substance along its girth. There it is denser, brighter, but its threads are less accessible.

Life begins with an explosion much like the one we postulate for the origin of the universe. Everything is blown out of an original moment atomistically and settles in the tensility of space. I can see now that at the beginning I was locked to my mother like a small satellite sun in a twin star system. It was not her exogenous presence that compelled me but her gravitation in the region of space in which I emerged. It was imprinted on everything I did. I was always shrinking from her, even when she was not present. But I was also drawn to her— profoundly and masochistically. I recognized her skitteriness and deviousness in me, a negative power passed through the blood. I even nurtured her alarms and false smiles, the melodrama that kept us occupied and distracted. As people often said, I was my mother's "picture image." There was never the possibility of pure escape.

Those years in retrospect grow faint and less complete: P.S. 6, Bill-Dave, the Yankees in their pennant races, World Series games against the Dodgers, dinners with Uncle Paul, walks around the reservoir, me pushing Debby in a stroller, check-ups at Dr. Hunt, haircuts from my mother's French barber on Madison, bus rides up and down the avenues, the Grossinger's car picking me up, Bridey singing while she cooked. . . .

I remember how I woke at times in the middle of the night, shivering, trying to hold the lost tendril of a dream. Finally, I would rouse myself, spread my sheets and blankets on radiator pipes, lie atop them in imaginary summer, aromatically steaming dry, until the sun itself rose through city stone.

Sometimes it will all come back in a flash of déjà vu: the walk to the barbershop, the color of light against a particular building at a time of day, Michel with his scissors, the hair all around us on the floor. I will feel the melancholy of then, suspended in a sorrow I will always have. I did not minimize the pain later. I simply engorged it. I changed it into something else, as *I* changed—into a numb, flattened ache so that now I remember only that it was desolate then. I feel the texture of what happened but not its subtle layers. Nothing will ever feel that old way again because, back then, I imagined my range of feelings and possibilities *was* the world. I had no reason to suspect I would ever be paroled.

The things I did during childhood do not seem as important to me as the overall mystery of it. I went from one event to another, as the Buddhists say, like a drunken monkey. Toys, games, comics, candy bars—these are what we are raised on in the West, and in much of the world they are considered the acme, worth rewriting history for.

Years later I look back on that childhood with dismay. What did I learn compared to peasant children in China who worked the farms and raised food for villages? What about the self-sufficient offspring of the Eskimo and other northern tribes? From the beginning of life they are taught where they are, the habitats of plants and animals, and how to find their way home in a blizzard. In New York City one is raised in an arcade without a sense even that survival is real.

Behind the scattered memories of childhood, a vast memoryless curtain covers my life. I can create names for that curtain, but they are intellectual constructs. The original sadness was an ocean. It wasn't even "sad"; it was sensual and rich, and I swam in its eternity—a planet of waters as large, in scale, as the lake into which *The African Queen* plunged in the movie. It too had lightning and demon cruisers. There was no opposite shore to that lake, but childhood was the process of sailing there anyway. Fear was my guardian, but fear was the same as timelessness—unrelinquishable, impenetrable.

Games kept me busy—toys, comic books, movies, waterguns—so that a yellow plastic Sorry token or a green Pennsylvania Avenue card brings back the whole enchantment.

COLOR WAR

In fourth grade Phil and I started collecting Superman comics and the Hardy Boys adventure series. The world of Superman was macabre and irresistible. Wearing his flying cape, branded by a red S, he was attacked by a giant Sphinx, rays shooting out of its eyes. He was forced to stand on his head before a row of dolls, a conniving man with a pocket watch controlling him. His other identity was newspaper reporter Clark Kent. Lois Lane not only sought to marry Superman but to discover his secrets. In another story Superman was wrapped in bandages; when they came off, what face would appear? He was selling his talents, an oil well on fire, blazing black-red in the background, his hand extended, asking for $5000 in cash. What had come over him? In a number of comics he lost his ability to fly, or was attacked by kryptonite, the only substance to which he was vulnerable because it came from the exploded planet of his birth. Adventures recalling Krypton showed diamond cities, exotic Kremlin-like towers. In one such adventure Superman was fighting a Clark Kent lookalike, actually Mala from Krypton. His thought bubbles wondered if people knew 'I am actually battling myself.'

Each Hardy Boys cover was a window into a mystery. The series started with *The Tower Treasure* (which I found covered with dust in Aunt Marian's abandoned library) and ended with *The Hooded Hawk* and the unpublished *Clue in the Embers* (which finally appeared the last month of sixth grade). When we got through all of those (to date) we moved on to Rick Blaine, Tom Swift, Tom Quest, and Ken Holt. The goal was to finish each set, adding new titles later as they came out.

These were more than just stories to me. When Frank Hardy or Ken Holt found an amulet or map, it was a real thing, part of a chain that led to sinister signposts, boats buried behind bushes, statues of Inca kings and grinning tigers, humming dolls (left by gypsies) that weren't dolls. I loved the sensation of suspense and irresolution, clues and characters hanging unsolved until I could read more. I would save my money and wait outside the bookstore across the street from P.S. 6. The silver-haired lady would appear around the corner, unlocking her door just minutes before the school bell. I'd follow her into a cranny of papyrus smells, pick the next volume from the shelf, give her my dollar, and run to class.

Eventually Phil and I began writing and illustrating our own mystery novels combining the familiar characters (Phil dreamed up one exotic plot in which Rick Blaine, Ken Holt, Tom Swift, and the others were unwittingly helping the crooks). Event after event was scribbled on yellow pads, an occasional full-page illustration with a caption like, "They had vanished without a trace."

Soon we went looking for clues at lunchtime. On such an occasion we found a silver watch on a chain with a small plastic skull attached to it—a remarkable object under the circumstances—and, by "deduction," attributed it to a nearby apartment building where we tried to decode the engraving on the watch to match names of tenants. We must have gotten in too deep because the police came, listened to our account, and told us that we could collect the watch from the lost-and-found if no one claimed it in a month.

Dr. Fabian and I remained great buddies; he even showed up with his wife for Christmas at Grossinger's and joined Aunt Bunny and Uncle Paul for drinks by the fireplace.

Our weekly meetings took on a character of interminable discourse. He was searching for a clue that would unlock my mystery. Since I had no idea what information he needed I said as much as I could in hopes of somehow hitting upon it. In fact, I began preparing my accounts on the subway and then skillfully rattled off tales of my mother, P.S. 6, Bill-Dave, dates with my father, and so forth. I expected one day he might leap from behind his desk like a scientist in a comic book and shout Eureka! Then I would be cured.

I brought him regular batches of dreams. I tried to capture the precise state that happened sometimes before sleep (in which I imagined my fingers and lips swelling into fat trees and my feet shooting out in the distance, so far beyond that my toes were as remote as a city seen from the sky). I told him my images of wedding couples while watching my pee swirl together in the toilet (as though the pattern of bubbles were a grail for the origins of the misdeed they sparked at night).

My life became a story I told—a primitive version of the one I am telling now. The members of my family were its characters. I was a character too (as well as the narrator): a boy talking to a wise doctor.

The fears—code-named as such—were *like* a character, for in our inquiry they became axioms, compliant abstractions. "I'm afraid of being poisoned," I said. "I'm afraid of dying and drifting forever through space." Yet inside me this was experienced as a gap, a place with no content, no defining boundary, no possibility of amelioration. I spoke hopefully but without real hope, for we never explored the gap; we just talked about one or another fear and its possible hidden causes.

Dr. Fabian couldn't begin to extricate me. "It's the sense that something terrible is going to happen to you!" was his solemn, reiterative pronouncement. But what did that mean? Was something fated to happen, or had something already happened?

In the end he settled on a surprisingly simple resolution: the terrible thing was the divorce of my parents.

This didn't seem sufficient, but in the context of our dialogue I became reconciled to it—the irrevocable mechanism behind my plot. The parental split gave me a mythology to identify with. I told myself that my troubles originated in a primeval Martha-Paul sundering that left me the victim of an embattled family and a tormenting half-brother.

Dr. Fabian never got past this interpretation. He applied it to wetting, schoolwork, friends, dreams, effects of Nanny, fears of diseases, and my relationships with my mother, Bob, Jonny, Uncle Paul, Aunt Bunny, and himself. All my emotions, he presumed, had roots in the divorce.

Still there was nothing that suggested this disclosure in the feeling of fear itself (or the tremor by which it enveloped me). What about

Nanny's goblins (abandoned because I could not remember them)?
What about atom bombs (that threatened us all)? What about death
itself? How could any of this be made normal, okay?

Traveling the subways myself, I saw Dr. Fabian less often as the years
went by, but I relied on his existence as proof of clarity and reason-
ableness in the world. As I got older, I continued to tell him "the story."
Precision and candor changed nothing. Only years later did I realize
how much I withheld: ungenerous emotions toward my friends and
family, escapades during interstellar daydreams, irritation toward him.
I was portraying only part of Richard and in a way that was comfortable—even self-flattering. Having already made myself his protegé
and hero, I could not abandon a privileged role.

It never occurred to me that I would rather hold onto my secrets
than disturb their roots. Nor did I let myself suspect, while I led him
on a merry chase all those years, that Dr. Fabian himself was baffled
and misled by the richness and complexity of my associations. He gave
an appearance of struggling to find the missing link when, in fact, he
was probably marking time until somehow he could reach me.

We were traveling different paths: I was looking for magic and revelation; he imagined a patient on the borderline of breakdown. I provided more and more bizarre material; he was searching for classic
etiology. I kept telling him there was something bigger, something different. He never understood its significance, so I settled for trips to
Grossinger's and Yankee victories.

Sometimes the haunting in me softened into a sadness, a sense of being
lost and forlorn (resonating in an image of Heidi's grandfather searching frantically for her through wintry villages). It was more than a sadness. It was a shadowing of limitless depth, of layers parting to reveal
other layers themselves parting, like the leaves of maples in an autumn
breeze. In this form sadness was not only not sorrow; it was secretly
the most joyful thing I knew. Not joyful like Grossinger's but joyful
like experiencing loss and then recovery, leaving home and coming
home at the same time.

The songs of the play *Finian's Rainbow* (performed by the older kids
at Chipinaw) bore shards of this sensation. I tried singing but couldn't

keep a real tune. Upon request (and with a little help on the lyrics) Bridey reproduced them in her brogue: *"How are things in Glocca Morra ... Does that leapin' brook still...."* Words and melody put their spell over me; the world itself seemed to drop a chord into slow motion and swim by in solemn, stately fashion. Yes, it was sad and fearful, but it was beautiful—shockingly beautiful. Then she sang, *"Look, look, look to the rainbow...."* I had no words to match it, but I leaned into the song like a sunflower into sun.

Jonny and I would run along the Nevele solarium, building little piles of snow on the railings in an effort to thaw some of the winter away in March. Debby splattered in puddles at our feet. Mommy sat on a lawn chair, her eyes closed, a silver reflector about her neck. Clump after clump of puffy cold was placed on rusty ledges as Jon and I called to each other to check the progress of melting at either end. This industriousness would arouse a sense of the profoundest well-being in me. I'd be thinking about where I was in my latest science-fiction book and how later I'd lie toasty by the radiator and read it—then we'd eat dinner; afterwards, chocolate horseshoe cookies ... and the song would seep through my veins: *"Follow it over the hi-ill and stream...."* I twisted the vowels in "follow" and "stream" until they were barely English in the back of my throat. There was a tenuous point, before they became ridiculous, at which they held the whole mystery, the fairy tale, Bridey's Ireland.

It was a book I read, maybe; a dream I had; or it was something else entirely, vast and incomprehensible. All the time, this mood dogged me, conveying secrets and masks—and also that strangely immense joy. *("So I ask each weeping willow, and each brook along the way ...")* Jon and I would buy candy bars and comics at Ivy's Store, go pinball bowling, and then sit in the lobby engrossed in Almond Joy and Porky Pig while languid crowds swept past. Smell, color, and mood combined in a wonder that we existed at all. Gradually the mood would fade, or it might call to me from the faint center of a dream.

Its nether side was sheer blind terror. The less there was to cause it, the more powerful its claim on me. It happened one night, as I came into the dining room for supper. I looked at everyone seated there at the table—Mommy, Daddy, Jonny, Debby. Bridey was serving halved grapefruits. The reflected ambiance of the walls was too pale. I thought,

'This is it, forever—no!' I couldn't relent to it, so I ran into my bedroom, hurled myself onto blankets, and dug my fingers into them. A black invisible light shot through my forehead.

I could tell later, from their judging looks, they thought it was that I'd rather be at Grossinger's, but it was more a feeling of having come into the wrong century altogether.

Jonny started kindergarten at P.S. 6 as soon as he was old enough, and from then we were dispatched to school together. Usually we would get off to a sluggish start and have to rush through breakfast. Bridey shoved us out the door to meet the Bill-Dave wagon. "Hurry, you two. I know it's going to have left this time." Often the cranky elevator ground to a stop just as Bert pulled up. Jon and I stood by the metal gate ready to dash, Ramon invoking his authority and ordering us back until he opened it. He probably wanted to eavesdrop on another exotic punishment.

One day the wagon just didn't come. Jon and I stood there in disbelief as the morning grew old and we watched a stream of businessmen heading off to work, a sure sign we were out of our realm. We dragged ourselves back to the apartment to Ramon's jests. "See, your mother was right! She told you, you gonna miss! She gonna beat ya!"

She was getting ready for the office and startled to see us again. We had no place being there that late in the morning. Saying not a word, still adjusting her collar with one hand, she herded us into her room and whacked us with the nearest implement, her umbrella. We were grabbing each other and trying to get away under the bed, but she followed us, slamming harder and harder.

During this improvisational beating, the phone rang and Bridey broke in.

"I'm sorry to interrupt, Mrs. Towers, but that was Bill-Dave to say the bus had a flat tire; it's on its way."

Mommy was undeterred. "The way they dawdle at breakfast they would have missed it a hundred times if it came when it was supposed to." And she continued smacking.

To my chagrin my brother quickly became the warrior-hero of P.S. 6: he was elected first-grade class president and had the highest marks in the advanced section. He was also king of the punchball court, regularly swatting the Spaldeen over the fence with his fist. He strode with a tough-guy swagger and won fights in the yard, surrounded by cheering supporters. I certainly didn't play punchball anymore, and I always had an eye out for where he was and shifted accordingly. At home he was a relentless, sweaty chunk, and often I had to wrestle him and hold on for dear life.

At the same time, we were intimate roommates, companions of necessity. We lay in bed at night watching the Knickerbocker Beer sign blink on and off in the northern distance over Harlem. Whispering across the room, we filled the interval before sleep with games—Animal-Vegetable-Mineral, Initials, Geography (as quietly as possible so as not to arouse the Cyclops).

When my brother saw ghosts at the window, he called aloud, waking me up. Adopting the role of Dr. Fabian, I walked to his bedside and comforted him, encouraging free connection in an attempt to locate the symbols at the bottom of his fugue. At first his ghosts were pure phantoms; their concrete bodies didn't exist. Gradually they became true adversaries, and he rose to grapple with them in the center of the room, punching the air and screaming at his tormentors. Sometimes he panted or whispered curses as he sparred.

Jonny, the schoolyard champion, never stopped fighting, even in sleep.

When I told my parents about these nocturnal episodes, they got angry at me. Jon was obviously normal; I was the crazy one. Daddy was very direct on the matter: How could anyone who threw three touchdown passes a game and racked up Honor Rolls left and right have problems?

Baseball continued to hold much of the glue between my brother and me: he was Mickey Mantle, the hero; I was Gil McDougald, the reliable sub. The Yankees were something always to come back to, a ritual beyond the disorderliness of our lives. I remember Daddy, Jonny, and me sitting on a park bench while Debby played on the seesaw, waiting in high tension for Irv Noren to take his turn as a pinch-hitter—two on, two out in the eighth. The season hardly matters.

Jon and I routinely carried a Spaldeen or a hardball and threw over and under obstacles on the street, widening our range as we hit the Park (Bridey said we had "ball-itis"). During weekends at Long Beach we held Ocean Ball contests, batting from more remote lines of dried seaweed and attempting to slug the Spaldeen high over the changing boundary-line of surf, making circus catches in the waves. Before the day was over, we were exhausted salt-and-sand outfielders.

How it filled my imagination when the Yankees and Orioles traded eighteen players, and both Don Larsen and Bob Turley came to my team!

Mr. Borrig was our chief nemesis, continually coming to the front door with complaints from the apartment beneath. That would lead to instant punishment—an early bedtime, a confiscation of the tennis racquet or some other toy, perhaps a whipping. Our tumbling catches and dives to block the socks from landing on a bed were often followed by a ringing doorbell. Once, in revenge, we lowered a warm red water-balloon on the end of a string slowly down six storeys and, as Borrig sat on his customary stool by the service entrance on 96th Street, set it softly on his bald head.

I remember a Monopoly match in which I was beating Jon so badly he was on the point of tears. I had all the reds, greens, and blues, and my properties were packed with hotels. I had thousands and five hundreds in abundance. With only a few hundred dollars and no houses on his properties he fought on, occasionally crying and biting his lip. In a moment of inspiration (that stands out over our whole childhood together) I invited him over to my side of the board to play against that bum Borrig. We slaughtered him. We took all his money. We forced him to mortgage his properties. We jumped up and down with excitement calling him names.

Our family went from nightmare to nightmare—my mother's rages and panics of disease, the goblin Hitzig arriving at strange hours, Daddy's arguments and setbacks at work, his battles with Mommy, plates and silver thrown across the dining room. She would burst from her vigil, heavy footsteps down the hall, a belt clunking menacingly, a voice so shrill it seemed to puncture the walls. But mostly there were lonely hours awaiting disaster.

One afternoon when I was about 11, Jonny 8, and Debby 4, we were walking with our mother down 96th toward the Park. Jon must have asked about his good points because she was reciting them aloud: "You're handsome ... brave ... courteous ... strong ... intelligent ... and you have this special quality of leadership."

Debby immediately chirped, "What am I?"

She was "beautiful, loving, and had a stage presence many actresses on Broadway would kill for. You're another Shirley Temple."

I refused to be part of this charade, but Jon was curious, as no doubt was I. "What about Richard?" he asked.

"Richard is. ..." She paused for a moment and then offered, with a curious smile, "Richard is loyal."

We continued walking, past the playground to the reservoir. I didn't ask for elaboration nor did they.

It was such a strange answer, given that I was famously disloyal. Was she being sarcastic? Or did she mean that I was loyal to Grossinger's and even in the service of the enemy it was an admirable trait?

Why was it my only virtue?

Looking back I wonder if she intuited (beyond time) who would be telling this tale today.

Before major highways were built into the Catskills it was a three-hour journey to the Hotel from the City, a stop for a snack always at the midpoint, the Red Apple Rest.

My clearest memory is of the arrival. I would bound from the car and go running down the road. Every tree and sign, even the dust I kicked up was special. It was Grossinger's! My sneakers tore along the dirt twice as fast as anywhere else. If Aunt Bunny wasn't at the house to greet me, I immediately sought her at the pool or beauty salon.

During most of my time I explored lobbies and underground passageways, every bungalow, office, plaza and path, until I knew their distinctive smells and ikons. It was more than being impressed by the scenery. I *was* Grossinger's. The flowers were my longing for beauty and celebration. The flood of guests through the corridors and feasts from the dining room evoked my imagination of galactic worlds. The various arenas and sites made up my itinerary of adventures. In my other life I was willing to be sullen and brooding, to live in prison, caricatured as the evil boy with the criminal doctor—as long as I could have this as my true home.

Depending on who was in town, I made trips to visit my relatives in their separate cottages: Aunt Lottie and Uncle Louie, Jay's grandparents; my father's sister Aunt Elaine, her husband Uncle David, and their children; deaf Uncle Harry and Aunt Flo who ran their antique shop next door and shouted syllables as they pantomimed a butter dish or china platter they were giving me for free to bring home to my mother.

Doing the rounds of family and friends was the heart of my Grossinger ritual. It was a chance to prove to myself I was not really a Towers. The sullen, morose kid from New York marched through lobbies smiling and waving at everyone. I prided myself on knowing all their names—clerks in their shops, waiters and waitresses, bus drivers and maintenance crew, Uncle Eli and his tennis pros, Uncle Abe and the athletic staff, lifeguards, shop-keepers, chefs and bakers, even janitors and dishwashers.

An ordinary day at Grossinger's began in the dining room with Jack Gallagher, the old Marine waiter with the Popeye face who, in season, would go over each Yankee game, adding his complaints about managerial strategy (as if Casey Stengel were a madman or in cahoots with crooks). He also growled good-naturedly about the mess left by any of us kids from the last meal. On the way to Jack's station I would pick up all four morning papers—*Times, Trib, News,* and *Mirror.* Sometimes I arrived so early that they were still tied in bands by the service desk. I would turn them over in suspense to trace line scores (as far as the innings went in the rural editions). Jack would still be in street clothes and suspenders eating his own breakfast, so I'd wait on myself.

In the giant pantry refrigerator I'd mix boysenberries, raspberries, and blueberries. Then I'd collect waffles from the grill and sneak a look at lunch desserts while waving hello to the bakers. In the summer I'd cut a giant slab of watermelon between meals and walk through gardens, spraying its seeds. This was my territory, free and anonymous. A voice inside continuously reminded me how incredible this all was, blasting it through images of kids at Bill-Dave and P.S. 6: 'Look at this, Freddie Meyers, Andy Pfeiffer, Phil Wohlstetter!'

During days I might get a ride to the bowling alley and stay there all morning, rolling game after game, comparing my numbers on successive scoresheets, or I might visit the stables and feed the horses, or sit in the audience at one of the lobby shows.

Often I stopped at Joy Cottage for a hour or so to keep Grandma company. I heard her odyssey, about how she came to America a poor girl, studied hard, learned English, and became God's custodian of the land. She taught her life as a Biblical proverb of rising above hardship. Although the contrast between our upbringings couldn't have been sharper, she imbued me with a sense of our affinity, as if we were unique among the family. "Our success should have bred vision and generosity among our own," she lamented; "instead it has bred envy and greed. You have suffered like me, so you understand this."

Near the end of each stay she produced a variety of gifts, not only for me but for Jonny and Debby. I got a blue and white Magnavox record-player with sequins on the case and a real tape recorder. Jonny got a set of battery-operated motor cars. Debby got the thing she wanted most—a full cowboy suit with a hat, a holster, and two pistols. Bridey even got a set of jeweled brooches. "We will shower them with kindness," Grandma said.

During one visit she recalled a treasure she had kept for years and summoned the maid to go to her safe for it. Wrapped in a piece of pink velvet in a bracelet box, it was a baseball autographed by dozens of famous old-time players, including Ty Cobb and Babe Ruth. She displayed it, rewrapped it, and then handed it to me. "Save this for your children. They will remember me by it."

I made friends with Herb Schwartz, the resident hypnotist, a man who knew much about symbols and dreams. In fact, he often lectured on Sigmund Freud to assembled guests. I'd watch him put volunteers into trances and instruct them to blurt silly remarks and kiss strangers. At meals he and I talked about therapy and especially the strange case of Bridey Murphy who, in hypnotic trance, recalled a past life in Ireland. *The New York Daily Mirror* ran accounts of their reporter's search for traces of the original Bridey Murphy in nineteenth-century Ireland.

"What could she have seen, Richard?" He seemed unwilling to admit it was really another place, another time, but at least he knew it was something. He agreed that stuff like reincarnation was more interesting than the stunts in his show, but he said he would get in trouble with my father if he tried it, and anyway the guests wouldn't go along. "This is a resort hotel, son, not CCNY."

The director of daytime activities was Daddy's much-maligned replacement, Lou Goldstein; he ran Simon Sez shows and other modes of participation comedy in the lobby. I'd try to observe him surreptitiously, for, if he saw me spying, he'd always embarrass me. "There goes the owner," he'd say, and everyone would turn around and look at me. "Don't let him fool you. He's a midget."

As James got older he joined Michael and me in adventures. The three of us spent one entire morning rolling tires down the main hill and chasing alongside them. For whole afternoons across the golf course and in underground passageways we played hide-and-go-seek. The main rule was that the hider had to keep moving. It would have been impossible if we could have dallied in the thousands of closets, alleys, and guest rooms.

One time, we set out a lemonade and soda stand, mixing exotic concoctions from the kitchen storerooms and the canteen to sell to passing guests. Any fruit with seltzer was a soda. Any fruit with sugar and water was an ade. This included watermelon soda and boysenberry ade. Uncle Paul ended that venture quickly, but not before we had made almost twenty dollars.

We collected sections of picket fence, truck tires, pipes, and other junk from the various warehouses and garages and constructed our own miniature golf in the backyard, digging tunnels and burying plumbing in them for the ball to rattle through.

I wrestled and ran with Boy, and spent hours brushing and feeding him. Then one visit during fourth grade, I arrived with Joe to hear he was lost, had been missing over a month. I went out searching the far reaches of the grounds, even into neighboring forest. But, in the last parking lot at the bottom of a hill with garbage, I found only another dead dog, and the horror of that ended my looking.

Milty Stackel was my best adult friend. He was at least six-foot-ten and two hundred and seventy five pounds. He had come to the mountains as a barnstorming basketball star and settled down at Grossinger's as the director of the canteen (the combination drugstore/coffee shop) and its adjacent TV room. There we sat with Al Rosen and a bunch of other Cleveland Indians watching the Dodgers play the Yankees in the 1955 World Series.

Milty was the source of ice cream and toys, free sports magazines and comics. We used to joke that he drank two milkshakes for every one he made us—and these were not ordinary milkshakes; he would throw scoops of butter pecan, vanilla, coffee, strawberry, peach, and whatever else we requested into the same canister. Even Bluto could not have sucked it through a straw.

Not only did Milty not object to our raiding his stocks; he encouraged us to dig into fresh-smelling stacks of every imaginable comic including those he was still unpacking from cartons. He had dozens of Heckle and Jeckle, daffy black birds with wide eyes and gigantic beaks: they were dentist and patient, hot-dog vendor and customer, twin waiters (one holding the other up by the feet as he took the order), bookends with sombreros, golfers playing with brooms, holding an 18 over a garbage can. Their colors were light pink, light blue, light red, dark blue, snow, ski trails, jagged black tree stumps.

Milty would throw me fly balls on the lawn outside the canteen for an hour at a time. Back and forth I'd run, diving on the grass, asking him to put them just over my head, just to the left, just to the right, high in the air. My side ached and my legs wobbled, but I kept pushing—one more great catch—one more . . . my whole mind and body primed for either a fling to the side or a dash backward.

"Don't you ever quit?" he'd say. "*You're* running and *I'm* beat." Finally, I'd give myself permission to collapse into the sweet throb of my heart and the grass.

Milty was a big kid. He read Little Lulu and Heckle and Jeckle avidly (he just loved the antics of those magpies) plus every sports magazine published. He played Baseball Initials at the drop of a hat but wasn't very good. After I got a camera I regularly badgered him for free film and developing. I went around the Hotel outdoors searching for compositions. New snow piled up atop wrinkled berries on bushes.

They looked like cherry ice cream sundaes, so I shot a roll of them and took the film back to the canteen. I photographed big Milty from down low aiming straight up into a distortion of his sad face.

When I was making my scrapbook of Mars, I wanted to get a picture of the planet itself. I went outside at night with a box camera. Milty came along with the longest flashlight he could find (five batteries). Although I told him it wouldn't help, he insisted on shining it up in the sky while I held the time exposure. "A little more light couldn't hurt," he muttered.

A couple of times a winter Irv Jaffee, the former Olympic speedskater, put on a fox uniform and whizzed along the ice with dollars, fives, tens, and twenties pinned to his costume. We had to chase him around the rink and try to pull off the money as he did amazing feints and swirls. That was followed by a Lou Goldstein-narrated ice show, with championship barrel-jumping—a speedskater leaping over fifteen or sixteen cylinders in a row, landing with a screech and spray of snow to great applause. I was wide-eyed and proud.

I would return to New York with gifts surpassing everyone's dreams, which made me a hero as well as a traitor. They could never quite acknowledge me because they believed *they* deserved what I seemed to have, more than I did—Daddy and Mommy because they thought they had made Grossinger's what it was, Jonny because he was so successful and good. Still I loved being Santa Claus, and Debby was always enchanted beyond subterfuge.

Throughout P.S. 6 I went to Bill-Dave Group and remained the friend and sparring partner of Phil. A list of our adventures would fill five hundred pages. Good old Phil—switch-hitting shortstop, grade-school hero, platoon leader, Tom Quest himself. Year after year he defeated me—in sports, in grades, in the esteem of our elders. But we shared the Yankees, the Hardy Boys, and a lifetime of cards and hardball. Our games ending always in his victories were a comfortably shared mythology. His role was as my leader and teacher, so I accepted his superiority and was as gracious a loser with him as I was a poor loser with my brother.

Most adults admired Phil's spunk and irreverence and laughed at his pranks, but to my mother he was a juvenile delinquent on the brink of serious trouble—another in my legion of errors in character judgment (that included Aunt Bunny and Dr. Fabian). Phil had been caught by Jessie in my company in the act of stealing. He had talked me into throwing my undershirt out the window to win a bet with Jonny Wouk. He had led us on nutty detective adventures that brought the police.

By fifth grade Phil had become a new kind of superboy; he was being tutored for prep school. He lorded that over everyone, quoting exotic formulas to prove his ascension to seventh and eighth grade math and bolstering his sassy slang with a new gentleman's vocabulary. He was suddenly the student-athlete, and Miss Fitzgerald, our teacher, infuriated my mother by saying she wished some of Phil would rub off on me: "He's just so energetic and creative."

"You follow her advice," Daddy said, "and you'll end up in jail."

"Daydream" was the word most used on my report cards. That didn't require great perspicacity from my teachers. But they thought I just didn't pay attention. They could have no idea of the things I was actually thinking. These weren't daydreams to me; they were "the story." So I ignored their complaints and learned barely enough to matriculate to the next grade each year. School just didn't count.

The years of my childhood embraced a dichotomy—Grossinger's and New York. It wasn't that New York was hell; in fact, it was real: it was long bittersweet days among my family and at school; it was Phil and the gang at Bill-Dave; my dialogues with Dr. Fabian; fungos with Jonny and Bob in Central Park; lemonades at the drugstore. It was the Yankees on the radio, boats in the bathtub, daydream planets rich as ripples across the Park reservoir where we fed the ducks. New York defined the me who got to go away. My brother Michael lived always in the magic kingdom at the end of the road to Oz; he didn't understand.

The feeling of being a culprit and a rogue was so basic it blended into the background of my City life. Even as I instinctively opposed the Towers' recriminations and censure, at heart I stood guilty before them. I fought back not as a good guy wronged but with the spirit of an outlaw. All Richard's victories, though they grandiloquently allowed them, were viewed as perverse and wrong—inroads of a family enemy. To this day I think of Richard as sly and conniving. I am compelled by ancient voices to play his role.

Yet it was never clear what my crime was. They tried forever to pass it off as duplicity and treason. In truth, it seemed more like something out of a Superman comic, as though I were the born adversary of my mother and Jon back on Krypton and now we lived on Earth.

I kept Grandma's autographed baseball in its box at the end of one of my bookshelves. I didn't think about it much, so I didn't notice at first when it was missing. Presuming Bridey had moved it while cleaning, I went to her. She shook her head and didn't want to discuss it. Then Jonny said, "Ask Daddy."

That evening, unaware of what I was about to invoke, I wondered if maybe Daddy borrowed it to show to a client.

"What do you mean, *your* baseball?" he exploded. "I brought those players to Grossinger's. Without Bob Towers, you don't have a baseball."

"But where is it?"

"He doesn't have to answer to you," my mother said, giving me her most authoritative and threatening look. Jon and Debby stared grimly. "You are insolent!"

"One Sunday we didn't have a ball," Bob shrugged. "Babe Ruth and Ty Cobb signed a thousand of those, and every clubhouse boy in America signed them for them. What did you think? You had something special? Richard, that ball was a big nothing."

I couldn't believe what they were saying. They had played with it, in fact the last time I was at Grossinger's. It was now just one more dirty hardball.

"It serves you right," my mother said.

It was never clear what she meant. Either it served me right for being at Grossinger's then, or it served me right for my general behavior. Then Bridey arrived with our plates. No one ever mentioned it again.

I spent summers at Chipinaw, moving up through the bunks with Jay, Barry, and whatever three other kids ended up with us. We became veteran campers, bored with regimens and activities. At the beginning of each summer I put a handmade calendar over my bed beginning with: "60 days left," and I tore off the top sheet daily until eventually everyone joined the spirit:

"Five more days of vacation,
Then we got to the station,
Back to civilization,
Oh how I want to go home."

Some years we had "good" counselors who collaborated with us—Sam Rosenberg spent half his salary on food and prizes for us in Bunk 9; he also gave up time-off to serve as commissioner for our All-Star Baseball tournaments during rest period and before dinner. That game had a spinner over which we fit disks with different sizes of home run and strikeout zones for each player. Other summers we were punished for our low grades in inspection and goofing off and docked dessert and movies—in constant strife with authority.

Jay and I became known throughout Chipinaw as the source of free passes to Grossinger's. Mine were usually limited to my own counselor and the group leader on their days off (my father ever vigilant against free-loaders), but Aunt Ruthie was quite willing to let everyone and their friends in, and Jay was the dispenser of her largesse. In partial bribery, counselors would slip into Monticello after Taps and bring us roast-beef sandwiches and knishes. We loved being awakened at 2 AM for such goodies wrapped in waxed paper. Sleepily we munched away while hearing them talk about movie stars, pro athletes, and beautiful babes in their swimsuits by the pool at the G.

I had a growing reputation as a prankster, and Jay and Barry often goaded me into providing entertainment. In fact, I developed a demonic streak I could ill explain. For instance, in Bunk 9 we were saddled with a kid even messier and more maladjusted than me. His name was also Richard, and he corrected mispronunciations of his last name so many times that we invented every imaginable pronunciation of it. Finally we settled on a pun using the "Or . . ." he hated the most: Orangeman.

I should have been his ally and sympathizer. Instead, one night long after Taps had sounded, I collected baseballs and shoes from our cubbies, tiptoed through the bathroom, and tossed them over the divider into the next bunk. Tearing back to my bed, I pushed Orangeman, covers and all, onto the floor. Then I pretended to be asleep.

The lights went on, and soon our bunk was filled with O.D.'s and kids from next door.

"Well, if you don't remember doing it, dammit, then you must have sleep-walked," said a frustrated counselor.

To my horror Orangeman agreed.

Years later Jay and Barry were still telling the story as evidence of my skill. "And that's why you don't see the Orangeman today," Barry would conclude ceremoniously.

Surely they have forgotten him by now, but I haven't.

The head counselor and ultimate authority in the boy's camp was Abbey West. A high-school principal and basketball referee from New Jersey, he was a stern, towering dignitary. Older than most of the counselors, he lived beyond the infirmary in a suburban cabin with his wife Dorey and two kids. On my father's coaxing, he had extended me an invitation to his dwelling back in my Midget days, and I continued to go there on my own, year after year, even after it was clear that it was regarded by others as the lair of the lion. (In fact, I found that the best way to deflect the lion's ire was to confront and entertain him during my most blatant truancies.)

Abbey's cabin was a camouflaged treasure. Blending qualities of Aunt Alice's yard and Dr. Fabian's office, it provided sanctuary in the midst of hazing and rivalry. Dorey poured lemonade and offered me cookies, as I discussed local events and even broached psychological ideas. I found Abbey usually (if not always) receptive, and willing to ignore my absence from where I was supposed to be.

When I was in Bunk 12 Jonny began as a homesick Midget. I felt sudden waves of tenderness for him, and I taught him Roofball and my armory game. It was strange in a way that he should suddenly be so close to Grossinger's—a place that had nothing to do with him and that he despised. My brother could only watch as an outsider as fruit, cakes, and chocolate chip cookies arrived. I was generous, but there was a subplot: I was telling a loyal Nevele fan about Grossinger's, rubbing his nose in it with my unreproachable magnanimity. I was showing him again how powerful and grand my other family was. He must have intuited that because soon he was refusing to eat "your rotten ille-

gal food." That was okay with me. Any connection between Jon and
Grossinger's bothered me.

(That fall, though, he actually shared my delight when we came
home from school to find that Yogi Berra had written me on the back
of a postcard of the ski slope to behave myself and do my homework!
"We should get Yogi Berra *here*," Bridey proclaimed as we danced
about, holding the card in the air. "Maybe he could introduce some
law and order before you wear your mother and me to death.")

Chipinaw was the liquored scent of its infirmary, the cracked paint of
its bathrooms, the smell of old pipes and cleanser. It was rabbits that
appeared at twilight and then darted away. They were not part of the
kingdom, though they lived on its grounds.

I remember our bodies crammed in together, in the bath-house at
the lake, the latrine where we brushed our teeth, lined up in the
armory—a kind of chubby fleshed aroma, childlike but clammy. I
remember the mess hall, the intricately eroded surfaces of its tables
like maps of other worlds, the pots of food with ladles, the game we
played with the salt and pepper, propelling them back and forth between
people on opposite sides of the table in an attempt to land part—even
a fraction of the glass rim—over the edge so that a flat hand pressed
against the table lip and then raised would dislodge it ... and how we
sprinkled salt on the surface for better sliding.

Meals at Chipinaw were a world unto itself, loathsome and sensuous both—dead flies inside the airy sections of the large sugar jars,
ice-cream-cup lids (off which a thin paper layer could be peeled revealing a round baseball card with the face of a player), a clatter of trays,
cheers when one was dropped, noodles and cheese onto which we
poured warm fruit salad, soggy chow mein, egg and egg-salad meals
from which I would go hungry.

Piles of comics collected in campers' cubbies, so I'd collect a bunch
of unfamiliar ones (a rocket blasting away as an astronaut floated above
Saturn in his space suit, a man and a woman submerged in test tubes
attended to by tentacled monsters with two tiers of vertical eyes, men
beside their rocket on the surface of a Martian moon under the giant
red planet crisscrossed with canals), lock myself in a bathroom stall,
and sit there reading about intergalactic criminals and renegade aliens

until I was going through them a second and third time each.

I remember the delivery of laundry every Friday in bundles wrapped in paper. They were heaved from the back of a truck into the center of the campus. Each bore a number in black crayon. We had to hunt through all the bunks for ours. They weren't Christmas presents, but there was a merry quality to the big paper blocks. The smaller ones could be lugged back by a single person, but the largest took two or three of us, and often they were busting as we carried them, leaving trails of socks and underpants, occasional mispacked bras and girls' underwear leading to slapstick and merriment. We lay on our beds for rest period, wasps whining at screens, a scent of grass cutters beyond.

The Yankees kept me company every summer. I would maintain my vigil even in bed at night when stations interfered and crossed, the radio on softly so that the O.D.s couldn't hear. As Mel Allen's voice waned and came back through the darkness I pieced together missing action until I clicked the knob just before sleep.

We wore our Chipinaw whites on Saturdays, which began with the morning services in the armory (the boys' camp on one side, the girls on the other). Counselors stationed themselves along the aisles, trying to keep apart brothers and sisters and boyfriends and girlfriends.

On rainy nights we converged on the same armory for movies. Boys and girls bustled in through separate doors in their yellow or orange gear, looking alike until they took off their round hats and the girls shook loose their hair. Rain-wear and moisture gave the room a sweet plastic smell. O.D.s passed around candy bars; then the lights went out and on the screen flashed the credits for some black and white spy movie or, on a number of occasions, *It Came From Outer Space*. The room was a racket of whispers and shouts. As the first pretty actress appeared, a bunch of girls hollered in unison, "Judy," and broke into giggles, then "Barry and Ellen," and, from the boys' side, "Tom in the shower" . . .whistles and hoots.

Dave Hecht, the unpopular owner, was regularly evoked. A fat, surly tyrant, he invaded events like a bossy cartoon mogul. He seemed to enjoy firing counselors for momentary indiscretions, often with a flamboyant gesture like an umpire banishing a player. During the major theatrical production one year, his teen-age daughter Lynne, acknowledgedly stunning, kissed an actor on the mouth, and Dave interrupted the play and came up on stage, where he reduced her to tears. The maiden appearance of the space monster always brought the same collective outcry of his name.

We performed skits and plays in the armory too, Dave portrayed by a camper with a painted mustache and a pillow stuffed under his pajama top. My bunkmate Barry put on blackface and blew into his trumpet, an imitation Louie Armstrong warble. A tiny girl with an enchanting voice sang: *"When you walk through a storm, keep your head up high, and don't be afraid of the dark."* The boys around me guffawed.

At the end of each day's activities we were summoned to the trademark Chipinaw ritual. Whether in the armory (moths rattling in ceiling lamps), or on an outdoor field at twilight, a counselor would announce it was time for "Friends" and "Taps." A few kids would always groan, but we put our arms around each other forming a long chain of all of us and then swung back and forth in place, our voices in and out of unison:

"Friends, friends, friends, we will always be."

It was ridiculous but irrefutable. No matter what we did to one another during the day, something about this comical, intimate song locked our hearts together.

The camp was pure blatancy, avoidance of anything inward or mysterious, denial of loneliness and sorrow. But joined in this chain of bodies against each other's boniness and weight, we were obliged to acknowledge how awkward and vulnerable our situation really was. The most competitive, aggressive athletes had to give up some of their bluff and join the others in a prayer that said that none of the rest mattered ... that we were all one. It may have been lip service, like good sportsmanship, but I experienced it as if we were all on a single spaceship, hurtling together through the big dark:

"Whether in fair or in foul stormy weather, Camp Chipinaw will keep us together."

Decorum never held up. People would be pulling too hard and parts of the line would collapse in heaps—or someone would stop swaying and we'd crunch. I would be yanked to one side and then feel no return tug from the other.

And when that was over we stood and sang the other song that made me think of the planet in space:

"Day is done. Gone the sun, from the earth, from the sky. . . ."

Later, we would march back to our bunks, get undressed, into pajamas, and lie in bed telling stories across the room; then "Taps" would resound wordlessly from camp to camp across the Lake. Mothwings flapped around light bulbs until counselors snapped the switches and hushed us.

"All is well. Safely rest. God is nigh."

Cozy in bed I broadcast my position to the gods and warned them—you sent me here, now please watch over me. This playful blasphemy (in place of the prayer the rabbi taught) eased my body and tucked me in.

Discipline and competition permeated Chipinaw. It was as though we were on a summer-long march under commanding officers. Many of these mentors were a type I met nowhere else. They were a blend of Park Avenue Synagogue piety and Marine drill sergeant (borrowed from TV shows and war movies, since none of them had been in the service). They spouted disdain for Arabs, fags, and "colored people" in a constant patter of jibes, imitation dialect, and jokes. (When almost four decades later a Jewish settler gunned down Palestinian parishioners in a mosque, I was startled to realize I had served under him those summers of my youth—not the same zealot of course, but his hysterical forerunners, boasting about turning rifles on Arabs and then aiming their imaginary weapons at us.)

Just past the mid-point of every summer the camp was divided into Red and Gray teams that competed singlemindedly against each other for points over a one-week period called Color War. Athletic contests were only a part of this competition. All of waking life, and to some degree sleep, were coopted by it. From the moment war was declared, the Reds and Grays were implacable enemies. Despite prior friendships opponents barely talked to one another (the bunks were rearranged with the beds of teammates together, and the mess hall was divided into team tables). The value of such activity was presumed as a law of nature. "Tough world, isn't it?" one counselor mocked.

Not only were campers all distributed to either the Red or the Gray, counselors were too. The sole noncombatants were the nurse and the doctor, the owners and administrators, and the elderly maintenance men (who lived in tents between the armory and the woods and were dubbed "the zombies"). The five head counselors served as judges, Abbey their commissioner.

One never knew when Color War would "break." In theory it could come at any time, though it never occurred during the early weeks. As we approached the end of July, campers were on pins and needles in constant expectation and speculation.

A dramatic event heralded Color War's outbreak. A bunch of costumed figures would burst onto the campus and throw around fliers with the division of Red and Gray teams. Or the bugle recording would suddenly blast out Fire Call or mid-day reveille and everyone would run to the O.D. shack to find team lists tacked on the bulletin board. The most spectacular breaking was a plane flying low over the camp dropping parachutes with the team lists. Back and forth it clattered, filling the air with them, insects materializing into objects, magnificent but also ominous.

With the announcement of the teams we were immediately summoned by our captains to strategy sessions. Any prior schedule of activities was terminated abruptly. I dreaded this moment; I knew its precise lurch of despondency. We now might be judged for points at any moment. The incompetence of our bedmaking and the state of our cubbies could lower our team's score. Every clean-up job at inspection, every appearance at line-up had the same potential of loss. Even famous slobs like Jay and Barry scrubbed and swept like demons throughout Color War. At meals we were expected to eat silently, with any spoken word charged against the team on whose side it occurred.

Color War encouraged a level of communal ill spirit I encountered nowhere else in childhood. The prison was turned over to the inmates. Athletic overachievers and militant counselors suddenly had free rein to keep everyone in line, the usual accusation being, "You prick, those points you're losin' I sweated for today on the playin' field."

All during the summer I could be a nonentity, half-athlete, half-eccentric, as I wandered between events with my books and radio. During Color War my rebellion fell under a microscope. The Yankee game cost points. My bedwetting became a public issue, team members unhappily having to help me with my sheets in order to be prepared for inspection.

During a packed week of competition the intensity climbed to a frenzy as campers not engaged in events came in crowds to watch and cheer for their team. It was meant to be Major League, but I felt like Alice in a court of playing cards. Even the sun met reveille with combat-zone light. All morning and afternoon and after dinner, battles were fought and adversaries glared. Night was a spy in an enemy camp.

Like generals of armies, Red and Gray captains carried around the unofficial tally on clipboards and, receiving messengers from farflung fields and courts, added in current points, but theirs was guesswork—the official running score was read by the judges to hushed silence at the end of each day at dinner.

One of the critical contests was a several-hour tag-team relay around the entire campus and requiring everyone's participation—a huge chunk of points at stake. Older kids sprinted the longest distances, for instance, from the mess hall to the lake; younger kids like us ran from bunk to bunk or armory to flagpole. A baton was passed from runner to runner, and the course of the race wound back and forth across the entire campus, building to a crescendo at the finish line. Those who had done their laps ran along anyway, urging others to go faster, to take the baton while in motion. The race disappeared into the woods and reappeared from remote trails. Fat kids strained at every muscle while seniors and waiters shadowed them, shouting for them to move their asses. The final laps were often hard to see, as waves of spectators surrounded single points of energy traced by batons. As the last runner crossed the line, the winning team danced and screamed.

The sing was worth even more points. In the first days after the onset of War the captains and counselors of Red and Grey stayed up late and wrote marches, alma maters, and novelty songs. Then all the rest of us had to learn their words and render them: *"The trees that wreathe our Chip'naw/the bunks along the hill, Abbey and Nurse Mary/the game our hearts do fill . . ."* and then *"The old grey mare/she ain't what she used to be. . . ."*

Whenever we weren't engaged in matches we were herded into the armory or mess hall for required sing rehearsals—top secret. No Roofball or Stoopball, no reading! If I was absent, someone found me and dragged me in. I remember a bossy senior smashing me across the face with his megaphone because he said I wasn't singing, and then putting his ear next to my mouth, giving me a short hard knuckle sandwich in the arm every time he thought my voice had gotten too faint.

Color War made my evasions useless. As in any win-at-all-costs situation, indoctrination and brutality became accepted norms. Even Abbey retreated to Olympus to let the battle run its course. He sat at the center table in the mess hall with Nurse Mary, the doctor, and the judges and, when I went to his house for the usual solace and conversation, Dorey turned me away, so no one would think she was favoring one side.

In past years I had tried to invent ways to dodge or at least mollify this event. The previous summer, at the beginning of July, I went around announcing that I was going to be neutral. I made sure every potential captain and judge heard me. But no one took me seriously, and for good reason. One early August night the team rosters were on our tables, and right away we were instructed to find our new places. Where could I go? My name was on the Red team list. There were no neutral tables; I had to eat dinner with them. Likewise, back at the bunk, symmetry required that my bed be moved into the Red zone.

Still, I was defiant. I didn't show up at any of my activities, and I didn't clean up my area. Some of the judges were as gung-ho about their roles as any camper and, to force the issue, points were deducted in unprecedented clumps. This created an uproar around me. Seniors and waiters made pilgrimages to my bunk to cajole me, but I held firm: I wasn't for either side, I hoped they had a good War.

They confiscated my radio. They woke me up in the middle of the night, marched me to the lake, and dunked me in my pajamas. They put me in wrestling holds and twisted my arms. But I wouldn't give in. I experienced in myself a stubbornness so firm and invulnerable it was astonishing to me. I felt that I was right and, though the entire camp stood against me, I wasn't going to back down. "Kill me!" I screamed, as they shook me in bed a third night in a row.

The morning after the dunking I stole the Sunday sports pages from a counselor and comic books from various cubbies. I got my copy of *The Way of All Flesh*, pocketed some bread from the mess hall, and took an unknown trail into the woods. I had eight never-read comics: space creatures with drooling green heads like external brains, emerging from a spaceship while in the background flying saucers streamed out of a larger flying saucer silhouetted against a huge yellow moon; Bugs flying a saucer with Yosemite Sam in a bubble beside him; Batman and

Robin holding their ears while attacked by Joker with bagpipes; an old-fashioned plane leaving trails against a purple-green sky, gold moon, Robin pointing to an impostor lifting off with strapped-on jets.

That evening Dave Hecht, leading three hounds on leashes, found me. He stood at leash length, staring with utmost disapproval. "Dickie," he said, which almost no one called me, "you have violated the basic rule of camping. In my forty years in this business you're the first person I've had to go looking for."

Crying, I stood up. I offered to come back if I didn't have to be in Color War.

"I'm not asking you," he pontificated, "I'm telling you. We're making no deals. Campers don't just walk off."

I was hungry anyway, and I wasn't going to argue with a two-hundred-and-fifty-pound lawyer with three dogs. I had to go through the motions for the rest of Color War, and I even won a rowboat race. Afterwards Abbey tried to explain: Color War couldn't be optional or it wouldn't happen. It was a big part of the camp, and many parents felt it was the single most important event in their children's lives.

In 1955 I started sixth grade with Mrs. Lewis. She was famous throughout P.S. 6 for not only her tough teaching but a flask of strong-smelling liquid masquerading as a water jug on her desk (the student who refilled her glass was known among us as the "whiskey monitor"). Her specialty, labor unions, was also not in the curriculum, but she diagrammed their history for two weeks on the blackboard, then let us in on the historic merger of the AF of L and CIO as it happened.

My mother set her heart on my going to Horace Mann or Riverdale, difficult prep schools on the edge of Westchester County. She had always admired kids in maroon Horace Mann jackets. In her mind her sons were scholars, intellectuals in the French tradition, like her brother Lionel who had run away from home as a teenager and become a renowned professor of history. However, the outlook for my going was dim to nil. Not only were my grades atrocious, but Uncle Paul opposed private school. He said it was a waste of money because it didn't prepare you for the real world.

One evening at dinner my mother startled us all by announcing,

"Richard's father agrees to send him to Horace Mann or Riverdale in the unlikely event he should be accepted."

"What's the catch, Martha?" asked Bob.

She smiled conspiratorially. "Just that his name be changed to Grossinger."

"What, Towers isn't good enough for him!"

"Well, Turetsky wasn't good enough for you."

"You needler," he retorted.

As a first step toward getting me into either school she made a rare phone call to Phil's mother and ended up hiring the young woman from Riverdale who had tutored him. She showed up at our front door, looking proper, and told us right away that Phil was the smartest child she ever met. She gave me two hours of her own impossible tests, looked at my results, and then informed my parents that I wasn't "Riverdale material." She would not even be my tutor. Undeterred, my mother called Columbia and got an older graduate student of history named Mr. Hilowitz. He arrived one night in a brown raincoat, handed his hat to Bob who put it in the closet, and then shook my hand.

"Educate this lad," my stepfather announced as we headed down the hallway.

"Your father has a sense of humor," Mr. Hilowitz remarked once in my room. We both laughed.

After the first exploratory session he took a deep breath and said, "You've missed a lot of basics, so let's go back to the beginning." From then on we spent two hours together three nights a week, redoing my education from first grade. It was all dimly familiar because I had watched it through a fog. Now I was captivated to see how it actually worked: the numbers carried over, the formulas enacted, the parts of speech forming grammatical sentences. He was a charming teacher, recalling the best of Miss Tighe, and it was elating to sweep away all the encumberances that had accumulated over the years. As long as I got it he kept speeding up the pace. In a matter of months I had reached sixth grade again. Nobody quite knew what happened—not Mrs. Lewis, not my mother, not even me.

I honor Mr. Hilowitz most for the day I had a panic. I was setting up a Sorry game with Jon. I stared at the yellow and red tokens in their zones at Start; suddenly I felt the disease. "I have it! I have it!" I screamed. My mother tucked me into bed, filled my nose with bitter drops, and smeared Vick's Vaporub over my chest. Then Mr. Hilowitz arrived.

I lay there, staring at the window, trying to keep thoughts at bay, ashamed to be so revealed. It was obvious I could do no work tonight. But he sat on the edge of the covers and told stories for the whole two hours, creating voices for historical figures as he went—Christopher Columbus, John Cabot, Roanoke and the mystery of Virginia Dare, Marquette and Joliet along the Mississippi, the French and Indian War, the Spaniards' unsuccessful search for gold. He lured me back into the world of real things and made life normal again.

That was my last panic for almost ten years.

The admissions interviews were stern and formal, so I volunteered little, answering only as I was asked. At Horace Mann the teacher read from a list of questions that included: "What are your hobbies?" None came to mind.

"Then what do you do in your spare time?"

"Watch TV, listen to ball-games."

"Couldn't you at least have told him you have a scrapbook on Mars?" my mother asked in the cab home.

"I forgot."

I failed the exam for Riverdale but somehow got into Horace Mann. Phil was unimpressed. "That's mostly for Jews and colored kids," he said. I didn't talk to him for the rest of the year. I saw him only one more time. During the fall of our first year at the new schools he called me about three out-of-print Tom Quest books I had found at a used bookstore near Grossinger's. He had never forgiven me that one victory, so I met him along Park Avenue halfway between our houses and sold the copies to him.

All that time I was doing something different with the hooded hawk and the clue in the embers anyway. Now I was done with the mystery story. In fact, I was done with Richard Towers.

Near the end of sixth grade I felt wild and unbounded. I tossed my cherished collection of cartoon, Flash Gordon, and other non-baseball cards into the air, free for all takers. They blew about the P.S. 6 yard, causing a commotion.

"The kid's a madman!"

"Totally nutso!"

I loved it.

And it was spring and cherry blossoms in Central Park, and something bigger, bigger than even me, was called for. So I dispersed my famous baseball cards too, six years' worth, an unexplained trail through the Park with the entirety of Bill-Dave following and fighting for possession a few hundred yards behind me as I ducked in and out of bushes—an anonymous Robin Hood—saving my Yankees for last, and finally, picture after picture, dropping even the hardwon years of every Gil McDougald. I had no idea why. I had planned to keep those cards forever. I only knew that I watched gleefully from a million miles away. ("It's Towers again," they all shouted as the last ones gave me away.)

One afternoon Mrs. Lewis asked me to stay after school for a conference. As I approached her desk, she congratulated me on my improved work and admission to Horace Mann. "You're going to have to work even harder there. I want to get you off to a good start, so try to be more alert in class." Then she extolled my new last name, which had been added to the record. "You must be related to Jennie Grossinger."

I nodded.

"What a marvelous woman. She does so much for charity."

When Mrs. Lewis taught us about apples a few weeks later, she asked for extra-credit papers on one or another variety and I wrote three of them: the pippin, the winesap, and the MacIntosh, the separate colors and tastes of which still have a sort of delicacy for me— they mark the moment of transition.

In the last weeks of school a few boys and girls began to go out with one another. A kid named Jimmy McCracken gave a studded dog collar to a girl named Annie Welch. She wore it around her calf above her ankle. Phil and I had no interest in this event other than embarrassed dodging. That Annie Welch had traveled with me to other worlds was something I would let no one know, not even Dr. Fabian. Though

Phil eventually proclaimed his intention to find a girlfriend too, it was mainly boasting. Neither of us was ready.

Then one night I dreamed that I had been hoodwinked in my pajamas, the very sheets and blankets still wrapped around me, back to the classroom. Only the girls were there, and three of them took my clothes off. They moved in a circle about me, silently, in a dance of animals. The room was thick with perfume and flowers.

And then it became ... walking in a forest, emerald moss beneath my feet. Long, light vines hung from the branches, exuding musty dew. I could actually feel their moisture and smell them. This dream was real!

I came to a log shack—the true one, the prototype of the place that Joey, Andy, and I had built on another planet.

Annie Welch was sitting there with two other girls. It was as though she were waiting for me. "I'm not Jimmy," I tried to warn her, but she didn't seem to care. She stood and approached me, put her hands on my shoulders and sat me down on a rock. Then she put a blindfold on me. One by one they kissed me on the face. I felt their lips in intoxicating sequence. Girls.

I began spinning. Then the whole world around me was tumbling. I awoke in great joy with my penis hard. I lay there in a kind of ecstasy. I did not understand what was happening to me, and yet I had experienced such complicated texture before, once in Westport when I was playing in the attic and hypnotic waves came from the aroma of trunks and old things.

My dream now bore the resolution of this childhood experience, not so much the intimation of sexuality as the power of being enfolded within a sensuous and opulent space. It was not just an image or landscape; it was everything I was, before Richard Towers.

Against that sensation my outer-space daydreams were faded postcards. It was one thing to fantasize settling on other worlds and another *actually to be there.*

The memory of that dream gave me solace for years—the fact that someone kissed me, the richness of the green, the scented moisture, the way I merged with everything as it spun instead of becoming dizzy and separate, how the throbbing filled me from the inside out.

I couldn't believe this had been there all along and neither I nor Dr.

Fabian had noticed it. I *was* that forest. Its familiarity was the sweet caverns of my own being. I didn't know it yet, but I had discovered that I was intact, that my body and spirit could still be recovered whole.

When I fell back asleep, though, I found myself in the vacant classroom at night. I ran down the hallway in fear of what might come out of such an emptiness, ran all the way to the auditorium where—in pitch black, just what I feared—a rude billowing voice arose from behind the stage and roared through the room like a beast. I turned and fled out the door. I raced for blocks, but the sound pursued me, persistent against the sky.

PART TWO

THE KID FROM GROSSINGER'S

1956–1960

HORACE MANN

The summer of '56, I went, as usual, to Chipinaw. Horace Mann First Formers were expected to have completed at least four books from an assigned list, so I arrived with instructions to Abbey that I be given time off to read. Taking advantage of this I chose more than four titles. While only *David Copperfield* was required I brought copies of two other Dickens novels, *Martin Chuzzlewit* and *Our Mutual Friend.* I lived that summer at Chipinaw partly in the fog along the Thames, musing about John Rokesmith's lost identities and following Martin Chuzzlewit back to England. Whole lives passed through me as I lay in the grass beyond the stridency of games.

Our counselor had to leave almost two weeks early, and an older redneck was put in charge of our bunk. It was rumored that they had found the guy hitchhiking. He carried a knife, drank hard liquor, and cursed us with four-letter words. He didn't care at all about our keeping things neat, but he liked to order us around like slaves. He raided our food supplies and, at meals, ate our portions. He also threatened us with his erect penis and invited kids to hold it. We imagined he was an escaped convict. Even Jay and Barry were terrified of him.

One breakfast, as our allotment of eight pieces of French toast was deposited on the table, Ralph grabbed the platter, lifted it, and stabbed four, leaving the rest for us to split. I didn't care that much for French toast (and I had stayed mostly out of trouble's way), but Ralph was insane by even Chipinaw standards and I was incensed that he should have been put in charge of us. When the platter reached me, there was one piece left and one more person to go after my turn. I handed it back to Ralph and said, "Here. Maybe you didn't get enough." There was a hush as he looked at me with wild eyes.

"Stand up!" he called out. That was the supreme embarrassment in the dining room—public reprimand. I sat there. "Stand up!" He rose and pointed down at me. The cavernous room was now soundless.

"Stand up!"

I stood and, with a quick sweep of my hand, turned over the pot of hot coffee on him. He let out a howl of pain and dove at me across the table. Three other counselors wrestled him to the ground. "I'm going to kill him," he screamed. "The little bastard, I'm going to kill him."

I never did understand why they left him in our bunk after that. I got little sleep, but I made it to the banquet alive. All that day we packed our things in trunks and suitcases. I felt so much excitement I could barely think it: we didn't have to sleep at Chipinaw another night!

At the end of the awards ceremony near midnight, cars arrived to collect us: me, Jay, Siggy, Jay's cousins from the girls' camp, and Barry. No escape by flying saucer was ever more thrilling or mysterious. We were lights moving along back roads toward civilization, toward the Emerald City. Everything was enhanced—boundless and utterly strange. Even billboards seemed gateways to other universes.

Jay, Barry, and I met next at the lunch buffet amid platters of roast beef, melons filled with fruit salad, and trays of chocolate cakes and fruit tarts. It was rapture, just to walk by the sparkle of the pool among the chattering crowds, to look up into the sky and watch the white cumulus exploding forever.

I had dreams of Horace Mann before I went there. Hiking up marble steps, I passed between pillars into a Greek temple housing a large industrial building. Once inside, I could find no classrooms—only hallways through which crowds of people rushed. I saw no kids there either, just preoccupied adults carrying papers and books.

My mother took me to Saks Fifth Avenue and had me fitted for an entire wardrobe of sports jackets, ties, slacks, and shoes. I was only an incidental party to the deliberations of her and the salesman, as though they were deciding how some abstract child might look if he were properly dressed. I could barely imagine attending a boys' academy where the teachers were addressed as "Sir," and I felt like an impostor in these expensive clothes.

On the evening before the first day of Horace Mann my mother and Bob marked the occasion by taking me alone to a fancy Italian restaurant. He spoke with accustomed flamboyance: "I hope you appreciate where you're going. This is your chance to join the archons of our society."

"I don't think he realizes how much work it will be," my mother countered. I was silent; I already feared the worst. "This is his last free night," she added, staring at me, "for six years!"

"Don't be ghoulish," Bob chided.

Lying in bed on the eve of a new life, I couldn't imagine Horace Mann. After all, I had barely been able to make it through P.S. 6.

Awakened by Bridey's cheery summons at 6 AM ("new school for the lad, first day"), groggily I put myself in costume, pulling pins and tissue paper out of a shirt and knotting a red-and-brown striped tie before the bathroom mirror. Doubt and exhilaration warred inside me—layers of sleepiness overlying tugs of unsettled remembrance: the Dragons of Blueland, Flash Gordon at the Martian court *(who was I?)*. Trepidation kept supplying guises of stern, unsmiling masters like the signers of the Declaration.

I glanced at a harlequin child in the mirror. Six years! I didn't think it would be possible to do this for a week.

By phoning the school my mother had gotten the names of two older boys who lived in our neighborhood, and she arranged for them to teach me the route. I left Jonny at the canopy and walked across the street. In a group Horace Mann students were gathering at the 96th Street bus stop. Boarding, we dropped coins into a box, found seats along the rear window, and began immediately playing a game with the numbers on paper transfers we had requested (though didn't need). We raced to be the first to make our digits end up at zero by alternate sequences of addition, subtraction, division, and multiplication. Meanwhile, Madison and Fifth flew by; then we zoomed through Park tunnels to the less familiar West Side, and finally Broadway where we disembarked and plunged into the tenebrous IRT.

First we bought fifteen-cent tokens from the lady at the booth, then wrestled through turnstiles to catch a parked train just before its doors closed. (In later weeks I would simply flash my pass at the agent as I raced through the gate.) In relief at beating the metallic thud we sat in mostly silent contemplation as—stop by stop—the car filled with students from all different schools, most of the later ones having to stand; then it emptied onto streets in the 200s as the train rattled out of the underworld onto stilts that wound above the northern city.

Horace Mann was the last station: 242nd Street. From there we hiked four blocks up a hill to 246th.

I was expected to report to Pforzheimer Hall. This sleek box hugged a slope below the ivy-covered upper classrooms. Designated solely for the Lower School, it was an elongated space station with zigzag entry ports. That we were its baptizers postponed the start of classes, and I was grateful for the hours before any distinct action, other than getting my schedule from an alphabetical stack, was required.

My first day as Richard Grossinger seemed an eternity among throngs of eager first-formers finding our way from room to room. Each teacher, though unexpectedly amiable, (without fail) advised us that his course would take *at least* an hour's homework every night and that we had better pay scrupulous attention in class. ("Every pearl of wisdom that comes from my ruby-red lips," warned Mr. Allison in American History when asked, "What are we responsible for?"). Maybe this *was* the end of freedom. But for one precious day I was snug and anonymous among the masses. The second morning, lectures began in earnest.

Almost immediately I decided I couldn't maintain my folio of planets and stay alert in class. In a series of protracted episodes I ended the adventures in space and hurtled my spaceship out of the Galaxy. Sometimes it crashed; sometimes it returned to its makers; sometimes it was swallowed into infinity—but finally it was put beyond reach. Although I made it up anew in later years, it would never again be real.

In jacket and tie, scrawling till my hand ached, I tried to capture the gist of lectures—arithmetic formulas, parts of speech, families of languages, interpretations of the Preamble to the Declaration. All around me, in jackets and ties, were other young scholars accepted to this academy. No one knew that Richard Grossinger had never been a scholar before, that he was dressed formally for the first time, that he was really Richard Towers.

Over the initial weeks I felt a mildly ecstatic respite from both my family and the premonition of a Horace Mann beyond reach. The math turned out to be no harder than what Mr. Hilowitz had prepared me for. General Language, English, and history were straightforward lessons exploring roots of words, sentence structure, and the laws of the Constitution. I assimilated diagrams of adverbs, adjectives, and prepositions; equations with letters; and the logic of parliamentary order. In Music we learned to identify composers and their symphonies. I loved finding the anthems and guns hidden in Tchaikovsky's *1812 Overture*, the aroused skeletons in the graveyard of Saint Saëns. Here were symbols wrapped in new latent forms. I even got Daddy to buy me my own record of *Danse Macabre*.

Yanking me out of this spell were two hours of gym capping each day. At two o'clock the whole First Form straggled from the separate classrooms of Pforzheimer around the walkway into the basement of a gray fortress on the far side of the playing field. There we were assigned a second set of lockers and ordered to get into sweat clothes pronto.

The coaches were fully credentialed deliverers of male authority whose gazes bore right through us. Calling us by last name only (often preceded by a scornful "Mister"), they gave instructions "just once" and then stood back with folded arms and squinched eyes to observe our performances.

We endured weeks of lifting barbells, counting sit-ups and push-ups, being matched with boxing gloves and on the mat. The members of the athletic staff attacked our isolation, exposing our bodies before one another, barking at us and calling us girlies. Ducking behind larger classmates, I prayed not to be noticed, not to have to wrestle, not to have my ragged sit-ups evaluated. But everyone took a turn.

I fluttered through appearances in the spotlight, straining and kicking my legs to pull my frame up, taking punches in the face, jabbing out a fat glove, trying to get my arms around the neck and legs of a huskier kid as we rolled on the mat, always amazed I came out the other end without some major embarrassment.

I survived these gauntlets, showered, bought a snack at the foot of the hill, and rode home on the el with my friends. Finally our P.E. group moved on to soccer, charging down an immense slope behind the school into Van Cortlandt Park where we squared off—vestiges of Bill-Dave in the autumn air, as I dribbled and then kicked at the goal. Volleys of oranged and reddened leaves gusted by, whistles from other games near and far. Discarded past and unknown future balanced seamlessly as Jeff Jones hit me with a pass across the field. "Go!" he shouted. "Go!"

Nights and weekends were packed with homework. I routinely started math on the subway and did not quit working until just before I dropped into bed. I handed in assignments and took almost daily tests. When Uncle Paul sent tickets for Daddy to take me to the two weekend games of the 1956 World Series at Ebbets Field it seemed like the revisitation of a childhood I had lost long ago.

To my mind I did okay. After all, I was crossing light years in months. I got plenty of things wrong, but I didn't daydream, and I understood. When the first report card came, however, it showed all C's, except for a D in math accompanied by a probation report.

My mother was frantic; she thought I was close to expulsion and blamed herself for not paying enough attention to my study habits. Soon she began scrutinizing me like a hawk. Her new injunction to study merged with her general outrage at me and gave her a *raison* for continuously reprimanding me. She had no idea of the real scope of the homework or of my progress. She was sure not only that I was way behind but that it could be remedied only by a constant threat of punishment.

Horace Mann had become my single identity to her. She had forgotten P.S. 6, Jessie's Jip Joint, and Bill-Dave as though they never happened. Even my apostasy at Grossinger's and Dr. Fabian's had become mere trifles. She judged me by one standard alone. As long as she saw me at my desk she was appeased. For years I was fixed in her brain as the single command to "get back to work"—no matter the time of day or circumstance.

I still taste the famished rush from the last morning class to the cafeteria line, piles of spaghetti in meat sauce, metal trays of white fish on

Friday—a block of ice cream or scoop of jello for dessert. After lunch we gathered at the bookstore to buy marshmallow bars kept in ice-cream lockers—so hard they cracked like stone in our teeth.

Before afternoon classes we stood in the pathway trying to catch leaves off giant maples, calling out each point. Cold squalls strafed the sky while, clad in jackets and ties, we twisted and grabbed at golden-red ghosts, colliding with one another and laughing. I played this game until a group of upperclassmen stopped to watch and I heard a whisper of "Fags!" Then a cool-looking guy grabbed the arm of the kid next to me and pronounced slowly through curled lips, "I just *hate* little fags."

One morning I awoke to see snow falling in the courtyard. I opened the window and put my fingertips into the fluff on the windowsill. Bridey had the radio on. They were reading the list of schools closed in the New York area. The names went on and on, so many Catholic schools and academies and colleges in Brooklyn, Queens, Manhattan. I was rooting hard for Horace Mann. I wanted a special day, a day from long ago when Jonny and I went out with sleds. "Adelphi, Hofstra, Horace Mann . . ." I cheered aloud. Bridey gave me a look of part amusement, part censure.

Central Park was an ancient village, snow falling so densely I could barely see. I clopped my perfect footprints and stared at figures materializing through the fog. Fifth Avenue was bare of cars. A few people skied down the long thoroughfare while others made snow statues and chased after the occasional lonely bus like some wooly mammoth.

The next day the sun shone on a new world, and I rejoined my comrades on the subway. I felt as though I were returning to Horace Mann from prehistoric Wales.

Naked in winter gym we stood by an unheated pool as Mr. Mathaner demonstrated the butterfly and side stroke. I sought radiator pipes along the wall, trying to avoid bumping into either bare bodies or the scalding metal, my arms hugging my chest.

Mr. Mathaner blew his whistle, and we dove a collective chlorine splash, raced to the other end, then got out, and jockeyed for positions near new radiators. "Mr. Grossinger!" Invariably he found me and redemonstrated the stroke.

I jumped back in alone and strained to imitate his rotating arms and chest.

"Better! Now work on it."

Through the entire period I longed for the steamy shower room . . . until at last I stood mesmerized in sweet, hot spray, spinning my body, letting the waterfall sweep and cloud over my shoulders.

Nakedness was a rite in which we observed our own bodies changing in the mirrors of one another. Beneath the mask of our shouting and ribaldry we spied on classmates' physiology, degrees of pubic hair and different-shaped penises. So many of them were men, and yet I too was becoming more of a man than I could believe.

In threadbare towels we raced across the stone of the locker-room, got somewhat dry (except hair), restored jackets and ties, gathered our books and papers, and headed home.

The subway bonded those of us who commuted from Manhattan (other classmates came by bus and car from Westchester and the general northern suburbs). The train taught its own internal clock. I grew to anticipate the feeling of the tracks between stops, how the snake lurched at each bend, where it accelerated, how it slowed down, and where the lights went out (so they didn't startle me). Some of my classmates became subway-map innovators and worked out complicated after-school routes, including ones that, skipping the bus, took us to the East Bronx (where we stared down from the platform at snow on the Yankees' field). Ultimately we came to prefer the long express stops and breakneck speed of the older, sootier IND, so we always switched lines at 168th Street.

For a whole month we held a contest of "IND basketball," shooting for the vents above sooty windows with crumpled-up notebook paper. One got two points when the "ball" was sucked out into the tunnel. It felt a little funny making our shots in front of an incredibly tall schoolboy across the aisle because he was supposed to be a famous player. It turned out to be young Lew Alcindor, but I doubt he realized the game we were playing was basketball.

When I got home I consumed whatever was there. I would make toast and layer on huge portions of apricot and grape jam, chomp half a pack of cream cheese straight, then devour bananas, oranges, cookies, and two or three little boxes of Rice Krispies or Frosted Flakes. Later I would get a light golden tan on slices of bread and coat them with melting butter. I alternated Arnold's "vanilla" and Pepperidge Farm Whole Wheat. One night I ate seven bananas; another night I went through a loaf and a half of Thomas' raisin bread with cream cheese. I would sit at my desk, stuffing it in as my reward as I worked.

Our schedules took us daily from one academic class to another to lunch, then later to Woodshop (supplanting Music), study hall, and gym. I was not much of a carpenter, but I made a rough facsimile of a stool for Bridey and began working on a birdhouse for Aunt Bunny. Impressed that the elderly teacher was missing three fingers, I was careful not to slip as I sawed choppily along my pencil markings. After another month, Woodshop students moved on to Theater Arts.

Twice a week the whole school gathered in the auditorium for Chapel at which we sang hymns and college songs. Words were projected onto a screen: *"A mighty fortress is our God"* and *"Stand and drink a toast to dear old Maine."* Every so often Mr. Allison led us in a rousing version of *"Give me ten men who are stout-hearted men. ..."* Soon the room rocked with male voices.

I liked being in the heart of such robustness, so I brought the songs home to the shower: *"We gather together to ask the Lord's blessing"* and *"To the Earth, to the stars, to the girls who will love us someday!"*

Staying on the train three extra stops after school and getting off at 57th Street was an alternative to going straight home. My favorite diversion was visiting PZ at the Grossinger New York office. PZ (never thought of as Paul Zousmer) was a short Danny Kaye lookalike, a longtime employee who preferred to work in the City to be near his ailing mother. He was a miscast journalist who handled details of Grossinger archiving, an unappreciated house historian in a cubicle stuffed with piles of photographs and yellowed newspaper clippings.

PZ's face always lit up when I arrived. I was not only a devotee of Grossinger memorabilia; I was a Grossinger myself and appeared in dozens of photos and press clippings from November 3, 1944, as a newborn, my mother and Uncle Paul, both so young and wide-eyed, holding me—the caption: "His Majesty, The King."

A fiery CCNY graduate named Bob Towers was also a mainstay of the 1940s lexicon, pictured with golfers, ballplayers, and stage stars, often a microphone in hand. Sometimes Uncle Paul and he walked arm-in-arm.

On the next block was a store called Photographic Fair where PZ went for film, equipment, and conversation at the counter. Our buddy there was a thin, balding clerk named Charlie de Luise who handed us expensive cameras from behind locked glass and let me adjust them for light and shutter speed. I wanted to be able to shoot close-ups and action photos, and I particularly admired a Minolta with a two-thousandths-of-a-second shutter speed. PZ promised to hire me after school was out so I could earn the hundred dollars necessary to buy it.

Grossinger's also had accounts at Womrath's Bookstore (next door to Photographic Fair) and Colony Records (a few blocks away), so I would bring lists of new science-fiction novels, reading for school, and songs I heard on the radio, and then charge purchases at both stores.

Just before Christmas our school routine was interrupted by final exams, which were scheduled one or two a day in the gym at odd hours. All the way to 242nd Street we quizzed one another, intimidated by how much our comrades knew, trying to digest a few more facts ourselves right up to the door. Cartons were sliced open and bluebooks poured out. The basketball court was coopted by desks crossing from window to window. Hearts thumping, we picked our exams from the correct stacks and took any seat along the sawdust-sprinkled floor (all grades were mixed). I scanned the printed pages, relieved instantly by the familiar, chilled by inevitable surprises. Then, my heart in my throat, I began scribbling for dear life.

These finals felt like ultimatums of life and death. For weeks beforehand I found myself having the same nightmare in which I looked at my test and could decipher nothing, as though I hadn't even attended the course. I still have these dreams. (Chuck Stein, a classmate then who's now a practicing Buddhist, tells me that even thirty-five years of meditation have not brought to an end his terror of the examinations in the HM gym.)

During the allotted two hours we expended monumental energy, drawing on hours of review and making a record of our partial mastery.

I pushed a pen until my fingers cramped. Near the end I rifled back to problems I couldn't get the first time.

Abruptly a command halted us: "Put down your writing implements at once!" I felt a moment of empty relief, then headed home to study for the next one.

After mid-terms Joe drove me to Grossinger's. To my surprise I arrived to find my brothers alone in their house, Uncle Paul and Aunt Bunny detained overseas. The living room was a mess—liquor bottles and newspapers on the floor. Michael filled me in: Beulah had gone to see a sick aunt, and Housekeeping had sent over a substitute maid who didn't speak English. "But she knows what that is," he said, pointing to the liquor cabinet. He led me on tour: "Empties in every room!" He threw up his arms in mock disgust.

When I first encountered the monster, she was brandishing a mop and chased me out of the third floor, flinging a bottle for good measure. It bounced crazily against walls and landed without breaking. This was great! Then she began throwing ashtrays and clothing down the stairs. I called the head of Housekeeping, but that was Aunt Rose, a tiny dynamo of spittle with no use for kids (and barely more sober than our guardian). She barked something indecipherable and hung up.

The three of us plotted. We took a human-sized stuffed monkey, dressed it in Uncle Paul's suit jacket and tie, and put him to bed in my room on the third floor. We spilled ketchup on his fine white shirt, knocked over some lamps, and led a string of knotted sheets from the bedpost out the window. Then we taped groans on the tape recorder and stuck it under the bed.

The noises engaged her curiosity. She edged her way across the hall, looked in the room, screamed, and went running down the stairs and out of the house. We had gotten rid of her just the way Bugs Bunny would have!

The day before Christmas, Michael's teacher came to talk to Aunt Bunny about his difficulties in school. All that afternoon, in preparation of entertainment, my brothers and I rehearsed *Curley the Talking Caterpillar,* which my Horace Mann Theater Arts class was performing. As the two women sipped tea in the living room we appeared suddenly in costume and put on a semblance of the script. In one particularly ad-libbed scene Michael ran around in a mustache and black derby, carrying a doctor's bag, yelling, on respective circuits, "If you think I'm Groucho Marx, I'm not. . . . If you think I'm Walter Winchell, I'm not. . . ."

This brother and I were connoisseurs of daffiness in general: leaving cryptic notes for a baffled Milty, hiding surprises in Jack's silverware drawers, doing parodies of fat, tongue-tied Uncle Paul, or parading to the dinner table chanting, *"The big baboon by the light of the moon . . .* and then *what became of the monk, the monk, the monk . . . ?"* We were volatile friends, inseparable for days (building snowmen, crashing sleds, playing board games, riding buses into town to explore shops)—but the Monk was unpredictably moody and, when he got angry at me, the worst insult he could think of was to call me by the name with which I arrived once as an outsider: "Go back where you come from, Towers." But how clean that was compared to the guerrilla warfare I conducted with Jonny!

My father was a Dr. Jekyll and Mr. Hyde. In the City he was my gregarious and permissive savior, but at the Hotel he was strict and distracted, always checking to see if we were violating rules. He made us tear down our golf course. He ordered us out of the Terrace Room at night. He hated ever to spot us cutting through the main kitchen: "You are never never to go in there again! We could lose our insurance!" Amid platters of food he looked fierce and dangerous as he approached, so we fled into pantry tunnels.

I was surprised how many of the staff were terrified of him: old men who washed the floors and directors of departments; Irv Jaffee, speedskating champion; even huge Milty, who would cringe if he were summoned to PG's office. "Your father wants me, Richie," he would say. "You suppose this is the end?" I assured him that Paul was a good guy and I would put in a word for him if necessary.

I tried not to notice my father's threatening side, for on me, generally, shone his protective face, and I was contained in his beneficent embrace.

Aunt Bunny was my main ally. She heard my tales of school and shared her own fears with me. We talked about symbols, literary works, and the various characters at the Hotel, yet never about Uncle Paul. In fact, one inexplicable aspect of my stepmother was how little she seemed connected to my father. I rarely saw them publicly together, and I couldn't imagine what they found to share. She tended to go to the nightclub alone and drink and dance. Once, Michael and I (with James in tow) sneaked over to see what she was up to. There she was, in her red dress and jewelry, the center of much attention. We were sure she was drunk. "You kids go home," she shouted. "Your mother's entitled to party without being spied on."

Grandma Jennie seemed to be running a different hotel from my father. There was rancor in the family about it, and my brothers were not encouraged to visit her and never did. Even Aunt Bunny had little to do with the world of Joy Cottage.

Every night Grandma would work her way through the dining room, table by table, greeting each group of guests as if they were the dearest of old friends. Because she was a celebrity they had seen on bread packages and television, grown men and women were thrown into a tizzy by her presence (sometimes she would summon me to be introduced too, and I would stand at her side trying to look appropriate; she always mentioned Horace Mann).

Her capacity for strangers was undiminishable. One night I heard Uncle Paul say (in response to her doting attentions to a particular group), "Mother, they're crooks; they've robbed us blind!"

And she answered, without irony or self-conscious sanctity, "Then we'll turn the other cheek."

I would sit on her bed, correcting diagrams of sentences her tutor had given her, debating mildly the futuristic visions of Orwell and Huxley. It was pretentious but guileless. She would urge me not to limit my vision to the Hotel but to move beyond it. "Your father is narrow. He doesn't realize that our good fortune has come because of the way we've treated people and the largeness of our vision. We have been blessed, but we must continue to earn our blessings with good deeds."

I could tell that she thought of Grossinger's as a cultural institution more than a hotel. That gave my own interests legitimacy, for I doubted I could do business like Uncle Paul.

Grandpa Harry was so alienated from Grandma that he had his

crew build a separate doorway onto his room so he could come and go without even incidental contact (in all my time there I never saw them together). He was out on the grounds at dawn and, if visited in the late afternoon, hunched before his TV. Piles of bird seed lay around stone slabs marking his entrance, bright jujubees in which a gaggle of pigeons, sparrows, and blue jays nibbled furiously. When I visited him, I remembered museum stones and chocolate silverware so long ago.

In Grandma's part of the house—which was all of it except that one room—I met the host of hangers-on my father stewed about: singers who no longer had managers, agents without clients, "doctors" who never practiced, boxers in long retirement, secretaries and cooks with foreign accents. To Grandma they were not freeloaders; they were gentlemen and ladies under her wing. Lonely women with academic pretensions became her tutors (they were the only ones who actually lived there; the others stayed at the Hotel—for a weekend, a week, or months, depending on their needs). They made up Grandma's salon, complete with two nasty Pekinese dogs and a mynah bird that shouted, "Ship ahoy!" and let out wolf whistles in the middle of parties. She invited diplomats, clergy, entertainers, and politicians to stay for free, so there was always considerable activity at her house. I was often the only child at these gatherings; once, for an ambassador from Israel; another time, Cardinal Spellman; then, the Lord Mayor of Dublin (whose autograph I got for Bridey, along with a promise to reunify Ireland for her).

Aunt Bunny didn't object to the idea of introducing Michael to this scene. "Your grandmother's quite the empress," she said, "but she never accepted us the way she did you and your mother or your cousins. You might as well be our Lewis and Clark." Grandma was delighted by these visits, though it was strange that I should be my brother's emissary given that he lived so close to her.

Soon we began to make regular trips to Joy Cottage, dialing in foreign countries on the short-wave, goofing off at elegant parties, collecting unexpected gifts and expressions of affection (the Monk would define these missions as "a quick twenty," which is often what we got). I remember the boxer Barney Ross throwing his great arms around me like a mother and hugging me much too hard while singing a lullaby in Yiddish. Ostensibly he did public relations, but he seemed to live in my grandmother's house and PZ's office.

I understood even then that the world at Grandma Jennie's was a mirage, her admirers the previous generation—my mother's time (which is why I was automatically embraced and had such stature there). Yet Grandma's graciousness and generosity, even if self-serving, were more appealing to me than my father's hard line. She upheld something I knew to be true—no matter how successful Grossinger's was, the world itself was filled with grief and poverty, and this was far more important. She told me she made certain that a portion of Hotel profits went to local orphanages—one of which the car taking me home stopped at in New Jersey, bringing leftover food from the kitchen.

In New York I carried around coins for cups of beggars and cigar boxes of amputees on crate stools selling shoelaces. I even took up collections at PZ's office for the amputee outside Carnegie Hall on 57th Street. Yet I still felt ungrateful and insincere.

"God bless you," the blind man would shout as my money clanked in his tin. I felt a flush as I tore the rest of the way to the corner. Something about this was terrible. He shouldn't be thanking me. I shouldn't be fleeing him.

I never fully understood why my mother and Bob as well as Uncle Paul opposed me so adamantly in this charity. To my mother, giving away money showed disloyalty to the family because the people were strangers. "You don't treat us half as well as you do the bums on the street," she complained. However, she often made donations to women who came to our door for cancer and other diseases. I told her they were strangers too and anyway that the charities were frauds. "Don't be a smart aleck," she said. She thought she might someday fall victim to a dread ailment and preferred to be on the right side of the ledger.

Uncle Paul was even more vocal in his rebuffs. Once, I was walking with him along Central Park South when a blind man with a muzzled dog approached us and I put some change in his cup. "You were just taken in by one of the oldest rackets in the history of the world," my father proclaimed impatiently. I bit my lip in silence, which disappointed him, so he continued, "I betcha he's not even blind."

"So what?" I told him.

"Isn't that why you gave him money?"

I shook my head. "I gave him money because he was sad."

"When you grow up you'll see that the world is full of crooks. You can't make everyone rich and everyone happy and, if you've got, those that don't are going to be looking for ways to steal it from you. Remember that."

But I saw only chestnut vendors in rags and beggars crouched in the alley.

I befriended a dishwasher at the Hotel canteen, a gentle old Hungarian named Ziggy whose shoes were so ripped that his feet were more out than in. I asked him about them, and he said his toes hurt. I told Grandma Jennie.

"I can't allow someone in my care to be in that condition," she exclaimed.

She had her driver take him to a podiatrist. When I met him next, he was wearing white therapeutic clogs. His eyes twinkled as he pointed down at them. Grandma was so proud of me that she told my father, but he wasn't of like mind. He called me into his office and told me gently but firmly that when I didn't understand things I should stay out of them. He meant it as a joke, but it had an ominous air to it: "I can't have you coming here if you're going to tell Grandma about every employee who needs shoes. Because if you do we're going to go bankrupt. She'll reclothe the whole hotel and send everyone to the doctor." He laughed. "That's Mother for you."

But it wasn't a joke to me: people *were* fired, and when I complained to my father, he was belligerent—it was none of my business. One day he would dispose of Milty too.

After the first term at Horace Mann it was not my mother who drove me. The competitive milieu of the school became my habitat. The fact that I failed six years of grade school had lost all meaning: I was Richard Grossinger now. Richard Towers was a fiction, and I didn't identify with his disgrace.

I imposed an attractively spartan existence on myself, and the rest of the family was compelled to respect it. No one was allowed to interrupt my studying—and I was always studying. So I could ignore Jonny with impudence. I didn't have to be a captive audience for his latest victories in the school yard or landslide reelection as class president. I simply excused myself from dinner early.

I had beaten my mother at her own game and won a haughty privacy.

Jon was infuriated by my new role. He tried to retaliate by ignoring me too, but I was a camel. I could go days, even weeks, without acknowledging his existence. No matter how loud he shouted or how often he imposed his body in front of me I acted as though I neither saw nor heard him. Even if we came face to face I would step around him and continue on my way impassively—a preoccupied student. Eventually he would attack, or tell on me, but I would pretend that he had been disturbing my homework. For once he became the recipient of their scolding ("Don't distract your brother when he's studying").

Determined to get revenge, he reported every slight and even began turning in notes to our mother, detailing my actions by the hour. Gradually she became suspicious of my devotion to schoolwork. Jon was ever her sweet baby; I was the evil saboteur from the other family. Suit and tie (and HM maroon) notwithstanding, she knew I couldn't have suddenly been reformed into a gentleman scholar. Finally she clawed through my ruses.

"He can't stand that child being happy and successful," she proclaimed. "He's jealous and wants to squash the joy out of him."

Bob suddenly stared at me as though his eyes had just been opened. "Mental cruelty," he said. "Is that what you specialize in, you silent instigator, you no good. . . . You're a real needler aren't you, a real tormentor behind our backs."

They were right of course, but I couldn't back off. Jonny was just too goody-goody, too boastful. I couldn't accept his kinship, and my feeling of repulsion toward him was one of the goads of my discipline.

At P.S. 6 I had been a loner, but at Horace Mann I seemed to be friends in some sense with just about everyone in my Form (except for a few spazzes and bullies). There was one group of intellectuals, much more articulate and world-wise than me, who held a forum during lunch and after classes. I would join them in the cafeteria and listen to their discussions of morality, politics, Marxism, and abstract mathematics. My only topic was symbols and dreams, but I established myself as an authority on hidden meanings and proceeded to discover them in everything we read, from Willa Cather and *The Martian Chronicles* to cigarette and beer ads (dreams on request). No one thought this was as substantial as Red China or Bach, but it gave me a standing among them as a trickster and entertainer.

Generally, intellectuals were not my milieu. I felt more comfortable with my buddies on the train. We gossiped about school and talked baseball and subway jargon. Yet I was well into my second year before I realized that my friendships with these kids were insubstantial. The rest of the subway crowd all seemed to maintain at least some contact with one another on the outside, but I never saw any of them except on the train and at school. In that sense I was still a child. I continued to join in my family's activities. I didn't think of calling up friends to see what they were doing. It was inconceivable to me that I would invite any of them to our household, for we never had guests anymore. During the whole of Horace Mann I think my mother's brother Paul came to dinner twice, her legendary brother Lionel once (en route from Paris to Pittsburgh), my grandmother Sally three times, my mother's assistant from work (Helen) once, Bob's friend Moe three or four times.... That was it except for a friend of Bridey's picking her up. Our apartment was taboo, a sanctum where only the bizarre privacies of the Towers family were carried out: the guerrilla sarcasm, my mother's facial packs and early bedtimes, her "palpitations," as she called her panics, and our relentless derision of outsiders.

The Manhattan kids had hangouts at East Side coffee-shops and movie-theaters, carryovers from P.S. 6 and other grade schools. I never met them there. When they talked on the subway about cute girls and parties, I automatically withdrew from the discussion.

My mother was little help on the subject. In retrospect I see that she was relieved I showed no interest in girls. What caught her attention, though, were the mailings from Horace Mann about formal dances. She wanted me to have the right social connections and decided that the appropriate next step was to learn how to dance. Against my wishes (though I secretly appreciated the possibility of meeting girls), I was signed up for Saturday classes at Miss Viola Wolfe's on Madison Avenue, to which I had to wear not only a full suit but white gloves. The elderly Miss Wolfe taught us the steps first by far-too-swift examples. Then she clicked her metal cricket, an assistant dropped the needle onto a record, and we each had to pick a partner and execute a fox trot or waltz, later the lindy and cha-cha.

The moment of choice was excruciating, worse than any Musical Chairs. I would set my imagination on a pretty girl or a friendly face and try to end up her partner. But I never moved fast enough.

Each time, with unimportant variations, the dancing was the same. We stood facing each other but not really looking, and then we put our hands on exactly the right spots of the other's waist and shoulders (the assistant checked us pair by pair). The music began, and we attempted to carry out the choreography for its duration. The assistant and Miss Wolfe walked around, correcting us.

Sometimes we alternated partners in sequence, so I even got to dance with the one I wanted, but it made no difference. I knew I was a poor dancer and an unattractive boy as well. Anyway, at Viola Wolfe's the other person didn't exist; there were only rules and steps, our partner an accessory. And yet the other person was everything—the look on her face, her scent, the cloth or velvety feel of her dress, the stiffness of her body in the dance.

I was Pip at Miss Havisham's mansion, with the bare longing of regret.

2

DR. FRIEND

Now that I attended Horace Mann, Chipinaw seemed particularly degrading. While my classmates went to arts camps like Bucks Rock, I was the only one still at a jock camp. After all my studying, I protested, how could I be required to go back to a place of anti-intellectuals and phony drills? My mother sympathized on this matter, but my father was intransigent. Chipinaw was filled with Grossinger's loyalists and patrons, plus he thought that it was even better training for the real world than Horace Mann.

The summer after my first year at prep school I became the editor of *The Chipinaw Chirp.* The camp newspaper—a one-page mimeographed collection of stories, jokes, and drawings—was put out weekly by a counselor as part of his job (it was too much like school for most campers). Though I thought of the paper as useless and silly, the new counselor-in-charge, a journalism student named Alan, enlisted me as his only assistant.

Trained in writing from Horace Mann, I also knew how to run a mimeo from my job at PZ's, so I was an ideal recruit. Right off, Alan was enthusiastic that we could do something livelier than usual. In our first meeting he sought my collaboration on figuring out how to publish a "real" paper. "Let's leave out jokes and dumbo stories. We can cover events instead," he said. "We'll load it with human-interest items too." The prospect of actually carrying this delighted me.

I began to attend random softball and volleyball matches, writing them up with interviews and box scores. Each issue soon featured a counselor's biography and personal opinions. I included a paragraph of Major League baseball notes and a question column—for which I went around the camp asking people: What is your favorite activity and why?; what meal do you like best?; what was your most exciting moment ever at Chipinaw?

In its new format the *Chirp* became so popular that we made it into a daily and, since Alan also had his own bunk and schedule of activities, I took over most of the writing and production. I sat in the O.D. shack, cutting the stencil with a typewriter, brushing on candylike correction fluid when necessary. Then I carried it to the administration building, a cluster of offices right at the edge of the girls' campus, usually off-limits. There I handcranked several hundred fresh-smelling sheets. I loved watching *Chirps* collect as the rolling cylinder hit a stack of coarse paper, transforming type, artwork, and corrections into a seamless page.

As the days passed I spent less time on camp activities and more and more on the *Chirp*. The question column became quite idiosyncratic. I asked things like: What is your favorite water fountain (of the three on campus—by the workshed, alongside the tennis courts, or at the stables)?; what is the best stoop for Stoopball?, the best roof for Roofball?; should Dave Hecht fire counselors publicly?; and most dangerously, what do you think of Color War? I asked these questions of not only campers and counselors but anyone I could find—Abbey, Nurse Mary, and many of the zombies. I even did interviews with the zombies about their maintenance jobs.

I composed descriptions, the first being a portrayal of a thunderstorm. I recreated the colors and movements of the clouds, the rain on the roofs, the rivulets behind the tents, and the different moods during and after. A number of counselors complimented me, so I wrote another, about sunset at Chipinaw. Then I did a description of the lake. I used lots of adjectives and drew heavily on the office copy of Roget's *Thesaurus*. I customarily closed with a statement about the great beauty of our camp. Soon the secretaries in the office were having me run hundreds of extras for promotional mailings. What had begun as delinquent behavior now had me in the service of management.

When Color War broke I was ready. An editorial appeared declaring the *Chirp* and its editor neutral. I printed lists of both teams (without my name) and announced that, for the first time, the newspaper would not suspend operations during Color War but instead would publish an enlarged daily edition, reporting on *all* activities and keeping an up-to-date tally. I ignored my own assigned competitions and ran around with a clipboard collecting results and interviewing participants. My product read like *The Daily Mirror.* Even the captains and most fervent counselors encouraged me; they loved the publicity.

Yet I had no reason to think that the judges would show me the sacred scoresheet. "Ask Abbey," shrugged Arnie, the chief of judges. I found the head counselor in his cabin. Not having yet pronounced judgment on even my neutrality, he offered only that he'd consider the request.

That afternoon, without comment, Arnie brought me a copy of the day's scores and points. I took it from him in awe. I was the first camper in the history of Chipinaw ever to view the official scoresheet during Color War itself.

By dinner my coup was complete: I was invited to eat (for the duration of War) with Abbey, Nurse Mary, the doctor, and the judges at the center table. I sat there, a child on Olympus. I had finally achieved neutrality.

After the last reading of the official score Abbey asked for a standing ovation for the editor of the *Chirp.* Both teams rose, clapped, and whistled.

Only with the passage of time did I understand the real accomplishment of that moment. Using the clichés of bigtime reporting I unintentionally parodied not only Color War, with its xenophobic rhetoric, but my own charade of superiority. I got other people to see themselves competing . . . for what? . . . the Red and the Gray!—and thus brought humor and self-reflection to the event. And I was exposed along with the rest of them—the imperious renegade.

In the second year at Horace Mann my courses included Ancient and Mediaeval History, an Earth Science class emphasizing astronomy and meteorology, requisite English and Math, and Beginning Latin taught by a man from Albania who warned, "If you do not study it will be too too bad for you—not for me, but for you." My yellow Roman reader had an allure and intrigue to it, as though I were entering a vast rebus of an extinct people. I was enchanted by strings of endings for nouns and verbs and vocabulary that bore English words in olden forms. These were not only puzzles and codes; they were real fossils.

I memorized *agricola, agricolae ... , porto, portas, portat ... ,* and the wonderful *hic, haec, hoc; huius, huius, huius ... ,* and translated simple sentences like "The man carried the water" and "The soldiers attacked the village." When Daddy quizzed me, we sang out the *"arum"* and *"orum"* of the genitive plural together with gusto (those were his favorites too from CCNY).

In science I learned the taxonomy of sedimentary, igneous, and metamorphic rocks, and cirrus, stratus, and cumulus clouds. I started a rock collection. My best ones were a piece of rose quartz from Central Park, granite gneiss from a trip with Daddy to New Jersey, an amethyst quartz cluster from Grandma Jennie, and chunks of dolomite a friend found at a quarry in Yonkers. I had an illustrated field identification guide from Womrath's, a scratch stone, and a magnifying glass. Those worthwhile specimens I couldn't identify for sure I took to a private room I found at the Museum of Natural History, where a man was friendly enough to look up from his curating and judge my attempts at classification.

We also studied the planets of the Solar System and heard a tape of inscrutable cosmic rays howling, energy (we were told amid weird music) that comes from the stars and penetrates the Earth itself, passing through even the cells of our bodies, responsible for the color of our hair and the freckles on a girl's nose.

With cotton, cardboard, and dozens of my own Kodacolors (courtesy of Milty) I assembled a cloud display for my project. (An ambitious classmate launched a three-stage rocket and landed it on the baseball field with parachutes—an event that inspires my imagination even yet.)

Down the hall from science I entered a world of Egyptians, Assyrians, and Persians, a classroom covered wall to wall with maps of their by-gone epoch. For homework I memorized names and dates of dynasties and battles. I wrote my term paper on the Phoenicians: alphabet, trade routes, shellfish dye, and how their descendants in Africa were the Carthaginians of my practice Latin sentences.

Mr. Hathaway added one full point to our final grades for every extra book read, so I bought volumes on Picts, Anatolians, Medes, and Creteans, read them at home, and passed his brief oral tests. He took out his ledger and made a red check after my name each time. Soon I had five full points, the difference between a B+ and an A–. I loved these ancient empires and their relics and rulers. They were like nations I had once invented or read about on Mars and beyond Orion.

When we reached *Life on a Mediaeval Barony,* Mr. Hathaway proposed possible projects, so I hiked the length of upper Broadway, visiting hobby shops for ideas, and finally constructed a castle of balsa wood with a moat, knights and horses, little rubber farm animals, and ducks for its "mirror" lake. We were dealt a three-hour mid-term that winter in which we were asked to describe the War of the Roses. I had charged Winston Churchill's account at Womrath's and read it for extra credit, memorized it down to its last details of lineages and successions. I got a clean A.

In fact, I spent much of the year memorizing: at the window sill overlooking 96th Street, alone on park benches, riding the subway, at restaurants while we waited for our food (filtering out my mother and the Towers drama). I kept it up even while we walked around the reservoir (a finger marking my spot in a book as I tagged behind them reviewing my progress and enlarging mnemonic chains in my head). I committed to heart the planets of the Solar System, their sizes, distances from the Sun, irregular verbs, verbs that govern the dative, the third and fourth declensions, ablatives of place and time, and chronologies of Old World civilizations. Each of these topics spun its own web. I wove myself into their spells and embraced their grandeur. Even Daddy marveled at my sophisticated dinner conversation and told Jonny, "I hope you follow in your brother's footsteps."

When Uncle Paul insisted I renew Hebrew classes in order to be bar-mitzvahed I objected strenuously on the basis of too much homework. My mother ridiculed his fake holiness but told me to go through with it so as not to anger him on Horace Mann and also to get plentiful gifts and money from his clients.

I was mortified at having to return to the Park Avenue Synagogue but took a perverse glee in hiding my Latin book inside the fat Hebrew one and memorizing my vocabulary and declensions while other kids chanted their Haftorahs. I set my sacrilege against their ethnic self-importance (and anyway, why should I lose time on my studying while someone else practiced irrelevant prayers?). I finally got caught, which led to a spontaneous sermon about the barbarian Romans. When I rebutted, from my new knowledge of the ancient world, the teacher was appalled. There was some sentiment in the office that I was an infidel and shouldn't be bar-mitzvahed, but the fact of being Jennie Grossinger's grandson outweighed being me. The compromise this time was that I learned my Haftorah at home with the cantor's recording and a tutor.

In the following month I memorized a long section of the Hebrew service by singing it over and over with the text before me. A tutor came three nights a week from Yeshiva to correct me. I was not much of a singer or a phonetic reader of Hebrew and, according to him, "a miserable excuse for a Jew." A week beforehand, I composed a bland essay on the teachings of the prophet Isaiah, which was then approved by the Synagogue.

My bar mitzvah was the first among my contemporaries. On the Saturday morning after my thirteenth birthday, in a state melded of terror and anticipation, I arrived at 7 AM at the Park Avenue Synagogue to await the fabled event. Gradually, a stream of figures from my life waded through the doors, each bearing gifts. Envelopes with bonds, watches, leatherbound dictionaries and prayerbooks, even shares of stock, checks, and cash piled up with Bridey beside the coat room. Despite her enthusiasm I would have nothing to do with such exhibitionism.

The service began. I looked out over a congregation packed with relatives and friends, rose from my throne-like chair, joined the cantor and rabbi, and swayed nervously at the podium.

This was a moment of truth, and I regretted not to be able to perform something meaningful (like the War of the Roses or the planets and their distances from the Sun). Instead, with my inability to carry a tune, I droned a replication of Hebrew characters as their shapes chugged before my eyes. At least, after so many rehearsals, the performance was at hand. Feeling more embarrassment than stage fright, as I sang I imagined myself expunging this deed forever.

The party downstairs seethed with melodrama and tumult. The figures of my life milled haphazardly about one another—schoolmates, family, and family friends. It was the first time I had experienced my worlds together. Bridey, Jonny, and Debby had never laid eyes on Aunt Bunny, or Michael and James. I pointed them out to one another and then presided over bashful introductions. Yet the actual meetings were nothing and passed in a moment.

Even Dr. Fabian was there (he gave me a dozen heavy books on topics ranging from the great explorers to Greek antiquities). I acknowledged him throughout the day with apprehensive glances, as he beamed his approval.

All these people did not belong together. Brittle and euphoric, I rushed from table to table accepting congratulations, but time was too brief and thin to contain the energy present.

To give the appearance of orthodoxy my father had not hired musicians. Instead the Yiddish comedian Emil Cohen told jokes for an hour. Bridey, having drunk too much champagne, laughed uncontrollably. Then Grandma Sally's brother Mooney did a slapstick comedy routine he once performed professionally (as a fake stumbling busboy).

To add to my awkwardness among my friends, not only was there no band, there were no girls. Actually, there was one. My mother insisted on that. She wrangled Vicki Berle, the daughter of the comedian, to join a dozen boys on the dais. The presence of a celebrity did not make up for the lack of a real party and, once Emil Cohen began his routine, all of my classmates left.

I felt the deepest pangs of loneliness, the one time everyone was there.

The subsequent bar mitzvahs of my friends were grandiose balls with bands, bars, and dancing, held in suites in midtown hotels or country clubs in Westchester. I either took the train or went in a car-pool. I was overwhelmed by the pretty girls, music, and crowds. I remember walking down a hallway of mirrors, the sound of a band fading into the distance: *"Non Dimenticar, though you've travelled far, / my darling...."* Nat King Cole's lullaby was too sad for words, and the feelings it generated in me were rich and tender—icicles on pine trees, liners crossing oceans, Judy in Westport long ago. . . .

Especially given the nightclub settings of these bar mitzvahs, my mood originated partly from an intimation of Grossinger's. Dr. Fabian continued to push this interpretation with his theme of the tragedy of the divorce. It was, of course, his preferred explanation for all my malaises: other kids' families were whole whereas I was a pariah in my own household. But by the time I was thirteen I had completely outgrown that depiction. Paul and Martha together would have been hellions. I didn't want that, even if it meant having always lived at Grossinger's. There would have been no Aunt Bunny, no Dr. Fabian either. My yearnfulness was remote and ineffable, as I watched kids from school dancing with unknown girls in a giant ballroom.

"Somewhere, beyond the sea, somewhere waiting for me. . . ."

I came home late at night, let myself in, found my bed and sleep almost simultaneously, got up the next morning and did my assignments. I even translated the Bobby Darin song into Latin, complete with gerund.

"My lover stands on golden sands, and watches the ships, that go sailing. . . ."

I stared out through darkening twilight over water towers atop buildings, the blown dust that was no longer organic let alone human, the pale replica of a night sky appearing.

"It's far beyond a star; it's near beyond the moon."

It was a mistake, clearly, all of this. But at last I was calm, unafraid.

I spent hours in the Museum of Natural History, going from mural to mural, gazing at animals in dioramas of the Rockies . . . Africa . . . the South American forest, the pygmy drawing his bow by a broken ostrich egg. Their stark, magnificent specificity was the only suitable representation of my moods. The Siberian tiger in his golden striped flesh against winter was a force, though stuffed and mounted in artificial scenery, a force I acknowledged but could not name. His majesty—and that of mountain sheep and antelopes—guarded my trance.

At school I fantasized that this kid Jeffrey, who commuted from Yonkers, would adopt me and I would come to school with him every day. His family, I heard, was having trouble paying the bills, and I imagined that the money from taking me in as a boarder would allow him to stay. I could share a room with him instead of the bragging ruffian. I was jolted each time I saw him in the flesh: his long thin face, black oiled hair, odd tan coloring. It was he I missed and longed for, not some original unity of my parents. It wasn't that I wanted to *be* him, but I wanted to stand in relation to him. I longed to hold out a hand and set my fingers gently on his forehead. His very existence was the feeling I wanted inside myself.

These were not things I could tell to Dr. Fabian, but he suspected their existence. We would discuss "diseases," bedwetting, my conflict with my mother and brother, but nothing more intimate. "You have to tell me what you're thinking if I'm going to help you," he would protest. I would agree and then pretend to be summoning deeper thoughts, snippets of fantasies but never their painful heart. Seeing him at my bar mitzvah and as a guest at Grossinger's, I realized he was not special; he was just a man with a wife at a party, shaking hands, smiling, drinking wine.

Before and after sessions I noticed his other patients more closely and recognized myself as merely one in a line of visitors, each with his or her stories and symbols. One time, I forgot my coat and came back in off the street for it. A woman lying on his couch leaped to her feet in embarrassment. He insisted that my return was from curiosity and not by accident. But viewing another patient in his presence drove me deeper into my pod, and I denied everything.

The last time I saw him he was irritable. He asked me if I had had any sexual fantasies. I bristled at the explicitness of his invasion and assertedly shook my head. He kept at me as he never had before, as though somehow he knew this was his final chance to solve my mystery. "You must have had some," he insisted, but I was tight-lipped. Then he missed the next two sessions. My mother told me he had gone out of town. It was mid-terms of my second year, and I didn't pay attention to the lapse. I was obsessed with studying and the moment of truth in the gym. I memorized so hard that by Sunday night I began to forget everything. I told my mother I was going to fail, and she ordered me to bed.

"You know there's such a thing as overstudying," Daddy chimed in. "You want to be in fighting condition tomorrow, not all worn out."

Two weeks later my grades came in the mail; they were all As except for a B in math. My mother was stupefied. She had no premonition of this happening, and she acted as though I had achieved something impossible. She was giddy on the phone with Grandma Sally and other relatives. She even got my father on the line and narrated my achievement to him with high suspense (asking, "Guess what Richard did?" in a tone of voice sure to solicit, "What now?"). I allowed half a giggle in acknowledgment of her joke.

When he finally spoke to me he asked, "What happened in math?" It was meant to be funny, but I didn't laugh.

As a reward, my mother invited me to her office for a special meal after school on Friday.

I took the subway to 57th Street and walked to the East Side. I sensed her unsteady mood as she phoned downstairs for a sandwich and then took me by the hand into the conference room. "Something I have to tell you. Dr. Fabian died." She planned this quick strike to avoid any dawdling. It was how she would have wanted to be told, and I appreciated her care.

I felt a shock of surprise. Then I thought confusedly back over the last weeks. "Was it on vacation?" I wondered.

"He never went on vacation. He died in the evening the last day you saw him. He had a stroke. I didn't tell you because I didn't want to disturb your studying."

Now I adjusted to the fact that he had been dead for three weeks. Morbidly I thought back to our last session and felt a rush of guilt. I didn't imagine I had caused his stroke with my intransigence, but I knew I had failed him nonetheless. I had failed the person who meant the most to me. And I was alone.

On the way home in the back of a cab with my mother, my tears faded into an uncomfortably impassive breeziness that said: no more prying into fantasies, no more long subway rides downtown. No more fears.

In numbness I had the illusion I could make it on my own, and I told myself a dark, shameful secret—that I wouldn't miss him. I locked it inside my heart.

If I could deal Dr. Fabian off so coldly, maybe I *was* the evil person my mother intuited. Richard the traitor! No wonder I had let him down.

When I tried to go to sleep that night I had nightmares. I saw figures tumbling off a tower atop a faraway mountain, disappearing into a chasm. Dr. Fabian was one of them, unable to help himself, falling, screaming too.

At another level of the dream his bodiless head came to the window of my bedroom; I screamed silently. His voice was everywhere. "See," it said, "I can't save anyone. It never really mattered, none of it. Not even symbols. Now I'm one of the dead too." His bones were in a garbage can. He was pale and rotted. He lay in a pond face down. Fragments of his body, rippled like cloth, wrapped around telephone poles.

I would wake, look around the room in the dark, remember where I was, and then try to go back to sleep. Every time I closed my eyes I saw the same tower, the figures closer and more human. Yet I felt that as long as they didn't see me looking at them I was safe.

For years previous I had had a recurring dream of going to see another doctor, a dull, uninsightful man who made a travesty of our sessions. It was always a relief to awake and remember good old Dr. Fabian. Now I had to encounter a daylight enactment of the dream. Not even my mother thought that I should stop my psychiatric visits, so, one afternoon two weeks later, she led me to a fancy apartment overlooking Central Park West. The proprietor was a man named Maurice Friend who saw only teenagers and had agreed to take Dr. Fabian's one patient in that age group. The final decision was mine.

He seemed an unlikely replacement for the tall, charismatic patriarch—this small, heavy man with a typically adult look, not as banal as in the dreams, but more than a step in that direction. He didn't seem anything like a wizard. Yet there we were, the two of us in chairs, facing each other, talking about a formal relationship. All through the trial session—as he explained his method of working and showed me on his chest a scar from an operation (he was also vulnerable to death!)—I sat there contemptuous, imagining I would eventually find someone more special. But then Dr. Fabian had stopped being a wizard long ago and, when the hour was over, the only answer I could think of was "Yes."

Right from the beginning Dr. Friend insisted I lie on the couch while talking to him. I balked at being forced into the psychiatric stereotype. I had imagined Fabian and me as engaged in something more sophisticated and personal. Since in all our years he didn't once ask me to use the couch, I had never considered its possible justification. Lying down made Dr. Friend disappear into a presence behind me.

For many weeks I dawdled there, numbly re-narrating my usual stories, his voice inserting only minor questions and redirections. I told my dreams of the tower and the other doctors, and I ran off the full version of "my crisis" that Dr. Fabian and I had collaborated on over the years.

At first Dr. Friend was able to squeeze me into his schedule only at six o'clock. I would take the subway directly from school to his building and sit in the waiting room doing homework for two hours or more while other patients, mostly surly, suspicious teenagers, came and went. At a table by the window I would work through math problems and translate Latin sentences while the sky darkened behind the reservoir and lights kindled the East Side. During that interval Dr. Friend and I maintained a code of invisibility. I wasn't supposed to be there, so I wasn't. He might sneak me the slightest glance of recognition while greeting the next appropriate patient; yet at my turn he welcomed me enthusiastically.

He spent many weeks just listening. When he did choose to respond at length his first comments were completely unexpected: "You're not as crazy as you like to make yourself sound. You've been in psychoanalysis from such a young age that you now think of yourself only in terms of problems." I turned to face him in his overstuffed chair by the horse-statue lamp. He smiled confidently as he picked up steam. "Dr. Fabian was obviously a great support and helped you through difficult years, but I get the idea he underestimated you. He made you into a sick child. You may have been then, but you're not anymore. I think it's an interesting coincidence that right after he died—even though you didn't know about it—you got As. Now you can't go back to the excuse that you're an invalid and nothing should be expected of you." He had little interest in my recitals of Nanny and the old fears. "They no doubt had an effect on you, but they're not active in the present. I can't do anything about the remote past or your mother's behavior, but I can teach you how to react in the present in ways that don't harm you as much."

As our sessions expanded he regularly cut off my narratives. "You tell me about being afraid, but I don't see you afraid. You tell me about your sadness, but you don't act sad or cry. I want to know what's happening inside you when you're here. I see you day after day studying in the waiting room, seemingly with tremendous patience. How do you control yourself? How do you create these rigid masks?"

He insisted on hearing fantasies and daydreams. When I balked and tried to substitute ideas he broke in abruptly. "Richard, I can't do anything unless you're here too. You're wasting my time, your time, and your father's money. I'm not prying because I'm nosy. I need to know what's going on with you, not what you choose to edit out for me." I could tell he was trying to appear stern. "I'm not going to be a second Dr. Fabian. I'm no friendly uncle."

Dr. Fabian had been a magus, appearing at the brink of the dungeon stairs, leading me away. Dr. Friend was the doctor of teenage years, demanding and concrete. Much of the time I would lie there irritated and silent, staring up at photographs of shell-like Grecian artifacts. "What do you feel?" he would ask tiredly. I was the last patient of the day, the smell of his dinner already drifting in from other rooms in the apartment, forcing me to withhold from him that I found him repulsive too.

His name was also ironical. It was because Dr. Fabian was too good a *friend* that I became unable to confide in him. Dr. Friend I found harsh, almost antipathetic, yet I eventually told him the truth.

The spring of Second Form I went out for baseball, but fast balls petrified me, curves were unhittable, and just about all the players were from the suburbs, so I rode the subway home alone in the late afternoon or, at most, with one other kid. It was the first time I understood the difference between the athletes—the jocks—and people like me. Bill-Dave and Chipinaw had left me with an unquenchable desire to play, but no intellectuals went out for these teams. The players talked mainly drinking and parties, and I felt like a baby beside them. I made my occasional great running catches, but I started only one game (against Riverdale when someone else was sick) and hit a line drive to the shortstop (with my eyes virtually closed), a real victory when twenty-five of our twenty-seven batters struck out.

Dr. Friend was right. It was hard to know what I felt because I almost didn't feel it anymore. An ancient wistfulness hung over those years, protecting them like soft rain. Coming home, I gazed out the window of the el before the tunnel at 200th Street. The world seemed to have grown even more vast and mysterious in my hibernation—a young mother, kids chasing a ball until a building blocked them, a cluster of men at a corner store, women hanging from windows shouting. Then the screech of wheels buried their images forever beyond swerving track. I yearned for something lodged inside the very depth and substance of the world ... wind dissipating through leaves ... sun glinting off surfaces ... a catacomb without an entrance. But intimations flipped by, not even like dreams.

That May and June through finals I studied into early morning hours every night. Latin was the most reassuring because I could at least translate all the texts and decode their grammatical twists. But science and European history were bottomless, and algebra always hovered on the edge of obscurity. No matter how many problems I solved successfully, I stared in the next one at numbers and letters in an absolute knot.

During those days Dr. Friend heard mostly stale dreams and petty frustrations. I not only lost all emotion. I forgot that I existed. Coursebooks and binders full of notes permeated me. I was determined to learn everything. Grades had become their own vindication: "A" was an ace in a deck of cards, a letter stolen from a sacred alphabet. I wanted to be defined by "A," to feel its tense explosion in my gut ... then its soft coils of relief. All of us shared that ambition to some degree—Chuck Stein, Erwin Morton, Jim Polachek, Andrew Schloss, Bob Karlin. We clustered before and after exams, alternately competitive and empathic, compelled to the ceremony.

After finals I returned awkwardly to who I was, a person with vague aches and yearnings, not quite the performer in whose behalf I imagined I was toiling. Formulas and forgotten facts thinned into vapor; only the imminent report card remained. I sat at my desk, listlessly crumpling my notes and shooting for the far trash basket, collecting my misses and shooting again.

Arriving in the mail like a holy epistle, the record of my grades coopted every prior essence, even seventh games of World Series. I could barely tear open the envelope my arms felt so weak.

It was As and high Bs—vindication! I was free; yet the sense of being on trial lingered. I didn't probe too deeply because I found only layers of recalcitrance and discontent. A premonition hid in the background of my mind—an obscure, unnamed malignancy.

I went to my annual check-up with Dr. Levine. I sat in his office, watching little kids build block cities on the floor. They were young and protected; nothing had happened to them yet. The muteness of that room masked a cataclysm, a silent white noise in which everyone went about their business as though we were invulnerable to what was at stake. Traffic roared by on the streets. One by one, the nurses called them in. Then me.

Was my heartbeat okay? Why did he listen so closely? Did he sense something Dr. Hunt had missed all these years? Why was he squeezing my belly again? I watched his face for a clue. But nothing came of it either, absolutely nothing at all.

I walked into a boiling-hot city, almost light-hearted, disbelieving my luck. The subway roared under grates, releasing summer stench and recalling my destiny. But what was it, now that there was time to live?

Suppose the Chinese suddenly invaded Quemoy and Matsu as they had threatened? President Eisenhower vowed to defend the islands with everything America had. I was sure I would never make it to Grossinger's. Bridey customarily turned on the news every hour from 7 AM till bedtime. I listened to its chimes, the voice of the global announcer an excruciating suspense. I glanced nervously at newsstand headlines. Every screeching sound and whine of machinery startled me. The testing of air raid sirens sent me searching for a clock to confirm it was noon. I couldn't understand why no one else was concerned—but then no one else had ever been concerned.

One day the sirens went off in the late afternoon. I thought—fire engines, no!; noon, no! Then this was it!

I stood there in the apartment listening to their unabated drone. Would I hear the bombs first or see the light? Would I feel the building ignite and crumble? My heart was beating so hard I almost could not bear its weight. But another part of me seemed to be laughing, as if to say, 'This is all crazy. This makes no sense at all.'

I tore to the radio and turned it on. I expected to hear the warning whistle, but there was music, station after station . . . music and voices.

Now I listened to the sirens with a different sense, one of mockery and defiance ... even though somewhere bombs were still mounted, missiles waiting to be dispatched.... The keepers of doom were imperfect, hysterical. And this time they were wrong.

That whole month I worked for PZ. I typed his press releases, sorted and cleaned his collapsing files back into the 1920s, and ran errands for the Grossinger office. Each day at lunch the gang of us went to the luncheonette and ordered soup and slices of the roast special.

After two weeks I had accumulated more than $100. In a mood of celebration PZ accompanied me to Photo Fair. Charlie was ready. He brought out a sealed box, cut it open, and took the camera from its packing. I held the cold, fresh-smelling metal to my eye and focused on people outside the storefront. Across the counter, de Luise pointed out the singer Phil Everly with his black pompadour. He was testing, then buying a Yashika. I pretended to take a picture of him, pressing the button at the highest speed and listening to the fine ping of the shutter. Kids at the Horace Mann camera club had said a two-thousandth of a second was a waste, but it made my Minolta special. When I took out my wad of bills, Charlie laughed. "No charge," he said.

I didn't understand.

"Your grandfather already paid for it."

Now PZ was laughing too. "He found out you were working in the office, so he decided to surprise you."

I spent half of my cash on a light meter and then hurried home with these treasures, testing the viewfinder on lights in the subway tunnel, people walking dogs along the park, silhouettes of water towers ... the whole superb world.

A week later, Grandpa's new driver, Ray, picked me up. Instead of going directly to the Mountains, however, he stopped in the Bronx because he had tickets from Ingemar Johansson for his second heavyweight match with Floyd Patterson, Jonny's much ballyhooed favorite. Johansson had trained at the Hotel, and Ray had become pals with him while taking him back and forth to the City.

I wanted to get out of the nuclear target zone, so this fight was one more frustrating obstacle. However, I was also involved in the Grossinger's fighter smashing Jonny's guy. After all, I knew he rooted for Patterson only because I had befriended Johansson.

In Harlem, on our way to Yankee Stadium, the Cadillac broke down and, while I stood alongside its open hood (Ray working underneath), an old man offered to start our vehicle by pouring liquor into its gas tank. Ray thanked him but said we'd manage. A crowd began to gather. I wasn't scared. World War was scary. This was an interlude in a strange place about which I was curious. What did it feel like to stand in these streets beyond the el, smell their different soot, gaze at their ripples of activity, watch their solemn faces? Twilight fell.

Suddenly Ray got the engine running. He was dripping sweat as we gunned out of there, but I was laughing to myself at what a great story this would be for Aunt Bunny and Michael. "Liquor for the engine!" Michael would roar.

PZ occupied the seat next to us. We had barely settled when he shouted, "No!" as Patterson sent the Swedish champion sprawling across the canvass. I was shocked. But at last it was over. Silently we found our car and headed north.

That summer at Chipinaw Jay, Barry and I graduated to the tents; we were seniors. Our habitats were actually large wooden platforms on which beds were set. Flaps of canvas arranged on ropes and supported by poles formed a canopy above each platform. When I was younger I was relieved to be in a safe and (by comparison) spacious bunk, but now a tent was an adventure of shifting sun and fabrics. I liked the sound of rain on cloth, the closeness of stars. I considered it one of the all-time highlights of Chipinaw when we were visited by three skunks in the middle of the night. Everyone in the tent froze in vaudeville while the creatures poked comically about, raising themselves on front paws to look into garbage cans and trunks, knocking over bottles. On the whispered count of three we rolled across our beds and scattered.

That was the summer of 1958 when kids first began to talk about girls and "making out." But we were thirteen years old, and it was all rumor and hearsay. I experienced my own sexuality mainly in fantasies and dreams. Bearing a trace of seduction was a rock and roll tune (single guitar plinks in the background) that went, *"Don't go home, my little darling, / please don't leave the party yet. . . ."* I would picture a girl in a slinky dress, wrapping her arms around me, keeping me there. . . .

Kids on the subway would report on girls who made out with them, exchanging information in a ritual of play-acting and slang. The vicarious sensations from their tales wafted over me like perfume . . . and then the song. . . . *"Can't you see I came to the party, I 'cause I knew that you'd be here. . . ."*

Chipinaw seniors had regular socials with the girls' camp. Walking with Jay and Barry to the first one, I hoped Viola Wolfe's lessons might finally be of some use, but it seemed as soon as we arrived at the armory older kids were dancing with all the girls and we were left standing along the benches making wisecracks to each other. Only one guy in our tent had any success—an unlikely red-haired sweet-talker named Al who was new that summer. He was a clumsy ball-player with a fake intellectual air. But he took up with a dirty-blonde named Joan Snyder, pert face and friendly eyes. I didn't remember when I became infatuated with her, but soon her image, recalling Judy in Westport, filled my life. I would sit by the side watching her dance with Alan, daydreaming *("I have waited long for the party, I 'cause I knew we'd finally meet . . .").*

In my main fantasy Joan was being persecuted by a counselor as dangerous as the one I had had the previous summer, so I snuck over to her bunk at night and called to her. She heard me and climbed out the window. 'Who are you?' she wondered, but she was happy to be rescued. We dashed for the woods, as I threw sticks in the way of pursuers. With counselors behind us we scrambled into the forest, found our way through grottos and glens—pursued for days while we hid. Through various twists of plot (including flying saucers) I transported us to the jungle where we made our way past waterfalls, along canyons, and over mountains to the Amazon. There we built an *"African Queen"* and fled down a tributary.

Every detail of this fantasy was luminous to me. As I revived it at night, the fictive grass became damp again; the sticks changed their location and shape; pools glowed in moonlight. I experienced these phenomena anew each time in my mind. They were always fresh—made real again by my evoking them.

Later in the summer, Seniors went on a co-ed field trip to Ausable Chasm. At the souvenir shop after our boat tour, on a dare to myself,

I bought a stuffed terrier and walked up to her outside the bus (where she was standing with other girls, Alan having just left her to board the boys' bus). I silently handed it to her. It was brash and foolish. We had never spoken a word, but I had thought about her so much I couldn't believe I didn't know her. She took it in surprise, thanked me, and hurried onto the bus in a cluster of whispering friends.

In another daydream we fled from the girls' camp to a waiting motorboat and then outraced pursuers to my camouflaged raft on the far side of the lake. We followed the bends of a previously undocumented stream until eventually we made it to Grossinger's. I saw its cottages through her eyes as if for the first time.

I lay in bed after Taps in a rapture of daring. I was cozy in my fresh pajamas, a wind in the forest, echoes of Taps, my mind racing toward Mars (red-tinged among glittering whites), voices of counselors passing in the night, the rescue barely underway. . . .

The next social after I gave her the dog I arrived with some trepidation. But nothing was different. She danced with Alan while I stared surreptitiously. Then suddenly she was heading toward me. I was dumbstruck. I tried to look away, but her eyes were directly on me. She came up and calmly asked, "You want to dance?"

I nodded. It was awkward putting my hands on her actual shoulder and waist as the record began, struggling to remember steps. (None of the dancing at Chipinaw was particularly intimate, for Dave Hecht would come around periodically with a tape measure and check the distances of partners. Six inches was the minimum.) She didn't evaporate; she was there and smiling at me. She told me I was very nice but that she was going with Alan, so she couldn't dance with me after this one time. I returned to my seat on the bench in a daze.

And Johnny Cash sang: *"I don't like it, but I guess things happen that way."*

And, yes, Phil Everly: *"Only trouble is, gee whiz, I'm dreaming my life away."*

At midweek movies I'd spot Joan Snyder across the armory, her presence instantly transforming me. I'd forget the film and sink into fairy-tale, leaving camp, starting again from the beginning . . . that very night, racing through the woods, an owl whistling, moths fluttering at her screen, the adventure still to happen.

Toward the end of the summer was an evening carnival at the girls' camp. I was holding my camera with its fancy Honeywell strobe, and she came up to me laughing, and said, "Goodbye," and "Guess what, I'm leaving early and going to Grossinger's. Are you going to take my picture?"

Yes ... and that snapshot, utter blackness behind her, was all I ever saw again. She never came back to Chipinaw ... and by the time I got to Grossinger's she was gone. I had that picture of her—head thrown back, wide-eyed, quixotic, laughing then—until I left for college and my mother threw the scrapbooks away. Now I have only the memory of it.

In later years, though, I had a recurring dream of returning to New York City and looking through old phone books for "Joan Snyder." She lived in a strange part of town. I finally had a date with her if I could find her. Depending on which version I dreamed, I would get off the subway at some deserted place uptown ... buildings crumbling, their numbers missing. I wandered through parks with small chapels. I walked up stairs of abandoned apartments to see only old hag women cackling at me. I fled over rock piles and skirted dangerous streets to flag the last bus going out. Even in my dreams about her, Joan Snyder never appeared.

3

ADOLESCENCE

In Third Form I moved on to Caesar, Tennyson and Sinclair Lewis, Geometry, and Biology with its bottles of white formaldehyde rats. We each had to slice one open and pull out intestines and other organs.

I was placed in mostly Honors classes. My competence was no longer a question. Horace Mann was my life—its classrooms where I earned my grades, its corridors where I met my friends, its auditorium where we sang hymns and heard senior speeches, its lunchroom where we gathered in groups to talk sports and politics, its teachers ("Sir!") now familiar elders to petition and beguile.

After the summer Dr. Friend probed me for fantasies about Joan Snyder. I offered scant approximations—and those reluctantly. He then startled me by asking if I masturbated. As he persisted his questioning, I realized I didn't understand the concept. I couldn't imagine more than my penis getting hard. He insisted that semen could spurt out too.

"Fantasies are only imaginary," I offered. "They're not real enough to make something like that happen."

"Oh yes they are," he said. "And you, of all people, should know that."

He didn't pursue it, and I changed the subject.

In the early years with Dr. Fabian I imagined Sigmund Freud as an immense occult system, towering above me, like the Parthenon in which

I imaged Horace Mann before I went there. The founder embodied the infinity and wonder I felt emanating from my own existence. By Third Form I was no longer a neophyte in an obscure system. I read *Interpretation of Dreams* on my own and discussed projection and sublimation by name in my English classes. "You had such an advantage," one teacher said to me. "You got to see the psychiatrist as magician at the only time such a thing could happen—the beginning of your life."

I was intrigued by Freud's accounts of Viennese ballrooms and museums of antiquities, followed always by the author's ingenious interpretations. Umbrellas and pianos became penises, laboratories revealed the actual situation of treatment, animals represented people or were transformed by puns into events. There were symbolic "puddings," "dumplings," "trellises," "chapels," "donkeys," "Turkish embroidery," "horse-drawn cabs," "Wars of the Roses," and "Kings of Italy." These trails were more furtive and mysterious than even the clues followed by the Hardy Boys, for they led inside the world.

In Freud's text, ordinary reality was represented by plain type and characters like Baron L., Professor R., and Otto. The deeper realm manifested in italics, their slant acknowledging that every image was as chameleon as wind dispersing clouds: *I am driving in a cab, and I tell the driver to drive to a railway station. "'Of course, I can't drive with you on the railway track itself. . . .'"* Nor could I ice-skate on water or levitate above the City.

I suspected that some of my own subterfuge was explained in a chapter entitled, "The Psychology of the Dream-Process." It was too sophisticated for me to understand, but I kept re-reading sections, trying to break through its rhetoric.

From the car heading to Grossinger's, staring out at a landscape of incomprehensible depth, I imagined a long, invisible sword extending from the near wheel, shearing away fences, trees, telephone poles, bird baths, and houses as we passed. Not knowing why I did that, I thought of luggage by rail (that wasn't luggage), blue plums concealing the number seven.

What was I transforming in my scythe?

During respites in the school day a group of baseball enthusiasts took to having catches on the campus. I heaved balls across the outfield and ran down return throws (often with backhanded leaps and dives) even late into November. It was exhibitionist (and meant to be, our audience made up of those walking between classes, including teachers, who didn't know I was that good). It also filled my chest and mind with ice for the next lecture.

A classmate named Fred played regularly with us. I knew him mainly from Latin where he was struggling (and frequently embarrassed by Mr. Metcalf's taunts at his butchered attempts at translation). I not only had sympathy for him; I liked his childlike face and freckles.

One afternoon, out of the blue, he walked up and invited me to his home in Scarsdale for a party. The whole rest of that week seemed charged and vulnerable.

On Saturday morning I left my apartment after breakfast and took the train from Grand Central, past Harlem, into countryside. Fred and his mother met me at the tracks with a station wagon and drove us back to their house. After Mallopuffs and juice, he and I trekked to the neighborhood field, joined some local kids, and took turns skying a hardball into the meadow. Everyone was confident and jiving, hitting the cut-off man.

I was attentive to the preciousness of the moment, in a funk at the thought of going home. My sense of wonderment transcended Grossinger's; it was more like—'This is real, and I'm only a figment.' If I could hang around these kids long enough I might become real too.

I gave the baseball all I had, racing at breath's end to intercept its pellet flight, rolling as I trapped it, jumping up and flinging it back in. My life was somehow on the line in that ragtag game, if only I could time my breath, the yearning, the arc, the infinity of blue. . . . As usual I felt hopelessly complicated and obscure. It wasn't just the dilemma of Pinocchio; it was that Dr. Friend did not even comprehend my feeling of being wood. He would lecture on about alienation and melancholia, trying to get me to acknowledge my feelings, but there was also that realm of untapped joyousness as big as the sky; it beckoned me right through the gloom. If he didn't perceive it—if Grossinger's wasn't it either—how would I ever find my way there? Only reading Wordsworth (for English class) made any sense. Could he have known something Dr. Friend didn't, born as he was, centuries before Freud?

"Whither is fled the visionary gleam? Where is it now, the glory and the dream?"

Anyway, I would be dispatched at day's end, back to prison. I sensed it would take half a lifetime to return to this dandelion field.

My song for those months was Cathy Carr's "First Anniversary." Her happy/sad tomboy voice spoke for Joan Snyder and for my lost, unlived self:

> *"Look at you. Look at me.*
> *See the way we glow*
> *You'd believe that we just met*
> *One week a-go-o-o-o."*

Though such sweet, perky simplicity seemed forever beyond me, it was secretly everything I was. I would sprawl on the floor against my bed, in touch with a reverence that, although not as familiar to me as terror, seemed equally to lie at my core.

After lunch Fred led me upstairs to his room and we sat, respectively, on couch and bed, practicing translations for the big test. I knew he was failing the course, so I played the role of the enthusiastic tutor, laboring to transmit the essence of the text. I carried my rhythm right from the ballfield through Caesar's Gallic campaigns, line by line, complete with citations of syntax. I was totally on. Latin just rolled into English. I was quite willing to give him everything I could in exchange for this day. Suddenly I noticed it was dark outside. "Hey, what about the party?" I asked.

"I forgot to tell you. It was cancelled."

It meant nothing to him. He changed plans without a thought. But my heart sank into oblivion at those words. I masked my emotion in a gulp.

I hardly cared when a moment later, with a mischievous smile, he pulled a tape-recorder from under the bed. He had made a copy of my Latin performance and was going to use it himself. For the rest of our time at Horace Mann he thought that's why he lost me as a friend.

I opened most weekends with a Friday night concert. Alone with my Magnavox I put on one 45 after another, and lay there suffused in the worlds of feeling they invoked. It was not so much their lyrics— although those sometimes paralleled my sentiments. No, it was that each tune-word combination was idiomatic and complete, a key to something faraway and of great tenderness. It was, as Bobby Darin proposed, *"Every night I hope and pray"*—it was a prayer:

"Dream lover, until then, I'll go to sleep and dream again...."

And the Everly Brothers, Paul Anka, Dion and the Belmonts:

"Now if you want to make me cry, that won't be so hard to do. And if you should say goodbye I'll still go on loving you...."

I melted my voice into theirs, participating in a force that supported and carried me along, as if melody were rich enough to fill creation. Even the brief silences between sounds resonated with undisclosed meaning.

"Each night I ask, the stars up above..."—my echo drawled out the "s" and "r" and "v" even more than Dion, in total agreement: that it was sad but that it was also wonderful ... that someday I would get to the bottom of it.

There was one song in which the deceptively simple words had no discernible connection to their power over for me:

"I've a-laid around and played around this old town too long,
Summer's almost gone, winter's comin' on."

Which winter? What town?

I saw a village out west. I heard the distant echo of "Winter Wonderland," my mother long ago in her black velvet overcoat, walking on the new-fallen snow of Central Park in a vastness that seemed before civilization, a panorama of childhood in a divining jar through whose opacity crystals fell.

But it was more than that. Just the word "winter" was evocative— the feeling of cold flakes on my skin, sleigh rides with Daddy, steering around titanic rocks, colored lights down street after street.

Dr. Friend would review the song with me by stanza:

"Papa writes to Jonny, but Jonny can't come home. Jonny can't come home, no Jonny can't come home."

"It's your brother, of course," he noted cursorily. I still wasn't sure.

"Papa writes to Jonny, but Jonny can't come home. 'Cause he's been on the chain gang too long."

Yes, Jonny it must be. So obvious. Yet it didn't ring true. The "Jonny" in the song was some sort of bandit hero. He was also *"Oh, my papa,"* Eddie Fisher singing a requiem, *"To me he was so wonderful ...,"* the sword of cancer shadowing those very words ... "another place/another time" (Bridey Murphy to Dr. Bernstein). Why such insistent associations, remote and obscure as to seem in different universe, yet almost palpable and at hand? Why such an unlikely procession of phantoms shrouded in jabberwocky?

"What about the chain gang, Richard? Do you picture your family in New York as a prison in which your brother is trapped? Your own father can call you home but not your brother who can't leave his family."

Maybe. Then, does that mean I feel sorry for Jon? Is there some other Jonny hidden inside my brother who would be my friend in another circumstance, another life? Does the ballad inexplicably call for him behind the mime of its jaunty cowboy voice?

Not enough! Still not enough! This was Planet Mars big, big as the ocean sending waves from out beyond itself, big as all the cities on all the stars in the night. Or, maybe it was the prophecy of escape, that someday I was just going to walk out of this place into my destiny. A dark November day bearing the amulet of my birth sign. . . .

"And I feel like I gotta travel on."

That year I made friends with the president of the Horace Mann camera club. His name was Rudy. He was short with a large owl-like face. I liked him because he was well-spoken and mature, so I began looking for him on the subway, hoping to find him before anyone else did and get his full attention on the ride home. He was the first person I ever met whose parents were also divorced and remarried, so that was a thing we shared even though our situations were so different. As we sat in facing seats, I blabbed on about my mother and stepfather, the family at Grossinger's, and the amazing scene at the Hotel itself.

The first time we got together on a weekend was a Saturday gathering of the camera club—a trek through Greenwich Village, each of us stocked with canisters of bulk-loaded film, focusing on debris and derelicts, framing car tail-lights into funny faces. That night I went to

Rudy's house for dinner, and his stepfather led a wide-ranging discussion about world events.

I couldn't imagine reciprocating at my apartment, so I came up with something more radical: I asked Aunt Bunny if I could invite Rudy to Grossinger's. She had already heard much about my new friend and was immediately receptive.

"I think you're old enough and mature enough to have a friend come stay with us." While conceding that my father would object, she drolly brushed that off, "Why not? PG probably won't even notice. He'd just be scared that your unregistered guest would trip over a rock and his parents would sue us."

My promise that wouldn't happen caused her to laugh out loud.

Ray picked me up after school on the Friday of spring vacation and headed straight downtown to collect my stepmother at her psychiatrist. As she emerged from the canopy I ran from the car to greet her. She was whistling quite loud and didn't stop for a while. Then she told me: Her doctor was leaving the building at the same moment, and she was letting him know I was her son too with a version of *"Yessir, that's my baby."*

I reminded her about Rudy, and she began to list the exciting things we could all do together.

Her enthusiasm drove me into a mood I had not expected. Right then I knew I had made a mistake.

The first morning in the country Michael, Jimmy, and I took sleds to the golf course and sped recklessly behind one another down the hills. We were daredevil clowns, challenging trees and tumbling into drifts as our sleds collided. Then, noisy enough to be hushed by the maître d', we hit the dining room at the peak of lunch, our hair covered with ice balls, gobbled down potato pancakes and pineapple blintzes, and ordered all four desserts (cookies, sherbet, strawberry shortcake, and date-nut slices).

Later in the week the air turned warm, the snow melted, and we took rowboats out into the lake, scouting for turtles on rocks and wading among lily pads to get close to bullfrogs.

Upon hearing I was taking biology, Milty produced an old microscope, and Michael and I kneeled on the floor, directing sunlight with its mirror, illuminating paramecia and other tumbling creatures from the Lake. I tested the water hole beside the willows and came upon one of the cute secondary phyla—thousands of whiskered rotifers spinning about. I collected them in a honey jar, then watched them bump among diatoms and plankton.

That Friday the event I had so casually set into motion came to its denouement. Ray pulled up at the house. I wanted the car miraculously to be empty. It wasn't. My subway friend got out and stood in the road, yawning. I observed him from the upstairs window: a diffident, self-conscious imp of a boy I hardly knew, a Horace Mann kid in a suit jacket and tie with a beat-up suitcase. Michael grunted in comic disdain.

"Are you going to show me the Hotel?" Rudy asked excitedly as I led him upstairs. I had talked about it enough; now it was there to exhibit in all its glory. I managed a nod.

Over the first two days I took him skating and skiing, as we tried to regain camaraderie. He stumbled along so embarrassingly at the rink I pretended not to know him, and then I left him in the beginner's class at the ski slope while I took the rope all the way to the top and sped down past him. By the next morning we were so alienated I didn't even want to be packed into the same toboggan with him, so I squirreled my way into a different group in the shed, leaving him alone to ride with a couple and their child.

Rudy was no hero, or buddy even. I was repelled by his style. His maturity was brittle and, against the diorama of Grossinger's, the gestures of his that once attracted me to him were affectations. Without the charisma I had projected onto him he was another sulky adversary who resented my indifference and took to priggishly demanding courtesies I withheld.

Instead I made things hard for him much in the way I did for my brother Jon—sneakily and irreproachably. I lavished more attention on Michael—on Milty, Irv Jaffee, and Jack the waiter. All along I kept up a clever, chatty front.

He kept asking, "What's wrong."

"Nothing," I snapped.

What I hadn't recognized was that through the years of coming unassumingly to my father's hotel I had turned into a tyrant. It had once seemed that, through a fortunate inheritance, I had escaped Jonathan and the Towers clan, that I was forever humble and thanked the Fates. But, even as I frolicked through the grounds, revelling naively in being Richard Grossinger, the owner's son, I reenacted the Towers stubbornness, their exclusivity and misanthropy, their dour condescension toward others.

I had told myself that Jonny was a bad guy, a tormentor, that I was his helpless victim. Now I realized I was a snob and a bully too.

I didn't *realize* it. I experienced its tawdry discomfort. I felt like a centipede exposed by a rock turned over, scurrying to dig back into my cold dirt.

The New York Richard was a shy, accommodating chap, studying religiously, seeking company, cultivating friends. The Grossinger Richard was a careless, slaphappy boss, an isolate trickster, lacking decency or congeniality. The two selves denied, even shunned each other. They didn't share the same desires. They didn't like each other. Together they had collaborated to fool Dr. Fabian, and now they kept their agenda hidden from Dr. Friend.

After three days Rudy and I had run out of ruses. Our grim silence marked the demise of another friendship. This time I was the turncoat and traitor.

Perhaps that's why I nursed the story of me and Rudy so long, drawing it out until even Dr. Friend was exasperated: it held an unpleasant truth which I could neither admit nor stop picking at.

"What are you *really* thinking?" he would ask tiredly, again, and again. My two selves, even as they hid behind each other's solitude, refused to become reconciled or answer.

The approaching end of P.S. 6 for my brother marked our departure from Park Avenue and the East Side. There was no longer any reason to hang on at the boundary of the school district. Debby was already going to the bilingual Lycée Français, so my mother and Bob found an apartment in a huge twin-towered building on Central Park West and 90th Street.

A small cubicle with its own bathroom adjoined the room deeded to Jon and me. It was made into my study in order to allow me to work late after he went to bed.

"How do you like it?" my mother asked.

I surveyed the room with its dark courtyard and answered, without thinking, that it looked a bit cramped. That sounded ungrateful, so she slammed the door, adding, "You'd better learn to like it."

A few days later she took me downtown to buy furniture for both my study and the "boys' bedroom," but she far exceeded their combined capacity—adding a desk and bureau for Debby, some chairs for the living room, and assorted tables. Then she charged it all to Grossinger's over my signature.

"They can afford it," she said, "and they owe me this."

Jonny and I didn't fight physically that much anymore. We had begun to appreciate our similarities and analyze our differences philosophically. Before sleep we lay in our beds, talking across the room. In our most familiar dialogue he took the point of view that the main goal in life was to have fun. "You have to agree to that, Richard!" he demanded. He thought I was denying it only to provoke him. How could I not admit something so obvious?

I, in turn, argued (time and again) that the point of life was to figure out who we were. He was sure I was just saying that to frustrate him. For the rest of our sojourn in the same household he challenged me on it, not accepting I might really believe my own assertion— though I could see he wasn't having much fun with his successes.

I would be awakened past midnight by him standing in the middle of the room, swinging his fists in the air. "Even if there are ghosts," I contended, "you can't fight them that way."

"You don't understand, Richard. They challenge me. They call me a coward."

I told my mother, but so vehemently did she accuse me of bad-mouthing my brother I lost any sense of why I was bearing the news. Did I perhaps secretly enjoy his haunted dance in the dark?

I remember a prank I played on him soon after we moved into our new apartment. I attached a ball of string to the cord of the ceiling light in my study and ran it under the door into our bedroom. I took the remaining core into bed with me and, after a suitable interval, tugged on the string to turn on the light. Jon propped himself up. "Who's in there?" he whispered.

"I don't know. Maybe someone's gotten in the back door."

I shook the string to create a rattling noise. Then I jerked it twice to turn the light off and on again.

He jumped out of bed. "I'm getting Mommy."

"No, wait." I hadn't meant for it to get that far.

I heard him wake them up. I was petrified. I pulled on the string to turn out the light, but it snagged. I pulled harder and harder.

They were walking down the hall. They were opening the study door. I gave one last frantic yank! The light went out, and the string came loose. There was a crash of things falling off my desk.

I pulled and pulled that string and, when I finally felt the knot at its end, I gripped it to my belly. When they came into the bedroom baffled, I was frozen in imitation of sleep.

Debby and Bridey shared a room at the rear corner of our apartment. On Bridey's nights off (when she went home to the Bronx where she kept a small flat) Debby would whimper softly and call for help: "Rich, come." Jonny and I were forbidden to visit her then. She was ostensibly being trained to lose her fears so she wouldn't end up like me. But I would creep down the hall, hush open her door, and kneel by her bed. I'd make jokes, cuddle her, hold her pudgy hand, and tell her stories. Sometimes I'd enact shadow cartoons on the ceiling, making animal shapes with my fingers—rabbits and foxes in the dim light from other apartments. She was Squizzle Drip, the baby I once tumbled with in the park and pulled on a sled, the one innocent in our family.

In the middle of such a shadow play—my whispering probably having grown too loud—my mother burst in and, with ungodly screams, chased me back to my room. Even Daddy was awakened to bombard me verbally until the walls shook.

After that it became necessary to work out a signal. Instead of crying, Debby would sidle across her room and rap softly on the wall, which was Jon's and my room. Even if asleep I would jump up and tiptoe to her chamber. These were what she and I called rescue missions. I didn't have to tell her I understood.

When both our parents were away I liked to surprise her and Jon with parties. At Cushman's Bakery I'd buy serrated cupcakes with lemon or chocolate frosting plus a container of ice cream. I would sneak these into the house and put them out on the table at lunchtime. Debby would prance in delight and, while we gobbled our desserts, Jon and I would tell her stories of the past, like the time we followed the wrong woman from the fish market. Our sister was astonished: "God, Mom was even worse. You guys got to see all the good stuff!" Afterwards, we did the dishes together, tossing plastic plates and cups acrobatically from the sink to the wiper to the putter-away.

We were such great friends at those times, but otherwise we were grim combatants, caught in an inexorable cycle. Under pressure they would tell on me, every last thing I had said. They never intended to; they always swore loyalty to our trio, but Mom was an enchantress and she could wring a confidence out whenever she wanted.

From our location on the West Side Dr. Friend was a mere four blocks away. I began seeing him at new hours, occasionally six in the morning en route to school but more frequently seven at night, dinner time. Setting a break in homework, I grabbed a jacket and rang the elevator. I was on an old familiar quest.

Leaving the apartment after my mother and Bob were home and Bridey was preparing dinner, then walking the streets along Central Park West at night, I experienced a breeze of cherry blossoms and old ball-games. It was an interlude when life was about to loosen its somber grip and become its own daffy topic. Even if Dr. Friend was a mercenary, I was his chosen cipher and I assumed that the heroism of our mission transcended the fee.

Dr. Fabian had originally characterized psychoanalysis as "a method of learning why one had certain feelings and behaved in particular ways." We were, he said, bound in habits by forgotten events. I long ago imagined the "source" as being like the pot of gold in a fairy tale, perhaps some explicit memory: the egg in the bush, the glass of apple juice at sunset, Judy in her yard, or something that had been lost so early it had no referent.

The demons I brought to the office on Seventh Street overwhelmed me once with their fathomlessness. Through Abraham Fabian's intercession they took on denomination. They were still shadow figments in an abyss, but I had confidence he knew (or at least intuited) the manner of thing they were. Ultimately, if I reached a crossroads or a moment of desperation and implored him, he would break his pact with the oracle and tell me.

Dr. Friend made it clear he didn't know and never would. There was no pot of gold in his office; there was in fact no rainbow. All the spooks and phobias were my own, as stubborn and insoluble as I was. "You expect to leave here someday with the solution," he said one day, "but, in this business, cure is called termination. When you feel able to terminate this relationship, that's when you're well."

On my way back from baseball practice one day, I told a classmate who also had trouble hitting the fastball that *my* problem was psychological. "I'm afraid of something that hitting represents."

"And what do you think it is with me?" he retorted. "Just because you go to a psychiatrist doesn't make you any more psychological than anyone else."

Danny had entered Horace Mann the previous year, and I got to know him in the camera club. He had subscriptions to both major photography magazines and was interested in taking a prize-winning picture with his Rolliflex. He kept track of contests and their deadlines and was prone to test his lenses by rendering random brick walls on Pan X film and then developing and printing for morsels of grain. Neither a notable student nor a jock, he spoke with authority in class and ran track. He had a James Dean look, a dense solid body with slightly wild, penetrating eyes. He cultivated a sneer and slouch and greased his hair straight back from a broad forehead. He was the embodiment of nasty charm.

I don't remember exactly when he became an infatuation because I seemed to have always known he was special. Since we shared history class I discussed assignments with him. Gradually we became friends, and he took it on himself to educate me in the ways of the world. My dressing, he thought, was abominable. "It's because your mother always buys your clothes," he insisted. I decided he was right. In fact, I realized, she had probably gone out of her way to make me dippy. So, in defiance, I visited Saks on my own and came home with loud black-and-white checked jackets and powder-blue shirts of as soft a cotton as Danny's. I imitated Danny's big dabs of Brylcreem and slicked down my hair. My mother was aghast.

One Friday Danny invited me to his home straight on the bus from Riverdale to Yonkers—no clothes, no arrangements. We left school with playful humor and were in high jollity by the time we arrived at his front door. I immediately called Dr. Friend to cancel my appointment. I expected that he would share my delight, but he seemed concerned only to remind me that my father would still be billed. "I'm at Danny's!" I enthused.

"I'll see you on Tuesday," he said.

My hero and I studied together in his room, ate dinner with his parents, and went to a movie just like real teenagers. This was an intimacy I had dreamed of with Jeffrey once and played at with Fred for an afternoon. We lay in beds on opposite sides of his room and talked past midnight—teachers, girls, summer camp, famous pranks played. As he described his successes with older women who found him attractive, I was like his younger brother, never daring to identify with him because his situation was so totally removed from mine. His contribution was to instruct me how to act cool, not to say twerpy things; he promised that, if only I came to camp with him next summer, I would meet a lot of girls and have a good time.

"We don't just steal panties there," he said. "We have real raids."

When Danny finally said, "Hey wow, goodnight," I sank into an effortless sleep and woke to the green light of his morning, birds of some other world chirping in the feeder.

Camp Orenda was owned by Danny's parents (his father was a high-school principal in Brooklyn, and his mother taught grade school in Rye); it was located far from Chipinaw, in the remoter reaches of the Adirondacks. A month later, when I came home with him again (this time by plan), his family was ready with a slide presentation. By then I couldn't imagine going back to my slapstick with Jay and Barry. I would have followed Danny to the North Pole.

My mother preferred to keep her three children together, and she pointed out that my father wouldn't allow a switch because the camp wasn't kosher and also because he didn't know the owners. When I raised the matter with him she turned out to be correct. "But *you're* not even kosher," I protested.

"It's the appearance that counts," he said.

Aunt Bunny thought it was a wonderful idea for me to strike out on my own. Since she was sending Michael and James to a non-Jewish camp in Maine, she didn't see why I had to be held to a different standard.

"What is it, Paul? Is he the only Grossinger in this family, so he alone gets to suffer?"

Not only did he give in but, when the time came, he drove me himself from Grossinger's, stopping at various hotels along the way to talk business. It was one of our best times together. I loved arriving with Paul Grossinger, president of the New York State Hotel Association. We were greeted by owners and given tours of their grounds. I overheard gossip about unions and regional trade plans. Then, back in the car, he encouraged my questions and answered with long discourses on the future of the Catskills.

One look at Orenda made me wonder if I had seen a slide show of a different camp. The bunks were flimsy, the athletic facilities nonexistent or in disrepair. Boys' and girls' camps shared the same fields. Color War would have been ludicrous here: there were virtually no activities at all.

On a hill near the dining room sat the social hall with its Coke machine and jukebox. The first night, full of anticipatory razzing, our bunk arrived together. The girls clustered along the far wall. Music blared away. I stood by the side, getting my bearings. Four or five songs played, and I was still mesmerized watching.

Danny strode briskly back across the room. "Hey, man," he said "this isn't the way it works. Nothing's going to happen if you park yourself here. You've got to find a likely candidate and dance with her."

"I don't see any likely candidates," I demurred.

He looked around and then, pointing into a crowd, said, "How about her?"

At first I couldn't tell whom he meant, but when my eyes fell on the right one, she was immediately made attractive by Danny's attention.

"Look at those tits."

I grimaced but maintained contact with his bravado.

"Now, go ahead," he urged me. Mission accomplished, he returned to the stunning-looking girl he had chosen.

The music played "Dream Lover" and then the music played "The Battle of New Orleans"; still no other guy approached the girl Danny had pointed out. She was wearing a tight sweater and I saw her obvious bustiness that had caught his attention. I waited until even waiting was unendurable, and then, on the next slow one, I walked over and asked her to dance. She nodded, smiled, and we walked to the center of the room. I placed my arms carefully around her, and we seesawed in a square while we said things to each other like, "Where do you go to school?" and "Oh, so you're Danny's friend. . . ."

Her name was Marian, and she came from the Bronx. When the record was over she sat down in her group, so I returned to my side. Danny swaggered across the room.

"I told you I was going to teach you how to act if you came to Orenda. Now here's your first lesson. You've got to hold your partner really close. Girls don't think you like them unless they can feel you up against them and your hand on their back. Then, after the dance, you sit down with her. It's not tag team."

I felt a pang of disgust. I found him boastful and crude, and I wasn't used to translating feelings into strategies. Yet I couldn't articulate my own position to myself, and I hadn't had any success acting my own way. I waited out a few fast dances for the next slow one: *"I'm Mr. Blue-oo-oo-uh-oo when you say you love me. . . ."*

I approached her, our eyes briefly met, and I put my arm hesitantly on her waist as we walked to an open area of the floor.

I had never danced close, but I saw everyone else doing it and I realized it would happen if I moved my hand to a different place on her back. With that one gesture I fell into total intimacy. I smelled her perfume, and felt her breasts touching my chest, our slight friction. My penis grew hard; a charge ran up and down me. What if she could feel me? I couldn't imagine how to get it to change back. It grew only harder, and holding her close was my only assurance no one would see. This time we said nothing at all. I could hear my heart beating. My throat was dry and becoming sore. There was a flow of awkward harmony inside me, memories of old ball-games, the frog at Swago, a bird against twilight.

She moved her arm along my back. I tried to picture Mickey Mantle's homers, one after another into the stands, deep into the bleachers, far back, against a pale sun; Bob Turley's fastballs, launched again and again out of his big easy pitching motion. These were the old rhythm, the familiar grace of a childhood suddenly lost.

For the next several nights I danced with Marian and sat by the side talking with her. I told her about Chipinaw and Grossinger's, and she described her school, her parents, and past summers at Orenda. The real event was the dancing, and I learned, like the others, to wear a large sweater to hide excitement.

After a few days I wasn't the only one asking Marian to dance. Bobby Sackett regularly beat me to the social room and, when he was late, he cut in on me and then monopolized her.

In order to recapture Marian I had to walk over to where they were sitting together and invite her to dance all over again. When I questioned her about this arrangement, she told me that we were both her friends, that she didn't favor either of us. Which I couldn't understand. . . . I had little personal confidence, but Bobby Sackett was as ugly as a crocodile and an obnoxious ass. Back in the bunk he talked about her, generally only her breasts, in the most blatant possible language.

But then how clean was I? Though I said nothing I would lie in bed imagining reaching inside her sweater and touching her, putting my head inside her sweater, licking her nipple. I would feel my erection pushing to the end of possible space.

On his home court Danny was despotic and sterile, ever preening, never deigning even to play sports with us. He prowled the girls' camp with self-appointed authority on the pretense of helping his father with maintenance. He had no intellectual interests; even his photography was a ceaseless competition. He obsessed over his impeccable enlargements, and at the same time used the darkroom for his trysts with Gloria, a black-haired girl from Montreal with a sad, Indian face.

Danny and I had one serious confrontation that summer. He heard that a dog had treed a cat and ran to get his Rolliflex. Moments later I heard too and came right behind him. He carried a tripod and set it at the base of the tree. As I arrived he exploded at me. "This is a prizewinning shot, you fucking asshole. Get outa here. I've had enough of your stealing my ideas."

I ignored him for the rest of the summer. He was easy to give up; he had become the enemy.

It was now Gloria who interested me. In my fantasies she was the one I rescued from leering boys. I reclaimed my childhood spaceship and set its opera in motion. Gloria and I built a house and sat out at night on our farm in another solar system. The Earth's sun was just a star in the sky.

As the summer progressed Danny seemed almost diabolic, combing and recombing his hair with Brylcreem, putting on layers of after-shave lotion, doing fake karate leaps half-naked and landing with his hand on his jock.

Then one night I was awakened by the creak of doors and whispers. This was the long-rumored raid. A bunch of girls had made it past the guards. They quickly matched up with guys, and I could hear them making out, giggling. I had no idea whether Marian was with Bobby. I pulled the covers over my head and burrowed deeper.

By then any relationship between Marian and me was tenuous. Bobby Sackett was so persistent that it was hardly worth the trouble. I wasn't even sure that I cared about Marian beyond the force of desire, which at times seemed so overwhelming it would dissolve me ... and at other times didn't seem to exist. In fact a large part of me was offended by both her herself and my own fantasies.

Bobby thoroughly enjoyed the competition and tried to keep our rivalry alive. Every time I danced with Marian he went through the ritual of allowing me a certain quota and then cutting in. Back at the bunk he loved to boast how he was winning, but he'd always add, as if genteelly, "Of course, we'll let her have final say."

One time, I asked her to promise to finish the dance.

"Not if Bobby cuts in."

"Well, would you rather dance with him?"

"Why don't you cut in on *him* then?"

I shook my head stubbornly.

When she responded to his tap a moment later, I turned and left the room.

Near the end of the summer Danny surprisingly asked another girl, not Gloria, to the formal dance. It was Monica, whom we had all come to regard as the sexiest woman at Orenda. Tall and lissome, she wore skimpy shirts, strolled with her whole body in motion, and talked like an ingénue starlet. Her face was pale and Cleopatran, and she smelled of spice. Although a camper, she dated counselors, and gossip had her sleeping with more than one. She reminded me of Jayne Mansfield, who once patted me on the head in the Grossinger dining room. ("She gives," Danny announced to his fans in the bunk.)

The moment when I could have appeared out of the blue and asked Gloria to the dance passed quickly. Spurned by the camp idol, she was in seclusion, but a fierce runty kid nicknamed the Bug must have had his eyes on her too because he found her, asked her, and got her to agree to go with him. He hadn't been to the social hall all summer. Now he kept saying he was going to get inside her pants, so I ended up in a fistfight with him. We wrestled on the ground until counselors pulled us apart.

Back at the Hotel I sat in the garden and told Aunt Bunny tales from the summer. "I feel badly for you," she said, "but you certainly make it into a great story."

Her big surprise was that she had hired a teacher from the local public school to live in the guest room because Uncle Paul wasn't around enough to serve as a father to Michael and Jimmy. His name was Jerry MacDonald, and he was a former shortstop from the Yankee farm system. Ten minutes after I met him I thought he was the greatest guy ever. We spent the afternoon on the ballfield, hitting fungos; then I led him on a tour of the grounds.

"This is some kind of place for an old Irish ballplayer to end up," he said with a laugh. "When do I get to wake up?"

In the fall my classes were Geometry and Chemistry, Pliny and William Faulkner, plus a second, deeper run at American History, using college texts.

I had naively convinced myself Jonny would go to a different private school, but his entrance into Horace Mann was like clockwork. I had to teach him the subway route the first day that fall. He tagged along with me and my friends.

At Christmastime Orenda held its winter reunion at a hall in downtown Manhattan. I took a break from Saturday homework and rode the IRT down Broadway, then walked to the address on my invitation. I spent an hour, munching cookies and drinking soda. I saw only a few friends and was on my way out when I got tapped on the shoulder. I looked around, expecting to see anyone but . . . Monica. She was wearing an Orenda tee-shirt and had on very red lipstick. "Richie," she said, though I had never talked to her, "guess what? I'm going to Grossinger's on Washington's Birthday. Are you going to be there?"

"Yes," I managed. There was no other answer possible. But I had never gone that weekend because it was my mother's birthday.

"Good. Then I'll see you."

I pleaded with Aunt Bunny. I told her I couldn't explain why but I had to come. After a week she let me know that it was okay. A driver would be there to pick me up.

For two whole months I wove fantasies. I tried to resurrect Monica's perfume in my mind; I imagined the slink of her torso and her red lips. I would hold her, undress her. There was no way to contact or release the sensation—it was irresistible and unendurable both.

When I told Dr. Friend, he asked again if I had masturbated yet.

"I don't know how to."

"There's nothing to know. You get hard. You keep rubbing. You ejaculate."

"But I don't," I protested. "Nothing happens. It gets hard; then it gets soft."

He merely smiled.

But he made me curious, so I would sit in the bathtub with the door locked, think of Monica, get an erection, and then rub harder. I would try to imagine her more intensely, invoke more intimate postures and activities, give her seductive words. Clearly I was missing something.

When the car left me off at Grossinger's I ran straight to the reservation desk to check the list.

Unbelievable! She was really there!

That first night I dressed up and went over to the Main Building. The dining room was packed. In recent years I had stayed away from it in the evening because I disliked its formality and gala atmosphere. It was a realm of extroverts and, since I was automatically a public figure, I drew all too much attention from waiters, guests, and assorted relatives. Tonight I moved quickly and pretended I wasn't me, didn't acknowledge any of the cries of my name. At the spinning rack of names I located her table.

"Hey, what! Looking for girls?" snapped the assistant maître d' all too appropriately.

"Nope." I wasn't looking for girls. I was looking for this one person ... and she wasn't at the table she had been assigned to ... and I was certainly too shy to ask the crowd there if any were her parents. After dinner I searched the lobbies again, hoping I would see Monica, hoping I wouldn't so that I could go home and talk baseball with Jerry. Then I caught sight of her standing by the dining-room entrance in a long white dress. I felt a dizzying rush. Each step in her direction increased the roar in my head so that I hardly knew what I would do when I got there.

She greeted me enthusiastically but said that we should make a date for the morning because she had to meet her cousin now. She stood there, taller than I, smiling bewitchingly. I turned and galloped back to the house. Standing outside in moonlight, I fired stones at a tree. My hits echoed like line drives.

In the morning I went straight to her table. She got up from breakfast and said, "Lead the way." We circled the downstairs lobby and watched indoor swimmers underwater through the observation window. I showed her how to see a rainbow by looking straight up toward the surface. Then, at her suggestion, we played ping-pong without keeping score. After that we tried the ice rink, where she struggled by the rail while I sailed through the crowds, waving or smiling each time I passed her. I knew that was wrong, but I couldn't bring myself to take her arm. We went from there to the toboggan, then the ski slope.

As ordinary activities filled the hours, my weeks of fantasies seemed absurd. Monica wasn't Danny's living centerfold. She and I were pals, exploring the Hotel, me leading her and her cousins through secret passages, showing them the inside of the kitchen, getting them cookies right from the oven. We watched the ice show ... and then she was gone, off to dinner and the nightclub with her family. I trudged back to Jerry, shaking my head.

"What's up, Richard?"

"Girls," I said. "Don't even ask."

"I know. Don't I ever know!"

In the morning Monica was the imperious actress again, aloof, preening. I was drawn right back in. Her allure seemed so obviously intentional. "Richie, I missed you last night after dinner. We had such a good time in the Terrace Room!" She told me she wanted to try swimming in the indoor pool. "Don't you think I'd look wiggly through the window?" I said I'd go with her.

"Good. I was hoping we could have some time together. I have to go upstairs and get my bathing suit. Come." She turned and glided toward the elevator, sashaying two fingers my way.

"This is it," I told myself, and the phrase echoed in my mind: ". . . is it . . . is it . . . is it"—like Mel Allen's description of a home run, only building in tension to something beyond imagination, wordless and final. I paced dutifully behind her, Pip again, all fated long ago. I had been in that lobby a thousand times, but now it was astonishingly luminous and immaterial . . . I felt it might all float away. I was weak; I had nothing left at the core. In her tight pants she swung back and forth. She was too old for me. I wanted to touch her anywhere, even gently.

In the upper lobby Herb Schwartz was conducting his hypnotism show, which caught her fascination ("Oh, look at that!" she cried out, stopping). I felt my tension snap and ease. I stood by her side in bored frustration. (Why had I never noticed how stupid it was, the same gags and stunts, year after year? Herb, do something different; help me!) As he held a match under a woman's hand I tried to devise a way to get Monica moving again. But suddenly her cousin appeared and asked if she wanted to watch a beauty show that was just beginning in the lower lobby. I assumed she had my same fantasy in mind (after all, she was Danny's alter ego), that she would say no, but she looked at me routinely and shrugged, "I guess we can go swimming later."

The let-down was worse than any embarrassment, so I asked if I could talk to her alone. A desperation was leading me nowhere as we walked to a corner of the lobby. I had not the slightest idea what I would say. She looked at me curiously.

"Can I kiss you . . . sometime?"

She seemed dumbfounded and didn't answer. I left my words there for a second, maybe another, and her face was still a mask, maybe an inkling of confusion. Then I said, "I've never kissed a girl."

"Ask Danny. I can't explain it. I'm a girl."

She smiled and turned, leaving the inappropriateness of her response in my mind. I ran fullspeed back to the house, tearing my nails into the back of my hand so that there were four red bleeding marks. Even with that I couldn't reach deep enough inside.

Then one night that spring I lay in the bathtub imagining the moment again, that she had said, "Well, come upstairs to my room, and I'll show you." And then.... And then.... I had this hard penis in my hand. I had a slidey bar of soap that I rubbed it against, back and forth. I was thinking ... and then the thoughts took over, making an episode. There were three girls walking toward me ... Marian and Gloria too. They were shimmying toward me, silently, diagonally, then straight, with terrible and terrific motion, in precise rhythm, oddly expressionless, two steps, then one, two steps, then one.... *"Don't go home...."* Then there was only Marian and her full body and breasts against me as in the dance ... and then she reached me ... but she didn't stop.

PART THREE

TEENAGER IN LOVE

1960–1962

WITNESSING

The next summer I went back to the tents at Chipinaw. Jay and Barry had graduated to being waiters, so I signed up to live with the campers who ran O.D. shifts—sorting mail, depositing laundry, answering the phone, carting candy bars around to bunks, playing the recording of the bugle for activity changes. It was a generally disdained job, like being the Joker in a deck of cards, but I didn't identify with the Chipinaw hierarchy in which waiting tables was the last rung before accession to counselorhood.

I had a new fervor for the Yankees after abandoning them for two seasons. I listened to every game and, during my shifts, posted Major League scores on the O.D.-shack wall (along with homers and winning and losing pitchers). Collecting little kids, I arranged games and activities around the shack, including treasure hunts and croquet. Some shifts I had a troop of six or more Midgets with me. I rough-housed with them, counseled the homesick, and told stories. They helped me put mail in slots and change painted wood activity tags on the bulletin board.

When girls had so dominated, baseball didn't seem as crucial. Now I found it where I had left it, bright and innocent, an alternate version of life itself. The 1959 Yankees I had skipped were the worst team since I had been following them; they didn't even compete for the pennant. After the disastrous season, a changing of the guard was in full swing: Roger Maris, Tony Kubek, and Luis Arroyo. Jerry's childhood friend Bill Stafford arrived mid-summer. Mickey Mantle, Whitey Ford, and

Yogi Berra were still around. In a back-up role in what would be his last season, Gil McDougald was playing great. His spate of home runs in early July marked my return from the Underworld.

It was a quiet, aimless summer. I wasn't alienated; I wasn't homesick; I just had no place else to go. My tentmates cultivated a social style much like that of Danny and the Orenda crew, though in a more jovial spirit. They talked cars and sex. These topics trailed seamlessly through each other in a ritual of swearing, jibes, and put-downs (called "ranking," as in "Oh, did I rank you!"). In another popular activity, one group, with much banter, would select a centerfold, form a circle, and then compete to masturbate onto her ("Man, your dick's got the pick-up of Pat Brady's jeep!"). I was too private to join them.

It was the only time in my life (never before and never after) when I could intrude upon three guys with their pants open racing one another to splatter a pin-up.

My bunkmates viewed themselves as suave hedonists with their collections of *Playboy,* their wardrobes bunched on hangers on the center pole, their personae of Jewish wise guys pretending to be Italian hoods. A tall Fitzgerald-looking kid named Eddie, who had impeccably combed hair, put us under his spell that July and August, relating sexual encounters, like how the kids at his school had paid a girl to beat them off, describing the satiny feeling of her hand on his cock. In the background Johnny Mathis sang "Chances Are," then "The Twelfth of Never."

"Unadulterated pleasure," Eddie said, lolling on blankets in a patch of sun. He was referring to the song.

One afternoon I lifted the flap and ducked into my tent. There was Elliot with his watch held out; he was clocking a contest. The target was a Betty and Veronica comic. "It's Kenny, Rod, and Eddie," he told me, "and all of them are going for Archie's record."

"You guys are sick," I said. "Betty and Veronica aren't even real."

"Not real?" Rodney screamed, as they all turned to glare at me. "Did you ever look at Betty? That long yellow hair. That pair of boobs. How'd you like to feel that red lipstick coming off on you?"

"I'm a Veronica man myself," added Kenny. "Rod and I have different targets. I'm taking that white sweater right over her tits. Oooh, man!"

I looked down at their inspiration. There was Archie with his combed pompadour, Betty wearing a red, busty sweater, Veronica trying to entice him away with Bambi eyes, Reggie lurking in the background in a sports car. On the adjacent page both girls lolled in bikinis at the beach, and Jughead, with his X eyes, overdressed (including his dumb crown), was carrying their lunch basket.

"What do you think Jughead's going to do when he gets home?" Elliot asked me.

"I can't guess," I sneered.

"He's gonna beat the meat because neither Betty nor Veronica got the hots for crowns."

Suddenly Eddie scored. Only problem was he splotched the "geiger counter for girls" in another comic.

It was actually perfect. Archie and Jughead were who they—the ones who made the comics—thought we were, or perhaps who they thought we thought we were. Infallibly our desires found their desires. We didn't know we could feel sex any other way.

When I returned to Grossinger's in late summer I was surrounded by teenagers in bikinis and shorts—younger than me, older than me. The Hotel was now a palestra of forbidden desires. Glances and innuendos bred a collective arabesque, flutters of allure exuding from tinctures of perfume, designs of swim-wear, even textures of shadow in the dressing rooms.

Yet my own body felt gawky and exposed as I wandered through crowds in my bathing suit. I was no longer a child but not ready to be one of them. I didn't know the way into the labyrinth or how to claim the icons of sex. Although I felt their incredible power and urgency, they seemed everyone else's property. My sense of lust remained solitary and secret, perverse I was sure. The "dames" from my father's mystery novels lurked in the cabana where he left them. I sat in a tin toilet stall, summoning my erection with visualization, spit, and soap. A mood grew: trancelike, sorrowing, hungering, blending rapacity and tenderness, compulsion and regret, always indescribably profound. I was lured by the teaser on a recent back cover: "Wearing nothing but too much perfume, she threw her arms around me ... and I acquiesced...." Behind my closed eyes the image dilated, intensified, became palpable, and then, against the fragrance of the soap, flooded me into a strange, irresistible montage. I too acquiesced, despite my wish to remain stolid and whole.

I would go to the Nightwatch, the new teen room overlooking the indoor pool, and hang out there. I thought maybe being a celebrity would help, but it didn't make any difference. The teen world was insouciant, vain, defiant. Girls would be amazed when they heard my last name: "No, really? You're kidding. Wow, I'm going to tell my parents." But that didn't make me desirable. It was all a light-speed stream of jive and double-entendre, guys and girls coming and going, gathering in groups, plotting strategy. I would see many of the girls again throughout the Hotel and attach myself to their periphery, but I was never more than a novelty. Then they were checked out, and others replaced them. I would have taken Betty or Veronica in a moment.

Meanwhile I relished the Yankees' culminating battle with Milt Pappas, Chuck Estrada, and the upstart Orioles. A tall lemonade with a lemon-tipped glass straw, sun streaming in the window . . . I stretched out on the couch and floated in the residue of innings past.

Existence was a tumult of nostalgia and obscure qualms. I didn't know what I felt. I was tragic and buoyant both, certain that I could not survive the wave and yet riding it in wonder. The Hotel was still a paradise of cherry-tart and chocolate-tree desserts, gardens filled with every color of pansy into whose tiger aromas I poked my Minolta, lobbies buzzing in excitement of the pennant race, a cloud of cigars and cigarette smoke and wizened men gambling—and I was still the child Richie, getting their handshakes and greetings, summoning Milty for a butter-pecan/peach malt. While everything else inside me ached, the sheer habit and density of existence bore me along.

One afternoon I sat with Herb Schwartz under a tree by the Lake, trying to explain my tangled emotions. He was charmed by my adolescent obsessions, but he refused to acknowledge their cosmic edge. To his mind I had intimations because I was feeling unfamiliar hormones. "You'll always want to remember this time," he added, "because love will never be innocent again."

I would watch him romancing guests, women not particularly pretty to me (but he told me I had no notion of what real beauty was). Once, I startled both of us when I came upon him a few days later beneath that same oak with a naked lady. He had the presence to pull a towel around himself, a blanket over her, get up, and introduce us. He was continuing to inform me, "No big deal."

Back at Horace Mann I entered Fifth Form; I was a junior. I had Cicero in Latin class, American History and Government, Advanced Literature, Chemistry, and French. I loved chemistry class, especially trying to solve for unknown compounds in test tubes. We used litmus paper, Bunson burners, and known substances as filters, then wrote our guesses on slips of paper: tin or zinc, potassium chloride or potassium permanganate.

At the start of the term my English teacher and advisor, Mr. McCardell, spoke to me about being one of the enrollees in the new creative writing program. Since the course was not for credit (and there was so much graded schoolwork anyway), few people volunteered; now he was recruiting in earnest.

"But I don't write," I protested.

"You don't have to. That's what the class is for, to teach you."

"I have too many courses already."

"It's not a time-consuming subject, and you have a study hall when it meets. You're one of the few people here who have done *any* creative writing. You put out a whole camp newspaper, plus you're a science-fiction addict like me."

Persuaded by magisterial flattery, I agreed at least to try the class, which turned out to be mostly very skilled and committed seniors. It was taught by Kingsley Ervin, a tall, young Harvard newcomer considered the best English teacher in the school. He met us relaxedly at the end of the day once a week, often outdoors under reddening maples. The mood was more coffeehouse than Horace Mann, as classmates read their most recent work aloud. I soon came to look forward to rounds of literary stars offering the next installments from their binders, Mr. Ervin commenting insightfully like Dr. Friend.

What I heard was truly dazzling: a science-fiction tale about armageddon as seen by an absent-minded God, a description of a circus and a whorehouse through the mind of a midget, a Civil War veteran recalling old battles on his deathbed. Chuck Stein, the only other Fifth-Former, read poems so elliptical and complicated I didn't understand them.

By the end of the first month everyone else had read twice while I hadn't presented a thing. In fact, I seemed to have forgotten I was there on the same basis as the rest. Then Mr. Ervin scheduled me for a conference. He prodded me with friendly enthusiasm. When I didn't provide any ideas on my own, he assigned me an imitation of Tennyson's poem "The Eagle." At the next class, feeling rather foolish, I recited my effort aloud:

"He grips the ground with grasping claws/Deep in lush weeds of tawny lawns. . . ."

No one had any comment except, "Glad you at least put your toes in the water." They were gentle.

From the early days of Dr. Fabian I had been a storyteller. My motive then was purely clinical. But by junior year of Horace Mann I had read so many novels I had bigtime aspirations. The weekend after "The Eagle," I felt the ancient call of narrative. It swelled in me as pure inspiration, but I was skittish and shy. I told myself I needed a fairy-tale setting to convey the strangeness I felt. After hatching a myriad of possible landscapes I decided to set my account in a family of moles (I was only vaguely aware that a classic such tale already existed). I spent hours that weekend laying its groundwork, describing the exotic scenery around the moles' village: the tawny fields in which they hunted, their outlying crocodile swamp, the serpentine stream curling past their hut. I even drew a map of the mole habitat. By then I had lost my impetus entirely and was involved in the laborious depiction of an imaginary village, adjective by adjective. At its conclusion I added, as little more than an after-thought, initial passages of dialogue among the moles to show where my story might lead. I planned to work my mother and other family members (as moles, of course) into the next installment.

On Tuesday I raised my hand and was called upon at once. I had the most free turns coming of anyone. I began reading with gusto but within two sentences was mortified and wanted to stop. I had produced mud. Words I had chosen so painstakingly from the *Thesaurus* lost even their ordinary meanings because no logic held them together. It was not a story; it was a crossword puzzle. Everyone agreed that the mole dialogue was promising, but "contrived" was the consensus word for the rest.

"You all share Mr. Grossinger's fault to a degree," Mr. Ervin said.

"You are trying too hard to be sophisticated and are not writing from your own experiences."

For weeks I backed off, but I was thinking about it. Something in me wanted to tell a story, but I didn't know what the story was. It was exploding silently in my mind like rock and roll. It was a tune I could almost grasp, palpable yet faraway. I felt a kind of prescient awe. The world was mysterious, was frightening, was vast, was downright bizarre, but how did I say these things?

The Yankees met underdog Pittsburgh in an epic World Series that year. In game one, the Pirates eked out a suspenseful win; then the Bronx Bombers of yore destroyed them in the next game—only to have the Pirates pull out the following game in the clutch. This was to be the pattern of the whole Series. While I could barely keep track of this drama amidst my class schedule, the confrontation went all the way to a seventh game.

I sat in Latin, suppressing wild curiosity, my ears straining for any trace of radio in the air. When I heard a roar out the window I tried to guess for which team. Dozens of radios blared in the hallways. While we passed between classrooms I pleaded with anyone for a quick recap. Finally I raced from an exam on *Moby Dick* to the gym TV to watch the climax.

Kids were crammed onto benches in serious contemplation. Forget *The Brothers K.* and algebra. This was reality—and we knew it. The Yankees had come from behind to take a lead, then held and increased it. The season was down to just a few innings. Bobby Shantz was coasting along when a ground ball skipped off a pebble in the infield, hitting Tony Kubek in the Adam's apple and driving him out of the game. When Jim Coates came in to relieve, the Yankee haters hooted in glee. I was sure the gaunt righty would show them, but a shocking home run by Hal Smith put the Pirates ahead. The Yankees made a valiant comeback to tie the game in their next at-bat. Then, as simple as nothing (and everything), Bill Mazeroski cleared the left-field wall off Ralph Terry. I rode home on the subway stunned.

Friday afternoon of the following week was a turning point. Indian summer tore at ocher leaves against a bottomless blue. 246th Street was a paradise I could not barter—fluorescent trees, ancient breezes, a group from Manhattan College singing doo-wop outside the station, a newly arrived train parked for its return downtown. *"Forget them all / But for goodness sake / For-get me not."* I was headed home to my pit. This time I vowed I wouldn't let the spirit die or pass unheeded. I nursed it on the subway. I reached the apartment with something still dancing inside me. It was the original feeling of my friendships with Rudy and Danny, the excitement of arriving at Grossinger's . . . and long before that, the surf at Long Beach. It was a hundred other obscure things. But now it sought a self-organizing form; I needed to grasp it as my own.

I recalled my day of baseball against the blue-sky clouds at Fred's, my inexplicable turnaround on Rudy, my crush on Joan Snyder. I perceived an emergent shape in my childhood melancholy. It wasn't unequivocal or boundaryless. If seen from another angle, it was rich and fissury. It had the promise of Willa Cather and William Blake.

My illusion had been that only my intellect could craft symbols and language, that I needed moles and thunderstorms as foils. That is, I could be a great writer only by the same preparation and hard work that had gotten me As. I tended to view my alienation and afflictions as flaws in me, mistakes. I had overlooked their texture. They were also the cloth from which art was made.

All those years Dr. Fabian and Dr. Friend had said only obvious things. They had talked about anger and guilt, depression and arousal, as if these were motivations in and of themselves. What about the fields of snow to the horizon across which Michael, James, and I pulled our sleds at dusk, the vastness of other worlds I looked into in the night sky. . . . Who was I? What was this all? And, then, the song:

"Oh Shenando'h, you rolling river. . . ."

More mysterious than life itself.

I sat at my desk and without drafting began to write.

"One Friday about the middle of last March I arrived home in such a happy frame of mind it was apparent I was feeling more than the natural relief the weekend offers at the end of five long days. . . ." I was describing the first time Rudy and I got together with the camera club. I retold our entire friendship right through the trip to Grossinger's, the sleigh rides with Michael and James, the rotifers, my friend's arrival with his old-fashioned suitcase. . . .

It was well past midnight, and Bob stayed up watching The Late Show. I had summoned myself into a storytelling spell, and I kept going even after he turned out the lights. In the morning my mother complimented me on my long stint of homework. I barely heard her. I was onto something.

All through Saturday I scorched memory into narrative. I would scrawl with a pen till I couldn't bear it, take a break, sit at the window, eat a snack, then come back, my capacity not only unabated but increased. At intervals I would rewrite my draft and type it into an accumulating pile I hid in the bottom of a desk drawer. I had no idea what I was composing, but I was addicted to it. I recreated my day-dreams of Joan Snyder, my summer at Orenda, my fantasies of Gloria. Then I took the story of Monica right to our humiliating encounter at Grossinger's. I described her as a clipper ship on the Nile, trailing Egyptian scents. I thought, 'I can't believe I'm doing this. I'll never be able to read it in class.'

But the deed had its own giddy momentum. By Sunday I was recalling Nanny, my early sessions with Dr. Fabian, my brother and our wrestling matches, and the first day of Chipinaw. Where was all this suddenly coming from?

I arrived at Mr. Ervin's on Monday with a sheath of thirty-five typed pages. There was no possibility of presenting this material in public, no chance at all. Right up to the last moment I was reassuring myself: "I will show him the amount of work so he knows, but I won't read."

"Mr. Grossinger, look at that. I never would have thought!" In fact, Mr. Ervin was so delighted he halted my protests with "Tsk, tsk" and summoned me to begin without delay. The class unanimously seconded him.

I balked. I had promised myself, under no circumstances. . . . "It isn't really writing. It's just about myself."

"Go on. It's your true maiden voyage."

"I'm not sure—"

"Read!" I pretended to be aghast, but something had changed imperceptibly. In my heart I had already made the leap.

I read it as one might a fairy tale to children—slowly and in wonder. This was not Dr. Friend's office. I was making a confession of a far different order, infinitely more dangerous and more powerful. I dropped my concern for how intimate and shocking it was, how it was stuff I would tell no one. In my reading it aloud, it seemed no longer to matter. Even as I invoked events I released their embarrassment. I was inexplicably vindicated. Merely by proposing my history I had already changed it. Now, as I reached page ten, I actually began looking forward to the more provocative sections with delight. I soared. I was in the fire.

When I finished I looked around at faces of people I had never seen. We had gone fifteen minutes past the period, past the end of school; still, no one said anything. Finally Mr. Ervin turned to the most accomplished writer, Mark Weiss, the one who had presented the Civil War story, and asked, "What do you think?"

"I think it's the best thing that's been done in the class all year."

I couldn't believe what I heard. My mind was tumbling. 'So that's it,' I thought. The path had always been there, and I had never seen.

I couldn't have known, but I may have intuited (even then) that the magic was not the writing or the telling of secrets; it was the realization that I had always been a witness to my own event, that I had never completely identified with the things happening to me. The witness was there in the courtyard of 1220 when Nanny pointed to figures blown across the night. I couldn't come close to perceiving it then, for I was a mere and mute embodiment of that dark. The witness observed someone else peeing on the floor and daydreamed in my body. The witness kept me out of trouble, but also kept me out of life. Compared to this, my symbolic renderings of dreams were cotton candy.

The years of dialogue with doctors had at last brought forth their antithesis—and their fruition—that my life need not be the raw material of dream work and psychoanalysis, need not be sustained only by symbols; it was real, by itself.

"It seems so simple," Mr. Ervin said, "but it's not simple at all. I dare anyone else in this room to try it."

For the remaining years of high school and beyond I wrote my story. I now go back to what is left of those first raw pages (the ones my mother didn't discard with the scrapbooks and other relics of childhood) and recover episodes I no longer remember. Here, for example, is a minor scene from a meal that winter:

"How's the food?" Bridey asked as she dished out my share.

"Okay," I managed weakly.

"Okay?" Bob protested. "I think the food is spectacular when you cook it."

"Yes, it is, Bridey," Debby added.

"You don't sound too talkative tonight, Richie darling," my mother said after the flurry ended. I nodded and did not look up. "Did school go okay today?"

"Yep."

"Are your grades okay?"

"Yep."

"Well, Richie doesn't have anything to say tonight. How about you, Jonny dear?"

"Great. We played football after school. I got an A on my history test."

"That's wonderful, Jonny."

"It is," Bob said. "Richard has compiled at enviable record at Horace Mann, and I only hope you can emulate it."

What strikes me now is how ordinary it all was. At the time I imagined a subtlety in my mother's inquisitorial misdirection, in Bob's hostility masked by flamboyant irony: that's why I recorded it. But the real issue was how I was always on the outside of a sanctum they sought to protect against me. Back then I assumed it was because they hated me; now I know they didn't hate me at all—that I was part of them, though not a part they wanted to see. I lived out an extravagance and terror they desperately—every instant in fact—struggled to conceal.

Only in those flickers of déjà vu does the person writing this memoir come back to me now. I realize I was his only hope, his excuse for persisting. He was writing to *me* as much as to anyone. I alone could rescue him from his empty world, and for that reason I reinvoke him and bring my imagination and healing back to him then, now—even as then, then, I called out to myself in some unimaginable future, to document the desolation and ensure that I survived it.

One afternoon, not long after my maiden voyage, I was sitting in the Horace Mann cafeteria, memorizing my Latin vocabulary, when a songful voice from the next table caught my attention. I looked up and saw a boy talking to his friends. He was acting an episode for someone, waving his arms, stomping back and forth, making pictures in the air. He flashed smiles, then took them away. What happened next was inscrutable. I knew it was him. Even then, at the beginning, the recognition was so precise, the feeling of longing so evocative of my memory of primal longing, I felt as though he had always been there and I had never seen him.

His face was deep and glyphic, yet pretty. His voice had a melody I craved, its swift flowing over the scale.

His name was Keith, and I knew him as a presence at Horace Mann from the class beneath mine, a student volunteer, a regular in plays and the glee club. I had already noticed something elfin in him as he strode through hallways delivering messages.

A day before, he had been just another kid; now I began to obsess about him. He became the reason for my existence. Every time I saw him I was startled, as though I had encountered a famous person. Lying in bed at night I wove fantasies around him. I imagined us as roommates in his cottage by the ocean. We stood on the shore and watched waves crashing in. We rode surfboards together and rolled and hugged in the foam after the waves. We dried each other off with towels.

There was a grassy front yard with wild blue flowers, a yellow table on which sat a pitcher of lemonade and different colored glasses.

Keith wasn't an athlete, so I instructed him in playing stickball. Afterwards, as we lay in the sun, he teased me about my obsession with the Yankees. We were sitting in the Stadium, rooting for them to come from behind. We were at the Hotel, rebuilding the miniature golf course, collecting empty pickle jars from the back of the kitchen, warped rackets from the tennis shop.

At my Friday concerts I crouched by the Magnavox, invoking Keith as gently and palpably as I could—his yellow court-jesterness, his farmboyishness along yon ancient Scottish burn, master of the lyre.

And the Platters sang "Twilight Time" and *"Oh yes, I'm the great pretender . . . pretending that I'm doing well."*

Then Brook Benton:

"Go on . . . go on, Until you reach . . . the end . . . of the li-ine. . . ." As music poured like honey I felt as though I could see a billion miles in my head.

When I went to Grossinger's that Thanksgiving I brought Keith imaginarily beside me in the car, viewing everything a second time through his eyes. "See," I said. "This is the route we take. It's the route we've always taken since I met my father and Aunt Bunny." Trees and houses near and far swept by in a gathering darkness.

I brought samples from chemistry class, and Michael and I soaked pine cones in elixirs, then looked for the faint reds of iron and greens of copper as they caught among logs in the fireplace.

My brothers and cousins had become obsessed with speedskating. They all had new long blades and looked so cool, crouched low to the ice, whipping around like Irving the Fox. When I told Grandma, she called the pro shop and arranged for me not only to get fitted but to receive lessons.

The rink had been a morose realm for me. With its ridiculous show music, stumbling fatmen, and prissy ballerinas, I had no reason (except boredom) to bundle up and glide through cold vapors. There was also the more recent debacle of Monica. But now I saw the ice in an entirely new light: it was a speed zone. "Look at these, Keith," I mimed as I sat on a bench and laced the boots. Then I stumbled along the rubber mat.

Though I had skated for years, I found it almost impossible to make headway against the extended fulcrum of such long runners. I was landlocked on the ice when my teacher, an Austrian named Kurt, initiated me with a spray of ice shavings, grabbed my arms, and guided me around while I developed a stride.

Practicing this motion quickly became the focus of that whole weekend. While my brothers whizzed around the empty rink after hours, I worked myself up to a moderate speed along the side. We began to appear regularly during guest sessions until Irving intervened, "Wait till we close," he said. "Otherwise, you three are going to kill someone!"

After the summer at Orenda, dating actual girls seemed impossible. At times, the lure of "acquiesce" would envelop me. I'd lock myself in the small study bathroom, a familiar darkness in which I transformed my Minolta shootings into negative strips of surprisingly lucid windows. These were viewed in the twinkle of alley light, then hung on the shower pole to dry.

Now I would follow some fantasy, a story of a girl either spontaneously invented, seen on the subway, or recalled from camp or Hotel memory . . . barely breathing, my lips half open, my heart thumping. I would go into it, through it, and out the other side, back into my body transformed. It was a journey of metamorphosis I never would have thought possible had I not experienced it in my skin. Its residue was a warm sap that in no way betrayed the blood and ecstasy behind it.

I actually spent a lot of time locked in bathrooms. I developed a series of contests for the larger bathroom, including a football one using a broken corner of soap as the ball, the squares on the floor as players, the lines that formed them as yard-markers, and the ring-handle of the hamper for finger-kicking extra points and field goals. A well-worn chip of soap would spin along grids and land perfectly in a distant square between the field markers—a forty-yard completed pass. Then, thump!, a flick of two fingers whacked the extra point against the hamper.

The days at school were interminable. In a new body-building program I was assigned to alternate periods of weight-lifting and swimming. I felt weak and defective as though my bones might break instead of the barbells go up.

My face became so covered with acne my mother took me to her dermatologist. From then on, every other week, I'd visit him myself to have the pimples popped. There was no gentleness to this process. He wrapped a boiling medicated towel over me and went pimple by pimple with a pin, scrubbing with gauze to get out the goo. As he worked he lectured me about diet, wash cloths, and Phisohex. Not only did it hurt like hell, it scraped my state of ennui and irritation. He was touching my very mask.

At home I'd work his white liquid medicine with its faint aroma of bubblegum into my skin. The constant soreness around my cheeks and eyes and a mottled appearance became part of me. My acne was not just an ailment; it was how I felt about the world.

When Uncle Moe came as a rare guest for dinner that December he presented me with an electric razor. I had hoped to avoid that deed forever, but as I checked the mirror I knew it was time. Later that night the three adults invited me downtown to a preview of the movie *On the Beach.* We were among a small number of people in an office room in a skyscraper, my mother having gotten tickets through the Fontaine-bleau.

After the Earth was destroyed by bombs (and ensuing radiation), the lights in the room went on, returning us to reality. I stood, blinked several times, and stretched uneasily. I had just seen the end of time. Now we had a reprieve, but for how long?

In a review of *On the Beach* for the *Horace Mann Record* I proposed that the chance event of a Coke bottle dangling in a window shade (sending out a signal drawing the post-holocaust submarine crew to Australia) represented the "accident" that might have set off the war to begin with—and might still. Friends complimented me on my astuteness.

But I considered nuclear war my birthright. The "bomb" was born when I was and had cast a shadow over my entire life. It would lie dormant for months and then wake me with a start: God, it could happen *right now!*

The previous summer at Chipinaw I had walked around in a daze after a vociferous red-haired counselor swore we would never get to be adults, any of us. "They're going to blow it all up one of these days! Just by accident! There isn't a chance in hell they won't!"

How had I ever lost sight of that cardinal fact? This whole unhappy parade was leading only to oblivion. It would be like *On the Beach,* the last straggling survivors singing "Waltzing Matilda." Would I get to be twenty, or even seventeen?

When I argued against Hiroshima my parents defended it aggressively, seeing only that it curtailed a horrid war and saved lives. "You didn't have brothers in the Pacific!" my mother snapped.

So I quoted by heart for them from *Night of the Auk,* the blank-verse play that I had watched over and over on TV: "We broke their back with one quick crunch/And cheered a reddened flag of sudden victory./But on their streets, and in their houses,/In the churches, schools, and hospitals,/In the dentist office, in the playground,/The flame of our treachery to humanity/Seared the flesh, the blood, the very genes/Of four ferocious students armed with all the terrible retribution/Of their abacus, textbooks, and lead pencils./ ... What have we done in all the intervening years,/We, high moralists, hope of Earth,/With that great treachery crouched upon our conscience?/What mass confessional has absolved us?"

As I glowed in my act of oratory, Bob applauded. My mother sat there silently; then she said,"He always has to be superior!" and, brushing angrily against me, left the room.

Soon after my review appeared, the whole of Horace Mann was addressed in the auditorium by a visitor from a group called Moral Rearmament. I had no idea what the name meant, but a number of classmates were outraged. A sour man in a blue suit calculated in chilling terms how vulnerable we were to an attack by the Russians. He said that they had submarines waiting offshore even as he spoke. "They mean to do it. Have no doubt about that, young men."

The fatal pronouncement having been uttered, time stopped. I sank deeper and deeper into my familiar holocaust gloom—a kind of defiant, numb paralysis—as he enumerated the massive weaponry we would need to defend ourselves. He had barely gotten into this explication when Bob Alpert rose to interrupt. "So what you're saying is that they can wipe us out four times over and we can only wipe them out three and a half times!" The auditorium erupted in spontaneous ovation.

"Are you a Communist, sir?" asked the speaker. He was drowned in hisses and catcalls. Each time he began again the uproar resumed. I had rarely felt so elated.

The next day Headmaster Gratwick reprimanded us about courtesy to guests, but it was unclear why this speaker, so different from everyone else Horace Mann had ever invited, should have been allowed to regale us with his misanthropy. I remember Bob's stand as a heroic moment. Not only were atom bombs horrendous weapons that could end our lives in an instant, their reign of terror was itself a lethal force. When one of us seized back the power (in all of our names), I realized that my fear of this man was greater than my fear of the bomb. I would rather not live at all than be in his thrall.

Even the holocaust had a human mask. Terror was mutable.

All that winter Keith was my amulet. When I glimpsed him in stray moments I would honor these as omens and signs. They would change the color of the day.

He was ostentatiously booting his schoolbag in front of him. With a heraldic flourish he was delivering a message to a class I was in.

One Monday I arrived at school feeling itchy and sore, every blackhead burning, subway stench in my pores. At lunch a voice from behind the desserts said, "What do you want?" I stared, for a moment, into the eyes of Keith.

In chapel choir his melodic Latin solos filled the auditorium. His being transmitted grace and consolation to me. In myself I found only Keith's foreshadowing—flat and unlivable. In him, it was realized and vibrant. His light brown hair combed in a self-conscious wave across his forehead, he was Puck, Hermes the boy. Hardly understanding the impulse, I honored his presence as that of a mythic being.

The name I gave this event when I described it in my writing or talked to Dr. Friend was borrowed from how I thought of Danny once: Keith was my "idol" (today I would change it only to its Greek root: *"eidolon"*).

One afternoon he starred in a Gilbert and Sullivan production. I brought along a small battery-run recorder.

That night, after everyone else had gone to bed, I took the machine into the bathroom. I was ready for a performance of science-fiction magnitude.

Most of the windows in the courtyard were dark. There was an old man reading a newspaper, a woman in a black evening dress, part of a body at a kitchen table with flowers—all made memorable by the fact that Keith was about to manifest, all frozen in time by the hissing blank at the beginning of the reel. Then, I heard him.

I have no idea what words he sang, but I made a lyric out of them and returned to the tape again and again that year for confirmation: *"They are, they are, the quarums they seek. They are, they are, and they are. They are, they are, the quarums they seek. Statitimski is hidden afar, yes afar."*

Speedskates weren't allowed in Central Park, so I had to wait till Christmas to try mine again. When I got to Grossinger's I discovered that my brothers had already moved on to other toys. But I was determined to race.

After breakfast, bearing blades in mittens, I headed to the rink and immediately sought Kurt. The morning was crisp and bitter, the night's near blizzard still crashing down from branches. A Catskills wind bit at my skin.

"Yes, I'll teach you but not today." He grinned and pointed, "I got someone better." He called over an older man in a Grossinger warm-up jacket. I didn't know who this was. Then I read the name over the pocket. Long ago I had watched him pass a pack of skaters in the last lap: Ray Blum was a hero from the dawn of my own memory.

I felt as though DiMaggio himself were coaching me as we stepped onto the ice at closing time. He got me to whip out my glides, to crouch perilously near the ice at the corners to pick up speed—his own motion silken and seamless as he swallowed the rink in great strides. Following behind him as best I could, I seemed magically to inherit his speed and grace. After a few days of unspoken lessons he was gone.

Now that I could zoom, I practiced in between sessions (after helping Kurt and Irv with the resurfacing). I was developing an inner rhythm and velocity I had long desired.

I continued to hang out at the Nightwatch and even twice asked girls to dance. Sooner or later there were older and cooler guys. So I took my frustration to the ice. At night it was a chapel. I turned on a few of the floodlights and fed the jukebox to the speaker. I could see constellations above the golf course. The choir sang: *"Tonight, tonight, won't be just any night...."* The lime rectangle was mine to inhabit and strafe.

It was just Keith and me, dark powerful circles seeking a tangent, ice hollowing my skull, blades rasping, tearing for a grip at corners. They were my voice. The threads I cut were my life. Almost mechanically I set before me figures who touched me: my mother and Bob and Jonny, Danny and Monica, Joan Snyder—I blended with them to enact greater swiftness, ripping the ice in quickening two-steps, pushing my tempo beyond limits of stamina—beyond breath, beyond agility, beyond desire. Those I wanted to defeat I defeated. Those I wanted to love became part of me, part of Keith. Those I didn't understand my feelings for, I tested. I was north of Horace Mann, north of New York City, north of Westchester and its parties, north of the subway.

I invoked and dispelled the cobwebs of studying, the wax museum of Horace Mann, the unrequited desires—all were translated into an orbital dance.

"Tonight there will be no morning star. . . ." This was the droplet at my heart—a faraway sun that gave light to unknown worlds.

In the days preceding New Year's Eve, gatherings in the Nightwatch took on the urgency of a search for dates. There seemed to be more and more guys all the time until there were no available girls at all. In fact, on December 31st the whole rock-and-roll group The Tokens, who sang, *"Hush my darling, don't fear my darling, the lion sleeps tonight,"* swaggered into the Nightwatch looking like a street gang and declared themselves in their Brooklyn accents, "Where duh girls?" The "girls" were totally snowed.

On New Year's Eve I sat at the teenage table, the only one without a date. When the lights went off and "Auld Lang Syne" began, I imagined time itself evacuating through the walls. These were famous seconds, rustling past like pages of old books.

I ducked through the fire door into sub-zero night. From roofs and trees, crystals glistened and blew into infinity. A sudden wind shook dry rattles at treetops. Icicles hung eternal in moonlight as if on the moon. When the Earth got this cold and black I was a mere ember, a random speck of carbon sustained by desire and melancholy. I took off my jacket and tie and unbuttoned my shirt. I ran. I ran even faster. The din faded behind me like a planet under my escape velocity.

Through frost flowers on my bedroom window the single street-light radiated a delicate grain. I lay there, engulfing Keith in my warmth, or was it I in his warmth?

I spent the winter pretending to try to call Keith's attention to me. I typed up slides for Wednesday sings, putting unusual songs on them, which I submitted anonymously with symbolic messages to Keith. I joined the carnival publicity committee and set up an exhibit, using a mechanical guzzling monkey with a beer can, a banana, and an expanding stomach. Keith came by, stood and watched, and then (his insignia) said, "Isn't that sexy" to a friend. Another time, I heard him mutter as he was walking down the hall, "Don't tell me he's done it again."

My daydreams began to change. I imagined Keith driving a car and picking me up outside my apartment building on Friday afternoon. He would laugh and look into my eyes. As I played with his wet hair, his smile melting mine, he became something that was neither boy nor girl and lay atop of me, swallowing my desire in the fragrance of his icon.

Beyond this vision a scenery formed on its own, a cornfield and haystacks, moon-yellow—a shade of straw I associated with him. He was wanton and luminous; he arose from the leather trunk in the attic; he played the panpipes. He held me prisoner in his room, drawing me unto himself. In this fantasy he was no longer Keith my friend and guide; he was the resolution of my troubled eros.

I wanted to lose whatever was left of myself in him. He could jump on me, beat me up, and that would be okay, for soon enough I would be burnt away and nothing more than part of him. I was a steel filing, and he was a dense raw, iron-smelling magnet, drawing me forever unto himself. He was still elfin, but gamy and seductive too. And now he knew my reckless hunger for him.

I checked the sperm from such fantasies to see if it was dark.

I arrived five minutes late at Dr. Friend's, so the door from the waiting room was open. I walked in and placed myself on the couch, fixing my eyes on the photograph of broken pottery.

"I'm sorry I'm late. The train was incredibly slow. It just took forever getting to 168th Street."

"There's no need to be sorry." His voice, always detached.

"Of course there is. I wasted some of your time." I was parodying a tone he often took.

"If I were you I would think more carefully about whose time is being wasted."

"Okay. One point for you."

"My, aren't we angry today. Angry, sarcastic, and bitter. What's all that about?"

"Nothing."

"Nothing?"

"Nothing at all."

"Well, what are you thinking about?"

"Only about how the damn train slowed me down."

"Was it all the train's fault?" I didn't answer. "Was it really all the train's fault." I stared at the second hand sweeping within the clock on the far wall. The radiator hissed, the odor of its steam musty and trite.

A few minutes passed and then I said, "I hope you didn't think I was going to sit around here and answer stupid questions about trains all afternoon."

"You were the one who brought up the train."

"Well, you always tell me what I'm thinking. You do, don't you? Well, if *you're* not going to talk, I don't see why I should."

I lay there quietly for a while and then unwittingly closed my eyes. A drowsiness engulfed me. . . .

I awoke with a start—it was dark outside. I was totally disoriented, my hour almost up. I felt instantly contrite. "Hey, that's the first time I ever fell asleep here."

"There's always a first time."

"I feel better now."

"Well, you escaped. You used up the whole session without talking about the thing that's bothering you."

"I feel sad."

"Good. Maybe we can use the remaining time and accomplish something."

"What should I talk about?"

"What did you dream? Do you remember?"

"Nothing really."

"Oh come now."

"I was in the country somewhere with Keith. Late afternoon. The light is very green."

"Any perceptions."

I saw the second hand erasing my last minute. I recalled an appletree, Keith beneath . . . as if Keith were me. Then I remembered. "It just faded into a bunch of cartoon characters dancing around and jumping in and out of the back elevator shaft of our building."

"Where were you?"

"Running around the hall trying to escape from them." There was no reply. Then the overhead light clicked on, signalling the end of the hour.

I heard him getting up. I turned and looked right at him. "I'm having fantasies about Keith. I'm thinking about him as a girl . . . and the fantasies are *so strong.*" I was pleading with him now. He was expressionless. I dropped my head and smiled at the wooden soldier on his desk. "I'm afraid I'm...."

"You're afraid of what, that you're a homosexual? Nonsense. Everyone who's ever lived has had those fantasies. A boy, a girl, what does it matter in the mind? You're reaching out to something unknown, something you want and don't yet understand. And you miss the obvious—that thought and action are two separate things. You can think whatever you want, and it doesn't mean you are likely to do it." He paused and considered. "It's really that you are so guilty—guilty of what you are, guilty of what you aren't. What you want you hate yourself for wanting. Perhaps that's the reason for Keith. He's not real, you know. No doubt you have created him in order to share the burden of your guilt."

I froze in sheer wonder. After weeks of sterile, boring sessions the face of the master shone, reminding me of the power of insight to heal and transform. In recent months I had become such a wise guy, a bigshot—Richard the writer, Richard the psychiatric pro. Now I bowed to the inevitability of the unknown, the power of the unconscious.

A realization born once of a chemistry set spilled in a dream had come again. The long, entangled mystery unravelled, exposing Keith for what he was—another semblance, cast against a lifetime of mystery visitors. He was a feeling I had always had, a vagrant figure encompassing the allure in everyone. No wonder I had chosen a magnificent child playing the flute to represent him. The Keith who bounded through Horace Mann and sang with the voice of the forest was my blond and wild twin in whose seductive grip, dark sparkly I became beautiful too. In my hunger to encompass him—and girls through him—he had become the captive side of desire, yet still always driving me toward who I was.

I couldn't say that then, so I said, "There's nothing bad about these thoughts? I'm not doomed?"

"Of course not," he smiled back. As I went through the door he added, "Why do we always accuse ourselves of the worst?"

"Because we're crazy or something," I laughed.

He looked up startled, then gave out his deepest-ever guffaw. "See you Friday, you funny kid."

MOON RIVER

It became spring. I wore light cloth suits. A sports fanatic from history class named Larry became my best buddy. We played hardball on weekends, and I awaited the baseball season with all the ardor of childhood. It was the year of American League expansion—there were two new teams (the Los Angeles Angels and a second Washington Senators), which gave the pennant race an air of magic. The number of teams had always been fixed. It was as if two new planets had just been discovered. What were they like? How would they look in the standings? From the first exhibition game I was clipping Yankee box scores and pasting them in a datebook with clear Magic Mending Tape, the piny smell of which still reminds me of that 1961 spring.

My mother generally did not get involved in my schoolwork, but from either a misunderstanding on her part or exaggerated rhetoric by Mr. McCardell during her annual parents-day visit, she got it into her mind that my entire academic career hung on my junior "Profile."

The "Profile" was meant to be the most challenging English assignment during our tenure at Horace Mann—a biography in the style of the *New Yorker* profiles. Right from the beginning she and I had a running disagreement about the topic. I thought that it didn't matter whom I chose, as long as I wrote well; she was adamant that I select a prominent man. She rejected all my more modest ideas and, through a newspaper friend of Bob's, lined up an interview with Dag Hammarskjöld. I fell months behind on my draft just waiting for the fabled appointment. A week beforehand, he cancelled. I was actually relieved. I couldn't imagine why the Secretary-General of the United Nations should take time out from trying to prevent nuclear war to talk to a high school kid, and I was glad I didn't have to be that kid.

The paper was due on the Monday after Easter. Now, with three weeks to go I didn't even have a subject. When Easter vacation came, my mother tried to keep me home to work. She was certain I would never find anyone suitable at Grossinger's, and she well remembered how embarrassed she was when I wrote a practice Profile a year earlier on Lou Goldstein. "Can you imagine it, Bob," she said. "He writes about that idiot and hands it in at . . . *Horace Mann.*" She always said the name as though she had a greater claim to the school than I did.

With Aunt Bunny's help I found a quick accomplice—Eddie Shapiro, an insurance agent in Liberty who looked like Paul Newman and was the husband of her close friend Connie. During the next two weeks I doggedly hung around him, transcribing his story in his own words, from direct interviews in his office to his off-the-cuff remarks to secretaries and clients on the phone. One Sunday he took me ice-fishing "with the guys," boasting all the way that he was the only one with a biographer. I stood on the lake, barely able to grip the pen to take down his jokes and off-color comments about his wife. Then I claimed one of the office IBMs and sat there among the secretaries, typing my notes into an "Eddie Shapiro Profile." On Monday I handed in the longest paper in the class. Eddie Shapiro had written it for me.

My mother was appalled. "His classmates are doing the Mayor of New York, the Editor of *The New York Times,* and who does he come up with: Eddie Shapiro, insurance agent from Liberty!"

Mr. McCardell agreed that he knew my subject better than any other profilee—far better, in fact, than he wanted to know him. Nothing else sounded quite like Eddie Shapiro saying, "Fuck them royally and fuck them all"—that from a section read aloud to the class. "But I'm not sure you followed the assignment," my teacher added. He then became the first to give me the grade that was to typify much of my subsequent academic career: **A or F,** written as such, on top of the first page.

Soon after the baseball season started I stumbled on a gold mine: Grossinger's shared a box at Yankee Stadium with Eddie Fisher's

Ramrod Productions. Not only was it rarely used, but the strips of tickets were kept in a binder in the New York office. From then on, every Friday that the Yankees were home, I would take the subway straight to 57th Street and call a number of friends depending on how many seats I had. Larry was always my first choice.

In our territory behind the visitors' dugout we were surrounded by hardcore ticket-holders with their pages of stats and scoresheets. They would bet and debate strategy as the game unfolded. If I added an opinion they might stop in curiosity, hear me out, and, usually to a one, dismiss it. But then they'd always invite me back into their wrangles. Once, I predicted that Johnny Blanchard, who hadn't batted all year, would get a big pinch hit. Mr. Glazer, the resident expert in the next box, was furious at the time that Ralph Houk had sent him up to bat with the game on the line. He said, "Aw, c'mon, kid. Ya don't know."

"Third-string catchers love third-string catchers," I snapped.

When I proved right he gave me an irritated swat, not concealing half a smile.

Through Fontainebleau connections my mother met a preppy camp owner who, upon hearing she had eligible kids, went into a song and dance about his facilities and so impressed her she invited him to our apartment to show his slides. We all gathered in the living room, and he narrated his Kodachromes past us. I meant to be a peripheral and uninterested observer, there merely to please my mother. But it turned out that our visitor had been coached on me because, after Jonny and Debby were signed up and I was headed back to my study, he made an unexpected offer: I could live with the waiters and be paid $500 to edit Kenmont's *Clarion* newspaper.

I had nothing left at Chipinaw, so I said okay.

My stop at Grossinger's after school ended was a brief one. Prior to camp my father and Aunt Bunny took all three kids on a tour of Massachusetts, including colonial villages and deep-sea fishing. When I didn't show enthusiasm for his patriotic commentary, my father called me "a socialist cynic"—but he did get tickets for the Yankees at Fenway Park, my first game out of New York. The next day, we didn't catch any fish initially; then PG [as Michael later told it] "slipped the captain a fifty, he moved the boat, and they never stopped biting." I was dropped in Connecticut on the way home.

Kenmont turned out to be a spiffy, upper-class, "country club"-style camp. There were no scheduled activities for teenagers, so most of them spent days at the golf course, sunbathing, or out in rowboats. A coffee shop was open at all hours for socializing.

My bunkmates were self-important jerks. Ranking each other out was just about the only interpersonal activity. Life was a constant battle to see who could put someone down hardest, then how the person would come back. They repeatedly said lines like, "You stupid iriot!" (imitating the comedian Buddy Hackett) and "How're they hanging?" (which I always blushed at when directed at me).

On the initial morning of camp we were given instructions by a short man about thirty:

"Now look here, you guys. I'm kind of with you the first week to make sure you obey the rules. I don't give a damn if you smoke, drink, or fuck around, but wait till after the first week. You see, the head counselor's new and—"

"What's his name?" interrupted a fat, curly-haired kid named Love, who carried an umbrella, though the sky was clear. He waved it in the air.

"His first name is Bob. He's from the U. of Florida and majoring in recreation. His second name sounds like a sweet-smelling flower, and I couldn't spell it if you gave me all the letters."

"Oh swell. Sounds like a real winner, doesn't he?" Love said, smiling at the group. "Let's give him three big cheers." And each time he yelled, "Hip, hip!" and waved his umbrella in the air, he was followed by a chorus of "Hurray!" from the group. Then he nodded sharply and sat down with a grin of satisfaction.

Two of us were outsiders. My fellow newcomer was immediately dubbed Spartacus because he was dumb and did everything Love asked him to. Love named me Lightning after the sluggish character on the "Amos and Andy Show" because I was so slow to respond to put-downs.

I had brought along a tape of super-realistic sound-effects and, before my bunkmates knew I had a recorder, I turned it on under my bed while they were up late drinking. One jet followed another, each one louder.

"Jeez, I didn't know there was an airfield around here," Craig exclaimed.

"Must be since last summer," said Randy.

A train sound followed ... first a remote whistle, faraway ... then closer and closer until it seemed about to crash through the bunk. "Christ almighty!" Randy bellowed, jumping to his feet and turning on the light. When they discovered the source they fired empties at me. After Joe drained his beer on me, they turned over my bed and kicked me.

"Lightning's asleep," Craig said. "Let him be."

"What do you mean let him be!" Randy retorted, and he jumped, knees first, on top of me. Joe kept whacking his pillow against my head.

I lay in the crumpled mattress and mass of sheets.

"It was an all-star prank," I wrote to my friend Larry the next day, "better than their dumb rank-outs, and not one asshole even congratulated me for it."

I was enchanted then with the Southern writer Robert Penn Warren, something about his lyric singsong and cosmic overlay that held intimations of my own raw prose. I read his novels one by one, memorizing favorite passages—for instance, about the moon borrowing its light from the sun in *All the King's Men;* and then a woman martyred at the stake in *World Enough and Time.* Midway through *The Cave,* in recounting the death of a man trapped underground, Penn Warren had a sequence of lines that became my benchmark of eloquence: *"... the handsome and generally admired carnal envelope of Jasper Harrick is, even this instant, as certain chemical changes begin, entering the great anonymous economy of nature. His soul, assuming that he ever had one, has flowed back to that burning fountain whence it came."*

My writing, albeit in a more adolescent form, hung likewise between epiphany and doubt, between nihilism and incandescence.

The fields ripe with blossoms, summer became a languid puzzle. Preoccupied with baseball, novels, and my imaginary friendship with Keith, I drifted through Kenmont's playland in a reverie of abstraction. It sufficed to have a catch with Jonny and find a meadow in which to lie and read. During part of each day I managed the *Clarion,* sending eager kids on assignment, editing and typing their articles, operating the mimeo machine, and dispatching finished sheets for delivery. The time slid by.

Sometimes at night I hung out in the coffee shop with a soda, lost in Kentucky towns, horseback riders, mulatto slaves. When there was a ballgame, I brought my radio shaped like a baseball (that Milty had gotten me that spring) and sat on the side, listening to innings, watching kids dance. I had no courage to "make a move," in fact no move to make.

Then one day Randy told us that he was breaking up with Tina. I had been admiring her for weeks—a petite sullen-looking blonde who had already gone on adventures with Keith and me. The next evening I decided to act. I left my radio and *World Enough and Time* in the bunk, showed up at the coffee shop early, and took a seat closer to the action.

Tina came in later than usual with a friend and claimed a bench in the far back, where they huddled, whispering. Invoking Keith for courage, I strode across the room as though through the separate cubes of a cubist painting, found myself at her bench, and asked her if she wanted to dance. With a look of adult resignation, she got up slowly, stared interminably at her friend, then walked well ahead of me toward the center of the floor. I set my hands on her back and waist. She was stiff and brittle, almost nonexistent. I hadn't expected that. I had imagined her as fiery and lynxlike. To all the things I tried to talk about, she repeated sarcastically, "Oh, isn't that nice!" After the dance, turning on a dime, she strutted back to her friend.

The main thing I thought, standing there for all to see, was that for the first time I was not afraid the Russians might bomb. In fact, I hoped if they did, they would do it quickly. Joe came running up to me. Ever since he had heard a song called "Paco Peco," he ended all his exclamations with an "o." "Lightning, why do you have to be such a shmucko? She's not the right type for you. She's much too fast. You make a fool out of yourself when you do something like that."

I left the coffee shop and returned through the forest to the bunk, the fading sound of *"Michael, row your boat ashore . . ."* in the air, the stars a bottomless whirlpool. Between the daydream Tina and candy-Tina with whom I had one dance were worlds I could not inhabit, and yet they seemed the only worlds everyone else was in.

Then on the radio pinch-hitter Johnny Blanchard, swinging two bats in the on-deck circle in my imagination, came up and ripped a grand slam in the bottom of the ninth to pull out the game against the Red Sox.

The Yankees chased Detroit all that summer while Mickey Mantle and Roger Maris hit unprecedented numbers of home runs. For a month I listened only on my radio. Then I heard that George, the middle-aged steward from the kitchen, was a fanatic Yankee rooter and had a TV in his room. But he was surly and unapproachable, plus he hated the wise-ass waiters in my bunk. After a few weeks, though, he must have recognized my legitimate interest, for he ceremoniously invited me to his "palace." I would stretch out on the floor while he sat on the edge of the bed in his undershirt with a beer. It was barely more than a large closet, but at summer camp a TV was major contraband. We would keep the silence of each other's company, discussing only the crucialities of the game. I remember how instantly alert we were whenever the Tigers' score was announced.

"Whitey Herzog has just homered for Baltimore in the first."

"Make it two on," George said.

"One runner on base, so Detroit's down 2 – 0."

"We'll take it."

One afternoon Joe happened to notice me pitching to my brother, and he signed me up for his team in the camp tournament. "I didn't know you had a fastball, Lightning." At Horace Mann and Chipinaw it hadn't been considered a fastball, but this was a different league. Later that week he caught my warm-up pitches and playfully snapped back curves. One tipped off my glove into my right hand. My finger became so swollen I couldn't grip the ball. I was taken into town for an X-ray and came back with a splint on.

The broken finger was the final blow. I didn't go to the coffee shop after that. I simply put out the camp newspaper and read Robert Penn Warren. At night, I sat with George cheering recklessly, as Johnny Blanchard rewarded us with a string of fabulous hits.

On one much ballyhooed evening the older kids visited the nearby Shakespeare Festival for a performance of *Macbeth*. In my wildest dream I would not have imagined ... there was Keith in the crowd. I had never talked to him, but now it was simple. I mean, we were the only two HM kids there. We chatted like any schoolmates about how each of us had gotten there, then ... good luck and goodbye. Dr. Friend was right; the real Keith was simply another person.

Summer reached its apex in mid-August. No dawn fog, at seven the sun was already a blazing ball. Grass-cutting machines perfumed the air.

My cast had been off a few days and, even in such daunting heat, I wanted to play. I found my brother, and we each contributed to a sack of hardballs. I ran to center field. He swung from the backstop.

I had the feeling I could never miss as I threw my body in the path of sinking liners and tumbled over and over with the ball. We kept changing places as batter and fielder until we were both soaked and exhausted and lay silently together in the grass. Then, I walked him to his bunk and continued to the coffee shop where I bought a cold orange.

"We've sold a lot of these today," the boy said as he dropped a cup over the bottle. I guzzled down the sparkling ice like drinking eternity. A fan turned ineffectually, as flies buzzed around rolls of gummed paper filled with flies. Over in the corner Craig was lying on his belly next to a tall, pretty girl I hadn't noticed before. He had his shirt off, and she scratched his back while throwing out witty asides. "What's this?" ... stopping and scraping a little. As he strained to look up and around at himself she sassed, "Oh, nothing, son," and went on in curlicues. She was so quirky and droll I couldn't keep my sideways glance from her. She had reddish brown hair, and there was something distinctly Keith-like about her—the theatricality, the playful intelligence, his melodic, showy voice.

Once again, an image of Pan had captured my wandering attention.

During the remainder of the summer, though I never approached her, I watched Jill in the kitchen where our bunk ate its meals. She was spunky and brash, more than a match for Craig. I would overhear him talking excitedly to Randy about her: "She french-kisses! She stuck her tongue in so far I thought I was going out of my mind."

Randy could barely contain his lust and envy.

The last week of camp I was standing with George in the kitchen before lunch, poring over the day's stats. Maris hit two more homers; we knew that, but had just discovered, to our chagrin, the Tigers won their late game. A familiar voice from behind me said, "Oh, don't tell me Maris hit another."

It was Jill. She moved in between us like a pro to scan the box scores. "My favorite player's Wally Moon. I want to see how he's doing. There. Not bad, not bad!"

"He's okay," I added unnecessarily.

"He's better than okay," she shot back. Her eyes were pale, transparent; she had on large earrings, and her hair was arranged in a complicated French twist. George went on studying the page.

The next day the boys played the girls in the annual softball game in which the boys batted lefthanded. Jill was the Yogi-catcher with a mask on. She fell to her knees and deftly grabbed an outside pitch on one bounce as I batted. Then I fouled one back; she threw off her mask, dove, and just missed it. Her lipstick and tight polo shirt notwithstanding, she was quite a player.

After Kenmont I returned to Grossinger's. Major changes were taking place. Jay and Barry were absent because Jay's parents, with Barry's father as their lawyer, were suing my grandparents over abuses of management. Aunt Bunny told me that they were justified. "But what can we do?" she added. "Your grandfather owns all our shares, and he insists on acting his whims without consultation. When he dug the first hole for the indoor pool he was warned that he would hit the pipes going into New York City. He said nobody was going to tell him where he could dig on his own property. He got one giant geyser, and it wasn't oil!" She flipped two fingers and her thumb in the air. "So then he had to fill in the hole and pay the fine too. Now he's off on some other hare-brained scheme and your father hasn't the guts to stop him."

Uncle Paul was mainly cantankerous—cursing the union organizers, avoiding his father, often bawling out guests for not being dressed properly in the dining room. And everyone in the family was choosing sides.

But Grossinger's was still my haven. I watched the Yankees, played ball with Jerry, shot rolls of Kodacolor, and wrote about the summer. As we came dripping into the cabana one afternoon from our swim I told Aunt Bunny all about Jill and, en route to lunch buffet, she responded with an outrageously direct suggestion: "You should call her and ask her out."

"I don't even know her," I protested.

"She'd be flattered."

"Sure she would. . . . Anyhow, I don't have her phone number or address."

"Call the camp office, dummy. What have you got to lose? If she doesn't want to go you're back where you are now."

"But what should I invite her to?"

"You know the answer to that. Invite her to a ballgame."

When she made the suggestion I was sure there was no way I would do it. She said it far too pliantly, without any real appreciation of the outrageousness of such an act—but she had opened Pandora's box. It was a simple, gutty plan, and it had the advantage of avoiding another long unrequited fantasy. It was also vintage Grossinger's—magical, daffy, overflowing with hope.

After evading the impulse for days, I called the camp office and asked for Jill's number. That was hard enough to accomplish gracefully. I kept it in my pocket like a stolen gem until the next morning, and then at nine-thirty I dialed quickly so that I wouldn't doubt myself. I listened to it ring and ring, mesmerized, every few seconds jolting myself to remember what I was doing, to prepare for the voice . . . and when it continued ringing I was totally relieved.

I grabbed *Band of Angels* and went to the pool. After lunch I hiked to the staff field and fielded for a group of Puerto Ricans shouting in Spanish as they hit fly balls.

I played at being the kid from Grossinger's that whole day. Observing myself in the role took nothing away from it. It was the great all-time gambit. I was young again, as I savored my daring ploy. I waited until evening. The phone rang, twice, three times . . . suddenly a click . . . and her voice.

"Hello."

"Hi. This is Richard Grossinger. Do you remember me from camp?"

"Oh yes . . . and how are your Yankees?"

"Okay, I suppose."

"Do you go to ballgames now that you're out of camp?"

"No. I'm not in New York. . . ." And eventually: "How would you like to go to the Yankee-Cleveland game this Saturday?"

"Hmmm, this Saturday? Let's see . . . How about next Saturday?"

"They go on the road Monday."

"Oh, no! I'd really like to go."

"There's one other chance. How about October 2nd. It's a Sunday, the last day of the season. And who knows how many home runs Maris may have by then."

"True, true. . . . Sunday the 2nd is fine with me."

I set a time and hung up the phone. Then I went tearing out the front door and ran around the house twice before falling into the tomato patch. I lay there in tall minty leaves, thanking them for being what they were, and the sun too.

"I told you it would work," Aunt Bunny said.

"It's because she likes baseball," I explained.

"I wouldn't bet on it."

I returned to the City with hopefulness, and my final year of Horace Mann began. I had Virgil, Honors European History, Honors English, Mr. Ervin's seminar, and advanced algebra.

My mother and I seldom spoke these days. As the years passed, we had enacted the semblances of a truce. Since it was clear that I had done something unforgivable once, we based our relationship on that and performed a masquerade of intimacy. She was my mother, which Aunt Bunny, however wonderful, could never be. There was something about this woman, the scarred, craggy landscape of her emotional realm, that made my life inalterably real. Even if she got there through grief and pain, she touched bottom and, through her, I gauged where my own texture was. We hung, in a figment of delicate balance, two trapeze artists, unable to look at each other, yet, while falling away, stretching the tension between us to the boundary of our existences. Richard at Grossinger's was a brief epiphany. Richard, son of Martha Towers, was the cartilage of my being.

During that fall my father drove into the City with Michael to take me on a trip to New England to look at colleges. Aunt Bunny had hoped maybe such exposure might inspire my brother to do his homework. However, it turned out to be a slapstick adventure. With Uncle

Paul's one good eye keeping us (mostly) on the road we crossed various mountain ranges going between Williamstown, Amherst, Dartmouth, and Middlebury. Michael and I kissed the ground on our arrivals (to our father's obvious chagrin).

With their rolling fields, colonial mansions, and ivy-covered masonry, these schools were imposing and majestic, on a scale above Horace Mann as much as Horace Mann was above P.S. 6. I could hardly believe I was close to attending one of them. In fact, the single payoff for my hard work and good grades was the privilege to apply to such institutions.

I knew I was a strong candidate, but my father thought he should grease the scales. At Amherst (which had the grandest campus) he arranged for a prominent alumnus, a priggish lawyer, to meet us at the Admissions Office. At Dartmouth, for some reason, we ate lunch with the football coach. Michael added humor by making a ritual of testing every water fountain we passed. "Now, wait," he would call. "I gotta taste the New Hampshire water, let my brother know if he should apply here." I was equally embarrassed by the lawyer and coach, but Uncle Paul insisted that getting into these schools was a matter of connections.

"What about my grades?"

"Lots of people have good grades. That doesn't mean they get accepted."

I paid little attention to curricula. I was looking for a landscape and a mood. At Wesleyan there was something about the arrangement of buildings and colors—sunny spots and shady spots in their patterns— that made me feel fearful and trapped. My first choice was Swarthmore in the suburbs of Philadelphia, which I visited myself by train. I loved its groves of trees and small-village ambiance. It was the bohemian summer camp I had never been allowed to go to. After my trip I was totally enamored, but the Director of College Admissions at Horace Mann urged me to apply to Amherst for early decision. "I'd rather just try Swarthmore," I said.

"Swarthmore is a second-rate school. You at least *apply* to the best school you can get into."

So I filled out the forms, and on my seventeenth birthday I got a totally unexpected letter that Amherst had accepted me. "What should I do?" I asked him the next day.

He had received his carbon copy and had a ready answer. "Write a letter thanking them and say you look forward to attending in the fall."

"But what about Swarthmore? I haven't even applied."

"Now you don't need to."

Everyone thought it was so significant I got into Amherst that I allowed myself to feel good about it. It was a cool place to go, and I imagined autumn meadows, New England houses, and wise girls at nearby Smith and Mount Holyoke.

Dr. Friend observed this whole process without comment. "I wanted to see what you would do," he said later. "I just assumed you would pick Columbia. I didn't think you were in any shape to leave treatment. But you never even considered me. You never considered that applying to Amherst *was* termination."

The Yankees held first place, and Maris kept hitting homers, not quite as many but enough so that on October 2nd he had 60—he had caught Babe Ruth.

I put on my powder-blue shirt and sports jacket and took the subway downtown to Jill's. She was waiting casually by the door and approached me with her winsome smile: "So we meet again, Yankee fan."

This October game had a World Series flavor, and we talked baseball stats all the way to the Bronx as crowds increased stop by stop.

Jill remained a blend of opposites, a pretty girl and baseball—I felt their energies awakening different parts of myself, waxing and waning through each other and never quite meeting. Our box behind the visitors' dugout was where I had sat with schoolmates dozens of times; yet it was as though I had never been there. Even Mr. Glazer kept his distance. Jill and I chatted about Kenmont and our classwork (she went to an all-girls' private school downtown). She had nothing good to say about Craig except that he was cute. "He's not someone I'll be seeing anymore." And then Tracy Stallard threw, Maris swung, and the ball sailed deep down the right-field line. The Stadium erupted into a roar. She threw her arms around me, and we hugged and cheered.

Jill became a regular phone friend after that. We wrote letters crosstown about baseball and literature equally. She rooted for the Reds to beat New York in the Series. When the Yankees won, she sent "a humble note of congratulations." Then I invited her to another special event—a sold-out Limeliters concert at Carnegie Hall for which I got tickets through Grossinger's. Afterwards, we went to a coffee shop and talked for two hours about Ibsen (whom coincidentally we were both studying at school).

Soon I realized I didn't have to invent excuses; I could just ask her out. We went to *Breakfast at Tiffany's* and Ibsen's *Ghosts* at a small Greenwich Village theater. Each time I would take the subway to her apartment, and from there we would call a cab. Afterwards, we would have dessert at a restaurant and sit around talking about the meaning of what we had seen. She considered herself an accomplished critic and thought I was undisciplined and too involved in psychology and magic. She playfully challenged me on every symbol and interpretation.

Sometimes we would go back to her apartment and continue discussion in the living room. If her mother was up she would join in. All three of us would jabber away for an hour or more. I would come home late on the subway and let myself in the back door.

The early darkness of the Solstice approached from a direction I had never known. City lights danced, and I was nearly happy. The song from the movie carried the ambiance of my life then:

"Moon river, wider than a mile, I'm crossing you in style, someday..."

Yes, she had been a "moon" figure from that first day I saw her with Craig. Even our initial point of contact was an outfielder named Moon.

In the shower I would sing at the top of my lungs, trying to capture the precise resonance. Occasionally Bridey would join in from the hallway, trying to steer me back into tune.

I remember Jill as Audrey Hepburn in the movie, curled on the living room sofa, blowing smoke in the air, conscious of each self-conscious motion she made. Part of me would be talking to her, and part of me would be looking at a remarkable girl: her face, her eyes, the formation of her breasts, her lips, her clothes, her pocketbook, her legs, her fancy gestures, her womanly movements.

I could never forget what Craig said, though I detested him for it because Jill had become my best friend and his words were always in the way, goading me, telling me I somehow wasn't as special as he was.

His description was a maddening abstraction with no relation to my experience. Once, I took Jill's hand in mine while we were walking. At first it felt ridiculous, too silly even to believe, but when she held my hand back I felt as though I held her entirely and was held by her as we walked along.

When I talked to subway friends, they were full of advice as to how to get started, but it was always the same advice, and it didn't add up to anything. "You know from that guy Craig she gives, so what are you waiting for?" They seemed concerned that I not lose my big chance.

One Friday, on getting home from school, I felt particularly gloomy and called her. We had been out together the past Saturday, so it was too soon to see each other again by our normal schedule, but I wanted to hear her voice and took the chance. When I asked her how she was, she moaned, "Dreary Friday." I was delighted—a soul-mate. "Yes," she said; "we should by all means go to the movies tomorrow night."

All the next day I hung around the apartment doing homework in distraction, wishing I could feel easy about her. I had become obsessed with what it would be like to kiss her. I imagined lying on top of her and making out, her long elegant frame moving with mine, her eyes, as always, teasing, bewitching. I forced myself to stop, tried to translate Virgil, and unfailingly came back again. It wasn't just that she combined all the fantasies I had ever had; it was that she was real enough I could imagine them coming true.

After the movie what had never happened happened as I had imagined it. On her lead we went into her room instead of the living room. I sat in a chair, and she stretched out on the bed, back against the wall. I heard my hollow voice talking, but my imagination was exploding. She was so exciting, smooth blouse over her breasts, thick teased red hair, adroit curl of her voice, alluring and friendly both. I tracked the lateness of the hour, later each time I glanced. In my mind all of time was draining away. I was numb with feeling; I didn't know what to do.

She began to show signs of getting up. I moved toward her, stood there. "What?" she said.

How could she not know? I made a gesture toward a simple kiss. She took a step back, looked at me bewildered, and said, "No."

"Why?"

"Because it would ruin everything."

Later—though only by years—I thought that perhaps she was telling me it had always ruined everything, that she wanted this to be different. But I was raw and wild then, and I couldn't bear the thought of Craig being allowed so easily, me not at all. That night when I left her I ran ten blocks down Fifth Avenue against a whipping wind, over and over calling Emerson's words in my mind:

"I am the doubter and the doubt, and I the hymn the Brahmin sings."

. . . ran past buildings and storefronts until I reached the apotheosis in myself, and its exhaustion.

I never called Jill again.

3

GRADUATION

Senior year brought its own privileges. We would sit in our lounge and watch "Amos and Andy" and "Bullwinkle Moose" during first-period study hall. From a closet at home I rescued a hockey game with a marble and tin men (which Jonny and I had played for years) and donated it to the lounge. Tournaments ran continuously. Then we voted to spend class funds on a new model with moving men in tracks and a wooden puck, and played non-stop all fall.

But our teachers were not going to allow a year in the tank. Mr. Murphy, whom I now had for the second time, intended his Modern European history course to be the *tour de force* of our education. Well over six feet tall with a mop of white hair and the fierce countenance of Samuel Johnson, he spent weeks filling us with an appreciation for the Church and the complexities of feudalism. Fascinated by the decay of worldly things, he would bring famous lives to an end always with the same declaration: "Death, as it must to all men, came to Charlemagne, Charles the Great. ..." Death later came to Ferdinand, and Magellan, and Philip of Spain, and even Martin Luther the reformer. After that we were so submerged in the details of the Thirty Years War that I imaged Gustavus Adolphus riding out of the woods behind Van Cortlandt Park, leading a Swedish army, his minister Oxenstierna at his side.

In the early days of Horace Mann I had mainly memorized historic facts. Now I was reading interpretatively like a college student. We spent weeks on Erasmus and the northern Renaissance and studied

Jacob Burckhardt on the Medicis and sixteenth-century humanism in Italy. For Murphy, the Church was the single great institution—humanizing and yet corrupting, simplistic and violent in its politics but profound in its ceremony. He lived the Church and enacted its Mediaeval passion in class. So convincing was he that Bob Alpert dropped left-wing politics and, to the horror of his parents, converted to Catholicism and began going to Mass.

There was a cult around Murphy. Rumors about his past ran the gamut from priesthood to Satanism to seduction. I remember how, after attending the funeral of an ex-student who had died young, he spent much of the next class describing the corpse in the open casket. "The difference between life and death is infinitesimal," he preached. "He was strong, strapping, handsome, a youth, lying there, but he had already entered the country from whose bourne (Shakespeare) no traveller returns." And then he wept openly before us, took out his handkerchief and sat silently sobbing at his desk for the remainder of class.

Another eccentric arrived in the middle of my junior year: Waldman was a strange-looking man, totally bald though young, flat thin eyes, and a fierce, sullen expression behind black-rimmed glasses. He ate in the student rather than faculty dining room and conducted sessions on the mystic Meister Eckhart and the Russian occult philosopher G. I. Gurdjieff. Chuck Stein told me Waldman was a member of an ancient Rosicrucian order.

Yet it was through my classmate rather than Waldman that I became involved in the occult. Since many of Chuck's poems were based on tarot cards, Mr. Ervin suggested he bring a deck to class. Colorful vistas of "The Magician," "The Wheel of Fortune," and "The Hanged Man" were placed on the table, as Chuck explained their arcane markings: "The wild red roses are our five senses. The Wheel is the Galaxy turning in seasons and epochs. The scaffold is the scaffold of Creation. The Hanged Man is really right-side up; he just seems upside-down from our limited perspective."

They were such vivid pictures: olden Flash Gordon cards with Alice-in-Wonderland knaves and queens, landscapes embodying the dreamwork of Freud. My favorites were "The Moon" and "The Star," two extraterrestrial vistas with creatures emerging from a pool, a pelican on a bare tree, an angel pouring water from earthen jugs, a sky bursting with yellow and white suns. The forces portrayed here, Chuck said, were perhaps even greater than all cosmic rays arising from the visible and invisible stars of the universe.

I wanted to learn more, so my friend led me downtown. I was flabbergasted that he knew the beautiful Spanish-looking girl who had ridden the same subway train silently with me for years (Julie went to Bucks Rock with him and greeted Chuck with a bear hug at 242nd Street). Together with her and a few other initiates we journeyed to Dr. Fabian's old neighborhood near 14th Street. Chuck took us beneath a used bookstore into Weiser's Basement of the Occult. There Donald Weiser removed hand-engraved tarots from locked glass cases and showed us the sacred landscapes in enormous luminescent versions. Then he talked of alchemy, reincarnation, UFOs, and the coming revival of the hermetic arts.

The first item I bought was the same modern deck of 78 cards that Chuck owned (drawn by Pamela Coleman Smith). The second was a book, *The Tarot* by Paul Foster Case. As I read Case's descriptions of the landscapes I felt as though I were passing through Robert Penn Warren's mere symbol into a glimmering of the fountain of souls itself:

"In contrast to the Magician, who stands upright in a garden, the High Priestess is seated within the precincts of a temple. The walls of the building are blue, and so are the vestments of this virgin priestess. Blue, the color assigned to the Moon, and to the element water, represents the primary root-substance, the cosmic mind-stuff...."

I stared at this magical woman in robes of gossamer indigo. She was seated between two pillars, an arras of unopened pomegranates behind her, the symbol of the Church around her neck. I thought: 'She is unconsciousness; she represents all that is hidden inside me.'

At different levels the tarot encompassed much of my past. It was an elaborate symbology; it illuminated gateways to worlds of Bridey Murphy; it was an anthology of science-fiction stories and an esoteric account of Phoenicians, Picts, and Medes; it was the letters of the Hebrew alphabet on the dreidel; it was also my first board games and baseball cards with their emblems and rainbow colors. It was "the clue in the embers" and Neil Sedaka, *"I'll climb to the highest star...."* Ghosts and panics now in my past, I considered myself a full-fledged pilgrim. I was determined to quest for the grail.

A week later I bought a second book, Arthur Waite's *Pictorial Key to the Tarot,* specifically for its appendix on fortune-telling. At home I set the cards on the rug and read my first fortunes—for Jonny, then Bridey (who was initially concerned that this might not be an appropriate activity for a good Catholic but finally couldn't resist). When I brought the tarot to Grossinger's, Aunt Bunny was so taken with her reading that she invited a group of her friends, and I read fortunes all morning, one woman after another.

"You should charge for this," said Marcia.

"I can't," I told her. "I'd lose the power."

I knew never to predict actual things ("abuse of the deck," Chuck had taught me), even for the Ten of Swords where the guy lay on the battlefield with ten huge blades piercing his body from head to thighs (bringing an unhappy gasp from Connie, who drew it). I spoke only of difficulties that could be overcome. I evoked the fear of exile (the Five of Pentacles), secret quarrels (the Seven of Swords), having rejected three things and awaiting a fourth (the Four of Cups), and loss of one identity before taking on another (Death, the Number Thirteen). My readings were a mixture of Freud, Waite, and intuition.

After so many years it seemed impossible that Horace Mann would end, but I was now an elder in the temple and the entering First-Formers were tiny pods. As I saw the end approaching, it was no longer possible to work with the same dauntless spirit. I didn't even understand how I had done it all these years. In English we went from *Hamlet* to the rage of *Timon of Athens* and his banquet of stones. I imagined Murphy a kind of Timon as he dragged us through the Industrial Revolution at breakneck speed, threatening and slandering us in comparison to seniors of other years. Mr. Metcalf drilled us daily in Latin, throwing chalk and hardballs at the unprepared (as was his style), and slamming paperweights on his desk to keep us alert. I looked for some concession or relief to acknowledge culmination, but it seemed as though he wanted to rush us through as many stanzas as possible before we got away for good.

I had peaked at mid-terms after my acceptance at Amherst. At that point I got As in Latin and English and an A+ on the famous senior history exam (said to be the hardest test in the school). I had mastered the history of the world up through the French Revolution and then written like a demon for two hours. Mr. Murphy extolled me as one of the best he had ever had. He even made out my desperate scrawl, my fingers cramping, the clock outracing me, as I noted Robespierre, the Jacobins, and doomed figures through Thermidor to the guillotine in the last five minutes, a mere list (because I had expended too much time on other questions)—but he had written, "Outline style excellent!" I couldn't lose.

Now, suddenly, that performance seemed contrived and pointless. I couldn't get my mind back on studying. The school buildings and their rooms no longer fooled me; they weren't the Sorbonne. They had become spooky and hollow without my noticing precisely when. I saw rust on the lockers, each brown clump of granules defining a possible universe. I noticed cobwebs in the ceiling corners of rooms, spiders crawling along cracks, chips missing from the moulding, sweaters and coats in classroom closets never claimed. Why was all this suddenly so lucid? Why I did care so much when for years I simply came and went with my assignments and grades? Something was happening to the very roots of perception. I was entering an alternate kingdom of matter.

In January I hung out with a group of jocks from Westchester who played hockey on a frozen pond Fridays after school. Shifting with the puck, I tried to dribble through clusters of opponents. Piles of coats formed the two sides of the goal, and missed shots rolled across the pond forever.

For that whole winter we tried to get hockey as a sport at HM, a difficult proposition at a school without a skating surface. Our hopes were based on the fact we knew there was a rink (visible from the subway) only a few blocks down Broadway. We spent months going through formal procedures . . . a signed petition . . . a willing faculty advisor.

Why this one victory, so paltry and late, should have obsessed not only me but thirteen others is inexplicable. Yet we threw our hopes into it. Finally, one of the coaches suggested that if we were so gung ho, we try flooding the tennis courts. Grateful to be let out of body-building, we spent an entire gym period on this enterprise. A hose was dragged out of its frozen coat, ripping up ice it had lodged in, until liquid toppled out in sputters and sloshed over snow. Drifts filled with water and caked. Those of us with shovels pushed their loads against the fence to build barriers to keep potential ice from running out.

It was an engineering impossibility and, though we were laughing, our shoes soaked and finally froze. Potential ice disappeared into the snow. The next day I tried gliding on the surface we had left, but after two strides I went right through it. It was like my old dream of skating down streets into summer ponds.

Then suddenly we got unexpected permission to hike to the Broadway rink with our faculty advisor. That afternoon we marched out of Horace Mann, down the hill, along the el, past the giant bakery, through the lands that bordered our hermitage. Carrying skates and sticks, bubbling with enthusiasm, we came to the gate only to find the rink had already been rented to a girls' school.

We peered over the wall at the scene. Half the ice was lost to warm weather. On the other half, girls, so many in different colored clothes like flags of different nations, were skating there—had, in fact, all winter.

My hockey friends had cars, and during spring vacation a gang of them came up to Grossinger's. Just like that! No formal invitation needed, I simply left word at the front gate, and they drove on through.

After the ice rink closed that afternoon, we taped our sticks and designated colored squares along the wall for goals, then played in every possible combination of four on four, using Irv Jaffee to round out the teams. He whizzed in and out of us, the old fox, teasing with the puck, ritually shouting, "Keep it on the ice, boys," which was hard for kids used to zinging it. But there was plenty of expensive glass around.

One afternoon near the end of February I bought a *New York Post* for the subway ride home. Whereas once I would have thought only of getting as much of a head start as possible on my homework, now I combed the sports for every last nodule of baseball. There was virtually nothing, so I read the hockey even though I didn't follow it. The Rangers had just traded for a defenseman named Pete Goegan. A perennially bad team, they had been in the upper echelon of the league during the early part of the season (after picking up Doug Harvey at the end of his career from the Canadians) but now had fallen into a battle with Detroit for the fourth and final playoff spot. That night they were playing the last-place Boston Bruins at Madison Square Garden.

I had never seen a hockey game, or, for that matter, any pro sport but baseball. Now I wanted to know how the game of tin men really looked. I stayed on the train till 57th Street and showed up at Bob's office. Hunched over drawings with his art director, my stepfather turned and looked at me. "What's up, Rich?" he asked impatiently, understatement hiding his astonishment at my visit. I showed him the *Post* and asked if he wanted to go to the Rangers game.

He scanned the article and smiled. "You know something—you and I have never once been to the Garden. I used to *live* there." Breaking family precedent, he called Bridey and told her not to expect us for dinner. We ate quickly at one of his accounts (across the street from the Garden) and then joined the arena crowd.

The rink startled me—how large its surface, the dwarf-size nets (not wide like soccer goals), the smoky crowd, the cold breeze. Carrying sticks like spears, the players skated around their nets, two different-colored circles grazing at their midpoints. After the anthem a referee dropped the puck; suddenly there was a swarm of players in front of the Rangers goal, the goalie fell down, and a red light went on as the crowd booed. Boston scored again almost immediately. Then the Rangers got to play with an extra man, a rule I knew nothing about. Andy Bathgate, the star, shot it from way out; somehow it went through the players in front of the net and bounced in. The light behind the goal flashed, and the crowd exploded.

For almost two periods after that, the Rangers surrounded the Boston net but were unable to put the puck in. The territory was always so clogged, and the rubber bounced zanily as ooo's rose from the crowd. There were only a couple of desperate minutes left when Bob's adopted favorite, Irv Spencer, passed to a player with slick black hair named Dave Balon. As I strained to see, the red light went on; the game was tied.

I loved the speed and chaos, the magic flash proclaiming scores. I talked about this event so much to my brother that he was suddenly as involved as I was in the fate of the Rangers. That weekend we got Bob to take us together.

The Rangers were beaten badly by Detroit, but an announcement during the game took away some of our disappointment: for the first time in ten years, hockey would be on radio—for the remainder of the season.

Several nights later Jon and I sat with our school books open, the radio beside us, the game beginning. I sensed trouble as my mother and Bob burst in the front door late, already in an argument. They went straight to their room and continued shouting. I knew from the cadence that her attention had finally scapegoated us. Sure enough, Bob came marching down the hall as her emissary. He directed his comments at me: "Just because you've stopped studying is no reason to drag this boy in too."

Obediently I took the radio into my study but kept Jonny posted on the score through the door.

A week later the Rangers and Red Wings met in a showdown. Jon and I kneeled by the radio: "Ingarfield and Ullman are ready. The puck is dropped...."

Detroit seemed to score at will and took a quick 4–2 lead. Then a Ranger defenseman slid in a long shot. We clapped. My mother screamed from her room. We lowered the volume. The Rangers scored after the next face-off, then again a minute later. We cheered with clenched fists in silence. But as the last seconds were counted off, the Rangers passed the puck around from player to player in victory; we couldn't contain ourselves. Our muffled shouts were still squeals. "You better tell those two maniacs I've had enough of this nonsense. You started this crap with your goddamned hockey, and you'd better stop it right now." I felt the familiar rush of guilt.

I awaited Bob's appearance. I knew so well the mixture of pain and anger on his face, his lips pressed in bottled emotion.

"C'mon, Richard," he almost pleaded. "Enough of this *chazerai*. Let this boy get back to his studies. What's wrong with you? Have you quit dead on the last lap?"

I seemed to have. I began playing a spinner baseball game in the bathroom, and after a few days I was inventing a whole season between the two new National League teams, the New York Mets and Houston Colt .45s, using their expansion rosters, making line-ups, keeping box scores of every game. I brought the stats from my made-up league into school, and Larry and his buddies perused them thoroughly. Guys even adopted favorite players. Mine was Elio Chacon. Larry picked Merritt Ranew of the Colts, and every Monday he came rushing up to me: "How'd my baby Ranew do over the weekend?" Once he even asked me to bring the game to his house in Yonkers. "C'mon, Merritt baby," he shouted, as I spun away.

Then the real Mets took the field in spring training. I loved Jay Hook in his New York uniform, blue letters written across the front, throwing Met curves. It was like a whole new country. They didn't have to win. Everything about them was fresh and wonderful. In the second exhibition game someone I never heard of named Rod Kanehl got a pinch single. All through spring training he continued to hit, and miraculously he made the team. He became my favorite player.

In Latin I was unprepared for the in-class translation for the first time in four years, so I got the punitive baseball thrown at me. In math I couldn't solve basic homework problems. Would I even graduate? In history the Nineteenth Century rushed by, a thousand details of the Industrial Revolution and its ensuing skirmishes. We were suddenly in the Balkans, World War I—hundreds of new names, dates, and battles unlearned, chapters of dense text, the coming exam a nightmare beyond comprehension.

Forsythia sprang up like fire. I heard birds outside the windows and saw branches thick with leaves and blossoms. A ball of sun blazed insect wings over the field. Physical reality was manifesting spontaneously, and it was pulling me away from the abstraction I had honored as Horace Mann.

Where had the time gone? My teachers looked gawky and sad, their authority falling into caricature. Underneath it all bubbled the anxiety of not being prepared, of slipping into the backs of classes, of praying not to be called on . . . and breathing a sigh of relief when I wasn't. This was so unknown.

I looked out the train window at landscapes and buildings and realized how many times I had seen them and how I was looking at them for just about the last time. Part of me belonged to them, and I didn't even know them—black children playing in parks, old men walking like beetles, shadows of my vehicle careening down through shadows of tracks onto people and cars and cobblestones—so complicated and ineffable. I felt them like a disease, a light growing in me, a poison through my limbs, making me weak and thirsty. I felt so much—loneliness, anxiety, hunger, impatience, desire.

I remembered how it used to be okay just to notice spring remotely as spring. But the wind was truly vast. The clouds were palpable and creamy. The air was filled with seeds.

Somehow I had missed the sheer enormity of existence.

I tried to remember old springs of childhood, the pastoral scenes in which I had played ball—Phil and me, snow in patches on the ground. I was in a stupor then, a dream without a landscape, without dirt, without twigs and leaf fragments, without cobble. Now an unearthly light invaded every dandelion, each stone ornament.

I was writing for my life.

Tillinghast Hall was dank and crowded. People pushed past. Seniors were still manipulating the tin men in the lounge. Chuck stopped me and read a poem about a girl in a sandbox. It was brief and silly but exactly right. "What's with you?" he asked.

"I'm trapped in the Six of Cups."

"Go 'way, breeze," he said. "Go back home."

"Don't you like breezes?"

"Yes, but I was thinking of it at the time, and it came." He made a silly face. "What are *you* thinking about?"

"How funny and insane this place that makes me come day-in, day-out, won't ever leave me alone."

Once, Chuck had stood blocking the way to Chapel, stomping like Rumplestiltskin, tearing dollar bills and throwing them at astonished underclassmen, proclaiming that money was the source of evil.

We walked around the track. Aimlessly I kicked cinders. I remembered the times I lay on this field studying devotedly before classes, other times I ran across it after fly balls. In my mind I heard Mr. Metcalf chanting Virgil's onomatopoeia, *"Magno cum murmure monte."*

I thought back to Monica and Jill, as if to trace the path of my downfall, but the feeling their memory left me with was already as ancient as my life. I had thought once to reclaim everything by simple narrative—therapeutic confessions and autobiographical prose—but even Mr. Ervin knew I had lost the thread (and the labyrinth as well) and was telling my story only from habit.

"Just because you were so successful with it doesn't mean the style will last forever," he confided one afternoon. Our class was filled with ambitious young kids already imitating me, and I was trapped between jealousy at their success and a weariness with the whole process. "You need to dig deeper now," he said. But what was inside me was hollow and insubstantial; it had neither a plot nor a name. Its feeling recalled the poisoning I had once associated with "cancer." In childhood when I felt this way I panicked; now that I could tolerate the sensations, they made me wistful beyond words.

I put aside what I had come to call the "novel" and wrote my first science-fiction story, about a man who unsuspectingly took an office elevator into higher dimensions; another about a Cheshire Cat Hunt on a distant world (and hunters who developed sympathy for their telepathic prey); then a fictional narrative through the mind of a child named Joey. I read them to the class on a day so muggy we were allowed to take off our jackets and ties. Branches brushed gracefully against the stones of Tillinghast. Chuck's tarot lay in the grass. Flowers fell from sky. I was marking time.

Every senior in Honors English was required to give a speech to the whole school, but each year some escaped for lack of enough chapels. Four of us were yet to go when the final slot was being delegated. "Any volunteers?" Mr. Baruch asked. All year I had made myself invisible at selection time, and now there was just one more.

In that slight interlude of anonymity, slinking in my chair, I recalled a feeling I had once, when I sowed my baseball cards through Central Park.

This speech was not a thing to be dreaded. It was a chance to meet estrangement head-on, to call out the shadow life I was leading. My hand shot up (to the amazed relief of three classmates).

Most chapel speeches were topical and neutral, a historical account, an analysis of a scientific problem, adventures in Europe, but I dug deeper, as Mr. Ervin had advised, and found exactly what I wanted. On the appointed day, I sat on stage beside Dr. Gratwick. I was going to spill the beans again!

My confidence lasted until my name was called.

I rose dizzily.

Dwarfed by the podium I suspected at once my resources were too shallow. I looked at a sea of faces and almost lost it. I stumbled in a false start, and then began for real.

I described the long years of work leading only to a world vast beyond comprehension. Without naming anyone I portrayed Danny's bluster and described the attitudes toward girls in an all-boys school. I told about my "idols" and how I feared falling in love with boys.

I certainly had everyone's attention—half in empathy, half in horror of what I would say next. I spoke my final words with a calm precision:

"How did we get here? How did I come to this difficult moment at the end of Horace Mann? I think back, and I am a little boy in a noisy playground. My nurse pushes me on the swing, up and down, in sun and into shade. I am lying in bed having sneaked back from the movies one night at camp to hear some wild, long-since-gone fastballer named Bob Wiesler try to win his first game of the year against Washington. The swimming counselor heaves the lemon-line over my head. I swim after, grab it from the water, and throw. . . . I remember a comic book I found on the beach, men on beds of spikes, tortured in steam showers, unable to change their fate. I remember listening to Allie Reynolds pitch and Walt Dropo get a hit in the second game of a doubleheader on a car radio so long ago. I am standing by the road on the last day of camp, waiting for my father to pick me up. I am only a baby, and warm summer shines on rotten apples beneath the trees. The world goes beyond us into things we cannot imagine. It is already too late, and I am about to become someone I don't even know. This is my moment to say goodbye, for all of us."

Then I ended by quoting Robert Penn Warren:

"Were we happy because we were happy or because once a long time back, we had been happy? Was our happiness tonight like the light of the moon which does not come from the moon, for the moon is cold and has no light of its own but is reflected light from faraway."

A gulp of silence ... return to the velvet chair beside Gratwick, then the applause, like the gathering rustle of that first Chipinaw rain.

Now I was ready to face the consequences. I made an appointment with Mr. Murphy and, at the end of the school day, climbed the twisting stairs to his lair. As I edged to the door I saw him sitting on the master's throne, playing with his belt a notch out from his belly, smiling and glowering intermittently. I confessed at once that I had fallen behind. He sat bolt upright in the chair.

"You, my star pupil? You dare to tell me this. You whom I trusted. This is horrible, Dickie."

"I'm sorry, sir. I just don't understand what's happening to me."

"Sorry, shit! You're going to be a damn sight more than sorry." His face changed like the sun passing through clouds. "You were one of the best I ever had. Dickie, you were like silver plate. Now what I see is silver plate covered with shit!"

"I tried—"

"I thought you had some depth to you, but I was wrong. You're all surface, there's nothing inside." A pause. "You let me down." He sat there in silence, his head bowed. When he looked up at me, his voice was so soft it was almost inaudible. "What have you been doing if you haven't been working in my class?"

"I've gone to a few hockey games. I've been following baseball. I went out ... with a girl."

"Girls!" he shot back. "Are you like all those other shits that sit there in class with their erections?"

I was shocked. "No, sir. I mean—" Why would he even say such a thing?

"Shut up. I'm talking to you. Would you betray my course?"

"No sir."

"Well, then you better catch up, shithead!"

I started to respond.

"That's it, you shallow shit. Meeting adjourned."

Murphy was more than I could handle, and the impact of our session was instantaneous. I went home, got out the history book, and fled him chapter after chapter, well into the next morning. I studied continuously after that until I was ready to take the Advanced Placement with a clear conscience. No all-star performance like at mid-term, but at least I got by.

On the last day of Horace Mann, Mr. Metcalf never let up once from the fury of his translation. Not a word of requiem after five years of daily meetings together. When the bell rang he said, "You're all good boys," and we left. Math class ended with cheering and hoots, English with a lecture on study habits in college. Murphy's class was the last; he greeted us with a scowl and said, "Take out a piece of paper and write about the period between the First and Second World Wars." Then he broke into a big belly laugh. He was still laughing at the end of class as we scurried down the hall.

One week later I left the gym after the math final, strode from the sawdust into the full sun of the afternoon, where it had been all day and was now decaying. The flowers were painfully yellow. They had waited six years for my first day of freedom, but I had grown old in the process, and now freedom was just a rumor of a childhood that had abandoned me. The air was damp as mud. I felt mainly its weight. I collapsed under the subway fan, oddly alone after the years of camaraderie. I changed at 168th Street and got off at 86th. I had an hour left before my last session with Dr. Friend, so I went into the Park.

It was already summer there. Mica twinkled from the pavement. My other lives were scattered about: the Hares and the Hounds, the orange-drink man with his waxed cylinders, Bob hitting fungos. These were severed by something opaque yet palpable. The world then was an agony, a melancholy beyond knowing, but it was simpler than it would ever be again. I thought once that growing up would help. I studied in order to become learned, to know the hidden truth. But vastness and ambiguity now stretched to each horizon, and dandelions everywhere both bid me back to Oz and locked me out of Oz forever. There were too many of them. They left trails to Chipinaw and Long Beach. I wanted to write so badly, somehow to capture this intimation, to justify myself, to declare the stubborn reality.

"Great is the truth and it prevails—" the motto of Horace Mann. I could say it even in Latin: *"Magna est veritas et praevalit...."*—"v" pronounced always as "w." And Wordsworth—I could recite him by heart as Baruch required: "There was a time when meadow, grove, and stream,/The earth, and every common sight,/To me did seem/Apparelled in celestial light. . . ."

I had become a scholar in the Grecian temple of my dream; I had reduced its arcana to ordinary events. Now ("Though nothing can bring back the hour/Of splendour in the grass, of glory in the flower. . . .") I wanted to return to childhood and make the journey again.

I began to compose an account of the customary walk home out the other side of the Park to the drugstore—recalling how, after baseball, I was so thirsty then I imaged waterfalls of pink lemonade and bubbling brooks of yellow lemonade topped with white lemon foam, until the soda-man poured it onto crushed ice, and I sat there sipping, nothing else of me. On the way home Jonny and I ran down the block catching make-believe fly balls, leaping beneath awnings, diving at the pavement, my left hand brown with glove oil.

I thought of the days at Bill-Dave when we finished playing and would sit under the cherry blossoms with Ranger and the Bully. I pictured the sticks of sweet colored chalk with which we drew our trails, and how we crossed the Park for hours in feint and counterfeint. I remembered Halloween at Pelham, when they hid the pumpkins, and I found the third and last one buried in a hole in a tree, packed in with dirt and leaves. But they wouldn't let me keep it as my prize because it was such a good hiding place they were sure I had peeked. All the way home Bert called me a cheater; yet all I had done was make a brilliant deduction. God, they were terrible; I walked among them in a daze.

I remembered the tombs of the Egyptians at the Museum and how we dashed through them, fleeing ghosts. I thought of how augural it was when the woman with absolutely white hair arrived to unlock the door of her bookshop, and I stepped into its antique aroma and found the Hardy Boys nook in the back. . . . And Gene Woodling's homer falling into the upper deck.

In sixth grade, I was the only one old enough to read who didn't walk to school, so on the Bill-Dave wagon I rendered the street signs aloud to the younger kids, making them laugh with my inflections: "Stellllaaa Doooro!" and "Prexy's . . . the eduuu-cated hamburger!"

Some days at P.S. 6 the rain would drip from the top of the window to the sill, the schoolyard damp, the benches soaked. We walked in gloomy halls, mud footprints.

Each item returned to be acknowledged and counted ... an Oh Henry! candy bar ... a Superman comic ... a red plastic water rocket ... a blue and yellow metal truck ... Tarzan rescued by the animals at the Trans-Lux theater ... my mother's hand patting Vick's Vaporub on my chest. Then I stepped into the elevator and pressed Dr. Friend's number: I had come to termination at last.

The final hour became a half hour, and then there were only fifteen minutes left, and still I lay there cold and untouched, objectively aware that the seconds were ticking off the end of this too. I waited without sorrow or pain.

"What do you feel now?" he asked.

"I feel nothing."

"Do you feel numb?"

"No, nothing."

"Think of it," he said. "After five years this is the end and you lie there emotionless. Is that possible?"

"I don't like to admit it, but it's true." I tried inside me to feel something, to cry, but there was nothing, only an irritation and a wish to leave. "I don't even know how I was ever afraid, how I ever panicked. I remember waiting day after day for our next session just so I could tell you something important. But now it's all gone."

"Then just talk."

"About what?"

"The rules are the same, even in the last session. Talk about what you're thinking."

I thought back to when Dr. Fabian died and how I had come to Dr. Friend for the first time. He now seemed so real, Dr. Fabian so dreamlike and faraway. Yet it was Fabian who had saved me at the brink. He was already a saint, but he had also become a mere legend. I began to say something, but I stopped. My throat hurt so much I couldn't talk. "How about that! My throat is too sore."

"Does it feel sore?"

"Can't speak."

"Describe the feeling."

"I can't."

"Where is it sore?"

I pointed. "Way back in there."

"Do you feel sick in any other way?"

"Yeah, sort of. My side feels weak, as though I'm out of breath. It's the old Saturday feeling."

"What are you thinking about?"

"I'm not thinking about it anymore." Then I realized I had to pee real badly. I told him that and began to squirm.

"You're not on a hot seat, you know."

"Isn't it sort of obvious why I'm restless? It's kind of natural when you have to go."

"You're stalling for time."

"That's not true. I have to go so badly. Can't I just go to the bathroom and then come back and finish?"

"You can end the session if you want."

"That's all?"

"Richard, don't you see? You confronted Mr. Murphy; you had a disagreement with Mr. Baruch and had to make up a test. You practically failed math. You wasted hours and hours trying to get to a skating rink that was already rented. Why? Because that was the only way you could express any feeling. Now school's over, and you're about to leave me. You want to cry, but you're unable to."

I searched inside me for the sorrow he was describing, but I didn't find it. I didn't find anything except the urge to pee. It was burning so I could barely think, but the paradox of the situation intrigued me. This was a Herb Schwartz hypnotism show.

"You mean I don't have to go?"

"Nor do you have a sore throat or a pain in your side. They're created for the moment."

"How can that be true? I feel them. They're real."

"Do you think I don't remember? Your head hurt; you were dying. You had cancer. Again and again you have come here seeking relief, imagining that if this or that feeling went away, you'd be happy forever."

"I still believe that, you know."

"So, you're not perfect. No one is. Maybe you'd like to convince me that you're so sick you can't possibly leave. But you've already made that decision. Something in you wants to go on. I imagine you'll have your problems, perhaps terrible ones, but you'll make it. And I'll always be here, thinking of you, rooting for you, here for you to come back to if it gets too hard."

I knew that I would never come back. This office, with its rich smoky aura, was the past. It was no longer me. The *tarot cards* were the future; the *writing* was the future; some girl I had yet to meet was the future. I could sense the movie camera panning away. 'Feel scared,' I told myself. 'Feel scared that this is it. You're on your own.' But I didn't get scared when Dr. Fabian died, and all I could feel now was the lingering soreness in my throat and the agony of having to pee. I counted out the blocks in my mind along Central Park West, imagining how fast I'd have to run to get home.

I had thought the ending would be so different, something like my glorious speech at school, but here I was, squirming on the couch, unable to get up and go to the bathroom because I didn't want that to be the last thing. I lay there watching the second hand. It was too late to recoup anything. It was done.

"Good-bye, Rich."

I got up and turned around. "I don't know what happened to all the great things I was going to say now."

"Well, have a good summer and remember not to fall into a rut in college."

"Good-bye," I said with a short nod. When I hit the street I realized I didn't even have to go.

4

TEEN TOUR

Months earlier, when a travel agency sponsoring a crosscountry tour for teens had made reservations at the Fontainebleau, my mother impulsively signed me up. I insisted I wouldn't go, but she held my slot and, with my attention on finishing Horace Mann and then getting ready for Amherst, it was suddenly mid-June, and I had no summer plans (she and Bob had always insisted on a childless household during July and August). My father refused to have me at Grossinger's for that long, and I had outgrown camp—so, on the first of July, Bob escorted me downtown in a cab with my suitcase. We were a bit late, and I was nervous.

"Don't worry," he said. "These things never get started on time."

"Maybe it will be a mirage, and I can go home."

"C'mon, Richard. This is a chance to see some of the great venues in the world: Niagara, Banff, San Francisco, New Orleans. I don't understand you kids. If someone had offered me such a trip at your age...."

He hadn't had breakfast yet, so requested a stop at the Automat. I answered by staring at a clock through a shop window. "Ten minutes," he argued. "Give a man ten minutes."

We pumped his coins into slots and took plates of food out. I quit on my slab of ham halfway through, but he seemed to dawdle forever with coffee and eggs. Finally he closed the *Times,* and we walked across the street into Grand Central Station.

We found the meeting place at once—a small circle of teenagers.

The tour leaders introduced themselves to my stepfather: they were a music professor from Rutgers (named Simmons) and his wife.

"My husband's very interested in this line of work," offered Mrs. Simmons, "because he's as fascinated by trains as most youngsters are by space ships these days."

"Looks like a nice bunch this year," he called out, approaching with his head half turned. He had square clumps of hair on either side.

"Yes, Sherman; it does."

"Excuse me," Bob interjected, "but your wife told me you were the expert on trains—"

"I am."

"Then could you tell me how soon this group will be departing?"

"We hope to get started in [pausing to look at his watch] about an hour."

"See, I told you," Bob said. "You lousy so-and-so wouldn't even let me finish my scrambled eggs." He gave me a friendly swat.

"Sorry. You were right."

"This looks like a young girl's nightmare," he commented as he scanned the group. "Any guy would give his right arm to be on this tour." In fact, when we finally all collected, it was twenty-eight girls and ten boys boarding a train to Buffalo (the 2.8 ratio, as tour members came to refer to it). "It shows how little some parents think of their kids," Bob concluded. "I would never send your sister on an unbalanced trip like this. She'd wind up with an inferiority complex."

With New York receding behind us, Mr. Simmons stood at the front of the car and struggled through a speech about not getting separated from the group, how to receive our food money, proper behavior with the opposite sex; then he concluded by promising us that the good experiences would outnumber the bad by two to one.

"Oh, you can give them a better score than that, Sherman," his wife coaxed.

"Okay. At least five to one. But only if you know how to be a good sport."

On the train to Buffalo a group of guys—total party boys—gathered with a cluster of girls from Florida and Georgia in the back of the car. They shouted and laughed, breaking into slapstick and group cheers. I heard so many choruses of *"Mi-a-mi Beach; our boys are brave and bold and true . . ."* that it seemed as if I had known the song forever.

I joined a different group up front. Harve was an immense, placid kid, headed to Yale. Barry was a tall, stiff, prep-school guy with dark-rimmed glasses. Stan was a prototype of the Bug from Orenda—snarly, sarcastic, combative. He paraded his street smarts, openly contemptuous of Harve's and my Ivy League ambitions. Alan was tall and handsome with a rugged face; he was amiable but with an edge, acting condescendingly more worldly than the rest of us.

Lucy, Laurie, Carol, and Dorothy sat across from us. Dorothy and Carol were from Atlanta and called each other "Bean." They kept busy playing a childlike game—"I See a Barr" (meaning "Bear").

I thought Lucy was especially lively and cute with long hair, pointed peg nose, and a wide-open doll's face. When we finally got around to telling the names of our schools, she announced dramatically, "Oh, what a school of cheaters. I go to Adelphi, and we played your school in soccer. Your coach 'reffed' and practically handed the game to them."

It seemed so irrelevant that I tried to make light of the matter, but she kept coming back to it. Each time her eyes met mine she snarled, "Remember, your school cheated." Yet I was still imagining her as a girlfriend on the trip.

After lunch Mr. Simmons stood and addressed us again, but he was continually interrupted.

"Hiya, Sherm," called out one of the party guys named Greg.

"I'll make the jokes," retorted Mr. Simmons. "You, I hope, will laugh at them. Now, first, you are Vista Co-ed Frontier Number One and will remain such throughout the summer."

"Bar mishap," inserted Mrs. Simmons, getting a laugh of her own.

He went on to describe schedules and events over the next several days, including a *"Maid of the Mist* Boat Ride" and "the earliest departure time of the summer, three in the morning. The operator will ring you."

"What if we refuse to get up?" Greg's friend Tony yelled back.

"Well," Mrs. Simmons interjected, "all I can say is: we'd hate to leave you at Niagara Falls, but it would be easier to lose you there before we get to like you."

Midway to Buffalo, Greg approached Harvey and me in the aisle and asked if we'd like to contribute to the ICF.

"What is it?" Harve asked.

"Never mind. Just contribute. It's a good and timely cause." Tony and Charlie stood behind him, stifling giggles. Harve seemed seriously concerned.

"Forget it," I told him. "It's a joke."

Greg turned quickly to me. "Can't you picture all those poor, sad illegitimate children you'd be leaving unfed by not contributing. You two should be ashamed of yourselves. Plus, if you don't contribute, you don't get—" he rolled his eyes—"any of the benefits."

Later in the afternoon Harvey and Laurie paired up, and I sat alone talking to Lucy. She was an avowed baseball fan, Mickey Mantle her favorite player. She had even written him letters (no answers yet). I kept a conversation going, answering her questions about Grossinger's and finally taking out my tarot and reading her fortune.

The train pulled into Buffalo at twilight. Noticing Harve carrying Laurie's suitcase with his own, I took Lucy's from her hand, saying, "Let me."

I was balancing hers with mine when Barry came swooping in from behind and, with a clutch of a hand, ripped the bag from my grasp. "It's okay," I grumbled; "I have it."

"No, that's my job."

I let go.

"Well, at least you showed him how to be a gentleman," she declared.

At the motel in Niagara Falls I was assigned to a room with Alan, Barry, and Stan. Dropping off our luggage, we surveyed the accommodations—three beds and a cot. I immediately agreed to take the cot, saving us having to do the odd finger. Then we headed downstairs for dinner.

Over the years most of these events have been erased or compressed in the scrabble of my life. It is only because I kept a journal that I am able to tell the story of the tour. I wrote down everything—dialogue, activities, observations. People utterly forgotten now leap out of dormancy. Barry and Greg, for instance, were erased companions until I found them again in my notes.

I am surprised by not only how mindless our actions were but how vapid even my literary narrative had become, the texture and originality I had cultivated a year and a half earlier now flooded with teen clichés and notions of boys and girls common to the time. Nothing I might compose now could more effectively convey the mood of how things were then.

In this journal I see the deep-rootedness of my compulsions. I am struck by my perversity, how I seemed only to return to the oracle again and again with the same question, yet never to hear its answer.

Vista Co-ed Frontier Number One camped in nightfall on the Canadian side—some of our group queuing into couples and making out. From hidden floodlights hues faded and reappeared, a light green so subtle I tried to taste it like a wafer against my palate, a tint of lake-top blue, a spring-day yellow. . . . It was as though the Falls were diluting the rainbow itself.

Barry rolled in the grass with Lucy. When did he lay claim to her?

"Color," I wrote in the faint light of a souvenir stand, "is what the Magician spills to make the world for the Hierophant and the Hermit. Without color this is all a cosmic void, realm of the Fool."

The next morning we donned black-hooded raincoats and boarded the *Maid of the Mist*. The Simmons stood in the prow, twin George Washingtons. Soon, fine droplets tinged my face. Memories of the Staten Island ferry flooded back. A loudspeaker blared: ". . . and numerous men have tried the much-publicized feat of going over the Falls with a wooden barrel as their mere protection from its mighty waters." I felt a mist over my face. Then the spume got thicker, and the Simmons led everyone back. Lucy shrieked, but Barry forced her into the mainstream. They were like a cigarette commercial—that breath of springtime—slightly out of control.

I stepped forward, threw off my hood, and let the Falls blow across me in sheets until my hair and face were doused.

On the way back to the room I bought a *Sporting News* and, as we straggled down the street, scanned International League stats, scouting Met and Yankee minor leaguers. Later, as most of the tour gathered at the motel pool, I claimed the empty chair next to Lucy. Putting on the Yankee-K.C. game, I began writing letters. "I wish I could send Mickey a postcard and tell him what a wonderful time I'm having," she mused artlessly. "Do you think he'll ever come to Grossinger's?"

"Maybe this winter," I lied. She was so irritating but so pretty, sitting there in four different colored squares of a bathing suit, each covering one quarter.

"You'll get me his autograph? Oh, please!"

"I'll try."

"And then maybe I'll forget your school cheated."

I dove in the pool and swam laps, the game in earshot. Maris hit a homer with two on in the eighth to tie the score. "What's Mickey doing?" Lucy called out, as I headed back to the room.

Changing into slacks and a sports shirt, I was looking forward to devouring *The Sporting News* on the cot, the tied game on. There was no way to have foreseen what would happen next.

I felt an eerie disquiet, a forerunner of panic. I turned off the Yankees.

I had come to a gap in reality. I had no desires, no sensations, no clear sense of my own being. I couldn't relax because I felt something profoundly uncomfortable. I paused, hoping it would pass. Then demonic sensations engulfed me. First I shortsheeted the beds; I unscrewed the lightbulbs. I set a glass of water on top of the bathroom door, a chair against the front door, dripped after-shave lotion on the pillows, and propped a note against the toilet paper: "Regards from the Unholy Four." Desperate not to get caught in the act, I accomplished all these booby traps in frantic succession. I didn't want to do any of it, but obscure emotions drove me along.

When my roommates came back I joined them, falling into ambush after ambush. They swore retaliation.

The phone rang in the middle of the night. "Oh hell," Stan groaned. "They must be kidding."

Our group filed out, past morning papers tied in wire bundles beside the shut souvenir stand, past a dozing clerk ... boarded a bus idling with its headlights on, traveled along bumpy backroads, then accelerated onto a highway ... falling asleep, awakened, onto a train, asleep, awakened again in Toronto to switch trains. Barely conscious, I was stretching in the aisle when a girl named Shelby asked me to carry her suitcase. "To where?" I asked.

"As far as we go."

She was tall and thin with tiny Oriental eyes, a long black dress; her hair sat on her head like an upside-down pineapple. She was really pretty, and I carried the bag proudly. Only later did I realize it belonged to her pudgy, neglected friend. Alan was already portering hers.

Afternoon rolled by—long rows of haystacks, children standing outside their homes to watch the train pass, cows resting in the shadows of trees. I dialed the radio in hopes of getting the Mets Triple A club Syracuse against Toronto (*The Sporting News* said they were starting their two bonus rookies in a doubleheader), but the dial was hum and static.

We were roused near dawn at Port Huron, divided into groups, and put in small cabins aboard a waiting cruiseship. Three shrill blasts of the whistle ... then the shore jerked away; black smoke poured against blue sky. Shelby stood by Alan on the deck, chic sunglasses, her orange kerchief whipping.

"It's quite a liner," he said.

"Well now it ain't the *Queen Mary*," she smirked.

As the lake stretched to horizons, we were set free, denizens of this floating hotel. I joined Shelby and Alan. We explored various sections of the deck, in the process being served tea and cookies by a maid and playing a few rounds of shuffleboard and quoits. Then we went to the piano room where Shelby performed tunes and sang witty flirtations to Alan: "Am I the one for you? For who? For you?"

He seemed amused, nodding with his fixed Bogart grin. I threw an imaginary sidearm pitch. "I'd play ball with you," offered Shelby, "but I didn't bring my glove."

Alan smirked.

"You don't believe me? I have a Marty Marion model, and I played shortstop for my camp. How about them there potatoes?"

As the tour assembled in the dining room, the god of tricks came back into me, and I was a cut-up at our table. With a spoon I fished a single very tiny worm of spaghetti out of my soup (which was nonetheless called "spaghetti soup") and stared hard at it. The table was in an uproar. I had already loosened the tops of the salt and pepper shakers so that Greg got a plate full of salt. I was out of control; things just kept popping into my mind while everyone else's humor fell flat. I told "The Shaggy Dog Story" until they were literally falling off chairs onto the floor. I despised my performance, but I just kept going: "Why that's the shaggiest, shaggiest, shaggiest, shaggiest, shaggiest dog I've ever seen. . . ."

"I've had enough!" Marcia screamed. "Enough!"

"No," Shelby insisted. "I don't think I've got it yet. What was it?"

"Why that's the shaggiest, shaggiest, shaggiest, shaggiest, shaggiest, shaggiest dog I've ever seen."

"If you don't shut up," Barry said, "we're going to throw you overboard."

Then Lucy got us going on "No Soap, Radio," the non-joke ending in a punch line without a meaning.

Alan and Barry stared in confusion. "I just don't get it," Alan complained again.

"No soap. . . .right?" I repeated. "No soap. . . .radio!"

Lucy erupted in fake laughter. Shelby was holding her hand over her mouth as though she wanted to laugh but really shouldn't. Alan shook his head.

Finally Lucy told him: "Don't you get it? The joke is that there's no joke, but everyone laughs."

"Ha, ha, ha," Barry said, grabbing her by the waist and giving her a sloppy kiss.

Then I reached for my ice cream, but someone had already stuck a spoon under the plate, and it turned over.

As people dispersed, I went to the cabin to get my radio and a pad and pen. Alan was my roommate, and I dislodged his bed from its moorings, so it would collapse when he got in. Then I propped a ladder against the door, to fall outwards when opened.

I hurried onto the deck. The sky was a planetarium. A cold wind slapped the waves. Foghorns and buoys sounded faraway.

As I turned the dial, ball games came from everywhere, Richmond-

Jacksonville, Indians against someone, Pirates-Colts. A long, thin cloud passed across the moon. Meanwhile, inside the cabin, much of the Vista tour was gathered in serenade:

"The sun shines bright on my old Kentucky home...."

I wrote: "The song with its minor chords haunts me. Stephen Foster, penniless and ill at the end of his life, imagined those words, that melody, in a place far from here. We are presumptuous interlopers, a bunch of wealthy kids on a fake journey. We don't have a right to his prayer."

"Someone sabotaged the whole damn room," Alan announced angrily, as I checked under the bed in a display of innocence. "There's a real wise guy somewhere!"

The next morning the Vista Teen Tour strolled off the boat at Port Arthur. I was standing hypnotized in the sun when Shelby grabbed a FUNERAL PARKING ONLY sign off the street and handed it to me to conceal under my jacket for her. I was scared of getting caught but hung on. Down the street she managed to charm an empty box from a department store clerk and then slipped the sign into it. On the customs form she filled out COMICAL SIGN, added her signature, and mailed it home.

"That's about the coolest thing anybody has done on the trip so far," announced Greg.

She smiled proudly.

A group of us wandered past Main Street into town. We stopped at a bowling alley, but it turned out to be tiny holeless balls and only five gigantic pins. Too bad. This wasn't my game. But it was Alan's. "Duckpins!" he proclaimed and proceeded to knock down more than the rest of us put together.

I felt sorry for the proprietor because it was a dark, old alley, and we were the only people there. He seemed so pleased to have us, but we weren't real. We didn't even acknowledge him. Finally I asked him about the history of the game and his establishment. He talked enthusiastically, making me even sadder. I felt sorry for the alleys too, the lonely alleys thinking they were called into operation for real people.

Outside, Shelby inexplicably turned to me. "Let's take in the sights," she proclaimed, grabbing my arm. "You and I'll hit *all* of Port Arthur."

We traipsed along Main Street, staring into pawnshop windows. In the back of my mind I held a detached image of myself on a pitching mound, throwing strikes, again and again my right arm around, fast ball down the middle, mirror image after mirror image. Shelby selected a hamburger place for lunch. The flag whipped in from left; I checked second and fired. The batter was way behind the thump in the mitt. I was a kid pitcher against blue sky, number 12 on my back, the quick feet of Al Jackson, the sudden speed of Art Mahaffey.

We were headed in the door when Alan came up behind us from nowhere and swooped Shelby up, putting his arm around her and turning the corner—identical to what had happened leaving the train in Buffalo (only this time the whole person was snatched away).

I saw the ball bunted down third and raced over, grabbed it barehanded, and fired to first—just in time!

From the train, my mind followed silos, trees, patches of forest, farms, a stately rhythm of endless prairie into sunset. Through a core of apple-clouds a gleam of orange shot; faraway on a hilltop, two windows of a house reflected that ray. Then nightfall. . . .

In small groups my trainmates began to pick up each other's songs, *"Michael Row Your Boat Ashore," "They Call the Wind Mariah,"* and *"Them Old Cotton Fields Back Home."* In a corner Barry and Lucy, Harve and Laurie were making out. Stan had his arm in a girl's blouse. Other couples more quietly nestled and kissed, the Simmons seemingly oblivious. I settled into memory, figments of long ago: Pine Cove, the Knickerbocker sign blinking over the city, Jonny fighting ghosts, all past redemption now. . . .

"The rain is Tess, the fire's Joe, and. . . ."

We traveled all the next day on the train. It seemed that the girls from Florida and Georgia never stopped playing a clapping song. They stood in a circle and pounded their hands in rhythm to: *"The spades* [pronounced "spides"] *go two lips together, tie them together, bring back my love to me."* Then the chorus: *"What is the me-ee-ea-ning of all these flow-ow-ers? They tell the stor-or-y of love from me to you—cha cha cha."* After that, they fell on the floor together, laughing. I alternately read Hamilton Basso, *The View from Pompey's Head,* and wrote. We reached Winnipeg at nightfall.

Drenched with train nausea, I collapsed into hotel sheets. I was fast asleep when Stan's voice jolted me. His breath was right up against me as he grabbed my blankets and tossed them on the floor.

"Hey!" I said.

"Shut the hell up."

"What's this all about?"

"I'm warning you. Shut up or I'll kill you." He stuck his fist under my chin.

"Maybe first you'll tell me what's wrong."

"Who said you could take the big bed and leave me with the cot?"

"Remember, it's your turn. I had the cot in Niagara Falls."

"You asked for that cot, goddamnit!"

"I'll trade if it means so much to you."

"It will solve only one problem. What's it going to do about Alan's bed? What's it going to do about our sheets and the water traps? What about the light bulbs? What if we had retaliated against those guys? I bet that would have been hilarious."

I felt both horror and remorse. This was the moment of retribution I had dreaded. I gathered all my rationality and candor, sat up, and said: "I meant to tell you. I don't know why I did it."

"Great. And what about your stupid jokes at supper? What about your interfering with Alan and Shelby? What's it going to do about the fact everyone thinks you're an idiot?" I stared in stunned silence. He was right, of course. "Going for that walk with Shelby was just so stupid, so obvious; how could *anyone* do that?"

I thought, 'She asked me!'—but I said, "I liked her, I guess."

"Well, that was the goddamn wrong way of going about it. Alan's trying to score with her, and you're getting in his way. He's so close. Do you understand that? He's gotten his hand in her pussy. She's using you against him. Don't you understand that? She's a cock-teaser. Do you know what a cock-teaser is? She's cold as ice, and he's working for the honor of all men."

I didn't really understand. I had been down this road so often before: Marian, Monica, Tina, Jill . . . Now I felt only emptiness and confusion. "I'm sorry. I'm guess I'm acting like a jerk. I don't know why. But I'll try harder."

"Will you keep your ass away from Shelby?"

I couldn't believe I was a real threat to Alan. "I'll stay away from Shelby," I promised.

Then Stan gave me a friendly shove. "You're taking this amazingly well. You make me think human beings are worth my trouble."

I thanked him and started to get up.

"Stay where you are. I'll sleep in the fucking cot."

Our instructions the next morning were not to leave the pool area because Winnipeg wasn't supposed to be interesting enough for sightseeing. I decided to take off anyway.

I had read in the paper that the Class C Winnipeg Goldeyes were playing Grand Forks that day, so I grabbed a map off the front desk and slipped out onto the street when the Simmons weren't looking. The ballpark was miles out of town. I boarded a bus along Portage Avenue. The signatures of Winnipeg roared by.

Hiking past suburban homes on Telfer Street, I playfully skipped in the outer edge of lawn sprays, admiring the newly cut grass. This place was a gem, Goldeye Stadium looming in the distance.

I arrived in the sixth inning, no admission fee, fans cheering for the home-team pitcher, "How you chuck, boy!" Minutes later I grabbed a foul ball ricocheting off a nearby seat. My Northern League treasure! From the stadium I gauged my distance back to Stan, Shelby, and the others. I was a needle in a haystack, beyond the naked eye.

From Winnipeg a train took us west to the Columbia icefields. There we clambered aboard tractors for a ride across a glacier, stared down through rainbow ice of potholes, and made snowballs of dinosaur snow. All day Stan and Alan kept joking about how much that glacier and Shelby had in common.

We journeyed from Jasper to Vancouver and spent an afternoon touring Stanley Park. At the zoo I saw penguins for the first time—little white, black, and yellow beings that inspired Shelby to do a penguin walk. She wore a tight skirt with a shiny black belt and a short-sleeved blouse with a man's jacket over it. For the first time she and Alan were apart, and she made a conspicuous effort to avoid him. He had found another girlfriend.

At the outdoor cafe she brought over a chair and set it next to me.

While we waited for our food she peeled back the cardboard layers of two matches to form stick figures; then she placed one atop the other and lit them. The torsos twisted and curled about one another, the stems rising in fire, flames crawling down the arms and legs. "See that," she said. A thin stream of smoke rose from the quivering ash.

I nodded.

"I'll bet," she added derisively.

Then she lit a second pair. I was silent.

"You and I are going to have a regular orgy tonight."

Then she asked me about what the boys and girls did on raids at *my* summer camp. I tried to be cute and evasive, but she would have none of it. "Did they do this?" she asked, raising her eyebrows, "or that?," raising them even higher. "How about some of this?" She rolled her tongue. The whole table was laughing.

Later in the meal she examined my jello and, pretending to find a contaminant in it, suggested I wash the cubes in my water glass. To please her I put a few lime squares in. Everyone was giggling as the jello floated about.

"Don't try to make me look stupid," I pleaded softly.

"Oh, don't mind the others," she retorted quite loud. "We can have fun, and they don't even have to notice."

After the meal I made a bee-line away from her, but she trailed close behind. We passed a stand with a sign above it: PO-BOY SAND-WICHES. "Boy sandwich," she called out to me. "Is that another way to have boy?"

She was taunting me with my interest in her. She didn't even know I was on her side.

I said nothing and walked faster. I passed Lucy and Barry, Harve and Laurie. The sky turned dark. I kept walking. I came to a fountain and saw the harbor lights of Vancouver beyond, as the Platters alone might have sung them.

Suddenly everything changed. Shelby and the teen tour were gone. I stood in a universe of stars, bearing nameless cities of ancient and future peoples. And the port shimmered, rough vessels carrying out human commerce.

Once again I had been recalled to witness a miracle, a world limitless and inscrutable, bathed in tarot light.

"Boats and buildings and stars and even the sound of the water have no feeling," I wrote; "they are cold like the wind. But I am their body. I can feel for them what they are."

In L.A. I was delighted to escape again, this time with permission. The old Grossinger's P.R. genius, Milton Blackstone, met me in the hotel lobby and drove us straight to Eddie Fisher's house.

The evening was high comedy. The three of us got lost trying to find Dodger Stadium and, after wandering between freeways, we caught only the last inning of the Angels game. "It's more exciting this way," Eddie said.

I sat by his pool the next morning, bringing my journal up to date— Seattle, Portland, San Francisco. Then I floated on an air raft while Eddie read some reports with Milton and hummed a few tunes. I wanted to ask him to sing "Oh My Papa" but didn't. After we finished corned-beef sandwiches, sodas, and fries, he sent his best regards to the Grossinger family and gave me fifty dollars from his wallet to "entertain the girls" (in his words) as Milton and I returned to the car.

That was the most impressive adventure anyone had to report. In Hollywood, where everyone had been searching for even a sighting, I had hung out all day with a real star. Lucy kept asking to shake my hand, whichever one "Eddie last touched." I stood in the lobby embellishing the story with every detail I could think of.

In the group around me was a girl named Betsy; she was in the Miami Beach chorus—one of those identityless cheerleaders. But standing there just then she seemed fresh and jaunty, such a sunny person that I struck up a friendship and sat next to her on the train to San Diego and then the bus into Mexico.

On request, she told me stories of her life, mainly about her boyfriend Brian who was a football player—All-City end, winning catch in the homecoming game. She lived in a Pine Tree Drive mansion. Her agenda was beach parties, sports cars, varsity sports, and motorboats. She heard my own tales of childhood with disbelief: "I can't imagine why you had such a hard time." She shook her head. "Well, that's at an end. You'll meet friendly people now, like me."

Lightly tanned, her hair gently flipped up in back, she could have been Cathy Carr singing "First Anniversary." I wrote of her first as

Neptune's daughter, Triton's sister on a shoal of a distant moon. She had tiny black berries of eyes and a bit of an Eskimo feel about her, plus a quiet, funny mouth, pointed out ever so slightly at the top.

We passed villages of lumber scraps and Coca-Cola crates. I talked about the politics of the Philippines and Ghana. Despite its irrelevance to her, Betsy listened with interest, no snide jokes. Our rapport was solid, but it wasn't as though I was a boyfriend or even a potential boyfriend. Big Brian was waiting back in Miami Beach.

Not only was Betsy not a potential girlfriend; she was never to become one, but she grew into the heroine of my book. Everything I had to say, everything I remembered about my past was transfigured through my sense of her.

Reading the tarot for her beneath a tree in Anaheim, I made her significator the Queen of Pentacles—compassionate and bountiful. After I set the cards on the grass, she held each one in her hand and took in my interpretations—the Wheel, the Hierophant, the Lovers. "Yes, these are special, quite special. I could never understand them like you. What do I know? I'm a cheerleader wondering which of these pictures is her boyfriend. Is he a Knight? Is he a King?"

"He could also be a Queen," I said. "Men and women are combined in all the cards."

"No, that he isn't."

At Disneyland she returned to her Florida friends, and I couldn't recover her in the crowds. So I took a banana-boat through Africa, a paddle-craft down the Mississippi, then played old-fashioned metal baseball games in an arcade for much of the evening. Suddenly fireworks erupted over Disneyland Castle; Tinkerbell was released from the end of a long, thin cord and, doll or human, soared across the sky past gingerbread peaks—one hour to curfew. I fell in with a group at The Wild Ride of Mr. Toad; in fact, I found myself standing next to Shelby in line, half-expecting to go through it with her, like the tunnel of love.

"Are you going to protect me from the monsters?" she asked.

I nodded suspiciously. I couldn't believe this was happening, and I hardly trusted it, but my heart was thumping as we reached the front of the line.

"See you later, 'gator," she suddenly snapped—a malicious grin—and she was gone.

I looked around for an escape, but the attendant was holding open the next empty cart for me. I took the seat. Immediately I was swung down a track into blackness, drawn through the machinery of the ride.

A glow appeared in the far sky, dark blue from the sun having just set. Then things got crazy. My car crashed through a wall; I careened wildly off the road; I was on a highway screeching past other cars, going the wrong way. I rammed a detour; barrels came tumbling down but froze in midair. I burst through an old warehouse. Suddenly I was in court; a judge jabbing his finger at me cried out GUILTY! Shrill cartoon characters were frantically pointing.

Next stop, Hell: devils roasting people, a scenery of orange-red flames, the chief devil laughing.

I couldn't help taking it personally. The verdict had always been against me.

Then I realized how much this stageset looked like The Devil of the tarot. I knew his alias all right: If only his prisoners could feel how loose the chains were about their necks . . . if only they could know that elsewhere in the deck he was a winged Angel . . . and they were Lovers.

("Geez, Richard," commented a friend years later, "can't you just go to Disneyland? Well, okay, so Disneyland really is only packaged archetypes.")

The next morning the air was sultry; the train station steamed. "Hey, Betsy," I called out; she turned from ahead of me on the platform. I ran and caught up. "Let me carry that for you."

"No, thanks. You've got your own bag." I took it from her anyway.

I sat beside her as we pulled out of L.A. She was wearing yellow Bermuda shorts and wondered how I could stand my hot black slacks. I promised to improve.

As we worked our way to the dining car together, the train stopped in Yuma and ended up being stuck there. She was talking about when her brother was born: "I kept saying to my mother, 'Whose little boy is he?' And my mother kept answering, 'Why, he's my little boy just like you're my little girl.' 'But who's his mother?' I kept asking. I couldn't get it, that she could be both our mothers at the same time."

It was this innocence she had. She wasn't childish; she wasn't naive. She was just so basically big-hearted.

She tried to recall how it felt when Brian kissed her for the first time. She described her moment of fear and then the rush of her own excitement: " 'Oh my my my my,' I thought. And then I worried that I'm only me, and me isn't really very much for him to love. But he knew who I was, just like my Mommy sometimes does, and that's really great from a boy."

Yes, even though she was a beach girl she embodied the moon. Because she was not a classically pretty girl, a Shelby or Lucy, it had taken me very long even to see her, but her sexuality was larger than anything I had previously presumed to approach. I felt an attraction to her that had no allure of fantasy in it. When I imagined being with her at one of those parties she described, even kissing her, I felt the pathos more than the sexiness, the texture of her personality that made her more than a teen mirage. She was a saltlike thing to me, as bottomless and blue-green as the sea, yet I was undiminished beside her.

I had wasted most of the summer. We had already turned the corner and were headed east.

When our ice cream came she said, "Yum yum," and I said, "Yuma," because the train was still there. She laughed, and my mind flashed to another dusk at 1235 Park when I was sent to the corner drugstore after dinner to buy a brick of chocolate, strawberry, and vanilla, a number-two combination for dessert. I was returning with the cold package pressed against my belly when the untracked spook caught me, the hidden familiar to my existence.

That originless throb had haunted my childhood—once a primal wave of panic, then a preadolescent sense I wasn't who I was, always a mournful other. It was the worst thing not because it hurt but because it went so deep without motive or explanation, with no hint of reprieve. It had to have been born with me, for its power lay beyond my American kid's body.

Betsy danced on Southern beaches then, calling to me to remember that one day in the future we would sit together at a train station in Yuma.

At least I had found her. Before, there was nothing, and now I had the whole of creation to dream of. So I thought, as I stared out the window at the Dipper over Arizona.

In New Orleans Betsy was kneeling alongside the pool, drying off, dark wisps of hair stuck to her neck. I drifted by, holding onto a plastic beach animal, my arms wrapped around it, my legs curled up. "I'm just a barnacle," I called out.

"You *are* a barnacle," she called back.

After I got dressed we broke the rules by hiking downtown together. At one point Betsy stood straight and tall on the street, doing what she called her "happy walk," half collapsing giggling, half marionette. It was contagious, and we began laughing and bumping into each other.

We spent the afternoon wandering in New Orleans. We visited antique neighborhoods, European parks, and a used bookstore where I bought an illustrated Hans Christian Andersen; we sat in a tavern recalling stories that went with the pictures, the tinder-box dogs with their saucer eyes. Then we raced each other across a park.

I forgot where I even was—that we were part of a tour, that I hadn't been her brother my whole life, that she was about to leave me for good.

The next morning we boarded for Florida—end of the line for Betsy. I was somber and train-weary, sick of the almondy steam, the sinuous motion. When the conductor came around for berths, I spent part of Eddie Fisher's money on a sleeping compartment.

Dusk turned quickly to night. As the train swerved and bumped, I watched lights passing outside, "lights of people"—I scribbled in the glow of a tiny bulb—"whom I will never know, who will live beyond me forever. And then, someday, I will pass a light in the darkness and it will belong to one of the people in this group. Everyone, including Betsy, is about to fall into the great anonymous void." Very softly I began mouthing a folk song to myself:

> *"Rockin', rollin', riding'*
> *Out along the bay*
> *All bound for Morningtown*
> *Many miles away...."*

It was a trance I used to put myself in, just before sleep; it was visitors in the courtyard at my own beginning. Now Betsy had come back to the beginning to claim me. But was she the mother tucking me in, or the mother of my child tucking him in?

> *"Judy's at the engine*
> *Tony rings the bell*
> *Seymour swings the lantern*
> *To show that all is well."*

The phrase "all is well" marched out of me like a cute little duckling, whisking off its fuzz of dew and standing there to be absolved. At dawn, billboards indicated we had passed into Florida, first only dense fog, then a faint butter sun bleeding through, trees along the tracks covered with Spanish moss. So I whispered a different song:

> *"This world is not my home*
> *I am bound across the river*
> *Faraway so faraway,*
> *'Cross the wide Missouri. . . ."*

I felt the chillingness in the words in my throat in my mind.

> *" 'Cross the wide Mizz-oour-ee. . . . ."*

I was calling on the presence of all beings, everywhere.

> *"Oh, Shenando'h, I love your daughter . . . !"*

"I'm so excited I'm shaking," Betsy said. "Do you think Brian'll get off work? Do you think my car will be there? Wouldn't it be great if I can drive my own car home?"

At the Miami station Brian was waiting for Betsy. She ran into his arms, and he held her against him and swung her back and forth like in the movies. And what did it matter, I thought, if *I* was happy. That was just me, one person. Betsy was happy enough for all of us.

But, as we walked into my mother's Fontainebleau, I chanted over and over the words I had memorized from Shakespeare's play, *Corialanus:* "The sorrow that delivers us thus changed. . . ."

The next time I saw Betsy was at the outdoor pool. I was having a catch with Lucy with a small rubber ball, the Yankee game on in the background. "Mickey goes back for it. . . ." I shouted with sudden excitement at seeing Betsy. I threw it straight but really high.

Splash!

"I guess I'm not as good as Mickey," Lucy said, "but thanks for calling me him."

Brian was with Betsy, tall and broad-shouldered, hardly any neck, soft blue eyes and a tough mouth. He swaggered as he walked. He was anxious to meet me. "How are the Yanks doing?" he asked.

"They're losing one-nothing."

"Great," he said. "I love to see them lose. But then again, I shouldn't get my hopes up. They always win in the end."

"Who do you root for?"

"Me? I don't like baseball too much. I'm from Detroit originally, so I root for the Tigers. But most of the time I just root against the Yankees. Betsy tells me you've got a box behind third base at Yankee Stadium. That must be cool."

He pulled a beach chair beside me, and Betsy pulled one over on the other side. She asked me to tell him about high school.

I seemed to astonish him with my most ordinary accounts. He wondered where I went when I dated and, when I told him that I didn't, he kept pressing me. "What! There were no girls in the school. You studied all the time!" He turned to Betsy in disbelief, glad he wasn't involved in such. She smiled knowingly.

Then he questioned me on whether she had been a good girl on the trip. "Oh, yes," I proclaimed.

He smiled proudly. "See, she's turning red. She's passionately in love with me, and I don't even know that I can stand her presence. Why, she walked up to me the other day on the corner and kissed me. Now what do you think of a girl who—" She had taken a glass of ice water and poured it on him. Then he said, "You're a good girl, Bets" and grabbed her legs. She dove away from him, then underwater. He followed. As she kicked and fought, he called back to me, "She's a regular tomboy, isn't she?"

"That's my hair, Brian," she said.

"I know. I know. Truce! I'll let you go."

Later I sat with her alone by the side of the pool. "You know, Bets, someday I'm going to write a story about this trip."

"Will I be in it?"

I nodded. "You'll be one of the five or six main characters."

"Thank you."

"You don't need to thank me. You're such a great character that there wouldn't be any story without you."

Brian was diving in the pool and surfacing, staring back at us, waiting for her to join him again.

"Why?" she asked. "What makes me a good character?"

"You're part of a theme I'm only beginning to understand."

"What kind of theme?"

"A sort of 'growing up' theme."

"C'mon," Brian called out.

"I'm just an immature little girl, and a lazy one at that."

"You're growing up in your own way."

"Brian won't even let me carry a balloon at a carnival because he thinks it makes me too young and silly. He doesn't understand that staying a little girl is part of me. Do you, Bree?"

"What?" He came climbing out and strode over with a look of mock impatience. Then he turned to me. "Betsy tells me you can get me Rocky Colavito's autograph at Grossinger's." I nodded. "Tell me; is he a decent guy? Some people say he's a wiseass and a show-off."

"My stepmother says he's one of the nicest of the players."

"You see that, Bets. Old Brian doesn't miss."

They headed down to the beach, so I went upstairs to watch the game on TV. I glimpsed them out the window, throwing a football back and forth. He sent her out on a long pass. Running through the surf, she muffed it but showed perfect form. Then they disappeared beyond my view. Tony Kubek had just come back from the Army and was in his first game of the season at shortstop. Yet that all seemed fake—the smell of sun-tan oil in our room, even the hallowed sound of Mel Allen.

I looked out the window. On a raft some girls and boys played diving tag.

"Stafford checks his runners, winds, and fires."

"Go to hell, Stafford," I said with a bashful smile. "I hate you," I added, addressing myself with the drama of a novelist transcribing his own lines. I recalled a spring day, robin's egg sky outside the windows of Horace Mann while I sat and worked from books piled beside me, no end in sight. What for? The last time I was in Miami Beach I had clutched the primal Easter egg; then I was sent into exile, following my mother into her life. It was too late to change such antiquities now. The hook was in me too deep. I was a castaway forever in my own land. I wrote, "I look upon a sky-blue, rose-red, sun-yellow world that is perfect, that I lost and now lose again."

On the next to last day of Miami Beach, Betsy invited the tour to her house. We went in separate cabs. Her mansion was even more than I had feared—fancy iron gates all around it, grillwork shaped like rays of sun. We followed a long winding driveway to the entrance.

For me it was just one more barrier: If I was already eight runs behind, bottom of the ninth, it might as well be twelve.

Betsy answered the door surrounded by two large barking poodles and a smaller one. "Don't mind the dogs. They're good buddies."

"Do we have to go through customs?" Lucy asked.

"Of course not," she laughed. "Come in and you can put on your bathing suits in that little house across the driveway. Wait. My brother will show you." It was as though we had been traveling the whole summer in a dark train to get here, where she had been all along.

Floats and balls were thrown into the pool. Servants were cooking frankfurters and hamburgers; platter upon platter of food arrived. It was pompous and syrupy, and Betsy was inaccessible in the busyness, but I loved just being there and watching her.

Later in the day she called me inside to meet a friend of my father. I was in the pool, so I dried myself off, put on my shirt, and walked through the living room. People were dressed in shirts and ties. My body seemed bare in that company, but I tried to be polite.

"There was a picture in a frame on a table inside," I wrote later. "It was a photograph of Betsy as a little girl. Her face was a bit awkward, with thin eyes, a half smile." Then I reached the epiphany of my book: "The wind blew gently, the tree leaves rustled slightly, the flowers dipping and rising in a ripple across the beds. It was famous warm, humid, sleepy summer. Hers was a face like the face on the rarest baseball card, that you would see in someone else's pack and then never again because there was only one. And you would open pack after pack looking for it, that face, the shade of blue in the sky behind, the home-team uniform."

I wanted to hold her, hold onto her, have her hold onto me. But I knew that I was leaving her company and returning to what I had been. I couldn't just grow here in her light like a vine for years on end. Her family would ask me to go away. She would get tired of this object trailing about her. She would want a man, a family, children. Could I ever be that?

I would have to grow up; there was no other path. Her body was real. In the end if I was to know her I would have to get down in the mud with her and fight it out. And it would be a fight, for I wanted to destroy the false aura that surrounded her, that kept me from her. In time she would have to change anyway, and the light would be different, but her Betsyness, that pathos and joy, would not break down like iron in fire; it was a part of her that would not ever be destroyed.

The following evening we had a last dinner and award ceremony. Afterwards Brian was pointing out Dorothy and Carol. "Now if I was on this trip and didn't have Bets, that's who'd get my attention. There's still one night left and plenty of girls," he winked.

"None like Betsy," I asserted. He laughed agreement.

"They don't come much better. She may not be as pretty as some of the rest, but she's pretty inside—and that's what counts. You say she was the nicest girl on the trip. Everybody says that. Everybody around here says she was the nicest girl at Beach." He shook his head in wonder. "When I first kissed Bets," he said, putting his arm around her, "I wanted it so bad. I don't ask no questions 'cause I don't wanta hear no answers. I just leaned over and kissed her." He paused. "I love this girl here. Even with football I was never important before Betsy."

Betsy came to see us off the next morning. Stan and Larry were kissing her good-bye, but I wanted no part of it. She was too special to share. I left the tour and walked five cars to the back, posting myself at the last dusty window. The train lurched sharply and then began to move. Her eyes and mine met, and I shouted, "Good-bye, Betsy" through the glass like in a movie.

Actually only my mind shouted. I said nothing. I wasn't even sure she saw me.

"Good-bye, Richard." I heard the ghost of her voice.

I watched Miami, tears pouring down my cheeks unchecked, my heart staring out into a void, streets sliding mechanically, surreally. I was too tired to imagine anything. But for once my desire was concrete and real. And I had Betsy looking over me, so I thought, 'I am coming home with an ally. They can do me no more harm.'

PART
FOUR

INITIATION

September, 1962–April, 1964

1

AMHERST

As I awoke I knew at once the day had arrived. 'It's over,' I thought, hardly considering whether I was relieved or sad. Dressing for the last time in the Towers family, I stared at an oblique ray of sun incising the top of our courtyard; silhouettes of pigeons purred against parapets. The world was hollow; yet my gut rang with unprobed emotion. Breakfast was a quick lump inside me.

Jon shook my hand with a shy grin. I gave Debby a kiss, hugged Bridey, then approached my mother. She held back tears; yet I had no capacity to comfort her. 'Just get me out of here,' the voice inside me screamed.

The elevator arrived with a noticeable clunk. "Hold it on eight, Jimmy," Bob said. "We've got a year's worth of Amherst College gear." A doorman met us with a rolling cart, and he and Bob helped me load suitcases and cartons into the trunk of his double-parked car.

The sky could not have been bluer, the vista of the Park more eerily serene in my departure. It was just another day igniting, like all the others, a blanket of taxis on the avenue, a pang of old history in my heart, an orange-rind of nostalgia. I tried to think and feel nothing.

We crossed bridges onto turnpikes, up through Connecticut into Massachusetts, tinges of russet in the trees, field flowers mostly blue. I set my mind to the speed of the highway. Eventually Bob was inspired to recall his own years at CCNY, as he invoked Amherst with reverence: "No Jewish kid from the Lower East Side would have dreamed of going to a real Ivy League school. This shows how far we have come in one generation."

So far that the issue was meaningless to me. The gap between my generation and his seemed almost a mutation of species. It was hard to imagine he identified with me in any way. One thing we had left, despite harsh words over the years, was our incipient friendship. We were in a sense both outsiders to a regime we didn't understand. Discussing my mother was taboo, but I could mention Betsy to him and get a rational, reassuring response: "The first one is always the hardest."

Amherst was a labyrinth of stone buildings around plazas and fraternity houses lining side streets. My dorm, James Hall, formed a central quad with three others like it. Across the quad was Johnson Chapel with its trademark white clocktower; it had been visible above the hills for miles. Now it rang out the hour, a welcoming troll.

The few campus thoroughfares were mêlées of parents and freshmen—wardrobes, trunks, hockey sticks, crates of records, lamps, stereos, libraries, item by item being carted inside. After we ferried my own things up the stairs, setting them on the floor of my small room, Bob and I took a walk around the quad to the War Memorial, an inscribed round slab overlooking ballfields so vast ten softball matches could have been played simultaneously on them without overlapping. The sun singeing grasstops in gold, it was a stunning vista to the mountains.

My stepfather took it in slowly and solemnly. Then we hiked back to his car and, in the fading color of afternoon, he extended a hand. As ever I felt the ambivalence of opportunity lost. We had done the best we could, and I wished I could erase the lingering awkwardness. He could see I was apprehensive. "You'll manage," he said. "I'd put my money on you in the clutch." He grabbed the car door. "I envy you, Richard, going to this school." Cranking open the window, he called out, "Be a mensch." And I was alone.

I had a single room on the fourth (and uppermost) floor of James. That had been my mother's idea. When housing forms came she warned me, if I let them assign me a roommate, I could "end up with a nut." I took her advice as gospel. Now I regretted it because just about everyone else was engaged in setting up their doubles and triples and getting to know the people they were about to be living with. Meanwhile, I sat in my room, unpacking gradually, hanging on to my old world in a Mets doubleheader on the radio. By the end of the second game I was totally depressed.

Then, just before dinner, I was paid a visit by two guys who shared a room down the hall. Sid was a tall, folksy kid from Portland, Oregon—talkative and cheerful. Alan was a poet, his diametric opposite—a husky, sad-looking guy with a scarred face, who came from nearby Massachusetts. In our first spirited conversation at dinner in Valentine Hall, Al confided that he planned to commit suicide someday because he didn't want to leave an event as important as his own death to circumstance. This seeming perversity sent Sid into conniptions. "How could you say such a thing, roomy? I didn't put 'suicide' down on the housing form, you know."

Al just chuckled. "How do you know what *I* put down?"

When Sid failed to budge Al on ontological grounds he tried to convince him that death wasn't really an issue now, certainly not when we were starting out at the beginning of our lives. "We're young. We shouldn't be thinking morbidly."

"Ah, but there you trick yourself," Al replied playfully. "I certainly hope it's not an issue, but the crux is—you don't know when you're going to be called on to make a decision, so you had better be ready."

Then we switched to hockey (Sid followed the minor league Buckaroos in Portland, Al the local Springfield team)—and romance (Sid wanted to marry his high school friend Barb as soon as he graduated; Al was "still looking"). The next evening Al and I sat in their room, reading our work aloud to each other—his metaphysical love poems and my narratives of the teen tour.

My single lay almost at the juncture of the two arms of the James "L." Down the opposite arm from Sid and Al, it seemed the entire freshman football team and their buddies were assembling a private fraternity by trading assorted roommates to other floors and dorms. On several occasions they asked me to accept a reassignment, but I had just gotten there and, anyway, changing rooms was against the rules. I could tell that my refusal made me unpopular; I felt a familiar embattledness and isolation.

James Hall itself was put on quick probation because a kid on the second floor named Marshall Bloom had been caught by a maid with a girl in his room. A gang from the football wing retaliated, scattering his belongings, hanging his bed out the window, and generally trashing his room and filling it with toilet paper. By Chipinaw standards this was heavy mayhem.

Most of the freshman classes took place in buildings surrounding our quad or just outside it. Thus we left for meals together and came back together. We also shared most of the same courses. Amherst believed in a quick, thorough indoctrination. All my courses (except for the one elective I was allowed—Introductory Philosophy) were part of a freshman required curriculum. I knew beforehand that this armada of courses was an admired benchmark in American education, a fabled initiation all its own.

Yet, compared to Horace Mann, at first the work seemed ludicrously easy. We had brief assignments with virtually no memorization. The priority was "analysis." In history class our inquiry began with interpretations of primary-source documents from ancient and Mediaeval times. We moved rapidly from the Laws of Hammurabi to Tacitus, Henry IV at Canossa, money and credit, early European cities, Cellini, Calvinism in Scotland, Machiavelli, and the Incas and Aztecs. We received hand-outs of laws, speeches, missives, prayers, and ancient chronicles and were expected to find their hidden protocols.

Physics was a course in rethinking the basic laws of nature (with the appropriate math in another class). English was completely a writing seminar—three times a week we turned in papers in which we considered "how one knew what they knew" in different ways. The first assignment proposed: "'I can make my past anything I want simply by thinking it's so.' What is your judgment of this remark? Does it not at first sight seem to you a fatuous statement? What is fatuous about it? But is there something in it? What 'truth' do you see hinted at?" This was the kind of game I enjoyed.

Otherwise, I deciphered David Hume and Charles Sanders Peirce, wrote enthusiastic papers, and struggled to keep up with physics equations that seemed to leapfrog in complexity as we rolled steel balls down chutes and dropped weights onto carbon paper on the floor.

In its own terms it was a thoughtful and tough-minded education that I look back on now with admiration, but at the time I barely noticed the artfulness. The ever-present landscape of New England woodlands, Ivy League classrooms, and colonial village was far more urgent and evocative. At the same time, I had to adapt to the male Amherst culture with its clan meals, obstreperous dorm life, beer parties, and strata of cool roles, none of which fit a daydreaming child from New York. Once again, I wasn't really there.

At World Series time I rode the bus through western Massachusetts and Connecticut back to the City to watch the Yankees take on the Giants. Our family had great tickets, direct from Bill Stafford, Jerry MacDonald's old ballplaying buddy—in fact, on the day he was the scheduled starter.

The first morning in New York, truant from college and an hour after the high-school rush, I rode a near-empty subway car and ascended the hill to Horace Mann. I walked its grounds like a time traveler— no trace of the Class of '62 anywhere. At lunchtime Mr. Murphy invited me into the faculty dining room. While I was regaling a number of ex-teachers with a description of Amherst, Mr. Metcalf strolled by, heading for another table. I popped to my feet and pursued him for a greeting.

"What Latin are you taking?" he snapped.

I froze. I started to say that we had only one elective and I had picked philosophy. I got out only half a phrase before he turned his back and walked away. I felt a flush of shame. How, in my sentimentality, could I have forgotten who this man really was?

The next afternoon, Jerry, Aunt Bunny, my father, and I watched the Yankees slip by the Giants, 3–2. It was an intense duel, ex-White Sox ace Billy Pierce matching Stafford with shutout innings until Roger Maris' crowd-erupting two-run single in the seventh. I stood and added my voice to the din. Stafford lost his shutout in the ninth on a sudden Ed Bailey poke into the right-field stands, but he got the last out on his own and, after the game, we met him by the clubhouse and drove to his home in Rye for a celebration barbecue.

For about five minutes I got to stand beside the Yankee star with my plate. I tried to be cogent as we exchanged prognoses for the rest of the Series. After a bit Billy teased me about my keen interest. "You care more than me 'bout whether we win or lose," he ribbed. "Either way, the season's over next week. Then it's women, not baseball—" checking to make sure his wife was safely out of earshot. (The previous winter when Jerry and I joined him at the Grossinger's bar I had been astonished that Billy didn't know the names of half the players on the Kansas City team. "But I can recognize them," he contended, "and that's all they pay me to do.")

I watched the seventh game of that Series in the basement of Mientka's TV repair shop in the village of Amherst, my brain a nubbin as I paced out Willie McCovey's ninth-inning at-bat (which would end in a terrifying line-drive out—the tying and winning runs on second and third—giving the Yankees a 1–0 win). I jumped with clenched fists and raced onto the street. But I was alone. There was no evidence of a climax anywhere in this Hawthorne landscape. Ringing with pride in my team, I headed back to James to do my evening's math and write my English paper.

Northern autumn came abruptly, blood-red and orange leaves, squirrels burying nuts on the quad. Nightfall began in late afternoon. Early snows covered it all. I sat in my room Friday evenings, singing along with the record player—sweet Johnny Horton, dead in a plane crash back when I was still at P.S. 6:

> *"Today I'm so weary,*
> *Toda-ay I'm so blue,*
> *Sad and broken-hearted,*
> *And it's all because of you. . . ."*

I'd turn the pages of my album through pictures of the summer and lie in bed waiting to fall asleep, imagining Betsy leaving Bob and suddenly showing up in Amherst, running across a snowy quad to meet me after class. She had a twinkle in her eye and a welcome heart as we hugged, oblivious to the crowds. She'd tell me she was escaping the madness of Miami Beach. We'd move into the village and make our home in one of those old cottages on Pleasant Street. In the end I settled for mailing her an Amherst sweater with a big felt "A."

On Saturdays the dorm floor turned into a nightclub—speakers in the hallway, replacement red bulbs in the ceiling sockets, guys carrying beer mugs, girls in purple-and-white Amherst scarves.... I sat in the sanctuary of my room, dialing in Ranger games from the scrambled airwaves, writing my stories, playing my records:

> *"Life was so sweet, dear,*
> *Li-ife was a song.*
> *Now you've gone and left me,*
> *Oh whe-ere do I belong...?"*

I did homework mechanically and tried to grasp the deeper intentions of my courses. Since there were none of the usual sorts of yardsticks (like how many details I memorized and regurgitated on exams), it was hard for me to gauge from week to week how my teachers thought I was doing. I was surprised to get Cs in history and philosophy and Ds in physics and math. I did well in only two courses: Humanities (in which we read and discussed Greek and Roman classics), and English (in which I was awarded one of the only two As among the entire freshman class). But then I was a pro: I had already written narratives that served for most of the assignments. In fact, many of the dialogues between me and Dr. Friend (written immediately after sessions) served as complete papers with only a paragraph or two of exegesis. I had always known that my past changed as I changed, that there was more than one truth.

My professor, Leo Marx (a renowned faculty member who didn't usually teach freshman English), was charmed by my blend of storytelling and psychological insights, though he warned me (in red) that mere psychotherapeutic interpretation had the effect of freezing events and oversimplifying them. He also chided me on sentimentalizing. Yet he thought my ideas were interesting enough to invite me regularly to dinner, a rare privilege for a freshman. I sat with him, his wife, and their son and daughter, and told stories about life in the dorms.

Professor Marx divulged the inner workings of Amherst. He and many of the other faculty were opposed to the fraternity tenor of campus life, and he appreciated getting my reports as ammunition for meetings. He also advised me on the correct approach to a writing career by recounting the literary paths of famous novelists he knew personally—James Baldwin, Norman Mailer, Saul Bellow. He did not think Robert Penn Warren was of a quality I should imitate. "A poet maybe, but he writes those damn novels just to make money." I felt quite deflated.

Every couple of weeks the Marxes invited me back. Their long hardwood dinner table and fancy silverware were an Ivy League replica of Abbey and Dorey's cabin at Chipinaw, and I felt the caution of an iconic presence. I ate slowly and courteously and tried to speak well.

Marx loved fireworks, so he'd invariably throw out challenges. An initial quiet round of melon before soup would turn into a rousing debate by apple pie. If he was the famous scholar and philosopher, I was his renegade disciple. Even as he routinely railed against my notions of mysticism (which he considered "ridiculous") and my associations with Grossinger's and baseball, he continued to praise almost every paper I wrote, and he went into generous detail when he criticized me.

Then—after years of false alarms and reprieves (and just when I had stupidly taken my guard off it)—the bomb was center stage again. Nuclear weapons were threatening to destroy the world. The Russians had assembled an arsenal of rockets in Cuba; additional Soviet ships were headed there. American destroyers awaited them in a blockade. There was no diplomatic way out. Though they would not target Amherst, I knew the sky itself would ignite and radiation would blow in with winter squalls. We would be dying on campus, amidst the "millions who . . . crawl the ashened Earth/Their flesh a ragged shroud around them"; so the old scientist screamed in *Night of the Auk*. Yet life at Amherst went on absurdly oblivious to holocaust. Sid was mainly obsessed with the fact that he hadn't made love to Barb or, for that matter, anyone. Al tried to convince him that it no longer made any difference, but his roommate was inconsolable (though in a comic way that didn't seem to take the threat seriously).

I poured my anguish into a poem:

> If they bomb,
> I will be lost
> in a frightened puff of smoke,
> my head whirling
> with questions about the stars,
> my mind fighting off visions

of its own burning vitals,
its own roast nothingness,
lying in a heap of blackbones....

My heart is sorry
knowing that
no more will the strawberry girl
give her first kiss
to the rusty boy.

One button
will still the sound
of every mandolin,
will fry the dream of love
into pale cold vapors....

If they bomb,
your violin of brown hair
will turn to straw
and blow as ashes in the wind.
Your wee eyes will melt
into eye juice, dripping
into the random mold of the ground.

The algaed pond will
snap, crackle, and pop
for centuries.
Clouds will sparkle
with strange water.
The land will phosphor
with electric dew.
And Orion will lonely pace
the heavens.

As the rendezvous approached, I felt desperate and powerless. Ancient ghosts stalked the planet. Not only was my personal being at stake but the meaning of all that had ever been. The life I had mustered these many years was forfeit, and ultimate Color War, with its rabid generals, was about to reign forever. I wanted to escape, but there was no place to run. I called my parents. Bob bargained well with Armageddon: "Don't be ridiculous. They're politicians, not madmen." I felt oddly reassured.

When the hour of the converging ships was at hand I went dutifully to the holocaust in philosophy (as everyone else in the class did). Professor Epstein opened by asking, "What is the most important thing to do now if this is truly the end of the world?" A titter crossed the room, but he deflected that with a confident smile.

He was maddening to me. Throughout that term I had summoned up all of my nonexistent psychic powers to try to make the overhead light—still glowing—descend from its socket to just above his head, to force him to give it one of his pat interpretations.

"I know what you're all thinking. You want to run over to Smith, right? Well, I believe we should spend our last hour doing the thing that makes us most human, that allows us to experience the highest form our species has attained—the philosophical discussion." Then he proceeded to conduct a normal class on the world-view of Peirce.

I kept glancing at the clock, the minute hand ... then the seconds ... five, four, three ... right through the assignation of ships. Class ended, and the ordinary world proved ordinary again. We had been living on borrowed time since Los Alamos anyway, and the real danger was probably buried so deep below headlines we would be oblivious when it came.

All autumn in physical education we were cudgelled through daily rounds on an obstacle course at the edge of the playing fields—a series of ropes to climb, bars to swing along, and hurdles to dive under. Some classmates mastered it and passed on, but most of us were left in our Amherst sweats, waiting in line to squirm through a tire and climb a fence, frost sticking to blades of grass pressed under our hands. Just when I had given up hope (the coach had said, "None of you get out of here alive!") we were set free unconditionally. I signed up for ice hockey and three times a week scrimmaged.

Amherst P.E. hockey was a rowdy affair, bearing little resemblance to the pond matches of high school. There were real nets and refs. I wore kneepads and a helmet, and every time I had the puck kids poked and pushed at me. I scored my first goal on a deflection through skates, raised my stick in pure ecstasy, and went to lunch ruddy and elated.

I suddenly adored being at Amherst—the snacks of french fries and creamy frappes (called milkshakes in New York), late hours in the reserve reading room, carting my clothes in a bag to the coin laundry, the quaint shops in town with proprietors who befriended me, my colorful hockey garb, Al and Sid and the gang at dinner. A sense of deeper alienation came on only gradually and unacknowledged.

Weekends were the hardest. The partying on the dorm floor got louder and wilder each week, with music and drinking starting as soon as Friday classes came to an end. I remember, prototypically, a kid named Jynx twisting up and down the hallway, whooping, shot glass in hand, to the big-band sound of Buddy Greco, *"This could be the start of something big!"*

Girls arrived from Smith and Holyoke, dressed in evening coats— and with them a female laughter and perfume. I sat in my room listening to the Rangers at Montreal, a staccato of rushes up and down the rink. The stridency of the "announcer" had kept me company all my life, meeting my hunger for cruciality with his own; now I clung to him for solace.

One evening there was a strip show with theme music and hoots, underwear and bras tossed into the hallway. I couldn't decide, even as in simpler times at Orenda, whether the girls were the guys' victims or their collaborators and counterparts. When I caught glimpses of their impassive, sad faces in the hours past curfew I felt an overwhelming sympathy, for they were drunk and helpless as they fought off (or hung onto) guys. Yet I was heir to the dilemma of Jeremiah Beaumont (in Robert Penn Warren's *World Enough and Time*), as he stared at a picture of a young martyr tied to a post. Sometimes he fancied he might seize her from the fire (and from the crowds cheering her agony); other times he imagined jumping in and perishing beside her. There were also times he imagined himself among those who bore the torches. I was overwhelmed by these same conflicting emotions—wanting to be one of the guys, hating them for who they were, and identifying more with female gentleness (however inaccessible it was to me).

The next morning James Hall sexual successes were scored on bathroom doors. First names of girls were listed in a vertical column alongside which guys put their initials or insignias and deeds. I hardly knew what to believe. The world around me was receding at light speed with consequences I chose to ignore. Leo Marx was appalled, but he applauded my isolation and tone of censure. Would that it had been that simple.

At vacation Ray the driver came to transport me to Grossinger's. It was an alienated Christmas that prophetically picked up the themes of Jeremiah Beaumont and James Hall. Donning the prestige of my purple Amherst jacket, I went to the Nightwatch where I discovered, pursued, and befriended a girl from New Haven named Mackey who turned every guy's head. She had a wiry body and seductive eyes, dressed in black silk ("no underclothes," boasted an older college kid who danced with her), smelled like mint and leather, and turned down my New Year's Eve offer: "Sorry. I'm gonna go to New York, find me a corner, and get drunk."

Back at college I sank into the quarantine of Ethan Frome winter. Coursework was meaningless beside the unplumbed turmoil in my soul. Math and physics had become little more than another obstacle course. The teachers seemed to delight in creating trivial quandaries and challenges. I felt estranged from their self-satirical egos—they were so witty and clever. Science had once been a viable alternative to writing and English for me—even a possible career, but I didn't experience the Amherst version as science; it was more like one-upmanship in which we tried to outsmart Newton and Galileo, in which Amherst men pretended to reinvent the laws of physics and were applauded for style more than substance. Even the lab atmosphere was smug and quippy (with members of the football team constantly forwarded as heroes to demonstrate laws of nature). My physics teacher ignited the homecoming bonfire with a Rube Goldberg-like contraption. I felt school spirit being shoved down my throat, so I stopped going to either math or physics and fell so far behind I was in no position to pass.

Amherst didn't have any Murphies or Metcalfs or Waldmans. My math and physics teachers were military commanders, and my rotating batch of history and humanities profs were young, erudite, and cynical. One of them responded to any astute or profound questions with lines like "I guess I just don't know that one" and "You've stumped me. Next?" We read Sophocles, Herodotus, Nietzsche, Peirce, Aquinas, Hume, and dissected their sentences and exposed them. There seemed a requisite hipness to all our discourse ("fine, fine, fine"—pronounced with breezy, detached enthusiasm). Everyone was smug and aloof. My classmates prepared to be doctors proficiently, played hockey proficiently, dated proficiently; were basic good guys. Amherst even had its own self-mocking slogan—"cowboy cool"—to set against Harvard's pretext of scholarship; fancy cowboy hats were favorite campus garb (though one upperclassman went through the day in monk's robes and sash carrying a giant flag—a lion's crest—of one of the German duchies).

Horace Mann had been a world of political passion and intellectual competition. Amherst was not even intellectual. Except for Professor Marx, none of my teachers showed enthusiasm for ideas; discussions were mere semantic hairsplitting. My wordy contributions were either critiqued or ignored. I had a few buddies—Marx of course, the poet Al, the guy whose room was trashed (Marshall), plus a small gang of politicos from Stearns Hall. But my friends and I were united mainly by our vague, unresolved resistance to the monolith. We called it "elitism," "jockdom," "anti-intellectualism," but we didn't have much confidence in our position. And I was the only one cutting class.

I no longer knew what I wanted to happen. At times I simply pined for Betsy; at other times it seemed more important to get out of Amherst, or at least out of James Hall, and become a full-fledged writer. It was the thing I did best, the main activity that sustained me. I also longed for the spirit of a collegium—something like the hours with Waldman and Stein, discussions of tarot and poetry, even Murphy's obscene zeal. One Saturday in disgust I wrote a description of the party down the hall; later I named my piece "Elmer the Cow" and sent it to the *Amherst Literary Magazine*. My title was a synthesis of "Elmer's Glue" and Eeyore the donkey, snow piled on his back (in *Winnie the Pooh*) because he had no home—a fusion of self-pity and rebellion:

> I went to the window, opened it, grasped the fluffy cold from the sill, and squeezed it into nothing in my hand. I looked straight down at a steaming drain-pipe, up at the hurried snow falling from heaven-black, out at where I knew the mountains and stars to be.
>
> The music droned and twanged in the hall, and I opened my door. I was looking at a messy-haired girl and a smooth-haired drunk boy. He had her pinned against the wall....
>
> My friend, I hate to be bitter, but Amherst was a snowdrift, doused in whiskey, beer, and perfume—smeared with lines of red lipstick

and broken brown glass, melting into a river of mud—clogging the delta into the great and endless sea (where a rowboat waits for me).

To my amazement, it was published. The day it appeared I found a copy nailed to my door, obscenities scrawled across it.

The janitors must have reported the condition of the bathroom doors to the administration because in early February a maintenance crew replaced the heavily illustrated scorecards with coated formica difficult to mark. The only one around at the time, I felt a manic glee watching the relics being hauled off. The moment called for action!

With a bunch of felt pens I quickly covered the new doors with grade-school pictures: penguins with party hats blowing horns, baby animals. For some reason I imagined no one would know who had done it.

That evening a committee of almost a dozen from down the hall appeared at my door and ordered me out of my room into the johns, where they presented me with Ajax and paper towels and told me not to leave until "every surface—every single one—is unblemished."

"Can't you let the school give us nice new doors without polluting them with your porn," chided Jynx.

Chastened by such a quick reprisal and truly frightened by a mob of adversaries, I worked assiduously for an hour, scrubbing the drawings fainter and fainter until they finally dwindled into pale scoured spots. As an inspection crew approved my work, I stood there trying to look contrite.

I skulked away and closed my door. The knob came off in my hand. My mind raced, sorting details, strategies: it had been rigged! I was locked in.

I looked hastily about and promised myself not to panic. A crowd gathered and began pounding my door and taunting. I felt strangely detached. The person they were assaulting *was* an asshole; he deserved it. I sat on the bed dazed, fascinated. Their epithets had no meaning; they were like the roar of a distant crowd.

Then a liquid began to flow under the door into the room. Before I had a chance to think what it was—lighter fluid! A curtain of flame shot up. I told myself that this was just part of the prank, that I still wasn't afraid. I opened the window to get rid of the smoke.

At windows elsewhere in James, kids from my floor had assumed positions and were chanting for me to jump. I felt a wild surge, like my fury toward Jonny during our fights, but there was no way to get at them. I looked for a weapon and found only my hockey stick. Good enough! Leaning out the window as far as I could I swung away, whacking at those taunting me, driving them back inside, busting windows. The feeling and sound of the glass was gratifying, but the world remained insensate. I could hear, as if faraway, Al and Sid arguing with the crowd. There was shoving and harsh words, and finally they crashed in, pulled me out, and led me down the hall to their room. I sat there in a kind of shock.

The next morning Dean Esty summoned me to his office. He had a one-sided version of the event and didn't want to hear another. He told me that I would be billed for the broken windows and that I was now on probation.

Back at the dorms word had spread, and a group from Stearns came that evening in support. When I recounted my penalties, to a one they thought I should fight back: "Those guys are football players, alumni brats; they do all that shit, and you get blamed." They told me that a lot of freshmen were on my side, and there were even upperclassmen who had heard about me and were angry. They offered to circulate a petition to get me off probation.

I was grateful for their company, but I shook my head. I was no hero; I was only crazy dumb Richard from the Martha and Bob Towers household: a jerk who had gotten his due. I had been wandering in a trance almost forever. The curses and flames, the broken glass, had woken me at last. I had no one to blame for my predicament. The dreams of Betsy and tales of Elmer the Cow were absurd, self-aggrandizing sentimentalities. They weren't who I was.

I declined their invitations to leave James; I rejected the idea of the petition. I remained in my room, isolate and repentant, wanting to feel what was happening to me. I was poised at last, ready to act.

There was one consequence of the mayhem I didn't hear about for twenty-one years, which is how long it took me to return to Horace Mann after the 1962 World Series.

Mr. Murphy was still there. When I was a student of his I thought of him as an old man. Yet, after two entire decades, he was young again. He welcomed me with tenderness and observable joy. At lunch we talked about the years gone by.

"Do you remember when you were locked in your room freshman year at Amherst and it was set on fire?" he asked abruptly.

"You knew about that?" I said, astonished.

"Knew about it? Dean Wilson at Admissions had the gall to call us up and complain about our recommending you. I gave him some choice words. His ears were burning."

Tears formed at the corners of my eyes. They had known? They had been my supporters? Horace Mann, in all its years of silence and rigor? "I was pretty crazy then," I admitted, "and I brought it on myself, but still, locking me in the room and setting it on fire—"

"Those prep school sadists. I know the quality of human being. I told Dean Wilson that. I shoved his piety right back up his ass."

In the spring I applied to both the University of California in Berkeley and Swarthmore as a transfer student. In April I took the bus down to Philadelphia to visit my true first choice. Blossoms were already on the trees, and boys and girls sat studying on the lawns. Compared to Amherst, this looked like paradise.

The Director of Admissions was blunt. "Your grades don't merit a transfer, and you're on probation. In any case, we consider Amherst the model of what we'd like Swarthmore to be."

In little more than a semester I had squandered six years of work.

On my way back north I stopped in New York, defeated. I went to my mother for sympathy. She sat in her bedroom as I will always remember her—by the window with her reflector, looking away from me into the sacred sun. She told me that I was missing classes, to go back to school. She didn't put down her reflector. She didn't want to look at me again until I got myself straightened out. She had had enough of my nonsense. My performance, she said, was an embarrassment both to her and to Horace Mann.

Math and physics were a lost cause. But otherwise I did the work and kept up the façade. I also tried out for freshman baseball, which meant practicing indoors in the Cage, carrying out drills and exercises in greenhouse air. I participated in long sequences with two other short-stops, fielding successive grounders and firing across the sod to first. Baseball had suddenly become as grueling and vacuous as math-physics. I was good enough to be on the field with them but not good enough to start. They wouldn't let me play in the outfield because they had too many stars out there, so one afternoon I gave up a career of com-petitive hardball going back to first grade. "You're quitting!" the coach snapped when I told him I wanted to switch to intramural softball; he insisted on hearing those words from me before he would sign my release.

"Okay, I'm quitting!"

But games were fun again. I played center, ran the bases with aban-don, made catches that had people shaking my hand at lunch, and even hit three home runs. I finally got to come down from a higher league!

That spring Leo Marx took me to lunch at the Lord Jeff Inn with a friend of his from New York: Catherine Carver, a senior editor at Viking Press. He had warned me ahead of time that she was exceptionally prominent, having worked with many famous novelists, including Saul Bellow. Her willingness to meet me just on the basis of the few papers he had sent her was itself a honor. A slight, dignified woman with a mannered voice, she skimmed through the high-school novel I now called *Salty and Sandy*. Continuing to peruse it during dessert and coffee, she asked for my car-bon to take back to New York. A week later she wrote:

> This is just to say how very glad I am to have seen you, and read some of your manuscript, on Monday. As I told you then, I think what you've written is clear evidence that you are going to be a writer; and although I can't say until I read all of it how much work this book is going to require before it can be published, I am cer-tain that there is a novel in those 600 pages.... Even the roughest of them has a quality of expressiveness that is very much your own; I am most hopeful about your future in this line of work—as you should be.

For the remaining weeks of the spring term I nurtured those words as my destiny. I had no intention of ever returning to Amherst. The day before I left for Grossinger's I received Miss Carver's special-delivery packet with section-by-section instructions for turning my book into a publishable novel. This was real! And I had a whole summer coming up at Grossinger's.

My father dismissed my scheme within thirty seconds. "You're living in my house; you work for me." As far back as the discussions about my going to Horace Mann, he had looked down on my following intellectual and artistic pursuits, but I had assumed the importance of Viking would transcend all such objections and he would recognize I was a true writer.

"You can't just study. You've got to prepare for life."

"But writing *is* a job. It isn't school."

"It's too competitive a field. You'll never make it."

I had waited all my life for him, and now . . . who was he? Expecting me to begin my hotel training at once, he had made up his mind that I would enter the bureaucracy at his own first job: assistant dead-letter clerk. Debate was pointless; he was presenting a *fait accompli*.

With Michael and James at camp and Jerry upstate with his family, the house was quite empty and I inherited Jerry's small room on the third floor next door to Emma. A large elderly black woman from Carolina, she had worked for Aunt Bunny's parents for three decades, and now had come out of retirement to help prepare meals and plan cocktail parties. (She called Hotel maids to do any serious cleaning and spent much of each day in her room watching TV—she never missed a Mets game.)

Major-league baseball had receded from me that spring in the ordeal of Amherst, but I lay on the floor of Emma's room many an afternoon and evening, watching the poor early Mets with their endless motley procession of new hopefuls while, sitting up in the bed without her wig, she moaned, hooted, clapped, and did her knitting. It was as good ballgame company as I had ever had.

The elderly woman who ran the mail room was assigned to train me. She spelled out the dreary parameters the first morning. I was expected to sit at a desk the entire day logging undeliverable letters in a ledger. Since the Hotel was a transient place, there were hundreds of such items: for guests who had left; staff who had been fired or quit, or never came; one-night-stand entertainers; even celebrities who hadn't been there for years.

After a few days it was clear that the only functional part of the job was re-addressing mail to those few who had actually left forwarding addresses. With an alphabetical list to consult and update, that took an hour, maybe two. The other six hours were spent going through ancient filing cabinets trying to match the names on envelopes to anything at all. In one full week we didn't find a single match; yet my supervisor thought it made sense to spend as much as half an hour trying to locate a staff member from ten years earlier—to forward a card that said: "Greetings from Tennessee" on both sides. Ultimately all this mail ended up in dead-letter boxes, the log books themselves piled in similar cartons, sealed, and stored. I explained the predicament to my father, expecting him to see that the job was a waste of time not only for me but anyone. He shook his head adamantly: "You'll learn discipline. And it's where I began."

My next ploy was to have Catherine Carver write him a cheery letter, but that had no effect either. "If she wants you to work for her, let her pay you."

By the second week I was no longer under direct supervision, so I took to throwing more and more of the unforwardable items into the dead-letter box without checking the files. Finally, I tossed all of them. By the third week I had stopped entering any letters into the ledger. I would finish after an hour and sneak back to the house to write. Aunt Bunny and Emma were my lookouts. If my father came home from work to watch television (as he did at some point almost every day), they alerted me and created a diversion so I could leave by the fire escape.

At Catherine Carver's suggestion I worked only part-time on *Salty and Sandy,* while beginning a new, more traditional novel *The Moon.* My characters were based on people from Amherst and the teen tour, with each chapter from the viewpoint of a different person. Every fifth chapter (assigned to "The Moon") was conceived as the mind-flow of a cosmic being.

Living at Grossinger's was the fulfillment of my oldest conscious fantasy and, although the experience wasn't what I once imagined, it was bounteous enough. During weekends I would haul my typewriter, a few makeshift paperweights, and a stack of paper to the family cabana at the pool and write sections of my books, taking occasional breaks to swim and talk to the other authors. For several mornings I typed next to playwright Paddy Chayefsky at the adjacent cabana. At one point he looked over my shoulder and pointed out false lines in my dialogue.

Aunt Bunny and I had plenty of time together, so we chatted like magpies, day and night, an intimacy my father barely tolerated. Seeing the two of us together he would snarl, "Richard, fix me a Coke on ice." I would stomp into the kitchen, prepare it, and set it beside him. Without a thank you he would bark the next order: "Go to the Hotel and pick up the evening papers and my crossword puzzle book."

Aunt Bunny had her own clan of friends, including journalists, quasi-sociologists, movie directors, pop singers—different adults who came and went all summer. I hung around with them, reading their fortunes and discussing politics and literature.

While I was passing through one of Grandma Jennie's parties early that July, who should appear but Milton Blackstone. He had recently startled the world by marrying late in life, and he was chaperoning two girls my age: one his new stepdaughter, the other her friend, a blond beauty-pageant winner from Miami Beach. In presenting her to Jennie, Milton explained that she had ambitions to be a singer and had come to Grossinger's hoping to be discovered; he reminded everyone (unnecessarily) that he had discovered Eddie Fisher here as a singing busboy.

After introductions the two girls chatted with me and, when Milton and his family departed, Rhonda and I were left standing together.

She wasn't a type I admired, but she was a striking woman, a *bona fide* starlet and beauty queen. At first, I treated her as an honorary adult, a celebrity unconnected to my own adolescence. I did ask one obvious question. And, yes, of course she knew Betsy—she knew both Betsy and Brian; Brian was a real close friend of her own boyfriend Spike. We continued the conversation through dinner at the family table, where she recounted the series of events that led her to the Hotel. (Unfortunately, Milton was no longer in the talent business, and the best that he could do for her was a job as assistant teen hostess and occasional stints with the band.) She didn't seem to notice that I was a pariah with girls, for after she got a room in staff quarters she called me daily and we began to see each other in the evenings.

I was amazed at our sudden exclusive companionship, but I rationalized it: she was ambitious; I was Jennie's grandson; and since she had a boyfriend back home, I was a good foil to keep other men away.

Rhonda dressed flashily: bright lipstick, loud blouses, high heels, lots of perfume. She was quite sexy in her lowcut dresses, throwing rehearsed smiles. But she wasn't magical to me; she was another melodramatic Jewish girl, a clever hustler. There was no enigma to her; ambition was always on the tip of her tongue. She equated my writing with her singing and considered us both talented teenagers waiting for the big break. Up in my room she would sit on the bed, I on the chair, and I would read her safe parts of both books, after which she would sing rock and roll. As I stared at this amazing-looking girl on my bed styling love songs *a cappella* and flashing the most fullsome look, I thought how she would have been a knockout on fourth-floor James!

Rhonda loved to review the precise parameters of our relationship: we were buddies, "platonic friends," not romantic partners. All the while she encouraged me to have hope for Betsy; in fact, one night she told me she was going to give me a present. She smiled coyly and then said, "Betsy and Brian are no longer going together." I knew from Betsy only that she was off to the University of Colorado in the fall. The news of her separation from Brian was a major omen, but I had no idea what to do with it.

That evening after dinner, as Rhonda and I were walking to the Lake, she stopped and kissed me on the lips before I could even think. "Don't you know what that is?" she said. "It's a pedillo."

I stared blankly.

A car wound around the crooked road and came toward us in the distance. "Only one headlight means—kiss your partner."

It was my first kiss.

The summer took on a pleasant dailiness, Rhonda and I enacting our non-romance night after night: in the bar, at movies in town, sitting in chaises at the cabana by the empty pool under stars, holding hands at the Lake. I played softball with the staff team, wrote new chapters and, slipping into my father's office at night, called Catherine Carver on the New York line.

"Exciting stuff," she said in praise of *The Moon*.

When Grandma Jennie got me a bike I raced childlike along Hotel paths, back and forth between my job and writing, the baseball field and dates with Rhonda.

I remember the evening Rhonda came to cheer for me at a game against another hotel. She was wearing an enormous panama with a pineapple on top of it and a dancer on top of the pineapple. Everyone stared, and some waiters whistled. Caught between secret pleasure and blushing I dove for a grounder down the line, trapped it in the webbing, and threw from my knees with all my might to first.

Late in July I got my grades in the mail: As in English and humanities, which, combined with my complete failure of math and physics, pulled me barely up into the Ds. The University of California wrote that my grade point average did not allow admission as a transfer student. Meanwhile, Amherst wasn't giving me up easily. A letter from the academic dean indicated that I could re-enroll for sophomore year, as long as I made up lost credits. New England suddenly looked friendly and tame, and I began to accept—and even look forward to—returning.

Aunt Bunny took off to visit her parents for a stretch in early August, and the next afternoon I came home to what appeared to be an empty house (except for Emma and the Mets upstairs). I was startled when my father shouted for me from the back porch, a place used mostly for storage. I opened the door to see his substantial bulk draped over a very young woman on the couch. As she raised herself I saw she was short, busty, and very made up. He had a broad guilty smile. "I just wanted you to know where I was," he said disingenuously.

Later that week he chose to pursue the subject he felt he had introduced. He wanted to know if I had slept with Rhonda yet. His fervor disgusted me, and I told him that she was just a friend.

"Let me tell you something, Richard; they're always your girlfriend when they hang around you. It doesn't matter why. Maybe she thinks you'll get her a break in show business; maybe she thinks she'll marry into this Hotel. You know you're not going to marry her. So why not get some experience. Just don't get her pregnant. And if you do, tell me, and I'll pay for an abortion."

"I don't think any of that is going to happen."

He wasn't listening. He told me how many different girls he had screwed in college. Then he said abruptly: "I think you need to get laid. I know some models, real high-class Rheingold girls." He smirked. "You tell me when you're ready, and I'll make the arrangements."

"How could you think I'd want that?"

"What are you—different from everyone else?"

We stood there, locked in mutual intransigence. He wasn't that far removed from the guys who had locked me in my room. When I was a child I could simply admire him and enjoy his company. Now, although he wouldn't have said it that way, he wanted my soul.

My rejection set a wall between us. His glances became always harsh and disapproving. I wondered if he knew about my truancy from the mail room. Once again, I was an enemy in a household.

Perhaps, years ago in their warnings, my mother and Bob had not been so wrong!

In past vacations I made friends with a disc jockey from Hartford named Gene Kaye and, when he arrived to host the big summer dance, I told him about Rhonda.

"So the kid wants an audition, right?"

I nodded.

"No big deal. Out of friendship for you, my man, and out of respect for your family who has done so many fine things for me, say no more."

The following weekend I sat in the back of the Terrace Room with Gene and his "buddy from the business" while Rhonda went through her set with a makeshift band. The guy thought she was fantastic and arranged for her to go to New York to cut a demo; he even gave her a new name: Francine Debois. "You found me my own Catherine Carver," she declared, hugging me with unabashed delight.

Late one afternoon I got a phone call from the highway outside the Hotel. Jay and Barry were passing through. I tore down the hill to greet them. They pummelled me delightedly as I slid in the back of their car; then Jay drove us along the backroads by Chipinaw. "You realize this is it," he cautioned. "Our families are at war. We probably won't see each other too much for a while. But I want you to know you're still my cousin and I love you."

I shifted awkwardly and said, as best I could, that I loved him too.

"It's terrible to admit this, but your grandparents and your father and aunt are common thieves. Do you think it's fair that they make all the decisions when we own shares?"

"No. They imagine they built the place and that your family is just taking advantage of the way the will was written."

"Do you agree?"

I shook my head.

"I feel sorry for you," he said. "Your parents are stupid and greedy. My mother and father want to preserve the fortune; they care about their kids. Your parents, if you don't mind the expression"—and he looked at me with a probing grin—"are idiots." We all burst out laughing. Then they left me back at the bottom of the hill. It was a decade before I saw either of them again.

On the evening of Betsy's birthday, Rhonda and I dialed her on my father's speaker phone. "Hello, guess who? I'm at Grossinger's. You know me, still trying to become a star. And guess who got me the big audition?" Before Betsy could answer I said hello.

"It's so nice to hear your voice after all those great letters," she said with her usual grace. Whatever else she was or wasn't, she was clear as a bell. I told her I had decided to stay at Amherst, and she thought that was the right decision. Then she said excitedly that she had pledged a sorority at Boulder before entering. I didn't grasp the importance of that, so I told her I was sorry to hear about Brian. She said, yes, she was terribly sad and hoped someday they would get back together because they had something special.

Afterwards Rhonda, full of excitement, was telling silly stories about Miami Beach, ostensibly because they involved Betsy in some manner. I was focused and sullen, which stopped her. We climbed the stairs to my room. I set myself against the backboard of the bed, and she surprised me by getting on the bed too, then leaning against me.

"I want you to hug me the way Spike does," she proposed, arranging herself at an angle so that her head fell back against my chin, my arm around her belly. We sat there quietly like that for a long time. I kissed her neck and moved my arm, but she stilled me.

"I saw the way you lit up when you talked to Betsy. I'm jealous even though you're not my boyfriend. I'm used to thinking I'm the one boys chase, certainly not Betsy. But I don't want to go any further with you because of Spike."

Still from that evening our relationship was closer; we were *almost* boyfriend and girlfriend. We danced in the nightclub and kissed on her doorstep, and I felt a kind of daily fellowship with her. After my father noticed me dancing with her one evening, he called me into his room past midnight and asked if I had gotten anywhere.

"We're still just good friends."

"You're not the only one."

"What do you mean?"

"She's doubledating you." I had never heard the term. "Don't you know? She's slipping out at night with other guys after you take her home." I shook my head defiantly. "Richard, don't be naive. What she's not giving you she's giving to someone else. She's not the innocent you think."

The next morning I arranged a ride for Rhonda to her demo in New York in the Hotel car. In the evening when she came back she was still flying from the thrill of it, but she said she had to talk to me about something. "Your father was in the car, and he told me, 'Give my son a break.' What did he mean?"

"Goddamn it!" I yelled.

"What?"

"It's not you. It's him. He meant what it sounds like."

"To sleep with you? Who does he think I am?"

"He's a jerk. Just forget him."

But one night that week I sneaked back to the Hotel in dungarees to procure milkshakes for Emma and me as the Mets went into extra innings. I shortcut invisibly through the Terrace Room and was astonished to spy Rhonda dancing with an older guy from the athletic staff. After that I avoided her until she came looking for me.

"I went dancing with a friend," she retorted. "No big deal, huh?"

That's right; no big deal. Betsy was the issue, not Rhonda. My friend

Sandy, the lobby portrait artist, was creating a lifelike pastel from a photograph I took in New Orleans, and I went every day to check on his meager progress (he preferred paying guests, of course). Yet I remembered the feel of Rhonda's body against mine, and I was trapped. I surely couldn't wait for Betsy, but I also couldn't imagine pursuing Rhonda. Go an inch more one way, and I saw my grotesque father grinning at me; go an inch the other, and I had this abstract love for a girl I might never see again.

When Aunt Bunny returned in mid-August I meant only to tell her about my dilemma, but our conversation was never constrained. Soon I found myself recreating the entire scene since she had left. She had surprisingly little concern about Paul's "escort."

"What's one more tramp with him," she sniffed. "It's my kids I care about. I won't permit him to destroy my children. What was he going to do when he took you to the whorehouse anyway, wait outside or go in with you? No, don't tell me, I already know. Well, sex with him is a crock of shit."

Spike arrived the next morning—a surprisingly timid, ungainly chap— to retrieve his girl. They packed his car with her suitcases and drove off together, back to Miami Beach.

Then one afternoon, just before Labor Day, I walked into my father's room. Out of nowhere he slapped me across the face, knocking me to the floor. Then he took a belt and began lashing me with it. I lay there, protecting my head. The pain was incredible, but the shock of it numbed me even more. I didn't believe this was happening—not Uncle Paul from the Penny Arcade! Only when he stopped did I get up. He stood there, breathing heavily, glaring at me with a venom I had never seen. He was a brute of a person, barely in control. "You don't ever go to Aunt Bunny again with stories of me."

As I left the room he shouted after me: "I won't make that offer again, you fag."

Michael and James were just home from camp, and at dinner that night my father was telling silly jokes and playing riddle games with us. We were guessing fruits. He had picked an egg—no wonder no one got it. When we protested it was unfair he said, "Richard should know that one. An egg is the fruit of a hen." Then he gave me a hug as he headed for the living room. "Come watch the Mets try to win one," he said.

As we sat there silently, they did.

I made a copy of my revised *Salty and Sandy* and mailed it off to Catherine Carver. Then, my bike in the trunk, the portrait of Betsy mounted in non-glare glass on the back seat, Ray and I headed out in the Hotel car—Route 52, the Taconic, the Mass Pike, back to Amherst for sophomore year.

2

PHI PSI

In the spring, when I was certain to transfer out, I had gone through the required rushing of fraternities. The way Amherst was organized (to Marx's dismay), there were no social dorms for upperclassmen— no living quarters in which women were allowed without strict curfews. Sophomores, juniors, and seniors who did not live in fraternities got spartan rooms identical to those of freshmen. Although independent organizations, the fraternities served as necessary housing for most of the campus.

Construction had already begun on a complex of social dorms that would alter Amherst forever, but in 1963 most guys disappeared into the system, essentially not to be seen again in daily life except in classrooms and, occasionally, the dining hall. The thirteen fraternities at Amherst were loosely ranked by status, in the minds of the students (if not officially). The top two or three had most of the student leaders, including those who were to become Congressmen, astronauts, chairmen of academic departments, doctors, and corporate executives. Two of the fraternities were "animal houses" (most of the kids from my wing of James ended up at them). The others were more subtly individualized by styles of behavior and regions of the country. One of the houses, Theta Xi, had a reputation as the "nerd house." It pledged selectively but advertised itself as a low-pressure "good guys" environment with inside access to such activities as the radio station and the yearbook.

One fraternity was totally idiosyncratic. Kicked out of its national for admitting a black in the fifties, Phi Alpha Psi subsequently abandoned rushing. There was no pledging—that is, no selective admittance by the brotherhood—only a voluntary sign-up sheet left on a living room table until the quota was reached. More by fortuity than design, Phi Psi became the safety valve of the system, admitting its rebels and outcasts. The membership was a potpourri of rock musicians, poets, political activists, motorcyclists, early conceptual artists and theatrical improvisers, running the gamut from Phi Beta Kappas to the first druggies and hippies of the sixties.

Through the mechanics of rushing, every freshman visited and was shown around each fraternity. Most of my friends either joined Theta Xi or, like Al, went into the dorms; however, Marshall Bloom challenged the system. By forcing a legalistic application of the quota rules he managed to con his way into one of the most prominent houses against their wishes. When I upbraided him, he mocked my parochialism: "Unlike you, I want to challenge the social status assigned to me. I'm interested in real change—in getting at the sources of power, not only here but after Amherst."

I was charmed by Phi Psi, which reminded me of Horace Mann. Since the house was well under its quota I expressed my enthusiasm by joining (despite my application to Berkeley). During the remainder of the spring term I spent many an evening in its public rooms, which were a general hangout for artists, including college dropouts and eccentric recent alumni. Activities ranged from debates about epistemology and campus politics to poetry readings, folk guitars, and string quartets. In fact, the Phi Psi fireplace had appeared in articles in *The New Yorker* and *Playboy* as the site of historic parties. At that time Amherst was still a small rural college town, and there were no other avant-garde institutions or gathering spots, so Phi Psi had developed a reputation in the national underground as a meeting place and hostel.

A three-storey Georgian Collegiate mansion directly across from the Valentine dining halls, Phi Psi included a large field along College Street and a parking lot in back. Down behind the lot was "The Glen," a small patch of remaining forest in a ravine with a stream running through.

The downstairs consisted of two large living rooms, a library, and two private student rooms. The basement was a social quarters with a ping-pong table and makeshift bar (complete with a Budweiser sign plugged in on Saturday nights). The darker rear section had tables and chairs and open space for dancing. The treasurer ordered a keg every weekend. A permanent stale-beer odor prevailed.

Most of the student rooms were on the second floor, including two singles and one big triple with a balcony. The third floor/attic had two real rooms but was mostly gigantic sleeping zones (it was the custom to keep beds out of social rooms so that there would be more space throughout the house). Both sleeping rooms were end-to-end unfinished, unheated sections of attic, rows of beds crossing them, each covered with an electric blanket. Their pale reddish lights dotted the frigid nights.

Phi Psi held only forty permanent residents, so when I realized I was coming back I wrote ahead and was remarkably fortunate to claim the last room on the second floor. I thought I was going to be in it alone, so I arranged it in my style from second-hand stores: a cheap coffee table, a butter churn to keep papers in, and Betsy's portrait on the wall above some ears of decorative maize. Then, just before classes began, a transfer student named Roger showed up out of the blue and joined the House. The verdict of the governing council was that I should share my room with him. A short, husky, Shakespearean with a booming voice, he was appalled at my sense of aesthetics and was piling my belongings in the closet when I laid eyes on him for first time.

"What's going on here!" I demanded.

"Just accommodating my stuff, that's all. You can't take up the whole room."

After we chose halves, he countered my Betsy/butter churn quadrant with a busty Renoir in a gilt frame over a straw hamper containing three bottles of French wine. As he stood there admiring it, I mused about the irony of our forced domicile. We couldn't have been more opposite in style and spirit. Together we bought used desks and a large faded green couch, probably in its twelfth or fifteenth student room.

Those last days before school I spent hours typing away on *The Moon*. Roger stormed in and out of the room in obvious irritation. "This is absurd. You think you can monopolize the space like a private studio."

"I'm finishing a book."

"I'm finishing the great American novel," he mocked.

Then he said he wanted to negotiate for private hours, in particular, Saturday-night use of the space, because, as he put it, "I need to get my social life going."

Since I wasn't dating I granted him the option indefinitely, a munificence I soon regretted, for he arrived early each Saturday with a different nondescript date and locked me out for the remainder of the evening. I sensed the event was usually a failure, for he developed a permanent bad mood. We kept out of each other's way.

Next door was Phil, the president of Phi Psi, a physics major with one of the highest academic averages in the school. He was elegant and handsome, with a bit of the Kennedy look, engaged to a pretty senior from Smith named Ellen. Further down the hall was an intimidating character: a very tall Rasputin-looking junior with fierce eyes and a long beard. Jeff Tripp played the guitar religiously and matched notes with records of Bob Dylan and Dave Van Ronk. His favorite song was "Don't Think Twice, It's All Right," which he sang so often and with such polish that, for a long time, I thought he had written it. I tried to avoid him because he was contentious, but I had a reputation and Roger was the younger brother of a friend of his, so he became an early inspector of our room.

At first he lampooned my reading tastes—Robert Penn Warren; T. H. White, *The Once and Future King;* Hamilton Basso; plus the other decadent American novelists I had picked up through Aunt Bunny and her friends. I was eager to learn, so I didn't defend myself. His chief amusement was to encourage me to confess my recent experiences in pop America. So he heard about Vista Teen Tours and the Nightwatch at Grossinger's and wickedly satirized them. He admired my talent with tarot (bumming a number of fortunes for both him and his girlfriends) and laughed aloud over my story of meeting Paddy Chayefsky. "The cat wrote one good line," he said. Then he performed it in perfect mime: "'I don't hate your father; your father is a *prince* of a man!'"

When, on request, I attempted to construe *The Moon,* I characterized it as being about a town in Florida, using cosmic and unconscious forces to describe inner worlds. Tripp couldn't stop laughing.

"This is the twentieth century, man. Next time someone asks you what your book is about, say it's about sex and death, because those are the only things it could be about and the only things worth writing about. If it's not about them, then it's about avoiding them."

Within a few weeks he had me reading Samuel Beckett and Vladimir Nabokov, as he tried to teach me the difference between sentimental melodrama and the radical modes of perception he saluted in these authors. "They're advertising men you're reading, not artists; they don't know anything about the mysteries." He would intone the word dramatically—"the missss-teries." He was quite committed to the minimalism of *Molloy* and *Malone Dies,* and he loved to burst into my room in odd moments quoting lines that turned the universe upside-down:

"The sun shone, having no alternative, on the nothing new."

"Come on, we'll soon be dead, let's make the most of it. But what matter whether I was born or not, have lived or not, am dead or merely dying, I shall go on doing as I have always done, not knowing what it is I do, nor who I am, nor where I am, nor if I am."

His soliloquies rattling the walls, I sat there in admiration and awe.

"Oh, Grossinger, you're so goddamn young," he said. "You know nothing; I have to teach you everything."

I wondered why he thought I was worth it.

"Yes, a little creature, I shall try and make a little creature, to hold in my arms, a creature in my image, no matter what I say. And seeing what a poor thing I have made, or how like myself, I shall eat it. Then be alone a long time, unhappy, not knowing what my prayer should be nor to whom."

Much of what Jeff taught me was social information: don't chatter; don't tell dumb stories; speak with style . . . just the right amount of irony. When I participated in house meetings he came over afterwards and graded me, telling me what I said that was good and what of it was horseshit. "Jive, man! Don't whimper. When you jive you're as good as anyone here. When you whimper you're fucking Elmer the Cow." He mocked my excitement over Grossinger's—my corny, naive sincerity— and he despised the portrait of Betsy hanging in my room. "You've got this two-bit American cheerleader hanging in a virtual shrine!"

Tripp drove a black Porsche, which was a sacred car in the house lot. He brought back stunning actresses and dancers from Smith, Mount

Holyoke, and even Radcliffe. So far as I knew no one else had ever ridden in the car. Once when Roger asked him for a lift to Mount Holyoke, Jeff stared him down hard: "Look here, man; this buggy is to tote cunt. Got it?" The beginnings of a smile froze on Roger's lips. Then he felt the full rush of shame and slinked away.

One night a bunch of us from the House collected at a table in Valentine where a senior named Dave, who was short on money for the weekend, mused about selling his post-mortem body to a medical school for a couple of hundred dollars. When Tripp challenged him, Dave kept saying, "What's wrong with it. Just tell me what's wrong with it, Jeff."

I waited anxiously for his answer, but he turned to me and said: "My student will respond."

I gulped, my mind raced for a second, and then I said, "Because it's making too big a separation between life and death."

He broke into a big smile, and, putting his arm around my back, said, "Exactly!"

Across the hall from Jeff, in the big triple with the balcony, was a senior named Paul from the Lower East Side. He was no older than me but had gained two years by accelerating through the public schools of the Lower East Side. A lumbering, storklike kid with thick glasses, Paul had no social poise; he was artless and endearing, and he became my best friend. We sat around evenings dialing in WWVA, Wheeling, West Virginia, country-and-western on a giant console I had claimed from the Grossinger's basement. Even Jeff approved of that, joining in on guitar: *"Will the circle be unbroken, bye and bye, Lord. . . ."*

At Phi Psi meetings I debated the stodgy seniors on policy. In imitation of Tripp I challenged bureaucratic protocol by suggesting we scrap our vestigial connection to the fraternity system and go it alone as a fully independent enclave. "We're just a bad imitation Phi Gam," I mocked. The seniors shouted me down, and Tripp strummed his guitar as a strophe between rounds. But I had partial success. Soon the House coffee hour on Thursday nights (at which we provided free doughnuts and beverages) was thrown open to the Amherst community, and we staged forums and poetry readings.

Virtually every night, Paul and I trooped to Valentine together, perfect company for each other on the topic of magical girls and rapacious men. Paul had his own Betsy—a co-ed from Bennington he had met the previous spring break at a work project in Springfield; they had painted the inside of a ghetto house together. Afterwards she had gone out of her way to drive him and a friend back to school. All last summer in New York they dated, but now suddenly she was being pursued by the millionaire heir to a chain of grocery stores. Her latest message to Paul was that their worlds were just too different.

"After all," he said, chuckling, "I'm the son of two people working in the welfare department of New York City, and I was almost tarred and feathered out of college freshman year for distributing *Socialist Worker* pamphlets at dinner. She's aristocracy with a social conscience, slumming."

So I wasn't the only freshman who brought the wrath of jockdom on himself! In fact, it turned out that Paul had heard about my "room burning" and had written a letter to the newspaper accusing Amherst and its faculty of snobbery, hypercriticism, and using its jocks to enforce an oligarchy. I missed that issue, so he pulled it out of a drawer for me. They had titled his column "Wasteland of Hypercriticism?"

Over the following weeks we filled in installments of our lives for each other. With the attentiveness of an Abnormal Psych major he listened to my accounts of my two families, and I interpreted his crises by tarot and dream analysis. When he was about to call his Bennington girl for a date, I suggested he go there by balloon, taking off from the Phi Psi yard, passing over the mountains, landing, visiting, ascending again, and leaving.

"Balloons are cool," he laughed. "I like the idea of going by balloon. Or even better: I could charter a blimp."

When she suggested instead they rejoin the work gang in Springfield and fix some more houses, he was totally deflated. "You did go by balloon," I told him. "Now you're back. Your next move is to hire a private army to storm the grocery chain with bows and arrows and catapults. Phi Psi could provide water-balloon support. We could flood them out."

His roommate Toby thought this was deliriously funny. "I can just picture the ice cream cartons floating down the aisles and everyone looking bewildered. That'd get rid of our turkey image on this campus fast."

Paul and I glanced at each other quizzically. Then he said, "You're pretty good at waking me up and making me look at myself."

"What do you expect?" I half-shouted. "I've been telling myself the same stories all my life. I'd like to send that same army down to Florida when they're done and blast the crystal and formica on Pine Tree Drive into the sea."

After I did a blow-by blow rendering of the summer at Grossinger's, Paul said, "Boy, your father sounds like a real winner. Just the type we imagine running corporations. It's too good to be true."

My buddy came from such a politically active family his parents had subscribed to the *Socialist Worker* his whole life. When he realized I was unsophisticated (if well-intentioned) on global issues, he began feeding me articles about how the U.S. robbed poor nations and oppressed its own lower classes. From friends like Bob Alpert I had some early political instincts, but I had never seen the facts so convincingly put forward. Communist propaganda had always seemed to me simplistic, like a "B" movie, but capitalist propaganda, I now realized, was far more insidious, for capitalism itself was propaganda, and it camouflaged its oppression in the deceptively innocent idioms of "The Free World."

"Of course the Russians fight us differently," Paul said. "They're poor; they have a less developed social system. The proof is in the results: how many fascist dictators do we support? How much of the resources of other nations do we consume through the fraud of a laissez-faire marketplace?"

All of this was spelled out incontrovertibly in issue after issue of the *Worker.*

From my summer at Grossinger's I was ripe for radicalized consciousness. My father had revealed himself as a prototypical capitalist—greedy, contemptuous of others, anti-union. But it wasn't just him. Seemingly the whole generation of my parents were as blind to our exploitation of the goods and labor of defenseless countries as they were to the reality of Hiroshima.

Those first months at Phi Psi changed my sense of the world. I suddenly saw the James Hall raiders, the Miami Beach playboys, and the materialistic and opulent teenagers at Grossinger's as masks of the same nameless conspiracy. Of course I had been uncomfortable all my life. It wasn't just the things Drs. Fabian and Friend had noted. I had been raised in decadence and corruption. My parents, my counselors, my bunkmates, even most of my friends were mindless oppressors of the poor and disenfranchised.

I was beginning to see beyond magic and symbolism, beyond Grossinger's as a fallback identity. I sensed something new, though it would be years before I gave it a name: our lives mattered! They weren't just foils for doctors or riddles with clues. They mattered for themselves.

As I began to speak out, my repertoire became more than pranks and psychological or literary performances. My verbalizing arose from the same place as my writing, except that it was more ideological and communal.

Paul's motto was "the greatest good for the greatest number," and I soon adopted it as my credo for myself. In early October I startled everyone in Phi Psi by proposing that the *whole fraternity* file papers to transfer to Cal/Berkeley as a political statement. I argued so persuasively at a House meeting that Paul and I were put in charge of a steering committee to draft a group letter of application. Most of the members signed it, though mainly as a symbolic gesture against Amherst. It was uncertain that very many would go to California in the unlikely event we were accepted.

Paul and I were intoxicated with our plan. We fantasized an article in *Time* explaining that the artists, writers, musicians, and many of the best students were fed up with Amherst's elitist social system and consumerist education, its gang-rapes and book-burnings.

Tripp was thoroughly disgusted with me. "It's bullshit . . . the wrong issue. You don't want to have to do with *any* college. Why draw the line at Amherst?"

But I was stubborn and zealous. I even took the dramatic step of requesting to make a farewell speech in Chapel. (The required morning chapels, like those at Horace Mann, were not religious services, but occasions for the school to gather and hear speakers of different persuasions, as at a New England town meeting.) When my time came I stood behind the podium and, with my new gumption, attacked the whole "cowboy cool" system in front of President Plimpton, the faculty, and the students.

In retrospect, my speech reads like the liberal clichés and adolescent utopianism of my generation—a disappointment to my memory of the force I felt running through me at that time (the sentiments were far less heartfelt and individual than those I expressed at Horace Mann). I thought of myself as awakened, liberated, no longer "Elmer the Cow"—a spokesman for the masses. I satirized Amherst's phony critical intelligence, the gentleman jocks, whom I characterized as provincial, anti-intellectual, anti-women, contributing ultimately to rape and war. I contrasted this milieu to Horace Mann, where Bob Alpert stood against the war-makers and Murphy and Waldman directed our attention to the veil of life and death. Then I invoked Swarthmore, where, I said, with stagey elegance, "girls and boys sat under trees dropping flower petals into one another's philosophy books." I closed by quoting the dying Malone.

At the time, the speech was well received. Marshall Bloom even printed up a version of it and distributed it on campus. Soon after, President Plimpton invited me into his office to discuss it. He said that I raised a number of good points, ones that were being considered by the administration, and he hoped I would stay and contribute to the change. He thought it would be character-building, and he offered his assistance.

"My office is open," he said. "Just come by."

I thanked him, but I imagined then that I had an appointment with destiny. I never pictured what it would be like to enter a large public university on the other side of the country.

With the freedom to choose my own courses that fall, I had expected things to improve, but Amherst seemed to confound me at every turn. I signed up for creative writing and found myself in a class that so little resembled Mr. Ervin's it might have been on a different planet. It was taught by an aged poet named Rolfe Humphries. He had been Amherst's only football All-American in the early part of the century, and he enjoyed filling the roster with current players because, he said, athletes were the best-disciplined students. Unknown to me before signing up, much of the team was in the course to pick up their gut A. Humphries disliked my work as much as it was possible to dislike anything politely. "You've got a lot of succulent imagery," he mocked, "but I doubt there's any meat on it." Everyone snickered.

After a while I stopped reading my work in class and simply listened to him adulate ballads of the locker room and fine-tune other students' translations of French surrealists.

My Shakespeare teacher, Mr. Baird, was a replica of Mr. Metcalf. At the first class he told us that all students were ignoramuses and he hadn't heard an original idea in forty years. He confined our written assignments to single paragraphs done in class: "The less of your idiocies I have to endure, the less crabby I'll be grading you." When he delegated us passages from *Hamlet* to memorize and then tested us on our recall, I couldn't resist commenting, as I handed in my transcription: "Sorry I didn't think of anything original."

He chased me out of the room with a quavering fist.

My European literature course had a great reading list (Camus, Sartre, Malraux, E. M. Forster), but another arrogant, self-enamored teacher, a younger man named Gutmann, wrote "No!" all over my papers and gave me Ds on every one. My formulations of symbols, cosmic mysteries, and communal justice were rejected in single red slashes, as though no explanation were necessary. Still I refused to tailor my writing to his pedant's notion of sociology and art. Freshman year had burned grade consciousness out of me. I thought of myself as a rebel in search of greater truth. E. M. Forster's soliloquy echoed through my life:

"Only connect! . . . . Only connect the prose and the passion and both will be exalted, and human love will be seen at its height. Live in fragments no longer. Only connect, and the beast and the monk, robbed of the isolation that is life to either, will die."

My other subjects were psychology, geology, and American Studies. Unfortunately, Introductory Psychology had nothing to do with Freud. It was mainly statistical. We read books on sensation, perception, and memory, and, for a term paper, were asked to make up our own personality tests. I devised a scale of "salty," "sandy," and "oinky" and proposed an evolution of individual consciousness straight out of Abraham Maslow (its ninety calibers included amethyst-salty, strawberry-sandy, papoose-oinky, tobacco-saltless, cellophane-sandless, buckle-oinkless, etc.). "On to the peaks!" was my professor's sole satirical comment.

Geology provided me with primordial images for *The Moon*—prehistoric volcanoes, rivers born in torrents and churning in stone for millennia to form canyons, overflowing their banks and dying into oxbows like the lake in Northampton. The class itself was sterile and formulaic and led only to the science of oil.

At his instigation I had Leo Marx again, this time for American Studies. In his real specialty he was not nearly as receptive to me as in freshman English. He told me, even before the first class meeting, that he wanted me to develop critical faculties this year at the expense, if necessary, of creativity. I handed in my poem "If They Bomb ..." for my assignment when he asked us to describe our political philosophy, but he rejected it ("Political, maybe; philosophy, no!") and asked me to try again. He also preached fervidly against Phi Psi. He had prejudged the fraternity as undisciplined and anarchistic and, after our first conversation, was sure I was being indoctrinated. "Richard, the only place for a serious student is a dorm."

Marx and I had another, more idiosyncratic point of contention. During the summer I had begun corresponding with my former classmate Chuck Stein (now at Columbia), and I was reading the work of his poetic mentor, Charles Olson. Olson was a thorny avant-garde writer. His poems were fields of seemingly discontinuous metaphors, but they had a spirit of bigness and cosmos about them. Chuck had been so taken with them that, during high school, he had actually gone to visit Olson in Gloucester. Back then I wasn't interested. In fact, I had dismissed the poetry as pointless, intentional obfuscating. I was an anti-intellectual baseball fan, spouting pop philosophy and symbolism. Now I was Tripp's disciple, a reader of Beckett, and a recruit in existentialism and beat literature. Discontinuity had become a mark of profundity, magic, and revolution.

I bought Olson's book *The Distances* and used my friend's notes to decipher my way through it. In just the first couple of pages I found kingfisher birds, the glyph "E," Mao translated into French, translucent eggs and fishbones, and a large gold wheel of 3800 ounces—all obscurely strung together in a mysterious rhythm. Unlike the admired Robert Lowell and Stephen Spender, this was a plunge into the unknown I could believe in.

I suspected what Olson was saying, though I couldn't articulate it.

It was a thing that lay at the core of ancient cultures, migrations, continental drift, and the tarot. It was the source of dreams and symbols. It was more complex and also more concrete than anything in the curriculum. To Leo Marx it was the last straw. "He's a lunatic," he shouted at me in his office one afternoon. "Even his own students don't know what he's talking about. Reading iconoclasts like that, you are going nowhere fast." He was so exasperated by this new sacrilege he could hardly think of anything strong enough to say. "Ask Katey Carver what she thinks of him," he screamed, throwing up his arms.

I did, and my editor at Viking agreed with my Amherst professor, instructing me to seek more suitable reading material. She sent me *Henderson the Rain-King* by Saul Bellow, marking those passages she herself had written. I read it, but the book seemed fake to me. It didn't have to do with real Africans, real madness, or the gods it seemingly invoked. By then I had come to accept Tripp's judgment of most American novels. They were advertising slogans dressed up in narrative. At least Olson offered the possibility of something radical and authentic, something beyond the controlling mirages of Western philosophy. His texts had no authoritarian or adult plans for me. He held out no promises, and he sought no adulation. It was as if he had said, "Find me, and you find yourself." One sequence of his called me back to the train station at Yuma in a different spirit. I posted it above my desk beside Forster:

> "O love who places all where each is, as they are, for every
> moment,
>   yield
>   to this man
>   that the impossible distance
>   be healed."

"Yes!" I shouted inwardly. Yes!

And *"Let the circle be unbroken, by and by lord, by and by."*

In the cusp of autumn 1963, I rode my bike along county roads, visiting fruit stands and lugging back bundles of grapes and apples. These were my harvest of images. At twilight, pedaling to keep the headlight on, I glided through pumpkin and tobacco fields. They spoke in the voices of *The Moon*. Unknown spirits hung just beyond me in the shades.

I sat in my room amidst corn and gourds and wrote:

The Moon was out, faint jigsaws on a faraway slice of light, the light pale down on the trees. And jigsaws were there if one looked closely enough. They were there as faint stains on a light that has been shining long enough to be stained, proof of mountains and valleys, deep and uneven, high and rocky, black as the space that separates planets.

On Earth, when mountains rise and valleys cut into beds, vegetation grows lush and deep, and in the depths of vegetation is the dirt and mystery of the world. There in the dampness insects live their whole lives; some emerge, flutter about for a while, then return. Down in the depths of vegetation, water flows and mud rots; pollen flies up, and leaves die and disassemble, matted down into rusty sand. There are worms and bugs and moles and fish. To the human mind, there is sultry heat and burning nostalgia, because we have lived something on this world. We are free from the beauty and harsh seduction of the land only as long as we keep moving. But when we stop, the land will swallow us like puppets. The insects will bite unhindered. The earth's rape will be whole, dissolving a body in its power and perfume and never-to-be-understood fantasy and mystery.

But the Moon is ragged and craggy and empty and cold. And it hangs in the sky, a lantern of emptiness, trying to tell us, playing its sterile fire on the burning vegetation, offering eternal life, an eternal answer.

It is unheeded; it is too ghostly and full of mystery, too faraway to be understood by such as us. Its stains are too faint.

Saturday nights at Phi Psi those guys with girls hung around the keg, a tape deck serving as continuous jukebox, the reels assembled from our various collections of 45s. I sat with Paul and the dateless others, listening to songs, sharing conversation, stuffing myself with pretzels, filling cups from the tap. These were the best friends I had ever had.

> *"Someday, when I'm awfully low,*
> *When the world is cold,*
> *I will feel a glow just thinking of you...."*

So sad, so finite our lives against the great secrets, but so warm and friendly in the Phi Psi basement ... until, weary and a bit high, I carted myself to the spaceship attic and crawled into my berth.

Early in the year, fraternities were invited to introductory gatherings (called mixers) at Smith and Holyoke. I joined cars full of Phi Psi members and then found myself in scenes in which a handful of girls were surrounded by guys from not only Amherst but more distant men's colleges like Dartmouth, Williams, and Yale. It was barely possible to cross the room let alone find anyone to talk to. A junior named Fred was generous enough to pack his Rambler full of us. He attended every mixer just for the opportunity to add names to his address book. He considered an evening a victory if he scored the phone number of one moderately good-looking girl. I would watch him snake his way through the landlocked masses, beaming and indomitable. I gave up after three outings.

From friends in the dorms I heard of another strategy. Many students had procured sets of freshman picture books from Smith and Holyoke. These gave home town and high school of each girl next to her photograph. Kids had gotten dates simply by calling girls from their mug shots and asking them out. I tried to interest my Phi Psi friends in attempting this method, but the response was a lot of horrified looks and "Not me's."

More than two years earlier I had simply picked up the phone and called Jill. Now the same inner voice would not let me rest until I tried this experiment. I wanted to risk my new articulateness. I considered myself daring and radical like Tripp, but unborn. "What's a phone call to get a date compared to the greatest good for the greatest number!" I taunted Paul.

He chuckled nervously but wagged his head.

I sat in the House library with him, turning Smith pages, and finally selected a sophomore from Music and Art in New York—someone more or less from my own background. Tripp, passing by, smiled beneficently. "Grossinger," he said, "I can remember when I took my own first puny chances."

Surrounded by muttering cohorts, I acted from an *esprit* of group heroism. I told them to give me space, then swallowed hard and dialed. When the phone was answered I asked for Amy. There was a torturous pause, then the clatter of her approach . . . a questioning "Hello?"

I said who I was . . . and would she like to go out Saturday night.

"Sure, why not."

Just like that.

When I reappeared in the hallway Paul was so excited he could hardly contain himself.

"Now," I insisted, "someone else has to try." But they all ran away.

That Saturday afternoon the first blast of hot from the shower was an epiphany. 'God,' I thought, 'so much has already happened.' I tended to drift numbly, hyperactively from day to day, to quell the past and its glimmerings. But a rush of anticipation and warm water sent images flowing toward my heart ... the street corner on which we first met Bridey, the shower room at Horace Mann, my last date with Jill, my dream of Joan Snyder. With sudden unexplained buoyancy I wailed: *"You're lovely / Never never change...."* And then Olson: "Hail and beware the dead who will talk life until you are/blue in the face...." Deep in myself I was almost happy.

I ran to the hitching corner of College Street and flagged a quick ride from an upperclassman.

Amy was redhaired and sprightly, a prospective painter. We kept up a conversation all the way to Amherst with many points of contact—subway routes and New York prep schools, aesthetics and school politics. We spent much of the evening in the Phi Psi basement, occasionally dancing, talking to my housemates. We went up to my room when Roger left, and continued our conversation, chastely and formally; then we hitched back.

The evening had been a success, but there was no tension between us—flirtatious or intellectual—no reason to go out with Amy again.

The second time, I went to the Mount Holyoke book. But the moment I saw my date in person my heart sank. She was duller and quite a bit chubbier than her picture suggested; she was also vocally conservative and patrician. We had a hard time finding anything to talk about and, on her suggestion, we hitched back at nine. I was so relieved to be rid of her I didn't try the picture books again for weeks.

On my third go-round I returned to the Smith book—and good old New York. I called a girl named Susan who had gone to Riverdale. "Since when does someone from Horace Mann ask out Riverdale?" she griped pleasantly. I was momentarily startled. Then she said, "I'll go out with you. I dig Phi Psi."

Leaping out of the stairwell I shouted, "I've tied Jim Brideweser's record!" He was a utility infielder who had gone three for three on the last day of the 1953 season for the Yankees—his only three at-bats of the year.

Susan was a field-hockey player—heavy-boned and sinewy; she was also witty and argumentative, her savvy and poise flowing faster than I could dodge. To her I probably seemed tight, infantile, and precious. She was ready for the world.

We vied with Paul and crew in the basement (Susan was the clear victor), had too many beers, and midway through the evening she took off on her own and I stumbled into the attic and fell asleep. I remembered her as a fierce, admirable girl I didn't want to be paired with again. I saw her next, fully realized, nineteen years later in Manhattan at a Doubleday book party for a baseball anthology I had compiled. She was a top-echelon publishing executive and had made a point of coming by after work to say hello.

"I hope you don't remember what happened that night," I said, shaking her outstretched hand.

"Only that it wasn't too good, but I have followed your writing ever since and always rooted for you."

Out of the blue, a writing teacher at Mount Holyoke invited me and two other Amherst students to read from our work in a dorm lounge. I was the envy of Phi Psi, Fred in particular. "What a golden opportunity!" he kept saying. "What great odds!"

In my fantasy I would read stirring, radical stories, and some folksinger girl would come up and talk to me afterwards, and we'd go to a cafeteria for lunch. She would play the guitar, have tarot blue eyes, long straight blond hair, and sing "Puff the Magic Dragon" and "If I Had a Hammer" (a younger, more innocent version of the woman in Peter, Paul, and Mary).

I accepted a ride to South Hadley from one of my fellow readers, but we got lost on campus and arrived barely in time; the other Amherst guy had already begun. He was hamming up some amazingly sexy love poems. Then he was followed by my partner, a short-story writer who was equally risqué. When my turn came, I felt totally overmatched. I was embarrassed to hear myself introduced as working with Saul

Bellow's editor at Viking (neither of the other, far more sophisticated writers had such a reference).

I took my place at the podium. I began to read, but my words mocked me. I sounded pious, ornate, precious. "The greatest good for the greatest number" was a ridiculous slogan. In the audience I glimpsed the faces of real girls—real people—and I understood this writing had nothing to do with them.

Once again, I was a fraud (or even worse, a con), proclaiming innocence and lofty ideals while seeking the same thing everyone else was—fame and romance. In any case, all of the interesting-looking girls flocked to the other two readers.

I ducked out quickly and stood on the highway, trying to hitch back. Of all unexpected people, Jeff Tripp pulled up in his Porsche. "Hop in, man," he ordered, ignoring his own rule (though I did feel a bit androgynous as I took my seat).

He was drunk and barely made the curves. "Don't worry," he said. "I may be out of my head, but I drive better in that condition than most people sober."

Instead of going back to Phi Psi he continued into town and parked outside a hamburger place. A sorority car from UMass pulled up next to us. Four extremely pretty girls in shorts got out.

"Well, lordy look here," Jeff said, standing up. "I wish I had my hat on, so I could tip it to the ladies like a good drunk." Then to my astonishment he called out, "Hey, cunt!"

I slid behind the door into my seat and stared the other way.

When I looked back, I saw they were giggling at this tall, gaunt figure with a long beard—as though they had been about to be offended but noticed a sacred fool. "You, you're the one I'm talking to. Baby, would you come home with me?"

She was wearing a busty tee shirt and automatically turned her back and walked away.

"Well, Grossinger, tell me if what my eyes see and my ears hear is true. The ladies will have nothing to do with me tonight. Is that so?"

"It's so," I told him.

"Well, I feel more like eating anyway. Shall we adjourn inside?"

Over a hamburger he portrayed his high days in Philly: debutante balls, blues and country groups, then a totally out-of-context scene of accompanying a woman to Boston, having decided to marry her when, en route to the courthouse, his car broke down. "I stood there, weepin' in the street over my goddamn buggy. And finally she said, 'Who do you care more about, me or the car?' I had no money, so I just sat there, weepin' behind the wheel, and she damn got up and walked out on me. I deserved it. That woman had every right."

"Did you ever see her again?"

"No, man, you mistake my point. I'd get married anytime on a whim. If something should happen to take me out of the mood, sobeit. Hey, Grossinger, why didn't you stop me there? It's not a 'mood.' I don't believe in mood. It's that there's a right time and a wrong time, always. Always! I certainly don't want to *be* married. It's just at that moment it's what I had to do."

"It makes sense," I offered.

He consumed big bites, then continued in a different vein. "I don't really care about my own death. It's boredom that terrifies me. I'm going to die like Malone anyway, my eyes shot, old fucks messin' up my prick, my mind indistinguishable from my ass, trying to write it all down with a pencil stub I keep losing in the sheets."

We walked back to the Porsche. He shot onto the road. "When I left Joanne," he sang, "she was standing still on the corner. I floored my vehicle and left her standing at sixty. And Grossinger, if you ever use her name in front of me, I'll never talk to you again. From this moment onward. Okay?"

"Sure thing."

Among the kids I occasionally went to dinner with was a fellow sophomore named Asher who lived across the hall from me in a single. Like Phil he was a prestigious type who could have joined almost any house, but he preferred the exalted bohemian life. He was the only one in Phi Psi with his bed in his room (along with a refrigerator and bar)—and a certain style of statuesque blonde regularly stayed over. He subscribed to *Playboy* and collected first-edition erotic classics. He was a ringer among us.

A somewhat plump Jewish kid from New York with an arrhythmic body, Asher was not an obvious stud, but he had a *savoir faire* and a wealthy family (plus a new Corvette and state-of-the-art stereo). He was smooth and well-groomed, with an insistent easy-listening personality; there was something seductive, almost foppish, about him, as though, male or female, he was always softening you for the kill.

Asher liked to debate literature and eroticism with me over dinner. He considered himself an aficionado and patron of the arts and insisted that I didn't have enough experience to be writing novels. He would come by my room and initiate a conversation just before mealtime with the goal of continuing in Valentine. He took our total intimacy for granted, pulling my working manuscripts off shelves and perusing several pages with an array of professorial expressions. "You think you're being daring, but this is nothing; it's not even sexy." He'd go back to his room and retrieve first-edition Henry Millers and read me passages. "Now this is real fucking!" he exulted with an almost beatific smile.

His selections were carnal beyond anything I had imagined, like a man cutting a woman's pubic hairs and pasting them on himself as a mustache.

"That has nothing to do with me," I protested. "It's sex for sex's sake."

"It be so!" Asher acclaimed.

Asher was the most obdurate version of a type I had known for years, so I fashioned a hybrid of him, including Danny (from Horace Mann) and Eddie (from Chipinaw) to form a Miami Beach playboy in *The Moon,* pursuing the heroine Peggy. In our conversations my friend would give me the villain's lines: "We went to the movies. I took her hand and placed it on my cock, and it just so happened she didn't take it away." He laughed. "Then we came back here and fucked."

"Fucking is pretty good," he pronounced one night, "but really only about—I'd say—a time and a half as good as masturbating." He loved to describe girls who had bathed with him and sucked his cock (and so on); he told these stories in thoughtful monotones as though searching in himself for a meaning, slightly troubled that he couldn't generate more charge but convinced he was on the right track. He seemed to require someone else's vicarious participation to savor his own deeds. I took every nuance down, and Catherine Carver thought it made for a very believable character.

Early in November, not long after my date with Susan, Asher mentioned a girl he thought I'd enjoy meeting. "I dated her freshman year, but we broke up. She's a writer." His eyes met mine meaningfully. "I think she dropped me because she's looking for somebody creative. Now I hear she's dating an architect from Penn, but she might like talking to you." He leaned forward in conspiracy. "I'm sort of curious to learn what she's up to. Maybe you could be my spy."

Her name was Lindy, and she was a sophomore at Smith. When I called she came quickly to the phone and had an immediately negative response: "I don't know you."

It was a wonder I hadn't gotten that before.

"Asher is not the best reference you could have, you know. One of the things I worried about when I broke up with him was that his friends would start calling me." Her voice was sharp and clear, full of personality. I explained I was no friend of Asher. I was a writer who happened to live down the hall from him. I told her I was working on a couple of novels and had a New York editor.

"I'd like to meet you; that's fine. But I'm not sure I want to troop over to Amherst. Why don't we have dinner together in Northampton?"

I agreed, and we set a time on Saturday night.

I hitched to Smith with the image of two writers getting together to talk shop. I precast Lindy as a Henry Miller sophisticate, like her ex-boyfriend, and I was mainly concerned to come off as a legitimate author.

I stood among the other males in the reception room at Laura Scales, waiting for my escort to appear. After a few minutes she came bounding down the stairs, tall and lithe with an open face, conventionally pretty—dark eyeliner, long light brown hair. She said perkily: "Where are we going?" I had no idea.

"How about Wiggins Tavern?" That was the classiest restaurant in town, old-fashioned and expensive.

We set out on the road that hugged the campus. It was just past nightfall, and Northampton had a brisk, sparkling appearance. As we crossed into the center of town we established our point of connection. "Asher is an egotistical ass," she declared at once—anxious to clarify her connection with him: ". . . a brief freshman flirtation. He was exciting, with his wealth and social poise. He'd score theater tickets, and it was one fine restaurant after another—a real gas for a girl from Denver." She flashed a "poor naive me" smile. "When he flew out to visit me at Christmastime I saw right through him. Even worse, so did my parents." I laughed at the image of Asher trying to appear like anything other than a hustler. "I learned my lesson. I'm dating an artist in Philadelphia now." We came to a curb with a puddle. "Jump," I said automatically.

"How chivalrous!" But she cleared it by a good amount. I jumped behind her.

There was a new playfulness as we strode past darkened buildings through the lobby of the tavern into its lantern-lit restaurant. The ornate setting evoked Towers family dinners in New York, but we were now the adults: me and this unknown person being seated at a table of silver and crystal. We shared quick guilty grins. After reading our menus and ordering, we each spun an epic.

I told her about my childhood, Drs. Fabian and Friend, Aunt Bunny, Betsy, Mr. Ervin's class, Chuck's poems, Charles Olson, Leo Marx, transferring *en masse* to Berkeley, and Katey Carver. She described growing up in Colorado, her family's summer cabin in a mining town, her two married sisters, years of ballet, her high school romances, her difficulty in science courses at Smith, her poems, her godfather the poet John Ciardi, her parents' rotten marriage, and her weekends with her lover Steve in Philadelphia.

We had an instant unplanned rapport that allowed us to go anywhere and confess anything without awkwardness. It was as though we were two very articulate members of an advanced species discussing the foibles of a lesser species, namely ourselves. We parleyed back and forth almost effortlessly through drinks, the meal, dessert, her coffee, and then afterward in the bar, a beer ... and another. It seemed as though we had been talking for weeks when we had to race back for curfew, stopping here and there at shop windows to catch our numbed breaths. She was a great discovery, even if not a possible girlfriend.

In the weeks that followed we spoke every few days on the phone. I gave her ideas for writing English papers when she was stuck, and she tried to think of girls I might go out with. We sent writing back and forth in the mail and commented on each other's work (she was a poet with a great deal of wit and a talent for the surreal). When she got back from an unexpectedly discouraging weekend with her boyfriend Steve, she called that Sunday night, and I commiserated with her at length. Then, as Thanksgiving approached and it became clear she didn't want to see Steve again so soon, I offered her a trip to Grossinger's. "You could meet Aunt Bunny," I added.

She rallied at the prospect and formalized it the next day by promising to write "your Aunt Bunny a letter thanking her for the invitation."

Then one afternoon, walking back from class, I saw people running with radios. President Kennedy had been shot, maybe even killed. . . .

I think now only of Phil Kaufman's movie *The Wanderers,* Richie the gang-leader at the end of his reign, aimlessly scouting Bronx streets, looking for a world that no longer existed, stopping in a crowd to gaze at a bank of TV sets in a store window—newsclips of Dallas.

And, on the soundtrack, words written by a young black soul singer working at his father's luncheonette:

"Oh I won't be afraid; no I won't be afraid. . . ."

In the City in which I didn't ever grow up—an esoteric moment, peeking from behind curtains into the obscurity of a new era. . . .

Of Amherst itself that day I remember nothing.

The next afternoon Lindy's letter came:

> This is a special, sad time. Now I think it is best I go and be with Steve, best for me, best for you too. Our friendship is good and means a lot to me, so I know you understand. Give my regards to Aunt Bunny and tell her I'll see her the next time.

I took a bus from Amherst to Grand Central Station and hauled my suitcase uptown on the subway. The soot and throngs were anciently familiar. I knew how to make my way home without even thinking, how to stand in balance on a train that was packed even before 42nd Street. I could no longer pretend that the stench and soddenness had nothing to do with me. It was the base mood of existence, and it subsumed me as much as it did these people returning to apartments from school and work. I had become merely another of those adult travelers I had stared at as a child without comprehension. But I wasn't sad or overwhelmed; I was pleased to be surviving, all the way to Central Park West.

My father had suggested at the last moment that I spend this vacation with my mother, mainly because his house was filled with guests. So, Thanksgiving had been downgraded from a chauffeured trip to Grossinger's with Lindy to a return to my haunted household. I balked, but he left no alternative. I did have one event to look forward to: Aunt Bunny had promised to take me and my friend Paul to dinner on her way up to the mountains from the City.

Even in the short time I had been away, the Towers family had changed drastically. Bob had more accounts and took longer trips. Bridey now lived full-time in her own apartment. Debby was taciturn and unapproachable. But Jon was the big story. It seemed that, almost on the day I departed, he turned into a delinquent, an event my mother paradoxically blamed on me—after all, he and I had become companions toward the end, and he had adopted *my* tarot cards and poetry.

He was no longer doing well at Horace Mann—on probation for bizarre, inexplicable incidents: shooting at his teachers with a water gun, throwing a rock through the auditorium window, staging fights behind the gym. He also came home suspiciously late, refusing explanation, and terrorized his parents with tales of how he would jump onto the subway tracks until the train was in sight and then climb back off just in time. I told Bob that they should find a therapist for him, but my mother refused to hear of such intrusion.

"One crazy kid is enough," she declared, as though the logic of that were obvious.

In her presence I froze. All the strength I had gathered at Amherst and during the summer shrank away. I sensed only an abyss and myself plunging helplessly into what I had been. She told me I didn't look well, that I had lost weight. She berated me for my grades, for the time wasted at Grossinger's, for the way I was dressed. She didn't want to hear about new friends and Phi Psi. "They must not be much of an influence from your performance at school . . ." and then turned and marched into her room. So I spent hours telling Jon.

He was a sadder, more somber kid now, more restrained. He wasn't interested in quarterbacking or grades; he wanted wizardry and wisdom.

The tarot was hardly my doing. Times had changed: he and his friends all carried around decks and were far more into magic and occult symbols than we had ever been. So he wanted to hear not only about Phi Psi but the legendary exploits of Waldman and Chuck Stein.

I put on my record of Bob Dylan singing, "And A Hard Rain's A-Gonna Fall." Bridey came in from the dishes, offended. "Who's that singer?"

I told her, but she had never heard of him.

"Is he an old man?"

I said I didn't think so. "That's probably him on the cover with the girl."

"He has a terrible voice. He should get someone else to sing his songs." And she returned to the kitchen, rendering the tune in her own lilting melody: *"Oh, where have you been, my blue-eyed son. . . ."* Right out of *Finian's Rainbow*.

The next morning I called Paul at his parents', then Bunny at the Plaza to confirm our threeway meeting. But all day a persistent snow fell. By afternoon the City was drear; a near-blizzard blew helter-skelter. The Park was barely visible, covered in oxide. Aunt Bunny called from a gas station; she was already across the Bridge on her way home. I was unable to reach Paul before he left on the subway, so I sat by the window watching the Park vanish in twilight as street lights popped on.

When Bob came home he was excited to remember I was visiting, and he extended an instant invitation. "What's wrong with our having your cohort to dinner? I'd like to meet some Amherst students, especially a Jewish kid from my own turf. Let your brother experience the Ivy League before he runs himself right out of competition."

So a half hour later the doorbell rang, and there was Paul, poking his way into this unfamiliar setting (about which he had heard so much). He shook hands with Bob and Jonny, and Bridey greeted him from afar.

Worlds were colliding.

I quickly apprised Paul of the change. He said, "So what. We'll do this instead." Then he whispered, "I actually want to be your guest here. I promise I'll take thorough notes."

We sat in the living room in anecdote. Paul's tales of his aunts and uncles set Bob rocking with laughter: "I know the guy exactly," my step-father parried. "No matter what you say, he's the expert, he has it all."

"Right," Paul continued. "And every day he's calling the patent office because he's got a new invention, gonna change the world."

Then they moved on to the *schnorrer*, the distant cousin who comes over every other night for dessert, and to make his suddenly pressing long-distance calls. After Bob provided his own Lower East Side cameos, the topic graduated to Marxism and trade unions. I expressed surprise at hearing him in such agreement with Paul's radical politics.

"Richard, you're talking to an old labor leader, a supporter of the oppressed. I love anyone who rebels, who attacks the establishment. I'm an Allen Ginsberg fan. I'm now a Bob Dylan fan. I'm an old Catskills rabble-rouser."

When my mother arrived she was flustered and then aggravated by both my presence and the unexpected company. She hurried into her bedroom and made a late appearance at the meal (so that Bridey had to serve her one course behind). Paul and I had been regaling the rest with accounts of Amherst and Phi Psi and, after being introduced to my mother, Paul continued. She cut him off at once and asked me why I was still here.

"Not at the meal," Bob said. "Have your heart-to-heart later."

"Would you rather I weren't here so you could all talk behind my back?"

I felt apprehension but also a twinge of pleasure. I was watching the family through an outsider's eyes, playing the most famous scene in my life, one that had been repeated with variations back to the dawn of time. I knew Hamlet's role; I knew the King's lines; I knew the Queen's responses; I knew the maid's foil. I had played every version and motif of this drama hundreds of times. Which one would we enact tonight?

"We're not talking about you, Martha. Paul was telling us about the Lower East Side—where I just happened to grow up. And Amherst—where he and Richard presently go to school."

It seemed right then everything would explode, but we proceeded without incident to dessert. There was no more conversation.

It was time for Bob to drive Bridey back to the Bronx, and, with a burst of surprising enthusiasm, he announced that he would pick up ice cream on the way home. "What do you people want?

"Chocolate," Debby said at once.

Then Bob responded with a line Paul never forgot, even twenty years later: "Chocolate? What's wrong with vanilla?"

"Now that's contrariness," he chortled back at Amherst. "He asked the kid what she wanted, and she told him." For the rest of the college year Paul would chuckle at appropriate times and say: "What's wrong with vanilla?"

My mother then asked that Richard's friend leave too.

"He can't have dessert with us, Martha? And you might dignify him with a name."

"He wasn't even supposed to be here. He was going out with Auntie Bunny."

I felt a surge of anger. "You can say her name without mocking it!"

I had lit the fuse. My mother's voice went up several octaves; she was breathing heavily. She began screaming at me for incidents going all the way back to childhood when—she proclaimed—I chose the Grossingers over her. Anyone could see I was a troublemaker; look at what I had done to my poor, innocent brother. Look at the kind of friends I brought home. She yelled at Bob, Jonny, and Debby, while they sat there staring. She ordered them to come to her support. Then she demanded we all leave. When Bridey, who was virtually her temple maiden, poked her head in from the kitchen, my mother told her to go too. She was planning to leave anyway, just not at that moment, so she had to run down the hall to retrieve her coat from the bedroom.

The six of us were standing in the foyer, looking away from one another with expressions ranging from Debby's icy stare to Bob's grimly pursed lips. As we awaited the elevator my mother reappeared at the door and began shouting. "You ingrates. You tramps. Go. Go. I don't ever want to see any of you again!" She was so loud that she roused Dr. Gordon, the psychiatrist who lived across the hall. We had spent years muffling our arguments so as not to attract his attention. Now that taboo was shattered too.

"You no-good crook," she hollered as he tried to calm her. "Don't try to tell me I'm crazy. Go back to your rich patients."

All our prior dealings with him had been courteous and neighborly, though no doubt he had overheard the "pogroms." He held his ground and told her maybe she didn't have to suffer this much; she slammed the door. He shrugged majestically, seemed to wink at the rest of us, and then slipped back in.

Out on Central Park West we split into groups. Jonny and Debby joined Bridey and Bob, while I continued to walk downtown in the snow with Paul as we constructed a plan: Chuck Jenkins, a member of the Phi Psi jug band whose home was in St. Louis, was exploring New York in his VW Bug; Paul had his hotel number. "If we can reach him he might be able to rescue us."

I suggested a drive straight up to Grossinger's, and Paul delightedly concurred.

Jenkins was holed up in his room, bored. He agreed to come at once and, after nursing him through directions, Paul called his own parents, told them where we were going, and asked them to pretend they hadn't heard from us. One hurdle remained—for me to reclaim my belongings upstairs.

We took the service elevator. I slipped my key quietly in the back door and tiptoed through the kitchen into the study. I felt such suspense inside me I thought I would explode. I could hear my mother on the phone in the bedroom, still hysterical, Grandma Sally apparently the audience now. She was denouncing the whole Grossinger family, saying how they had cheated her and ruined her life. Over and over she mentioned Bunny and blamed Jonny's problems on her, this woman he had never even spoken to. She had plenty to say about Richard: an ungrateful, lunatic son who was flunking out of college because he cared for no one but himself. A thoroughly intimidated Paul hid behind the garbage can by the elevator.

Twenty minutes later Jenkins' green Bug swung around the corner. Paul and I cheered, and Paul patted him frantically on the back. We fit my suitcase in, slid into seats, turned the corner, and headed through driving snow toward the George Washington Bridge. I was jubilant, the stream of thick flakes only adding to my adrenalin rush. I was finally fleeing the Medusa.

Crowded into the Bug, the wipers barely keeping the road visible, we coasted up the Thruway—mere snow matted with tire tracks. We arrived after midnight.

My mother's barrage of phone calls through the evening had led my father to guess I was coming; either that, or I had gone to my friend's house (but his parents had no idea where we were). When we arrived he was hardly welcoming; he said we looked like three revolutionaries about to join the Cuban army. He put me in the basement (since the house was full) and sent Paul and Chuck to staff quarters.

As he pieced together the event in his office the next morning he grew increasingly miffed at Paul's parents. After reprimanding the three of us he called them on his conference phone and righteously berated them: "I don't believe in parents collaborating with children against other parents." But they held firm (while Paul smiled at me), and my father ended the conversation as politely as he still could and then released us for the remainder of the weekend. Fittingly enough, he saw one advantage to my unexpected presence; he realized that, as a worker from the summer, I could cast a timely vote in the Union election. "But for which side?" I asked Paul and Chuck playfully. The Union had me disqualified anyway.

The three of us paraded through the Hotel for the next few days, delighting in the food but assailing the displays of bad taste and decadence. Everywhere we looked we saw blacks and Puerto Ricans sweeping and polishing windows, wheeling carts of laundry, while grotesquely overweight, overdressed Jews flaunted jewelry and barked crudely at wives, husbands, kids. How had I missed it so completely!

On the mail table at Phi Psi was my mother's response—a carbon of her letter to my father, disowning me and turning over full responsibility to him. "That's the way Richard has always wanted it. So now I will grant him his wish."

"No one is responsible for a nineteen-year-old," he told me coolly. "I wrote her that if you can't take care of yourself, then heaven help you."

My weeks into December were dominated by tests and papers, but we held a Thursday pre-Christmas literary event at Phi Psi, starring my freshman friend Al, Stephen Mitchell (the best writer from Humphries' class), and Jeff Tripp. I invited Lindy to read too.

"Sorry, I'm off to Penn this weekend."

In fact, she said, she was so overwhelmed with schoolwork during the next month that she asked me not to call for a while. I became busy too and gradually forgot about her.

My best friend during that time was a kid named Schuyler whom I met inauspiciously during hockey. One game, while trying to pass, I mistakenly whizzed the puck by his shins. Shaking his stick over his head, he threatened to castrate me if I did that again.

I knew him only from afar as a surly rebel in my American Studies class, but his remark had the curious effect of melting the distance between us. Walking back to our lockers we dissected Leo Marx, then continued to lunch at Valentine. Schuy knew I was one of Marx's favorites, which he considered a *de facto* betrayal (after all, he was Marx's daily whipping boy). I assured him that the professor was now down on me too. "He doesn't like my reading material, he doesn't like Phi Psi, and he wants me to imitate him and his buddies."

"He's supposed to be one of the good-guy teachers," Schuy complained, "but he's just another authoritarian 'my-word-goes' *bwana*. He's all for revolution and protest, but in his own class he can't listen to someone else's opinion without losing his cool. Just because he's teaching *Growing Up Absurd* doesn't mean he's on our side."

Schuy was a paradox. A virtual prep-school icon in style and appearance, he was also as bright as anyone I knew, a natural athlete, and strikingly handsome—a mop of sandy hair and classic features. But he was fiercely independent and alienated from every peer group at Amherst, including Phi Psi ("just another social club," he snarled, "a lot of ignorant guys practicing reverse snobbism"). He was not even trying to date girls, though he was very into them in his mind.

He was mainly on guard—furious at being hustled all his life, determined not to be taken in again if he could help it. One Saturday night we hitched together to a mixer at Smith, talking up our excitement all the way; yet in the follow-through we both hung in the crowds along the side. Whereas I was paralyzed and frustrated, Schuy was noble and defiant. I thought he was far and away the most attractive guy in the room, yet he offered only a volley of churlish remarks. "They're so damn good-looking, but that's what they're playing at. I'm just not gonna go for it. Let one of them act like a normal human being and come over and ask *me* to dance." No one did.

Rhonda had invited me to stay with her at Christmastime and, after a dicey round of diplomacy, my father agreed to take me to Miami with him and Aunt Bunny. I rode the Trailways out of Amherst, met them at the airport . . . and suddenly stepped off a jet in Betsy's city. Sun throbbed through listless air. I kicked a broken coconut shell along the ground. Harbingers were everywhere, but I had little hope.

The first two days were a throwback to "Uncle Paul," the guardian of my childhood. He took me on a tour of his haunts—the Grossinger Pancoast he once owned (now the Algiers—"but it's on lease; we get it back in ninety-nine years," he joked), the restaurant in which he and Grandpa Harry were partners, even the house where we had the Easter egg hunt. I enjoyed being under court protection again: dinner at an elegant French restaurant with him and Aunt Bunny, a fishing yacht with their associates, lying on the beach drinking rum cokes with Bunny. My image of Betsy was a constant prod, but I put a mask around it and walked in my father's ancient shadow. Then, on the third day, I moved to Rhonda's.

I expected a normal Jewish family, but I found another cliché: a sardonic, abusive father; a sluggish, oppressed mother. After one meal I wondered why Rhonda stayed here. After all, she had cut her record and was singing regularly in nightclubs. She had also broken up with Spike and very recently rejected a marriage proposal from a much older, carrot-haired lawyer (who still didn't want to hear no for an answer). She was relieved to see me, and asked me point-blank if I'd be her boyfriend now. "Don't you see," she pleaded. "We're both going to make it. We should make it together."

I refused to discuss the subject. The anticipation of seeing Betsy obsessed me.

It wasn't until my fourth day in Florida that she returned from college. I called. We arranged to meet on Pine Tree Drive the next morning.

I got off the bus and walked for blocks under the tropical sun, manuscript under my arm. Coconut palms rippled eerily. This was almost Long Beach. This was almost my whole life in a cameo. Movie cameras tracked me from across the street.

Internally I knew better. I could barely separate Betsy herself from the character in *Salty and Sandy* or Peggy in *The Moon;* she was a kind of illuminated being. Rhonda had told me she was back with Brian, and there was nothing in Betsy's and my infrequent newsy correspondences over the year to suggest that she in any way considered me a boyfriend. But this was the conclusion to *Salty and Sandy.* Catherine Carver and my readers-to-be were waiting.

I was led into the mansion by a black butler. Betsy met me at the edge of the living room and reached out with quaint tenderness to shake my hand. She was the same plain but charismatic being whose cameo had hung on my wall all year. Her voice was disturbingly familiar; it had been in my head, in my dreams so long. We sat there, she on the couch, me on the adjacent chair. We had nothing in common except an old feeling of rapport, and even that was a superfluous memory by now. She was already a sorority girl headed for bigtime cheerleading, and I was quoting my friend Paul and Samuel Beckett. But I had to speak for myself:

"I really looked forward to seeing you. You look great." I had broken the lull with a pair of stilted lines I couldn't rescind.

She saw what I was carrying, so she said simply, "May I see the book?"

For the next hour I sat there skimming magazines while she turned the pages. My mind raced through an inventory of what she was reading—my descriptions of her, my transcriptions of her words, my fantasies of her coming to Amherst and us going off together. It didn't matter any longer. It was a hundred-per-cent-total confession.

I stared at every last thing in that room many times, each piece of kitsch art, each painting and statue, the *Reader's Digest* books on the shelves, the view through the sliding door to the pool. I had come, like the troubadour, to the castle.

She straightened the pages neatly into a pile and returned them to their box. In her eyes I could see the answer, or perhaps it was the question, searching my own piercing look in order somehow to understand—but, in any case, it was final, and I knew it. "You should go," she said.

I got up and walked to the door with her behind me. "I had hoped—" I started to say.

"You'll find someone right for you," she interrupted. "Thank you for letting me read it. You didn't have to."

I strode down the long driveway, out the iron gate, past the coconut palms, into my life, which was waiting painfully in the Miami afternoon. I encountered something almost prehistoric, but it had no name or meaning. I felt drained and feverish. I tasted slightly the memory of toasted almond ice cream. I walked for miles, past houses, fallen coconuts and oranges, lamp posts, stores, trying to harbor every breath of flowers in the air, to record each feeling and its echo, singing the old songs in my heart, and telling myself, with feigned drama, that it was over.

I have not seen Betsy since, nor have I had any communication with her; yet periodically I dream of that mansion with the iron gates and palms. I come long distances through the South or find myself in Florida (to my astonishment) and decide to look her up. I go to the front door and am told she doesn't live there anymore . . . or that she has died. Or she appears, hopeful and shining, as she was then, in some version of that living room. Or she is an old woman, sad and defeated. . . . And I long to recover the purity of the feeling I had for her once.

The dream grows and changes with my own aging. In one version she is divorced and caring for dozens of young children in a slum; in another, she is on her way to the beach with no apparent appreciation for how far I have come. She says hello and hurries on.

For years we never spoke in dream, but now we do and, though I don't remember what she says, it scalds new light and sensation over the perimeters of my unlived life. I experience a Pacific wilderness, fragments of an Australian Aboriginal dance, a beach far older than Miami where she shows me patches of glacial ice and gullies exiting from the planet's core among the ordinary sunbathers and palm trees; then she vanishes in the crowd. Or she comes from a room in an old Hardy Boys book and discloses the answer to their mystery, a sinister question mark floating through a Viennese ballroom into the dream-work itself. Since I don't know the plot I don't spot its resolution.

When I awaken I feel a tremendous loss but also a wonder and freshness for having been there. I am forever regenerated by that dream.

I know Betsy wasn't an appropriate girlfriend and that she is kept alive in me in the form she first manifested: as the anima, the mirror of my lost female being. At a moment of life change—of leaving my mother's bewitched household—she appeared in the guise of a Dade County cheerleader to lead me into the caring and lightness of the world, to insist that I fulfill her potential in me . . . to open my heart ahead of time to women who *would* love me. Without her I would have been stumbling across the threshold, from darkness into darkness, however adroitly I faked it.

Yet "anima" is merely a name for a symbolic transformation of many masks. Her form of appearance changes as we change, bringing lost parts of ourselves to consciousness as they are needed, discarding familiar reference points so that we become estranged to ourselves. We think we are dying, or in love. That's where the rest of our lives *always* emerges.

But just because Betsy was the projection of a force inside me does not mean she was not a girl. In truth, eros failed, and our lives twained without either of us understanding who the other was or could be for each other. Perhaps such broken romances are absolved by the universality of the feminine and masculine (yes, we are all the same woman, the same man, acting out the same metadrama). Perhaps our losses are healed recurrently in later love. But there remain holes in the dreamtime, things ever needing mending: it is through their eternal return we experience that we will never be made whole.

That night Rhonda and I went to a drive-in. She leaned against me as I put my arm around her. She giggled uncontrollably at the atrocious comedy on the screen. I felt apart and disinterested. On the way home I slid back across the front seat, but she told me it was proper in Miami Beach for a date to sit flush against the driver. I felt that was silly and would make me an obstruction, so I stubbornly angled myself against the door. We didn't talk. She pulled into the driveway, and stared at me. I longed to be on that jet going home. "It's over for you with Betsy," she said. "Why don't you take me seriously?"

"I guess it was something special with her. It's nothing against you; it either happens or it doesn't."

"How would you know?" she said. She leaned over, put her mouth on mine, and kissed me long and hard. At first I felt like pulling away, as though from a gushy relative. But she put her tongue inside and rolled it up and down. I felt a wave of excitement begin at my roots and rush straight up, flowering over my whole body. I held her and kissed back. I was trembling, and she sucked me further into the kiss. Then instead of continuing, she pulled away and looked back at me probingly. She said, "Let's go inside. There's time."

Not really. Her parents were sitting up, so she went straight to her room. The next morning she rushed out early for rehearsal; she had a date with her lawyer friend that night. I left the following noon, and I didn't see her again until five years later in Detroit, when she had three children by the lawyer and was no longer singing.

3

LINDY

I returned to college after Christmas with a new strategy for changing schools. A dissident English professor named Roger Sale had departed Amherst with a rousing chapel speech two years earlier and had gone to the University of Washington to teach. He had become memorialized as an underground hero, and now people were comparing my own speech to his. On that basis I had written Professor Sale before Christmas and, when I got back, there was a letter from him, encouraging me to apply and offering to help. I sent for the application and filled it out as soon as I got it.

At the start of second semester I signed up for predominantly new classes (only American Studies and Geology carried over). I added a seminar on D. H. Lawrence; an Abnormal Psychology course taught by Roy Heath, a visiting professor from Pittsburgh (where he was a colleague of my mother's brother Lionel); and a survey of modern European drama.

The latter was inspired by Tripp, who was directing an Amherst production of *Waiting for Godot*. I began to read Anouilh, Giradoux, and Cocteau and, with Jeff's rehearsals going on night and day in the living room, I developed an allegiance to the theater of cosmic irony. Men stumbled across minimal stages calling out to gods who were their own inventions. Antigone and Oedipus were reincarnated as Europeans enacting Freudian myths.

I had a sympathetic teacher named Stephen Coy, who was also a great admirer of Tripp, so, for once, there was free rein. I wrote sixty pages of an Anouilh imitation of *Hamlet* in which the ghost of Hamlet's father cried out, "Stop in the name of Jean Cocteau!"; Hamlet read a baseball magazine on his bed after delivering a soliloquy; and America's role in Vietnam was satirized in Denmark's "Norwegian crisis."

Passing the old Shakespearean tyrant, Professor Baird, one day on campus that spring, I let drop a "Hello, sir."

"Watcha doing?" he snapped automatically. This was the man famous for his canonization of the Bard and utter disdain for student work.

"Most recently I rewrote *Hamlet,*" I deadpanned.

It would be impossible to imitate the startled grunts and outraged syllables that followed.

Jeff told me that in America not being able to drive was "tantamount to not having a dick." When I heard that, I immediately looked up "Driving Schools" in the *Yellow Pages* and enrolled in a series of private classes with a man who turned out to be the Northampton High football coach.

"That's who *should* teach you!" Jeff roared, as he leaped into his Porsche and bombed onto College Street.

Once a week I hitched to Northampton where the coach took me out on back roads as I followed his rat-tat-tat instructions. Jeff was right: the car felt like enfranchisement, adulthood. Despite one bad outing (when I confused left and right and ended up in a tobacco field), a month later I got a Massachusetts license.

In Psychology we began by studying the etiology of neurosis, which revived memories of my subway-guide Neil quizzing Dr. Fabian after my sessions. My coursebook could have been Neil's graduate text, its opening pages christening the famous id which discharged torrents of primal stuff until the nascent ego contained and bound them into personality. Such was the psychic energy of our lives—cathected and transformed as "fantasies, daydreams, conflicts, object relations, the self, and social roles." No more statistics to parse—this was true "inner sanctum" stuff.

Dr. Heath was a mild, reassuring professor, much like a psychiatrist himself. Because of my psychoanalytic history and his connection to Lionel, he and I became out-of-class friends and ate many a meal together.

Early in the term Heath took us on a trip to the Northampton State Mental Hospital where patients flocked around our class, pleading for attention. One young man cornered my Phi Psi friend Paul and me and showed us a sketch pad of his fabulous inventions, page after page, meticulously drawn, men with wings, elaborate pulleys and windmills. He told us that they had imprisoned him for his genius, and he asked for our help in escaping. Another man confided to Dr. Heath that *he* was the psychiatrist and the doctors were his patients. A grotesque elderly woman took both my wrists in her hands and told me that she knew my grandmother. Surely that couldn't be true, for she didn't even know my name. But people had tossed that line at me ever since I became a Grossinger, and I hated it to the point of being uncivil. Now suddenly I felt as though a madperson had read through my pretension and was flouting my paranoia.

In class I questioned whether these patients had real diseases— neuroses and psychoses—or whether they were simply victims. In truth, what I had observed were women too weird to find husbands, elderly people without homes, exiled prodigies who couldn't adapt. I applied the sociological arguments of my American Studies reading to the terminology of my "Abnormal" textbook and wrote interlocking papers for both courses.

Paul Goodman's *Growing Up Absurd* became my link between Freud's theory of insanity and the sublimations and addictions of our rat-race civilization. Goodman implicitly connected the threat of nuclear holocaust to the vapid materialism of Kenmont and Beach High. No wonder Godot never came. No wonder Betsy, Rhonda, and the rest ... Barbie dolls, chimeras. Even our sexuality didn't belong to us anymore. Schuyler was right: "Growing Up Absurd" was the least of it.

The book almost gleefully assaulted the very world in which my parents had spent their lives: "human beings working as clowns ... thinking like idiots ... Alternately, they are liars, confidence men, smooth talkers, obsequious, insolent...." If this was my heritage—

and it fit Bob, my mother, and their colleagues to a T—then my so-called craziness, my inability to conform was actually a badge of honor. "If there is nothing worthwhile, it is hard to do anything at all. When one does nothing, one is threatened by the question, *is* one nothing?"

Exactly!

The hero of these discoveries, Mr. Goodman himself, visited Marx's class (he too was a friend of the professor). A group of us went to lunch with him afterwards. I had expected a thoughtful, compassionate scholar, so was unprepared for the gruff, belligerent elder who made speeches at us and pushed aside our questions by saying that kids our age cared about fucking and nothing else. After he made that asser-tion the third time—seemingly oblivious to the fact he had already said it twice—Schuy and I stomped out.

Goodman's book was still important to me, but, in my mind, I appropriated it from its author. He was right, of course, that we were trapped in adolescent fantasies and probably useless for more subtle discourse. But that didn't make us libidinal animals without discern-ment. It wasn't sex itself that drew me; it was the texture that seduc-tive feelings invoked. It was *"Shenando'h, you rolling river ..."* and the way things changed and were changed into each other in the depth and tinder of masturbation. I was called not just by the lure of girls but the seemingly bottomless labyrinths of feeling in myself where *all* things were entangled, one covering another. I saw, on a smoke-thin arras, a Sphinx, a sun in an extraterrestrial tarot. I felt, fleetingly, my own skeletal existence.

For Beckett and the existentialists this ancient vision had been shat-tered in despair, in the disillusion of eternal waiting; even the won-derment of life had become part of the crap of the world—discarded in the garbage cans of Tripp's stagesets. In the end, these prophets warned, we will find our hearts and souls empty; we will be unable to go on. Perhaps, I thought, that's what happened to Goodman. But I was still brimming with hope and grief.

Catherine Carver spent many months with the finished draft of *Salty and Sandy* and my completed sections of *The Moon,* and she finally wrote back that, although I was very talented, I had not yet written a book publishable by Viking. She trusted that by continuing to work with her I could get to that point, and she presumed that we would talk the next time I was in New York.

My fantasy of the future was tied up in the publication of my books, so I skipped a Friday of classes and took the bus into snowy Manhattan to meet her for lunch. She picked a distinguished literary restaurant where she told me right away that *The Moon* was going in a dangerous direction, from sensible narrative into occultism and arcana, and she warned me again about continuing to read Olson and Beckett. "You are no longer making believable stories or creating characters who are real. Some of the writing in *The Moon* is truly inspired, but I think it belongs in essays, not novels." She wanted more Grossinger's, more of my clever metaphorical devices, and more sex—in general, more action and less philosophy. She was asking me to abandon the part of my writing that was closest to my heart.

My father was in the City that afternoon, so we had dinner in his hotel room. He was interested in the career implications of my lunch with Catherine Carver and, without forewarning, he picked up the phone and dialed the popular novelist Harold Robbins.

"Harold, Paul Grossinger here ... yes, you can do something for me this time." In the course of the conversation he wrote down an address. "You meet him at his place; he'll read your work and tell you what it's worth; then you'll know whether this woman is just leading you on."

It had the crudity of all his offers, but I too wanted to know what Harold Robbins would make of *Salty and Sandy*. The next morning I took the bus downtown and rode an elevator to a penthouse where a middle-aged man in a silk bathrobe led me into his living room and ordered me lunch while he sat on a sofa rapidly flipping through my manuscript. After fifteen minutes he let me know he was finished by taking a deep breath. Then he said:

"You're a writer. You've got a ways to go, and this stuff isn't ready to publish, but these editors, they're frustrated college teachers; they want to latch on to some young kid and indoctrinate him. I don't know what kind of writing you're going to do, but keep going and it will work itself out. Don't change for her, for the promise of publication." As I left he added, "When you're ready, come see me; I may have my own publishing company by then."

The next time Catherine Carver wrote me I replied candidly, telling her the gist of my meeting with Harold Robbins. She had a markedly unhappy response—carbon copy to Leo Marx.

"How could you even listen to such a hack!" he berated me after class. "First Charles Olson, then Schuyler, now Harold Robbins. I put myself out for you. You taught me an important lesson: never get too close to students."

But Tripp enjoyed the Harold Robbins affair. ("Serves Marx right," he chuckled. "The fatuous dictator!")

Between semesters Roger had left Phi Psi for the dorms, so I had my room to myself. In his abandoned corner I hung an ancient horse from Lascaux alongside Paul Klee's knight in a rowboat. As the comic figure speared at three crooked fish dilating through a bent shaft of opalescence, the glow lit a universe of more and less deeply-bathed cubes from white azure to blue-black.

On weekends, freed from the burden of making a novel for Viking, I wrote tarot-card poems and passages for *The Moon:*

> Even the word has a strange and undiscovered past: *mone, mona, maan, mana, mond, luna.* Does it describe the timepiece, the light, or both? Is its real meaning yet to come, hiding shadows *in* shadows, creating letters on the ground where geese lay eggs, forming arbors and lagoons, burning slow hieroglyphs in rocks, and, in each turn of the river, leaving a *sweord* without an "e"?

I called a girl out of the Mount Holyoke picture book. Jane was a tall pixie who discovered my scratchy, old *Alice in Wonderland* and insisted we dance to it. Giggling compatibly and stomping like puppets, we acted out the "Lobster Quadrille":

> *"'Will you walk a little faster,' said the lobster to the snail.*
> *'There's a porpoise right behind us, and he's treading on my tail.'"*

Despite our shared admiration for the mock turtle, whenever I called thereafter she said she was busy.

Then one night in February I made a "picture book" date with a girl at Smith and on Saturday hitched over to meet her. She was late coming downstairs and, as I stood by the desk, the striking-looking blond girl on duty asked where I lived and what I was studying. She was also curious why I was dating this person and, when I told her, she smiled and confided that I was in for a surprise. A little later she told me she was herself a poet. We were talking about our writing when my date appeared.

Nancy was a small energetic girl who was already practicing the twist on our way to the highway. She was looking forward to an evening of partying and announced right off that Phi Psi was the pits and we should go elsewhere. She talked so incessantly about a new British rock group that it was years before I was willing to listen to The Beatles with an open mind. All evening I looked forward only to getting back early enough to see if the poet was still on duty. She wasn't ... and I hadn't even gotten her name.

But I was friends with a senior who dated a girl from that house, so I asked him to inquire discreetly. Her name was Ginny, and I called her the next night. "Of course I remember you," she said.

I started to explain how she had been right about my date.

"Do you want to go out this weekend?" she interjected. It was like Tripp saying, "Stop chattering." As simple as that.

What I saw the second time was a lean, medium-height girl with a complicated, mature face and a mien of sadness. Her dress had lots of lace, and she wore a pearl necklace. We caught a ride to Amherst and, after a visit to the basement (where she was much awaited by Paul and a curious crew), we went upstairs where I sat on my desk and she took the couch. I read to her from *The Moon* and Olson's *Distances*. She continued with her own poems and some favorites from a book of D. H. Lawrence I had.

Ginny was from Wisconsin, though she had spent lots of time in the South; she was a sophomore like me and was also thinking of transferring. She bore the same sorts of grievances toward Smith I did toward Amherst, decrying the atmosphere of constant dating, materialistic values, and antipathetic teachers. Her depth was ungaugable, but she was certainly a kindred being.

After she had finished her last poem, there was a silence, and I asked abruptly if she wanted to dance. It was so obviously a request for contact I instantly regretted it. "Maybe that's not such a good idea," I added with a bashful grin.

She said she didn't like to dance but gestured for me to come by her on the couch. I did. We looked at each other, and I saw in her a mirror of my wanting, a mouth opening, and I met it. We kissed long, repeatedly. I reached out from my heart and held her against me. This was what I had waited for, so many tangled years from the dream of Annie Welch. It wasn't just a single kiss, or a feint in a game I didn't understand. It was a time and place to do nothing else but feel someone and be kissed, and kiss. And there was so much to it—hair, a neck, a back, a backbone, a face, lips, a tongue, pausing for a breath and looking at each other, beginning again simultaneously.

We walked silently back to the College Street hitching corner and she said, "I could feel it that first time I saw you. I knew this would happen."

During February and March we went out each Saturday night, sometimes to dinner, sometimes to a movie, but always to my room where we took up kissing and caressing. I was in a waking dream. Loving was not some elusive thing in my future; it was as intrinsic as the desire that led to it, in fact more so, for not being fantasy.

I was astonished to hear Ginny had a boyfriend in law school in Virginia whom she was thinking of marrying. I couldn't imagine why she was becoming so involved with me. She was open about that. "You're very wonderful," she said, "but I don't know who you are. *You* don't even know. You're the original 'ugly duckling,' and I have no idea what you'll become. I'm the first person to reach you, so I can touch only so much. But I love the part of you you let me touch."

I wasn't nearly that articulate emotionally. I couldn't communicate or even understand my absorption in her, but I clung to it compulsively. I wasn't infatuated the way I had been with Betsy or even Joan Snyder. Ginny seemed dainty and fragile. Yet I felt the magnetic flow of my attention onto her, a passion that seemed to dissipate right through her. She was opaque and ulterior to me, but it didn't matter because the weekends had become their own intoxication.

My Lawrence course had built slowly, and now, in this spring of the birth of eros, *The Rainbow* and *Women in Love* infused me with images of the lives of men I might yet be. Paul Goodman may have seen only adolescent lust, but Lawrence detected a spirit drawing souls together beyond discourse. It was a force lodged in our hungering cores, transforming not sublimating, spawning the miracles of domesticity and children. Mutual attraction was as natural and unconscious as fields of flowers and wild rabbits, but it was not discardable as mere instinct; it was the basis of civilization, of church, of art.

Lawrence meant regular rough and scarred men and women, not just playboys and dandies; in fact, he mocked the big talkers and had his women prevail over them, their eros actual and boundless rather than an adjunct of male fantasy:

". . . her limbs vibrated with anguish towards him wherever she was, the radiating force of her soul seemed to travel to him, endlessly, endlessly, and in her soul's own creation, find him. . . ."

. . . so that desiring *was* the mystery. I felt that profoundly with Ginny. It wasn't something that came to an end in fulfillment; it went on forever. And then . . .

"There is only one clue to the universe . . . the individual soul within the individual being. That outer universe of suns and moons and atoms is a secondary affair . . . the death-result of living individuals."

A secondary affair? How incredible to think and believe and then be able to say that! Certainly my physics and geology teachers wouldn't agree. Even my Lawrence teacher considered it mere rhetoric.

Ginny said one night that she wanted to smother my pain. She put her arms over me and hugged me and rubbed my back, but I still felt untouched and wanted her hand to go to my penis. She resisted the hint. Wordlessly I asked why. She said, "It's too soon," and gave me a long kiss. She was so luminous and saintlike I wondered where I made touch with her seduction—or even with the ragged edge of my own desire. My attraction toward her was sinuous and indirect, like an old, old cloth bearing some of her lace and elegance but also a gap across which I could feel nothing. Finally I let my yearning go and plunged into the heap of affection she provided. Down the hall in another universe the Phi Psi jug band was closing out the evening, Paul sliding the base, Jenkins blasting guitar, Bob rapping with thimbles on the washboard, Paul's new girlfriend blowing into a jug. I observed Ginny moving, eyes cast upward, in her own quiet, beyond me.

My only guide was *The Rainbow:*

"Suddenly, cresting the heavy, sandy pass, Ursula lifted her head, and shrank back, momentarily frightened. There was a great whiteness confronting her; the moon was incandescent as a round furnace door out which came the high blast of moonlight, over the seaward half of the world, a dazzling, terrifying glare of white light. They shrank back for a moment into shadow, uttering a cry. He felt his chest laid bare, where the secret was heavily hidden. He felt himself fusing down to a nothingness, like a bead that rapidly disappears in an incandescent flame.

"'How wonderful!' cried Ursula, in low, calling tones. 'How wonderful!' And she went forward, plunging into it. He followed behind."

A Saturday night later, I picked a handful of flowers in the Glen behind Phi Psi and brought them to Smith. Ginny strolled downstairs, short sleeves and a skirt for the warmer weather, a quixotic smile. Delighted with the gift beyond any expectation of mine, she insisted on finding a jar and taking them upstairs to her room. Then we hitched a ride and arrived at a boisterous Phi Psi.

We spent an hour downstairs, talking with Paul, Phil, and Ellen ... drinking tap beer. Ginny was buoyant and flowery, and we danced to (Patti Page) the "Tennessee Waltz," so that I felt like a character in a Hamilton Basso novel *("I remember the night, and ...")*. We went upstairs. I noticed the blossoms-on-peach fabric that made up her dress, how it swooped in and under to follow her shape, framing the line of her breasts. We immediately fell into our tryst.

I experienced the thing between us like a pale, unexamined amber, a glow fluttering alive at the slightest friction. I was straining against my boundaries to contact her, to come to a resolution of this, to know what followed next. She was telling me stories of her brothers in Baltimore, her summer in France where the family she was living with broke apart before her eyes.

I reached under her blouse for the first time and felt the band of her bra in back. She continued to clench and kiss, and I moved to the front and softly held the frilliness covering her breasts. Waves rolled through me, and I rubbed against her with my groin and pulled her onto me. She responded effortlessly, as if she were already there. Our bodies, though clothed, wound in frictioned counterpoint. At junctures I felt flat, as though the current had stopped, but the spark kept reigniting.

Again I noticed her face in the semi-darkness as a vague almost inhuman mask, floating in its own space, its own romanticism. Something older than even desire was pushing me.

I couldn't touch her presence. I kept reaching out through a feeling in my penis that was spreading throughout my body, trying to hold her on it, hold me in her ambiance. I pulled her hand against my hardness, but she took it away. I was frustrated, not sure—if that was the wrong thing—what the right thing was. I tried to rub against her, but my attention was broken. I sat upright and looked at her with questioning eyes.

"We're still not there yet," she said. "We can't force it."

"Why aren't we there?"

"I don't know. There's something missing. It's not you. There just hasn't been enough time."

I trusted her insight, but I was also suspicious. "Is it because of your friend in Virginia?"

"I'm going to see him next weekend, and I want to be clear. Yes, I sleep with him. But he's not the problem I have with you. I'm overwhelmed by you. I care terribly for you. But you're more than I can deal with."

I turned on the light, and we sat there in silence. She felt my sadness and put a hand gently on my face. In my smothered fierceness the openness of her gesture was too much.

I bounced to my feet and left the room. I went upstairs, through the attic onto the roof. I stood in the night air. At a distance I could appreciate her again. As a fantasy, she filled me with desire. I climbed back in through the window and lay in my bed fully dressed. I wanted to cry, but my throat and eyes were hardened against it. I reached for my genitals and rubbed them. I spat on my hand, then rubbed harder. There were no tears there either, only the dull side of disappointed lust. I strained to summon the scene in my room back into my mind so that this time she took hold of my hardness. And staring blankly into her face in my mind I pulled the current up through my surging breath and shot out a bitterness into the sheets, my fingers instantly on top of its warm film, rubbing it into the surface in some meager extension of pleasure.

Then I went back to the room where she was reading, and we talked idly for half an hour—my evasion now a block between us because I couldn't tell her the truth. We left in time to hitch back before her curfew—a thoughtful goodnight kiss at the doorstep. She said she'd see me soon. There was no cloud between us, just a deepening of the puzzle. I assumed things would go on as they had. In the rear of a car full of kids hitching back from Smith to Amherst I stared at the night, over and over in my mind the words of a blues song performed by Tripp on the guitar:

> "I ain't no iceman, no iceman's son,
> But I can keep you cool till that iceman come."

Two days later I got a letter from her:

Dear Richard,

Thank-you, thank-you, thank-you for the flowers. They've made me so happy. My room has been warm and cheerful because every time I've looked at them I've thought of you and that wonderful part of you that I can't understand but is so important & must survive even if transplanted in Washington. I know what you mean, Rich, about losing the words & the experience—the derivatives. I suddenly realized that everything you say means something. It is all so important and I wanted to cry out to you & ask how you understand & what you understand. I wanted you to pull me out but you can't & I can't and now that my panic is passed I wonder if I want it.

The flowers are dead now. There was no fuss or anything. They just died without a whimper. I couldn't stand it—that they should die & be gone and everything would go on as usual so I write you as nearest of kin to inform you of their passing. They lived well and died bravely—not losing their dignity when their beauty faded, leaving behind a vase and a brown paper bag. More than most.

I express my—I'm overdoing this. Well Rich, thank you again. Have a good weekend. I have an exam tomorrow, then, am leaving for U.Va.

'By
Ginny

I didn't realize it then, but that letter was farewell. I came upon it again ten years later while cleaning out old files and was moved to tears. How thoughtful and clear she had been, how heartfelt her statement, and generous! I was a stubborn child, twisted up inside. In all my bravado of complexity and themes within themes, I couldn't hear her simple rightness and respond to her as she deserved.

So I tried to answer ten years late and say "I'm sorry." I wrote to Smith for her address and found out she had left after sophomore year; they had an address for her under a married name in Cochabamba, Bolivia, care of the Peace Corps. My letter came back "addressee unknown."

The last time I saw Ginny was a summery April Saturday a few weekends after her trip to Virginia. I hitched to Smith in high spirits and went to her house and asked for her.

"Hi, hi," she said excitedly, poking her head out of the kitchen. "I can't see you today. I've got lunch duty and then a big paper to write. But call me—we'll set another time."

As a child I read lots of science fiction. In fact, when we were asked to write our first research paper in the Second Form at Horace Mann, mine was entitled "Themes and Symbols in the Work of Robert Sheckley and Theodore Sturgeon." It was that long ago that I incorporated the notion of alternate probabilities into my life. I never let go of it.

Sheckley's argument was that the present is made up of infinitesimal minutiae such that the movement of a single object by a careless time-traveler could alter the whole course of world history. (What if a rock had been seized as a weapon, at a moment of life—or death— by the chief who was to unite the American Indian tribes into a nation that discovered Europe? What if that rock were suddenly kicked out of his reach a thousand years earlier by a time-traveler from a 22nd-Century Indian Empire? If the chief were then killed for the rock being just beyond his reach, the traveler might find not only that he had no country to return to but that he himself was impacted in time and space, unable to be born.)

"Worlds without end," Sheckley had written, "emanating from events large and small; every Alexander and every amoeba creating worlds, just as ripples will spread in a pond no matter how big or how small the stone you throw. Doesn't every object cast a shadow?"

Ever since my Second Form paper I played a game with such shadows, tinkering with paths to alternate universes. Periodically I would take an unplanned route to test if it made any difference in my life. While I could not (of course) know what I missed by my detours, I never succeeded in altering fate in any obvious way. On this morning, however, as promising as blue sky and dandelions, I was disappointed in not having Ginny go with me—I did not want to return to Amherst.

What I failed to see was that she was receding from me anyway at light speed, already a faded memento in a scrapbook. Upon reaching the likely turning-point to the highway I decided to cast my lot with the ripples . . . and turned the opposite way.

Whether by accident or unconscious design, I came to the back end of Laura Scales House and remembered Lindy. I marched in and asked for her at the desk. A few minutes later she appeared in the stairwell.

"What a surprise! I was sitting in the smoker feeling depressed and sorry for myself, not able to do a stitch of work, wishing I had some wonderful visitor . . . and then you just arrive." I asked if she would like to go for a walk into town, maybe a glass of lemonade; and she nodded. "Wait, though," she added. "I want to go upstairs and change."

She came back wearing a blue and white striped polo shirt, a light sweater, and tan pants. After a hiatus of almost six months we took our second walk into Northampton. Stopping at an outdoor cafe we picked up our narration over sweet rolls and lemonades.

It hadn't been working out for her in Philadelphia; she felt used on the weekends and then cast aside—no good conversation, no real emotional contact. So, she wasn't going there for a while, and Saturdays were particularly lonely. Her classes were also discouraging, the teachers uninspired, even vindictive, mainly concerned with a narrow sort of critical thinking.

I could make the same generic complaint about Amherst, but now at least I had a few good courses and was surrounded by exciting people at Phi Psi. I told her about Tripp and *Godot,* about Paul Goodman's visit, about Schuyler, D. H. Lawrence's *Rainbow,* and a bit about Ginny. I even recounted how the ripples had led me to her doorstep. She found that remarkable and foolhardy.

We headed back up the hill, a charge of ideas and rhythm between us. Everywhere sun, birds, flowers filled the air, and my mind and heart. I told her a sudden inkling—that Freud had discovered only the *method* of symbols, but nature itself from the beginning of time had been creating reflections and replicas. I identified them wheeling about: the speech of blue jays, patterns of clouds and leaves, signals not needing interpretation or criticism. "The trouble with our teachers is they think they can explain things. But there's nothing to explain. There's only the breeze, the Wheel of Fortune, those dandelions, and billions of stars."

Then Lindy moved the conversation to *Moby Dick* (the subject of the paper she was trying to write when I arrived), and I pointed at the sun that Ahab said he would strike if it insulted him. "That *is* the White Whale," I said. "Its primal force is there. Ahab wanted to strike at the heart of nature itself. The Whale was just a passing snare."

"I can see that," Lindy said. "So much more powerful than a symbol to be a real breathing creature, a real sun." She was lucid and sparkling, tall and strong, challenging me with a forcefulness like my own. She spoke not of magic and literary allusions (as I was wont to) but of emotions and feelings and how hard it was to reach people. "For me they always seem to skitter over my surface like bugs. The shallowness of people even betrays this lovely day. Maybe only the trees and fields can be touched, and they don't speak. Certainly I couldn't touch Steve, or Asher before that, and it doesn't appear as though you could touch Ginny."

I adored her directness. Her face conveyed an Athena-like intelligence, and her eyes were filled with sensuality and compassion. This was the beginning—we both must have known that. I felt that afternoon like the Magician presiding over the First Trump, spinning out worlds without diminution. She was the High Priestess of the Second Trump, deepening them, weaving them together, making the universe calm and lovely. We found a place on the grass and held court there until late afternoon. Then we hiked back to Wiggins Tavern for dinner.

The following Saturday I met her again, downstairs in Laura Scales. She was more dressed up, in a blouse and dark skirt and perfume, and we hitched to Amherst together. I felt uncertain about who we were as boy and girl. To me she was as perfect as anyone could be, present and contacting, sexy by her force of personality alone but also stunning with a Circê look I could never resist. Her mouth was large and sensuous, her light grey eyes intense and focusing under dark brows. Her body was a dancer's, elegant, poised in its movements, strong and yet light, large hips, full but delicate breasts. Was this a date?

We sat downstairs at a table, drank beer, ate pretzels, talked. I felt so pleased to be with her even if she wasn't a true girlfriend. There was a brief predicament when Asher peeked in with his consort, but he saw Lindy and was quickly out.

I asked her if she had noticed him, and she nodded. "He's still chaperoning around *les* selected *femmes* like some sort of mogul. He's pretty gross."

"He's also a fake. For all of us still, it's our parents' money," I said. "We haven't done anything yet. It's so easy to pretend and lose who you are."

"For girls it's especially easy. You're taught to please men, to be what they like, and you get to do that so suppely you don't even realize you're doing it." She paused. "This friendship is a great relief to me, like a break from the whole tyranny of dating."

A small part of my heart sank on that comment, but I didn't back off. In the first chapter of *The Rainbow* Tom Brangwen was carrying a load of seed in his cart out of Nottingham through Cossethay; that's when "she" passed him on the road—the unknown woman who carried off his mind and soul. "The load of seed" was both a cargo and a symbol, not just for the male gamete but the germinal force itself: tiny seeds, which having borne us blindly into being, in their ripening bear us toward fruition. We don't have a choice, Lawrence warned. When we least expect it, nature summons men and women from obscurity to be each other's lovers.

There was a silence between us, and she said, "let's dance," and I said "okay," and I held her almost fragilely as if to preserve every molecule of our contact, its different weight, scent, her blouse, the feel of her head against mine, the tightness of her bones and muscles, her sweet, gentle angularity. She was so much denser and springier than Ginny.

I didn't know what was proper—dance close, dance chastely apart—but she automatically danced close, and I felt myself transported, as much by the sense of our fitting together—the solidity and definiteness of her—as by a sexual feeling. I was inundated by her whole intelligence and bearing. It was the first time a dance did not feel self-conscious.

It was my own tape playing now, from the movie *The Alamo* ... the Brothers Four singing, but I heard it as the theme song of *The Rainbow:*

> *"A time just for reaping, a time just for sowing,*
> *The green leaves of summer are calling me home...."*

Oh, everything.

In that moment every intimation I ever had filled me. I didn't have to know the answer or articulate the mystery. Just as I was, I was complete.

In the song I experienced the generations of life on Earth—single men and women—each come into being, grow, find lovers, have babies, plant their crops, die. I had spent my time on dream planets. But Lindy was the grace of the whole West—and I was holding her.

> *"A time to be courting*
> *A girl of your own...."*

And then she did something startling. She playfully blew in my ear, not just once, but continuously, a soft, sustained breath. I had never felt anything so tender and tantalizing. My body froze in rapture, as though all my attention had to go into perceiving this before it passed. She blew harder, looked at me, smiled, then blew in my other ear. With adolescent awkwardness I felt myself become hard and extend out against her. She acknowledged that with a smile, and then shifted her head and put her tongue in my ear and rolled it there so smoothly and deeply I felt as though it were passing through my brain. I drifted in bliss trying to make that ear even more available to her. And, for once, my feeling sustained the feeling in the song:

> *"Twas so good to be young then, to be close to the earth,*
> *And to stand by your wife, at the moment of birth."*

Now I glimpsed the pathway to the center and saw how rich and complicated the world was. Everything I had both feared and wanted had an existence, an autonomous tangibility. In my senses I tumbled through primal symbols, fragments of memories ... the relic of an Easter egg hunt, a tulip garden at the edge of creation, into the forest of my sixth-grade dream. The moisture from those aromatic vines coursed through my ears. I saw a friend a child once had named Phil, a magician Dr. Fabian, kids from Bill-Dave baseball, from camp singing in a chain, all combined in me, all once, all briefly, because in my heart, which was full, I wanted to acknowledge them each and thank them, for being alive, for me being alive, for sustaining me to get this far, to this large a reckoning.

The sense of doom was gone. I saw my freedom. We left the basement and went to my room, and she lay atop and freely kissed me and laughed, and put my hands on her bare breasts. And then she jumped up like a sprite, and said, "Enough of this stuffy place." And we went onto the roof overlooking lit fields between fraternities, sounds of the Saturday night bands drifting together. It was peaceful just to lie there and look at stars—in the breeze feel as though the planet itself were rolling in space. I hugged her more tightly and she began to breathe harder and run her hands along me, feeling the lines of my waist, and then my chest—that secret territory, realm of imagined diseases in childhood. Her touch opened it to feeling, and I took my shirt off under the starlight and felt warm.

"You look great, alive," she said. "Beautiful. You *are* beautiful. Don't you know that?" she demanded, shaking me with a smile. I held her silently, feeling her shape against my chest, thinking it was her that made me beautiful, and then she lay on her back and sighed, and I sat lightly on her waist and rubbed her breasts and along the lines of her body, trying to feel her without violating the dignity with which she opened to me. It *was* like praying.

And then she put her hands on my nipples and felt my torso, undid my belt. She pulled me on top of her again, and putting her tongue in my ear, reached down with her hand and held me and gently played with me—all the time the link between us lucid and real, the point of contact unbroken. "Don't be afraid," she said, though I didn't think I was. "It's a fine thing. It's a lovely full hardness."

And then we stopped and went no further. I lay there, her hand on my chest, exposed and joyous in this open place. This was the extent of it, as much as I needed in order to feel absolved.

That night, at bedtime, I read Olson's "Moonset" poem from Gloucester, December 1, 1957, 1:58 AM:

> "Not
>   the suffering one you sold
>   sowed me on Rise
>   Mother from off me
>   God damn you God damn me my
>   misunderstanding of you
>   I can die now I just begun to live."

My mother, Mr. Murphy, Abbey, Betsy: I could reach back to each of them and tell them, forget it, whatever happened, it's okay. The kid is going to survive.

PART
FIVE

THE CEREMONY

April, 1964–June, 1965

THE TAROT

Two nights after Lindy's visit to Phi Psi, Asher came into the bathroom as a few of us were brushing our teeth. Purposely ignoring me, he turned right to Dave and said, "Did you see? My former live-in whore was just by here the other night."

I whipped around. "You fat bastard!"

"You're going to take that back," he growled.

"Like hell I am!" I stared right at him. "Pretentious jerk!"

He charged at me like a rhinoceros and, as I swung back, he tried to pin me against the mirror. I slid out of his grasp. He pounced again. Toothpaste, shaving cream, and sundries crashed along the shelves. Then Dave grabbed him and, with Phil's help, pulled him out and led him back to his room: "Cool it, man; cool it."

A week later Asher moved into the dorms.

Life had followed the script of a Lawrence novel—an esoteric undertow that carried me through the veil of plot and character into the heart of a sacred text. Betsy had stood at its outer gate, a guardian spirit. Then I had a date with the wrong girl ... and someone else was sitting in the alcove.

Where Ginny led me (or I her) we followed as though Star and Moon trumps were themselves our guides—until we were blindfolded down separate paths. Lindy was waiting at the ripples of the Stream of Probability. What was elusive with Ginny was now as simple as breath itself.

Lindy and I made spring into our continuous study date: alongside Paradise Pond at Smith, on the Phi Psi lawn, in Valentine between meals. The tableau of Phi Psi faded—Paul, Jenkins, and the rest. We still hung around, but we were no longer confidantes or collaborators on changing the world. What I needed were Lindy and my two most demanding male friends, Jeff and Schuyler.

During that term Schuy became buddies with Larry and Chip, obstreperous juniors from my Lawrence seminar. The four of us maintained a running satire as we spoofed and flaunted Amherst fashions (sitting in the dining hall, noting "cowboy cool," "big man," and pseudointellectual). Larry and Chip were actually cowboys of their own ilk; decked out in jeans and leather, they shared a souped-up old sedan and spoke in periodic Laurentian and Keatsian mime.

One Saturday Larry drove us all to a swimming hole up north near Vermont: Chip, Schuy, me, and our dates. I felt an ancient wistfulness, as Lindy and I lay on our backs in the grass . . . clouds blown apart in the jetstream. I was chasing the bare eclipse of a form, itself a shadow. Beyond the hill, the land dipped precipitously into the unknown, an obliquity that masked a dream. Something indelible was lost; something equally remote still beckoned.

Then we dove into the water, smashing sky.

That evening Lindy, Tripp, and I took a walk along backroads— he delivering speeches from *Godot,* she improvising with surprising aplomb. Then she spat from a bridge into headlights—a Colorado method, she said, to gauge the speed of cars. "Pretty tough girl," he confided later. And he was the ultimate judge.

Schuy's friends turned out to be more than collegiate rebels and cowboy poets; they were rogue revolutionaries. After keeping their alter egos secret for months Schuy finally confided in April that Chip (known as Axis, a near-homonym of his last name) was king of something called "guerrilla warfare," conducted on Saturdays after midnight at the Psi U fraternity house. "It's beyond description," he said. "If you could just see it you'd realize that Phi Psi is a bunch of wimps."

Later that month he extended a guarded invitation: Axis had arranged for me to witness a session of war as a noncombatant. He couldn't a hundred percent assure my safety, but I would be under his protection. If he prevailed no one would bother me. If he were defeated it was every man for himself.

Just after midnight I met Schuy at his dorm. From there I followed him along College Street to Psi U. With unnecessary bravado he shoved open the front door, pointed the way down stairs, and led me through catacombs to an unlit sector. It was crammed wall to wall with bodies. A single lantern shone. Occasionally someone let out a shout, but mostly we jostled one another.

Suddenly—with a scream—Axis leaped onto the bar. His chest was painted in blocks of color, American Indian style. He stared down the group. Then he danced in place as others threw objects at him—mostly their cups of beer. He retaliated with the hose from the keg, its spray singeing even Schuy and me.

Gradually the repartee became more frenzied. Axis goaded the others with taunts. People tried to yank him off his perch, but with the help of allies he beat them back. Skirmishes broke out, and Schuy whispered, "Stay close . . . just watch. Do you see *The Plumed Serpent?*"

He meant Axis' favorite Lawrence novel, in which males transcend their mediocre social condition and enact soul-magic. But this was an Ivy League fraternity not a kiva, and I was unwilling to concede such prestige. The ritual at the bar was Psi U's attempt at primitive courage, a way of striking back against the allure of women. Here in the basement, after curfew, after their dates were dispatched, they could be godmen (and literary critics) at the same time.

Some of the brethren raised hand-made torches. The room shimmered. The keg nearly empty, Axis demolished it with a hammer. He poured kerosene on its pieces, and Larry applied a torch. Spinning before the fire, brandishing a lance and dislodging challengers who came at him with sticks and ropes, Axis became a visitor from Aztec myth. As the Psi U basement resounded with chanting, a chorus of males in round dance, it was actually a parody of late baroque Lawrence, fascist and primordial:

"Now she understood the strange unison she could always feel between Ramon and his men, and Cipriano and his men. It was the soft, quaking, deep communion of blood-oneness. Sometimes it made her feel sick. Sometimes it made her revolt. But it was the power she could not get beyond."

While Axis was still king, Schuy and I slipped out of the war-zone—

though we had to shove past a few "enemies" to clear our way. (And nowadays I smile when I read in the *Amherst Alumni Magazine* of the "king's" appointment to boards of psychiatric hospitals. I wonder what his colleagues would make of his reign in the Psi U basement.)

Later that spring Paul and about half of Phi Psi threw themselves into planning an anti-segregation march through the South. As students from various colleges showed up in our living room, Tripp was a scornful spectator. "It's a waste of time. What are these jerk-off college kids going to do against the resident rednecks. Protests don't bring change; they just generate conflict. Only acts of radical art bring big enough shit into the world."

Our guests bristled in umbrage, and Paul was facetiously gracious. "Count on you, Jeff, to stand in the way of social justice."

"I certainly hope so."

Jeff, as it turned out, had a more personal stake in our loyalties. He had invited an avant-garde film-maker he long admired to show his work the weekend of the political congregation. He wanted Phi Psi—and especially me—at *his* event. I was ambivalent and told him so.

"Well, get your priorities straight, guy. This is a crossroads, and what you choose, you just may become."

The film-maker's name was Stan Brakhage, and he arrived as a guest of Phi Psi a few days ahead of time. After spotting him, Jenkins warned Paul and me to expect "a cross between a water buffalo and a Spanish revolutionary." It wasn't a bad description. Aloof and humorless, Tripp's gunslinger prowled the second floor, snubbing the rest of us en route to the bathroom and stairs.

My ambivalence came to a head on Friday night when Brakhage's lecture coincided with a meeting for march participants. Right up to the last moment I intended to go on the march. I was angry at Jeff for pressuring me otherwise. Had he no appreciation for the Dylan of *"The Times, They are A-Changin' "*—this selfish bully with his Porsche, guitar, and private acting troop? But then I found myself walking from the dining room to the theater with Schuy, no clear motive except that this was where my heart had been all along.

On stage in front of a screen, waiting for the room to settle, Brakhage paced, hands behind his back. Schuy admired the snarl: "He's a tough guy all right!"

Then Tripp's hero launched into a discursion of aesthetic theory, punning and undercutting his own meanings, to stay free (as he put it) of the patterns of literal speech: "Howsomever being then whom?-soever with whatever lets it be. . . . A film more filmically than script, than art, than arc-key, than spiri-spherically? . . . a fil, a fi-fie-foe-fiddle-di-dum." I looked at Schuy incredulously.

Brakhage warned against any expectation of conventional visualizing, offering instead the color of non-colors, the shadows of angels, the blackness behind the sun: "I serve the fates, the actual stars, not their Hollywood imitations." He meant the sunstars of creation, the tarot, which he then contrasted to the imagistically depleted decks of card games.

Twittering or smirking, much of the Amherst audience left even before the projector was turned on, their catcalls echoing down the hall. But I had no doubts any longer. This man was not Tripp's ornery house guest. He carried the torch of Beckett and Olson. He was telling us that he had survived by refusing conventions, by inventing his own forms and confronting the universe head-on. In fact, he was showing us how to live on the roller coaster, both of mind and heart.

In the first film a man in slow motion struggled up a snow-covered mountainside, his dog running beside him . . . light distorted, mirrored, scratched, twinkling, eroding, reconstituting, floating disjunctively in layers that seemed to dissolve through one another into new images at different scales and perspectives. Sudden flares of the sun's corona shot through a black silhouette of a tree . . . then both were gone and we saw the actual surface of the film cracking, a baby being born . . . snow falling . . . wild flowers . . . unfinished spirals . . . night traffic . . . fragments of faces . . . actual constellations . . . waves of colored fish . . . a brief moon with clouds crossing . . . he and his wife naked as lovers . . . nothing . . . a door opening to a house . . . a woman's breasts . . . candlelight. This irregular chorus rose and fell in visual harmonics. *Dog Star Man* was more than science fiction or surrealism; it was pulsating, irreducible montage.

The second film was made from moth bodies pasted on mylar, so that one saw a dance glinting through the actual texture of wings. ("As a moth might see from birth to death if black were white," Brakhage said.)

The next film was pure night interrupted only by widely separated strokes of lightning. Suddenly a syncopated double-star appeared, as if to remind us that our life takes place on a strange world under inexplicable circumstances—then a single unearthly cry: the slowed-down recording of a child being born (this was the only sound in any of the films). *Fire of Waters,* its maker called it—fire of the light of which we are made, waters of the birth canal in which we are washed ashore.

Schuy was thoroughly won over. When Brakhage stayed in the front answering questions he remained there even long after I got sleepy and returned to Phi Psi. The next day at lunch he reviewed it for me:

"We're completely enslaved by these advertising images, all the crap we're supposed to be—so that we can look like soapsuds men, so that girls will like us, so that we can get jobs. He's outside of that, and so he's able to make his own things—and without the derivative academic language of Marx and his buddies."

In truth, there was no resemblance between the life Brakhage embodied and that of my teachers or parents. They came from two different civilizations. And his oddly was the more familiar to me.

Frustrated at having missed such an epic event, Lindy devised a plan on the phone. Since Brakhage lived in the mountains outside Denver, maybe I could come and visit her at Christmas and we'd go find him.

Later that week she and Schuy joined my Abnormal Psych class at the movie *David and Lisa.* Lisa was this mute, schizophrenic girl-child, darkly beautiful; David was an uptight compulsive teenager, obsessed with clocks and death, phobic about being touched. They were residents of the same mental hospital and, gradually through the story, drew each other out. At first she talked to him in rhyme, saying things like, "Hello, kiddo" and "Today I'm low, low; so, David, go, go, go." In the culminative scene she walked right up to him, her hand extended . . . and he finally allowed her to touch him.

Schuy was enraged at this resolution. "What's wrong with David's alienation?" he demanded. "He didn't want to be touched. He understood clocks were the enemy. Why couldn't they leave him alone? Why did some pretty girl come along and invade him?"

But Lisa was my icon. Soon after the showing, a classmate with literary ambition—who now writes for *Playboy*—tried to mock me at dinner by reciting her rhymes in a dopey voice. I picked up my plate of spaghetti-and-sauce and dumped it on his head.

On a Saturday morning in mid-May I was sitting in a cloister of sun in the Phi Psi stairwell, reading *The New York Times* and eating by hand from a box of Corn Kix into which I had poured half a carton of currants. There were complete Yankee and Met articles to devour, plus seasonal averages. Lindy and I were going out that night.

Suddenly the ocher hue on the rug seemed to flicker and change. The world deepened by a layer, and I felt something oppressive inside me. I took a quick breath and put my interest back into details of box scores.

There was a brief hiatus; then the deepening came again—a tremor followed by a series of tremors. Their sheer output was incredible. I felt disoriented.

I bolted from the stairwell and took an immediate protective stance on the floor of my room—feet up, arms around my knees. The biggest one yet swelled . . . right out of my center, visceral, primeval, bottomless.

I told myself that nothing was happening; it was some sort of passing sensation like heartburn or a headache. It would subside.

I was astonished how solid and fixed it was. Everywhere I turned I felt *it* coming at me, nameless, remorseless, looming up from the background of existence—neither simple nor manipulable.

I reached behind and around my neck . . . and contacted a string of odd lumps. Had I developed tumors overnight? In alarm I jumped to my feet and grabbed for the top of my backbone. It was hard as stone!

Racing to the bathroom mirror, I ran my fingers frantically up and down my skeleton. I had always had a backbone, but what was that floating bump above it? It throbbed, as I twisted and pressed it.

There were times at Grossinger's I was overcome with a homesickness that made no sense given I was "home." Some mornings, coming down the stairs to breakfast, I would get a dose of color of sun on the walls.

The light was too pale. I felt suddenly as though the joys of the Hotel and Aunt Bunny's household weren't that at all, and that I didn't belong there.

Usually this melted into something remote and wistful, too vague even to tell Dr. Friend. I tried to explain it to Aunt Bunny. She assumed it was a form of anxiety, or thought maybe that I really did miss my other family.

A flurry of Hotel activity always swept away the mood, but a part of me knew it was there and someday would return.

Till that morning sophomore year of Amherst, though, I had not had a panic since Mr. Hilowitz charmed me out of the last one at the end of sixth grade. The occasional flutters I rationalized as vestiges of childhood. I had grown up like a weed through debris—intrepid, stubborn, tough. But Dr. Friend had seen the other side of the coin; he expected me to apply to Columbia. He knew that Amherst was pure bravado. He saw, all along, panic had been biding (not diminishing), disguising itself in my boundaries, driving me into daydreams and compulsive rituals. For all my vigilance I failed to recognize their truth. I had been masking a fugue in heroism and romance. No wonder my friendships were thin and substanceless. Even my pranks had sinister roots. For years I had been a centurion, keeping at bay wolves who weren't wolves, who wouldn't be held off indefinitely.

Time passed; colors restored; life began to take hold. The lingering pangs became an attack from which I was separating. I sensed them in the near distance, their premise absurd. I summoned Beckett and Camus to my defense. *They* knew about the darkness of infinite spaces, the void left by an absent god. They were not afraid. In fact, they sang in the darkness. I could sing in the darkness too.

Although the universe was an agent of death, it didn't select me alone as its victim. We were all in this together. The goblin was cosmic not personal.

Thus reassured—even a bit hopeful—I joined the human race at lunch and spent the afternoon studying geology.

Lindy and I met for dinner in Northampton and afterwards sat on a Smith lawn; she stroked my suspect backbone, felt nothing odd, and reassured me. The anticipation of seeing her—and then the logistics of getting there—had sustained the day till then. In her presence the world was soft, sensuous, just a fraction out of orbit. I thought maybe I could outrun it and live.

But panic came the next morning, synonymous with my awareness of waking; its dread waves rolled through the overbrightness of sun. I heard a distant radio, like a foghorn. Getting dressed, I caught a glimmer of spring outside, guys beyond the window in tee shirts and shorts—so much easy-going activity it was intolerable. Just two days ago I was one of them—baseball, banter, classes. I was normal, a bit of a rebel and a nut but an okay guy. Now I walked like a zombie, going through a pretense of conversation and meals.

Why was this happening? I searched inside me for anything that felt mutable, capable of humor. Instead I recalled the lobby of the Y with its fruit machines, as real as yesterday, more real for its mucid gloominess. I saw the natal sun come up through swamp vines from a whining train. Those images were lethal, cold as radiation. I thought: I can wait this one out.

I couldn't. For it wasn't just a matter of minutes, or hours. Every second, my heart beat . . . and I took another breath.

It would have been manageable (I thought) if the panic were the trauma of my wound from my mother, but once again she seemed a pathetic accomplice to forces beyond my lifetime. This must have been the evil my parents saw and feared in me—that I was the carrier of darkness. I might contaminate others. I should be quarantined from the whole human race. Even as I thought that, I thought, 'Down the dungeon stairs, into the darkness, forever.' The threat was a million times worse than the Cuban Missile Crisis, for nuclear war would incinerate all life and thought. I would be blasted into nothing. This, on the other hand, would go on forever, waking me up from every life and every death, to experience it again. I was truly and utterly terrified.

I bolted.

She was studying for an exam but took time off and walked around Paradise Pond with me. We sat on its far edge. "You'll be okay. You're really a wonderful person; you've just forgotten. It's as though your mother put something inside you—a curse—and you have to find it and defeat it. Ghosts are so much harder than daylight. But you're courageous. You'll do it."

I returned to Amherst heartened.

Days passed interminably. I wrote Dr. Friend for the first time since high school. He sent back three sentences of cheery encouragement. I could tell he had no inkling or, if he did, nothing resembling a solution.

I hitched grimly back to Laura Scales.

"You show up here looking spooked," Lindy snapped, "and what can I do that I haven't done?"

I stood by her, sheepish and agreeing. She had too much school-work to spend any more time on this, but she made an offer to study together by the pond. Beside her I was in a state of grace and finished a day of assignments as the sun crossed the sky.

We headed back in late afternoon, holding hands. She grabbed my arm and wrist together, as though to snap me out of it, coaxing me with lines from *David and Lisa:*

"Your face is nice; not like snow, not like ice."

I laughed appreciatively.

"Haven't you been this bad before and gotten out of it?"

"Never this bad. Never like this."

"Well, maybe that's just because nothing has been at stake before."

I nodded.

I promised to give it a week before I called again. During the ensuing days at Amherst I let the tremors build and disperse. I tried to defuse them by reasoning against their hysteria, tracing the semblance of their origin in me. I packed as much mundane life as I could between fluc-tuations.

Saturday afternoon, I looked back through the years and saw nothing, just thousands of meaningless ballgames on which I had wasted my life, staged psychiatric sessions, family melodrama, pages of nervous-energy writing rejected by Mr. Ervin and Catherine Carver anyway. It was a wasteland; it passed for a life because no one had looked at it closely. I had never really met the challenge of having been born. Now I had no right to live. I wasn't a scion of magic and vision. I wasn't a spokesman for my generation or novelist-in-training. I wasn't funny or capricious. I wasn't even good. I was nasty and selfish—my mother's

bane, Jonny's tormentor, Dr. Fabian's traitor, a petty prankster, a mindless tyrant. I had been grade-hungry at Horace Mann; now I was sloppy
and narcissistic: both were vacuous states.

All the time telling myself, no! retreat!, I went back to Laura Scales.

"I can't keep doing this, Rich! You've got to solve this yourself.
You're not some special case. We're each of us alone with our own
ghosts."

We went out again. "Just a short walk this time," she made me
promise. She loped beside, withholding comment, in warm sun then
shadow. I wanted to be regular like her, to stand up and live the damn
life.

Yet ordinary existence seemed a sham, like play-acting. I couldn't
fake or carry its weight. Nothing except the fact of us interested me.
Everything else was a life sentence. I thought, 'I'm destroying this, this
one possible thing I've made.'

"I'm weak," she said. "Don't you see that? I can hardly save myself,
let alone you. The world is not ugly; the world is good and beautiful."

I trudged silently as the sky proved her right, showing its last sienna
hues before twilight. Couldn't I just give this up and disappear, never
have been? A cat stared up and bounded across the path. She smiled
and extended a palm in its direction. Everything was so studied, so flat.

We reached her house. "End of the line, kiddo."

How did *anyone* live?

For lack of another option I kept going to class, almost losing hold of
Geology because I didn't have the patience to sit through labs with
rocks all over the floor imitating a landscape. I wrote my term paper
as a script, with the monadnocks and mountains and rivers announcing their roles aloud. At least I got a bemused C.

Abnormal Psych was my one solace, for I could pore over the textbook for disorders that seemed to apply to me. I wanted to be an episode
like an oxbow lake or continental drift, something explicable that Dr.
Friend could cite from years of work with me. But I sensed the reti-
cence in his response, his unwillingness even to admit that we were
the blind being led by the blind.

I had fallen down the dungeon stairs, past Nanny's ancient grasp,
into the darkness, forever. But now—I understood—it wasn't a dun-

geon of granite or stone. It had nothing to do with matter. Yet even the wildest volcano had a cause, a force behind it:

"Anxiety attacks are acute episodes of emotional decompensation usually appearing in a setting of chronic anxiety, and exhibiting to an exaggerated degree the characteristics of normal fright. The fright usually comes from within, from a sudden upsurge of unconscious material that threatens to disrupt ego integration. The anxiety attack often climaxes a long period of mounting tension to which the anxious person has been progressively adapting, but with ever-increasing difficulty. Finally the limits of tolerance are reached, he can compensate no further, and the continued stress precipitates a sudden discharge into all available channels."

"... *into all available channels!*"

My diagnosis was that I was plummeting through the entirety of my unconscious childhood, recapitulated as blind terror at this turning-point in my life. On the path to my freedom, I had met my shadow head on. And it was bigger than the whole universe!

"Whether or not the patient is able to verbalize what he is doing and what attracts him, the basic situation is the same. He is impelled to repeat his futile, frustrating behavior—in overt action or in fantasy or daydream—because of the relentless pressure of unconscious infantile urges, fears, temptations and conflicts."

The next time a wave of panic came I ran to Roy Heath's house. He was hurrying down the front stairs to class. He looked at me.

I tried to explain, clenching my fists, running fingers through my hair down over my face, grabbing my arms.

"What affect!" he noted instructively, never breaking stride. His observation cast a quick mirror; I saw myself absurdly in our textbook, then laughed at both of us and accompanied him to class.

The next night I dreamed of an unexpectedly immense wind. It blew across the darkness, carrying images, image fragments, scraps of paper down avenues of the City. Fierce, unformed animals—wolves and cats and curs—tore off the dream shroud, led me through its scar into a hollow, a true void. There, UFOs patrolled an outer sky of too many planets and moons.

This counted. This was real too. This was an actual place—always had been.

They never spotted me as I ran through high grass and hid in vines. The wind was frantic, bracing. Everything that needed to be changed it ripped apart, swallowed into its momentum without distraction or regard.

In the morning I felt both better and worse. I was dizzy and hungover but, paradoxically, not as afraid. I went to geology class without fully appreciating the change. I had a spark; I felt normal!

I finished lab by working through half my lunch hour. Then I ran back to Phi Psi in glee. It was over! I knew that implicitly, even as I knew when it began. There was no reason or resolution; it was just gone. In its place was something like the dream wind, carrying the most beautiful images across spring morning—shards of an unwritten ode. The shadow of doom had been replaced by an ebullience that had so much melody and hope it was absurd. Was it ever a stunning day—such blue heavens, so many blossoms, such wondrous insects and birds! I didn't have enough music for it all, but I found a patch in the Glen and took those lines that came:

> Day of blind flies, lethargic clouds, tardy stars.
> Once again you have come to haunt me dead. . . .

Four sheets of paper later I came to a crescendo:

> And for the first time you asked the only question
> That you could never stop asking
> Until weary with wrinkles and questions
> You stood by another fence,
> Eons apart,
> And knew that the sun of the tarot,
> That Apollo,
> That the golden blood of susans
> Were born before men
> And planted in men's eyes
> To pull men back
> To the honeyrod fields of time.

The lines translated themselves from nature as lucidly as stanzas of Virgil. Nothing eluded me, nothing fooled me; subjunctives and strings of participles were right at hand in the breeze and grass. All I needed was to decode the words of a slightly unfamiliar dialect "swim-

ming in arcs of separate selves/Out of concentric circles of öo-births."
Images flew by, everywhere I looked: a back-up first baseman from the
old Yankees (Don Bollweg transformed into granite-gneiss pinstripes),
daisies across fields of childhood, the haunted land beside a cobblestone road, "a tiny dead bug/drifting across a marsh moon/into the
black/forever," "the fleeting blackbirds from maple pies" ("four and
twenty in four and twenty speckled swarms"), "the Spaldeen rabbit
bouncing home." The sky's deepest blue finally spoke; the stream
through the Glen uttered the ancient proverb of my life:

> Depart this dawn-haunted house.
> Depart this laughing kitchen. It is
> A tide of the rising sun,
> A spooking hole
> For the dancing yellow heart.
> ... run out beneath the long sky
> Before it mellows
> To the purple wine of twilight,
> Comes supper comes terror!
> Comes terror if you have not sweated, loved, or sung a song
> On a day of the haunted dawn.

By mid-afternoon I had entered the realm of the planet Jupiter:

> ... a sea of Jovian pomander
>   of squashed gases,
>   of methane-smoking caterpillars,
>   of purple electric breezes
>   That come with the ozone rain
>   And the neon rainbows.
> With spring I am launched
> From the quiet frozen moon
>   Of Io
> To the dense bosom
>   Of swirling clays. . . .
>   The prehistoric wish,
>   The Cro Magnon sperm,
>   The weeping willow of Om,
> All lost   All not lost:
>   The ancient baby of Tigres
>   The young ageless of Atlantis. . . .

After twenty pages I dropped my pen into the grass and looked around at the calm summery world that had arrived in my absence. I was starving. I felt as though I hadn't eaten for eight days. I ran to the snack bar and ordered two cheeseburgers, a plate of fries, and a maple-walnut frappe.

Before the end of the semester Lindy went to Penn to see Steve again for the weekend. I was dismayed, but I figured rather than wait this one out, I'd put myself in motion too. The previous summer I had made friends with one of the hotel drivers, a kid about five years older than me named Jimmy McAndrews. He had told me any time I'd like to phone in a trip from Amherst he'd be thrilled to come and get me and see that part of the world. So instead of petitioning my naysaying father I called Jimmy directly at Traffic, and on Friday afternoon, like magic he was sitting in the black Cadillac in the Phi Psi parking lot.

"I don't think anyone really knows where the PG went," he told me, naming the car by its license.

On the way to Grossinger's he heard all about my new girlfriend who, sadly, was checking out her past guy in Philly—even that scenario so deliciously American compared to panic. As he let me drive my first 200 miles, we mustered a plan. Coming back on Sunday we'd intercept the last bus from Philadelphia in Hartford. Ideally she'd be on it; then we'd drive her back to Smith.

Sunday evening we filled the PG with sandwiches, fruit, cookies, and Heinekens and timed our departure so that three hours later we actually beat the bus by fifteen minutes. Lindy was astonished to spot me from the window and immediately debarked. She claimed her suitcase and jumped in.

By the time we reached Smith we were all three jiving and drinking beers.

The following week I received an acceptance letter from Seattle, but that now seemed a remote fantasy. I couldn't imagine not returning, so once again I went to the Phi Psi room committee, hat in hand. They assigned me the large double on the first floor, to be shared with a wide-eyed sophomore-to-be from Boston named Marty.

The last date with Lindy was agonizing; we were already planting the necessary distance between us and, as we strolled by the boathouse holding hands, we argued about where our relationship would lead. The time apart would be good for us, she said. Now that I was strong again I should build on my strength. "We can date new people and write each other wonderful intimate letters as confidantes." Her jovial mood made me sullen, and I accused her of tearing down what we had.

She said we would always be good friends but could never be more than that. I didn't want any limit on it, didn't see any reason for a limit now that we were parting.

At the airport I kissed her quickly. Our goodbye passed without lingering—a girl with a suitcase merging into the general crowd.

Upon my arrival at Grossinger's my father told me (with a hint of iron- ical fanfare) that I had been promoted to desk clerk. I gave him a codliver-oil look. Playing hotel was not what I wanted and, in such a visible role, there was no chance for a repeat of my escapades of the previous summer. After thinking about it for a day I told him I'd pre- fer to get my own job.

He was momentarily speechless. "Okay," he responded with a series of perturbed nods. "I'll give you a week. If you don't find one by then you're washing dishes all summer."

My impasse of transportation was solved almost immediately. On a visit to Grandma Jennie the next morning she offered to lend me her white Lincoln Continental (the JG) for the whole summer! It was not what I had envisioned (ostentatious for a nineteen-year-old with 200 miles under his belt), but there were no ready alternatives. I knew my father gave her regular grief about it, but apparently she held her ground because, other than continuously making me repark it, he never interceded.

Lindy was going to intern at *The Rocky Mountain News* in Denver, and I figured a newspaper was the most promising opportunity for me too. Setting off in my chariot, I turned east onto Route 52 and drove fifteen miles to the relatively large town of Ellenville, site of the Nevele. No luck.

For the next three days I tried newspaper offices from there through Monticello, Liberty, and even smaller villages, filling out employment forms that probably no one has yet taken out of the files.

Then I worked my way west on 52—the less populous direction out of Liberty along the Delaware River, across train tracks into Hortonville, past old farms and covered bridges. This was even worse: no newspapers at all. On my last allotted day I came to the Pennsylvania border town of Callicoon, thirty miles from Grossinger's. Right on its main street was a classic storefront: *The Sullivan County Democrat.* I poked my head into an alcove dominated by galleys and stacks of metal type.

The proprietor was a mountain of a man named Fred Stabbert. He extended his hand to the young stranger and, with a friendly bark, grilled me right at the doorway. He said he'd hire me once he determined I wasn't running away from home. "The last place I need trouble from is Grossinger's."

The *Democrat* was the one anti-hotel paper in a conservative Republican county, and it struck Fred as odd that the son of the owner of the largest resort should come to his door looking for work. He no doubt took pleasure in his phone call to Paul Grossinger. I imagined their dialogue all the way home. My father said nothing in the living room, but at dinner that night he seemed genuinely pleased—though he added quixotically, "So you don't want to go into the hotel business?"

"You know I want to be a writer."

He agreed he knew that.

I sent Lindy an account of those events, and I began work on Monday.

For the first week at the *Democrat,* I sat at a desk proofreading county news and writing captions for photographs of car wrecks, retiring supervisors, and high school swimming stars. Fred kept teasing that he was working me up to bigger things, but I enjoyed the time regardless, especially the bag lunches with him, his sister, and the staff by the Callicoon River, luxuriating in the sun and talking trifles. Each day I tried to bring everyone a spectacular dessert from the previous night's meal at the Hotel; my folded cake boxes were much awaited, their contents eulogized.

Finally Fred dispatched me across the Delaware into Pennsylvania to cover a town meeting about snow removal. I mailed my subsequent front-page article to Lindy.

Her job in Denver was similar, except that she was an intern at a big-city daily. She proofread too, and rewrote other people's articles. She was sent to cover veterans' meetings and hundredth birthdays. Her first letter detailed all that and then stated explicitly everything I most feared:

> You will unfortunately get to know me much better in letters. Unfortunately in that what I write in these always has and will be too truthful; whatever last trace of a gossamer mask there was is now off because we have started letters. They are the great disarmer; I'm stripped now because they are the first and last source of communication. Your letters I prize too much, perhaps even more than many of our conversations which were distorted by fear on both our parts. What *will* happen is that I will end up talking about you a lot more than you will about me in these letters, which fact *is* a fact and deserves to be wondered at. I think you're interesting but I also think I'm interesting—but in the last ding dong ding dong of the world it will be you we'll go down discussing because I am uncomfortable under the glare of the operating table light. . . .
>
> I am not so secure that I don't love love when I see a little of it flowing in my direction. I think I am horribly idealized in both your and Aunt Bunny's eyes now, and probably to see me again in flesh and blood would wreck the beautiful image that has somehow been created. Connect now with the moments when you hated everything I said during the last times, as I do, but then always give the exquisite rationale that I do, that those angers were because I was leaving. All this makes me tiptoe and not count on a thing—people or you seem to be so changeable that I'll be wary and fly back up my tree before eating out of your hand.
>
> I'm very ordinary. I go to work every day and am a cub reporter on a Scripps-Howard tabloid. I write crap well and they like it and me. . . . I see Steve as often as I can which is infrequently. I was in Aspen with him when you called, and there is no sense in playing games, leading you on, or worst of all, having you build images of me (too positive or too negative). I don't want to be another Betsy; idealization is not flattering to me. Steve is the end of a long quest and search. I have perhaps found him prematurely because now no

one else will ever really do in his role. You and he play different parts. I play a part to you which is not sufficient for you; you will need someone else to play the part that Steve plays in my life. The role is indefinable—it's not exactly that of a lover but perhaps that of a stronger person. I'm too weak for you in the end, and you are too weak for me. This is maybe too much honesty, but I would rather knit alone than have any sham falsity. What you are is perhaps the closest friend I have and have ever had. I can't *depend* on you but I can write you with this candidness and not be afraid of losing your friendship. . . .

I dread next fall in a way (and this will hurt you, but don't let it) because we will either split or change. I dread having to face you because I will have to be freer than you let me be. If I can't be as free as I want I'll just fly from you, try to get away and out of your pocket. I'm only good when I'm free to study, grow, explore, and develop on my own and the only people who have ever held me have been those who let me fly. I'm nobody's parent, wife, lover; only friend.

Fred sent me to Ellenville to talk to a Japanese man who wanted to saturate the Hudson and Delaware Valleys with cherry trees. I took down his story in his own words: immigration to America, homesteading in rural New York State, now vowing to spread this gift from his homeland throughout his new country. I posed him stiffly in front of his orchard. Fred loved the photo and article and decided I was more valuable hunting up human-interest items than proofreading. I was given free rein to come and go.

I drove to small socialist hotels—diametric opposites of Grossinger's—where I interviewed guests and staff. Then I met with Kurt Shillberry, the main critic of the hotels and opponent of their tax breaks. He thought that resorts like Grossinger's should pay for County social services at a scale in keeping with their revenue. My father read my article (shifting restlessly) and concluded, "You're a dreamer!"

Fred heard about a community of black Jews called the Gheez living in the woods by Callicoon. He thought they might be too dangerous to approach, but I edged the Lincoln to the end of the last dirt road and then walked the rest of the way to their encampment. They were delighted by a guest and took me on tour through their huts and temple, all the time spieling gospel and Biblical history. They had a gigantic queen whom they carried on a litter, but I saw only pictures of her and the throne. Fred published the main sections of my account.

Next I went to a remotely situated boarding school called Summer Lane, modeled after the radical Summer Hill schools of England. The director, a young minister, met me at the gate and escorted me past clusters of suspiciously-staring boys. A Civil Rights activist who had been on the recent marches in the South, Reverend George von Hill-shimer was an elegant pedagogue, well over six feet, looking like a frontier priest in his collar, or perhaps a charismatic gang leader. He officiated over teens in leather jackets and bracelets, clusters of them smoking cigarettes around classroom-sheds. In the hour that followed, through our picnic lunch, George proved capable of spontaneous oratory alongside bursts of startling ferocity (when something untoward caught his eye). In fact he seemed more dangerous than the kids.

Many times after that I left the newspaper office at noon and drove the backroads to share Grossinger sandwiches with him in his grove. We talked about Lawrence and James Baldwin, and he read to me from his own radical writings. "It is crucial," he admonished, "not to live the typical American adolescence, self-indulgent and conscience-less. Go through life as a hero. James Baldwin dreamed of 'another country' without this prejudice and pain. Well, he knew, and we all know—it doesn't exist. Your generation has to make it from scratch."

My clippings delighted Lindy. "I am of course jealous you get to range through such exotic and meaningful territory. And they support you? I'm astonished."

Well, not all the time. I sent her my editorial about the Presidential candidates. I compared Lyndon Johnson to a man driven by an exogenous force, as the tides by the moon (the moon being Barry Goldwater, whose war-mongering had triggered LBJ into sending troops to Vietnam). I closed: "It is nightfall in America!" Fred refused to publish it.

"You're too damn radical for me, boy," he said. "This stuff is downright depressing."

To the amusement of the staff, Fred and I engaged in constant political polemics. Head of the county Civil Defense agency, he insisted that atomic bombs were no big deal. "It's just one more weapon," he told me. "It's been the same since the cave man. You invent a weapon; then someone else finds the defense for it—so you build a bigger weapon. You can't stop that. Atomic bomb's just a big bomb, but it's not *more than a bomb.*"

I was glad it was only the Civil Defense Fred ran; still his rhetoric terrified me. I imagined instant holocaust if Goldwater were elected, and the fact that a "Democrat" like Fred could be so close to his position on armaments was disconcerting to me. Leo Marx had tried to convince us that the liberal tradition of Thomas Jefferson *was* America, but outside of Amherst and New York City I never seemed to encounter it.

While driving country roads I visited antique shops and, on my salary, bought old jugs and lamps which I used to redecorate my room. Rescuing scenery left over from Hotel banquets I formed a shrine of plastic trees and birds behind which I hung Klee and Miró prints. I lay in my bower, reading Olson and Nabokov and listening to the music of the Phi Psi year: Bob Dylan, Jim Kweskin, Dave Van Ronk—the folksong/jug-band axis.

"Change or lose me," Lindy had warned. And since she had gone back to Steve I did not feel disloyal noticing a pretty waitress at a station near our table. She was a heavy-boned girl with a Central European face. I slipped into casting subterfuge glances her way. A riveting actress with rolling hips and a pouty stare, she lugged trays more fully loaded with platters than any of the men. She served these in a sullen, airy manner. She was totally charismatic, impossible not to look at.

We seemed to catch each other's eye more than I would acknowledge. I assumed those self-conscious smiles were just part of her act. Then one night in early July, after the dining room had closed and she was cleaning her station, I approached cautiously until she looked up (with perhaps a twinge of "Finally!" in her pout). My role at Grossinger's had become totally ambivalent to me. Whereas once I took my identity from being the owner's son, now I was mostly embarrassed by the family and tried to downplay the affiliation. Yet it was also part of the courage I drew on in approaching her—that, plus pure attraction and the reckoning in Lindy's letter.

Her name was Joanne (nickname: Smokey). Polish Catholic, from Pennsylvania, she was working for her college tuition and thoroughly despised the Hotel and its guests.

"Yes," she said, she'd love to go out to dinner.

Through July, Smokey and I saw each other regularly, going to movies, driving backroads, listening to records in my room. After several times together I kissed her while dancing.

We hiked to a meadow on the edge of the woods and wound in the grass. Her dress was shiny over her large butt and hips, her perfume medicinal-smelling. I was encouraged by her sighs and rough hugs, but she broke off, jumped to her feet with a hearty laugh, and brushed away the weeds.

Meanwhile Schuy had gone with his family to their summer home on Martha's Vineyard to race his sailboat, and he was working (with Larry) as a dishwasher:

> Thanks for your two letters and I'm sorry I didn't write before. It sounds to me like the best thing about this Joanne is that this all gives you a chance to get Lindy in some kind of perspective—get some of your power back, speaking 'Davidwise'—which turns out to be the same problem I have here. The first day on the job I saw this interesting and thin attractive girl—after a day made an Axis-like remark to her about how the people around seemed all to be so affected by the bureaucracy and so forth, took her out to coffee, etc. All was nice—she turned out to be a Smith grad who writes poetry, hated Smith, didn't date Amherst, is earning money to go to Europe, and anyway I really like her.
>
> Her name is Diana, and I'm kind of relieved to be going out with someone with such a derivative name, like in the song, 'Oh, please, stay by me, Di-ana'—you know, the embarrassing mushy one. I have been dating her a lot. I can't stand her being a waitress right there and me washing dishes. I don't understand what my position with her is, and what I'm trying to do is make her change her mind about her being 22 and graduated and me being 21 and (I lied to her) a senior—and I really do think she is 22 (and I'm not really 21), but I don't think it should make such a difference. Anyway, I'm trying to act tough—you know, the way Axis does—to try (I guess) to shake her up. But I'm pretty weak about it. I guess I've been seeing her quite a bit. A week ago we had this big moment at a party, and it was 'I do love you, but I'm not in love with you; I want you to be a friend, even though I know how ridiculous that sounds.'

I have been sailing every day now for three or four days, since I got the boat in the water. In the first race I did well till we got lost in the fog and had to be towed in. Larry is my crew, and we are living together in this little sort of shed-garage apartment. There's a bunk for you if you want to come visit. . . .

Coaxing a few days off from the *Democrat,* I took the Thruway north along Albany to the Mass Pike, drove most of its length, and veered south below Boston. The Atlantic and its beaches filling the horizon to my left, I smelled snatches of salt air. I parked at the Terminal and caught a ferry to the Island.

Larry met me at the dock, and we went straight to the fabled restaurant. When I saw Diana I fell in love with her too. She was brown-haired and sun-tanned, her 1940s Ivy League style purveyed in a sassy banter. Schuy poked his head out of the kitchen in his dishwasher's costume and greeted me clownishly.

After closing, all four of us went to hear Jim Kweskin's Jug Band. It was a small club; the performers were breathtakingly close—thimbles on washboards, honking jugs: *"Washing-ton at Valley Forge/Freezing cold and up spoke George. . . ."* Between sets I edged over to Kweskin and mentioned Phi Psi, where he had played before my time. "Hangin' out with Mr. Tripp!" he proclaimed. "Well, give him my best, and maybe you guys can come up with some bread and get us back to Amherst." Then he sidled away.

The next afternoon while Schuy raced, Diana and I sat on the beach trying to spot the faint image of his sails. She knew I was a writer, and she had brought along her black binder of poems. She read from it— clean lucid lines, playful and insolent—like suggesting to a lover that they spend their lives together scraping off the insides of Oreo cookies with their teeth. She invoked a landscape of ancient summertimes, toy boats, and shiny pebbles.

I had only the cards with me, so I laid them in the sand and read her fortune of felicity, strife, and sudden bounty (wands everywhere).

All the next day Schuy seemed to ignore both of us. When he wasn't washing dishes he was working on his boat. Diana and I used his car to drive the single road to the cliffs at the end of the island. She pointed out the sights as we traversed Freud, Sartre, and Lawrence. Then she questioned me about Schuy, asking why he had to pretend to be so tough. "It's really quite silly," she remarked. I tried to explain the reasons.

Yet I hardly understood Schuy. Since his letter he had become involved in a highly disciplined game of pretending not to notice Diana except to snap criticisms and commands her way. He smashed the copy of Paul Anka singing "Diana" that I brought him as a gift, saying, "That's exactly the kind of sentimentality that destroys relationships."

He was not amused by my suggestion that the song's words could be reversed from *"You're so young, and I'm so old"* to *"I'm so young ..."*

And later he added: "I have to break her, like a horse."

He was growing a mustache; he had changed his name to Scotty; he thought he was going to become D. H. Lawrence.

That evening he threw Larry out of the shed, telling him to find another place to live. When I tried to intercede, he said, "Just fucking leave. I don't want you around anymore either. You're both children. I've got enough problems." I asked Larry to take me to the dock. It was late, and I had no fallback position, but I caught the last ferry by a minute.

I still had one day left before having to return to work, so I took it in New York City, the first time driving there myself: rock and roll on "Double-U A B C," gleefully hitting the George Washington Bridge and rattling across. I shot down the Henry Hudson Parkway like Bob Towers of yore, crossed over at 96th Street, and parked in the basement of 300 Central Park West. Without warning, just like Grandpa Harry, I appeared upstairs in the hour after breakfast. After my family got over the shock (and I finished distributing pastries and lox), I was welcomed by everyone, even my mother.

"How about some old times together," Bob said, finishing off the last of the salmon with an appreciative smile. "Feel like doing the reservoir?"

"Of course."

As we walked in the past (Debby tossing crusts over the fence to the ducks, then as now), my mother took my arm, causing us to straggle behind the rest. She confided how difficult my brother had become. "I can't control him anymore. You were impossible, but at least I could reach you." She intended a backhanded compliment.

"Right, I was the loyal one."

She nodded. "He's beyond me."

I smiled grimly, but I had always known that.

In the afternoon I drove uptown to meet Chuck Stein. It was the first time for us since Horace Mann, and I was startled to see how he had changed into a magus with a pipe and bushy beard. Seeking the hour before sunset, he led me to a bench along the Hudson. There I quizzed him on Olson poems, as he interpreted difficult lines and explained why it didn't matter whether one got all the references or not. Then I paid careful attention while he showed how to use the tarot as a meditation tool. He laid my deck, card by card, on the grass, demonstrating that their vistas weren't just matrices of individual symbols, they had relationships of energy among them and could be structured in a pantheon representing the formation of the universe.

The Fool sat atop the rest, idle source of all substance and form; he carried the *materia* of the universe in his prodigal knapsack, its atomic ignition borne heedlessly in a single white rose between the thumb and forefinger of his left hand. The other cards lay in three parallel rows of seven representing the successive stages by which cosmic vibrations become molecules and cells and are translated into worldly designs.

There in the evening glow, Venus bright over the Hudson, the twenty-two buds of the Major Arcana forming a magnificent foliage, Chuck taught an esoteric tarot.

I saw Miss plump, naive Empress in her watery robes, candescent diadems on her head. Conductress of the streams and blossoms of memory, she spun paramecia and diatoms; she fed chlorophyl its DNA. In the next card sat a grim, uptight Emperor wresting a granite-fortress realm from the Magician (who wanted only to spin and disperse phantasmagoria till time immemorial). At position five the Hierophant engirded them both, oscillating the kingdom of matter indoors and founding the first temple. While the Emperor was busy holding three dimensions in a cube and locking the stars and planets in their courses the Hierophant was inventing astrology. He conquered the Emperor with a single eclipse.

In the sixth trump a man and a woman (Adam and Eve perhaps) arose in a mirror of dreams that cast all kings and queens, magicians and priests, into background dimensions. Looking into each other's souls, the Lovers saw the faint replicas of gods reflecting . . . the frontiers of substance . . . beyond those, the Magician's golden sun. Even as they gave themselves to each other and transcended false personality, beneath them in the matrix fell the more universal transcendences of ego: Death, the card thirteen, creating by transforming, preserving essence while destroying appearance—below thirteen, the number twenty, Judgement—not, the Day of Judgement slandered by biblical literalists but the simultaneous presence of every creature on Earth, all arising from coffins of three dimensions floating on an unconscious ocean, tearing down the limitation of form, as teeth break up food.

Back at the end of the first horizonal row the Charioteer of the seventh trump established his ancient city, the Persian or Mayan city at the dawn of civilization. Beneath a fake cloth sky, dangling the ecliptic of the zodiac at his belt, he incorporated the passion of the Lovers through the cyclotron of the Magician, the dark imago of the Priestess, the garden of the Empress, the laws of the Emperor. Rooted in language, he rode along, unaware that his armor was a symbol, that his words had no roots in objects, that his vehicle was motionless.

The lion of spiritual Strength initiated the second row. Controlled by an angel holding his jaws open, he roared all the atoms, elements, cells, and letters of the first row into history. Such a lion could not be mastered; he could only be charmed. Then (at position nine) the Hermit, bearing a single cookie-like star in his lantern, stood at the snowy mountaintops. Having wandered through all the integers, he was an old man with a beard, though far younger than the Fool. He had no generic power. All his potency and wisdom came through his acceptance of the forces that made him up.

It was nightfall (Suns and Moons and Stars later) by the time Chuck reinvoked the Chariot city, flanked by black and white sphinxes, as we entered the modern metropolis, the World as cosmos—the last and twenty-second trump. This city needed no sphinxes; it spun so fast its inhabitants were not even aware of its motion. The zodiac ripped open, the cube melted, the anagram of the Wheel of Fortune decoded (tarot . . . tora . . . rota . . .)—Bull and Lion faced each other no longer, and a new dimension tore trillions of galactic years into the future.

In this amazing circumstance we hiked back to the avenue of the Western edge, down the lamplit street. Creation shimmered with magic and surprise. Then Chuck declared that the gossamer intensity of our very thoughts was merely another manifestation of the gravitational fields around stars.

The dancer had become the dance.

One midsummer eve Aunt Bunny and her compatriots packed wine and towels and hiked to the Lake. The men took their clothes off and dove into chilled water. Afterwards we lay in the sand philosophizing—Johnson versus Goldwater, the bomb, bad marriages. Sam the revolutionary wished he had died there in the hills with Castro on assignment for *Time* because everything since had been downhill for him. "Is that what our lives are: one flash of brilliance and then it's over?" he mourned, struggling for articulation against the stars. An art-film director couldn't believe Bunny would stay with Paul and, perhaps facetiously, proposed to her, but she turned him down.

"You'd tire of me," she said.

At about that time I made friends with one of the few black guests at Grossinger's, a regular named Bitty Wood who was in residence all summer because his wife, Damita Jo, a nightclub singer, used the Hotel as a base. He lived there with my grandmother's—if not my father's—blessing. A lanky middle-aged musician, he would sit in the lobby talking bop and poetry, rapping fingers in constant rhythm and laughing with great good nature at the decadence around him.

"Lose that freeloader, will you!" my father said one evening. His threats were not empty ones. Milty Stackel, Irv Jaffee, Jack the waiter ... had all been fired, long ago. Each time I'd come back after months away and someone else would be missing: Herb the hypnotist, Abe the athletic director, Kurt the ice-skater.... "Crooks," my father would say.

"All of them?" I would ask, disbelievingly.

"They stole from me." His eyes were riveted in revenge.

When I arrived at the beginning of the summer Jimmy McAndrews was gone too. He had made the mistake of phoning some friends in California from Traffic and then joking about it. "Big deal, a few calls," I said angrily.

But my father couldn't get over the fact I had known and hadn't told him. "And I don't want you hanging around with you-know-who," he said, not willing to dignify Bitty with a name. "It doesn't look good."

In my letters I brought Lindy up to date on Chuck, Schuy, Diana, my job, the Hotel, even Smokey. These delighted her, and she was sorry to be so slow in answering. Her only mention of Steve, after the original one, was an embarrassed aside that he had dumped her. But now there was someone else:

> I date police reporters and get depressed by their views, and for the first time in my life went out with a married man the other night. I must have been totally out of my mind to think that all he wanted was intellectual companionship, but I didn't know so found out. I don't want to do reference work in sin; there always seem to be bigger and better sins just when you think you've exhausted the list. He was interesting, as people are. . . .

Smokey and I continued to spend evenings together, enacting our flirtation in my room. Our making out was almost a wrestling match. One night she began to grab at me and pull me into kisses that were mainly bites. I squeezed her and rubbed her body under her dress. She sighed, returned my hug, and clawed my back, first seductively, then like a lion. Suddenly she sat up hard against the wall—thump! She put her hair back in place. I looked at her.

But she said nothing.

Likely if she had been a boy (or I a girl) we would have been enemies. I was the wiry, innocent youth; she the bruising, worldwise trucker. We necked as much out of sublimated antipathy toward each other's types as out of attraction, but we never went far enough to reveal our contrary passions. (We were also perhaps combatants from thousands of centuries of our ancestors' wars.)

A short, swaggering assistant cook at the Hotel had taken a real liking to her. Not only did he ask her out, but he followed the JG on his motorcycle, buzzing us during our dates. One time we slipped away from him to a diner but, when we came out, the car wouldn't start. Suddenly—in a sequence of unnarrated gestures—he appeared from behind a tree, threw open the hood, plugged the distributor head in and zoomed off on his cycle. She shook her head sadly.

The next morning at breakfast I blabbed a version of the event to the Head of Security (who happened to be nursing his last cup of coffee when I arrived with my berries and cereal). Some guy wanted to date the girl I was going out with and had messed with the JG. No big deal, just a story. But that night Joanne shot over from her station to confront me at dinner, eyes like guns. "You shouldn't have done that!"

I looked at her blankly, imagining, out of guilt, something sexual. "I would have handled it," she fumed. Then softly: "There wasn't any damage done."

The house detective had apparently approached her courting cook and threatened his job.

"But I didn't mean for that to happen," I protested, truly shocked.

"Sure, you didn't!" She turned and marched away. I saw myself suddenly from afar, sitting at the head table among the bosses—the owner's son, a model of false innocence.

I went to apologize to him in the kitchen, but before I could speak he spat out his challenge:

"You can do anything you want, but it's not going to stop me. Do you know that I've given her my mother's ring. That ring is sacred to me!" He was almost hysterical. "I'm going to marry her. I just want you to know that."

"I'm not your rival," I said. "Smokey's just a friend." But, even as I spoke the words, summoning all my imagined earnestness, I remembered the sensation of us rolling on my bed, her bra open, my hand inside her dress.

That night I tried to write her a letter. I was a muddle of mixed motives. I said—of course, we should stop; we could still be friends . . . I felt badly for what I had done.

I wanted to feel noble and pure.

False innocence again. Her answer was combative and contemptuous: "You think just because your father owns this place you can set all the rules and push everyone around."

We never spoke again, so we parted enemies. We had indulged in a brief erotic encounter before returning to our ethnic stereotypes.

Lunchtime at the *Democrat*—everyone else around the presses—I sat at a lone desk in the copy room, laying down the tarot as Chuck had instructed me: three equal rows, The Fool at their top. In the sun in the window they were beautiful, their colors, the faces, the Hebrew glyphs, the white pillars of temples, the stream-of-unconscious waters.... I followed the azure rivulet that materialized out of the Priestess' robes, pouring across the downed oxbow moon at her feet, bubbling behind the granite cliffs of the Emperor ... between edifices of the Chariot and the City, until it drained through galaxies and civilizations into the pools of Star and Moon and became an ocean of many dimensions.

An actual blue seemed to trickle across the cards. I looked up and saw the water along the rocks of Callicoon Creek. Matter, phenomenon, and symbol were one. I had known that intellectually; now it was perceptible.

Leaves rustled against dusty windows, sunlight through them (and dust) breaking into thousands of coins on the table. Around me was the yellowing rag, the decay of material history. All this lived and would die, as Beckett had observed, but it wasn't empty or, more accurately, its emptiness was precisely its fullness.

Our lives posed no danger to the real creation. Even the atomic bomb was the handiwork of the Magician; so was Fred's fallout shelter. The skeleton of the Death Card stood near the center with his scythe, mowing down every living form, but obliterating nothing, transforming only so that new cells were born from the paring of old ones.

I could hear the ripple of the Priestess' robes outside, the water also of my senses and memory. Callicoon Creek rushed along. I stared at its twinkling rocks. I looked up through the trees at a disk in the sky. Even the so-called hydrogen of its formation was a mask, concealing a Magician. I turned down to the deck and saw suns exploding everywhere, in alien skies against dreamlike arrases. I saw wheels turning and currents manifesting deeper and deeper into substance. I realized that these figures of men and women wandering through the deck were the same man and woman, not at different moments but all at this one moment.

I stood in a daze. Tears crinkled the corners of my eyes. I rubbed them away and poked my head into the next room. Fred, his sister, and the others were at work. I wanted to shout, but of course I couldn't. They were standing in spirit fire and didn't know it.

That night, filled to the brim, I had no doubt anymore. I sent Lindy my joyfulness in a poem:

Do you listen
To the burning of the stars?

I am the burning of the stars:
Listen to me. . . .

Do you search
For the silent sandy people?

I lead them:
Follow me.

Do you hear
Sometimes a distant lonely whisper?

I hold one promise:
It is there.

Do you want
The rainbow flock?

I am one of its sheep:
Want me!

"Some long overdue letter here," she wrote back a week later. "I thought your poem was beautiful and good. It sang, as they say here, and the song it sang was good. You are doing good things still, are amazingly productive and active politically and writing-wise."

We were more than halfway through the summer and headed toward reconnoiter.

2

HALLOWEEN

In early August Fred assigned me my grandmother's Senate testimony on a prospective Sullivan County Airport ("This way I'm sure to get the inside dope," he teased). I flew to Washington with her and Milton Blackstone. We were checking into our hotel when Grandma was paged. Minutes later Milton whispered the news: While we were en route, Harry Grossinger, back in New York, had died of a heart attack. Standing there, Grandma barely noticed us; her gaze was fixed. "At last!" she whispered. "He lived too long, the bastard."

It was a mask I had never seen.

We rushed back to the airport where Milton hired a private plane. He would stay and testify; I would accompany her home.

We squeezed into a cabin with two young pilots. They taxied, took off quickly, and headed north. We flew inland from the coast, then over the New York line (as one of them consulted a map) . . . finally to the vicinity of Grossinger's.

Enormous thunderheads loomed directly over the Hotel. I saw them floating like a luminous three-D Ektachrome, violet, amethyst, and black. As the pilot was descending to land, we floated into sudden darkness. Hail slapped against the windows. The plane rocked and jerked. The pilots rode the bumps and howled in delight. Their confidence kept me unafraid. Yet each time we approached the Hotel runway, we were buffeted so hard we were forced to pull away.

"It ain't gonna work, buddy," conceded the pilot.

All the while my grandmother stared into empty space, chanting bitterly, "It's him. I can see him. He's trying to keep me out."

We had left ordinary time—but if it was Grandpa indeed, I was confident he would spare me.

The storm was brief and concentrated—by newspaper accounts the worst flooding ever recorded at Grossinger's. It washed out Harry's two recent scaffolds and blew down trees that had stood for centuries.

The pilot searched in nearby sunshine for an alternate site, finally picking a meadow outside Monticello and radioing its position. By the time we came bouncing along the pasture the Hotel limousine was waiting in the far weeds.

My father retreated to his sister's house. Aunt Bunny left her group of friends to enact the required Orthodox mourning. I watched her become more and more morose. One evening she was sitting on her bed, arms tucked in against herself, fists clenched.

"Jeez," she said, "this is a big one. I don't know if I can make it." She braced herself against the headboard. I set up camp beside her bed. When ordinary words ran out, I invented koans, from Beckett and Keats combined:

"Was I sleeping, while the others suffered? Am I sleeping yet? This is the court's eternal session, the courtiers crushed by the golden weight of their robes. Tomorrow, when I wake, or think I do, what shall I say of today?"

"Thank you, Richard. You bring me the best company, the kind that recognizes who I am."

We had gone together earlier that month to see *Night of the Iguana,* so she paraphrased Tennessee Williams: "I see twilight through the branches, the coming dark. Like the iguana I am one of God's creatures at the end of its rope."

And Jimmie Rodgers on the stereo—plaintive, accordionlike notes: *"... someday some old familiar rain will come along and know my name...."*

The next weekend, putting her hopes in a change of scenery, she had a driver take herself, my brothers, and me to her parents' house in Atlantic City. This trip coincided precisely with the Democratic Convention, so instead of asking for time off I arranged with Fred to cover the event.

In reality there was nothing to report. It was like a stadium with no game. I could barely see from the back of the hall. Only the belief that this bedlam was a rally against the warmongers made any of it worthwhile. Bunny's friend Sam had warned us that that hope too was an illusion. The years would prove him right.

Bitty Wood was also in town for the Convention, and one night he picked me up and drove us to a nightclub where we sat at a table listening to jazz. The comedian Dick Gregory sneaked up and embraced Bitty, then, after much laughing and riffing, accepted his offer to take the empty seat. The two men chanted stanzas back and forth.

"Something big's coming down in Philly," said Gregory. "The people is angry."

"Amen, brother. Amen."

I couldn't believe that a kid from Grossinger's was privileged to be in their company. But Bitty put his arm around me and said, "He's my man."

"If the heart of human existence is sheer terror on one side, the power of the Magician on the other (and real politics in the ghettos, Bitty Wood), then what are thousands of people cheering and waving their placards for?"

I sat up late writing these insights to Lindy and sent off a fat packet—Atlantic City postmark—the next morning.

Our letters crossed, and there was one waiting for me at the Hotel. She was delighted I got to go to the convention and wanted a full account. Yes, she was seeing her married police reporter fulltime—and afraid her parents would find out. She told me not to worry about her.

I went out driving at night on backroads, closer and closer to the realm of Chipinaw. In droves along the sides were camp counselors—guys and girls my age—hitching. I would zoom past in the ridiculously pretentious car. College kids waiting tables at the Hotel had told me the main way they met girls was by picking up hitchhikers. But I was moralistic and shy.

I came to a mysterious moonlit meadow, if not the precise site, then a replica of where we had gone for haywagon rides. I turned by pulling onto the shoulder. In the air I smelled sienna hay. My headlights, crashing through branches, illuminated the whole field. I stared into the darkened speculum. In front of me hung a web, the stony silhouette of its maker in the center.

I had come to a warp in my own fabric. I knew that spider. This was a moment of eternal return.

Back at the house I began pouring myself glasses of vodka. Geoff Muldaur was singing "Wild About My Loving" on the stereo. I was probing the depth of my blues, my right to be this romantically askew yet unafraid . . . and suddenly I was dizzy. I called out to Emma who thundered down the stairs: "Oh, Lordy, you damn drunk."

I was glad she lingered. I could discern the edges of a black hole floating just beyond me.

"You haven't watched a single ballgame with me all summer," she pouted. "You just fussing about girls. No wonder you're drunk. You'll be good and drunk until you forget about women, mind me." I followed her back upstairs and collapsed on the floor before the Mets game. And when it was over I stumbled into my room and fell into dreamless sleep.

George von Hillshimer and I had talked at length about my brothers, in particular Michael because he had been to a number of schools not dissimilar to Summer Lane and was as academically marginal as the students there. A victim of Grossinger's and its moneyed, erratic lifestyle, Mike had little use for authority or the formalities of schoolwork. He lived, it seemed, in rage, paralysis, and slapstick, watching TV sometimes for entire days—from cartoons to comedies to Westerns to "Little Rascals" to more cartoons to old movies. I thought of Summer Lane as his hope, a community acknowledging alienation without trying to crush it—and fortuitously just down the road.

George was candid about his own motives. If a Grossinger kid attended Summer Lane, it might generate income and get the County off his back. When I told Aunt Bunny, she reluctantly agreed to an audition. "I trust your judgment," she said, "and we have just about run out of options. But Summer Lane sounds much too far out for your brother." On her okay I invited Reverend von Hillshimer to dinner.

I warned him about the depth of ethnocentrism in my family, but George was a wildman and wouldn't reconcile himself to anything less than a gladiatorial triumph. Despite the incredible longshot, he became megalomaniacal, preparing eloquent speeches, thinking ahead

to the spoils of his certain success. Everyone at Summer Lane was saying prayers for this gambit.

At lunch the day before, I gave him directions and, with a preda-
tory smile, he promised not to wear his collar.

On the evening of the dinner I called the Front Gate and left word
to let Mr. von Hillshimer through. Then I paced the top of the hill,
scanning for his car. His wreck rumbled incongruously up the main
drag. He parked beside a row of Lincolns, patted each of them on the
fins, and bowed before me. I grabbed his hand in delight.

Aunt Bunny seated him on the side of the table beside Michael,
James and me on the other, her and my father at the heads. Emma
served salad as George introduced himself to my brother. He quizzed
him about his present school and then began to describe Summer Lane.
Listening with interest, Michael finally met his glance and asked: "So
how much work do kids really have to do at your place?" Before George
could answer, my father interrupted.

"I should tell you, Reverend, I attended military academy myself
in Peekskill and I don't like regimented schools." George started to
respond, but PG raised his hand imperiously and asked to be allowed
to finish. He proceeded to say that he and his wife had put together a
list of schools for Michael to consider, and he thought it was best that
he stay within his own religion.

He lectured so long and insultingly that I cringed. He wasn't even
going to give Summer Lane a chance.

I knew that George had a lot at stake here and also that he would
not stand to be humiliated. I watched him lose and then regain composure. When my father ran out of steam, he summoned fresh energy
and answered all the objections one by one rather brilliantly. Then he
turned back to Michael and asked him what he was looking for in a
school.

My father jumped in. "Reverend, the matter has nothing to do with
Michael; it's Michael's parents who are making the decision. If you
have anything to say, please address me."

I could barely keep from exploding. This was a man of learning
and achievement. He was rightly honoring my brother's opinion. He
didn't have to be subjected to bullying and rudeness. I turned to Bunny
silently for help.

"I'm afraid what happens to Michael is his father's decision."

"Do you agree?"

My father was glaring at me as she replied: "I don't think Mr. von Hillshimer's school is for Michael."

Ostensibly victorious, my father then decided to lighten things with a series of jokes about his experiences with "men of the cloth." Reverend George kept any subsequent thoughts to himself.

No matter how angry I had been at my father in the past I had always thought of him as a basically decent person, reliable when the chips were down. Now I saw him as a willful, spoiled child, ordering around a black maid and, under the thinnest sham of dignity, boasting and brandishing his wealth. A part of Bunny was wed to this man irrevocably.

After dessert I accompanied George down the stone path through the garden. We were silent most of the way as my mind raced for something to say. "This place is a menace, my friend," he suddenly offered. "Leave quietly, or it will cannibalize you." Then he crouched low and collapsed on the lawn. I didn't know what was happening. I thought he was sick, so when I saw him rolling there laughing I was relieved. He pulled his body up to its full height slowly, like a giant cricket. "You'll have to pardon me," he said. "I was holding all of that in."

I smiled nervously and assured him it was okay. I apologized for my parents and for bringing him there with false hopes. "They were worse than I ever imagined."

"So it wasn't a bad evening," he consoled, "because you learned something." He walked a few more steps, and as we reached his car he turned to me and, with a sudden fierce stare, said, "Forgive me, Richard, but at my father's house in Germany your father wouldn't have been permitted to eat with the hogs."

I heard him say it, shook his hand, and waved to him as he drove off. Then it sunk in. He knew, as I did, that he spoke as a German less than a generation after Hitler. He had reduced my father to a piece of meat. I felt the coldness of his glance. I was a Grossinger too. Would I have been fed (or even denied service) with George's father's hogs?

At the same moment, another part of me met him in his brutal assessment. My father was not just a clown; he was a ruthless boor— I had to know that. I stood there looking out over his Hotel, the glowing glass cupolas of the indoor pool, the luxurious façades of new guest buildings. For virtually my whole life, even in the worst of times, I had considered this place a paradise. I may have mocked it, or decried its elitism and lack of social conscience, but I considered it an important locale in the universe—a haven, almost a shrine.

Now I realized it was nothing. It was the cheap passing vanity of Jewish peasants, arrogant and graceless in their fortune (as Grandma Jennie confided, so long ago), oblivious to the Wheel of Fate whose turning brought them to this perch and would crush them in a flicker, even as it had crushed dynasties and nations.

I didn't get to keep Bunny company during her next panic. My father wouldn't even let me see her. "Not after the damage you've done," he accused. "I told you two to stop talking. You just upset each other."

A doctor came from New York and dispatched her at once to hospitalization. My father said she would be "incommunicado." "Indefinitely," he added.

And then just before I left for college—when I was most alienated from him—he called me into his office and said he had a surprise for me. "Go to the front of the Main Building," he grinned. As he watched from his window the head of Traffic handed me the keys to a small yellow car parked there, a brand-new Ford Mustang.

"You won't be monopolizing the JG anymore, I guess," he called down.

I packed it for Amherst with my jugs and plastic vegetation, plus cans of twilight-blue paint, a discarded stained-glass lantern from the Nightwatch, and a bright yellow Mexican blanket I had bought in New York. I loved the car's new bowling-alley smell and the way the miles climbed into their first hundreds as I drove into Massachusetts. This was a magnificent, unjustified gift.

I spent the days before school painting my room into a night sky and arranging all my artifacts in a semi-jungle diorama. It startled Marty when he arrived. "But I guess it's okay. It's, well, uh ... different."

I formed a couch in the corner by draping the sunny blanket over a mattress. Then, with screwdriver and tape I put in my first electrical fixture by trial and error.

"I can live with it," Marty concluded. "It looks a little like an oasis at dusk."

As a junior I had to declare a major, and English was the only real possibility. In order to catch up on credits I signed up for courses on Yeats, Faulkner, and Sixteenth-Century literature, plus a writing class, this one at Smith with a visiting novelist named Stanley Elkin.

Lindy called me as soon as she was back, and I sped over to Laura Scales. She sprang downstairs looking vibrant and strong. We stared at each other; then she said, warily (as Lisa), "Hello, kiddo."

We smiled, kissed quickly, and walked outside. I pointed to the car: yellow baby with a red, white, and blue LBJ/USA bumper sticker.

"What! They just gave that to you?"

I nodded, grinning.

"I hope it doesn't spoil you," she said.

I gave her a look of—how could you think such a thing?

"We can't repeat last spring," she said after a while. "I'm in love with Jim."

He had left his wife and, in a month, would be moving to New York to take a new job with an advertising agency. From then on she would be seeing him regularly.

"I'm not really for you and, by pretending, I'm making it hard for you to find the right girl."

"How do I fail?"

"I have no way of making it sound nice. He's so much older. He's a man."

"What am I?"

"Not yet a man."

"Can you wait?"

"It's you who can't wait. You think you're in love with me now, but you'll find so many nymphet girls who will fall at your feet you'll forget I even existed. I don't want to be around for that."

"I won't do that," I insisted.

A cat came out from a yard and wound around her legs. "Maybe if I had a cat, I wouldn't need to get married. You want to arrange that?"

After dinner I lingered in the car outside Laura Scales, asking perversely if she had slept with him. She avoided the question ("None of your business"), but I persisted, until she said of course she had. Long after she had gone upstairs I sat there in my funk.

I was at Smith each week for my writing class. Some days Lindy and I went to lunch together. Much of our exchange was playful and low-key, but I had lapses into solipsism. One time, I berated her for her taste: Who would go out with a police reporter from a second-rate newspaper, some guy who would leave his wife and kids for a college girl—plus a job in an advertising agency of all things? She defended herself in a letter:

> Cut the shit, kiddo, about the dilettantism. Just like everyone else you go along saying great things and then just fall on your face every once in a while by saying something like that. I've thought about the journey that's ahead of me and of us. Because I am in love with a man who is more bound to the earth than I am does not mean I am a dilettante. For all my haziness, I am damn sure of what I must do to stay alive in this world by preparing for the next (and I don't mean heaven), and if anyone or thing becomes a threat to that aim, he will fade out, as Steve did. Let me be free, and cut the "I told you so's" and the "You'll be sorryies."

For two weeks after that I kept away, not calling or visiting, trying not even to think about her . . . until, one day, walking from the parking lot to my class, I passed her riding her bike and waved cheerily. She looked at me, burst into tears, and then sped off.

'She must care,' I thought; 'I must be special to her.'

With the graduation of seniors and the entry of a new class under us we were now elders at Phi Psi. Tripp was back, but not as a member. He had dropped out of school, and his family wasn't paying any bills (although he had an old credit card that still seemed to work, so he would fill my car with gas and I'd give him cash). He lived in the woods east of Amherst in a cabin with another well-known renegade, Eric the Red. From there he was casting a new play.

His Porsche had fallen into disrepair, so, throughout that fall, I would pick him up on the dirt road and drive him to his appointments with actresses. "I knew it was worth cultivating you, Grossinger," he said. "You're a man of compassion."

Schuy returned as Scotty, with a full mustache. I rarely saw him, for he worked hard all week (graduate school now the goal) and on the weekends drove into New York to see Diana.

"I've got to make every moment count," he told me in a moment of candor. "I've got no more moves to spare."

I was relieved not to be there yet.

Most of my course material seemed magically to replicate my tarot vision—the alchemical metaphors of the Sixteenth-Century poets, the mindflow through *As I Lay Dying* and *Absalom, Absalom!,* the lunar pulses of William Butler Yeats. In an evening full of cricket songs and linnet's wings, I drank from the fountain of "I will arise and go now, and go to Innisfree" and imbued (William Faulkner) "who even at nineteen must have known that living is one constant and perpetual instant when the arras-veil before what-is-to-be hangs docile and even glad to the lightest naked touch if we had dared, were brave enough (not wise enough: no wisdom needed here) to make the rending gash ..."

This was not only vaguely but precisely my life, the motto I needed in order to act—brave enough, no special wisdom needed, the arras-veil hanging quite docile and even glad to my lightest naked touch, if only I dared. At nineteen I too was living in a constant and perpetual instant, fluttering before a mystery (within another mystery).

Faulkner's rhythm and lyricism struck at my heart; they alone bore my sense of peril, of Lindy, of imminent revelation and disaster, of a dark and coiled ancestry: "the prisoner soul, miasmal distillant, wroils ever upward sunward, tugs its prisoner arteries and veins and prisoning in its turn that spark, that dream which, as the globy and complete instant of its freedom mirrors and repeats (repeats?, creates, reduces to a fragile evanescent iridescent sphere) all of space and time and massy earth. . . ."

"And what rough beast," warned Yeats, "its hour come round at last/Slouches towards Bethlehem to be born?"

For years I had been eyeing the large black volumes of *The Collected Works of Carl Jung*—ever since Horace Mann friends had posed them as an alternative to Freud. Back then I tried to imagine what manner of symbols could be in these books, how they could possibly be different from the authoritative *Interpretation of Dreams.* Loyal to my lineage, I wasn't ready. Now, thumbing through *Archetypes and the Collective Unconscious* and its section of colorful mandalas, I was totally won over and entranced. This was Chuck's tarot in a honeycomb of Freud's dreamwork.

I was returning as a neophyte to Dr. Fabian's library, except now the system was ancient and vast in all directions. Beneath the old familiar personality symbols was a whole other layer of images, not limited to our individual experiences or even our lifetimes. Jung called this "the collective unconscious," primal material given shape by archetypes and appearing spontaneously as creatures and forms in fairy tales, myths, and dreams, as well as in the texts of alchemists and astronomers. Such lineages stretched in unbroken chains of symbols from the equivalents of constellations in the Babylonian sky to their break-up into fragments of particles at the inception of modern science. Not only do we suppress, as Freud claimed, our instinctual libido, we conceal (Jung) our connection to nature itself, our inherence in the universe. Thus, the soul of each of us tries to restore that connection through primal mythic acts, a process he called individuation, which was just as real as trauma or the Oedipal complex. We are transformed, ultimately, by a deepening of all our experiences into a cosmic frame and by dreams (whether we heed them or not).

This meant I was no longer doomed by Nanny's ghosts or my mother's curse. I could transubstantiate them into allies, like in the alchemical nigredo and albedo. I could turn their venom into vitalized wines. Psychoanalysis was more than people and neuroses; it was a record of the presence of psyche in creation—an act of synchronicity beyond symbol. Traumas aside, I could try to encompass my larger, archetypal self.

Jung joined Yeats, Faulkner, and the tarot that fall in providing me a realm to inhabit. Their collective landscape became my solace.

Then I bought a second volume, *Symbols of Transformation,* which interpreted journeys of rebirth from New Guinea to old Cambodia, from Tlingit Alaska to India and Rome. I read "The Hymn of Creation," "The Song of the Moth," and "The Battle for Deliverance from the Mother." I saw jackal-headed Anubis bending over a mummy; beneath them the sun in the teeth of the alchemical lion dripped blood. These images were unique enough to serve as my personal totems. They were so much fresher and more seminal than baseball or the moons of Jupiter.

While reading *Symbols of Transformation,* I found a volume of Grimm's fairy tales, then my old childhood favorites, *Nine Tales of Coyote* and *The Dragons of Blueland.* I read these stories again and gazed at their artwork with new appreciation. Talking crows, winged dragons, learned spiders, wish-granting fish—these were not only imaginary beings and visitors from other dimensions; they were our own unspoken selves. Rapunzel and Sleeping Beauty, the Indian maidens Coyote courted—I had known them unconsciously long before I awoke to their representations at camp dances and on teen tours. Nor were planets and stars only distant alien worlds attainable by voyages in rockets. They were obscure parts of me. When I daydreamed them in grade school it was not a maudlin yearning for some impossible alien connection. It was an expression of a magnificence and mercy I could reach no other way, things that already existed and were cosmic in me by birth.

Instead of bowing to Miss Tighe and Bill-Dave I maintained a child's version of the ancestral spirits and archetypal sky, the only version I could have invented and believed at the time. I stubbornly held to it, not knowing what it was, only that I experienced its hypnotic joy. Joan Snyder was not only a cute girl; she was as old as the moon. Night after night at Chipinaw I had to rescue her again to give birth to myself.

Revelations swept over me continually that autumn. They softened and healed me. My dreams took on luminosity, etched in cosmic and leprechaun figures. Neither Fabian nor Friend had suggested that such nocturnal journeys were possible. Their interpretations had languished in social symbols and relational conflicts. Now the entire Museum and Planetarium were breaking through.

In one dream-event Chuck's "subway girlfriend" appeared as an editor at an occult publishing house in New York. I went to her offices with my manuscript (as to Viking Press to see Catherine Carver). She led me into a deserted ballroom where mammoth tarot cards hung on arrases. A priest sat mum on a pedestal before a buffet, like those at Grossinger's except that the carved ice figures at its center were alchemical symbols. She said, "We are the Sixth Trump, the Lovers," and embraced me. I looked up, and on the ceiling I saw a painting of a giant angel smiling, embodying us in her deck.

The ordinary world had become mediaeval.

After classes one Friday I drove into Cambridge to meet an old friend from Horace Mann, James Polachek. I knew him mainly as a buddy of Chuck's and a member of Waldman's circle: a tall, shy kid with a large-featured but intelligent face, who played the violin and carried its imprint on his personality. Now he was studying Chinese and philosophy at Harvard.

To enter his abode—ashen spice tinting the air, the sound of sequential bells on his stereo—I ducked through a bamboo curtain. A low desk and a Japanese frame with pillows served as furniture. Two silken hangings and a shell screen formed a room within a room. Jim had spun his own spare web.

Together we wandered through Cambridge, visiting bookstores, talking texts and our so-called lives—in an olden city, no longer tied to the boundaries and curfews of prep school.

After a while I told him about Lindy. I took comfort in representing my grief as a passage through the Underworld. "No way to arrive at the full moon without the dark moon behind it," I mused . . . all my life a Scorpio born in the rubble of November, fighting to survive millennial darkness. "Regenerate," I boasted. "That's what Scorpios do best. Just when you think that they're dead and gone they awaken with almost magical powers."

I did a fair job of convincing myself, but the flood of obligatory insights exhausted me. By dinner time I had become silent and morose, as we hastened through drizzle to an Italian restaurant. Wetter than I realized, I accepted a towel from the maître d'. Then Jim and I sat, warming in pleasantly mute surroundings, a crackling fireplace making the scene indelible. This was no Bob Towers account. I had no homework, no mother, no brother. My sadness was eternal and merged with creation itself.

Finally I sank into the sheer texture of life. It was all okay, even if it wasn't. I sipped wine. Neither of us said anything for a long time.

"Look around you," Polachek offered suddenly. "We are in the material universe, but everything is magnificent beyond words. No matter how cheap and poorly made, it all has a sacred property; it's all beautiful." I followed his eyes to the ceiling candelabra. It was a multicolored electric wheel.

"Even here," Jim continued, pointing to the empty Chianti bottle on which a candle dripped blue wax over the yellow and pink wax of prior candles. A timeless awe settled over me. "No surprises. Exactly the way it should be." God, was the universe deep!

Jung's color plates showed a succession of such mandalas: a man and woman standing in a lotus, within another lotus, within the phases of the moon and cycles of the planets. Three rabbits chased one another's tails. These patterns were transposed sequentially onto nighttime New York, riverside church steeples, gold vestry windows. An amoeboid glow broke through stone armaments and blossomed over Fifth Avenue. In Waite's Five of Pentacles two beggars—one lame on crutches—traversed outside a chapel. As they hobbled barefoot through snow, yellow light poured through a stained-glass oriel.

This was the card of exile, of finding oneself beyond the sanctuary, unable to get in.

The Chianti bottle was the hearth. The plate of lasagna was an offering, red and alabaster, from the belly of Ceres. Suddenly I felt safe. I wanted to cry. The world had revealed itself, and I was home. Even the ghost of the brick of ice cream I carried back to that apartment, even Lindy's defection were redeemed, were part of the simple excitement of being here, the privilege of being alive at all.

I had lived till then as a mendicant in the Five of Pentacles. Now, in the blues of a lost girlfriend at an Italian restaurant with an old friend, by name at last I acknowledged the gods.

Nelson was one of the sophomores who hung around Phi Psi. A studious squire who looked like the artist Andy Warhol—pale glasses, a mop of blonde hair, and an elegant, flowing voice—he was a poet who had lived recently with the writer Thomas Merton at Gethsemani, a Trappist monastery in Kentucky. In September when we met I found him narcissistic and boastful. He had never paid House dues, yet he was coming around all the time, using the facilities, ever the preening expert. I also heard from the other sophomores that he considered my literary reputation "a lot of fuss over nothing."

But people who knew both of us used to tell me we were dead wrong about each other. They kept bringing us together, and we kept ignoring the occasions. Then one afternoon we came face to face in the Glen where we had both retreated to study. With no one around to observe or encourage affinity we looked at each other's eyes clearly.

Neither of us spoke it, but we said silently, "Let's get this over with and talk."

He told me about the monastery, its regimented life and perverse sexuality, and how that left him uncertain of his own feelings toward either men or women. He worried about the ease with which he could be a "character" at Amherst, the way other kids just bought his act, as though he were a priest or some sort of oracle. "I didn't fool you, though."

I apologized for holding it against him and told him why it was a hard time for me. I described my panic of the preceding spring and how I blasted out of it with a poem. I quoted the lines I remembered.

He whistled acknowledgment. "I would call that a text of madness. *You* didn't write it. You *received* it. The beings who watch over you decided that your fugue had gone on long enough and they sent you instructions on how to solve it. You wrote those down, but of course they are in the language of the angels not of a psychology book." He paused for a moment. "Or, maybe the panic *was* the poem, and you resisted its message until you had suffered enough to be allowed to speak it."

I couldn't have been more wrong about Nelson. He was there with Polachek and Stein.

He told me that his own revelations were in the form of angels. "But they're not—you know, 'angel' angels, cherubim or the like. 'Angel' is just the Greek word for messenger," he explained as we crossed the street. "Those kind are everywhere. They are messages from divine beings. This rock is an angel. That bird is an angel. Even that asshole over there is an angel. The forms of the world are merely the clothing angels adopt. Without those markings we wouldn't know they exist. We ourselves wouldn't exist." He stopped walking just before the door and looked carefully at me. "Don't you see—we pick our angels. Lindy is your angel. You chose her willingly. Now you are doing a grateful penance."

"But you chose Thomas Merton. That seems a little more intelligent."

"Even you know better than that, Grossinger!"

Through the mail Chuck had loaned me a book called *Magick in Theory and Practice* by Aleister Crowley. I had heard that Crowley was a dastardly figure who cast spells to defeat rivals and seduce women, but there were other more traditionary aspects to his work, notably his theorems for a "magickal" science that included—hence transcended— physics. He asserted that, through our wills and desires, we ourselves conducted the primordial forces shaping earth and heavens. Like Nelson he urged me to regard all events as messages from higher masters to my soul (for nothing that happens to us is arbitrary). So I carried Crowley's axioms around with me like the debris of '50s rock 'n roll:

"Every intentional act is a Magical act."

"A man who is doing his True Will has the inertia of the Universe to assist him."

"Every force in the Universe is capable of being transformed into any other kind of force by using suitable means. There is thus an inexhaustible supply of any particular kind of force that we may need."

"Every man and every woman is a star."

On a night in mid-October, while driving home from dropping Lindy off at Smith, I gazed across silver pumpkin fields and imagined an archetypal connection. Lindy was Persephone, imprisoned in the underworld by a police reporter. I was her animus-warrior, rushing to save her before she swallowed the fatal pomegranate seeds. A litany of old songs and coyote tales blew over the car. I felt a wild and invulnerable joy, warm and cozy, yet spread to the ends of space and time.

"Done laid around and stayed around
This old town too long. . . ."

Scorpio within awoke and reclaimed his dormant power. He identified himself as my erstwhile trickster self—or made it impossible that I mistake his pranks for anything less than alchemical leaps of magic— and he proposed a new prank, a transforming one: I would conduct a ceremony in the Glen on Halloween, three days before my twentieth birthday.

I was so convinced of the rightness of this event everyone in the House blended with my exuberant energy. During the next week Nelson, Marty, and I mapped out how to do it—candles, mandalas, fairytales, slides of galaxies, a flute and a xylophone, jugs of apple cider. I personally invited acquaintances from all over campus. I called Polachek and Chuck; both agreed to attend. Chuck said he would bring his friend Josey (who, I had heard, was a witch with psychic powers). Even Tripp accepted:

"Staging a Halloween happening in the Glen demonstrates an excellent sense of theater, man."

But Persephone would be absent in the land of Pluto. Lindy told me that, ceremony or not, it was the first weekend Jim would be in New York. I pleaded with her in the names of angels, magic, the forces of destiny, but she said they would all have to do without her. She wrote:

> I can't come to Halloween with you, kiddo, as you know, because my Jim needs me and I need his closeness and love. There is a price to pay, and I pay it by missing Chuck and Polachek and the whole world of talk that I'm dying to hear, souls over Fifth Avenue, and Pegasus and Persephone myths. It seems ironic as hell to me and absurd that some other cute thing will hear the magic you have to say, but that's my price to pay, for not being clever enough to do two things at once, to fleece the gods completely. . . .

In her last letter the week before leaving she told me to "speak softly with the spirits and respectfully, and they will know that you feel the connection with the past and them acutely. I hope that time past and time present merge, gradually, for then you will have the essence of time."

"I guess you'll just have to do your ceremony without her," Tripp said. "A worthy challenge for you."

I answered him by writing a quick jingle based on a well-known radio station's ad for itself:

> N E time
> N E place
> in New York,
> any double you, there's
> always something happening in
> Neeeewww Yooorrrk.
> jesus yes!

"That shows spirit, Grossinger," he said. "It's a battle cry."

On Friday we began serious preparations. Nelson suggested that we each create a personal mandala. Most participants painted theirs on slabs of plywood; I used a detached black tabletop. On it I did my own version of Jung's Fifth Avenue scene. I stained a baseball with stitches, the buildings of Central Park, symbols for Lindy and me reaching across the baseball and touching, while—a nod to Crowley—in the lower lefthand corner a stray voodoo figure (a police reporter) was banished.

On Saturday morning Polachek sailed into the parking lot in his VW, bearing two records of Chinese temple music. He immediately set to work painting an enormous, impeccable High Priestess on a piece of plywood, a veil of pomegranates behind her. The basement was soon filled with mandala painters from all over the campus.

Chuck appeared mid-afternoon, trailing not only Josey but a short, flinty kid from Bard College named Harvey Bialy. He looked like a cartoon of a fiend, and he spoke in an ornery self-promoting way. As far as he was concerned, Bard was the center of the universe, at least for colleges, and he let everyone know at once that it was a "bad joke" he should be dragged up to Amherst "for a Crowleyite ceremony of all things." The three of them huddling together in the living room were a vintage cameo of beatniks.

Tripp stood by the side, smirking at my designation of Josey as a witch. "She's a sweet, tubby Jewish girl from New York; that's what she is," he whispered, but once I led them to the basement she did paint a beautiful abstract Moon on a thick square board, vibrations of Hebrew letters rising from the crayfish in the pool to form a pulsating lunar node.

The outcome was totally in the air as we marched to the Glen. But Nelson really came through! He had arranged our mandalas amidst ten torches, placed five long candles and two squat ones on an altar, and set metal railroad poles towering into the heavens. Marty had hung speakers in the trees, and Polachek's bells and flutes filled the universe with its own music of the spheres.

I carried an extension cord and boxes of slides I had culled from the Astronomy, Biology, and Geology Department files. We set the projector going in a loop—galaxies, flowers, amoebas, rivers, volcanos, craters of the moon, mountains, birds, the planet Jupiter, glaciers— one after another, enormous and rippling on sheets Nelson and crew had strung among the trees. Torches made our mandalas shimmer, the true sky was stark with constellations, and from the darkness came the notes of an Oriental temple.

"Now this is a real party, Grossinger," Tripp exulted, collapsing back on the grass. (I had bored him in the past by bringing back Grossinger steaks and desserts, barbecuing in the fireplace, and declaring a banquet for all.)

After a while I moved into the candlelight of the altar. "Why are we out here?" I asked. And I offered the explanations of archetypes, planets of science-fiction universes, old trick-or-treat Halloweens in ghost costumes. "We have come," I said, "finally to what we are. Through this ceremony we deny the false carnival colors and adolescent rituals of America, the neon and gloss that douse our lives with fake significance and blind us to our true natures. . . ."

> It is a belief that we are something more rather than something less, that we are being robbed of that something more, that belief, if any, that should make us listen more closely tonight. Not that we will find it, certainly not in one casual evening among friends, as hardly in one casual life among warmongers. We are merely to be reminded that it is still there, to be stirred again with the haunted fairy tales of a childhood that once seemed filled with a secret and a majesty that the world never became. . . .
>
> What bothers us are the forces that pretend to know something they don't. What bothers us about the too-blue Sunoco sign or the over-ripe can of red paint is that they are filled with energy but sourceless. . . . They are as bright and sparky as anything lit before our eyes, yet directionless, lacking any sense of the ghosts that fill each of our daily existences.
>
> And there *is* a source, a great pull of mind-stuff, resting in electric calm out in the bends of the universe, the stars, Orion, Sirius, Vega, Alpha Centauri, cutting loose forces that fill the forces within us. . . .
>
> You *are* the stuff that the stars are made of; all is not bleak existentialism; there *is* a temple, a sanctuary. . . . There is a second self in you like an eagle locked in the belly of a pigeon—and it is incredible if you have not noticed him kicking to be free, to be off and back to the sky. . . .

Having delivered my speech I fell silent. Then others read poems and offered blessings, after which we sat mesmerized by the slide loop in its chapel of billowing images. Nelson served cider and cookies.

Harvey was visibly transformed. "I want a copy of that talk," he declared back in the House. "There are people at Bard who will be very interested. Very interested indeed!"

On Sunday night Lindy called to find out how the "great event" had gone. I talked a blue streak ... incident after incident, trying to make my speech over again to her ... until she told me to stop because she wanted to say something: "I had a terrible weekend. I don't know what I ever saw in him. It was a fantasy, I guess. Will you forgive me for all I've put you through, kiddo?"

I received two invitations which now fit together on my twentieth birthday. Aunt Bunny was out of the hospital, and her friends were holding a welcoming party in Manhattan. Then I got a special-delivery packet from Harvey's teacher at Bard, the poet Robert Kelly (an associate of Charles Olson), who made a gift of a batch of his poems and said that he would like to meet "the author of that wonderful Halloween prayer." So I presented Lindy with the offer of a trip to New York and Bard, stopping at the Hotel overnight in-between.

She nodded excitedly.

I woke on my birthday and drove to Smith lightheaded, an old vigilance taunting me with a terror that she wouldn't be there. But she was standing outside Laura Scales in her down jacket with her suitcase and looked at me with her gray wise eyes, hugged me and handed me a package and a poem: "Happy birthday, honey."

> "Who is the spooked left-over wind scaring
> on this third day of November?
> It's only herding stray leaves—they keep close
> to one another in circling, then open out for
> the long stretch down the lawn...."

She started to get in the passenger side, but I handed her the keys. She splashed along snowmelt highway, whizzing down Massachusetts into Connecticut while we talked about a thousand things—her breakup with Jim, Aunt Bunny's homecoming, Kelly's poems, Jung, Crowley, her terrible teachers at Smith.

My own class there had become a travesty. Elkin was a thickset, sarcastic man who told us at the first meeting he could never get dates with

Smith girls when he was in college so he was going to take his revenge. It was a joke, of course, but the seminar consisted of little more than his parodies of our work. He claimed that all stories were about obsessions—no exceptions—and he dared us to prove otherwise. Since that seemed a cheap gimmick I took him up on it. The first piece I wrote was in the style of Beckett, about a man walking down a hall, which was on the Earth, which was in the Solar System, which was in the Milky Way. I described the hall in great detail, but nothing happened:

"Hiya," said a man on his left.
"Good day. Bad day tomorrow, though," said a woman on his left.
"Hello," said a woman on his right.
"Pleased to see you again," said a woman on his left.

Elkin was incensed and called it a fake.
"I guess the obsession is my trying to fool you," I teased.
He snarled in the affirmative.

The day before in class, I told Lindy, Elkin had been tearing down a girl's story. I jumped to her defense. When he said, "You have an antiquated view of literature," I began to quote out loud the Nobel Prize acceptance speech of William Faulkner, an author he admired. Lindy and I both knew that speech well—an artist at a moment of public honor proclaiming that our true work was a statement of undying faith against atomic holocaust. At first Elkin tried to shout me (and Faulkner) down, but when I kept going, he conceded, "So the man was a promoter. He had a fine sense of theater. Give him a platform, and he knew what to do. But don't believe a word of it. He didn't."

Why was it such a crime in these institutions to claim that a work had meaning and touched the soul? Why an almost pathological denial of emotion and spirit? These things were not the enemy. Quite the opposite—they were the source of everything that mattered. Without them, why exist? And yet our teachers, puritanical in their sophistication, mocked these paths as if naive and puerile indulgences.

We were beginning to see that we had always been taught nihilistically. Witty progressive liberalism was the only acceptable mode of discourse—a tyranny of fashion that Lindy, with her sense of humanity and associative mind, suffered even more than I.

Such conversation lifted our spirits and, as we neared New York at night, the years rushed through me like so many alighting birds. Road signs proclaimed the familiar Westchester towns from which Danny, Jeff, and Keith once commuted: Mamaroneck, Larchmont, Scarsdale, Yonkers.... Across the fields I saw a lit subway train, the one I had taken, its unknowing passengers looking out toward the highway. Despite everything, this was the egg out of which I had crawled.

I took over driving and wove my way through the maze of streets to a midtown apartment. We parked in an underground garage and rode the elevator up.

It was a fashionable affair: people standing around with drinks, Bunny in the center, her attention splintered dozens of ways. She seemed as I remembered her, maybe a bit more subdued. She acknowledged our arrival with a beaming smile. Later she joined us, and she and Lindy talked about her illness, and then Smith. I stood beside them, delighted at bringing two great women together. When Lindy left to get her coat, Bunny used almost the words Lindy herself had written me during the summer (about Steve), "I hope you haven't found her too soon."

It was the portent she would leave me with. A month later she was back in the hospital, and I would not see her again for more than a year.

I drove the old trail: up the Henry Hudson Parkway to the George Washington Bridge. New York drifted against the River, a galaxy of fixed and moving stars. We whizzed into the uncluttered woodlands of the Palisades, then onto the Thruway, fifteen miles to Route 17 and the Catskills. Lindy handled the final fifty miles, her breezy Colorado eighty. A familiar cluster of gingerbread Victorians appeared down over the hill at Exit 101. The intervening years seemed an illusion through which I again viewed the shining kingdom to which I had come as a waif.

We parked in front of my father's house, beside the (otherwise) NO PARKING sign and walked straight to the indoor-pool building. It was past midnight and the coffee shop was closed, but I scaled the wall and opened it from inside. We sat on the reverse side of the counter, and I made us Milty-Stackel milk shakes, mostly ice cream (six different flavors), malt, vanilla syrup. The machine eventually beat them into froth, and we drank straight from frosted metal cups with straws, feeling foolish and delighted. Then I gave her a quick tour of the night-club, the enormous empty kitchens and dining rooms, and the lobbies.

Emma had left the house unlocked, so we went upstairs to the guest room and lay on the bed quietly kissing. Her whole being was so lovely and sweet I could not imagine stopping, but then she asked me to show her to her room. "Honey, this is not the time. We're both exhausted. We've had a wonderful glittery day; let's not force the fates."

She was right. It was only desire that held me to her body, whereas necessity bound me to her friendship. I led her to my room from the summer. She returned in a nightgown, hugged me in bed, then slipped away in the dark.

3

10

It was a red-blue autumn morning, November 4. Lindy and I walked to the main building, grabbed a *Times* at the service desk, and headed down the aisle of the dining room. Grossinger regulars waved at me as though nothing were unusual. I was with a girl. I had been with a girl before. That was how it looked. But Lindy was a totally different girl. She wasn't just a girl found there. She was a girl who represented everything I was that had nothing to do with the Hotel.

Chill morning we walked the grounds, out across the golf course to the Lake, back past the skating rink and greenhouses along the ball-fields, leaves gold and red on the trees of eternal return. Afterwards I led her on a second tour of the kitchen, past steaming grills and lines of waiters and waitresses; in the process we collected fruit and cookies for the road. We came back to the car and filled it at the Hotel pump.

"The Big Rock Candy Mountain," I joked. "Next stop, Annandale-on-Hudson. You drive."

She zoomed out the gate and, at my instruction, turned left on 52. As she opened a window and lit a cigarette, I got out my mimeographed stack of Kelly's poems and began reading aloud:

> "Raven   in Chiapas. . . .
> wings tensed back
> it has swallowed its tongue
> in hunger to eat
>   hunger to cry out loud   into the sky   I am here
> feed me unmerciful gods

who made us feed on shit
>   feed me because I cry louder. . . .
because I can crack the cheap bowl of your cry with my
shriek. . . ."

"He *is* amazing," she said. "It's hard to believe we're going to see him."

There was a wonderful ordinariness to the day: familiar scenery scooting by, her snappy turns on the backroads, lying against the cold sunny window and reading aloud (despite a touch of carsickness), a right turn onto 209 in Ellenville.

Passing the mansions of Stone Ridge, we crossed the boat-filled Hudson over the Rhinecliff Bridge and continued along wooded thoroughfares.

Robert Kelly lived on the Bard campus and, when we inquired for his house, we were directed to a small parking lot with a driveway ending in a cluster of barracks-like apartments. As we pulled up close to them, I checked his letter for the correct number. We knocked on the last door. A woman answered; short and stocky, she stared back and forth at us so intently it was almost rude. She was so oddly garbed in shawl and robes she might have been a dwarf out of Norse mythology. Taking stock of these two naive college students, she proclaimed at last, "You must be Richard Grossinger. Come in. Robert has been waiting for you."

Already I could hear his voice bellowing from the back rooms: "Joby, is it Richard Grossinger?"

We stepped into another reality. It was the den of a wizard, packed floor to ceiling with every imaginable size, shape, and age of book and manuscript. Esoteric tomes and black binders, some lying open, others with feathers and paperweights marking the place, rested on all the tables and were scattered as well over the faded Turkish carpet. Walls were decorated with occult icons, alchemical posters, tarot cards, and horoscopes. Every table bore unfinished cups of coffee and ashtrays overflowing.

There was no heat; the apartment was stone-cold. A large mechanical furnace with a pipe up through the ceiling sat silent. Across the archway leading to the entrance from which Kelly himself appeared was a hand-made sign with the words: TOMORROW POSSIBLE BECAUSE IT IS.

Though we had been forewarned about his appearance, nothing could have prepared us for such a giant or his manner of entering. Well over three hundred pounds and six feet, an unkempt red mane, he transformed scale itself, inhabiting the room by gasping between breaths. He continued to alter space as he walked, like a boulder coming through water.

"Yes, yes, Richard Grossinger—wonderful speech you gave—and—" He turned to Lindy, whom I introduced. Then he scurried us to chairs like a man feeding pigeons. "Is there anything happening these days at Amherst and Smith? I had thought nothing. And then Harvey Bialy returns with a story of an unlikely ceremony and carrying this magnificent piece of sacred oratory." He grabbed it from one of the tabletops and shook the daylights out of it.

Collaborating on our response and filling in each other's details, Lindy and I lamented that there was in truth little going on at Amherst and Smith. We told him what courses we were taking and what we were reading. He listened patiently and then indicated he would supply the remedy.

While delivering an impromptu sermon on Sufi music and cosmic vibrations and citing texts he presumed (quite wrongly) we knew, he seemed to gloss over the evident gulf between our spheres of learning. Even as he spoke, Joby interrupted constantly. We had to pay close attention not to slight either of them.

At one point Kelly retreated to the back room and remanifested bearing piles of colorful mimeographed sheets he stapled together by virtually crushing a tiny machine as he walked. These made up a magazine he called *matter*. We each got our own copy. I turned through my pages, which were filled with poetry, notes, diagrams, and epigraphs. Right away I saw an essay on film-making by Stan Brakhage, and I told Kelly all about the screening.

"Brakhage taught you an important lesson," he remarked. "You see, when you are young, you think you can live on anything, like junk food, and you can, and seem to do all right—you two are testament to that. But in order to grow into men and women you need real things, real imagination, not just symbols, or the ideas of some professor who hasn't been out of the university in two hundred years."

Kelly asked Joby if she was hungry and, when she responded with a growl, he decided to take us to town for lunch. Outside the apartment we were chaperoned to an old sedan. "Named Bloisius," Joby informed us with a maternal smile. As she and Kelly occupied positions in the front seat (which was decorated with postcards and amulets), we obeyed her instructions to pile up books strewn across the back and made enough room to squeeze in together. A smell of decay was indigenous to the vehicle (reminiscent of parchment, so not unpleasant).

Kelly hugged and rolled the wheel like an octopus with a crystal ball as he followed the bridge across the Hudson into Kingston. I had driven past this town many times but never seen its interior. We came down a surprisingly busy main street and pulled into the parking lot of a Chinese restaurant. Inside, we continued to talk.

In the course of egg rolls and spare ribs Kelly made headway through an invisible list of issues, quizzing us on them one by one—where we came from, what we read and imagined we wrote, what our relationship to each other was, in general who we thought we were. He certified each answer with a smile that was sometimes approving, sometimes quixotic, but never condescending. He cited important poetic and Gnostic masters and urged us to supplement our meager, modernistic educations with real texts, the titles of which he continued to compile on the back of an envelope he carried throughout the encounter.

"What planets do you think are inhabited?" he suddenly asked, recalling my interest in science fiction.

I gave a considered response, favoring Mars and Venus.

"But I think they are all inhabited," he attested, "inhabited on their own planes and by creatures indigenous to those planes. We think of life only in three dimensions, but beings might live on worlds in other dimensions while at the same time the surfaces of those worlds would appear barren."

"Even Pluto?" I asked.

"Don't be fooled by its size. It's a planet, the same as any other, and we know nothing about it, except as we have seemed to discover and name it." He gulped a full demitasse of green tea. "You ask about Pluto. I say Pluto may give birth to the present epoch. I say that the Sun itself is inhabited. I think its core is teeming with creatures, all in an exalted spiritual state. Not necessarily higher, though. Souls exist on the Sun in their own occasion. Souls come to all worlds for specific reasons. Ours is the green planet, the realm of growth; here, uniquely, creatures can transform themselves by work. That is our desperate situation, the reason we cannot dawdle. Your professors don't see it, so they fulfill their etymology. They profess. They go on and on as if we had time unto eternity." He paused to order additional food, choosing for us too, and then he picked up exactly where he left off. "We have very little time, almost no time at all, and the Moon itself is waiting to swallow us, to trap us in habitual motion. In truth, we live our lives in an instant, effect a transmutation (or not), vanish into darkness. That is the next task for you two—to live—now that you have declared yourself apart from the monster."

Then he asked us about dreams, and I answered with interpretations from Jung and Freud. "Good basic training," he said, "but this is still the Western dream you are talking about, the dream that stands *for* something. I am talking about a pure act of dreaming that does not have to be subservient to any system of symbols. Remember Blake: make your own system or be enslaved by another's. Unfortunately, Blake was enslaved by his own system. Dreaming in fact is no different from 'lifing'—that's an American Indian testament. You need not ever think of yourselves as bearers of artifice or requiring interpretation. Dream is its own mystery, its own logos, not the product of some professional establishment."

"But don't dreams carry the meaning of past events?" Lindy asked. "Do you think Freud is all wrong?"

"What about the archetypes?" I added. "Don't they shape dreams at a primal source?"

"We don't even know if there *is* such a thing as an archetype. Jung is seductive, hence dangerous. He offers candies so delicate they are hard to resist, but he too was enslaved by his own system. Meanings and symbols are only accoutrements of a dreaming. But they are not the fact of the dreaming. Dreaming is its own fact."

The arrival of main dishes interrupted our talk. Kelly dished out generous helpings for all.

"It is charming to be children when you are children," he opined while counting out his cash and assuring us we were his guests. "But in America they want to keep you children forever." He downed another cup of tea in a gulp. "Your professors are children—I mean, in terms of the wisdom of the universe. Your parents likewise." He looked around the room as though perhaps to include its inhabitants in his indictment. "You have an opportunity to be more than that. Already Richard's Halloween vision speaks to a deeper truth. I see it in both of you. Stop writing fiction. Stop making up things. It's not cute and inventive; it's clever and evasive. Do you want to live lives of gossip? Do you want to dream and breathe this fraud of a civilization? Grow up!"

Back at his apartment he offered to read to us from his work. In a hurry to get back to school, we politely resisted, but he chided us for being Amherst and Smith drones and mesmerized us back in our seats. "What would your good professors think if you refused a reading from William Butler Yeats?"

I disliked being a captive audience, but he read like a jinni. Yeats was an understatement.

He closed with a long poem called "The Alchemist" with lines as good as any I had ever heard:

> "& if we do not get up and destroy all the congressmen
> turn them into naked men and let the sun shine on them
> set them down in a desert & let them find their way out,
> north, by whatever sexual power is left in them, if we do not
> seize the president and take him out in daytime and show him
> the fire & energy of one at least immediate star, white star. . . .
>
> we will walk forever down the hallways into mirrors and
> stagger and look to our left hand for support & the sun
> will have set inside us & the world will be filled with Law. . . ."

We sat in silence, in humility. Each in our way, we realized that we had been blessed. Then Kelly told us to stick together and protect each other. He handed Lindy the reading-list envelope and bid us "God's peace" with a mantra of his left hand: "Until the next time. I'm sure there will be many."

We left him copies of our work, and he promised to read it and discuss it with us the next visit, which he hoped would be soon. We found the Taconic and followed its gentle hills up through New York to meet the Thruway just before the Massachusetts line.

"Give me a few days to get my life together," Lindy said at the door to Laura Scales. I nodded and drove back to Phi Psi.

Several times a week over the next months she and I met at Smith and set out looking for new places to have dinner: a tavern in Hadley, an Italian restaurant between Northampton and Amherst, a diner in Florence, a steak house in Springfield, a local Howard Johnson's. We wove an emotional and artistic world within the limitations of the Amherst-Smith system.

Yet the relationship was also a struggle. I had no doubt found "her" too soon, but it was too late to do anything about it. We were in a trap—in my blue room on the yellow serape, not able to escape by becoming lovers. Our different histories precluded any ease of sexuality, so we argued it nightly like teenagers, one more cigarette for her in the car before curfew, trying to patch it together before saying goodnight. Like Schuyler I was trying to leap the abyss of my failed adolescence in what amounted to a single act. Lindy was as helpful as another person, with her own life at stake, could be. She was clear and acerbic and embraced the confident good-humored person when I became him but teased and dismissed the perverse child. When I kneeled on the mattress looking wounded and distraught, she would say, "Enough," and go for a walk in the Glen, or sit in the living room talking with other people until I gave it up. I despised that child too, but there was no place to hide him.

"That's okay," Lindy said. "So, we hate each other now. It will all come out in the wash."

She decided to go to a friend's house outside Boston for Thanksgiving ("Remember, familiarity breeds contempt," she warned). I went to the Hotel and used it as a base to visit Bard. It turned out Kelly was not seeing people on the day I chose, but Harvey led me to the house of a married student poet. Beside the fireplace after dinner I experienced an evening of Bard gospel and poetry after which I answered questions about my life. Harvey sat smoking his pipe, nodding.

I visited Kelly the next afternoon. He expressed surprisingly appropriate concern about my "traveling without Lindy." I acknowledged the warning and promised to return together, but he was already on the next topic.

"Why did you tell Harvey and Jonathan your story and yet never a word to me, even about Grossinger's?" I was dumbfounded that he knew and then mortified as I pictured myself chattering away while the disciples prepared their report for the master. But was he saying that I should have told him the tales too, or that I made an ass out of myself telling them at all?

"It didn't seem appropriate."

"You're right. It wasn't. I caught the attention of the part of you that is awake, and you didn't think to waste my time on that nonsense. Having Lindy with you helped; you were in too serious a situation to dawdle. With those others it was just nervous energy, nothing at stake. That's okay. You defined them too. Nothing lost." He had a very definite opinion about my relationship to Grossinger's. "You must have accumulated good karma in a previous lifetime. Grossinger's is the universe's way of rewarding you. Don't reject it. That would be ungracious. Try to put it to good use. Since it is a blessing to you, try to be a blessing to it. Not in a culturally ritualistic way, as everyone will insist at the waste of both your time and theirs, but in the true sense of magi bearing gifts. Respect the karma of your family members too. Don't deprive them of your knowledge and compassion out of second-rate political claptrap."

Then he handed my manuscript back to me.

"The speech you gave at Halloween was, in a sense, your first piece of writing. What comes before it is gossip, social chatter of the sort you did last night." His eyes were solemn and piercing. "Confession is a trick we play on ourselves. It is the least personal act of all."

I nodded, so he went on. "We were all mistreated in childhood; do we want to make that the talisman of our lives? We all have fantasies and daydreams; they're not of essence. It's the energy they generate that matters. It is far more difficult to face our uniqueness, to speak of what is truly in our hearts."

I had waited a lifetime for Fabian and Friend—or even Leo Marx— to speak with such impeccability and precision.

"Your Halloween speech was personal because no one could have spoken it but you; it expressed your destiny. These Betsies and Peggies are everyone's fantasies, which means no one's." He closed by reading from a poem by Olson:

> "This, is no bare incoming
> of novel abstract form, this
> is no welter or the forms
> of those events, this,
>
> Greeks, is the stopping
> of the battle."

On the afternoon of Christmas vacation I drove Lindy to the airport outside Springfield. I already had my own ticket out of New York and would meet her in Denver by week's end. I passed through Grossinger's like a stranger.

Aunt Bunny was now getting shock treatment. "How can you allow such a thing?" I demanded of my father.

But he was beyond reach. As far as he was concerned this was a matter for experts only.

"It's her life," I pleaded, but he stared blankly back as though I were just another hysteric. He was a vintage male of his generation, capable solely of counterfeit gestures and sentimentalities. He liked children and animals. Actual emotion left him cold as poison.

I came to my mother only for sentencing—an unspoken judgment far more complicated than simple banishment. The second night I was there she was yelling at Jonny about some misdeed. He swore back, so she said, "Don't ever talk to me like that."

"Fuck you!" was his answer.

She slugged him. He shoved her on the couch. She ran him down and pounded him with her fists, scratched at his face and neck until he was bleeding. Then he swung really hard and sent her reeling across the room.

The next morning I flew out. My head against a window, looking down at the snowy checkerboard, I sang on and off in my head the silly New Christy Minstrels song about *"got me a woman in Denver, Lord. . . ."* and then on the other side of sky, mid-afternoon, she was standing there in the crowd in her blue puffy winter jacket and an ingenuous face that melted through me.

"Hello, kiddo."

It was rhapsodic to be taken into a whole family at Christmas, and I lost myself in the adventure. Lindy and I toured her city by day and night—coffee shops, old neighborhoods, late meals and beers in Larimer Square. One afternoon I went around the house photographing vignettes of her life, collections of objects on her desk, clothes thrown over the chair. She stood out in this family as a jewel in the desert, and she was also my whole family too.

I was in flight over the abyss. My only hope was to land on the other side.

When I called Brakhage in Rollinsville I left out mention of Phi Psi. I did not want to be implicated in Tripp's excesses. Happy to have unexpected visitors courtesy of Kelly, Brakhage gave me directions on how to find his cabin. Lindy and I set out on a pilgrimage the next day after lunch.

The highway to Boulder was easy, but on subsequent mountain roads we got lost several times and had to keep winding back. Then we found a hopeful unmarked lane, much like the one he described. It was a matter of plunging blindly into the wilderness, but we followed it to the end.

I stood in the snow, clearing my head, staring at a relic: a log cabin amidst drifts, piles of wood and splitting blocks, a very old car, an axe in one log. . . . This was the stageset of *Dog Star Man*.

When we came in the door I had the same giddy sense as when entering Kelly's.

"Greetings," said Brakhage, extending his hand.

We followed him in and immediately met the real-life Jane. Dressed in Colorado work clothes the Brakhages were imposing: the renegade couple of the avant-garde film world.

The hearth of their cabin was spacious and sunny, filled with books, canisters, and other paraphernalia of film-making. Small kids scampered in and out, mostly without pants. If Kelly's was a basement of the occult, this was the wild West out of Denver and, although we were both babes in wonderland, Lindy at last was on her home turf (Jane in fact looked like a bigger-boned, huskier version of her).

Stan asked if we were hungry, and Jane served up a bark tea and goat's milk cheese. Then he began talking, just as at Amherst, partly from the generous impulse of his own thoughts and partly in resentment for what he felt was his mistreatment at the kinds of Eastern colleges we came from. He railed about being poor and unappreciated and not having enough money even to buy film stock. Since Amherst and Smith were red flags to him of moneyed elitism, there were moments I thought we were about to get evicted—for instance, his initial rage when he figured out my connection to Tripp—but he concluded merely that Jeff should sell his beloved Porsche if he cared about art and, if he didn't need the money, there was a film-maker in Colorado who could always use it to buy another year's groceries.

We sat studiously as he took us on tour with a rowdy cast of characters: Sartre, Cocteau, Gertrude Stein, Ezra Pound. Once again, we were woefully underinformed. When he realized Lindy hadn't seen his films he brought out a projector and showed a section of *Dog Star Man*. Then he told us about the death of the dog, Sirius: Other dogs found his corpse in the snow and rubbed themselves in it. "The origin of perfumes is the body's decay—you know, John Donne: the nearness of death and sex."

Day became night. I was exhausted and felt myself slipping back into the languor of childhood. Wind blew snow against the cabin. I felt faraway from anyplace and wanted to go home, if only I knew where.

They fed us from the soup they were making for dinner. Afterwards, Stan posed a riddle: One night he and a friend, happy and peaceful, sitting under the moon with beers, asked each other, "Why can't it be like this all the time?"

It was a wonderful question, but we couldn't guess the answer: "Why *can't* it be like this all the time?"

"It *is* like this all the time," Stan said. "It's just that we don't know it."

They walked us back to the car, and we chugged into the wintry black. As Lindy worked her way down the mountain I got dizzier and dizzier. It wasn't just carsickness; it was the whole day, perhaps the life. I rejoiced outwardly in my baptism, but my guts rejected it. I felt chilled. Finally I was too sick. I had to get out.

I stood under stars, shivering but refreshed, breathing Rocky Mountains Orion, nauseous with goat's milk cheese and pages of Gertrude

Stein and strange tea, Stan and Jane's marriage and children, now the twisting road, the intimacy of Lindy herself. I was terrified that I didn't have the strength to pull this thing off. I wanted to rest. Enough bravado. Enough radical art and transformation.

The bitter air gave me a brief hold on reality, a remnant of the Chipinaw forest I could cling to. I came back into the car and put my head in her lap. I hadn't the strength even to focus—let alone identify—the constellations I saw upside-down.

I refunded my plane fare so we could take the train east together. We tried to arrange it so that we would go to New York, claim the Mustang, and drive it back to school, but her mother caught on at the last minute and changed her ticket right there at the station.

"It's totally inappropriate to travel together," she grumbled. "Let Rich go fetch his own car."

At dawn we lay against each other half-awake on a littered bench in the Chicago station . . . bookends. My train came first. I kissed her and boarded. I shot through the Midwest, across New York State, down Harlem, into the tunnel at Park Avenue and 96th. I took the subway up to Central Park West. There in the basement garage I found my car all shiny yellow—Bob had had the mud of winter washed off. In the warmth of that gesture of his I drove the turnpikes back to Amherst.

On Lindy's suggestion I signed up for Watercolor and the History of Art. I also took History of Film, Cognitive Psychology, Hindu Philosophy, and Seventeenth-Century Literature. While needing credits to make up freshman year, I was also aware for the first time of having virtually no cultural background. Lindy's world included Monet, Klee, Satie, Prokofiev, Poulenc, Merce Cunningham, and Yvonne Rainer.

I began dressing in the way she wanted. I bought dungarees and turtlenecks, learned to drink coffee, tried to smoke her cigarettes and finally compromised on a pipe. It was an unfamiliar ritual, stuffing in the tobacco and igniting it, but it created a fiery aroma that I associated with Dr. Friend. I was not a smoker. The venture lasted only a month.

Unfamiliar rituals were precisely what I needed. The past offered only a sense of smallness and loathing. Soon enough my mother would meet Lindy and thank her—with nothing short of amazement—for going out with me. That's how they thought of me: a weirdo, a misfit, a reject. Troubled little Richie. But to myself I was a maker of ceremonies, a radical artist, a grail quester. No wonder I wanted to rebuild my associations from scratch—Joan Miró: "Courage in a dragonfly"; Charles Olson; Charles Ives; dark coffee; *Dog Star Man;* Gertrude Stein; Robert Kelly; the writings of Sufi dervishes. Every day new. Tomorrow possible because it is. . . .

Rhonda wrote me a letter pleading not to drop her. Rhonda? For a moment I couldn't even remember who she was.

I was now midway in my leap.

I stopped writing novels. I stuck my reams of confessional prose into cartons and forgot about them. I wasn't Hamilton Basso or Leo Marx's precocious upstart. It didn't matter that I was at best an amateur poet. I wanted to remake myself through Kelly, Brakhage, and projective verse. I wanted to run as fast as I could from Saul Bellow (or Catherine Carver pretending to be Saul Bellow):

>miró
>>using brightest colors on
>loops of the infinite, stars
>>were made blue, gods were made
>>yellow, and where
>one color crossed
>another, a
>message was born.

>lindy hey
>>lindy hey come
>>>to the window babe
>>smile babe

>grey sunless
>>>>>air
>>driven by
>isobars
>>>>into
>sky wind.

today when i was not thinking of you,
  a lean bike figure
drove softly by, i
    was 2fingering an acorn,
      so I sidearmed it happily in your direction, you
arrived
blue, your reindeer skijacket powder
   blue, your thinking notebook marble
blue, your bike scratchy with Donald Duck
  blue, its silent eye a filament of ozone
blue, i
following
  to catch you soon,
soon, kiddo.

On weekends Lindy and I ranged farther. We began with the art museum in Worcester, then Boston. We picked up Polachek at his apartment and went to hear Harvey Bialy read with Allen Ginsberg and Harvard poets. Afterwards everyone was invited to Ginsberg's half-empty apartment building. A party was in progress; a dog was giving birth in the corner. It was over our heads, so we stood by ourselves, aloof and innocent, then fled back to Western Mass.

Next we drove to New York and stayed a night at my mother's. For all the angst I put into that meeting, the weekend was mostly uneventful. Bob took us out to lunch and did most of the talking. My mother and Lindy had their *tête à tête*. We visited the Museum of Modern Art for much of a day—a treat to see giant canvases after only slides. Then at a raunchy theater in the East Village we went to a late-night Kenneth Anger retrospective. The crowd was testy, police cars up and down the streets. The films were violent homosexual fantasies, motorcycle orgies, Crowleyite masques, but Brakhage had assigned them and we were under the protection of our quest.

During spring vacation we drove to the Hotel. My father's house was empty except for us. As we studied in a rowboat, puffy clouds floated above the golf course. The air was barely warm, a few turtles visible on rocks along the shore. It was a luxurious idyll, mixed with beers at the bar and dinners of matzoh ball soup, steak, and fries, capped with different flavors of sherbet and chocolate or lemon cake.

Io

We continued to Bard. Kelly had tendered an invitation to visit him when school was out and he had more time. He provided us a bare room in the infirmary. That night she stared down at me like a rider on a horse and said with a cheery laugh, "There, Rich, no longer a virgin." I felt oddly clinical, a post-sensual coldness and a wish to get myself back. I had wanted this for so long, but it was another thing entirely, not the tantalizing forest of vines (though I experienced them all around me in her body), more a combination of mythical sex and actual intimacy, a dance of man and woman bones I hadn't yet learned.

The next morning, driving across New York to Connecticut to see Brakhage show his films at Yale, the experience opened inside me. A calm, almost pleasurable nausea blossomed from my belly like a lotus, so that I had to be neither powerful nor well, just cozy as she bounded the car through sun-shade patches of trees and houses. I felt less as though I had become a man, more that I was a kid again, safe and whole, the heater blowing warmth, the sky an unreal robin's egg blue. I even turned on the Mets opening game . . . an extra-inning single winning it for them.

Why *can't* it be like this all the time, Stan?

In the weeks that followed, unhappily I discovered that it can't. We lived out the prophecy that making love would become an obstacle not a touchstone in our relationship. We were back stuck in the blue room. I wanted to have that closeness always, not because it was easy and pleasurable but because it sealed the promise. I was already running five years ahead of myself, hoping to escape the risks that lay in between. I didn't want to be grim and militaristic like Schuyler. I made her a map of the house in which we would live: the bedrooms of our children, the darkroom, the attic with its telescope, the garden. I should have heeded Scotty's warning. She began talking about how we were getting too cozy—that I was assuming the relationship rather than letting it develop. As she stomped out of the blue room one night, I lay there, drowning in my ashes. She returned, furious at my self-pity: "I hate men who drool!" It certainly all would . . . in the wash.

The blanket of childhood crept over me like a spell, not then, once upon a time—because that was all dead and gone—but now, in the present, in the form of the strictures and agonies it gave rise to. I knew

445

deep down I couldn't just keep climbing; soon enough I would tumble back down the dungeon stairs. I knew this, and yet couldn't help myself.

She wanted to be free again—it happened so fast I didn't know where it came from. I wrote apologetic love poems.

She said, Whoa! Let's stop seeing each other for a while. I need to breathe. You're holding on too tight.

Familiarity had bred something akin to contempt.

Earlier that spring, provoked by unrelenting criticism coming from Phi Psi, the Amherst Fraternity Council had issued a series of punitive citations, requiring the House to make more conventional uses of its budget, including a regular homecoming band and a fraternity publication. We welcomed their interference as a gauntlet. At our next Wednesday meeting the money for the band was voted to the House jug band, and $100 for a publication was turned over to me to put out a literary magazine. At first I said no, but Lindy thought it would be a great idea to launch a four-college publication together. So we found co-editors at Mount Holyoke and UMass. Then, since the money was hardly adequate, I enlisted Phi Psi members to join me in traipsing from shop to shop in Amherst (and later, Northampton), begging ads from bookstores, clothiers, art galleries, optometrists, gas stations, and of course the Lord Jeff Inn and Wiggins Tavern. All of these establishments had budgets for student publications, so we were able to gather $500 in a matter of weeks.

We laid out some thirty pages of writing and artwork, including poems from Chuck, Harvey, Lindy, and Diana; the text of a pamphlet (handed to Lindy and me in Greenwich Village) blaming all mankind's woes on an innocent comet; and a cheery greeting from science-fiction writer Ray Bradbury in response to a query from me. Then Nelson convinced me to open with my Halloween speech (for which he wrote an epigraph).

All we needed for publication was a name and a cover. This confounded us until, re-reading my poem of the previous spring, I saw the moon Io circling Jupiter. The idea of such a short title delighted Nelson and me—him as a minimalist and me as an old crossword-puzzle/"moons of the solar system" buff. Using discarded window screening from the attic, he made a surface of mesh, sprinkled it with mothwings from the bowl of a lamp, added washers and nuts, smeared the whole thing with India ink, and imprinted it on a piece of paper. He thought that the resulting image was perfect by itself, but on my insistence he took a fountain pen and etched a pictograph of Jupiter in the wet ink. "Ever the literalist, Grossinger!"

In order to have the magazine done inexpensively we mailed it to the Grossinger's print shop. Lindy and I had planned to go together and drop the first copies at Bard, but by the time it was ready she was off at Williams, dating an old friend from Denver. So, that Friday after classes, I drove four hours to the Hotel.

In stacks beside the rooster-clad breakfast menus, *Io* sat, Nelson's raw image fully realized a thousand times on its front. It was a minting of rare baseball cards; it was an occult *Chipinaw Chirp,* covers floating slightly above the pages, artwork perfectly tattooed among words. I kept resniffing the fresh ink as I filled the trunk and back seat with cartons. Then I drove the fifty miles to Bard.

Kelly heard out my woes and suggested we go to the Chinese restaurant for a private session. As we clanked across the bridge, his body draped over the wheel of Bloisius, he gave the oracle's answer: "This is life and death to you, isn't it? At least you recognize that. Most people in this country think it's all fun and games." His words were always startling and on target. "America has teeth, you know and, if you rise up and become what you are, it will try to destroy you. But all the while it will smile and pretend to be innocuous. Ah yes, that great American sense of humor that will surely someday kill us all."

I said that Lindy wanted to date other people and I wondered if maybe she was right and we weren't good for each other any longer. I said that I didn't know why I hung on. Perhaps it would be better for me also to meet other girls.

"Those are just notions. You don't know where the gods are leading you. Simply follow. Forget the past. Be what you are now. Lindy— and you likewise—are involved in an old image of ecstasy, but 'ex' is always outside. We need to invent a new word—call it 'enstasy,' the pleasure of staying within a growing form no matter how painful. The form itself will sustain you and tell you when it is time to break off. You have only the vulnerability of your being with which to face the world. So expose yourself and be blessed."

On a walk in the Glen the following Monday, Nelson cautioned me not to forget the angels either: "You can't write their script for them. They write for you. They write so much better than you could imagine. When you get too involved in making things happen you get in their way. Simple prayers are everywhere—like those bird sounds."

"Kywassik!kywassik!kywassik!" shot from the distant trees.

The primal obscurity of that code cut through me like a knife.

Then one evening in May, Lindy called and asked me to bring her some more copies of *Io*. We went for a drive in the country and parked by a tobacco field. I looked at her face, no more anger in it, only a mirror of what my love for the world had become, my nostalgia and my hope, because I had cast it all into her. I kissed her teary cheeks as she said, "Okay, Rich, so we try again."

Now the summer faced us—and how to get to be together. Lindy had her own crisis with her family. There was little good feeling left at home: her sisters grown and married to professionals, her mother and father in middle-age misery.

More radical and zany than her sisters, she had grown up nonetheless a cheerful, compliant daughter in a Colorado Episcopalian setting, Mayflower Society on her father's side, Denver society on her mother's, trappings of upper class but the money gone. These parents meant to sabotage her, to keep her powerless and eligible. They never considered who she was, or that she might contain energies and dreams not in the other girls. With adolescence she was transformed from debutante and family clown into a rebellious teenager, throwing her clothes down before her and then slipping out the window on late-night dates, hanging around with "wild girls" at marijuana parties. Her parents felt outmoded and unprepared; they couldn't rein her in.

The last weeks of high school were open warfare, though when she left for college, the conflict was papered over with niceties: "That couldn't really have been you, dear. It must have been those boys you were dating." In this family they didn't shout so much as conduct a mincing debate of sins and apologies. Most recently they engaged in escalating confrontations over Lindy's view of the shortcomings of Smith, which to them was flawless. Smith was the sanctum from which her mother had failed to graduate, the nest from which her sister Polly had flown to Yale Graduate School. They expected her to worship the place; they wanted to hear the words "eternally grateful" again and again. She could no more return to that world than I could to Grossinger's.

We played with the notion of both working in New York, but when she sounded her parents out they said they wouldn't pay for Smith unless she came back to Colorado. So we evolved another plan. We would each go home; then she would head to the Rockies—Aspen— and get a job. I would drive the car out and meet her there.

With a healthy sense of the hurdles before us I took her again to the airport. At least we were of one mind and heart and our difficulties were merely practical. We said goodbye, and I headed to Grossinger's.

When I told my father that I would get my own job again he froze: "Absolutely not. This summer you're working for me." I nodded silently.

The next morning I visited Jerry at his new home in Grahamsville. I told him what I was about to do. It seemed sad that he and I couldn't have another summer of playing ball and sitting in the backyard with Aunt Bunny, but that pastoral was over. He understood my wish to be free if not the irreconcilability of my condition.

I had been under the influence of the gods so many months now that nothing was innocent—they were hurrying me on my way. I was lucky to survive even that simple encounter with a friend. A large blue car that sped past me twice (going into town and then back out at perhaps ninety) was involved in a hit-and-run accident moments later. A witness said it was the one that "came back through town," which was also me. Jerry got a disquieting phone call about his guest while we sat on the porch. He questioned me closely, figured out my degree of jeopardy, and then sent me home at once on a backroad.

I had done nothing, yet I was in peril. I felt the malevolence of the thing that pursued me. Some stranger, on a whim, could take away my license or force me into court for the summer. I could lose Lindy. I could end up like Bunny. And my own father was laconic, barely conscious. I had no time left.

PART
SIX

NEW MOON

June, 1965–November, 1965

ASPEN

A t nightfall of my third day back I wrote a brief note to my father, packed my car, and set out west on 52. Harvey had left his Bard room unlocked and empty for me. I slept there, then got up at dawn and went north on the New York State Thruway. I drove the entire day, west into Pennsylvania, then across the Ohio line.

Gradually my excitement subsided into the boredom of the road, the imagination of long miles ahead. The radio became tiresome. Only currents of memories held any interest. Ceaselessly they bubbled up, contacted my mind, and fell back away: Bill-Dave Group, punchball in the P.S. 6 yard, Dr. Friend opening his door, June Valli singing "Applegreen," the Callicoon River.

I was driven by rage for all that had been done (to the world as well as to me), but also by a tenderness I felt for Lindy and the vastness itself of time. The morning was cool. A big sun cleared the last stars. Little by little the tincture of hue changed, traffic increased; I opened the window. Repetitive thoughts raced, disappearing, returning. I became quicker and more coordinated, darting in and out of lanes clogged with trucks, breaking again and again into the clear. By the time I pulled into the driveway of my old roommate Roger in Hudson the world had become an oven.

I stepped into a locust invasion: they were crawling across the ground, flying up and buzzing in swarms, rapping against the window as I showered and fell asleep in the back room.

Noon (awakening) was Ohio balm, floating in zephyr-fragrance blossoms, inviting me (through Roger's parents) to stay on a few days. *("And all the world seemed applegreen....")* I saw kids lined up at an ice-cream truck, a softball game in the choose-up stage. There was so much life for which I felt a fathomless nostalgia: the things I had not been as well as those I had. I wished that I could disappear into their sweet opacity, smash vigilance and lie exposed and anonymous, a frog again in the sun.

I left the next morning and set out west on the Ohio Turnpike. A year ago I had borrowed Fred's clunker with Ohio plates to take Lindy to the airport. Now I was in Ohio itself, following, at a snail's pace and five days after, the wake of her plane.

I crossed the line into Indiana, then Illinois. My speed increased; my mind ground miles into pebbles. I began to notice police cars as I fantasized my father collaborating with my hypothetical accuser to bring me back. But moods came and went in a tedium of driving; only the mileage made progress, now less than a hundred to the Iowa line.

Habitation became sparser, landscapes rural—farms scattered in near and far distances, corn dust in the air. I crossed the Mississippi at Davenport. I was surprised to find Iowa Highway 80 posted for seventy-five. I coasted.

I stopped in Iowa City at nightfall. Sitting in a restaurant with a slice of pizza I sank into *Lord of the Rings:*

"Whether the morning and evening of one day or of many days passed Frodo could not tell. He did not feel either hungry or tired, only filled with wonder. The stars shone through the window and the silence of the heavens seemed to be around him...."

Having left the Shire, Frodo was traveling through its outlying districts, all of them fraught with dangers human and half-animal, also allies he had yet to identify. He was led by a gray magician named Gandalf. On the deepest of esoteric levels this was my journey too.

I chose a motel on a sidestreet; signed the register; then lay in fresh, stiff sheets, reading till I couldn't keep my eyes open:

"When the Elves passed westward, Tom was here already, before the seas were bent. He knew the dark under the stars when it was fearless—before the Dark Lord came from Outside."

Yes, the Dark Lord, so long ago.

In the morning I explored. Along the spine of the town ran a bounteous river, houses on its banks, children in their yards. I imagined
Lindy and me living there. I even found the offices of the Iowa Writers' Workshop on campus. A British faculty member visited with me
for a half hour, let me babble on about my writing, shook my hand,
and encouraged me to apply.

Sustained by that fantasy I returned to the speedway and zoomed
through the swelter of cornfields. 'Salt flats, salt flats,' I encouraged
myself as the expanse of stone whipped beneath, syncopated by blips
of cars in the other direction. At sunset I came into giant Nebraska,
swept past Omaha, then the tapers of Lincoln at dusk. One more full
state to go.

Through night, old Yankee and other farm teams (Kearney and
North Platte) approached at 50 miles, dwindled to digits, exited, and
passed. I slept in the car at a roadstop and awoke at the dawn.

Light revealed a foreign landscape: brown and sparse, a few farms,
pigs and cattle, brief azure ponds. I was an astronaut fleeting through
badlands, dependent on my vehicle. At a gas station I patted its hot tin
reassuringly. The nearness of Colorado, recalculated every few minutes, kept my brain interested through the endless empty corner of
Nebraska. By the time I crossed the state line the sun was on top of
me; then the miles to Denver melted across the plains. The last three
hundred were nothing at all.

I came in through ranch suburbs, the urban radio on news and rock.
I found my way to Lindy's street, parked in front of her house, and
emerged like a snail from a shell.

Her parents regarded my arrival with immediate suspicion: Did I
plan to spend the summer with her? Where would I live? I tried to be
matter-of-fact.

Lindy was already in Aspen and, since they had her phone number, I called. She was both astonished and delighted: "I knew you'd
try, but I told myself you might never get out of there."

She reviewed her situation. She was staying in a dormitory/motel
and had gotten two part-time jobs already—one writing for the *Aspen
Illustrated News,* the other as a bartender-in-training at an Alaskan restaurant decorated with dogsleds (she could begin on July 4th when she
was 21).

From Denver it was a gradual ascent into the mountains, curvy roads up and down passes, occasional straight stretches across high-altitude valleys. Woods became evergreen, sky spackled with cumulus that descended multidimensionally to timberline. Finally, after more than five hours, I came out the steep chute of a pass into a small Western resort town, its main street teeming with college-age kids. I got directions to her apartment complex, found her door along its dim hallway, and knocked. The flight from Grossinger's had brought me home.

Her face and presence were famous by now, but I was surprised by her actuality. In driving so many days I had frozen her portrait and forgotten her subtleties. For a second I found it hard to respond; then we hugged and sat together on the bed telling our tales. I relived the journey: the imperilled escape, the locusts, Iowa City.... But after a while she pointed out the obvious: I needed a place to stay and a job.

She had heard of a ski chalet on the eastern side of town where there might be inexpensive rooms. In fact, she had thought of living in it herself but couldn't without a car. We drove there, and I rented the last room for a few dollars a night. It was a gloomy basement cubicle without a window, but I happily unpacked: typewriter, clothes, books, baseball glove....

For the rest of the week into the following one I hunted for a job, answering ads (with Lindy slipping me the classified before it was printed) and going door to door. A roving horde of college students had the same intention, and I was routinely turned down at restaurants, the other newspaper, the bookstore, two rock and mineral shops, and various assorted establishments. In order to get away from the crowd I offered to tutor Latin at a private school in Carbondale. They thought about it three tantalizing days before declining. Lindy meanwhile found a third job, cleaning house and babysitting for a postal clerk whose wife had just had a baby.

I was running out of money, so I called my grandmother and tried to give her a quick account of my situation. She didn't need to know—she wired $200 the next morning.

Meanwhile Lindy and I discovered—from a poster on a lamppost—that we had literary company; there was a writing program with East Coast people, including two poets we knew of through Kelly: Paul Blackburn and John Taggart.

The Aspen Writers' Workshop was located in a cluster of apartments downstairs in a ski lodge. We found it by attending a reading there; we introduced ourselves and passed around copies of *Io*. Although not paying members, we were invited by Blackburn to join his classes. With Lindy working and me hunting for a job, there weren't many opportunities, but the hours lying in the grass, listening to student poems and Blackburn's street-smart critiques, became our favorite activity.

We ate lunch and dinner regularly with the Workshop crowd at an open-air restaurant in the center of town. On our meager budget we developed a passion for bowls of soup mixed with oatmeal or Wheatina (the house speciality), followed by after-dinner philosophy over tea.

Our main friend was Mitchell, a tall, spacy kid with curly black hair and glasses. A onetime student of George von Hillshimer at Summer Lane, a graduate of the bohemian Music and Art High School in New York, he now attended experimental Antioch College in Ohio. Intellectual and hip, he was a master of deadpan cosmic comedy. His favorite topics were Jungian synchronicity, sacred alphabets, and an avant-garde philosopher named Marshall McLuhan who had turned the world upside-down by placing the medium before the message. From topic to topic Mitchell always had to clarify whether we were talking lineal typographic reality, phenomenological reality, tribal reality, or radio-TV electromagnetic waves. He soon had me reading his copy of *The Gutenberg Galaxy*, Gaston Bachelard's *The Poetics of Space*, and Robert Graves' *White Goddess*, which transposed the origins of alphabets back to primeval tree names.

I had long sought such a companion, a gentler, goofier version of Chuck Stein, someone who, like me, wandered unabashed from science fiction to alchemy to Dakota lodges, with baseball history, subway stops, and other New York trivia thrown in. Mitchell and I lay in the yard by the Workshop, endlessly rapping Olson's projective verse, pre-Giotto Christian paintings, the totem poles of audio-tactile cultures, and the mysteries of the letter Q (from which came *quis, quod,* and the "quest" itself).

Our summer banter, behind its nouns and syllables, brought an ancient arbor of glyphs to life. The Rocky Mountain landscape dropped into oneiric immensity and, at the same time, cast four-dimensional diamonds of focus everywhere, pulling images out of the dialectics of space. But I still needed a job.

Toward the end of the second week Lindy met me at lunch with a hot new listing: A restaurant named Sunnie's Rendezvous was opening underneath the bookstore in the arcade—they needed a busboy. "Say you worked at Grossinger's this time," she advised. It wasn't honest, but it worked like a charm.

Sunnie was a platinum-blond ex-showgirl from Manhattan. On the magic of my name she hired me at once, and I began work the next night. It was an intimate dinner-only saloon—menu on a blackboard (trout, sirloin, fondu, etc.). The whole room was serviced by just one waiter and busboy.

Sunnie featured the live jazz of her new boyfriend Ralph, who had just left his wife for her. He was a serious bespectacled man who sat at the piano all night, playing whether there were customers or not. I imagined him both celebrating and doing penance for his romance and, in any case, he probably had nowhere else to go.

In addition to being the busboy I was paid $25 once a week to scrub the kitchen floor with commercial detergent and another $20 to come in every other morning and clean the bar. With tips I had more than enough to live on.

"Why pay two rents?" Lindy volunteered. "We should get a place together."

Gleefully I concurred, and spent my subsequent afternoons checking on listings. Most apartments were too expensive, but Mitchell heard about some log cabins on a road outside town. "They're really beautiful," he said, "and in the woods." Such a dreamy resolution seemed improbable, but I drove west anyway and, four miles down the trail, along the Roaring Fork River, came upon Aspen Park Cabins. The owners were school teachers from Denver; they had one unit left.

For $50 a month we got a room with a wood stove (management providing firewood), a desk, a table, shelves, two double beds, a sink, silverware, plates, pots and pans, and a refrigerator. All the cabins shared one outhouse. "The only requirement is that you have to be married." I swallowed hard and signed "Mr. and Mrs. Richard Grossinger," then hurried back into town.

"You did it, Rich!" she exclaimed. Collecting our belongings in two trips, we planted our typewriters on stacks of crates, clothes on shelves (the overflow on hangers along a center pole). Books were set on small half-logs we hammered above the beds and over the sink. The second bed served as a couch.

After arranging our dwelling, we returned to town and wheeled a cart up and down aisles picking out cans of soup, boxes of cereal, shell noodles, milk, butter, eggs, parsnips, carrots, lettuce, and cellophane-wrapped lamb chops and ground beef. Back at the cabin, it was wonderful to discover the plates, cups, and silverware and make our first lunch.

That night Mitchell was our guest. We three lay on the porch at sunset in the music of the Roaring Fork, talking Hindu illusion, tarot, and the sacred yew—a fire snapping inside, boiling water for noodles and vegetables. As the sky darkened, Mitchell blessed our cabin with an epigraph from a French poet:

"All these constellations are yours, they exist in you; outside your love they have no reality! How terrible the world seems to those who do not know themselves! When you felt alone and abandoned in the presence of the sea, imagine what solitude the waters must have felt in the night, or the night's own solitude in a universe without end!"

"Mitchell," Lindy said, "that's a beautiful, perfect prayer. I only hope we can deserve it."

After the meal we sat silently on boulders over the Roaring Fork. Shooting stars filled the universe. While I drove him back to town, Mitchell and I played with the radio, hunting for ballgames. From the Rockies we could pull in the whole continent.

Dressed as an Alaskan maid, Lindy served drinks to a courtyard—she joked—of garnished fowls, but the Toklat traineeship never materialized into a full-fledged job, so she wrote her articles and twice a week vacuumed and dusted. Meanwhile Sunnie's Rendezvous was perhaps the least popular restaurant in town. I would arrive at 4:30 in jacket and tie. Chester, the old cook, would feed the waiter Bob and me scraps from the menu, odds and ends of fish, fondu, and assorted fried vegetables. Then we would sit in the alcove and wait for customers.

My partner, Bob, a cowboy freak from Wyoming with a healthy tuft of hair growing out of each ear, was a career waiter and ardent supporter of Barry Goldwater. He was dependent on tips and, like

Ralph, had left another "situation" to launch Sunnie's enterprise, a mistake he now regretted nightly.

No more than four of the fifteen tables were ever filled, though I found it a distinguished crowd. I made friends with two priests from Oklahoma City to whom Bob was rude because he thought they were fags and probably wouldn't tip us ("Would you give the same compliments to Jesus Christ?" I asked). My friends not only left a generous stack of bills and coins but bought a number of *Ios* to send home. Throughout one meal I kept reigniting a discussion with a NASA executive about their Mariner spaceship headed towards Mars. He took down my name and Phi Psi address and promised to send photos. He came through (and years later was appointed Secretary of Defense). Bob thought he was a Soviet spy. Meanwhile Sunnie told me to stop pestering the clientele with "your college-boy routine."

On most evenings it was hours before even the first customer appeared. Chester stared dolefully at the ceiling. Bob eventually went into a stupor. And Ralph's witticisms had more and more empty space between them until he fell silent. I spent my time on tenterhooks over the fate of Frodo the ring-bearer.

"... he looked eastward and saw all the land of Lorien running down to the pale gleam of Anduin, the Great River. ...

"'There lies the fastness of Southern Mirkwood,' said Haldir. 'It is clad in a forest of dark fir, where the trees rot and wither. In the midst upon a stony height stands Dol Guldur, where long the hidden Enemy had his dwelling. We fear now it is inhabited again, and with power sevenfold.'"

"I don't care if there ain't no customers," snapped Sunnie. "I don't want you educatin' yourself on my time. At least *look* like you're ready to serve."

After my reading was abolished, Bob and I stood in the empty alcove debating politics and our boss's dementia.

I came in to clean around 10 AM, pushed open saloon doors, turned floodlights onto the bar. I counted empty whiskey bottles by brand, hosed the walk, put in fresh ice chips, rotated the warm beers under the cold, swept away crumbs, polished tables, emptied ashtrays, checked toilet paper, and refilled bowls with pretzels and potato chips.

Sunnie had told me to amuse myself by playing records; she meant *hers,* but one day I brought in T. S. Eliot reading the *Quartets.*

> "What is late November doing?
> With the disturbance of the spring. . . ."

She had forgotten to shut off the speakers by which recordings of Ralph (at dinner time) ostensibly lured customers from the arcade above. So I was serenading the town of Aspen.

> "Scorpion fights against the Sun
> Until Sun and Moon go down
> Comets weep and Leonids fly. . . ."

While I poured potato chips in the semi-darkness, unknown to me a merry crowd had gathered on the street.

> "Whirled in a vortex that shall bring
> The world to that destructive fire. . . ."

Rumors of this performance soon roused Sunnie and, just as Eliot was intoning about "the movement of darkness on darkness . . . " (the panorama of blue sky and aspens being stripped away), she burst in.

"Turn off the sermon, boy! It ain't Sunday!"

Our life in the cabin was the heart and soul of the summer. We would wake into ice-cold mornings and cuddle there in bed until one of us got up and put newspaper and kindling in the stove and lit a match. Smoky tree alphabets warmed the room with their blood. We hiked in bathrobes and moccasins across pine needles to the outhouse on the hill to brush our teeth in ice water and then take a quick hot shower. Back at the hearth we cooked either french toast or pancake batter on a ring of wood heat.

We collected suns: the low orange sun on the morning table, the cold white breakfast coffee sun, the dishwashing sun in gray-water, the noon sun when we lay and read in high grass, the grocery sun, the golden sun of supper beans, the sunset of bats and smoke. It was a dream of apple trees and cloud forests I had never known.

Moths fluttering on the screen, an owl singing the prehuman notes behind "Wynken, Blynken, and Nod," Lindy and I submerged in a huge bed that seemed a raft among constellations . . . onto "a river of crystal light/into a sea of dew."

One morning I rescued Ralph's eight-year-old son from Sunnie's basement (while his father practiced the piano)—drove him to the cabin and tossed him pitches and pop flies in a clearing. Later, he looked up at the dresses and sports jackets hanging together on the pole and asked, "Does your wife live here?" Tears welled in my eyes as I nodded. Male and female clothing mingled magically to make a home.

Our other close friends were Welton and Elsie, a black poet and his Jewish wife who lived otherwise on the Lower East Side. Welton was a scholarship student, the star of the workshop. A small trickster with twinkling eyes, he liked to tease Mitchell and me.

"I'm a street poet," he declared, "a man of the people. I'm Malcolm X and Che Guevara. I don't go for all this crazy shit about angels and alchemists and electronic higgledy-piggledy."

"Welton's a closet sorcerer," Mitchell whispered, quite loud enough for him to hear, "but we'll keep his secret."

Welton smiled in collusion. "We're at Yankee Stadium," he said, "waiting for the word. Maher-shalal-hash-baz. Will the real Martin Luther King please sit down."

Mitchell and I could not stop laughing.

"Hey, I'm writing this poem for you guys—Dar es Salaam, Key West, Antigua, Azimuth. The number of conditions required to determine a curve is equal to the number of independent constants in the equation of the curve."

"What else, Welton?" I managed.

"What else! Sinai, Phoenix, Zajecar, Paoting, Harlem, Toulouse, Minsk. The case, the gender are irrelevant!"

In mid-July Lindy answered an ad for "kittens" and came back with a little gray tabby we named Frodo. She tore around our single room and pounced on our bed in the morning, chasing the covers as we shifted. A perfect hobbit, she would prop herself on hind legs poking her head under the curtains to watch birds and rippling branches, her attention a ceaselessly moving bump of striped fabric.

The summer is preserved in a single image: Lindy and I with our cups of coffee in the high grass and dew after breakfast. Across the road the Roaring Fork is milling stones. Frodo runs from tree to tree, grasping the white bark with her claws and pulling herself up like a lemur. She drops, dashes again. I lie back against the sky.

I grew my hair long, wore blue work-shirts and dungarees, and wrote a new style of philosophical prose—clipped syntax like that of Olson but narrative nonetheless, combining images from physics and astronomy with Graves' tree alphabets and Kelly's alchemy. I gave my essays titles like "Aspect," "Syntax," and "Quantum."

We drove to meadows and mining towns and, mid-summer, bought tickets to an outdoor performance of Holst's "Planets." The orchestra tuned in the pavilion, then burst into melody. Above timberline, meteors scraped an astrological sky. Mars danced with the ghosts of Indian warriors; Saturn brought fullness and old age; Uranus arrived as a magician; Neptune finally settled the revelry, a mystic and sea captain accompanied by all the dream-folk of childhood come true, sprites and nymphs and brownies.

"If we lived on Uranus," I wrote that night, "there would be five moons: Miranda, Ariel, Umbriel, Titania, Oberon. Imagine wandering in a gaseous body in a methane breeze, Oberon setting, having nothing to do with Holst or *A Midsummer Night* ... except the sound 'oberon,' pulling green gas in spouts back and forth across a sea of green gas."

On Sunday I imagined the thumping jollity of Jupiter in thunder's rain, washing mud and leaves, twigs and pine needles into gullies while Frodo hid under the bed. Neptune rinsed the forest in "a riot of unspoiled beauty." Afterwards I smelled quixotic Mercury in the air. Life had lost its narrative structure and was becoming a dance.

When Lindy was sick I brought her cups of tea and sat by her bed. We talked tirelessly and sometimes argued fiercely but always loved each other again. I had never suspected life could be this way—the kitten-cat, chortle of the fire, meals together, forest, evergreen air, big night sky—and my memories of all of childhood resolving through bitterness into wonder and compassion.

One mid-August day Lindy and I rose in darkness. Freezing ... no time to set a fire ... stars still out. We collected Mitchell in town, then drove on backroads for miles. He pointed up a dirt road toward an edifice—the Snowmass monastery. Against a violet sky, shadows pushed plows. It was a landscape from another century.

Through stone portals we made our way into the nave. Bumping into each other in the narrowness, we finally found our morning's repose on benches.

The resident monks, one by one, came into a stone pit, across the ember of sun, chanted in Latin, left ... until only a fly buzzed in the patch of yellow, projecting a glyph of itself onto silence.

Months later, thinking back to that morning while drowning in nostalgia on Xenia Street, Ohio, Mitchell wrote "there is a honeysuckle vine which comes in our window; it makes the air so thick and sweet it is hateful."

And that was the dilemma: so much feeling, such texture of sadness from the past, such tenderness for Frodo, the twinkling dance of Holst's Neptune ... all without remittance. Lindy and I sat on the porch, late afternoon, glasses of ice water, each working on our typewriters. She drove me to Sunnie's, came and got me at ten. Her poems followed the path to the river, Hans Christian Andersen, the magic of children actors ... and Lindy-Rich:

> "It is partly because
> he has this kind of courage that i don't have
> it is partly because
> he has this kind of courage
> that allows him
> even commands him
> to open the latch of the door and flash the
> light around on the high green weeds blowing
> and the swaying trees/ old men/
> flash the light around through the wind
> blowing out there so hard and rushing
>
> partly because of that courage
> which i don't have
> so that when he left to go into town
> i stood awhile looking around the room
> and thinking where to begin again
> and where to begin and where to pick up and begin

to make order in my mind
picking up i thought of what he
had said afterwards/ that i am
4 people and what negotiations and wars

there are, and the same for him
well after he left as i say i played with
the kitten which was a distraction from
whatever distraction i would pick up next
the kitten curious and unafraid, bounding
finally asleep in the woodbox from which
i removed him, thinking of spiders
aware that it was so quiet picking up
threads trying to make order thinking
what kind of courage to have met him here

on this summer's night's battlefield—
the sky so porous and wind lightly through
moon shining shafts between the trees
and thinking and thinking and thinking
until finally lying again on the bed
the field opened, wind blew the flowers
gently, softly around all our feet as
four against four met, capes blowing and
standards locked in stirrups, flags unfurled
bearing signs and messages moon shining between
shafts of trees/the wind blew, ruffling
his hair and across the field mine, how
we charged
wind streaking in my ears/horse under me
swelling full with a fast thrusting of muscle
again and again we clashed/throwing each other
tossing each body into the air until
exhausted almost/we reached up past the porous sky
with one hand each, clasped a sweating hand there
each other's

after he went into town after
after that and that i stood in the room
fixated, and picked up things and lay on the bed

and finally heated up some coffee which was too bitter
i thought and thought, thinking
of that and then made some instant
which was better the kitten asleep
i put more coal on the fire, settled
down to write this about the making of
new boundaries and old wars, settled down to wait."

And I wrote:

Rolling off you dark and tarotesque against moonglow ... what
colorless alchemy is drawn from my dreams through this awakening flesh?

Our original passion had been replaced by an intimacy so riveting
and solid, so delicate I hardly noticed how we had become a couple.

But by mid-August, living together was living with ghosts. We
stopped making love. We argued. After dinner she would leave, and I
would find her later at the edge of the river. She kneeled there, crying,
oblivious to words or touch. Our pasts were reclaiming us. I crouched
in silence too, the starry heavens suddenly a glittering shroud, the Roaring Fork scraping the horizons of sound.

We reached the last quadrant of August. The Workshop disbanded.
We were going to drive straight back to Massachusetts, but Lindy's
parents demanded she come home for the three weeks before college.
We packed at night and drove down the mountains at dawn, Frodo in
a cage, Welton and Elsie in the back seat, their luggage tied to a rack.
They would share the driving east. Frodo would stay in Denver and
then come to Phi Psi with Lindy on the plane.

We set her down in the sunshine of the backyard. She bounded
across the grass and stopped at the fence, sniffing, considering the new
setting. No aspen bark, no chipmunks, no porch. She charged back
through the glass door, reentering the dining room as she had our cabin
hundreds of times, like a bull in the ring. It was excruciating to watch.
There was nothing I could do. Summer was over.

Lindy's parents were visibly uncomfortable with the three of us, so we
returned quickly to the car. "Drive carefully, and I'll see you back at
school," she said, a parting kiss. My heart sank as the bigness of the

highway and flatlands east of Denver absorbed us. Something vast and hollow was sucking us in. A thunderstorm blew atop the car; the blankets covering the luggage began to flap, the vehicle itself veering. I pulled over onto wet dirt. We stood outside, drenched, tying knots where buckles had snapped, retrieving odds and ends inside, tying the rest back down. We drove until rain ended in darkness. The moon was out by the time we began looking for a place to eat in McCook, Nebraska.

"I'm not hopeful, but we'll take our chances," Welton said, as we pulled into the first decent-looking restaurant and ordered hamburgers. We were exhausted and disoriented, having been up since sunrise. Before we realized it, a bunch of hoods had surrounded our table.

"Who are you all?" they asked. "Where're going?"

They didn't overtly threaten. In fact, they invited us into the back room for "the show." We followed, Welton remarking, "Just a little bit now 'cause we gotta get on the road."

The makeshift theater had an audience of about two dozen people, young farmer types. On a small stage a guitar player, visibly drunk, struggled through a song.

"He used to be with the New Christy Minstrels," someone told us. "How do you like him?"

"A whole lot," Welton said.

Then he flashed Elsie and me a sign. Five minutes later he tapped my knee; I tapped hers. We stood and marched out of the room, quickly through the restaurant, the guys breathing down our necks.

"Hey, the show's just starting. You haven't seen the best part. Don't you like it?"

We hastened into the car. I turned the key at once. As we hit the highway Welton sighed, "Guess seeing a nigger's 'bout as much recreation as they've had for a while. But I didn't want to entertain 'em anymore."

He told me not to stop unless I got too tired. "Or you hit Iowa City," he added with a laugh. He was afraid the guy who had sublet their apartment was going to sneak out without paying, so he wanted to arrive early and unannounced. He also wanted to put about a thousand miles between himself and McCook.

I had all the energy of the summer behind me, and night was friendlier than day, so I drove until the sun wrote its signature in a frieze over cornfields. In the rear view I caught a sudden glimpse of the stranger

I had become. I saw how the summer had begun to shape a man who might really exist. I had always feared looking like this—wild, unshaven—and yet I had waited, seemingly forever, for such a self to be born. Exiting as requested, I pulled into a parking space and announced, "Iowa City!"

"You must be kidding," Welton coughed, rubbing his eyes.

He had a friend there, a black professor who taught "Shakespeare, of all things," Welton scoffed. We spent the day with him, a tour of the town, then lay out by the river.

"It's fine, man," Welton told him, as we shook hands after dinner, "but you gotta lose that cat Shakespeare."

Now Welton was driving, and I collapsed on the back seat, having been up more than twenty-four hours; I didn't wake until Indiana.

We sped through Ohio into Pennsylvania. The land got greener, more familiar; the radio songs were "The Eve of Destruction"; The Toys, "Lovers' Concerto"; then The Four Seasons: *"Let's hang on to what we've got...."*

We were suddenly in New Jersey, approaching the City at light speed. I was wearing jeans and a work-shirt. I was still in Aspen as we pulled up to the first traffic light beyond the Lincoln Tunnel. And stopped.

I saw New York from our cabin. Through Frodo's eyes—Frodo the hobbit, the cat.

Stone and filth. Madness. Claustrophobia. People sitting on ledges outside brick buildings, portables blasting, torn billboards. My return was as miniscule as a piece of soot.

"Abandon all hope," Dante had written, "ye who enter here." So the City fused and filled my heart with dread, not of the people presently living there but of what I had been. I balked. No more sweet nostalgia of origins, it was so malignant I couldn't bear it. This *was* the panic; it always had been.

I left Welton and Elsie downtown, perhaps a day too late: the sub-letter had flown the coop. Then I drove to Central Park West and 90th, to the people who had once been my family. My mother approached in astonishment, her hand frigid. "What's happened to you?" she said, as though staring into my coffin.

I told her I was fine.

"You're pale and gaunt. When did you last have a check-up?"
I stayed overnight and fled just a hair's breadth ahead of the shadow.

Grossinger's was in full flower, buffet tables crammed with meats,
the lobotomized crowds moving from cabanas to coiffeurs, Yiddish
comedians on patios rattling through microphones, a haze of perfume
and tanning oil. It may have been paradise once, but George von Hillshimer was right: it was a gaudy and devious hell ... especially after
a life of coming home to Lindy at her typewriter with her cup of tea,
Frodo bounding across the floor.

I dressed as though in Aspen and walked the grounds unshaven.
Aunt Bunny was still gone, and my father wanted no part of me. I figured I'd get a sermon, but I hoped he would at least be pleased to see
me. He was indifferent to my return; he reprimanded perfunctorily,
then stared right through me. I knew there was no way to explain where
I had been. He said he would pay my college bills for one more year;
that was it. He could not forgive me for running away.

Michael was in a state of constant rage, tearing in and out of the
house with druggie friends. James had become a deer hunter whose
carcasses littered the basement. Both boys strode macho in their boots,
shouting out orders. The vultures were finally coming to the feast.

At least a dozen times that week, guests, executives, and assorted
relatives told me I looked haggard—but I was alert and liked the feel
of myself. Their real grievance was the fierceness with which I guarded
my new shape. I wasn't confident enough to relax in it, so I strode
around, bristly and unyielding. I had become Schuyler at last.

I drove to Woodstock to hear Kelly read and afterwards went to
dinner with him and his two "wives" (he was living with a young girlfriend as well as Joby). He was delighted with my tales of the summer,
and he hoped Lindy and I would be by to visit him. As I left he called
out, "You are finally beginning to look like who you are."

Lindy's first letter was dated August 30th and came to the Hotel:

Dearest Rich,
    Things are okay. I miss you a hell of a lot, more than I thought
I would. . . . I am terribly aware of things. I have sat and talked with
both of my parents for each night, telling them about Aspen and

what's wrong with it and all the funny stories I can remember....
Almost no mention of you by them, but frequent mention of you
by me, of course. They are mainly wary and afraid of what they
don't know about you, as they would be with anyone.
    I MISS YOU, BABY.

She told me her plans were to head east as soon as possible and join
me, and she closed with: "I'll write again soon. I love you, honey ...,"
the stick figure of a happy dancer sketched beneath her name.

That letter is now a torn, refolded relic: I carried it in my pocket for
weeks, reading it again and again to remind myself that Aspen really
happened. A second letter came only a few days later. She said that
she had to be frank—people who argued as much as we did could
hardly be appropriate lovers. She had found Steve again. She was going
to be staying on in Denver an extra week.

I drove back to New York, but bad things were happening there too.
Welton and Elsie, it turned out, weren't really married, and Elsie's
father had come to their apartment and chased Welton onto the street
with a gun. "A guy from Great Neck in a 1936 Volkswagen would like
to murder me," he announced as he let me in and quickly relatched
the chain. "I can't feel lonely anymore."
    Elsie was hiding on the upper West Side, and Welton had his TV
playing nonstop upside-down. "Maybe you and Mitchell know something," he explained. "I need that McLuhan magic now." It was an
old Western, horses and riders galloping off the top. He had finished
his poem for us and handed it to me:

> "richard feels angels battling over our heads
> discharge the froth that clouds our lives.
> the number of conditions, the case, the gender,
> are irrelevant...."

He left the TV on as we went onto the street, found a beer hall, and
ordered a pitcher of draft. The room was so smoky I could see particles shifting. I read his poem and shared my lamentations while we
drank.

"the number of conditions required for my murder
is equal to the number of independent constants
remaining at the end of vesper...."

"What Lindy is we call 'Phat!' " he suddenly offered. "Some girls are
like that; they got your soul. You don't see any other girl. You've either
got to get with her or get your soul back."

"What if I don't do either?"

"Then you won't live."

The jukebox was "Eve of Destruction." Barrels of peanuts lined
the walls. We ate those for dinner—like everyone else, throwing the
shells onto the floor. And Barry McGuire pounded out the theme of
the hour:

> *"Don't you understand*
> *What I'm trying to say!*
> *Don't you feel the fears*
> *I'm feelin' today!"*

There was a cinematic beauty to my situation, its music a soundtrack of angels, a tree alphabet veering by indirection toward something that could not yet be alive. The words, I thought, must mean
exactly the opposite of what they were saying, yet they gave me a grim
satisfaction:

> *"If the button is pushed,*
> *There'll be no running away.*
> *There'll be no one to save*
> *With the world in a grave!"*

Welton peered up and down the street to make sure no Elsie's fathers
were following him. Then we hiked from the bar to a nearby loft where
a poetry reading in progress featured Paul Blackburn and two young
writers—Ishmael Reed and Ed Sanders. We sat in the crowd along
the wall, taking it in for over an hour. "Enough about the effect of the
second crusade on the uses of alliteration and assonance in poetry,"
Welston finally snapped. "It's my turn." He waved to his friends and,
on their acknowledgment, took his place at the pile of coats that passed
for a podium:

> "this
> is a note
> to an old black couple
> in a backwood mississippi church
> shouting   happy   stomping
> sending their songs
> shining their light . . ."

I could see the fire and hope in his eyes, the desire to establish his legitimacy, to have his moment. His voice danced with jazz and harmony. I thought he was beautiful and proud, a combination of Dion and the Belmonts, Bob Dylan, and Ray Charles:

> "in me
> in the san francisco streets
> in me
> in the new york high glass
> in me in my time."

I looked around and so wanted Lindy to see this, to hear Welton come home to New York . . . be chased out of his home by a honkie with a gun, then appear in the loft and stop the show with his song.

> "in harlem in black hands
> holding red roses
> in the fibers
> of my hair in my breath
> in me   flowing
> thru the world
> in me to another backcountry
> child that i see
> on the sidewalk
> shouting   black   happy . . ."

I called Lindy afterwards, across the time line, to tell her about Welton and Elsie, Kelly, and the great reading that night. She gave me her flight number and said I could pick her up if I wanted, but—no trips to Kelly's or Grossinger's—she was going straight to Smith. She added that Frodo would stay in Denver and have a decent home.

The next morning I drove back to Amherst and moved into Phi Psi. My room was the same single Asher had had sophomore year.

ANGEL*S*

needed two more English courses to fill the requirement for a major, so I signed up for both Romantic and Modern Poetry. Otherwise, I followed Kelly's admonition to study only real things: Biological Anthropology, African Folklore (at Smith), and Attic Greek. In beginning a new language, I plunged right into memorizing its alphabet, taking delight in the ancient letters—alpha, beta, gamma; xi and psi; mu and omega. Prehistoric trees were embodied in these hieroglyphs, not only the aspens of the summer but the original appletrees of childhood, the "querts" whose "Q" was shaped from the mysterious apple of Eve's first question. Behind the alphabet, behind the origin of speech in the man-apes, lay only an atomistic chaos, not unlike the moments of sleep before dream.

Next I learned words: *"Logos"*: speech; *"anthropos"*: man; *"hodos"*: road; *"angelos"*: messenger; *"thalatta, thalattes"*: sea; *"klopes, klopos"*: thief. Greek declensions bore the templates of Latin ones to which I had devoted years of study. Their chains of endings became mantras in my mind.

From Kelly's reading list I selected *The Holy Kabbalah,* by which yet another alphabet, an artifact of my childhood, was restored to me. Hebrew letters, wrote Arthur Waite, emanated from God's mind in the creation of the universe. Beth, gimmel, and lamed were a church, a camel, and an ox, were the lights on the menorah Jonny and I once lit. They spelled words only on one level; on another they embodied the ongoing genesis of matter and spirit. They continued to spill into the world moment by moment, as molecules, as cells, as quanta of light.

The shapes of these esoteric letters were originally entrusted to Adam by the angel Raziel. In Eden Adam studied them clandestinely and, when he was banished, he smuggled them out. Later he lost them in the wilderness. The angel Raphael restored them to him, and he passed them on to his son Seth.

On Mount Sinai, Moses was given two sets of laws: The External Law and The Secret Doctrine. The first he communicated. The tablets bearing the latter, under the ruse of the Golden Calf, he smashed while transmitting to the elders as the *Zohar.*

Yods were shattered yellow sparks dancing in the air of the Moon card. Kether was the crown of creation, the first octave of matter. Yesod formed its base in the autonomic nervous system.

In that one text of Waite my failed Zionist training was redeemed. I understood that Eden was a state of being on the other side of perception. We were kept out of paradise not by some Biblical illustrator's sword of archangelic steel but the sharper blade of the firing of our neurons. Our very bodies—nerve by nerve and membrane by membrane—were our state of exile, but they were also our way back in.

Through the summer Lindy and I had been living an ancient ritual, not only as lovers but as adepts building a man-woman double, a *Shekinah.* Despite our present separation our dyad was still alive in the upper spheres. According to Waite, a bond of real love contained the Supernal Work, the Union of Jehovah and Elohim. The mystery of eros reenacted the Divine Mystery, the Union with God; that's why it felt so powerful. With his usual archaic pomposity, he pronounced that "when it is said that the Blessed Vision is the sight of *Shekinah* and the contemplation of her Divine Face, we are to understand apparently that the union of sister-souls is under her eyes and in her presence."

Elsie was back living with Welton, so when I returned to the City she loaned me the keys to her empty apartment. I went straight there so as not to encounter my family. Night fell:

> How wild and soulless
> Is the wind,
> Driving through yonder helium towers,

> Dense metropolitan vats of subway cider,
> A pinwheeling purple sky?

All the next day I memorized Greek, read tales of African gods, and awaited the plane's arrival.

My sister-soul appeared down the Kennedy corridor with her handbag. I ran to intercept her. She hugged me quickly and then stared. "Babe, you look as though you've been through hell."

I nodded with a bashful smile.

I told her about Elsie's place. She snapped, "Is everyone on your side?"

"They're on *our* side."

"But I'm not an appendage of you."

So we didn't stay in the City overnight. We drove up through Connecticut, arguing. I thought she was being belligerent to prove we weren't any good. She claimed we were naturally contentious.

We argued about the events of the summer and even about how much we had argued. Then we argued about the war.

"We don't even share the same opinion about Vietnam." Steve had raised some salient points which she now itemized: What about the Red Chinese? What about stopping them before they got the bomb? What about the spread of Communism through Laos, Indonesia, and the Philippines?

"The famous domino theory," I announced with sham surprise. "How original!"

My attitude, she said, merely demonstrated how different we were. "We don't have the same politics. I'm not a pacifist. Are you? Would you refuse to fight in any war?"

"Any but this one," I joked.

As we ate at Howard Johnson's on the outskirts of Northampton, she made a case for remaining good friends without being lovers. We could still do things together, but not as often and much more low-key. On that gray evening I left her at Laura Scales with her suitcases and drifted back to Amherst.

I translated simple sentences, the very sound of which lifted my spirits: "*hoti kai ho anemos kai he thalatta hupakooay aitoo.*" I learned the names of the Ice Age glaciations (Gunz, Mindel, Riss, Wurm) and the sites from Olduvai to Lascaux where the bones of ancient primates and the earliest humans were found. I imagined a long mute dream at the beginning of our species—the dream of the grasses and animals—transformed through tree alphabets and Greek stems into the songs of Shelley: "And the green lizard and the golden snake/Like imprisoned flames, out of their trance awake."

On Kelly's urging I read P. D. Ouspensky's *In Search of the Miraculous,* the tale of his meetings with the Russian master Gurdjieff. Gurdjieff described a scale of musical vibrations crossing the cosmos, leaping octaves, exploding zones of stars and planets into landscape realms. Our world was merely one of these frontiers, a regional tonation in a vast, multidimensional cosmos. The master seemed to be telling Ouspensky—as Kelly me—that we had been born into a trap. If we remained there, we would be sold into fire, doomed to light the void (as stars do) at our bodies' extinction, eternal photons, never to be transmuted to spirit.

There was no choice. We had to become aware of the direness of our situation—and change, or be exterminated.

I was bursting with this new knowledge, but there was no way to use it, no way to give it life in the world. What could I tell my friends—that we risked being turned into nuclear particles unless we acted at once?

Then one night at dinner Lindy confided that Steve had abandoned her again, noting indignantly, "I guess I was just another end-of-the summer fling." It didn't mean that she and I could pick up our romance together because she stood by her negative view of Aspen. "It took us such a long time to learn to do love, but we do hate rather easily. Can't you see—it's perverse to try to make something happen that's not there."

She called it "love," but she meant that we didn't have the quick and easy chemical attraction she shared with Steve and Jim.

"I don't see hate," I said. "I see only anger, frustration, and the pain of transformation."

In anthropology Don Pitkin assigned an unusually Kelly-like book, *The Phenomenon of Man.* Its author, Pierre Teilhard de Chardin, described a primal esoteric fire—an incandescence of souls in the Sun. These embers (with all of us in them somehow) endowed the newborn Earth (flung long ago from the Sun's body) with a latency of consciousness. In the global ocean, atoms and molecules, already cooling and liquifying into myriad shapes, charmed out of dormancy the archetypal forerunners of DNA helices. All the solar spirits came rushing into being as plants and simple animals. The Sun was awakening as a living creature on Earth—first a worm, then a fish, then a shaggy wolf, each of them a fragment of Sun. The primeval humanoids, Australopithecus and Pithecanthropus, were roused by visions of their own prior lives inside the star. Consciousness was a more interior part of themselves, singing so deeply within that at first they couldn't hear it, or could *only* hear it. The early man-apes were premonitions of ourselves, ancestors of the Greek *anthropos* (from whom even the name "anthropology" came). When Stevie Wonder sang, *"There's a place in the sun,"* it could mean only the *real* Sun, the dense cocoon of hydrogen souls:

> *"Every branch on the tree*
> *just reaching to be free...."*

Right! Because what else would give them shape, would extend them in a delicacy of twigs and flowers?

This vision was my solace. As long as I believed it I was safe, so I carried it with me, reinventing it every hour. I kept salvaging anew all that was lost, all that had sunk into the poison of painful memories. And Bachelard asked: "From what intimate valley do the horns of other days still reach us?"

"Imaginal reality!" I answered him. "The unknown God is striving to know himself through creatures of his making, to become through us what he has eternally desired to be."

I wrote my first Romantic Poetry term paper on "Blake, Gurdjieff, and Hopi Indian Verbs," citing Navaho sand-painting, alchemy, tarot, and theories of etymology. Bill Heath gave me an A.

Then I picked up a science-fiction novel, Arthur Clarke's *Childhood's End* (in which dreaming children open an evolutionary detour and, guided by the Oversoul, cross galactic dimensions into a new universe). For Pitkin's topic I synthesized their quantum leap with Hopi myths of the Fourth World and my own theories of the origin of speech—and got another A. I was amazed. Then I submitted "Religion as a Coded Language" to Bill Heath under the playful epigraphs:

'if Barbara were an angel,' sang Coleridge
'i'd pray she'd watch over me.'
a nightingale
flew right up to John Keats   and sang
'only trouble is
gee whiz,
        i'm dreaming my life
           away.'

Heath wrote at its end: "You have moved from your prior papers to a more comprehensive view and closer to the burning center and point of origin. I have enjoyed reading what you have written. I cannot and will not dispute your vision. I salute you."

Not only was my state of revelation sustaining, it was backed by my teachers.

Earlier that term I had reminded President Plimpton of his offer once to help. He responded with swift, unexpected generosity: an Eastman Kodak grant to encompass both publishing a second issue of *Io* and running an arts series from Phi Psi.

We launched the series right away, selecting and ordering favorites from an experimental cinematheque catalogue and inviting numerous poets from the Kelly/Olson circle. After setting up two months' activities, we mimeographed an events calendar, which we posted throughout the campus and at the other three colleges.

Our first event was an evening of Kenneth Anger films. The Phi Psi living room was packed with visitors. I couldn't believe we had spread the message so widely. Folks continued to stream in, and the place buzzed with excitement. Nelson, Marty, and I finally had to borrow chairs from Chi Phi next door.

After I made an announcement about coming events, the audience quieted, and Tripp set the projector running. Up on the House screen flashed Anger's motorcycle classic, *Scorpio Rising,* Rickey Nelson backgrounding credits studded on a leather jacket:

    "Fools rush in
    Where wise men fear to tread,
    And so I come to you my love,
    My heart before my head...."

In New York I had been intimidated by the implacable male attitudes and violence in this film. Now, after Gurdjieffian octaves and sacred alphabets, I saw things quite differently. The cyclists of my birth-sign were not only the fascist warriors they imagined themselves—the willful actors of Anger's ceremony; they were the unwilling planets of astrology, blind meteors cast through the cosmos at uncontrollable speed. *Fools rush in,* for sure ... all of us, always ... *my heart before my head.* What other choice was there in a universe that was not only about to explode but had exploded to become—in a prison formed by the illusion of time and matter and the speed of light?

Anger had perceived our fanatical need to break out, which he presented as sex, drugs, revolution, swastikas, bikes, magic spells, and death. That was why he led Christ on a donkey to the sounds of Little Peggy March, *"I love him, I love, I love him, and where he goes I'll follow...."* It was all the same rush to get high—the orange cocaine surge of the cyclists, their homosexual orgy in Halloween drag, their Nazi checker game, their fatal race, Christ restoring sight to the blind man ... these were all ... *"I will follow him!"*

Yes, my heart shouted. Yes, Scorpio. Yes, Teilhard, Stevie Wonder, Pithecanthropus!

At the party after the films a bearded boy named Black, a bigshot writer two classes behind me, came up to Lindy and offered to publish her poems through a small press he was starting. She drifted off, talking with him.

I had always thought of Black as a devil, his writing metallic and pretentious. He was the prototypical snazzy dresser, self-proclaimed new wave. We had turned down his nihilistic fiction for *Io.* He was living plutonium. Now he was in direct competition with us.

I heard about him next when I called Lindy to tell her that Kelly's reading was set for November 3rd, my birthday. Suddenly she had a visitor and asked me to hold on. It was Black; he had come to pick up her poems.

"Maybe they're just a ruse," she wondered. "Maybe it's me he's trying to pick up."

A week later I drove to Smith to ferry her to the reading. She was waiting downstairs with a birthday present. I read the card first. It told me
to be gay, not tragic, to enjoy what we had together, not to ruin it by
wanting it to be more than it was. The gift was a bedspread with a
brown print of ancient armies moving across it, plus a tan knit tie and
a gold oval tie-clip.

Back at Amherst she insisted I put on the tie, so I did. She hugged
me, gave me a quick kiss, then laughed, pulling churlishly away. "Let's
not be late for the reading. I couldn't bear to miss their reaction to the
first sight of Kelly."

A wall-to-wall audience had gathered upstairs in the Octagon, a
small tower overlooking the highway on the edge of the campus. Almost
a hundred people filled a formal lounge used to host visiting poets.
This was the home field of Robert Frost and Archibald MacLeish.
Most members of the English Department did not condone Kelly's
visit, but they felt obligated to attend.

The background murmured with conversation and humor. Our
guest was late. He was ten minutes late ... twenty-five minutes late
and counting. I tried to soothe the audience by giving an extempora-
neous talk on his connections to esoteric traditions, couching everything in somewhat academic language. Their looks ranged from hauteur
to bemusement. Lindy waited by the highway, hoping to flag Bloisius
and save precious minutes.

After my speech the mood became noticeably more discordant. I
peeked outside to check. Lindy met me halfway up the stairs, pointing frantically behind her. Near the bottom the master was huffing and
puffing step by step with Joby right behind him—and behind her, Button, his tall, elfin girlfriend. He peered up through the spiral railing
and waved as though there wasn't a care in the world. I glanced down
and smiled in relief. Two minutes later, under a full head of steam, he
burst into the room dangerously out of breath. While people gasped
at his appearance he lit a cigarette and dragged away as if to restore
his oxygen.

He looked around at the portraits of famous poets who had visited
Amherst, his eyes alighting on the one most associated with the school.
"After all, Robert Frost *is* dead!"—his opening words. The shock was
audible.

Kelly had introduced himself with a sacrilege, and before anyone could react he began reading:

> "When he was an old man
> Williams spoke of the 'female principle'
> & to it made
> his last appeal
>   still feeling its lure. wch we call
> a lure
> & so
> degrade it
> thinking it draws us
> for its own ends
>   but it is endless
>   & without end
>   & draws us.
> That we may learn
>   all patience to be drawn,
> for there are men
> who rush so rashly toward woman
> all of their own hunger
> all of their own need
> that what womanliness
> lures them
>   is lost in their rage
> to pursue & possess. . . ."

Not everyone thought he was as wonderful as I did. A good portion of the audience straggled out between poems. When the reading was over, the rest of us adjourned back at Phi Psi for cider and doughnuts. Then Kelly signalled "Finis," and he and his two women drove us to a restaurant in Bloisius.

We sat at a booth together where he ordered dinner for three and we got dessert for ourselves. "I don't apologize for my opening remark," he said immediately. "I knew you would present an overly generous version of me, and I preferred to destroy that quickly. It is useless to read to people who want to be polite." Then he took out his Camels, gave one each to Joby and Button, and offered a third to Lindy.

She shook her head. "If I'm going to smoke, I might as well stick to my filters."

"Do you believe they're less dangerous?"

"Of course."

"Who are you to allow the Surgeon General of this nation to make important decisions for you? Do you know that filter-tips have the most carcinogenous tobacco?" She stared at him silently, lighting her Newport. He held up his package of Camels and gently stroked the emblem. "Does this little animal look as though he could harm you?"

She blew smoke coquettishly across the table.

On the way back to Smith she was friendly and excited. She held my hand as we walked to Laura Scales. "I enjoyed tonight. You were alive, more yourself." We stood holding each other, then a long kiss, and, with a skip, she was off and in the door.

A week later Diane Wakoski read, and I drove over to Smith to fetch Lindy again for the event. She was worried she was going to be late for a nine-thirty babysitting appointment at the home of her modern-poetry teacher. In the car she let me know right off that she was coming under protest; then she complained all the way.

"But this is *our* series."

"Don't kid yourself whose series it is. This is Amherst, Phi Psi, Richard Grossinger. I'm a girl along for the ride."

I tried to revive the mood with jokes about Kelly's reading.

"I guess you're the only one who has prerogatives," she finally retorted, "the only one allowed to dispense magic."

Schuy and Diana arrived at the last moment. They were now married and living together in Belchertown, and Diane was their favorite poet. "She rules over our marital discord," Diana joked. "She always gives me new excuses to dump this guy."

To their delight our visitor read her "Six of Cups" poem:

> "I guess we want the illusion of what we want more
> than what we want
> because we think we are wise and know
> it's harder to destroy an illusion
> than what the illusion stands for:
> the star, burning the flowers in those gold cups,
> held and exchanged by the children."

Afterwards, Lindy and I rushed back to the car and sped to Northampton. Her teacher was standing on the porch, checking her watch. "I'm not amoral," Lindy said in conclusion, as she patted me on the knee. "It's just that I'm like Diane. There's more than one of me. Remember, it's harder to destroy an illusion than what the illusion stands for."

"But also don't forget the flowers in those gold cups," I called out, "the star held and exchanged by children."

"Just because I don't tell you every second doesn't mean I've forgotten!"

Driving back to Phi Psi I sang the end of Welton's poem aloud like a rock song:

> "sending light
> and the fragrance of flowers
> thru me like a great
> soul coming
> from the backwood
> in me in my time
> smashing like shouts
> against the stone and glass
> of all the cities
> shouting   happy
> shining great light
> in me...."

And then the last line that filled me with such hope:

> "i believe *as* you believe."

The following weekend Lindy and I traveled to Cambridge for Brakhage's lecture and film-showing at Harvard. We had dinner with him afterwards and drove home late. She was cold and proper the whole time, slipping defiantly from my affection as though it were a first date. There was nothing left on the surface, so I had to go deeper.

I didn't shave Sunday or the next day. I watched myself change. The roughness was what I felt like. I wasn't going to fake it anymore. My hand reached instinctively for the fur. I was no longer a stagehand; I too could wait for Godot with the big boys. After a week, dark beard had begun to cover stubble.

I still carried her letter of August 30th. These were the days I reread it most often, when she seemed irretrievable. I couldn't have made it all up, I told myself. She had to be there, the person I had loved, somewhere inside.

A few nights later we met at Smith for Cocteau's *Orpheus*. "I may be quite fed up with you," she teased, "but you're still the best company I know for Cocteau."

Appearing in a brief cameo in his own film, the director set the stage, telling the handsome hero Orpheus (just before a riot at Café des Poets), *"Etonnez nous!"* ("Astonish us!"). Then two motorcyclists rolled in (the very ones Kenneth Anger, back from France, lying under the Boardwalk at Coney Island, transposed into *Scorpio Rising*). They felled the poet Cegeste. Death, a fashionably dressed woman, got out of the back seat of a sedan that trailed the cyclists. She ordered them to put Cegeste's fatally wounded body inside. "Why are you standing around, staring?" she suddenly demanded. "Get in!"

"Who me?" asked Orpheus, looking around.

"Get in!" she gestured.

Then the angel Heurtebise chauffeured them away.

When Orpheus awoke in Death's room, she was gone. All that remained were the chauffeur and the car. Now the hero madly sought this woman, Death. Since he did not know how to look for her, he sat in her car, obsessively transcribing the message fragments that came over its radio, written (in truth) by Cegeste in her company.

Orpheus didn't realize that Death had also fallen in love with him.

Without permission of the authorities, Death then took Orpheus' wife Eurydice. Even so, it was Death Orphée grieved after (as mystery, as lover), not his lost partner. *"Etonnez nous,"* indeed!

One upon another, the characters in the movie, wearing special gloves, touched and passed through the liquid surface of a mirror into the Underworld. There they spotted salesmen carrying panes of imaginary glass through ruins.

"Out of sheer habit," Heurtebise told them.

Finally Orpheus made it to Death's boudoir, only to learn that she was not all-powerful, that her love for him would salvage nothing, that they were petty criminals and would be seized, separated, and punished.

Cocteau's Death was not a ruler or goddess. She was but one of the faces of an eternal form. She acted from her orders. When Orpheus asked her who gave these commands, expecting like some Western hero to charge in and stand up for his lady with his fists, Death shrugged and told him, "No one knows. The messages of creation are carried from dimension to dimension, region to region of an invisible bureaucracy like so many tom-toms beating across *Afrique.*"

The only remaining, desperate hope was for Cocteau to run the movie backwards, against the force of a cosmic wind, to undo the damage and restore Orpheus and Eurydice to their myth. The backdraft of time rippling their hair, the characters traveled motionless toward the beginning of the film—Orpheus and Eurydice in a trance, Death and Heurtebise laboring against gravity itself to achieve a single ember of free will (no doubt Cocteau's joke on Sartre, Camus, and existentialism). "We must, we must," Death shouted. "Without our wills we are nothing."

Afterwards, sparked by such overt magic, Lindy and I experienced a resurgence of our old fire over tea on Green Street. We chatted away excitedly until moments before curfew and then had to run back to Laura Scales. Shivering as the November wind cut through us, she lamented not being able to afford a good coat.

The next morning I went to a store in town and bought her the bushiest overcoat I could find. My heart beating with both empathy and terror, I showed up unannounced bearing its enormous box. She was furious at my intrusion, but I jauntily handed it to her.

"Think twice now," she said. "Are you sure you still want to be giving me things?"

I nodded perversely. From the outside I could see how foolish I looked, how quickly she was becoming someone else. From the inside I could only blunder on, led by my feelings.

That evening she called me. She told me how mortified she was to open the box and find the coat.

"I can't stand you, Richard. This is the end. This is really the end."

I stood there in the stairwell holding the phone. My body rang with shock waves. "Do you realize how low it is to try to buy back someone's love when they don't want it?"

I said yes.

She described in agonizing detail how she had to take it into town on her bike, return it to the store, ask that my money be refunded. I told her that she had been freezing, that we were old and close friends, but she said I was making an ass out of myself and, additionally, that she had another date that night. I shouldn't call her again for at least three months. It hadn't worked, she added, just being friends.

I went back to my room, cried briefly; then pulled myself together. I was curious to know how much of me was left. There was something there in the center, thin and quite stringy, a rag perhaps, but at least I could feel it.

Sometime afterwards I heard a knock. I opened the door and was astonished to see my old sophomore-year friend Paul, the one who had witnessed my New York family at Thanksgiving. He was visiting from Clark where he was a graduate student in psychology. He heard my woe and said we should walk. I nodded and put on my coat. We traversed the railroad tracks, across the bridge where Lindy and I had accompanied Tripp the previous spring.

I tried to salvage the summer in a description of it, to probe it for a flaw, a clue. While I entertained both of us, I dreaded the conclusion of my narrative.

We continued to Valentine and got in line. I would have a life, I told myself. I would eventually find someone else. In fact Elsie had mentioned introducing me to her "very beautiful friend." I tried to picture who this other woman might be. She was a chance to start over. I had a moment of fragile elation. With our trays we crossed the dining room and found a table. Then I saw in the far corner Lindy sitting alone with Black. I jumped to my feet. Paul glanced over his shoulder, whistled, then frowned. "Let's get out of here," he said.

We abandoned our meals and crossed the street to Phi Psi. I chose its roof as refuge. We sat there watching the males stream toward dinner in the twilight. "It's not that important," I said finally. "If I could see all this differently it would be a vision; it would be beautiful, absurd."

"But that's the whole of psychology you're dismissing," he protested.

"Yes, I know; it's why I'm in this state." I lay back and stared at the early bright stars, musing as though from a million miles away. "I used to think back then, when I was a kid, an infant, that my family scared me by something they did. I went through all those years of analysis trying to find the one event."

"The trauma," he chimed in.

"Now I think it's just who they were—my mother, Bob, Bunny, Paul—each in their own way."

"It always seemed that way to me," Paul agreed. "Just as an objective observer I didn't find anything about them I think of as parents."

"The thing with Lindy, you see, is that she was the one who taught me about family. She gave me that in Aspen. And now tonight—it's like finding my family, being born, having to grow up in a summer, and then losing it, all in one year. That's why it's hard for me just to take it as it is. I don't have anyplace else to go."

"That seems a fair picture," he acknowledged. "So what now?"

"I either jump or try to live."

He shifted half-facetiously, as though to stand in my way. We both laughed. "I don't think you're going to do that, but I'm not sure it's a good idea for you to stay around Phi Psi either. You sound dangerously like someone trying to prove he's sane and rational."

"I know. I'm speeding on the strangeness of tonight, but it's gonna run out."

"And you might not plan on killing yourself, but one way or another you're going to crash."

"I gotta walk that lonesome valley, aye, Paul?"

"Yep. And the Four Seasons too: *"Walk like a man from her!"*

We chuckled. He asked me for Schuy and Diana's number. We went downstairs, and he dialed them. He wondered if I could stay there for the night. Diana said they'd come and get me.

I grabbed a toothbrush and some clothes, and we sat in the parking lot waiting. The omnipresent Andy, who had been kicked out of school for LSD, came by and, as usual, tried to convince me it was all ego, illusion. He said that his serum would cure me of whatever was troubling me, would expose the world for what it was.

"Tonight I'm just trying to be human," I said.

"But it's all illusory anyway."

"It may be illusion, but it's also a myth, and unless we live it and make a stand, it will repeat again and again."

"Your choice!"

"That's right," Paul said grumpily. *"His* choice."

Schuy and Diana came, looking harried. I started to explain, but she headed me off. "It's not so good where we are either. We're talking about getting divorced."

That surprised me, but after Schuy went to bed she stayed up and explained. "Don't believe his shit about being a tough guy. He said that making love was like breaking a horse, and I'll tell you, I feel very much like a horse that was broken. We've got all of that to work through now, and I doubt that we're going to make it."

"Would you rather be where I am?"

"I'm getting there." She gave me a hug and showed me the unheated back room of the cabin.

I slept on a mattress, their collection of blankets and quilts thrown on top of me. Rain blew against the window and walls. Smothered in homeyness, I drifted off to dream—only to awake with a start. The first birds were chirping. I couldn't get them out of my head. I didn't want to know or think anything. Then I heard Schuy and Diana arguing, so I scurried to get dressed, went outside, and edged into the woods, trying to pick up a sign.

It was all pain, in all directions pain. There wasn't a clue anywhere. The natural world seemed to stretch unabated in every direction, forever. This was the heart of Mordor.

I came back. We ate breakfast together while they jousted black humor about their divorce.

I told them I thought their life was very beautiful, even their arguing was beautiful. I warned them there wouldn't be anything better. They smiled at my naiveté, and Schuy drove me back to Phi Psi on his way to class. A few months later they were divorced, and a year after that Schuy was dead in Illinois, apparent suicide on a motorcycle.

I packed my things that mattered and set off in the Mustang. In my head was Lindy's song once for her lover Steve: *"Try to remember a time in September...."* I rehearsed its haunting tune. *"... when life was an ember...."* The minor chord was an epode, ringing down a corridor, illumining perhaps another life, another world. It was magnificent, and it was hollow; it was exquisite, and it was vast beyond knowing.

It was all September, going back to the dawn of consciousness. The cabin in Aspen was as old as Welsh alphabet trees and the Central Park autumns of my childhood.

All I wanted was to get inside this damn thing—the song, the mellowness—the dreary, streaked-rain, gold/red world, to become even its sadness and old age. And sing it someday from within.

I established a single plan. I would go once more to see Lindy. I would try to recover the girl from Aspen. If that failed—as surely it would—I'd continue into the City (the necessary phone calls already made) and go out with Elsie's friend.

Summoned by the Laura Scales switchboard, Lindy stormed downstairs. "What in the world lets you think you can browbeat me!"

But the anteroom was no place to talk, so we automatically went outside and sat on the curb. I told myself melodramatically that at least our unborn children would want me to make this one last try.

"I don't think that we're the only people for each other," I told her. "It wasn't set up that way. But we had something special once, and if we're going to drop it I want us to drop it together." I looked up, but she didn't interrupt me. "I feel as though I haven't seen you since Denver. I've been carrying around this letter—" I held it out for her, but she shook her head as though to say she didn't need to see it. "A different Lindy came back on that plane. I can say goodbye if that's what you want, but I don't want to abandon you." Her response was a gasp of outrage followed by a haughty frown. "I don't believe that kind of stuff," she said, "and you are very unperceptive to keep trying it."

I let the resonance of the car absorb me. I accepted finally that it was over. But instead of going straight into the City I detoured via Kelly at Bard. He sat in the outer room, the sybilline Button at his side. I came as the knight to the throne and told him I was sorry to intrude, but I had two questions to ask and then would be gone. "Go ahead," he said.

The phone rang. As he reached for it he handed me a piece of paper, a poem of Chuck's.

"See if this takes care of the first one."

> "The world (or a world)
> is complete

by that I mean
there is no other
world from this vantage but
where the hills cut the scene off
is the end of it there
are no towns
to the west of those mountains
imaginable voids of darkness
black gulfs of myth where anything is. . . ."

When he finished his conversation I told him there was no need now to ask the first question.

"Why don't you rephrase it anyway. Tell me the answer you have gotten."

"Where is the other world that shadows this one? The answer is: There is no other world; everything is here."

He nodded. "Your pain is teaching you well. Your education is accelerated in this extreme state."

"What about Lindy? That's my second question. I think I have given up and am going into New York to see another girl." I was sure, especially in his own condition of infidelity, he would concur.

"Richard, are you going to be the troubadour all your life," he said, "singing to women on balconies? You must abandon such a role and speak to the consciousness of the woman. Tell her what you have to tell her. Right now you are wasting your dwindling energy in groups of people living dreams, sitting around coffee houses discussing irrelevancies."

His words surprised me. I imagined back at Smith that I was telling her the truth, but now I realized I was merely greedy for confirmation, impatient. I was playing games with her, keeping my stupid magician's role.

"Listen closely," he said, "for what I am about to tell you almost everyone would miss.

"You must not make this woman into a star you cannot reach, although, God knows, you may have an easier time waking in the morning to a clear star than the rest of us having to put together a day from scratch."

I smiled.

"But that is also the astrology of hell. If you can free yourself, then take her away with you and face the risks that come your way. Better those than the meaningless risks of the troubadour."

"And what if she won't follow?"

"And what if we knock and the door doesn't open? And what if it won't close? What if the world is destroyed tomorrow? We all live in dread."

I nodded.

"Go to her and tell her what you have to say. That's all there is."

"Is it like breaking a horse? Is that true?"

"No. Sometimes a certain strength is necessary because of the tyranny of words. They *do* fail or, rather, we fail them. But I wouldn't liken it to breaking a horse. It is more like the electron seizing a positron in the heart of matter. Isn't that what lies at the creation of all things?"

"Yes."

"You have happened upon Brakhage's old riddle: everything is as we want it, if only we knew. That's what Chuck is telling you; he didn't realize he wrote it for you. But he sent it, and you and it arrived minutes apart."

"And what about the girl in the city?"

He shook his head. "Richard, don't *ever* try to cut your losses. Go back and tell Lindy what you have to say. You have no other course."

"This endless cycle is wearing."

"We're meant to be worn."

Then he raised himself slowly and turned toward the inner rooms. He instructed me to talk to the sybil. "I'll be back."

Button spoke in ellipses, so I told her about the Maori arrow-soul, the *waiura,* that stays connected between people even when they are apart. Then, as twilight fell, old things began to creep across the room.

"I sense a fright," she piped. "There's a fright in the room."

"It's probably mine."

"She's not a bad girl," she said, an utter *non sequitur,* "just a bitch. We need bitches, though. They cut through the shit we create."

Just then Kelly returned and asked at once who had dispelled the ghost. She pointed to me. He pondered and then restated his message: "All people are not interchangeable. Lindy is a girl in Massachusetts. Go back to her."

Then he cast a sign over my head and bid me farewell.

491

"How does he know?" I asked her.

"Because he's him."

The ghost had not been dispelled, but it was also no longer the enemy. I took it with me into the car and instead of heading for either the City or Massachusetts I turned toward Grossinger's.

It was night-time now. A disorientation like carsickness came over me. In it I felt something alive, something with barely a mass or shape, but it was solid and at my center. I saw Kelly in my mind's eye— Orpheus in the room with Death—and shouted aloud, "He's right! He's right!"

I had solved the sphinx's riddle at last: Lindy was addressing me *directly* by picking the one person she knew I most abhorred. She hadn't broken off our connection; she had merely changed its language. This was the final test. She was parading before me a specter of existential nihilism in order to see if I was strong enough to break through. That was the only possible explanation for going from the failed relationship with Steve to an irrelevant jerk like Black. She had cast a gauntlet/grail and was waiting to see if I responded. It would prove nothing if she gave it away and simply yielded to my entreaties.

A summons from the White Goddess herself! What an honor!

I warned myself that this might be wishful thinking. Certainly that was how I had been taught: Don't give money to blind men; don't trust strangers. But I had no choice: I must commend myself to angels and act.

The lights of traffic suddenly fizzed and bloomed into melody, a supernatural order of particles of which I was the core and ordering principle. I turned on the radio just in time to hear the confirming song:

> *"Hello darkness my old friend,*
> *I've come to talk to you again. . . ."*

The Hotel loomed on the hill ahead, welcoming me always, its wayward son.

> *"Because a vision softly creeping*
> *Took my mind while I was sleeping. . . ."*

I was aswirl with messages. The doom I had felt was merely the veil, always had been, all my life. I was at the heart of a myth, and

492

there was nothing except these lights and suds exploding all around me.

"She is my moon," I said aloud, "and he is the Blackness of my moon."

At the Hotel I stayed for a night and a day, asking nothing more than the thing it was. I walked the golf course at dawn, sat by the glitter lake . . . ate in the dining room, greeting everyone with warmth. There was no point in hiding or skulking anymore; I had to act with humility and honor every sentient creature from here on in.

In my heart I was back in Aspen, at last with Frodo, unafraid.

I found my father by the ice rink. I told him that I might quit school. He stared vacantly at me, his bearded son—stared without recognition: "Do whatever you want. It doesn't matter to me anymore." Then he turned and walked away, though he looked back over his shoulder to add: "Go let those phony father figures Borkage and Kelly take care of you."

It *didn't* matter to him. It never had. It wasn't ever a matter of two families fighting over me. I was orphaned to both of them.

I drove back to Amherst the next morning, telling myself to be true, to stay conscious. I had reached the edge of the abyss and would make it or fall.

I called Lindy several times that afternoon, and the next day, but she was never in ("And what if the door does not open. . . ?").

In the evening I went to hear a lecture by Timothy Leary, the messiah of redemption through drugs. I sat upstairs in Johnson Chapel and saw her down in front with the Black one.

"Maps," Leary announced. "Someone must go out into the wilderness beyond the Mississippi of the mind, like Lewis and Clark, and tell us where the Indian priests are and what lands are inhabitable, what sorts of plants grow and what wisdom animals dwell there." He was talking about the world of LSD, but I imagined other interior worlds our courage might find for us. The medicine herb by itself was nothing; in our flesh too, fantastic realms lay unexplored.

He reminded me that while our elders were worried about the Russians and Sputnik we had ignored equally vast interior hemispheres. I thought, 'Yes, all the years wasted on fizzled Vanguard rockets and visionless accelerated science courses, no care at all to real science—that any force in the Universe can be made into any other—the singular truth of our existence.' I imagined our whole troubadour civilization paying homage to a goddess of masks and rings.

Then I took the magic of Leary under the moon and ran across the playing fields. I tumbled in the grass, climbed the rope, dove through the tire. I called to Welton: "i believe *as* you believe."

I awoke the next morning on the cusp. I could see my beginning clearly from here. Nothing at all separated me from Dr. Fabian's office or 1220 Park Avenue. I had no images, just the terminus of a line with two ends. That span became the locus of points between two towns, Amherst and Northampton. There was no extraneous scenery, no impedance. I set the stream of matter flowing from one point to another. The whole cosmos rushed by me in a karma of trees and houses and people, a fluvial loom. It swallowed landscape and led me to the next node.

I parked near the library and went loping across the campus, seeing everything in flashes and blobs, feeling the air as a force, respecting the presence of gravity. I imagined myself a leopard, with no mentality. I went to the magazine room, linguistics section, took down a journal, and opened to a page in the Xhosa language. I intoned its syllables silently.

"Hello, kiddo," she said. She was standing beside me, smiling. She had come to the library also in response to the lecture, but she was looking in the parapsychology section for a journal of psychedelics.

I told her that I had heard Leary. I thought the answer was not drugs but myth and prayer. She nodded.

I suggested we get some coffee and we walked onto Green Street, into a cafeteria. I had been through the rite of eight moons, the last one Black, and now a fine delicate crescent lit not the night but the astral sky.

The jukebox played, *"Sloopy hang on,"* from my quarter. We ordered coffee and pie. She sat there looking at me and said, "Honey, I don't know where I've been, but I missed you. I'm just glad you came back."

PART
SEVEN

THE ALCHEMICAL
WEDDING

1965–1970

ANN ARBOR

A few weeks later we were sitting in Lindy's room, trying to decide which of several graduate schools to apply to. She was planning to go on in English. I was considering linguistics and anthropology. As we read through a sample application, she wondered whether to say we were married in order to have a chance at a better scholarship. I didn't know what to answer.

"Should we just fill it out that way?" she asked.

Her pluck emboldened me. "Why not!"

"Can I take that as a proposal?"

I nodded assertedly.

And so it was.

At Christmas we replayed our strategy of the previous summer. Again each of us would go home first, she to Denver, I to New York. We would let our respective parents know about our plans to get married in June. Then she would take the train and I would drive. We'd meet in Indiana at the Bloomington station and spend the rest of vacation visiting graduate schools.

As soon as I left her at the Springfield airport I felt a ghost. The past was too cold and dark to sustain life, let alone this little shoot of hope.

"What the fuck does that mean?" my father said upon hearing my news. "Are you using your asshole for brains?"

I didn't expect approval, but his total lack of empathy shocked me.

"Not on my money," he continued. "You don't get a penny from me." He paused to reload. "What do you think she's after anyway? This hotel, that's what. You think there's any other reason she'd marry you?"

"That's not true," I responded. "The hotel's not even an issue in our relationship."

"It shows what you know. You've been listening to all those phony father figures so long you don't know your ass from your elbows."

I stared out the window at distant crossing highways, the rattle of my brother's cartoons on TV. Protective spirits were there also—the wind through trees, the sun a living being guiding consciousness upward.

By the next evening I was in a shouting argument with PG. I called him a destroyer of people for what he had done to Bunny. He so little understood that he thought I was blaming him for the massacres of the Vietnam War. He didn't know whether to defend government policy or to deny his complicity in it. "I don't have anything to do with that," he finally spat. "Go protest somewhere else!" Aunt Bunny stood numbly by his side, a wafer of her former self.

He had reduced our relationship to an ideological battle and her to a mannikin.

But Lindy wrote: "Much love, dear thing . . . life is definitely better with you than without. I woke up this morning and knew the most important thing was to leave and not get stuck here. It has been like crashing through 5 roadblocks." She sent regards from Frodo who, she added, was in fine shape and looking forward to the reunion.

I drove to New York to tell my mother. She had an almost identical response.

"What money?" I argued. "When have I ever had money from the Hotel! Maybe someday a hundred years from now."

She flashed a wicked grin, false consolation in her voice: "You know your father won't allow you to marry someone who isn't Jewish."

I shrugged off that irrelevancy and asked her to trust me.

"When have you ever given me reason to?"

It was not their opposition that unnerved me; it was my reflection in their eyes. I saw the old "Richard" they had stage-managed. Schuyler had reported the same dilemma a year earlier from his own parents' reaction to his engagement: no reasonable, intelligent girl would marry him unless there were an ulterior motive. "That was unendurable," he said, "so I told them, 'Fuck you!' and we eloped."

It became another automobile Western. First I left New York under leaden skies. Windblown flurries in Pennsylvania were ominous, but night was warmer than day, snow blending with rain. I barreled through slush.

After a restless stop at an Indiana motel, I tried to bite off too much in the face of grim weather reports across the Plains. St. Louis caught me at rush hour, five hours in traffic, chasing my mind. I found myself hurrying across Kansas past midnight in hard, sticking snow . . . promising only a few more miles, one exit more, and suddenly . . . the world was spinning. I slammed on the brakes. The car rotated—a full circle . . . then another. The *best* outcome I could imagine was flying into a snowdrift. But I stopped, facing forward. In that crucible, prior life had passed. At the next exit I collapsed into a motel bed.

Out the morning window, sun covered snow in mounds, trucks scraping away frost. The stage was clear: wet roads across the rest of Kansas into Colorado, checking into a motel on Colfax. I dialed Lindy's number before I could think.

"What, you're here! I can't believe it! You're in time for Christmas. I haven't dared mention the wedding yet. Now I can say you've come to ask my father for my hand."

I lay on the bed watching icicles melt time against the blue sky forever.

Yes, it had always been a circus.

Lindy's father asked me how I intended to support his daughter (I mentioned graduate-school fellowships), but otherwise our meeting went smoothly. Even though her parents regarded Lindy as their black-sheep daughter (and hardly approved of her wild suitor), they weren't engaged in atomic warfare. With two older married daughters they knew how to act.

Reading poetry, science fiction, and Sufi tales aloud as we covered the long miles, Lindy and I retraced my steps across the Plains, visiting Indiana and Michigan, doing graduate-school interviews. We ate at restaurants and thruway cafeterias, then sat around motel heaters, imagining life in these somber, snowy towns. Outside our Ann Arbor room I waited in ambush, then charged her with snowballs as she came into the day. She let out a Harumph! and came after me, whacking powder off the branches, all the way to Howard Johnson's.

As senior year moved into its last term, I signed up for Plato (in Greek), Mediaeval Latin, and Physical Anthropology. Several of us in Phi Psi initiated an independent course in the Anthro Department, combining linguistic theory, abstract topology, and Indian ceremonialism. My buddy Greg, a lanky, asocial math genius, used the fourth and fifth dimensions and the morphology of toruses to analyze dreams, patterns of Navaho sand-paintings, and the music of Bach. We read popularized quantum theory, Buckminster Fuller, and Benjamin Lee Whorf. There was perhaps an academic work here, something about the phenomenology of non-Western symbols and alternate views of time, space, and matter:

> "In the Hopi view, time disappears and space is altered, so that it is no longer the homogenous and instantaneous timeless space of our supposed intuition or of classical Newtonian mechanics. . . .
>
> "Hopi imposes upon the universe two grand cosmic forms . . . we may call MANIFESTED and MANIFESTING (or, UNMANIFEST) . . . The manifesting comprises all that we call future, BUT NOT MERELY THIS; it includes equally and indistinguishably all that we call mental—everything that appears or exists in the mind, or, as the Hopi would prefer to say, in the HEART, not only the heart of man, but the heart of animals, plants, and things, and behind and within all the forms and appearances of nature in the heart of nature, and . . . in the very heart of the Cosmos itself."

Unfortunately—as I discovered well after applying to graduate programs—Whorf was not the present voice of academia.

Although Lindy and I both got into Indiana, it was in linguistics for me—and no scholarships for either of us. Then I alone got into Michigan—in anthropology, a scholarship pending.

"Let's accept it," she said. "You're better off in anthro, and anyway I'd like a break from heavy-duty academics."

With my father and her parents both refusing to help us we decided to gamble on Michigan.

There were no fields of study in what we were about, so it hardly mattered that it wouldn't be ceremonial topology or nonlinear iconography. We knew that graduate school was a smokescreen, the cover story for our marriage.

On Brakhage's inspiration I ordered a used 8-mm. Bolex, two plus-ten lenses, a splicer, and a Wollensak projector. While we were in New York picking these up, my mother invited the local relatives to a party to meet Richard's fiancée. Lost cousins, aunts and uncles of childhood—a decade older—returned.

"You're restoring the family," my brother told me. "That is why they once called you 'the loyal one.' I serve different gods. That's why, someday, they will know me as 'the ferocious one.' You started the war. Now you've become a civilian. It's up to me to finish it."

Walking Times Square the next night, Lindy and I took turns shooting signs and marquees, phalanxes of flashing bulbs, and streams of traffic. Then I tried the zoom lens, going from smoke puffed through the mouth on the Camels billboard to the whole illuminated vista.

Back in Massachusetts I filmed children walking home from school; Australian bark paintings; a dead squirrel, its tail blown by passing cars; newspaper burning; and, for an entire roll, a journey through night fog, the arrows and rings of traffic beacons floating like C. S. Lewis' eldils on Perelandra. With some of it double-exposed, I had no idea what I had actually put on film. Weeks later the mail brought my first reels. Running them into the projector, I watched red Kodak letters flit by in an opening banner, then a kinetic, grainy flow—a changing field of shapes and rhythms, textures dissolving: squirrel fur through bark, marquees through rose petals. I was elated. Much of it was kaleidoscopic and clear.

Through the tiny window, using the blade of the editor, I cut away the junk and spliced the remainder into a film, "Sounds of Silence" for its soundtrack.

In the spring we produced a second issue of *Io,* premiering Robert Kelly's "Week 86," his poem about the female principle. Diane Wakoski submitted "Serious Poem for Serious People" and Stan Brakhage an essay, "Making Light of the Nature of Light." The Aspen crew provided John Taggart ("Christopher Columbus and the Cigar Factory at Key West"), Paul Blackburn ("Hesper Adest"), and Mitchell Miller (on McLuhan, Olson, Yeats, tarot, the White Goddess, and Gestalt psychology). Then I convinced Chuck to send "Assisi," which I had seen at Kelly's, and "Reading Basil Valentine in a Mountain Cabin." We added a few of my prose pieces and Lindy's "Poem About Magic," "The Quadrants," and "The Path to the Stream."

Nelson served as art editor and, in addition to his own images, he procured ink drawings of celestial creatures from Philip Terry Borden, a New York window-designer, plus the rights to an original Jean Cocteau "Opium" plate—a kneeling man, fat head, long braids, iconographic genitals, one hand disappearing in his shrunken body, a hole in his other hand. Chilean artist Eduardo Zalamea, another contact of Nelson's, sent us a surrealist text ("The space between things seems to be reserved for another universe./Light is the nerve of an invisible being ... Only statues can hold the soul's hand")—plus a dermagram, his face covered with black ink pressed on a sheet of paper, so that, curly-haired and eyeless, he looked through page 75, alongside his poem.

Panned in *The Amherst Student*, *Io/2* sold briskly for $1.00 on college dinner lines. Copies discarded in Valentine were recovered by Phi Psi members and resold. Most of the interest, however, came from literary bookstores around the country and in England, ordering five to ten copies each. Kelly made sure *Io* was well publicized. "A magnificent new journal," he declared, "the best in years." So the Bard Bookstore restocked twenty-five copies a month.

He even accepted my invitation to visit us when Lindy and I were staying at Grossinger's spring vacation. "Now that you're about to make a formal Shekhinah," he mused, "your father should get to meet your 'phony father figure.'" I was apprehensive, but the poet charmed PG in his office. Then he caused a commotion by strolling down the main aisle of the dining room. When I had suggested the side door, he looked at me askance: "What! You want to deprive paying guests. Let me be displayed. Otherwise, they might get indigestion craning to see." He ordered blintzes, whose every nuance of flavor he extolled. Lindy and I glanced at each other, beaming with pride and vindication. Soon my father was treating our guest like the Pope, though Kelly remarked, "I'm just another rabbi—albeit an Irish one."

Both sides of my family came to graduation. High school had been all accolades. Here I had no honors for them; I had barely made it. Beard, unruly curls under square cap, I joined the third of the class who wore black arm-bands to protest the awarding of an honorary degree to Robert McNamara (although he was *humane* compared to Senator Paul Douglas, who, in the speech to graduates, directed us to prepare for war against the godless Communists; it was our duty, he said, even as his generation had handled the Nazis).

The elders were notifying us, "You've got no life at all in our world; we're taking it from you right now."

That Douglas was an immodest blowhard did not mean he was not chilling. Through his glass darkly we were deeded a horrific future: a battle to the death in Vietnam for the next ten years, twenty or more years of war in Asia, prison camps of conscientious objectors, devastation of the entire planet. Did he have any idea what he was saying? This was supposed to be a celebration of our academic degrees, a gracious initiation into the world of adults. And yet his words, in bullets of oratory, rained on, long after there was nothing left alive.

As McNamara was introduced, I rose with a scattered twenty-five others. Causing a temporary commotion, we squeezed our ways to the aisles and exited at the rear. It made the front page of *The New York Times*.

Afterwards my father was speechless with rage; he said grimly he had paid to see me graduate. He said nothing after that, except that he intended to boycott my marriage as *his* right to protest.

Ostensibly because of the expense of the upcoming wedding, Lindy's parents cancelled a trip east. I was her lone observer at graduation. I sat among parents and siblings and watched her bouncy stride in black gown, reaching gracefully for her diploma.

Getting a trailer bolted to the back of the Mustang, we filled it with the remains of Amherst and Smith—in fact, all of childhood—and reached Ann Arbor by nightfall. We took a motel room and, in the morning, procured a student rental list and a map of the town. Two days of unsuccessful hunting in wooded suburbs gradually led us back to the core district, and we finally settled on renting the upstairs of a small house on Mary Street, a few blocks from campus. The landlord himself lived in the lower unit. He was a pleasant if brooding Midwesterner who offered us a beer on the porch that night as Michigan melted into stars. We sat, backs against wooden posts, young girl, young boy. He told me he didn't like long hair or beards, but he didn't press the point.

The next morning we picked up our driving help (and first wedding guest)—my friend Greg who had helped organize the American Indian/abstract math independent at Amherst. A Phi Psi loyalist and avowed fan of our marriage, he met us, as promised, at the Ann Arbor train station. Greg carried the spirit of Halloween in the Glen, Tripp's *Godot,* the birth of *Io,* in fact, the whole zany mythology out of which Lindy-Rich was born. Likewise, we were his hope and ideal, a generic couple melted down and tempered in the unpromising cauldron of Phi Psi.

Lindy's parents were unhappy that we showed up so far in advance of the wedding, so they refused to let either Greg or me stay at their house. "It's improper," her mother declared.

They didn't want to hear about difficulties with my father or our need to find a place in Ann Arbor. Perhaps they were hoping for a wedding without a groom.

Greg accepted their invitation to stay in the family cabin, a hour away in the old mining town of Central City. Meanwhile, I found my classmate Marshall Bloom, who had parlayed his Phi Gam initiation into a senior-year editorship of *The Amherst Student* and (more recently) had plotted the graduation walkout. He invited me to camp in his basement where he and his fellow college editors were founding the Liberation News Service.

I spent the first few days in the cabin with Greg, watching shadows of clouds run along timberline, walking the cowboy/ukelele streets.

I spent the next days in Denver, admiring ceremonial artifacts in Colfax shops, meeting Lindy for raisin-apple pie, picking out wedding-gift settings and silverware at department stores, getting a haircut and trim in a barber chair adjacent to her father, and buying a rare Navaho grammar from Fred Rosenstock's Trading Post (while befriending the owner, who took me to tea with a local occultist). Old Colorado territory, vestiges of mining and timber exchanges, Indians filling its thoroughfares, Denver was country-club suburbs around a hub of banking and Western shops, pale commercial buildings rising to low-flying planes. Its aura was clear and free.

I inhabited the unencumbered space between dreams, a wind blowing through the big sky, the Rockies white and rough beyond. In my mind I kept coming back to who I was, who Lindy was . . . and the West. It was unreal, and it was happening.

Then Greg and I drove all day through the mountains to Gunnison in search of a perfect Galaxy valley:

> no sleep rolling
> against the side of the tent . . .
> in half-dreams
>
> i meet you i touch
> you
> each time under different bowers
>   about to be married about to be
>   and spin away . . .
> on top of colorado
> colorado torque the universe . . .
>
>   meteors drop
>   all thru colorado
>
> speeding out of the open universe
> threading themselves on air . . .
>
> back and forth
> i walk
>
>   hope
>   despair
>
>   love
>   lust
>
>   fear
>   energy
>
>   free
>   compelled
>
>   certain
>   doubtful

full

empty ...

second by second
the open universe burns

me ...

An orange pre-dawn ball among the stars overwhelmed me. I had
no patience for any more high-octane, bachelor conversation. I knew,
as Greg and I fried bacon over coals, it was time to go back to the city
and await my wedding.

Two years later this apolitical violinist and mathematician would be
in Canada, a draft refugee living among Leninists, and Marshall would
be dead—suicide by automobile exhaust in a Massachusetts garage.

Propriety won out. They all attended—not only my mother, Bob, Jon,
and Debby, but my father and Aunt Bunny (without Michael and
James), Grandma Sally, my uncle Eddie and his wife and daughter
from San Francisco, and Grandma Jennie. Earlier in the day she had
gone with Lindy and me to Fred Rosenstock's to purchase a large
Navaho rug as a wedding present—old Fred had offered a great price
if Jennie Grossinger came in person.

My mother was pale; years later I realized she thought of her own
mortality rather than my wedding. She could not believe life had come
to this and left her behind.

My brother Jon was my best man—"Frodo, the ring-bearer," he
called himself. He confided that my father and his father had "con-
spired against the heathen," concealing yarmulkes in their pockets to
don "if anyone showed up in a collar."

It wasn't necessary. The wedding was in the backyard, with a judge
marrying us, mostly her high-school friends in attendance, the sermon
from D. H. Lawrence—an event having curiously little to do with the
woman I knew. She seemed a stranger in her white Spanish dress and
tiara of lace. I was a character in my own play. My private odyssey
was over, my eccentric presence and maleness suddenly center stage.
I hid out and let destiny take me. Then at dinner time we left the gathering and drove to Shiprock, Arizona.

That night, on the porch of our motel, a public-health worker shared his last bottle of chianti with us. We sat toasting the Corn Goddess and the moon.

It wasn't a typical honeymoon. For Lindy it was revisiting the Four Corners of her childhood. For me it was a continued search for Indian talismans. On and off till it practically drove us crazy I played the Navaho-language radio station. We gave one old hitchhiker a ride, and the stench of his life startled us.

We parked on the desert and walked through an impoverished, esoteric landscape. We saw their wide Asian-plateau faces, adobe structures, eyes both of the Buddha and North American mammal.

Following the tracks of Frank Waters' apocalyptic writings we made it to the heart of Hopi territory, the windblown Third Mesa and outlaw village of Hotevilla. It wasn't the fancy mandala or sand-painting cult Greg and I had celebrated at Amherst; it was stark and impenetrable—clay houses on dirt paths, men with empty eye sockets, terrific heat, and obscure herbal odors. In our haste to get out we trapped our car in the sand and, as twilight fell, we were marooned on a planet as alien as Mars.

The people were indifferent—they ignored our presence, let alone our plight. Then a boy, maybe ten, approached, offering help: he would drive straight down the cliff—he pointed—and then around the edge (showing us by rotating his finger). It was foolhardy and perilous, but there was no other offer. I handed him the keys. Either he knew how or would go flying over.

Wheels spun; the car jerked forward. He lurched and bumped to the edge of the rocks, swerved perfectly at the last moment and brought the beast yawing through the sand onto the road, then jumped out with a magnificent grin and a whoop.

Our apartment was down a small hill between campus and athletic fields. When we had rented it the landlord apologized for its condition, explaining that his wife was in the hospital and his grown son had left the place a mess. It looked idyllic even so. On our return, as he turned the key and let us in, we sniffed the must and stared at falling plaster. He offered to reimburse us for materials if we would do the necessary work. Then he took off for the country.

Through hundred-degree days we scraped, spackled, painted, showered, made dinner, and rapped away on our separate typewriters. At dusk we sat on the porch watching students zoom by on cycles. Later I kneeled in the attic, splicing 8-mm. strips, listening to Mets games. I was young again, playing stickball and frisbee with neighbor kids, reading Beautyway ceremonies and Jung on flying saucers. I wrote poetic narratives and science-fiction essays:

> We are things across night, and across day. We are dreams, dreamed; we feel our bodies, feel like holdfasts; it won't hold. . . . Each flower, face, song is a separate, a new touchstone, Blake's system washed out by saline earth, the Assyrians invading from a higher more northernly order, the wheats extinct, the priests slain, and the costumes of women, the coinage altered, a new race following the glaciers, the Victorian poets, Bill Haley and his Comets, an unknown flower, a flag with strange markings. We awake in the morning and rip the sacrament, the muscles apart; the sunlight pours in through the nightmare, the old language forgotten, the old words unwritten: not that we speak in tongues but . . . wind through the trees, trilled 'r,' the b-s that goes along the park.

We were a study of innocence and young naive intelligence. She was alternately endearing, alluring, and infuriating. We fought continuously and on occasion debated how long we had to stay together to make the wedding gifts not a scam. We were different types: her elegance and dignity confronted by my bursts of energy and pranks (a cup of cold water over the curtain into her shower). Her dinner recipes led to spiced mush she called casseroles, and I presented what to her were inedible sculptures of potato, stringbeans, and a hamburger, usually overdone.

We posted the words of Lawrence over the kitchen table: "You don't find the sun and moon playing at pals in the sky. Their beams cross the great gulf which is between them. So with man and woman. They must stand clear again. They must fight their way out of their self-consciousness: there is nothing else."

Our union was intellectual and reasoned—we were so verbal anyway. Self-consciousness made sex awkward, a haste to get through to an ease on the other side. Flirtation was impossible because we were together all the time anyway. We met our similar lithe bodies in the muggy afternoons, my dark unruly curls, her made-up blue eyes and pigtails. When a cool breeze rolled over us afterward, it was sweet, it was sad, but it felt like home. For once, I didn't want to watch too closely; I simply wanted to be.

Suddenly the heat broke, and rain sealed us inside a cone of sound; thunder clapped eerily. I was on the phone with my mother when I looked out the window to see Mary Street underwater, cars floating, kids and dogs putting on a show of makeshift rafts and floats. I got the camera, went outside, and filmed them at twelve frames a second. When I presented it later in the attic—and again and again, on request—they were speeded up, racing around like cartoon characters, water sloshing up behind them as they dunked and throttled one another with brooms. Each re-run they'd explode with laughter and start kicking and pushing right there as though to bring back that madcap afternoon.

The details of us two in the summer of '66 are engraved in my memory like scenes on Persian parchment: visiting coffee shops and occult bookstores, accompanying each other to graduate-student picnics where a pig and a lamb were roasted by bare-chested returnees from New Guinea and Peru, UFO lectures in the basement of a suburban Detroit bank (an Air Force pilot promising this whole planet would pass into the fourth dimension by 1980), Winnebago drumming ceremonies in Quimby, a rainbow fountain in Jackson (providing glow and silhouettes for double exposures), driving home late and tumbling into bed.

We played ceaseless games with Frodo, Lindy peeking inside one sliding door of a bureau while she went into the other, saying, "'ello," then—as she looked around—closing it and saying, "'ello" at the opposite end. We took her on walks around the block; she darted in and out of bushes, always racing ahead and rolling on the pavement, scratching her back like speech between us. She was the bright alter ego of our marriage, and we made a haven of shoeboxes and pillows for her in the attic.

Finally, in mid-August, I wandered up to campus to start classes. I was told to make up my lack of undergraduate anthropology with Introductory Genetics. Ethnology was a required seminar. Plus I chose Linguistics and a Middle Eastern survey. About the time my first Fellowship check came, Lindy found a graduate assistantship at Eastern Michigan, one town away in Ypsilanti. Twice a week she drove there to teach and then went back one evening to take graduate classes.

In early September the landlord returned with his wife. Remarkably she hadn't known that her husband had rented the upstairs, and now she said she didn't want anyone in her son's room. A scowling gel of venom, she sat on the porch swing, tossing cigarette butts and beer bottles into the yard (all summer, as we gradually cleaned these up, we had assumed the litter was from passers-by). They drove an antique polished Cadillac which they parked in the yard even when there were spaces on the street. When we played our record of Navaho music she began pounding on the ceiling. Her problem was not that it was loud—it was "anti-American."

He came one morning to inspect our work. We were whimsical enough to think he would be delighted by our reclaiming the attic, but he insisted he had never rented it to us. Then pointing to a "No pets" clause in our lease, he threatened to poison Frodo if we kept her. He also refused to reimburse us, saying the paint job was "a piece of shit" and my shelves were "junk."

"You might as well take them down," he declared, waving a quivering hand—so I did, right there, tearing off chunks of plaster in the process.

I thought of the apartment as our asylum and was ready to fight for it. Lindy understood the battle wasn't ours and ended the confrontation without even telling me. Since her job at Eastern Michigan gave us twice as much salary, she rented a modern basement duplex about a mile further from campus. The kids of Mary Street helped us pack and then rode in our U-Haul, throwing themselves into its padded walls and singing beer commercials, squealing as we went around corners.

Brooklyn was a quiet residential street. Our home comprised three unfurnished, newly painted rooms and a kitchen of spiffy appliances. For less than a hundred dollars we bought all its furnishings from a consignment store called The Treasure Mart—filthy but sturdy pieces we painted Chinese red, yellow, maroon, and sky blue. At a Kiwanis Club sale we got a $4 couch with a Beardsleyesque print of eagles, some Chinese rural scenery showing through, plus a few overstuffed chairs, one on wheels with stringy frills.

The bathroom was aqua green—walls, tile, and shower curtains. Since the floor had a complex pattern, I devised a coin game while I sat on the toilet, using different-sized squares and rectangles as targets and bouncing a dime high off the walls. It was like a flat, dispersed skeeball with box grids instead of circles. The smallest square counted for six; the rectangle, three; and the large square, one. I had twelve shots to get twelve points (or lose) in a series of best four-out-of-seven matches. No skill was involved. Despite some amazing streaks—the dime bouncing off the tub and walls and spinning or rolling crazily— the game was pure lottery and spectatorship. Although I never named him (or kept a cumulative score), my imaginary opponent was the same one against whom I played my childhood numbers game in the synagogue; twelve was Gil McDougald's number, long ago iconicized and made the duodecimal basis of all games in my cosmology.

The ladder we climb to reach the roof goes down to crabgrass. The neighbor's dog barks beside an abandoned motorcycle, unable to climb toward us. Frodo comes out the kitchen window, walks along bushes in the yard, slinks from a dog across the street (that does not see her), and rests beneath a clump of low budding branches. Upwards a commotion of birds . . . she scans them, laying as far back in her body as she can. Then she climbs a pine tree and jumps to a nearby roof. We call to her, asking her to come. She rubs her nose on a branch and lies in a patch of sun. . . .

Shrieking children fly past. One of them is pulling four of them in a red wagon down the street. . . . In the next yard a tiny boy and girl are having a tea-party. Yesterday they were married on a stack of firewood. Now little fat Sophy pours his tea and he sits at the table enjoying married life.

You have baked a rich pie, sir, and we like it. You have planted dandelion candles in your pie, and it lies cooling beneath the sky. And you have baked four and twenty blackbirds in with us and now they are looking for homes. . . .

My nine-year-old friend Steve arrives with a glove: will I play? I come down the ladder onto the street. I stand snapping the ball. The dog, released, chases the shadow of every throw. You have baked a rich pie, sir, and though I will not be fooled I am always fooled and would have it no other way. . . .

You have baked your richest pie, and each day I eat a little more. You have baked me into your pie, and here I am, throwing with my right hand, catching with my left. The first planet appears on the horizon.

A graduate wife taught us to cook rice with pomegranate seeds, then painted a Scorpion on a doorknob for my birthday. An Asian specialist talked decades of Pittsburgh Pirate baseball while Lindy was stuck in the kitchen trying to understand his Laotian wife. A lonely classmate came over for dinner and departmental gossip, then asked Lindy to help him find a date. A North Korean scholar brought amazing tales of his homeland to coffee and dessert. A British film-maker introduced us to the works of Merleau-Ponty and Robert Indiana while trashing Kelly's poetry as kitsch.

The narrative was over. We had started public life again as Lindy-Rich.

That fall I memorized details of meiosis and mitosis, solved workbook problems in African and Pacific languages, and was a sales clerk Saturday afternoons at Bob Marshall's Bookstore. At Halloween I used the light of pumpkins to film kids trick-or-treating, then spliced those shots together with close-ups of larvae inside rotten chestnuts (the ghosts!).

One evening Lindy was late returning from Eastern Michigan. An hour late . . . two hours late. I paced all three rooms and then ran around the block. I sat on the bed with the lights out. More time passed. I jumped up and vacuumed the whole apartment. I washed every dish and piece of silverware. I alphabetized the bookcases and fed Frodo a second dinner.

I had so few resources. Without my wife I was trapped in an antipathetic Midwestern town, and even more dangerously, in a nascent identity I could not maintain by myself. I threw on my coat and circled the block again, peering ahead for her car lights. The night was immense and void, blind vehicles rolling on. My mind rang in frantic thoughts.

At the sound of our car in the driveway, roots of memories streamed over me. I bounded out to greet her. I felt her woolen coat and smelled the winter briskness of her skin that was once so strange. I stared as though I had never seen her before. This was my wife. It wasn't just some girl or girlfriend. My relief at her familiarity transcended any other attraction.

She explained she had taken someone's parking space by mistake. When the car wouldn't start, this guy came out from behind the bushes and threatened her. He told her he had removed the distributor head. Then he opened the hood and reattached it.

I felt crosswinds of emotions: rage at this asshole, terror at the thought of losing her, guilt at being unable to protect her. From then on I accompanied her to Ypsilanti, sitting in her office doing my anthropology assignments while she took classes and taught. It became a ritual—a delight at her return, lunches and dinners out. A part of me knew this was crazy—I couldn't guard the whole universe—but another part of me had returned to the watchtower. Barely outside the forest of an incomprehensible childhood, in this first year of marriage, I was utterly compelled to stay awake.

Jonny had begun college in Madison at the University of Wisconsin. He came monthly to visit us by bus or train. On a high-school diamond, once again we fielded each other's hits.

Almost without notice my brother had become my disciple—my one-time blood enemy and tormentor, the golden boy to whom my life had been but a shadow. All his ancient animosity seemed to have melted into devotion and admiration, as he propounded a mythology of our early years in which I had blazed a trail, first of rebellion against the corrupt elders, then of initiation into magic. He read my writing avidly and worshipped Frodo as a great warrior incarnated in a cat. Brothers at last, we applauded her leaps from roof to roof, her sly reconnoiters at our rear.

In a marathon of old 45s we sat up late talking Towers family lore: Mickey Mantle bunting with two strikes, Sam Cooke singing "Wonderful World," the Fox Den of Uncle Wiggily, the Knickerbocker Sign, baseball in Central Park, the Fool and the Hanged Man. We were both refugees from the kingdom. Our nightmares and legends were the same.

"I dreamed," he told me, "that I went to Doctor Hitzig to have him give me a check-up. It was an old mahogany, spiral-polished-stair place. He found that one of my testicles was diseased and gave me a new one, so I had three; he would take out the bad one later. The new testicle has a genetic memory of only 9,000 years plus some, while all the other parts of the body have infinite genetic memories back to the beginning of the world."

In our separate University libraries we had discovered Indian texts. We began to address our family legacy through the vigils of shamans, the rites of Osage and Navaho. Our parents suddenly seemed pathetic and self-aggrandizing before the true American prairie.

"Do you think the cards are real?" Jon had asked me even back at Amherst. "Can prayers turn lead into gold?" He was desperate for me to tell him, since he couldn't imagine how.

My brother and I had always had two mysteries in common—baseball and rock and roll. Now, in our rapidly changing world, Mickey Mantle and the Prince of Wands had fused; Dion and the Belmonts and Elvis recalled Meister Eckhart and Parcelsus in some eternal cycle of pop and esoteric wisdom to which the whole of America was suddenly turning. Columbus' voyages to the New World became connected at some obscure but intrinsic level to pennant races against the Cleveland Indians and Chicago White Sox and the epic Yankee-Dodger World Series. *The Tempest, The Prairie,* and *Moby Dick* were magical books which disclosed, beyond what we had been taught at Horace Mann, adventures of migration and transmigration. It was *"Dream Lover, where are you?..."* the sky blue and eighteen and Hopi forever—rain dance and star chart, kachina on primeval ball diamond, numerology of old Bering Straits League now playing at the foot of Orinoco, meeting the Yankees of John Dee and William Blake.

"Gil McDougald and Mickey Mantle," Jon intoned with the reverence of a chant. "It was but yesterday that Casey Stengel said in Los Angeles something good about these two players only."

"He did?"

"Yes, but you and I always knew that it was the combination of McDougald and Mantle that made the Yankee teams. You rooted for one and I the other."

"What did Casey say?"

"That you could play McDougald anywhere, short, second, or third. Instead of buying two players you just shift McDougald over to one of the vacancies. And he said about Mantle that he never saw anyone hit them further in any park, and from both sides, not just one. I have both parents, but you play all positions by having two families."

Jon was lonely and sad, his yearning bottomless. A lifetime of being enemies would not go away that easily. However compliant my brother was—and despite claims he was now my loyal pupil—I sensed his

submerged rage and charisma, his capacity for violence. This was someone who knew my secrets and observed my flaws. I could permit him
only guarded access to my world.

The trouble was: I heard my own ghosts and superstitions in Jon's
cry, felt my own anxiety in his visionary urgency.

My brother and I were joined at our mother not like Siamese twins
who shared a body but plants whose roots drew from the same
unknown soil. We both had nightmares of Doctor Hitzig taking apart
our bodies, finding (or causing) teratologies, chasing us through rooms
of an unknown hospital.

We did not know we shared another phobia until one morning during childhood, lying in bed—each thinking the other was asleep—we
kept half-open eyes on a pigeon that had stuck his head in the crack
of the courtyard window—just its head . . . then part of its neck and
body . . . then—we knew the exact moment when it crossed a failsafe
point—suddenly, racing to the door I crashed into him.

Neither of us could bear to be trapped in a room with this wild
bird, its wings beating the walls.

"It was her, our mother, it had to be," we told ourselves one night,
reviewing the incident in Ann Arbor, hooting over the memory of how
fast we had bolted, how shocked we were to meet each other at the
door.

By the third day of his visits Jon would grow totally melancholy and
intense and begin ranting about Arthurian knights, Hopi queens,
Apache warriors, and turning base metals into gold. I couldn't keep
up his ghost-dance grail. "Richard," he chided, "where is the alchemist
who taught me? Now that I am finally ready to go to battle beside you,
don't abandon the grail!"

What could I say? I didn't want anarchy or the fourth dimension;
the dark side of the occult frightened me. I clung to domestic life and
hoped the Aquarian apocalypse wouldn't harm us. I was satisfied with
small hints of magic. Lindy's company and the high clouds telling
nothing—those I loved more than any chant or prophecy.

It was always a relief to take my brother to the train station. His
departures lurched between his bashfulness and fury. "You're holding
something back," he snarled. "There shouldn't be any problems

anymore between us. Man, my head is really in the stars and planets, just where you told me to put it."

When my mother learned of Jon's visits, she was furious. She informed everyone who would listen that we were exacting some sort of revenge on her by turning Jon into a lunatic. To Lindy she assigned Aunt Bunny's old role—seductress and saboteur. Yet she would call me regularly, sounding conciliatory, even cooperative. "I hear Jon was there again," she would begin. "Do you have anything new to tell me?"

She sought analysis and advice, so I would explain my brother's beliefs and actions as best I could. It was a short rope: Psychiatry was out of the question. She also did not want to hear that his ideas were brilliant (even if grounded in emotional disturbances). She thought they were crazy and, if pressed, she reminded me that I was their major source.

She had concluded (beyond appeal) that Jon was possessed by something exotic and renounceable, and she wanted me to convince or compel him to renounce it. I argued that he was a combination of brilliant occultist and scared child. I wanted her to accept his grail and to see me too, a husband and a graduate student, to abandon the mystique of the past so that we could all breathe. But she was immutable.

I tried to simplify Jon's cosmology to her in terms she might understand, but she had always considered me a con-man. My strained if sincere lessons in Aquarian morality were viewed by her as mere chicanery and disingenuous sophistry: "You're trying to put something over on me, Richard. I know this isn't real. This isn't a thing anyone else talks about. It's just the newest trick up your sleeve."

She abhorred anything that originated with me. Once upon a time she even railed against *Camelot*—which was to become her favorite musical. This was after my father Paul took me to see it and bought me the record. She condemned it first before she had even heard the songs—then again, with self-righteous vehemence, when I proudly played one of them on the stereo for her. "What trash!" she proclaimed, turning her back and leaving the room. These were the sort of robust romantic lyrics she normally adored—*and did* once she forgot I was their source. Whatever I brought into our home was tainted, even if it was Robert Goulet singing, *"It wouldn't be in summer, knowing how in summer...."* Now it was Nicolas Flamel and Chief Joseph. I had ruined

516

my brother's mind and derailed his career, and she pleaded with him to stay away from me "and that woman" I had (like my father) married.

We were collaborating on a plot as complex as *Hamlet,* tracking a troubled hero, imposing alternate interpretations on his epochal acts. I suspected that Jon was the true realization of her own complexity, her fright and passion both, as—through tarot cards, alchemical codes, and Indian myths—he tried to rip open the curtains and peer down into hell. No matter how visionary and farout these exploits, he was always grim and miserable in their aftermath, as she was in her own compulsive rituals.

I couldn't tell her how she haunted Jon's dreams, how excited he was to see us, how he worshiped Frodo. The mere mention of animals incensed her.

In truth, my brother's revolutionary fervor and mythological fantasies left me the amateur. I was simply trying to make a home. He was undomesticatable.

As time passed, these positions hardened. Jon became wilder. He battled with his landlord, got evicted, dropped out of college, and returned to New York. His parents rented him an East Village flat. He invited hobos off the street to stay with him (seeking, in each, a replica of Dickens' convict-benefactor in *Great Expectations*). He smoked marijuana ritually and ran his life wholly by tarot divination and an esoteric interpretation of the Apache vision-quest; he took to preaching on the streets. He never returned to the ordinary world.

My mother blamed me for this forever. Debby was forbidden even to admit I existed, so all of her teenage years passed with no contact between us. As these positions became more entrenched, Bob decided to boycott Lindy and me too.

Yet for all these same years I remained my mother's confidante. Never asking about Lindy or what I was doing (ever), she turned our filial relationship into an exegesis of her other son.

Years later I was led to reevaluate the pigeon who peeked in the window. That bird was not really our mother. Trapped indoors, it might have flown about frantically like her. Yet *she* was not incoherent and panic-stricken like a pigeon. She was not some alien force. She spoke

THE ALCHEMICAL WEDDING

English; she made demands. Her attack was concrete: claws in our flesh, fists against our bare bodies.

No, the bird was not her hysteria. It *was* our internalization of her hysteria, fashioned into a nameless hysteria of our own and projected outward onto a plump, winged animal caged in an alien castle, throwing its unconscious being against the geometry.

The terror was that it was us, not her, that in us it felt more like a mute pigeon than our mother. Flying blind and panicked inside our bodies, it could no longer be exorcised or set free.

The second term I took Advanced Genetics, South American Indian Cultures, Phonetics, and more ethnology (with a heavy dose of tribal politics, Big Men, chiefs, and Stone Age economics). By then I was immersed in a lingo of blood groups, phonemes, jungle polities, slash-and-burn agriculture, and Eskimo kin classification. My writing blended totems, Palaeolithic migrations, shamanic rituals, and dreams. Our favorite albums were Smokey Robinson and the Miracles' *Greatest Hits* ("You've Really Got a Hold on Me"), The Rolling Stones' *Flowers* ("Ruby Tuesday") and *December's Children* ("You Better Move On"), *The Best of the The Lovin' Spoonful* ("Summer in the City" and "Do You Believe in Magic?"), and Donovan's *Sunshine Superman* and *Fairytale* ("To Try for the Sun" and "Belated Forgiveness Plea"). I added my voice to Neil Diamond singing, *"Red, red wine. . . ."* and *"Girl, you'll be a woman soon, soon you'll need a man. . . ."* These songs were the sounds of the Earth moving through 1966 into 1967: *"who could pin a name on you?"* and *"the seagulls they have gone."* When town ponds froze I played pick-up hockey with local teenagers, dashing up and back, dodging litter as I chased the puck-carrier, chest burning. Stick over my shoulder, *"my heart both young and old,"* I strode home under an early moon.

> Gunz
> Mindel
> Riss
> Wurm
>
> step by step
> moving east with the ice age
> swarming and sweeping

518

thoughts of a world
moving south into the rich caves
passing over land to Britannia and Java
Alaska the New World

carrying a word of bone
dancing
horned masked—
that one man
                a universe
lives
is dug from the earth
every bone every tooth   tested   to know what
moved this man who he was what
touched him . . .

seeing as the earth was then the earth
                        making that earth

dying before the next hill
the first night of stars rolling over him. . . .

My last year at Amherst, anthropology had been the opening into a non-Western code of colors and totems masking primordial rituals (themselves masking symbols and archetypes). Ojibwa thunderbirds and Cezanne's essential "blue" pointed to the same missing link as the poems of Olson. I imagined initially that if I learned enough Indian and African cosmology I could synthesize native shamanism with Gurdjieff's octaves, Jung's collective unconscious, and the paradoxes of quantum physics. Yet, after a term and a half, graduate anthropology was a total disappointment. It seemed only to homogenize cultures into social and economic grids, making Australian Aborigines and Iroquois Indians sound like practitioners of the same formal system.

My faculty adviser Roy Rappaport, a prominent ecological anthropologist in his early forties, had been a hotelman in Massachusetts and knew my father. When Lindy and I arrived he adopted us at once, though he soon came to view me as a challenge. Tirelessly he debated the occult with me, trying to win a wayward student over to the more conventional point of view. "Richard," he insisted, "graduate school is about being an objective scientific observer not becoming a practicing magician." When I mentioned Rodney Collin's "theory of celestial influence" at a department party, provoking an eminent physical anthropologist, Rappaport took me by the arm: "There are certain things you don't discuss with some people. It's not duplicitous, just good politics. After all, you *are* on a Fellowship."

"I thought it would interest him."

"Interest me?" called out the offended party. "What interests me is 'where's the evidence?' then maybe a theory!"

"Please don't make me have to defend you to my narrower-minded colleagues," whispered Rappaport.

Throughout my first term, he urged me to be patient and unprovocative, things would get more interesting. In January, hearing my continued frustration, he suggested I apprentice myself to the last of the great old-timers, Mischa Titiev, the man who had written the definitive book on the Hopi in the '40s.

"It will do you some good to stop romanticizing Indians and learn some facts," he scolded, somewhat facetiously. "Also Mischa is quite ill and needs help, and graduate students have been ignoring him for years."

Titiev had actually visited Hotevilla not long after it was founded in 1906 by 298 religious conservatives of the Fire, Sun, and Spider Clans seceding from the village of Oraibi. More than any Westerner, he was a "member of the tribe." Barely able to communicate now because of Parkinson's disease, he sat behind a cluttered desk and directed me to organize his papers and books. He assigned me standard ethnologies of the era and was dismayed—even insulted—by my fervor for the esoterics of religious life.

For my first report I spent weeks half-skimming, half-reading thousands of pages of nineteenth- and early twentieth-century accounts of Hopi ceremonies. Travelers and ethnographers had recorded and illustrated every detail of ritual preparation they were privileged to attend (and the Smithsonian, Bureau of American Ethnography, and University of Chicago Field Museum had graciously published these in massive volumes complete with sketches of rattles, kachina dolls, sandpaintings, sacred shields, and color plates of feathered prayersticks). I proposed subliminal codes linking myths, rituals, and the cyclical practice of agriculture, but Titiev scrawled across my paper, "Diving deep into shallow waters."

"Shallow waters," he gesticulated wildly with his good arm. "Nothing there!"

The founder of the department, Leslie White, had taken a stand against collectors of pure data, arguing for scientific, evolutionary laws of culture. Although he had become an irrelevant ideologue among his peers—evicting nuns from the classroom for being inappropriately attired and slandering his deceased opponents—most of the Michigan professors had been hired because they were sympathetic to some form of anthropology as hard science, whether statistical theory, homeostasis through native ideology or, like Titiev, religion as social glue.

I wrote mostly orthodox papers and learned the foundations of anthropology. It was my job. Meanwhile Lindy and I put out a third issue of *Io,* featuring not only my brother, Diane Wakoski, Welton Smith, and Harvey Bialy, but also the elders at Old Oraibi and Hotevilla.

My heart was in my pilgrimage with Lindy; I marked it in 8-mm. films (snow covering the garden, wind strewing crisped leaves, the moon through bottles of cider), walks along the snowy Huron River, dinners in town followed by movies.

I cast my deeper intimations into experimental prose, transforming daily life through semes of crushed stars, wild pigs, and chromosomes. I named my writings: *Solar Journal, Book of the Earth and Sky, The Alphabet Book,* and *Spaces Wild and Tame:*

> Matter that is drowned or dwindled bubbles up in another part of the universe, or another universe. The collapsing star is a temple, as dense as a holy place, hot spot, as a sun-shrine is lit by exusion of law and candlelight and gold, the hymnal hydrogen, Hebrew or Inca, crushed by invaders, the altar demolished, the lights put out, the treasures sacked, the spirit driven into the forest. The actual energy is sucked through the tail by the mouth, the snake disappearing that it may return to natural matter and begin once again its journey to text....
>
> In the spring the queen leads a swarm of bees from the hive to another territory; the second queen awakes from the galaxies, finds herself in the kettle, quacks and is released. The court swarms around her. She emerges into a Ptolemaic universe, her winged harmonies dead center, the sun quacking, and as she flies into the microcosm its fields are filled with light.

In the early spring Robert Kelly came through Detroit to read at Wayne State University (which put him up at a spiffy hotel). We joined him there for dinner. The conventioneers were not used to a four-hundred-pound poet with billowing red hair and a scraggly beard, so when the elevator stopped, the crowd turned and gasped. Kelly raised a finger above his head and then brought his arm down like a slow guillotine until it was aimed at them through the moving doors. He howled in Celtic.

"What was that?" I asked.

"Just some poor devils won't sleep for a few nights."

Two days later we returned and fetched him and Button back to Ann Arbor, having arranged for a reading that evening in our living room (since there was no University support). Rappaport alone came from the Department, and my two "fathers" sat there afterwards agreeing with each other that I should learn academic graces and how not to antagonize the heathen. Their facile collaboration surprised me.

After our friends left, Lindy and I gave Kelly and Button a private reading, and he praised my montage of anthropology and literature: "You've found the path. You will never go backwards from here."

He left us with an odd, lengthy manuscript of his own, "Alchemical Journal," insisting that *Io* was the only place where it could be "published honorably." It was filled with aphorisms like: "To answer my earliest question: it would have been enough to see the sun rise."

Entrusted by him with a mission, I spent many subsequent afternoons hunting through rare volumes in the Michigan library, selecting Amerindian and Mediaeval texts to contextualize "Alchemical Journal" in a fourth *Io:*

> "A fire is laid under the Sun, which is burning, and much smoke
> is ascending. An old man has in his hands an urinal, in which is
> the Moon lying on her back in blackish water. Out of the vessel is
> flying a green Dragon, holding the Moon in its mouth by the navel,
> and placing its fore feet on a black rock. Beneath the rock a green
> Dragon lies dead on his back."

This was, on the one hand, completely obscure; on the other, the story of my life.

Because of my work with Titiev, the Anthro Department Chairman recommended that I begin research in a Pueblo field area, so for the upcoming summer I submitted a project: to go to Oraibi and Hotevilla and compare Frank Waters' *Book of the Hopi* (assembled from Hotevilla informants) to the more conservative monographs favored by Titiev. Through the linguistics program I would also get paid to collect Arizona dialects for a dictionary of American Regional English.

In June we sublet our apartment, then picked up our Aspen buddy Mitchell and his girlfriend Joanna in Ohio. Packed in the Mustang we headed west, Frodo panting in her cage by day—at night, paws on dashboard, gawking at headlights . . . smuggled into motels. Hot Missouri afternoons were followed by incredible displays of lightning over Kansas ("all that we can see from here/in light/all that we cannot see in darkness"). Colorado was clear as glass.

We left our passengers sublet-hunting in Boulder, stayed with Lindy's family a few days, then drove to Tuba City, Arizona, where we rented a trailer. On the first desert morning we went back to Oraibi, looking for English-speaking Indians. This time it was really no honeymoon.

We were astonished to find lines of young professional interviewers at every Hopi home. Graduate students were flooding in from field schools, cash in hand from Government stipends. Delighted Indians were setting rates to talk about kin ties and tribal myths. We didn't have a chance. Even Sun Chief would not receive Dr. Titiev's greetings without an informant's fee—Sun Chief of all people!—the great warrior-dreamer who had visited the Upper World.

"Heepees," shouted children, my beard alone enough.

"Heepees and Hopis," I wrote in my journal. "And *I* cannot tell the difference between *Book of the Hopi* and *Book of Mormon.*" In fact, the more I read of the plates of Nephi and Enos the more convinced I became that either Waters or the Indians were merging Hopi and Christian theology. I imagined lost migrants of some global Atlantean nation, skirting the Antarctic in their triremes, having mapped the Earth before Chaldeans mapped the sky, building the Sphinx and the solar temples of Bolivia, erecting their castle on Guantánamo Bay, etching the secret routes Columbus used to rediscover the New World. Actual sociology was useless. This was Ghost Dance time.

And did it matter? Especially among vans of people headed through these villages to Haight-Ashbury and the summer of love . . . with talk of Atlantis, UFOs broadcasting the end of the world in cataclysm—

same prophecy as the Blue Star kachina, same North American Indians visited by the Irish sailor-saint Brendan in the Sixth Century, even if he didn't make it west in body to the pueblos and Mesa Verde. The flower children bore his millennial message.

Outside in Hotevilla by the kiva (where there were no students) a hawk was tethered to the roof by a rope—flapping outraged wings, each time yanked down. I was carrying *Book of the Hopi,* and a local noticed it and summoned us to follow. Inside a house an old woman brewed black medicine sticks over a fire. Her husband's face was the most rugged I had ever seen; it was ripped apart, one eye socket open. He sat there like Geronimo, impassive and inconsolable, a prophet of doom.

He had been in prison, he said. He had been forced by Americans to work with gangs on rockpiles. They had let his eye rot out. All because he refused to fight in World War II. Smearing his muddy finger across his name Paul Siwingyawma in my book he cursed the White Man and Navaho and proclaimed: "Hopi people will rule the next Earth, the Fifth World. Wars in the Holy Land are beginning. The Blue Light kachina is the first of our prophecies. It visits the Mesa every night"—his voice emotionless, as though dictating from tribal memory. "There will be whirlwinds, dust storms, lightning, meteors; whole planets will fall."

A teenage boy hunched in the corner read a porn novel. The steam from the pot was profoundly acrid. The floor was dirt. On the radio: the Monkees.

Back in Tuba City we lay in our trailer exhausted—sky empty of clouds. The preacher next door blasted the radio, narrating the Arab-Israeli War aloud, praying for Endtime. "We'll be fightin' the Russians and the French and those Scandinavians," he said with a howl of delight. At least he wasn't charging by the word, so I wrote it down. "People think war is a bad thing, but it's only prophecy. In a week I'll be sitting on the Lord's right hand." Someone played one finger on a piano, a ghostly sequence of notes, over and over. Across the row a Hopi child was pounding the head of a kitten against a stoop. Then he dropped it from the roof of his trailer. Dogs came out of the desert to fight over wet catshit ... "and I sit on the steps reading the Qabbala again because it alone makes sense. Because where there is no water its glyphs touch things and make them wet. The sun pours onto its pages, blinding the words. It finds Lindy's hands splashing with soap-suds in the sink. . . ."

The only person in Old Oraibi who would speak to us was Chief Myna—and then only to beg us to go home "if you really love the Indians. It's crazy, people just getting in the way, even taking notes watching me hang my wash." She stood in her standard American living room by the fireplace. "We have nothing to teach."

In the morning we fled Tuba City for Snowflake, a dictionary-assigned town in the mountains. Checking into a motel, we celebrated dusk with a picnic. Playful in the breeze, Frodo charged recklessly into nearby woods. By then our hobbit was so skilled at adapting to new bases we let her wander. She always adventured and returned.

We went to the drive-in that night and saw *One-Eyed Jacks*. It was Marlon Brando, surrounded on a hill by Mexican police, deserted by his only friend, bullwhipped and his hand smashed by the one-eyed jack, stealing the sheriff's daughter with a lie, conceiving a child, shooting his gun at the cliffs with the wounded hand, pushing aside the form of the soul of the woman of the temple of the wise Chinamen who fished in the salt that finally healed the hand and the Moon and all things in time, breaking out of jail, rescuing her, riding off to Oregon.

Back at our motel Frodo didn't come to greet us. Hours passed. We called for her, walking to the woods. In retrospect now, our laxness seemed ridiculous, a myth of this animal's theomorphic stature. We wandered under stars, around blocks, making cat noises Lindy whistling her most familiar calls.

In the morning there was still no sign of her. We dressed, ate a quick breakfast, then searched the neighborhood. We widened our territory, spending most of the day—and the one after—going street by street, checking deserted cellars, meowing to the tops of trees, finally hiking through fields and forest beyond the town.

> You slipped out so quietly, a moment without denotation or meaning, and were gone in the night . . . the blank fury of a bobcat, torn from her garden and caged to the rhythm of traveling. . . . Now you might be starving, chased by dogs, meowing under an unfriendly window, pursued and shot by Arizona teenagers. . . . .
>
> Though we call in abandoned buildings and look under the railroad station, though we are led by children to a spot on the road

where a dead cat once lay, we begin to drag our feet, to awake at night to the howls of dogs, Lindy with nightmares of stuffed cat furs.

Our cat clearly gone, we continued to Prescott, the next assigned town. I sat in people's kitchens, reciting the questionnaire with Lindy's help, taping usages and jargon of housewives and retired school teachers.

Military jets flew overhead. A parade marched down Main Street. My beard drew angry shouts.

I visited a dying cowboy. The night previous, this old man had dreamed he trod a rocky landscape—vast beyond imagination, inexplicable lakes in the desert, fifty thousand head of cattle or more stampeding loose. It had to be the Afterlife, he thought. "There ain't no country like that anymore! The only place like that I ever knew of was over on the north side of the Grand Canyon—what they call the Strip up there, right along the line of Arizona and Utah. There was a big outfit in there at one time. And it was a wild outfit—and I guess they was runnin' quite a few men killed on that ranch. Well, that's the only ranch that I can *even picture in my mind* that'd be anything like the dreams I've had.

"The other night I had a dream about—I got into a country, and I come to a stream of water—*big* stream. I was on horseback, and I didn't know where that stream of water went to, and I had to cross it, and I didn't know whether my horse would swim that stream of water or not. I figured maybe I could help him and get across it because I *had to* cross. Well, I rode off into it, and we jus' swam across it—without a bit of trouble and got on the other side, and got out and went off into the mountains there. It was only jus' rough country, *real* rough, *rocky* country. I thought, 'What good is this country, ain't nobody want country like this. There's nothing here; there's not even a bird here. Couldn't nothing live here because there's no feed.'"

But this was also Yesod ... the eternal pools and herds of the unconscious ... the prehistoric inland sea.

We had encountered an even more profound law than those of Hopi legend: the angels wait where you least expect them, where you do not consciously seek them. For all our journeying through aboriginal country looking for sacred texts, we had found one at last—an old cowboy remembering the Turkey Track Ranch in nineteen-nine, a bad man with a gun singing "Sweet Maggie Jones."

When they received my tapes, the Dictionary of American Regional English was not equally enamored. By special delivery they rejected my Snowflake and Prescott transcriptions and told me to stop. We took that not as chastisement but release from Arizona. Fieldwork had become an affectation (Chief Myna was right). Forget dialects; forget academia. I spent my last afternoon in Prescott chasing fly balls in a Navaho hardball practice. Just dust and sun, lemon sodas, dripping adobe sweat, agreeing to play in their game, lying in the dust with them by the batting cage. Finally the pre-Columbian chatter was real.

Returning to Colorado, we spent structureless days in Central City, hanging out with Mitchell and Joanna in town, then acquiring a fluffy ball of kitten we named Quis. And Donovan sang, *"There's nothing left for me now, but the seagulls they do. . . ."*

And Kelly: "Life is preparation for taking leave of the work."

One morning I awoke to the presence of something ancient. I had lived with Lindy inside a dance of love and hope; now a thing beyond hope and diabolic was pushing on the boundaries. Hot and achey, I fought it all day.

Mitchell and Joanna came for dinner. They were sitting in the living room. I was telling stories of our time in Arizona, Lindy was cooking. . . . My voice became the chirp of a distant being.

It wasn't any one thing, the loss of Frodo or the prophecy at Hotevilla. It was more like the cowboy's dream—crossing a stream into disturbingly wild country, the sudden disappearance of everything that had once been familiar.

These molecular walls, this macabre lamplight, were the skin of creation. In my scant physical form I was incapable of dispelling their impermanence, their intimacy. Mitchell sat across the room, foggy eyes and curly hair; Joanna a dark hierophant lady—they were classic New York figures, allies both. Yet the very pans hanging by handles on the wall terrified me. "They're the cooking apparatus of this world," I said, "and it will go on forever."

Mitchell nodded plaintively.

I reviewed my paths to this moment: New York childhood, Amherst, the courtship of Lindy, Mary Street eviction, my wild brother, Arizona territory. I was just entering the world, but everywhere glaring people—Indian and Baptist prophets—prayed for Endtime. Now Frodo was lost.

Sitting on the bedside in the dark, Lindy urged me to try to sleep. Even with my eyes closed I kept seeing a light across the mountains blinking blue and red, opening into a negative universe, its eye sucking at me.

But there wasn't any eye behind that light; it was *inside* me, shimmering dizzily up through childhood memories of sun and stone, the glowing Christmas trees, the Cropsey Maniac in his shroud, the fields of Grossinger's, rain falling into a valley somewhere, blue sky/marble clouds, potatoes on the stove, an insufferable tide of daylight....

And then for a hesitation of a second I looked at her Modigliani face and wise eyes, moths against the window fluttering ... and I began to laugh. She was alive, light and energetic—was laughing too. I followed her into the living room, a shy giant.

Frodo was found—a week later, sixty miles away at a funeral. She had shocked the mourners by jumping onto the casket meowing; someone read the name and phone number of the motel on her collar and called the manager. We paid him to have her flown to Denver and then drove to the airport to collect her. They brought her cage out of the baggage room.

She was not as we remembered—more a feral grey beast. "Is it really Frodo?" we asked, astonished that we couldn't recognize a being so dear and familiar. But this growling animal in a cage was a hero, so we initiated her back into our marriage. That weekend we made her homecoming official by driving from Central City to our former cabin along the Roaring Fork.

In the morning we fixed our favorite wood-stove pancakes with cups of coffee. Then we sat in the grove and watched her tracking chipmunks, climbing white bark, plunking to the ground—a hobbit returned from the dead.

2

ROBIN

I had a full slate of classes that fall: Old World Archaeology, Evolutionary Theory, History of Anthropology, South American Indians. My writing teemed with hominids, ice sheets, totem poles, and millennial rains. I transposed the Mesolithic realm of stilt houses and boat people to Venus and framed a Cytherean Genesis using Hopi myths. The mechanics of plot overwhelmed me, but not before I got a hundred pages into a kula ring and tribe of hallucinating magicians.

Drawing a chalk square for balls and strikes on the house, I played stickball with friends—the sting of fastballs hitting the corner of the box, the yard across the street our outfield. Lindy and I baby-sat for the couple next door (and got to use their washer and dryer and watch their TV). We acquired a brindle cat with injured back legs we named Puddin'; she and Quis charged each other in the backyard (an unamused Frodo observing, from her perch atop the fence). A favorite afternoon jaunt was to take the neighbor's neglected collie in the back seat of our car to run by the Huron.

Finally I assembled enough material to put out the *Alchemy Issue* of *Io,* a fat 164-page book with a naked man and woman in a water droplet on the cover (courtesy of Nelson's window-designer). Around Kelly's piece I gathered my alchemical translations as well as sixteenth-century texts by Edward Kelly ("The Theatre of Terrestrial Astronomy") and Janus Lacinius ("A Form and Method of Perfecting Base Metals"), transcripts of the UFO lectures we heard in Detroit, Hopi mythology from Government field reports, and Earth, Fire, and Chain poems by Ted Enslin, a lay physician in Maine and friend of Kelly's. Our bookstore customers doubled and tripled their orders.

Meanwhile the '60s, as they were later iconicized, hit their florescence: anti-war rallies, dope, psychedelic imagery. These seemed, curiously, to have everything and nothing to do with us. After all, Kelly's salon and our wedding preceded and overshadowed this carnival even as constellations of the night sky dwarfed the traveling amusement park I filmed on the outskirts of town.

Local artists and astrologers admired *Io,* so we attended their gatherings, but the realm of "free love" and cosmic vibrations—its dark dens, naked bodies, paisley hangings, incense, and flirtatious innocence—seemed decadent to us, even kinky. Holding ourselves aloof and innocent, we shied from invitation.

SDS initiation among our peers was full of macho posturing and counting coups. One weekend that fall, Mitchell and Joanna came through town with a tough-talking politico named Les—her new boyfriend (it turned out), an upper-echelon SDS guy. They were headed for Detroit to join an underground explosives factory. Les was talking tough and told us "we'd better start swimming or we'd sink like a stone."

Mitchell said nothing. We tried to get him alone, but he pushed Lindy away, saying, "Don't even start. I've got no business with you guys anymore."

Les was there only to use our phone. While he made touch with cronies, Joanna at his side, I asked Mitchell how he could let this guy take his girl and his life, why he wanted to blow things up.

"The people," he stated deadpan, "always come first." Ten minutes later, the local cell arrived. In boots, these Vietcong fraternity jocks tramped down our stairs and pounded until Lindy opened. They stood at the door, affecting aloofness and impatience. Without introducing themselves, they grabbed Mitchell by the back of his sweater and dragged him up the stairs. Les and Joanna were laughing. I stood on the street watching their indecorous departure.

My sadness was like staring through the zodiac at the occlusion of an epoch. The interlude with the tree alphabet was over. Music and Art was over. "Teenager in Love" was over. That was the last I ever saw of Mitchell.

Robin

One evening outside Lindy's office I found a wandering white cat with a raccoon tail. It was still sitting on her desk beside me when she returned. We debated, then took it home and, when no one claimed it, added it to our family (calling her White Kitty). Four daffies now dashed in and out of our bedroom window. Though we didn't quite understand it, we seemed fated to nurture this zany crew. Three gave birth on the same day (all except Frodo whom Lindy's mother had had spayed)—twelve kittens meowing, the adults so confused they were frantically stealing babies back and forth from one another's litters until we locked them in separate rooms. We kept two of the kittens, naming Puddin's charcoal gray one Spindle and White Kitty's calico Prunella.

When Gary Snyder arrived in Ypsilanti that November from Japan to read his poetry we showed up early to introduce ourselves and give him *Io*. He was an authentic elder, a character from a Kerouac novel. He spun landscapes of Asia and Kwakiutl, rivers and mountains without end that seemed lifetimes beyond as he took us (finally) "down the smoke-hole" of the kiva into Hopi chambers.

"What a fine little magazine you two have got," he declared afterwards, putting one arm around each of us. Two days later we accompanied him into Detroit to meet his buddies, the Trans-Love/White Panthers. These working-class artists made the Ann Arbor radical crowd look preppy, but because we arrived in the company of a shaman they welcomed Lindy and me and, upon learning we were local, invited us to read with them sometime.

We made it back on a Sunday in December—a rundown neighborhood, urban smells up the stairway, into a living room decorated with psychedelic posters, audience either backs against walls or lying eyes closed on throw rugs, a pot of aromatic tea on a table cluttered with mimeo broadsheets.

The men all had beards, and everyone wore beads. Our greetings were in the language of revolutionary brotherhood, bear hugs even though we hardly knew them. They were neither sympathetic nor unsympathetic, but I could tell they expected us to be raunchier. They seemed in fact so much older, as though already evolved into post-Marxian bodies (years later when their leader John Sinclair went to jail, the Beatles held a benefit concert for him).

531

Sinclair opened the proceedings that day, reading his jazz poems. Alan Van Newkirk followed with prose riffs that were intense, discursive, and weird, mixing African mythology and political diatribe. Then Sinclair gave Lindy and me a generous introduction. I rose in turn and performed my pieces on Hotevilla, Vietnamese warriors, Black Power, and sacred agriculture. They nodded in agreement and asked us to stay for dinner. When they passed around a joint later, Lindy and I both shook our heads and then sat feeling totally dumb while everyone else spaced out and chuckled. (We were in fact so out of touch that when Gary Snyder asked us if there was any grass around town I remarked, "Not in the winter.")

Gary had taken a few of my Indian essays with him, and he delivered them in person to *The San Francisco Oracle,* which published one in their rainbow-colored American Indian issue. The summer before, we had gotten only as far as Tuba City, but my re-creation of the Blue Star kachina made it all the way to the Haight. With "Richard Grossinger" headlined in psychedelic script no one could have guessed how guileless and unhip he really was. (One night soon after the edition appeared, I dreamed of Lindy and me asleep like babes at the bottom of an alchemical flask, the editor of the *Oracle* enfolding us, arms wrapped in a circle, casting a prism of soft light.)

Gary had been an anthropology student once and, after his performances starring Asian and Pueblo priests, it was clear that at Michigan the "real" stuff was missing: myth and comparative religion, philosophy of Tlingit and Australian Aborigines, plant and animal lore. The curriculum was dominated by kinship systems, theories of economic exchange, mathematical analyses of artifacts at Stone Age sites, and interbreeding of genotypes. It was as though our modern milieu alone counted, their ancient realm mattered not at all; yet it was them we were studying.

Not only was I bored; my status hung in jeopardy. I had had an unproductive research project in Arizona. I had exasperated an emeritus professor (Titiev). I had openly discussed Teilhard's concept of spiritual evolution on the Sun. And I was studying the most forbidden text in the field.

On his visit Kelly had insisted I read that book in particular—*The*

Savage Mind by Claude Lévi-Strauss, a scholar most members of my department refused to acknowledge as a "real" colleague. In ethnology we had been assigned some of his early social essays, but his later work systematizing native myths and taxonomies was considered the epitome of "diving deep into shallow waters"—hundreds of pages on native systems of classification. In *The Savage Mind* I found parrots and jaguars transmuting into stars and plants to form dense topological systems, multidimensional structures that would have delighted my friend Greg. This was the sort of advanced non-Western cosmology I had been seeking all along!

It wasn't that I was *trying* to be provocative. I had a conviction about some innermost truth and imagined that the mysteriousness of existence was obvious and everyone was feigning academic protocol. After all, wasn't that the real basis of fieldwork, the reason why people studied Indians and Africans in the first place? To learn disparate realities from other cultures ... to see the universe through other eyes not so dissimilar from our own, and yet have it become as strange as if viewed by inhabitants of another planet ... the Australian Dreaming, the Sioux war party, the Dogon realm of ancestors, the Mayan calendar.

Rappaport differed. "You may be right, Richard, and you may be wrong, but you're talking religion, not science. And you know what you're going to accomplish?" he chided; "you're going to make enemies gratuitously. You're going to lose your Fellowship. You're going to let some idiot take his revenge by keeping you from getting your degree. What you're going to accomplish is making my life miserable."

During all the time at Michigan I never really got the point. It seemed that everyone was involved only in the most perversely limited interpretations, students as well as faculty. I could learn the assignments and do well on exams, but I couldn't authentically mimic their opinions and styles. Plus there was an overall tactless competition over grades, grants, and fieldwork sites. (It was bad enough that, unless one got to the reserve room quickly, key articles might be razored out of books—not so someone could study them at home but so that no one else would.)

I signed up for Rappaport's ecology seminar and arranged my Hopi research into a paper on "The Role of Religion in Sublimating the Calendrics of Farming Arid Land"). I also tried to interest my advisor in an ethnoscience reading course, but he felt I should plunge in deeper by taking an independent study in ethnobotany and, concurrently, the famous Systematic Botany graduate seminar taught by Dr. Warren Wagner. So, after trying to cram in the gist of textbooks all the way from Introductory Botany to Plant Morphology in a month, I entered a class of advanced botany students, a neophyte again among insiders.

All that winter I dissected cones and stamens and drew their parts in my lab manual—spike mosses, horsetails, the primitive magnolia, and the occult subspirals of the periwinkle. These plants were the real matter of the universe: the sword, the wand, the club. Petals and sepals, cymes and umbels, in numbers and combinations of numbers represented the oldest mute codifications on our planet.

As our class hiked the Washtenaw countryside, spring spilled out the distinct characters of legend. They appeared as tiny florets bursting beside a log, young blossoms among last year's dried fruits, marigolds and skunk cabbages in mud, fields exploding with violets and mints. Nature, I realized, had mostly been subjective and nostalgic for me; black-eyed susans and rose bushes were remnants of Proust. Now I was handling objective creation.

Alchemy led me to the Doctrine of Signatures—a Renaissance principle of occult affinities between macrocosm and microcosm, between stars and plants, also between resemblances and virtues. To fulfill my graduate language requirement I began reading Michel Foucault's work on signatures, *Les Mots et Les Choses,* which joined the meanings of the bestiaries, herbals, palmistries, and physiognomies of olden Europe to the totemic orders of plants and animals among the Arapaho, Xhosa, and Aranda. My Table of Contents of an emerging *Io/5* mixed a friend's translations of Foucault with work from Kelly, Stein, Enslin, Brakhage, and other contemporaries, plus a gaggle of such "library" authors as Timotheus of Gaza, Oswald Croll, C. W. Leadbetter, Albertus Magnus, Ibn Qutayba, and Henry Cornelius Agrippa. Its topics were signatures, sigils, signs, and talismans—occult chemistry, astrological botany, and herbal medicines.

Enslin also introduced me to the signature-like Doctrine of Similars and the homeopathic medical system based on it. Accounts of plant and mineral remedies taking on the personalities of patients and their diseases astonished and charmed me. Doctors had always seemed sinister and authoritarian, their teachings nihilistic and disenfran-chising, their drugs the potions of an alien science. But homeopaths did no surgery and sought no dread diseases. Their only diagnosis was to find the signature of the life force in the patient (much as Freud had found the dream symbol). Their sole treatment was to bolster one's inherent healing capacity through the introduction of a similar-acting subtilized substance, a *doppelgänger* running along a parallel track.

Ignatia, Silica, and Lycopodium were simultaneously "drugs" and spirits. They bore no material, so could be neither pharmaceuticals nor toxins (they left only their quantum footprints in water—nary a molecule—and water somehow retained the memory of their having been there and transmitted its similar to the body). They were char-acters from literature, benign wizards capable of by-passing ordinary Newtonian law and sparking a vital force in sick people. They inhab-ited the world of supernatural allies that Don Juan the shaman had shown to Carlos Castaneda in the new anthropological best-seller that typified the type of fieldwork they *didn't* want us doing.

One afternoon I sat on the carport roof reading P. D. Ouspensky's short novel *The Strange Life of Ivan Osokin*. In 1902 in Moscow, after leaving his wayward girlfriend Zinaida at a railroad station, Ivan real-ized he had reached an impasse. Nothing in his life was right or would ever be right again. It was a dull, profound depression. He considered simply ending his existence then but chose instead to go to a magi-cian. The magus sat by the fire, a black Siberian cat on the back of his chair, an hourglass on the small ivory table beside Ivan:

" 'If only I had known what I should come to,' Ivan says. 'But I believed so much in myself, believed in my own strength. I wanted to go my own way. I was afraid of nothing. I threw away everything that people value and I never looked back. But now I would give half my life to go back and become like other people. . . . I can't fight any more. I've gotten myself into a sort of bog. I can't make a single movement.' "

Upon request—though against his own better judgment—the magi-cian makes it possible for Ivan to return to a chosen point in child-hood, to live his life over from there. With the knowledge of what is to happen Ivan gets a second chance to avoid the *cul de sac*. He reappears in his grade-school dorm full of resolve. Memory, however, has tricked him: events which he had imagined as easily redeemable were actually more complicated, their enactment deep-seated in ways he had forgotten. Initially he finds himself doing the same things for different reasons; eventually even his motivations are the same and it becomes uncertain to him if this is his singular life or if he faintly remembers living it once before. He finds himself back at the magician's, making the same request (Chapter XXVI is identical to Chapter I)—if only he could have it over again he would do better so much better the next time:

"The old man smiles and nods. 'I can carry out your wish,' he says, 'but it will not be of any use; it will not make things any better for you.'

"Osokin throws himself into an armchair and holds his head in his hands.

" 'Tell me,' he says, 'is it true that I have already been here with you before?'

" 'It is true,' says the magician.

" 'And I asked you the same thing?'

" 'You did.'

" 'And shall I come again?' "

Yes, in essence, the magician tells him. Or, at least, you can do no better than that. If the best of circumstances befall you, you will come again to my door, again and again, universe after universe ... until you realize that it will work out exactly the same every time. " 'In that there can be no difference and no change.'

" 'But this is simply turning round on a wheel!' says Osokin. 'It is a trap!'

"The old man smiles.

" 'My dear friend,' he says, 'this trap is called life.... You ask me what you are to do. I answer: *live*. It is your only chance....

" ' ... if you still want to go back and begin again I will send you back even to the day of your birth, if you like, but I warn you that you will come here again—if you can.' "

This tale resonated with my own unclaimed journey. It showed me myself in cosmic time. How did I awake from childhood to find Lindy an instant before it was too late? How could any of this be arbitrary?

(Even Kelly and Button discussed not only past lives together but a day in a restaurant on the Lower East Side when he as a teenager had glimpsed her briefly as a precocious child.)

The next evening Lindy and I went to see Dustin Hoffman, a campmate of hers from Perry-Mansfield, star as Benjamin in a new movie called *The Graduate*. It was a totally American melodrama, riddled with exaggerated humor and slapstick; yet I saw another film too, a life-and-death quest to break out of the trap of materialistic culture. In the morning I hauled my typewriter up to the carport roof and wrote past lunch, weaving the two plots together.

I portrayed *The Graduate* as an occult document. I interpreted Mrs. Robinson, Benjamin's seductress, as a tool of the Devil, luring him to trade his soul (and ultimate soul-mate) in advance for a tawdry affair. I gave her Faulkner's great line from *The Wild Palms:* "... between grief and nothing I will take grief." I cited Miss Havisham in *Great Expectations,* Lord Byron and the neo-Platonics, syntagmatic language chains, and the word that can bring back the dead that Carl Dreyer spoke at the end of his film *Ordet.* I compared Benjamin's "astrological binge" to the sprees of Kenneth Anger's motorcyclists and Christopher Marlowe's *Tamburlaine the Great,* also to the mayhem of the characters in another contemporary film, *Bonnie and Clyde.* I mailed my review to Clayton Eshleman, the editor of a well-regarded literary magazine named *Caterpillar.* He said that he would publish the whole thirty pages.

The mere act of stopping birth-control pills brought its own metamorphosis. All Lindy's life, love-making had had one goal—not to get pregnant. Now suddenly we were full-fledged lovers—a man and a woman.

For months, nothing changed. Each time her period came, she informed me in the same half-embarrassed tone. We began to doubt ourselves: maybe the countless x-rays shot through her as a child had damaged her ova (her parents had put her in a research program to get free medical care); or maybe my father, the product of cousins marrying, had passed on sterility. Then, after three months, the seed was planted.

At this inopportune time Rappaport decided I needed a field area and, because of my twin involvements in religion and botany, he suggested the Cuna Indians of Panama. A woman on the faculty of Northwestern University was already doing research among a Cuna tribe, so we were dispatched for an interview with her.

We drove to her apartment in Chicago one Friday and after dinner looked at her slides—informants posing, community dancing, costume-making, boats being built. Listening to her talk as though my continuation of her work were a *fait accompli* I felt mainly a desire to vanish. How could I repeat the Hopi sham? What about six cats and a baby? What about the improving Mets next season?

Crossing through Indiana into Michigan the next day, we decided to say no. Our life was still our own.

Back in Ann Arbor—a heavier period than normal—Lindy lost whatever was there.

> "An old man is pouring blood out of a urinal, together with a winged child, into another urinal, which stands on straw and contains the Moon lying on her back. Near the Sun a jug is pouring white rays, or drops, into a urinal. On the hill stands a Phoenix, biting its breast, out of which drops blood, the same being drunk by its young. Beneath the rock a husbandman is scattering seed in his field."

It was a familiar premonition. How could "Richard" really make a child? He was a dream man trapped in a coin game, inventing Palaeolithic planets, paying homage to a decanter four centuries old. He lived in his mind aloof from the awkward bearded figure who attended his classes and argued occult visions with real anthropologists; his sexuality was an aura of fantasies sublimated into Lindy.

It was only an alchemical wedding. It wasn't flesh and blood, or as real as the SDS couples in their matching military jackets.

But in September Lindy missed another period, and gradually her rounding belly became a fact of our life. Embracing her in bed—the substance of our cells woven together—I felt a new sensuousness. It might be only a dream, but it was a dream with a very real egg. It didn't matter that I hadn't reached this point yet in my mind or didn't believe I carried a live seed. As she lay on the floor in natural childbirth class, rocking her pelvis, I timed her breaths. Among the couples in that room I was a mere husband at last.

Then I got a notice from my draft board in New York City, summoning me to Fort Wayne for a physical. I knew it was coming (graduate deferments had ended), but it was still a wraith. Hands shaking, I tossed it on the kitchen table. For months I had fantasized simply showing a letter from a psychiatrist and being excused. Now that the skull-and-crossbones had arrived, I remembered how other graduate students—even with notes of major physical disabilities—had been required to go by Army bus and been kept there overnight and hazed.

The centurions were closing in, and they were as old as my life and had as much claim to it as I did. I had been living an ostrich's mirage.

I wrote Dr. Friend. He responded on medical stationery saying that I had been in treatment with him and Doctor Fabian for eleven years for "a paranoid character disorder" and "incipient schizophrenia." It was all I could have asked for, a pair of powerful, concrete names— just when I needed them most but (in another sense) just when I wanted them least. They might also disqualify me from fieldwork, marriage, even fatherhood. But I wasn't choosy; I wanted to survive. On the phone to the Selective Service, Lindy spoke with authority and composure, not only getting me out of the bus trip but gaining the right to accompany me to the physical. (One part of me certainly knew why "we" had married her.)

When the appointed day came we left the house near dawn and exited I-94 near Detroit. Fort Wayne was a bunch of institutional buildings—soldiers at the gate to look up my name and present me with documents. I was sent to a line that fed down a hallway into assembly rooms. There we were handed IQ tests. My entire age group in America was in attendance, my years of school and experimental writing, my long hair and wife notwithstanding. I thought, 'They will finally nail us to the common denominator and kill us all.'

After two hours of word riddles, reading comprehension, geometric objects to assemble and disassemble, and simple arithmetic I fled (without permission) to search for Lindy. As long as no one stopped me, I kept moving. I saw what my serial number was headed for— shirtless lines stretched down hallways around corners, all the way out into courtyards, barely moving. Lindy had noted that too and was waiting just beyond them.

"What do you think this is," shouted a commanding officer from around the corner, "a peep show, lady!"

Scanning my doctor's papers, he was exasperated enough to march me all the way down the line, corridor to corridor passing thousands of potential draftees. It was an escort through hell. I couldn't believe I was accomplishing this, that I was getting away with a disruption of martial process.

I expected to find someone enlightened at the end of our journey, but the psychiatrist was just another hassled military man behind a desk. He read my note only because it was handed to him. He growled impatiently. I felt certain I was about to be tossed onto the lines. But he looked up like God, flipped the letter and my papers back across the desk, and snapped, "We don't even want you!"

It was hard to keep from breaking into a smile, no matter what cosmic debt I was compounding. I acted contrite while he completed and signed my papers. Then we roared back through the gate into the Michigan day.

My review of *The Graduate* appeared and, soon afterwards, I got a letter from John Martin, the head of Black Sparrow Press. He wanted to publish an entire book of my work. I had finally made it back to where I left Catherine Carver, on my own terms.

Then the man himself wrote. Charles Olson had been a magical figure to me so long he seemed to dwell on Olympus—his scrawl on an irregular scrap of paper seemed a Minoan fragment that should instantly be in the antiquities locked case. He acknowledged an earlier poem of mine in *Caterpillar* (about a shipwreck in the Bay of Fundy); then he praised *Io* and inquired about the next issue topic.

We began a correspondence on migration routes, ancient calendars, crystal and plant morphologies. These were eventually to form the basis of an *Ethnoastronomy Issue*. Olson broadcast the word so widely that we soon received pieces from many of his associates: Edward Dorn ("This is the way I hear the Momentum"), Robert Duncan (a section of *The H. D. Book* on Chaldeans, Mayans, Assyrians, Persians, and Ezra Pound), Charles Doria ("Introduction to The Phoenician

History" and a translation of Sanchuniathon), and Nancy Blecker (on Vikings, Shoshoneans, and Druids). My Amherst friend Greg sent notes on topology from exile in Canada, and Harvey Bialy, now a graduate student of molecular biology at Berkeley, offered an essay on "The Molecular Basis of Change, DNA & the I Ching." Kelly's contributions were entitled "Daidalos was the father of our interplanetary confusions" and "The princes in their masks come carrying wheat." In the library I found Ralph N. Buckstaff's "Stars and Constellations of a Pawnee Star Map" and Alice Fletcher's "Pawnee Star Lore." Then by mail I interviewed Charles Hapgood, a New Hampshire cartographer who had discovered ancient maps of all the continents, including Antarctica, redrawn during the Renaissance, but perhaps originating from an unknown people as long ago as the Pleistocene.

With one more term of graduate work I took courses in material I had missed for not being an undergraduate major, notably kinship terminology and social structure. Meanwhile, I tried to construct an alternate project to the Cuna. Rappaport was no longer in town: he had left for a year's sabbatical in Hawaii, and I inherited the new statistical anthropologist, Joe Josephson, as an advisor. Although on the surface a friendly rotund man with spectacles, he was in fact quite pugnacious. He considered himself one of the premier activists in the country, yet my cavalier attitude toward academic initiation rites irritated him.

To prepare for a North American regional specialty I took an independent study with him in which I tried to cram years of ethnographic coursework into months, from pre-Iroquoisian bands, Basketmakers, and Southern-cult temples to Osage, Choctaw, and Eskimo social systems.

I also began to organize my study of homeopathy in hopes of writing an ethnomedicine thesis. I spent afternoons taking notes from rare volumes in the University library (Michigan had been one of the final schools to retain a homeopathic program). I loved these forays into the dusty stacks of vitalistic science. Here was a real medicine operating on a psychic and energetic level. Here was a noninvasive remedy that could go back to my beginnings and heal Nanny, heal the blue lights in my lungs (no matter whether they existed or not), heal the vigilance in my heart. Here was proof of a habitable world. These doctors ridiculed all Hitzig's prognostications. They were defiant, feculent, immune.

Finally I submitted a grant application for "Ethnography in Maine" with the specific goal of studying the last homeopathic physicians still in practice, colleagues of Enslin.

Joe signed my paperwork with avowed misgivings about not only my choice of topic but my viability as a graduate student. He believed that I was a poor representative of his department and that *Io* was giving Michigan a soft, hippie reputation. Being a well-known supporter of Indian rights he had a copy of my issue of *The San Francisco Oracle* in his office. I thought it best not to draw his attention to my own contribution (unnoticed probably because of the gaudy calligraphy embellishing authors' names), but when he showed me his souvenir one afternoon, I couldn't resist turning to my page and handing it back to him. His vain grin turned into an astonished scowl. At the time, he recovered to compliment me on my publication, but our antagonism would erupt during a different, seemingly even more innocent exchange.

In Ann Arbor I had adopted the football Jets as the one New York team televised there. I had never been a football fan before, but over two seasons I had developed a rabid loyalty to the broken-field runs of Emerson Boozer and over-the-shoulder grabs of Don Maynard— in fact, the whole renegade AFL. In 1969, when these guys somewhat flukily made it to the third Super Bowl against the invincible Colts, no AFL team had yet beaten an NFL opponent. I fantasized Don Maynard diving for impossible catches, Matt Snell breaking the tackles of the Cyclopses from Baltimore. This was more than a game; it was one civilization against another, like the Irish discovering America before the Vikings, bearing game relics of a different texture and shape.

When Joe told me that it was *"absolutely impossible"* for the Jets to win I countered with an enthusiasm for statistics I had never shown when ethnography was the theme.

"You apparently know as much about football as you do about anthropology," he snarled. Then he thought about his comment and decided he liked it well enough to go on: "You don't ever study facts, do you? It's all ideas to you. Somebody must have made the mistake once of letting you think you were smart."

"It's all just numbers to you," I fired back. "No Indians, no cultures, no real lives."

"And you're a great defender of Indian rights, I suppose?"

"I don't have your international reputation, but then I don't play at being radical."

"Why don't you get the fuck out of my office?"

I couldn't sleep on game night. Over and over in my mind I pictured Namath to Sauer, to Lammons, to Bake Turner, to Maynard. I got up at 4 AM in an excitement reminiscent of Christmas mornings at Grossinger's, took a hot bath and awaited the game. Kickoff had the ambiance of a spaceship approaching the Martian canals.

It seemed at first the Colts were going to run right through the young Jets, John Mackey galloping at will into their secondary. I resigned myself. But the defense began stopping them. Then Snell carried the ball. He picked up yards in chunks, shattering the Colts . . . and history. The Jets led 7–0 at the half.

I went for a walk. A fresh snow was falling. I watched my bootprints form—how clean and facile the world, the many houses and rows of streets. I walked for blocks, TVs lit everywhere. At this moment of epic importance the event itself seemed to fade before the density of creation. Then I came back and stood before the vindication.

My Fellowship in Maine was granted by the National Institutes of Mental Health. Then in March, with only three months left in Ann Arbor, we were evicted. Our surgeon-landlord, who showed up personally each Friday to collect coins from the washer and drier, had noticed the fall-off after we began baby-sitting. He had asked us if we were taking our wash elsewhere and then ordered us to use his machines. He also warned us not to plant any more parsnips in the backyard, not to sit on the carport, not to play stickball, and not to spoil the upstairs dog (the neighbor had complained). We had failed on all of these. Now he offered the apartment back on the promise of good behavior and at twice the rent.

Turning him down, we took what we could find—an old country house on the outskirts of the city. As part of the deal we were required to take care of the owner's senile mother upstairs (who not only didn't understand why we were there but didn't want us). She screamed in

German down the laundry chute in the middle of the night, crying for Adolph—the landlord—and his (dead) brother. She lay in wait for the postman and hid our mail. She spat curses at Lindy for getting herself pregnant. "And no father," she muttered.

Yet our Crestland Road dwelling was idyllic in other ways. The cats roamed a small wooded meadow. Lindy and I had our breakfasts in a glen and lay on our bed under blossoms of quince, baby flush against her skin. All my coursework was over. I studied advanced kinship terminology, political structure, and New World archaeology, and prepared for doctoral exams.

Each evening we practiced birth ceremonies on the living-room rug. We washed and shelved the purple Arabian dishware from the wedding. Time continued—dinner, classes, Mets games through static on the radio at night, walks through fields forever long ago.

> Where are the lost sparks of Adam Qadmon? Where are the particles of anti-matter that bombard our hidden planet?, the missing letters of the alphabet?, the twelve clans, who were the original Basketmakers of the Animas River, maize farmers living beneath the earth, planters of flint corn, amaranth and sunflower collectors, the pre-Cochise, Temple Mound Builders of Illinois and Ohio, leavers of arrowheads on the Moon? Where are those tribes whose temples we dig up in Wisconsin and Delaware, who controlled a continent, leaving plazas and roanokes, star-queens and sun-circles and bilobed arrows and forked eyes, baseball cards of Whitey Ford and Mickey Mantle, at Etowah and Moundville, the Southern cult of the Mississippi, and the old New York Yankees?

I took my exams over three days—a massive disgorging of two and a half years' information into bluebooks. There were no difficult questions. Each prelim was an invitation to write at length on a topic—ethnological theory, myth and religion, social structure of Indian tribes, and so on. I was so full of Lévi-Strauss's mythological transformations and Foucault's mirrors of resemblance and difference that I guilelessly ran Nuer, Yahgan, and Australian Aborigines through them. When one question asked for an explanation of the Aboriginal Dreamtime, I drew circles to illustrate phenomenological realms and their hingepoints, trying to pinpoint the precise behavioral components of living in two universes simultaneously. I left the room on the third day, brimming with confidence, and that evening Lindy and I flew to New York. Bard College had paid the fare. Kelly thought Lindy's reciting her poems to the students while eight months pregnant was a perfect lesson.

Then we drove to Maine to look for a place to live.

After getting back I went to check on the results of my exams and was summoned into the Chairman's office. He told me somberly that although some of the readers loved my exams and had given me unprecedented tens—perfect scores—Joe had made a compelling case that I didn't belong in the program, and enough others had gone along with his absolute zeroes that I ended up barely above 50%. I protested on the basis of the widely varying scores, but all I gained, finally, was a joint hearing with the Philosophy Department to which I wore a jacket and tie and at which a distinguished Professor named Bergman asked me impossible questions and then said that what I had written was gibberish to him.

"But I've never had a philosophy course," I protested.

"Exactly," Joe snapped. "So you have to please us anthropologists."

I was mortified, but in another sense the whole affair was irrelevant. Helping Lindy up the stairs and lying beside her in maple and quince light I remembered that *this* was what we had come to Ann Arbor to do. I had fieldwork money, so the coming year was covered. And Black Sparrow Press was already typesetting the "Oecological Sections" of *Solar Journal.* I imagined I could write books and teach college with my M.A.

I put anthropology out of mind, read histories of the Vikings and Polar explorers, and went back to the unfinished *Ethnoastronomy Issue,* taping a discussion with a crystallographer and interviewing a professor of radio astronomy about the Jovian bursts incited by the moon Io (he was amazed we had named a weird journal after *his* moon). I filmed my wife opening curtains to daylight, belly silhouetted, tattooed flowers and skies. We picked spring weeds, brewed jugs of dandelion wine, engaged in cat gambols—and waited.

> A wind blows thousands of seeds across our dinner table, seeds in the iced tea and potatoes, genes of multiple lineages crossing in storm. There is no light, but the spores are light, or contain it. . . . There is no light but for our two candles—and lightning in the dis-

tance. Then the flight of cells is swallowed in heavier rain. We go inside, the cats rush to the window, wet ... lie on the red rug licking their fur.

I wrote a new series of pieces beginning with Mediaeval sign magic and leading through Viking explorations and dreams of a North Atlantic Highway to "the ice itself," the North Pole:

> ... here Erik looks North North North into a mirror of continuous blinding daylight, uninhabitable as the sun is or interstellar space, in a way that makes Baffinland look like paradise, for Baffinland is within the circle of the lands. Here he floats among the peaks of sunken mountains, the fragments of olden worlds, the glitter so bright he cannot see, where all languages and landscapes mix in the polar scramble of atmosphere and solar wind, closer to Thor than he has ever been ... ; he sails out of Disco Bay, calling this place Snaefells (Ice Fields), rounds Cape Desolation, and returns to the quiet waters of the Julianehaab fjords.

On the evening of June 18th her water broke. We had practiced this so many times we moved with numb mechanical precision, timing contractions. I sat in the hospital in an empty room waiting for her to be prepped. Police cars sped past en route to student protests, their lights distorted in wrinkled glass.

> The answer to the question—who were those who came before us?—is that we are those who came before us, the ones, ourselves, the same. I have come again, like Osokin, in my twenty-fifth year, to the body of light. ...

Lindy lay on the mattress, an eternal moment disguised by the doctor with his mirror, nurses in bureaucratic garb.

I reenacted our rituals, coaching her movements, helping her slow down her breathing, bringing crushed ice for her to suck.

But there was a distance between us. Who was this girl I married in her Spanish gown?

It was too advanced for either of us, plus she was in pain. The hours streamed past midnight.

She cried out. I reminded her to pant and blow. I took her palm and talked a blue streak. She told me just to hold her.

Near dawn the doctor reached deeper and more deliberately; then, before I could comprehend it, he bore a giant head in his hands.

He comes into the room, wriggling and wet, gleaming with blood. He glimpses us all, smiles grandly, then sputters and cries. His name is Robin, as in Christopher Robin, and Robin Red Breast, Cock Robin . . . a young magus, crashing this sphere as the sign itself, 19 June 1969, 6:19 . . . He glows, is alive . . . magic inseparable from body, animal inseparable from man, fish and lizard, red tarot. . . .a sun, on high, towering over us . . . the fat wrinkled testicles of a male. Doctor, nurses, parents, all these tiny beings, work to bring a giant into the world.

He arrives in a craft of his own making, handicraft of the upper spheres, not the metallurgy down here. Master of an alien science he has come to learn our customs. His power is zero, Fool, full. He has all of time on his side; it is we who are measured and named.

He enters the delivery room with a majesty and dignity that stuns us, that we reserve for those of greatest learning. Though we fear for him, how could he possibly have fear for himself? (Mitchell said that if we wouldn't have conceived children, they wouldn't have to come here to suffer, to be slaughtered in a nuclear war. We have no such power, to make something out of nothing. If for some reason it did not come here for its experience, it would have had to go elsewhere, to suffer and learn.)

Aged husk falls away from fruit, red creature dripping of the sea it has lived in. Robin, a Gemini, descends through the spheres, wrapped in robes.

I called my father from a booth downstairs. He came on the first flight— the only time I ever knew him to leave the Hotel unplanned. I met him at the airport, and we went straight to the hospital, arriving ten minutes past closing. He couldn't convince them to change their rules.

"Let's get some food," he proposed. We stopped at the Kroeger and picked out dinner. As I began to cut stringbeans, he interrupted, insisting on his prerogative as a onetime chef in the Army. He showed me how to trim the meat, what temperature to preheat the oven, how to tell with a fork when the noodles were done.

The birth of my son had seemingly reconnected us, bypassing my beard, my politics, and my lack of interest in his business. We shared one other thing: after dinner he asked if there was a way to get the Mets on the radio. I nodded. We dialed them on the Phillies clear channel. It was 1969, their best season ever, but on that evening Nolan Ryan failed to hold a five-run lead. We shut it off after the last out, were silent for a while; then he began a line of thought.

He started with an old ritual of pretending I had asked him about his courtship of my mother, "When did you know you had made a mistake?"

"The first night," he answered himself. He loved to savor that he had stuck it out six years even after this discovery. "Your mother was a beautiful woman," he continued, "but you ask Bob sometime what sort of wife she is."

When he inquired what religion Robin would be, I responded with vague notions about teaching him spiritual and moral values rather than anything Jewish or Episcopalian. "That's philosophy, not religion!" he complained. So I argued, from my anthropology, that *his* religion was really ethnic chauvinism. I got out Emile Durkheim's classic on religious life and read him the passage about group soul. "Your anthropology's only useful when I ask you for help in crossword puzzles," he teased. But the Durkheim inspired him to ask if I believed in life after death.

I said I did. "I think we get reborn, but it's something deeper, not the personality that returns."

"What does that mean?"

"Perhaps we don't remember earlier lives; only their imprint remains on us."

"But that's like not getting reborn at all," he objected. "What good would it be if I couldn't remember Babe Ruth, or find out what happened to you, or what Robin became?"

I was embarked on a long, probably pretentious response when I realized he was snoring in his chair.

That single exchange from the heart marked our meeting as men.

Back home I washed this new thing, his tiny soft body in a plastic tub, and stood over his crib filming him, his hands (as he slept) making little arcs over his face. (On TV, men walked on an igneous, prearchaeological Moon.) I cradled my son in his rubber pants like balsam apples (so we called him Waddo). He slept beside us—sputtering tears, sudden burps and bowel movements, smiling on Lindy's dripping breasts. Soon he remade daily life into tiny shirts, jars of baby food, and deliveries from the diaper service.

My father presented us with a Pontiac station wagon we picked up at the factory. We hired a carpenter to build crates for the cats, put our belongings into a U-Haul, and set out onto I-94 amidst mournful meows.

As we drove through New York in August the Mets caught and passed the Cubs in their great closing run of 1969.

On our earlier trip East a folklorist at the University in Orono told us that if *he* had a free year he'd spend it by the ocean. And he directed us to Mount Desert Island.

From outside Bangor we followed the highway straight to the coast, crossed a bridge over the sound, then took a room at an old inn in Bar Harbor.

In the sun-bright morning we checked on an ad and were shown a cottage on the road between Bar and Bass Harbors. At one time it was the servant quarters for an estate situated on Green Island just offshore. The woman who presently owned the island wanted someone there for the winter, so rent was negligible. Beyond the meager formality of the fenced yard was pure wilderness, no houses for miles on either side.

Now, after years of suburban life, we were by ourselves. We lay in the grass and crawled with our baby through clubmoss and weeds, up to lichen-covered boulders on which he rested his hands. He smelled so pink and new, his warm cheeks next to mine, his bundle on Lindy's shoulders.

I played game after game of solitaire Roofball, diving after impossible bounces of the Spaldeen into pine needles and autumn leaves, matching all-time Met and Yankee teams against each other. At night I followed the last days of the pennant race on the radio while reading histories of colonial Maine and the Maritime Provinces. The cats raced in and out of the forest, carrying occasional moles.

Day after day, we explored boat harbors and village squares, wandered along craggy beaches. The ocean was an immense horizon, populated by sails and motorboats and dotted with the mysterious vistas of islands. At Green Island Landing we pulled clams out of the mud with our bare hands and then steamed them and dipped them in their own water and butter for dinner.

I stood in a cove among abandoned sheds and remains of sawhorses, staring out at patterns of lobster buoys and primitive fishing weirs. So hungry was I for the brine and chlorophyl I scooped strands of icy seaweed out of waves and held them dripping over my face and hair.

3

MAINE

From our cottage it was a short hike through forest to the shoreline. The sea, with its gulls and rocky vistas, was a cut of larger cosmology—backward to Phoenicians and Vikings, forward to Aquarius. Not only did the key to poetics lie here (light cracking off waves, the wind in my beard) but my own uncertain manhood.

"Send me any flashes from Somesville," the voice of Charles Olson on the phone, welcoming us to the Atlantic.

To hell with academics! I was being enlisted by the gods.

> The Cranberries hang in medullan medulloid medullific space, just as sun in trees, stone in lower water, or Photo Number 14 of the Planet Mars. . . .
>
> The flashing from Somesville is unenumerated, innumerable, *sine nombres,* is the clear historic present past of our condition—the glaciers moving as the sun in its place also moves, sashweight to ice (the axis shifting every 25,765 years . . .).
>
> With child in backpack we head through the woods, along the gulley, the cats coming to what they have never seen . . . sniff the salty mussel beds, tiptoe on rocks, and stare into absolute space. . . .
>
> We see islands in time, in utter sunlight, in humpback splendor, in broken field dashes. Everywhere we look there are more than three dimensions, for tongues of land go out into ocean, and ocean penetrates lacunae, lagoons of shore. . . .

The debacle of prelims had changed the terms of fieldwork. When Rappaport returned from Hawaii, he pointed out that, since any folk-medicine project would have to be read by Joe (assuming I were readmitted), I should switch to something ecological so he himself could head my committee.

The next week I visited the Southwest Harbor green where retired fishermen gathered. While Lindy explored shops I approached the men commandeering park benches. An ocean breeze blew, but the sun was warm. Gulls dipped and squawked overhead. One of the men could have been the convict from *Great Expectations* or Charles Olson himself, a giant with tufts of white hair under a cap, pipe at a jaunty angle, his newspaper folded into a tiny square. Pigeons pecked crumbled bread at his feet. He was reading about the Mets' game, so I took my chances. He introduced himself as "Enoch Stanley, retired sea captain." He joked that the "Maine Mets" were his team. Since he was willing to answer my questions, I transcribed his account of venerable runs for cod and hake, the famous crews, the subsequent demise of fisheries into motorboat runs.

"I bought from vessels on Great Cranberry for my uncle's place, Stanley Fish, in Manset. Thirty-two cents a pound for cod then," he added, blowing tobacco into frosty air. "Now you can get six cents for it."

> Robin. This morning. Raised himself up on his arms for the first time. In his crib. And for the first time looked out the window at the sun and wind in the trees, the blue sky in which he was asleep. the green earth. he took a long look, a serious look. like an instant deep image for later endless realms of nostalgia. Robin all his life at the window looking out into the sun at an older age.

In the Bar Harbor newspaper I read about a priest, Jim Gower, who was starting an experimental college. When I phoned him to hear about it he invited us to dinner at the parish house in Northeast Harbor. There we sat in the elegant cloister of a backyard garden, exchanging interdisciplinary gossip. Eventually he told me two of his parishioners were lobsterfishermen; in fact, Wendell Seavey's family had been trawling in the New World "since barely after Columbus." This was a great lead. First thing the next morning I drove through Bass Harbor to the head of the town of Bernard.

Gulls dominated the wharf, landing on roofs, boats, each other, clustering and fighting. Their calls rang out amidst static from radiophones. A swill of rotting brine salted the breeze. I poked my head into the shed and asked for Mr. Seavey.

"You should know better"—someone replied; "he's out haulin'." So I climbed a hill and stood alongside stacks of knitted traps. Dozens of small boats crisscrossed the harbor, carrying arsenals of these artifacts. This was no tourist village.

Wendell turned out to be a square-jawed pugilist with intense, twinkling eyes and fancy peaked cap, a bit older than me. He heard out his querist without a word, then responded slowly, as though presiding over court. He agreed to answer my questions only if I would answer his too, so we made an appointment at his house in Southwest Harbor the next evening.

At the appointed hour Lindy and I pulled up the driveway of a Colonial house and picked our way through logs and old tires into a mêlée of children, clown music, an overfriendly giant dog. A chubby Sue Seavey, preparing five dishes at once, waved hello from around a corner, and Wendell appeared, thumbs in suspenders: "Sue and I thought we'd serve you the famous tongues and cheeks of cod as an introduction to our way of eating."

When Wendell said, "Shoot," I asked three questions for every one of his and got the general intro on territory, gear, trap wars and finding directions at sea, with additional commentary about the greed of the yachting crowd and the decadence of lobster eating. Meanwhile, I told him about anthropology wars at Michigan and the tourist scene at Grossinger's. By then we were seated at the table, and Sue was tying bibs on her older children. Even Lindy, who was not a fish eater, found the breaded chunks delicate and yummy.

"Since I'm mostly out to sea," Wendell concluded over apple pie, "I imagine you'll be spending your time at the wharf, so I want to introduce you to Jasper Merchant and the men. Maybe they'll talk to you, most likely not. But they'll be more prone to if I give the say-so."

Jasper was the sullen, bespectacled proprietor to whom Wendell sold his catch each day. During those first weeks I got up early, had breakfast, then drove the eight or so miles along the ocean to Bernard and spent my mornings in the shed, which was a kind of fisherman's lounge. For lunch I'd buy hake or a couple of lobsters (at cost) and bring them home to share with Lindy. Then I returned in the afternoon and continued writing down dialogue and events at either Jasper's or nearby wharves.

As short afternoons sank into quick dusk behind the mountains, the men began to appear, one by one, lights puttering across the harbor. Following Jasper down to his floating dock with my pad I tried to place myself strategically, then unobtrusively note the men's catch and how they were paid. Although such blatant intrusion was hardly popular (Jasper lamented inheriting me almost as much as Yaqui shaman Don Juan lamented Carlos), my patron's stature paved the way. Many were willing to be interviewed, though others stormed by as if I didn't exist.

Lodged in their favorite chairs the older non-seagoers at first tried to stare me out, but I hung tough, being charming and ingenuous, until they reluctantly restored conversation. During times Jasper wasn't handling boats or bitching I kept up such a blatantly artless interrogation of him that he gradually took to answering my questions as a means of making jokes at my expense. In fact on my first day he advanced the idea that I was an IRS agent checking how much cash the fishermen were really taking in.

"But do I look like a Government agent?" I asked.

"You're just the way they'd disguise one a' them," a fisherman in the corner snarled.

I tried to explain my situation. A "thesis" didn't mean anything to them, and the word "anthropology" sounded like something Gladstone Gander might have made up. Only the plea that I was writing a paper for school had credibility.

"I can't believe a school'd send someone so ignorant down here to study fishermen."

"But you're going to *teach* me," I proposed.

I was quite candid about my preparation for an abandoned folk-medicine study. Their knee-jerk response was to blame the Government, somehow, for my misassignment.

One of the first things I had to figure out was why some of Jasper's men sold to him every day while others sometimes used wharves across the harbor.

"Does Marlon always sell here?"

"Far as I know he does," Jasper said. "But he can go anywhere he pleases, and I'm sure he'll tell you that if you ask him."

"What about the men who don't own their own boats?"

"I should hope they would sell here."

"If they don't?"

"If they don't!" he said, raising his voice so he had the largest possible audience. "Well, I'd think they'd find themselves walking on water!"

Still, it was a lot easier than the cargo cult at Hotevilla.

After studying the basics for three weeks I was ready to expand my bailiwick. First we drove to equivalent wharves in Bar Harbor, Northeast Harbor, and Deer Isle. While I conducted interviews Lindy sometimes joined and sometimes explored the town. Each new establishment we invaded with trepidation, but the stacks of different-colored buoys and lobster-traps became welcoming insignia for me, even as alchemical drawings and Hopi shields had been in the Michigan library. These talismans identified the text I was inventing, its growing authority inside me. I would march into surly and indifferent groups and enthusiastically begin asking questions about trap quantity, territory, and price. Lindy and baby were my allies. Their presence made everything normal and gave an escape valve of polite conversation (although Vance Gove made a point of obliquely answering a question by telling me *his* wife was home "where she belongs!").

Small outer islands were accessible only by craft. Deposited by a ferry or mailboat, we would troop down antique roads, every buoy-covered shed and stained glass window leaving its glyph in my mind—as Swans Island, 1969:

> ... a giant series of fields up to shoreline forest, several rows of apple trees bare in autumn, and four old buildings, held back up by fresh birch bark, and stuffings of rags, newspapers, burlap and plastic. Wesley Spurgeon stands in front of the barn, working over an old car.... He beckons us to follow him. We peek: a dozen kittens run in and out, winding through legs of an old stove and into the corner among cans and sacks....

Anthropology provided the excuse, but collecting this data was more than an exercise; no one in my various lineages, anthropological or poetic, had been here to collect such freemasonry yet. I was making my own Lévi-Straussian *bricolage*.

The Mets' run carried them to the pennant. I listened to their games at night, each one a classic. Then, with mythic plays that have become baseball icons in the years since, Wayne Garrett, Tommy Agee, Nolan Ryan, Cleon Jones, Al Weis, and crew disposed of the imposing Orioles in the World Series. The great elder, Casey Stengel (representing also Enoch Stanley and Charles Olson), spoke a deeper, aeonic truth when he said: "The Mets have come on slow but fast." It was true; we all had.

The old novelists and corporate academics were dying. A generation of Woodstock and Haight-Ashbury was being born. Tom Seaver, Wendell Seavey, George Sauer, and Ron Swoboda were not only my players but my contemporaries.

The Yankees of my childhood may have been my archetypal team, but I would never root for them again. The Mets were the Cranberry Island Mets, the rebels of Phi Psi, Welton with his TV upside-down. They were a kid driving a Mustang to the edge of the Third Mesa, Emma's team, the moons of the Jovian planets. They were Neil Diamond singing, *"The boy's no good . . . ,"* and all the minor leaguers of my Chipinaw armory game, redeemed at last.

The next day I got a surprise call from my one-time introductory psychology professor, now a dean at Hampshire, an experimental college in Amherst that was planning to begin classes the following fall. I had heard of the school and even fantasized teaching there, so his invitation to be interviewed was like telepathy fulfilled.

Two weeks later we left mid-morning and by dinner reached the site of the unfinished campus. They put us up in the fancy Lord Jeff Inn, and the next morning three well-dressed deans joined us on a veranda for muffins and coffee. They wanted to hear my philosophy, so I was willingly evocative with fresh courses—Jungian alchemy and Heisenberg's philosophy of physics, Olson's North Atlantic and the colonization of New England and the Maritimes, the whale in literature and ethnography. We adjourned to a tour of their construction zone where I was introduced to an assortment of faculty on the run. At lunch I continued my rap with astrophysics and language structure, the poetics of space-time, ecological anthropology, and *Io* as campus journal. By dinner they were brainstorming how to develop my own curriculum called Earth Mythology. "To hell with liberalism," exulted Dean Smith. "Let's shoot for the noosphere."

On the boat back to Mount Desert from Little Cranberry it begins to rain, a soft drizzle off the sea. Robin enjoys the mist on his face—rocking on the deck, gnawing his rubber ring. Two women make their sentiments heard: "Not fit to be parents. Someone should take that baby away from them."

Later that afternoon, back home, he awakes in his crib from a long nap, and I am so delighted to hear his whimpering I run into his room whooping and shouting, "Ding dong, Rescue Squad Number Nine." He graduates to a howling tantrum.

Lindy, close behind, whispers, "I think Rescue Squad Number Nine was a little boisterous."

Father Gower's second fisherman parishioner was Buddy Hooper, "as different from Wendell," the priest said, "as night is from day." For a month it was impossible to track him down. Though he fished out of Mount Desert he sold his lobsters in Stonington, a sociologically significant violation of community. He was so universally disliked that Jasper said he wouldn't buy a boatload of selects from him if he were the last fisherman at the height of tourist season.

I found Buddy pulling out of a Bass Harbor store, in a hurry. He stared me down from the cab of his pick-up, rifle mounted behind beady eyes. "Come back tomorrow. What d'ya want to know?"

"Just fishing."

"Tomorrow."

It was November 3rd, my birthday, twenty-five years ago, and a driving rain kept the boats in. A gale tore against their figments in the harbor. As I edged along the wharf my umbrella was suddenly blown inside-out, then back. My feet slid on crushed fishbait. Even the most intrepid stayed indoors, painting buoys and netting traps.

I had this gnawing, compulsive fear that I would be killed on the day I was born. Yet I flaunted the omen and tested its edge.

When I tried calling Lindy from Jasper's, there was no answer, time and again. Manson murders in my head I sped the eight miles, skidding around curves. I burst in the door to find her quietly changing Robin. It was just that she had the vacuum cleaner on and didn't hear.

I thought: 'My wife, my life. My son, my one.' I looked in wonder, 'They really exist.'

But I had made a date with Buddy and, after a bowl of soup, I got back in the car ... four o'clock at his shed out on the Duck Harbor marshlands. I parked just off the road and ran through drenching gusts to a hut at sea's edge.

He opened the door for me; I crouched through. A fierce-looking, ugly son-of-a-bitch, he shoved an immediate shot glass in my hand. I didn't drink hard liquor, but this was fieldwork; I had no choice. He barely let me test-sip before he refilled in front of my mouth. He told me it was his first day off the sea in months, as if we shared the blame.

A fire snapped in an iron basket, casting uneven light on shelves, buoys, nets, gear, pinups. The sun which I couldn't see all day anyway was setting. Wind and waves crashed into Duck Cove. This was it—as he forced the door shut. But I was too soaked and cold not to appreciate asylum.

Buddy bragged on his scallops, how they were the only ones on the island "without shit on 'em." He added up his enemies and imagined they'd be his friends tomorrow. He proclaimed, "Anyone's welcome in Buddy's shed"—breaking wood over his knee and tossing it into the stove.

"I'm a real rough guy. There aren't many like me left," rubbing his hands. "In the old days a bunch of us'd have tied you down and given you a shave and a haircut."

When I joked nervously about my reception at Jasper's, he snarled at mere mention of the wharf, cursing its fishermen and their dealer. He said he'd been told who-knows-how-many times to take his lobsters and shov'em, and had, "except," he added, "for the shovin'." Then he boasted, "When I go through Blue Hill Bay, out by the Ducks and Cranberries, I take no prisoners. I tear up other pussies' traps like hell." He was the maniac riding the atom bomb bareback at the end of *Strangelove*.

We generated a renegade rapport, as he kept filling my glass and pointing to it (and I kept drinking), so the tension burned and broke until I was laughing on my birthday, and Buddy put his arm around me and started preaching: "Is there any other way? I mean do you know any other way? It's not that I'm a hog. I give twenty dollars a month through Catholic charities to some kid down in Mexico, or New Mexico. But you can't save the world goddamnit. You can't save everything till there's nothing left for yourself. I can't take these pussy-assing fishermen here. There just ain't time."

Then he said, "If you want a name for me, call me a weirman. I'll take that. Because Buddy Hooper's the best damn weirman left."

Weirs were beautiful Mesolithic fish traps, Stonehenges at sea, so I came back with "Why is it we do whatever we do, and fuck it, Buddy Hooper, don't you agree there's just one thing in this world and there's nothing else you can do a thing with or about and nothing else that counts, and that thing's the use we make of these lives."

"Goddamnit, yes!" he says. "The best makes the top."

Slow but fast for sure.

I felt as though I were struggling against the dross, the haze and armor over my whole life, whatever had held me down, consciously, blindly, or both, to know that nothing matters because nothing can be kept from happening.

Pitch black, the wind and rain around us, our single light in Duck Cove an altar—I told Buddy my wife had cooked dinner and I had to go home now, so he poured another drink and said, "You ain't scared of your wife, are you?"

It sounded like *life* to me again, as I pried open the door and got a face full of rain.

He blurted in protest but didn't try to stop me as I burst into blackness, an enveloping roar of waves and trees. I was stumbling over buoys and traps through gullies, trying to flee the warden, and I thought, 'He could take his rifle and shoot me down.'

He stood at the door, the only manifestation—a bright rectangle against the sky. "For chrissakes turn on the headlights there, so you don't kill yourself. And come back after dinner. My house! ... with your wife and kid. You can't tell what a man is like without his wife."

I looked about.

"On the pickup, pussy!"

"What about your battery?" I yelled back solicitously.

"No damn light's gonna burn out the battery on Buddy Hooper's truck."

I reached in across the dashboard, pulled—and suddenly saw mud rolling down into the cove.

"And if it does, who says Buddy Hooper can't afford another?"

Every six weeks or so we took a break from the tundra and made the eight-hour journey to Grossinger's. For years I had been the family hippie. Now I was the father of Jennie's great-grandchild and a respectable Grossinger again. The Hotel, once larger than anything in my world, was smaller than my marriage. Yet it provided a haven. We got free jars of strained food, new stuffed animals and toys, bags of shirts and jammies, sweaters and bib overalls. On our departure we filled the car with sacks of fruit, cookies in bakery boxes, banana boxes packed with steaks and chickens arranged by Jack the steward (always asking after the mother I never saw).

There were times we visited the Hotel to find occupancy so low that sections of the dining room were roped off. Facilities went unpainted. History was happening all by itself, and Grossinger's had become an antique. More and more guests wore yarmulkes, until there was the sense only the most orthodox, who had been left out of the previous era, still came.

Grandpa Paul crawled along the rug with Robin and hoisted him up on his shoulders, then paraded through the Hotel dining room, showing him proudly to guests and colleagues. He loved to remark publicly how he thought once to oppose the marriage but then changed his mind and now was glad "because I already have one dividend." He would nod at Robin and chuckle. I reminded him that he didn't actually change his mind until four years later, but he only stared incredulously.

As the Hotel sank deeper into debt, he was very much the threatened monarch. His hasty redesign of the grounds had been mindless and sterile, mere justification for borrowing more money and creating the illusion of progress: a tinsel renovation of the coffee shop, a needless second golf course around the Lake wiping out the last expanse of wilderness, the concrete shell of the Harry G. dwarfing the charming old Main Building, a false front melding old-fashioned villas into one long "Howard Johnsons." Grossinger's was becoming crowded and junky, not only less palatial but less real.

But I didn't need the Hotel to be more than the place that I came with my wife and child, where Robin could roam the grounds with some of the wonder of my early years there. Lindy and I would stroll from PG's house to early breakfast, set Robin in the highchair, and order from among hot cereal and waffles as we orchestrated the constant fuss over him. In the afternoon we made a snowman, putting Paul's hat atop, and Grandpa suitably played the fool on returning home, demanding to know who was standing in front of the house. When Lindy and I met at the bar for beers after dinner, the bright lights of this failing resort town were just flashy enough to be romantic.

That January, the switchboard tracked me down to my father's bedroom to receive a call from a "Mr. Olson." Astonished, I stood there, the TV blasting, straining to hear the poet's words. Olson was praising the "Cranberry Islands" text I had sent him, while a jealous PG kept insisting, "Who are you talking to?"—probably because my smile seemed so subversive.

"Who's that?" Olson snapped at the audible interference.

I had to admit that it was my father and that he was both curious and impatient, a comment which aroused the attention of the men on either side of the line.

"Then put him on!" Olson bellowed.

I handed PG the phone. Baffled, holding it to his ear—"Paul Grossinger!" he announced. He didn't say another word. Half a minute later he gave it back, turned off the set with the clicker, and lay there silently on his pillow.

"I told him who the hell he was dealing with," Olson growled. "Not me. But you. You, for Chrissakes, his son."

I explored different establishments: a sardine factory (women in assembly lines), a boatyard, the bank loan office (a link to economic anthropology), the shrimping wharf (where men's catches were loaded right from the shipboard onto trays into an oven). I stood in tasty steam interviewing a foreman, pink slush condensing and dripping into snow. I was sweaty and cold at the same time, overwhelmed by the mass death of creatures, yet glad to discover such a sociologically crucial moment—fishermen setting up their own dealership. Old '40s songs followed me on the radio, echoes of white Christmases.

Chuck Stein came to visit. We sat on the porch with tea, backs against the house (Frodo beside me), him reciting his newest poems and me alternating with sections of *Book of the Cranberry Islands*. Beside his quick zen lines I sounded ornate and ponderous.

"Maybe you should read Olson instead of trying to write him," Chuck suggested. After he left I transferred the master's drunken, ecstatic soliloquy at the 1964 Berkeley Poetry Conference to cassette, and his voice became the cosmic radio of the island as I drove among wharves: "far away from the rules of sea-faring far far from/Gloucester/far by the rule of Ousoos far where you carry/the color, Bulgar. . . ."

Then one night Chuck phoned—just like that, Olson was dead.

Cold and isolation. Ocean frozen onto rocks. For days, wind screeched; snow covered the windows. I drove to the wharf at ten miles an hour or less, talked to the men in their workshops. Afternoons I sat in the house, reading science-fiction novels and playing Scrabble solitaire on the living room rug.

We awaited the mail jeep each day until . . . finally . . . the Hampshire letterhead, torn open to find—Dean Smith: they have decided not to offer me a position.

It was half a day's drive to the poet Gerrit Lansing's house in Gloucester. After a while Lindy fell asleep in sun against the car window. She awoke to the procession of houses and lights into Gloucester. A note on Gerrit's door: "Richard and Lindy: Went Shopping, Back in a Half Hour."

I loaded Robin in the carrier on my back and explored the backyard, bouncing him like a horse. He laughed and pulled down my woolen cap so I can't see. We galloped about, making hoofprints in snow—then got warm by turning on the car fan.

That night we sat in the house library beneath an alphabet-tower painting. Gerrit showed us his Aztec herbal with the habitat of the roots of each plant in color code (blue rivulets, red bugs). "There are no pure foods and drugs anymore," he said, "because our planet is so polluted. Just fifty years ago actual fish swam these waters." Then he looked into baby's eyes and asked, "Robin, Robin, is there the spark of an ego there yet, a spark?" Robin pounded on the chair and squealed. The cat hopped after a string caught on itself, and Gerrit said, "Cat, cat, are you a cat? No, this can't be a cat. This must be a rabbit."

In the morning he took us on a tour of Olson's Gloucester: Fort Square where he lived, Maximus's harbor full of vessels (dwarfing Bass Harbor as New York does Poughkeepsie), his haunts by Stage Fort Park. I thought of the biopsy that doomed him as against this photo Gerrit had of a bare-chested young man shoveling hay in the North Carolina sun, another of him as a child in a mailsack on his postman father's back—so quick the years ... so lucent the mirror through which we sail.

After lunch I got lost leaving town. We drove back and forth, in and out of Gloucester, and finally settled at a diner in Saugus where Robin charmed the woman in the next booth, tearing apart a roll while we ordered. The music was Neil Diamond, *Holly, Holy;* then the Beatles, *Come Together*—imbuing a relentless American elegy of moods and faces, villages and restaurants, all suggesting something profound, yet brief and superficial.

We came the next day to Hampshire and parked in the construction lot. No Lord Jeff this time—I was an outsider—even an outcast—and I viewed their utopian masque with suspicion.

Waiting for Dean Smith I was momentarily elated to find my name in their catalogue. An oversight no doubt, for the meeting with him was pure doom. "You're not what we want," he said from behind his peace medallion. "You confuse the faculty. What will happen when there are students?"

He sent me to the professors who made the decision. "See if you can change their minds. You shouldn't feel disappointed not to come here. After all, ours is an unusual lot: we have been commissioned to select the best faculty in the nation."

Hampshire may have been pretending to put together a radical, interdisciplinary curriculum, but the staff were ordinary academicians: the puffed-up, acerbic folklore lady who belittled shamanism; the Harvard Americanist in his plaid flannel shirt; the lanky, well-spoken descendant of Franklin Roosevelt; the blond, famously interdisciplinary dean—each cold as ice. The first time they could be amused by my intensity and even incorporate a rendition of my ideas into their curriculum. Now they were the "experimental college" version of my nemeses at Michigan. My fantasy of Earth Mythology was a gaudy overassessment of my stature. All his life they kept Olson out of the academy—and I could not hold a candle to the master.

In New York Chuck said: "Forget experimental colleges. It's near the end of the world. We don't have that kind of time." He pointed to the stream of cars at our red light, Fifty-Seventh and Broadway. "It's no longer between those who know and those who don't. Everyone knows it's happening. It's between those who think something can be done about it and those who know it can't." He told how in great pain of cancer Olson named his medicines War Spite and Yellow Jacket, invoking Zeus-Typhon and the black Magellanic storm-clouds (that interrupt the Milky Way) . . . and awoke only once from his final coma to say, "Wonderful!"

Lifetimes from such wisdom, such courage, I retreated to the car at dusk, looking for some sort of shelter. It couldn't be our time yet to prepare for death! But on the way to Grossinger's, we stopped at Bard, and Kelly concurred, "We are living in the darkest West, in the dark that does not precede the dawn, the utter darkness, before the birth of a radically different order of things."

No wonder I had spent my life in the watchtower. No wonder my panic was autonomous and contentless. The light at the end of the tunnel was somewhere like summer in the twenty-fourth century, after all the wars, an entirely different planet, clouds of insects rising and sinking about an unimaginable city, perhaps not even human.

At my father's house I was startled to face myself in the mirror. Uncombed curls, a child still, a bearded father, intense and earnest. I could see why they turned me down.

Robin called out, "DaDaDaDa."

And I said, "DaDaDaDa." We exchanged these dark cows of recognition—back and forth. We didn't have to use words I wanted to talk to him so much.

Freed of Hampshire I wed myself to Maine and the outlands. We drove East along the coast, stopping at wharves in Corea and on Beals Island, into New Brunswick and Maces Bay. This was a vaster and more desolate landscape, the Atlantic rolling in on all horizons. The beauty of its winter was fathomless, a fairy tale set in Mediaeval Europe. Fishing sheds were unadorned clubhouses; their occupants, though not pleased to welcome a woman, stopped card games and made space by the fire.

I discovered how on Beals almost everyone was a Beal or an Alley. I assembled kinship charts to discriminate owners of boats from clam-diggers. The people were barely removed from the Mesolithic: merely transported from one side of the sea to the other.

We explored the more colonized direction too, from the libraries of the State Fishery office in Augusta (where catches were recorded by species back to the 1900s) to the immense tidal flats of Newcastle and Damariscotta where we walked the exposed seabed and interviewed men as they hoed through dirt smooth as mirrors. We crouched into limy basements where they brought their trays of booty. Our bundled baby in his carrier grabbed at bloodworms and weeds, held a sea urchin and was fussed over by daughters and sisters of fishermen. I was writing "Cranberry Island" ledgers, as though intercepting a lightspeed rush through my mind would recover everything and restore a habitable world.

I stood in the spreading cataclysm of Ben Hasbrouck's woodlot, in the luminous snow of 1970—chlorophyl girding the sky, chainsaws dislodging it, crashing to earth, one by one. The rich smell of resins marked the advancing line of planetary death.

> The wood is piled with a thickness, the logs stacked, that can only recall time itself—the girth—the volume of a three-dimensional world. The thickness of, I am speaking of a cube. X, Y, and Z are all there, have always been there. X times Y times Z, imbedded in time. Sits in sunlight, 8 feet long, 4 feet high, and 4 feet wide: cordage, cordwood, core. World-space. We are not two-dimensional beings in a two-dimensional forest; we do more damage than that. We are men.
>
> I thought once that if this planet were as large and dense as Jupiter we would be still within a million years of using up its resources. There would be unknown islands, tribes, plains of buffalo and kangaroos, wild genetic pockets. Not true. X times Y must also be taken by Z. 128 cubic feet....
>
> Saws snap and penetrate, sounds arising unevenly from different parts of the forest. It is simple and invisible: we are cutting away at the heart. Sunlight falls shallow and empty. A dirt road leads past piles of wood to men operating at twelve points, backs to the forest, branches separating from heaven....
>
> The wind crackles, the trees fall. More and more of the surface of the sun is exposed, just how thick a three-dimensional solid, how many generations, cords its history, how deep its corm into the soil, its cork, corn, cornucopia, cormorant....

When my Amherst friend Paul came looking for land and left behind his Strout Realty catalogue, Lindy and I read about "85 cheap acres" downeast across Washington County. Though we had no money, we called the agent (ostensibly just to hear about it) and were talked into an inspection. We drove all morning through snow to his office.

> It is the old crumbling inn of the ancestors, overlooking Harrington like a postcard of 1910. Woods stretch to blueberry hills and a stream.... Orrin has forgotten the key and can't budge the cellar door because it's frozen.... Together we force it open, rise into an abandoned castle, large empty rooms sprawled in the late afternoon sunlight, dozens of them, indoor plazas and hidden hallways....

This was perhaps the true Hampshire decades from being born. Staring out the window across tundra I found myself wanting to replace Grossinger's by a place so remote it could be 1665, or the future on a moon of Saturn. Even though the inn was collapsing, the temperature below zero (and dropping), sparsity and disrepair were themselves reassuring. But Lindy shook her head as we put Robin back into his car-seat. "We would never be able to get a job there," she said, "and we don't have the ingenuity to start a commune or farm."

"If you change your mind, call me," Orrin shouted after us. "Don't bother the owner. I'm his only agent. Nothing you bid could be too low."

On the way back, my mind making wild passes over the land, I became carsick. Lindy pulled over. Taking medicinal sub-Arctic breaths, pissing into the gravel, I looked up into the Dipper and Orion. As sad as childhood was, at least the ball of yarn was tight. There was some hope of holding it together. Now the meaning of everything, even myself, had changed. Far from my own beginnings, I had become a father at the start of a new unknown family.

We were approaching the edge of winter. "The March hill," the men called it, the sea too stormy even to unload traps—five pennies and three screws a fisherman held out to me as the total remaining wealth of his pockets. My informants built and fixed gear, sat by the stove for a tale or two, then headed home.

Jasper was working over his ledgers, a lifelong project he never finished; he just kept turning the pages, writing things down. It was such a trivial succession of small events, which is why it was so important. After plying him for some forbidden facts about men's catches, I grabbed a Hershey bar and tossed a nickel on the table.

"Well thank God for that!" he announced. "That just about puts me over the top for the day."

He got up and walked to the window. I stood there beside him— big round Moon, the trees and wharf posts across Bass Harbor mere sticks. Then he put on his coat and muttered something about five minutes left to vote for selectmen.

Sparkling morning, stiff Northeaster—we entrusted our child to Sue Seavey and hiked to Jasper's pier. Wendell collected his gear. We got in his dinghy and rowed to where his lobsterboat was anchored. Singly we stumbled on deck.

"Don't worry," Wendell said; "once we start the engine, the motion'll even out."

I sat on the prow and monitored the sloshing of the waves, the rhythmic bumping. Bass Harbor. Back Beach. Big Heath Forest.

We passed into open waters, the sound of the motor steadying chaos, and in the sky: blue, for the last three billion years.

The old man fishing on rocks by the lighthouse washed past us, then Placentia, Black, the Gotts—Mount Desert sprawling behind, its limbs the legs of a Sphinx.

We stopped inside the Ducks, Greater and Lesser. By its distinctive salmon and blue buoy Wendell located one of his traps.

The sudden cessation of the engine brought the feeling of a carousel. Up and down we went, tumbling over invisible mountains. I cried out.

"Do you want me to go back?"

I shook my head. I propped myself against the lobster crate and anchored my vision to an armadillo cloud over Swans.

Wendell pulled the twine through his hauler and ignited the pulley. Wet rope came flying, its length confirming immense depth. Then a form burst through—a cage filled with sea urchins, baby lobsters crawling around them, too small for the measure Wendell hooked behind the sockets of larger ones as he tossed them back.

Lindy moved about nimbly. She helped him throw out urchins and crabs. A horned sculpin, warty and spiny, twisted in his hands, eyes protruding agog. "Ugly thing," returning it too. He brought me a cunner to hold, thin lips, spiny dorsal fins. "It won't hurt you," he promised, "but no one brings them in." I grasped its cold slime, then dropped it into the water. It lay on its side, slight movement of a fin. "It must have popped its insides coming up," he sighed.

Ebb tide pulled one way, wind another. Choppy, slatty waters. Rotting bait bags were emptied back into the sea, silver shards eclipsed, as invisible mouths snapped at them. Fresh ones tied in, trap back overboard.

The wind tugged, the boat bumped, I sprawled on the crate. 'Limits,' I kept saying to myself, 'are what we are inside of.' As Olson said at Berkeley. Nausea was clearly more than just the rocking of the boat and waves. It was the sensation of everything I wasn't and couldn't be. It was Egyptian too, the faces of gulls staring back at me. I would live and die in this body. I would never visit Mars or fly beside Don Juan as a crow.

The waters became even rougher. Wendell explained he was running Schoodic Mountain out by Little Duck Island and putting Gooseberry Island on Placentia Head—two points on either axis marking a shoal into which he dropped anchor. The boat was rocking so much I swallowed sun.

Shutting my eyes and turning onto my belly, I listened to lines being cast out, the hoisting of fish on board. I opened a single eye and saw cod thrown onto the deck—massive fish, flapping on one another's bodies, three and four off each line . . . from the dark ocean that bred them through the mute veil of mutation into the sun that fathered them, all brilliant and unforgiving.

Lindy offered me her line. Still lying there I pulled on a shoal "no wider than this," Wendell holding his hands apart . . . intercepting their impact, creatures of the abyss plopping like lumps into flatland, silver coins shattering as they are minted, imagos of the Portuguese *bacchales,* each one absolutely new as it crashed onto the deck, drowning in air.

"The New World was fed off him," Wendell said. "Without fishermen the pilgrims would have starved."

Near sunset we returned. While Lindy steered, I sat on the tarp watching Wendell sort the fish, his hands into their eye sockets as he cut open their mouths, tossed innards into a bucket, threw flesh into a pile by our end of the boat. In his bright yellow oilcoat, blood splattered grenadine on the deck. The gulls were going crazy to get at it. He dumped a bucketload overboard; midair, they tore organs from one another's beaks.

After dinner, Father Gower joining us, the women in the kitchen, Wendell asked what I thought of him then: "Richard, did you imagine me a murderer? Did you consign me to some Hindoo or yogi hell?"

As Father smiled, I said, "No, of course not. I empathize with the fish, the suffering of all life, but I am also American. I eat the food."

Pleased with my response Wendell felt encouraged to add that humanity is not perfect, "and I don't know what the Father would think of this, but I believe Christ died so that we could be fishermen."

The pastor nodded. "In confession you receive absolution, release from obsession. You can fish again in the morning. No point in faking it. Men just don't have the power to save their own souls." He stole a bite of Sue's huckleberry pie.

"I can't keep from taking their lives," Wendell continued, "but I'm different than Buddy. I can keep from destroying their homes. I can be a steward. God gave us dominion over the animals. That was his promise. The fish know. They would not break that promise. Right, Father?"

"Wendell here is struggling to find the meeting place between the world of ecology and the world of spirit," the pastor opined. "He may not quite realize it, but he is asking famous transcendental questions. He is trying to understand social and natural law."

"I'm just a fisherman. I don't have the knowledge or the philosophy you two have gotten through book-reading."

"Well, at least you can stand up in a boat," I said. "I feel like a coward and a fool."

"Not so," Wendell replied. "You knew you were going to get sick and yet you went out anyway. That takes courage. You knew you were going to get sick as death, but you smiled and made good humor of yourself; you didn't ask me to turn back, and you even helped pull in the last line of cod. You went to Buddy Hooper's boathouse at night. That alone should prove it. Right, Father?"

Wendell poured us each another glass of wine, and Father lectured on the difference between Christ the Savior and the Tibetan view of many lives in which men may yet come back as lobsters. He said he was a priest because he believed in the single Christ, in redemption through faith. Then we sat in silence.

"Right here is the closest that men can ever become," Wendell finally offered. "Saying what's in their hearts. I've heard tell that a man and a woman in intercourse is the closest, but I'll have to question that. I doubt if any human beings are closer than we are now."

In March my book arrived from Black Sparrow Press—*Solar Journal: Oecological Sections,* sandstone brown cover with chalk-white figures of man-apes. The big surprise was that Robert Duncan, an elder San Francisco poet and colleague of Olson, had written a preface:

"Pound, at most, in the *Cantos* had proposed a poem that contained history. Olson went further: the poetic was the primary knowledge from which the truth of history must spring; only the mythopoetic could reach the heart of the matter. In Grossinger the old arguments of these poets, men in transition, battering often at the walls of old institutions of mind that they might have let go, the old polemics are gone, or rather swept up in a new order."

Then he quoted from my Halloween speech at Amherst and concluded: "Grossinger has opened for us a new era. . . ."

It was an ancient fire that lit the writing once at my heart, a song of inexpressible beauty I tried to sing along with Dion beside the Magnavox so long ago. Shredded newspapers from the package on the floor—sunbeams shimmering in dust—Duncan had foreseen me. The exile was over.

I visited the two southern campuses of the State University—Portland and Gorham—an afternoon of interviews arranged by my anthropology friends at Orono. The event was as straightforward as Hampshire was duplicitous. It wasn't the noosphere; they didn't care about *Io* or Duncan; they were interested only in hiring an active ethnographer of Maine (to replace the video version of anthropology they piped in from Orono). A few days later my contract came—a lecturer at $10,500.00. Lindy celebrated this passage to adulthood, while I was wary of cultural yardsticks (though that afternoon at the wharf Wendell and the others shook my hand, and Jasper joked about how I was going to work for the great State of Maine).

For two days spring seemed finally to have arrived, Prunella dancing mock entrapping patterns in snow on the garage roof, Spindle making whining sounds at a blackbird whose wings shook the tree. Frodo came from damp shadows with a flat decayed bird, her wet paws picking up grit in the road. She rolled and scratched her back with gravel, stone against fur, stirring dust, releasing pine.

The landlady's painters showed up (unannounced) and began rapping on the outside of our sleep with their ladders and brushes. But the weather changed rapidly, and that night wet flakes fell, covering trees, crashing onto the mud from overloaded limbs. At nightfall the sky was as clear as I had ever seen it—a million stars. I stood in the front yard, firing at a fence post—soggy, easily packed snowballs. I hit it 217 out of 300 times. It was time to leave Somes Sound.

The next day we drove four hours to the University of Maine and, after lunch, began collecting listings from rental billboards. A history professor who had interviewed me, locking his office for the day, stopped to explain that country houses were quite scarce: "You might as well *buy* something. In Portland it's cheaper than renting."

That very night we met the embarrassingly eager agent he recommended—another unrehearsed plunge into secular life. In her red sports car she gave us a sunset tour of Portland and suburbs, including a series of run-down houses representing *her* version of our description of the old inn. The next morning while driving through Cape Elizabeth I pointed to a green farmhouse with a barn as an example.

"That?" she asked, surprised. "That one's for sale from my own office."

The property on Mitchell Road was $19,000. A downpayment for this could come only from my untapped bar-mitzvah presents, which had been held in my father's bank until I was of age. I was approaching 26, but he fussed and stalled. He preached debt and ruin, mocking, "Since when did you become an expert in real estate!" Finally he hung up.

A few days later it came without comment—a cashier's check for a little over $10,000 plus another $7,000 in shares of IBM (from the gift of a single share half a lifetime earlier).

My childhood and college years had been shadowed by expectation of vast wealth; yet here was all I needed: milkweed, marsh berries and rhubarb patch, apple trees, a barn full of hay.

As soon as the house was available we loaded a U-Haul and drove back from Mount Desert. In subsequent weeks we visited second-hand shops and warehouses, assembling an array of wicker rocking chairs, cabinets, and tables of various vintages and shapes.

Kids from across the road came by to visit. They walked our baby to the play equipment, six fisherman's daughters holding out fingers for his hands, pushing and catching him on the swing, bringing him toys, incorporating him in make-believe with dolls and stuffed animals.

Our first guest was Roy Rappaport. He came mid-July, looked at my fieldnotes and, that night, while buying us dinner at the local steakhouse, tried to convince me I could still write a decent thesis (about the assemblage of gear, market price, wharf hierarchies, the inheritance of territory, and trap-cutting wars). There was a new, more lenient set of rules for doctoral candidates, he explained, in the aftermath of "the Grossinger affair."

I told him that I didn't need a degree; *Book of the Cranberry Islands* was so much bigger and more important than a thesis.

"If you don't get it," he warned, "the prelims will be an issue your whole life. Get it and trivialize them." He shoved cup and saucer in my direction with some gusto. "You don't have a choice. You either can trivialize them or portray yourself as their victim for the rest of your life."

When Lindy and I found each other we were barely out of our original households. We began dating and, almost without fanfare, passed from childhood together. Robin literally emerged from our dark, a being of cells bred in love, a spirit propped up in his small plastic tub in our yard in Ann Arbor, carried to the islands of Maine, borne to our house in Cape Elizabeth where we surrounded him with stuffed monkeys, a swingset, and colored jammies. Lying in bed listening to him babble to himself, pulling him on a sled under the evening stars, we were brought back to being children again ourselves.

We lay upstairs together in the late afternoon, looking out at what was once farm, what was once forest (and still resembled them in the late-afternoon light). Half-asleep on the mattress he had been weaned to from his crib, staring out the window at branches high above him, Robin said over and over: "Birdies, lil'girls."

At Crescent Beach, he and I built tunnels and castles and led the edges of waves into them. In the movies we took I was astonished at my own brown body swinging him in the surf. I looked radiant, beyond omen, holding my child with golden hair. Then Lindy and I grabbed him and ran along the edge of the surf, water splashing against our cutoff jeans, throwing him back and forth between us, "He's your Robin!"; "No, take him, he's your Robin!"—as he giggled uproariously. ("Me and my hippy-dippy parents," he would laugh later in his own college days, viewing the old 8 mm.).

We bought wicker furniture, a pot-bellied woodstove, and an aquarium of soft-shelled turtles clawing through pebbles and floating weeds. We learned to boil young milkweed pods and make desserts from the rhubarb patch. Our cats roamed the fields.

Ordinary time imbued me, and though in my rationale it had to have arisen from my devotion to alchemy, poetics, and magic, it was more than that—it was the ritual of each meal, of changing and washing diapers, of putting our child into his colored jammies, of taking our cups of mint tea under the stars.

Returning from Portland with a headache, late afternoon, I dropped, coat and boots, onto the bed into a drugged sleep. Hours passed until I felt Lindy's hand on my shoulders. She was slow and gentle. When I sat up she told me that Frodo was dead.

No!

But she said it again.

It seemed impossible that such a creature could be obliterated by a crappy hit-and-run car—she who had quested heroically across Arizona—and found us again; who vanished on Mount Desert, was missing two weeks, then recovered in a barn twenty miles across the island. Frodo the wanderer . . . ever returning to the shire. (In fact she defined the shire, the hearth Lindy and I had lit in Aspen.)

That night I dreamed of her appearing in the field behind the house near where we buried her. She was running up to us, trying to speak, but something muted her. Twenty-five years later I still dream of Frodo. I see her gray body bounding across the grass, an icon heralding our marriage, an upraised tail, guiding us to Michigan and Tuba City, then to the edge of the Atlantic. Other times she comes as a person in a fur suit, meowing. Her figure emerges alternately from old bushes by forgotten houses, basements of abandoned buildings, mine dumps, excavation sites, primeval forest and caves—sometimes fat and healthy as though nothing has changed; sometimes gaunt and dusty, beyond death, making dry sounds. As the years pass I am a bit afraid of her because she is now thirty years old, too old for anything but a zombie from a tomb.

My child drinks the last of the grape juice; his toys are collected. Frodo is buried beneath the appletree, and with her all of Colorado, and time, as I said, lies like the whole moonworld on the other side of us, a green light through berries and blossoms.

I dream of seeing down onto a planet—a colossal shipwreck. My body smashes overboard. I try to drown, to shut off sensation.

I am flung by a wave into a hole where the timbers have broken away. There I lie, for years like a beetle, my arms stretched to the ends of the world. Water flows over my torso. The question eventually comes: If it is only wood and water and moonlight (and these are eternal), why do I want to live?

An island woman speaking an exotic lingo enters the hull. She begins to teach me her language. She is not human, but she distracts me.

The end of the dream is as obscure as its beginning. A piece of clockwork stretched on tidal flat while its hours turn on a giant zodiac; above, infinity packed with monkeys. I fight my way up through the water. I cling to a sandbar.

"One last glimpse in the mirror, father."

"No," he says. "Go through."

EPILOGUE

L indy and I lived in Cape Elizabeth two years. At the college we called PoGo (Portland-Gorham) I gave lectures on Melanesian tribes and chiefdoms, Kwakiutl potlatches, and African fossils. I organized film-showings and poetry readings, played in an intramural softball league, and assembled *Io*s on Dreams, Baseball, and Earth Geography.

Since I could offer only subjects based on the limited State University catalogue, I converted "North American Indians" into "South American Indian Mythology," with the class reading a single book, Lévi-Strauss' *The Raw and the Cooked*. My enrollment of seven was made up of business majors, nurses, and secretaries who needed to earn credits in the time slot after lunch.

The Raw and the Cooked evoked the flora and fauna of the South American jungle, the life and customs of the Bororo. At first the students wanted to know why they should even care about these things, so I demonstrated their equivalents in American culture. Using colored chalk I portrayed etiological relationships among stars, ornaments, diseases, and tobacco in terms of history of science, business, and other affairs closer to their hearts. On a few occasions, in order to show them the underlying structure of myth, I converted the diagrams left over from an economics class that preceded and succeeded mine, so that its bewildered professor returned to find his grids and flow charts intact but his dollar amounts and gross national products replaced with armadillos, marsh plants, and intestinal gases.

Primitive cultures were mind-boggling to these students. Some of them didn't even believe in the non-Western world. When I showed ethnographic films, they took it for granted these were actors in costumes. Many were scandalized by one particularly long sequence on the preparation and enactment of an Australian Emu Dance. How could anyone waste so much time? How could they get any pleasure out of lives like that? Weren't they deprived?

I turned the tables and asked them what *they* looked forward to— a grade, a basketball score, a new dress—these were symbols too. At core, I told them, there is just a human organism, and to the body it makes little difference whether it's a colored feather, the bone of a kangaroo, or a trip to Boston Garden.

Winter deepened. I scraped my windshield for work, took off my coat, knocked ice out of my hair, and stood at the lectern.

In sleepy introductory lectures I guided them into the Mesolithic, the time of prehistory when the big ice melted and tribes of ancient hominids crossed land and sea to populate the old continents.

> The hunters of the Stone Age awoke to find the world disappearing, in storms of a sort they had never known, a black forest no one had predicted, no soothsayer of their peoples.
>
> The Earth was getting warmer. The middle ages of the universe were passed.... Africa remained Bantu; China was logjammed; Australia was discovered in waves of seafarers. In Europe: lakewomen, fishermen—Maglemosians, or bog-peoples who found their way out of darkness and recovered the classic wisdom of the Magdalenian, built the first Mediterranean cities.
>
> We were raised by a witch of the forest, who in the dark hours of night examined her own body for signs of illness, fled from imagined terrors and passed that legacy on to us. Our culture must be at least as deep as our fear if we are to survive it. This is the only answer to the Maglemosian underground....

On Gorham days I drove the backroads, often slowed by school buses en route to my early class. On Portland days I sped over the bridge through downtown, past the lake with the swans. After my first class I held office hours in the Sociology cottage and then met faculty friends for lunch—a Fordham philosopher studying Whitehead, my sociologist colleagues, the self-conscious English faculty. They came from the usual colleges—Boston University, Case Western, some from Orono—and except for a general small-town mood it was not that different from Ann Arbor. Even eating in the faculty dining room seemed festive, holding forth on my favorite topics from the Mets to Black Mountain literature to Gurdjieff. Day after day of this activity had its own metabolism.

During the two years at PoGo, Lindy and I were invited to give readings from our work, so we traveled to Kent State, UC/Santa Cruz, California Institute of the Arts, and elsewhere. This star junket was dazzling. People around the country knew our writing, read *Io,* and were interested in other far-out stuff, from Druid mythology to Reichian orgone to esoteric cowboy literature. We fantasized living and working in a more exciting situation.

Then the president of Goddard, a small experimental college in northern Vermont, called and offered me a job there. He had read and liked *Solar Journal.* It wasn't quite the bigtime scene we had fantasized; it wasn't even as lush as Hampshire. But it was close to Maine and within the Vinland sanctuary we had come to consider home.

We moved in the summer—Lindy driving the station wagon with a U-Haul attached, a friend following in a rented truck, me in the rear in a used red Mustang we had bought for $200. This remains Robin's oldest memory: branches crashing against the top of the twenty-four-footer, neighbors standing on porches waving, a sudden downpour followed by a rainbow. Everything which lies on the far side of this fugue for him is forever a forgotten dream.

In Plainfield we got a white, green-shuttered farmhouse connected to a barn—steep tin roof, a grove of maples in front, a plowed field with stick sculptures and psychedelic flags along the side. The acre of land, twisted complexly around a hill, dropped off as much as 65 degrees in some directions, down slopes of blackberries, apple trees, and chokecherries.

Once upon a time the trains from Burlington to St. Johnsbury ran through the yard. Their abandoned ties were later used to wedge stairs up the hillside to the entrance. These rotted chunks of wood had become sanctuaries for toads almost too fat to hold in one hand, whose piss left visible puddles the cats sniffed. The path the train took was still delineated by rows of tightly packed horsetails and raspberry bushes leading up to the giant concrete foundation of what was once its bridge across the Winooski. Beyond the gap its discolored mate sat.

The dominant sound was the river, a continuous stream of water from the surrounding hills. The minor chords were vehicles shifting gears on the bumpy road, muffled rock music from the onetime-feed-store (now apartments). All summer we put the house together, another in our sequence of abodes following Ann Arbor apartments, Mount Desert cottage, and Cape Elizabeth homestead (a nesting pattern become familiar). This one was not in the suburbs, except maybe of Free Quebec. From our window we saw a constant crowd around the feedstore, sharing a joint, kicking a small leather sack heel-to-heel, working on cycles and disassembled cars. Students and townspeople freely crossed our yard and coopted its outskirts for games and conversations (though we discouraged motorcyclists from doing tricks down the railroad bed).

We had another garden plowed, watched river ice form, and waited for spring melt. Dressed in his bib overalls, Robin attended funky co-op Center School in the hills above town. His first peer group marched down Creamery Street, gathering bottles in their wagons, trading them at the local store for candy. Around our hill he collected colored leaves in his pail. In the mud of the driveway he carved roads for his match-box cars. In November we sledded through rows of maples, me holding him in my arms.

Goddard was an experimental college without a catalogue or formal classroom buildings. Topics were announced by mimeo; students and teachers met in dorms. The campus population represented different left-wing factions, from blippies (black hippies) and anarchists to social progressives and Maoists. Astrology and tarot were virtually required subjects, and students practiced ritual magic and read the *I Ching* the way those at other campuses might throw fraternity parties (one dorm even ordered its food according to the principles of the Yellow Emperor). Consciousness drugs, improvisational softball, and ten-speed bikes comprised an informal athletic program.

Gradually I began to organize my field notes into a thesis which analyzed the economics and ecology of coastal Maine—how men catch lobsters (and different species of fish, worms, crustaceans, shrimp, crabs, sea urchins, and the like) and turn them into cash while forging a mythological and social order. Finally I wrote it up and got my spurious Ph.D.

> Robin and I climb the hills into the woods beyond Plainfield. We pass through evergreen trees along an old stone fence. I carry him over its barbed-wire boundary to the edge of the sugarbush. He discovers wild strawberries, each so tiny it is only a sip. When I pick him up, his cold face smells strawberry.
>
> I stare at the vastness of forest and valleys, mountains ringing them in, clouds active across sky. It is more terrible than beautiful. Chamomile grows sweet in the hardpan of our driveway, a traditional tea, but here are hundreds of budding and unbudded herbs, large and sour leaves, nightshades and vines, poisons that no doubt contain medicines, if our wisdom were deeper, if our fear of being reborn, or even of living this time, were not so great.

Book of the Cranberry Islands, The Provinces, The Long Body of the Dream, The Book of Being Born Again into the World, The Windy Passage from Nostalgia, The Slag of Creation, The Planet with Blue Skies: my unruly narrative ran through graduate school in Ann Arbor, fishermen on Mount Desert Island, two years at the University of Maine, five more at Goddard. My readers tended to be hippies or artists whose lives were weirder than mine. Awkwardly I fulfilled the requirements of my public, even as Duncan has proposed them. I maintained correspondences with aspiring magicians and revolutionaries and gave readings across the country (Lindy and Robin always in the audience, he kneading a corner of a blanket as the hour got late).

For the years I taught at Goddard we inhabited tundra winters and swam in moraine mudponds, *roches moutonnées* stretching to cumulus skies. Our daughter Miranda was born in Barre in 1974. That same year, we converted *Io* into a publishing company which we named North Atlantic Books. We started with a half dozen small volumes of poetry and experimental prose, the first two our own, the rest from writers we published in *Io*.

> Winter flu swallows mind, and I float in a world beyond space, beyond the recoiling fractions of time. The nihilism of war, violence, metals fades through mocha, dwindling to inevitability.
>
> I have fallen upon the living room couch into a realm between

sensual memory and memoryless sleep. Lindy has put Donovan's children's record on, first time I have heard it since Michigan—his voice merging nausea into gold coastlines, eggs bursting magenta clouds, seaweed and starfish, *fill her sails.* . . .

I am a child buying yellow-frosted cupcakes for my brother and sister, riding home from baseball practice on the subway. . . .

It's all that was, what I thought then, and what I imagined I was doing, and would become. And it's gone, not like silence, but into the mystery, as old Horace Mann classmates come before me in a hypnagogic vision: Frank Haynes, Carson Eoyang, John Coffee.

I awake to a softness within, Robin building a block city, Lindy bringing me a cup of lime jello, snow out the window, a cold I rest my forehead on.

In 1977, with Goddard about to fold, we packed a U-Haul truck and moved to Oakland, California.

We lived a year in Oakland, then the next five in Richmond, another San Francisco Bay city. For the first two of those years, I worked on an advance from Doubleday, assembling a text on the history and philosophy of medicine.

When I began writing this book, I thought of it only as a job (that was how I fooled myself then). But *Planet Medicine* became an act of self-healing. It was *Io* grown up. It was the doctoral thesis I was never allowed to write; it was also a homeopathic poem. In it I found a voice closer to my heart than the experimental prose I had been doing for years; at the same time, I taught myself the rudiments of shamanic practice. Right from the beginning I asked: what has been damaged? what needs to be cured? who is left with medicinal power? And then, on the excuse of the manuscript, I went out looking for healers and found not only bodyworkers and homeopaths but acupuncturists, chiropractors, yogis, herbalists, alchemists, and anthroposophical physicians. My sessions with them broke through my hangdog attitude—my sense of exile—and gave me back my heart.

Once *Planet Medicine* was in stores, I got invited to lecture on healing and ethnomedicine at various local colleges, a brief career that culminated in my being hired to develop a course on the epistemology of medicine at Pacific Naturopathic College in San Rafael. I drove the Richmond bridge on Mondays and Wednesdays and conducted a seminar in a room of prospective practitioners. Unfortunately Pacific Natur-opathic College lasted only two months.

Then Sierra Club gave me money to write a mythocosmology of the stars and planets. I went from *Planet Medicine* to *The Night Sky* because I intended to launch my remedy as deep into creation as I could (that is, into my internalized image of the cosmos)—to send the poetics of healing into the most primordial, life-threatening wound of all: the intimation of an amoral, spiritless Big Bang that scientists had set at the birth of the entire universe. The night sky had always been a more primeval place than the Earth, so to look among human images of fiery stars and planets (which is all we ever have of them) was to search for ultimate beginnings, even my own.

Olson and Kelly once sent me back to the roots of Western civi-lization, the birth of consciousness in acts of ritual sorcery. In gradu-ate anthropology I had studied the origin of the human species and the genesis of language. But there were dozens of thresholds between the unconscious and the unknowable Jungian archetypes—quantum particles, aboriginal creation myths, Celtic alphabet glyphs, even the cellular imprint of life itself in the primal ocean. All of these could be submitted to the same oracle.

During those years I drove once a week to Charles Poncé's study on Uranus Terrace in San Francisco for an hour of dream work. Charles directed me away from symbolic interpretations (even archetypal ones) and toward the unknown life of the soul.

"Traditional psychotherapy separates you from the novelty of expe-rience," he warned; "it teaches you that your pain and growth are not your own."

He was a dark-complexioned man (half-Panamanian, half-Greek) who had written popular books on the *I Ching* and Qabbala and picked up street wisdom in coffee houses of the Lower East Side (of which his pony-tail was a reminder). "A doctor is no priest or soothsayer. Sometimes things just are. Pretending to know more than you do is useful only for keeping clients. Maybe it's because in this business they're too hard to come by to part with them easily."

As I wrote down each night's dreams, I excavated a familiar but bygone self, one trapped in a seemingly interminable cycle of exams

I passed (or failed) long ago, graduation ceremonies for which I always forgot my robes, Mets games in megalithic ruins against extinct teams or teams that never were, school auditoriums and extensions of Bronxes searching for camp friends, alien versions of Grossinger's under new owners (our family either surreptitious or evicted)—over and over these same journeys, sometimes layered through extraterrestrial and Atlantean landscapes, emblazoned with luminous objects and magical forms of *t'ai chi ch'uan.* Twice in such a setting, while demonstrating Cloudy Hands and Single Whip, Chuck Stein taught me to fly.

> I am returning to Dr. Fabian's dark brownstone in Greenwich Village. I have to pee very badly, and I stumble into a bathroom so dark I cannot see the toilet. As the urine hits the "water," I smell sulphur and then I hear hydrochloric acid bubbling in the bowl. I rationalize that it is not my pee but a substance in the toilet. In any case the gurgling stops. Then, as I am leaving the room, I hear the sound again, like sizzling rice soup. I realize my upper lip is burning from having been splattered. I am wondering why there is a scalding element in my urine, and I think I must tell this dream to Charles.

"You know what it is," I remarked. "It's a new version of the first dream I ever had interpreted by Dr. Fabian. It's going back to him not *with* a dream but *in* the dream. His office is part of the dream. Back then the incident involved a chemistry set. Now it's sizzling rice soup."

Charles knew the old dream as well as Fabian's interpretation, so he offered a deciphering:

"You dreamed once of a chemistry set that spilled. You brought that dream to a doctor who told you that the substance in the test tube was urine, that you were dreaming of wetting your pants. I think this can all be viewed another way: You brought your first harvest of symbols to a wizard. He recognized the symbols. He said, 'What is happening in this dream stands for something else. It is not a chemistry set. It is an act of peeing.' He said, 'Another meaning is speaking through you.' But then he limited that meaning to a representation of the asocial act of wetting. He grasped only the aspect of wetting associated with misbehavior. He failed to grasp the mercurial waters, which you now bring back to him thirty-five years later to remind him that his earlier analysis was lacking."

"So I am dreaming now to change the dream then."

"You are dreaming the same dream in order to change the authorized interpretation of a dream you have been carrying around your whole life. Back then you dreamed of mercurial waters too, but Dr. Fabian, like your mother, could see only a wet bed. He could explain your wetting only as a form of rebellion, of primitive consciousness. You came to a magus with a primordial dream of burning waters, of consciousness wanting to be born. He told you the burning waters were urine. But you were telling him they were the seeds of a sorcerer. He couldn't see that magic. He couldn't see the alchemist longing to create. He could only see a child needing toilet training. So now you want to show him the real dream in a way that can't be missed."

"Even then it was an alchemical dream," I continued, "because the important part of Dr. Fabian's interpretation was not that the chemical was urine but that it was a symbol at all, that it stood for something else—anything else. Before I brought him the dream I had dreamed as a child dreams, never thinking of my dreams as commodities or texts, never naming them. His act of asking me to bring him a dream changed the way I thought of my dreams, perhaps even the way I dreamed. So I went home and dreamed alchemy, if there was alchemy in me to dream."

"And this is what your present dream is saying: 'I was a magician then, and you didn't see it. I gave you the gift of my first dream, my first magical act. And you thought I was just peeing, you thought I was just dreaming ordinary stuff."

"Yet I got the mercurial seeds by the sheer fact Dr. Fabian exchanged the dream for symbols. He *was* a magician and didn't know it. Then I dreamed the new dream in order to salvage him, and also, I guess, to reestablish the act of interpretation in the present."

"Not interpretation," Charles interrupted. "Consciousness. The problem of 'keeping dry' is also an alchemical matter insofar as 'toilet training' requires bringing consciousness to the autonomic realms of the body. You were peeing not only antisocially, but in a struggle to free yourself from unconscious elements. Your dream, by casting wetting in a mirror, cast again by Fabian's interpretation, was a step up the ladder."

While we lived in Richmond I continued to explore autonomic realms—dreams, Chinese medicine, *shiatsu* massage, zen, bioenergetic breathing, and *san shou* and *ta lu*—two-person sets of Taoist martial arts. In a phone conversation with Bunny one night I offhandedly remarked that I wished we had done *t'ai chi* and meditation at Chipinaw rather than exercises and sports.

"But you weren't ready," she answered wisely. "You guys would have giggled and goofed off. You wouldn't have even tried."

She was right of course, but I wondered if it was we who weren't ready or the culture itself that held us in such a deep trance.

I volunteered every day at lunch hour to supervise games and tell stories at Miranda's school (some Cloudy Hands and Needle at Sea-Bottom thrown in, mostly for circus, perhaps proving Bunny's point). With the poet Ishmael Reed I wrote a grant to start Barbary Coast Distribution Company, through which we then sent out students to place multicultural literature in stores. I also published many books by different writers under North Atlantic (not only literature but *t'ai chi ch'uan,* homeopathy, Peruvian shamanism, Ponce's alchemy, and Roy Rappaport's "ecological and religion").

Meanwhile I searched for replicas of an idealized Hampshire at schools ranging from coastal Washington and Tennessee to suburban Philadelphia—a quest that included a brief chance at running a writing program in Colorado and a lecture/job interview at the New School for Social Research. Everywhere I seemed to "just miss"—A or F my final "final" grade.

The publishing company and Lindy's jobs in arts management and technical writing became our means of support. I never taught again.

Grossinger's lasted until its financial demise in 1985. Then the plant fell into ruins, its golf courses alone maintained, first by yuppie time-sharers, then by a Korean corporation.

PG died penniless in New York City in 1989.

Bunny emerged from it, lucid and wise, the Hotel a fading mirage.

My brother Michael wandered like Ishmael, teaching art to convicts while trying to raise wild daughters who kept fleeing a reckless ex-wife. James tried to run Grossinger's, then (before its collapse) cast his lot with the apocalyptic future—Atlantic City and Las Vegas—before yielding the hotel-casino profession and going into hibernation with a wife and two sons in Pennsylvania.

My brother Jonathan joined forces with a Polish witch-woman he found at a Manhattan bookstore. In 1969 they bought a used station wagon and migrated to Colorado. Two years later, in Boulder, he escaped her hexes and became a disciple of marijuana—an avowed warrior with his own sacred dagger. He was teaching Apache chants to a gang of Chicano teenagers when ghosts hunted him down and almost killed him. His mother flew out and retrieved him, then incarcerated him in a facility in Towson, Maryland.

She jumped out her apartment window the day after her birthday in 1975, leaving behind an even greater mystery than the one she lived. At her death Jon was released from the hospital to become one of the first street people in America—in Baltimore initially, then for a decade and a half in Central Park (though his father always kept a flat for him on Second Avenue).

Over the years my stepfather and I tried to redeem our relationship, but it took till 1991 (three years before his death) for us to meet at a midtown Italian restaurant, bear witness, acknowledge, mourn, and embrace in parting on the street.

My sister elected (for the duration) to bear our mother's cross.

In 1992 Jon escaped the City, appointing himself poet and custodian of the marshes of Southeastern Connecticut and making his home in a motel built on the site of the last Pequot Indian slaughter. He had written a letter to Bridey from Madison in 1967, which she gave me before returning to Ireland:

> The house at the beach sounds fine. Hearthfire and the sea is better than buses and elevators, especially for you, I guess, who has lived all her life near the sea. Bridey, this wish for you—may you ever be what is best of Ireland. May you always carry its myth and mystery in your spirit and its love that is an elf's love riding the wind through old castles, lighting night's land into twilight and when settling on the child's face whispering of the dream and its brightness. It is by this I will always feel you best.

California's seasonless time occluded the passage of our children's years. We drove them to schools and friends' houses, heard their stories at dinner, tucked them into bed. We organized birthday parties: pitching pennies in floating cups, pinning a tail on a pig, shooting out a candle with a watergun (while Lindy struggled with recipes for cakes and frosting). With a menorah from the Hotel we attempted to perform *"Vitzyvanu l'hadlik nair."* Dripping wax and flickering shadows added their own mystery. At Christmas we decorated a tree with Lindy's old-fashioned Denver ornaments and strings of lights. Then we drove through El Cerrito, viewing the exotic displays—statues of Santa on ceilings, dioramas of babes in mangers among flocks of sheep.

We played Sorry and Monopoly, our attention riveted on tokens, cards, and strategy. We invented games, bouncing balls into cardboard canisters for points, rolling marbles to knock over each others' armies of plastic statues. We held regular rough-housing sessions, tearing from room to room, jumping on beds as Lindy feigned protest, me always the monster, swinging pillows as Miranda squealed and Robin whooped.

Seemingly overnight our son turned into a woodworker. He carved a set of dollhouse furniture for his sister. Then for her birthday he designed and assembled a tall dresser in which to hang her clothes. His most special gift, though, was a round mirror imbedded in a piece of fine sanded wood with a curved handle. She ran ecstatic circles, hugging him.

Some Friday nights I'd put on old rock and roll and we'd prance about, amazed at the distance our life now spanned. Lindy and I formed partners, she showing off how she used to do all the dips and turns in the dance of her name. Miranda clamored and raised her arms, so I seized her up and did my steps holding her on my hip. Robin would crowd in too, so all four of us were swaying together—Rickey Nelson singing "Poor Little Fool," Jimmy Jones "Good Timin'," and then "You're the Reason God Made Oklahoma." This was our once and ever family—Lindy and I the parents, honorary adults—everything we were, everything that was beyond us too.

In the years ahead Robin became an ecologist of tidal marshes, Miranda a playwright and performance artist.

)

In 1983 we moved to Blake Street in Berkeley, just below Telegraph Avenue. North Atlantic Books occupied the basement. Almost immediately, Lindy took a new job, writing grants for an educational laboratory in San Francisco, and then was hired at Cal/Berkeley to teach writing in the Engineering School.

In Richmond we lived in a collusion of a neighborhood that was actually a trailer camp/suburban mall. Blake Street was apartments and condos—we had the only single-family house on the block. Transiency was global: Africans, Arabs, East Indians, Asians from every country, all manner of Continentals mixed with the usual student and jock crowd.

Within a block of where Blake met Telegraph (a minute or two on foot) was a Middle Eastern grocery, a bagel bakery, a combination photocopy center/dress shop run by Punjabi Hindus, a herb apothecary, a store selling natural lotions and soaps, an Ethiopian restaurant, two Thai restaurants, two used bookstores, and a national center for handicapped people. The rest of Telegraph was a combination of bookstores, restaurants, street theater, and college life—hordes of craftspeople lining the curb with their stands of Aquarian wares. Up and down the Avenue, students flowed in near gridlock, along with shoppers and sightseers, motorized and hand-propelled wheelchairs, beggars and alcoholics, plus the homeless who lived on the street, sometimes with pets.

One could see every variety of humanity. (Until the police took the animal away from him, one man stood on Telegraph for months, mindfucking a dog with sounds and gestures, claiming that the mind of Hitler in the creature was trying to control him.) Our kids quickly learned that the Avenue meant the ever-present possibility of confrontation and that being a child didn't provide the usual amnesty. The state of things had gotten way beyond such a consideration—for instance, a haggard man running up and down the street shouting "Fuck you!" to everyone as loud as he could. Or a black woman calling everyone else "Nigger!" Preachers came in every guise—hippie Christians, tarot soothsayers, riffing guitarists and tomtom players, John Lennon conspiracy freaks. Their speeches ranged from surreal madness to kitsch mediocrity, but the energy was world-class. For Robin and Miranda, Telegraph Avenue was a kaleidoscope, and they loved to walk it with me.

Both kids' schools let out early on Friday and, given the gauntlet they had to pass through, I came to regard their arrivals (Robin by city bus, Miranda walking from the local public school) as a major festivity: Everyone was safe and sound. A ritual of ice cream cones on Telegraph soon expanded to full meals in the center of town. Preferring to be starving for the occasion, the kids stopped bringing bagged sandwiches and yogurts to school on that day. Near two o'clock we rushed to catch the end of the lunch special at the Taiwan Restaurant. Months later we switched to the more elegant Mandarin Garden. Robin and Miranda never varied from Cashew Chicken and Mandarin Beef, carefully dividing portions with each other like scientists carrying out experiments, Miranda always nursing hers to make sure that Robin finished first. He brought *The Sporting News* (which usually arrived on Friday); she countered with at least half a dozen comic books. It was total blissout.

"You spoil them," Lindy complained half-jokingly. We encouraged her to join us one day when she was home early. At the restaurant she was shocked to view the actual scene and immediately demanded better manners—no reading after the food came, no eating directly out of the platters, more frequent use of napkins.

"We want just Rich," Mandy snarled, and I slipped Lindy a guilty grin.

It took a little more than a year for me to write *The Night Sky*. Even before I finished, I began *Embryogenesis*. That is, I took the cosmic question from the sky into the oceans where the shapes of living creatures evolved. Because my previous two books were evocative and expansive I felt compelled to go through one specific act of creation. Something in me had always wanted to return to the physical beginning, ontogenetically in the sperm and egg and phylogenetically in the first animals of the prehistoric broth.

What made simple molecules clump into cells? How did the cells know to weave tissue, tissue to organize in layers and shape not just geometry but functional organs, then all of it to assemble its own nervous system and mind? Was it, as scientists swore, an accident of cosmic chaos regimented by the chance associations of genetic code—or was there something else, hidden in matter?

There were obviously no answers, so instead I tracked my imaginary embryo through its metamorphoses in the womb, bringing a companion creature down generations of sea worms and squirts, emerging finally onto land where they lost themselves in the guts of the mammals and primates. It took almost four years to write this one (beginning in Richmond, finishing on Blake). Then I sold the book to Avon, a mass-market publisher in New York.

Finally I was ready to return to my own story. I had explored for seven years (and over a thousand pages) how we got here, who we were, and what medicines could cure our disease. I was now trapped in a universe vast beyond contemplation or redemption and with two young kids growing up. My work had become an entanglement of stars and cells and shaman doctors. But I wanted to dance again in the open field with Robin and Miranda. I wanted to play games and tell stories before it was too late. So I went back to the narrative Katey Carver loved and rejected. I opened the carton that held *Salty and Sandy*. Robert Kelly's warning about confessional prose had kept it sealed for twenty years.

ANCILLARY MATERIAL

The following books and journals described and/or used in this text are still available at the time of publication (some in limited quantities):

Solar Journal: Oecological Sections (describing the years in Ann Arbor)

The Continents (describing the years in Ann Arbor and the first weeks in Maine and containing the sequence from Indian and Viking explorations of the New World through the Moon landing and Robin's birth)

Book of the Cranberry Islands (describing the first five months on Mount Desert Island and including dialogues with fishermen)

The Provinces (describing the last three months on Mount Desert Island into the first month in Cape Elizabeth; includes dialogues with fishermen, loggers, worm-diggers, etc.)

The Long Body of the Dream (describing the subsequent full year in Cape Elizabeth)

Io, issues one through seven, and issue nine.

Io/#1 contains the full text of the 1964 Halloween speech, and *Io/#9* contains the full text of the spring 1964 poem ("Day of blind flies, lethargic clouds, tardy stars"). *Io/#4* contains "Alchemical Sections," and *Io/#5* contains *The Alphabet Book.*

The following books and journals covering the five years in Maine and Vermont immediately subsequent to this text are also still available:

The Book of Being Born Again into the World

The Windy Passage from Nostalgia
The Slag of Creation
Io, issues ten through twenty-four.

Although the books were originally released by a number of different publishers, both they and the issues of *Io* are now available solely from North Atlantic Books, Post Office Box 12327, Berkeley, California 94712. *Planet Medicine, The Night Sky, Embryogenesis,* and *Waiting for the Martian Express* (including the full text of "Sea Wall") can also be ordered from North Atlantic Books. Please write for a *New Moon* price list.

The following books and journals are out of print and available only in libraries:

Book of the Earth and Sky (parallel material to *Solar Journal*)
Spaces Wild and Tame (parallel material to *Solar Journal*)
Io, issue eight.